Also by Virginia and Lee McAlester

A Field Guide to America's Historic Neighborhoods
and Museum Houses: The Western States

Great American Houses and Their Architectural Styles

By Virginia Savage McAlester, Willis Cecil Winters FAIA,
and Prudence Mackintosh; photography by Steve Clicque

The Homes of the Park Cities, Dallas: Great American Suburbs

A Field Guide to American Houses

The Definitive Guide
to Identifying and
Understanding
America's
Domestic
Architecture

ALFRED A. KNOPF
NEW YORK
2013

A Field Guide to American Houses

Virginia Savage McAlester

With drawings by Suzanne Patton Matty
and photographs by Steve Clicque

Revised and expanded from the original edition
written by Virginia and Lee McAlester

With drawings by Lauren Jarrett and
model house drawings by Juan Rodriguez-Arnaiz

THIS IS A BORZOI BOOK
PUBLISHED BY ALFRED A. KNOPF

Copyright © 1984, 2013 by Virginia Savage McAlester

All rights reserved. Published in the United States by Alfred A. Knopf,
a division of Random House, LLC, New York, and in Canada by Random House
of Canada Limited, Toronto, Penguin Random House Companies.
Originally published in the United States in different form by Alfred A. Knopf,
a division of Random House, Inc.
www.aaknopf.com

Knopf, Borzoi Books, and the colophon are registered trademarks of Random House LLC.

Library of Congress Cataloging-in-Publication Data
  McAlester, Virginia Savage, [date]
    A field guide to American houses / by Virginia Savage McAlester ; revised and expanded
    from the orginal edition written by Virginia and Lee McAlester ; with drawings by Lauren
    Jarrett and model house drawings by Juan Rodriguez-Arnaiz ; revision drawings by Suzanne
    Patton Matty and photographs by Steve Clicque.—Second edition.
      pages cm
    Includes bibliographical references and index.
    ISBN 978-1-4000-4359-0
    1. Architecture, Domestic—United States—Guidebooks.   2. United States—
    Guidebooks.   I. McAlester, A. Lee (Arcie Lee), [date]   II. Jarrett, Lauren,
    illustrator.   III. Rodriguez-Arnaiz, Juan, illustrator.   IV. Title.
NA7205.M35 2013
728.0973—dc23   2013018432

Jacket illustrations by Juan Rodriguez-Arnaiz and Lauren Jarrett
Jacket design by Linda Huang

Manufactured in the United States of America
First Edition published June 12, 1984
Second Edition

TO

Carty Talkington

Martine McAlester

Amy Talkington

Keven McAlester

Clementine Adams

Virginia Adams

Contents

How to Use This Book

Each chapter treats one of the major architectural fashions, or *styles,* that have been popular over our country's past. The chapters are arranged roughly chronologically, with the earliest styles first. The opening page of each chapter features a large drawing showing the three or four most important *identifying features* which differentiate that style from others. The most common shapes, or *principal subtypes,* of each style are also pictured on the opening page, along with references to pages of photographs in the chapter that allow the reader to see quickly the common features in a range of examples from each particular style and subtype. Most chapters also include drawings that show typical smaller details—for example, windows, doors, and roof-wall junctions—that cannot easily be seen in full-house photographs. Text supplementing the drawings and photographs discusses the *identifying features, principal subtypes, variants and details,* and *occurrence* of each style. Concluding *comments* provide a brief introduction to the origin and history of the style. A few later chapters have a less detailed treatment of a style or styles. Generally these cover either revivals of earlier styles or less common ones.

Confronted with an unfamiliar house to be identified, the reader may approach the problem three different ways. The simplest is to thumb through the many pages of house photographs, looking for examples similar to the unidentified house. Here one should pay particular attention to such large-scale features as roof form (gabled or hipped, low or steeply pitched?) and facade balance (symmetrical or asymmetrical?). When a similar photograph is located, the unknown example should be compared in smaller-scale features of architectural detailing: windows, doors, roof-wall junctions, porches, etc. The additional photographs and drawings provided in each chapter will aid in this process, which can be repeated until a final identification is made.

A second and more systematic approach is to turn to the Pictorial Key and Glossary on page xiii. This illustrates a variety of different types of such common architectural features as windows, doors, and roofing materials, with a listing of the styles in which each type commonly occurs. Using the Key, the reader will find that a house with a red tile roof, for example, will most likely be found in either the Spanish Colonial, Mission, Spanish Revival, or Italian Renaissance styles. Photographs and drawings for these styles can then be compared with the unknown house as in the first approach.

A final approach is to become familiar with the relatively few historical precedents on which American house styles are based. These are reviewed in the introductory chapter on *Style*. With this background, one can learn to quickly determine if a house is of Modern, Medieval, Renaissance Classical, or Ancient Classical inspiration. With a bit of further practice, it becomes easy to distinguish between the half-dozen or so principal American styles that have been based on each of these traditions. With this knowledge, style identification can become almost automatic. The book then becomes a useful backup reference for identifying stylistic subtypes and subtleties.

Preface

Looking at houses today is even more interesting and challenging than it was in 1984, the year this guide was first published. Almost 80 percent of the houses in the United States today have been built since 1940, the date the first edition concluded its full coverage. Surprisingly, during the last twenty-five years there has been a reinterpretation and new building of most American house styles that existed before 1940. Knowledge of earlier architectural styles—both traditional and modern—is now a necessity for understanding new houses, not just historic ones.

The first edition of *A Field Guide to American Houses* ended very naturally at 1940. The Great Depression of the 1930s had effectively ended construction of Eclectic house styles, and when construction resumed at the end of World War II, both house styles and lifestyles had shifted dramatically. An appendix to the original book gave a brief overview of styles built from 1940 to 1984. It was my intention at the time to expand the 1984 publication to fully cover these, particularly the mid-century modern homes gradually reaching their fiftieth birthday, making them eligible for National Register listing. This updated revision intends to fulfill that original goal. While many of the homes built soon after World War II are now eligible for listing on the National Register of Historic Places, they are nevertheless among the most endangered of houses—primarily because of their choice locations and generally smaller size. With this book I hope to help in their preservation.

Two additional topics were added during the course of revision: an overview of the extraordinary variety of styles built during the millennial housing boom (1990–2008) and a section on neighborhoods that covers the typical ways American houses are grouped together. The new chapter on neighborhoods provides a brief introduction to typical American communities. Just as *A Field Guide to American Houses* concentrated on typical homes, not architectural landmarks, the neighborhoods section of this new edition concentrates on typical neighborhoods, not landmarks of planning. It presents the simple patterns of development repeated in cities throughout the United States, rather than offering a study of mostly one-of-a-kind planning icons.

When it came time to write a preface for this expanded edition, it was suggested I might write an entirely new one. However, after rereading the original I found it so concise I could see no way to improve upon it. Thus, it follows here, because I believe it is as relevant to this new edition as it was in 1984. In updating this work, I have tried to adhere to the same approaches to research and presentation as the 1984 edition, described below in the original preface.

This book grew from the authors' efforts to identify the houses found in typical American neighborhoods. Many excellent guides are available to detail the features of our country's monumental dwellings; other works deal with the everyday houses of specific towns and neighborhoods. What was lacking, we discovered, was a guide that related the architectural landmarks to their far more numerous cousins throughout the country—the common houses that make up most of our nation's built environment. Our book attempts to fill this gap by treating the entire spectrum of American domestic building, from the most modest folk houses to the grandest mansions, but with a heavy emphasis on the familiar dwellings that lie between these extremes. It is intended not as a scholarly treatise on architectural history, but as a practical field manual for identifying and understanding the changing fashions, forms, and components of American houses. In treating this broad subject we have imposed certain limitations on the coverage. Because it emphasizes field identification, it concerns primarily the *exterior* appearance of houses. The important subjects of interior planning, design, and detailing are given only the most superficial treatment. The book also concentrates on *styled* houses built before 1940. Unstyled folk houses and post-1940 houses are included, but are treated in considerably less detail. The principal focus is on *single-family houses,* which may be either detached or, like attached urban houses, built with common walls. A few duplexes or triplexes built in the form of single-family buildings have been illustrated, but larger multi-unit dwellings are not included.

The book is organized chiefly by the chronology of changing architectural styles. In one sense these may be considered a merely ephemeral and somewhat superficial series of fashions. More fundamentally, however, they reflect the tastes and sensibilities of our forebears over three centuries of dynamic history. Looking still farther, most have deep roots in European history, whence they draw on Renaissance, Medieval, and Classical models for inspiration. An understanding of these stylistic traditions as they have repeatedly reappeared during our nation's history is, we believe, the most practical framework for identifying and understanding American houses.

A principal difficulty in stylistic analysis involves recognizing underlying similarities in style when buildings differ in size, shape, and degree of formality. Many Greek Revival houses, for example, bear little resemblance to Greek temples, but almost all show certain key features that can, with a bit of practice, be easily recognized. Such features are emphasized in schematic drawings placed on the opening pages of every chapter. Beneath are placed sketches of Principal Subtypes, usually based on roof form, to which the characteristic features of the style are most commonly applied. Photographs provide a variety of typical houses of each subtype as a further aid to recognizing a style in its many guises, while drawings illustrate typical architectural details.

The many photographs of typical houses are, we feel, the heart of the book. In choosing these and preparing their descriptive captions, we have attempted to follow certain guidelines for consistency. Most of the houses illustrated are still in existence; photographs of examples known to have been destroyed are included for only a few rare styles of subtypes. All houses are identified by the state and town (or county for rural houses) in which they are located; where possible, the year construction was completed, the last name of the first owner ("Johnson House"), and the architect are also noted. We have usually relied on secondary sources for this information and have not attempted the enormous task of documentation from original sources. Precise addresses have been omitted to protect the occupants, since most of the houses illustrated are privately owned and not open to the public. Where secondary documentation of the date of construction was lacking, as was the case for the bulk of the examples illustrated, we have estimated the dates, using the forms "late 19th century," "1920s," and "ca. 1905" to indicate increasing certainty of attribution. Familiar names of landmark houses (Biltmore, House of Seven Gables) are sometimes used instead of, or in addition to, the name of the original owner.

Most of the styles of American houses have been previously recognized and described, and we have thus drawn heavily on the works of others in preparing the book. Defining stylistic subtypes and characteristic details has, however, required much original research. To this end we have reviewed and analyzed photographs of more than a hundred thousand houses. In addition, we have traveled to almost every state to study and photograph the spectrum of American houses first hand. Even so, we can only claim to have scratched the surface of stylistic analysis. Most styles, we discovered, provided problems enough to occupy the energies of architectural historians for many years. We very much hope that our preliminary efforts will lead to such refinement and correction.

It has since been very gratifying to find a great deal of research that was not available while working on the 1984 edition of this book. Much of the new information has been included here.

For readers wishing to know more about houses that interest them, internet research has made much new information available to even casual observers. Of particular value are several websites that offer information on most houses, including when they were likely first built and much more detailed information derived largely from county property tax records. Or one can directly use the county property tax records available online. The ability to quickly and easily research these most basic facts for something approximating 80 percent of the houses in the United States built after 1920 has led to simpler, yet far more informed, house watching and house watchers. Do a web search on a single address and see what you find. You might be surprised.

Pictorial Key

Roof Form	IF YOU SEE	TRY THESE FIRST
side-gabled	steep pitch	Tudor, Gothic Revival, Stick, Queen Anne, French Colonial, Postmedieval English New Traditional
	moderate or varied pitch	Colonial Revival, Georgian, Federal, Early Classical Revival, Folk Victorian, Neoclassical, Shingle, National Folk, Pre-Railroad Folk, Minimal Traditional, Styled Ranch, New Traditional, American Vernacular
	low pitch	Craftsman, Spanish Revival, Italianate, Monterey, Greek Revival, Dutch Colonial, Spanish Colonial, Federal, Minimal Traditional, Ranch, Manufactured, Contemporary, New Traditional
front-gabled (also tri-gabled)	steep pitch	Gothic Revival, Stick, Queen Anne, less commonly Tudor, New Traditional
	moderate or varied pitch	National Folk, Shingle, Folk Victorian, Neoclassical, less commonly Colonial Revival, American Vernacular, New Traditional
	low pitch	Greek Revival, Italianate, Craftsman, less commonly Spanish Revival, Manufactured, Contemporary, New Traditional

Roof Form	IF YOU SEE	TRY THESE FIRST
cross-gabled (or gable front and wings)	steep pitch	Tudor, Queen Anne, Stick, Gothic Revival, Millennium Mansion, New Traditional
	moderate or varied pitch	Shingle, National Folk, Early Classical Revival, Minimal Traditional, Ranch, American Vernacular, New Traditional
	low pitch	Craftsman, Spanish Revival, Greek Revival, Monterey, Minimal Traditional, Ranch, Contemporary, New Traditional
centered gable (or)	steep pitch	Gothic Revival, Millennium Mansion, 21st-Century Modern
	moderate or varied pitch	Colonial Revival, Georgian, Federal, New Traditional
	low pitch	Italianate, Italian Renaissance, Beaux Arts, New Traditional
hipped (with ridge)	steep pitch	French Eclectic, Chateauesque, French Colonial, Millennium Mansion (with many added roof elements), New Traditional
	moderate or varied pitch	Colonial Revival, Georgian, Federal, Early Classical Revival, Folk Victorian, Mission, Neoclassical, Minimal Traditional, American Vernacular, New Traditional
	low pitch	Italianate, Federal, Greek Revival, Italian Renaissance, Spanish Revival, Prairie, Ranch, Minimal Traditional, New Traditional

Roof Form	IF YOU SEE	TRY THESE FIRST
hipped pyramid	steep pitch	Chateauesque, French Eclectic, New Traditional, Millennium Mansion (with many added roof elements)
	moderate or varied pitch	National Folk, Colonial Revival, Neoclassical, Folk Victorian, Mission, American Vernacular, New Traditional
	low pitch	Prairie, Italianate, New Traditional
cascading hips (hip-on-hip)		Millennium Mansion
mansard		Second Empire, Beaux Arts, Richardsonian Romanesque, Mansard
gambrel		Dutch Colonial, Shingle, Colonial Revival, Georgian, New Traditional
pent or visor		Georgian, Colonial Revival, Mission
hipped with cross gables		Queen Anne, Richardsonian Romanesque, Shingle, Millennium Mansion, New Traditional
flat roof without overhang	symmetrical	Beaux Arts, Italian Renaissance, Federal (rare), town house subtypes, New Traditional
	asymmetrical	International, Modernistic, Pueblo Revival, Spanish Revival, Spanish Colonial, town house subtypes, New Traditional
flat roof with overhang	roof overhang on entire house	Contemporary
	roof overhang only on specific sections of house	International, occasionally Contemporary

slanted roof section (shed roof)		Contemporary, Shed
roof extends to ground (forms A-shape)		Other 20th-Century Modern: A-Frame
segmental vault		21st-Century Modern: Segmental Vault

Dormers	IF YOU SEE	TRY THESE FIRST
hipped		Prairie, French Eclectic, Shingle, Tudor, Millennium Mansion, New Traditional
gabled		Craftsman, Colonial Revival, Federal, Georgian, Shingle, Queen Anne, Stick, Gothic Revival, Tudor, Chateauesque, French Eclectic, Millennium Mansion, New Traditional
shed		Dutch Colonial, Craftsman, Colonial Revival, Tudor, Shingle, Millennium Mansion, New Traditional
arched top		French Eclectic, Second Empire, Beaux Arts, Millennium Mansion, New Traditional
round or oval		French Eclectic, Beaux Arts, New Traditional
pedimented		Colonial Revival, Georgian, Federal, Millennium Mansion, New Traditional, American Vernacular
wall dormer		Gothic Revival, Chateauesque, Richardsonian Romanesque, Mission, French Eclectic, Mansard, Millennium Mansion, New Traditional
eyebrow		Shingle, Richardsonian Romanesque, New Traditional

shaped		Mission, Queen Anne, Tudor, New Traditional
through-the-cornice window		French Eclectic, Mission, Mansard, Millennium Mansion, New Traditional

Other Roof Elaborations	IF YOU SEE		TRY THESE FIRST
towers	square		Italianate, Stick, Second Empire, Spanish Revival, New Traditional, Millennium Mansion, occasionally Queen Anne, Mission, Italian Renaissance
	round		Queen Anne, Richardsonian Romanesque, Chateauesque, Shingle, French Eclectic, occasionally Spanish Revival, Millennium Mansion, New Traditional
	hexagonal		Queen Anne, Richardsonian Romanesque, French Eclectic, occasionally New Traditional, Millennium Mansion
gable-on-hip roof			Ranch, Styled Ranch: Character
hip-on-gable roof (also called jerkinhead)			Tudor, Craftsman
roof-top cupolas			Italianate, Octagon, Second Empire, Greek Revival, Ranch
decorated vergeboard (also called bargeboard)			Tudor, Gothic Revival, Queen Anne, Exotic Revivals, Styled Ranch: Character
trusses in gables			Craftsman, Stick, Gothic Revival, Queen Anne, Tudor, Ranch, Styled Ranch: Tudor

beams exposed at gable end (may be fake)			Craftsman, Prairie, Contemporary, Ranch, New Traditional
flared eaves			French Eclectic, French Colonial, Prairie, Stick, Dutch Colonial, Craftsman, New Traditional
multi-level eaves			Tudor, Shingle, French Eclectic, Millennium Mansion, New Traditional, occasionally others
tile roof		rounded tiles (more often red)	Spanish Revival, Styled Ranch: Spanish, Millennium Mansion, New Traditional
		(more often green)	Mission, Italian Renaissance, Prairie, New Traditional
		flat pantiles	Tudor, occasionally Neoclassical, Colonial Revival, Italian Renaissance, Prairie, New Traditional
exposed rafters			Craftsman, Stick, Mission, Ranch, American Vernacular, Contemporary, New Traditional, occasionally Prairie, Gothic Revival
pinnacles			Chateauesque, Richardsonian Romanesque, Gothic Revival
battlements (also called castellations)			Gothic Revival, Tudor
roof-top or roof-line balustrade			Neoclassical, Colonial Revival, Federal, Georgian, Beaux Arts, Early Classical Revival, Italian Renaissance, New Traditional
metal roof cresting			Queen Anne, Chateauesque

Roof-Wall Junction	IF YOU SEE	TRY THESE FIRST
parapet on flat roof (wall extends up beyond roof edge)		Beaux Arts, Italian Renaissance, Pueblo Revival, Spanish Revival, Mission, Modernistic, International, Spanish Colonial, New Traditional
parapet on gabled roof		Tudor, Queen Anne, Richardsonian Romanesque, Mission, French Colonial, Millennium Mansion, New Traditional
no eaves (little or no overhang)		International, Modernistic, Spanish Revival, Postmedieval English, Minimal Traditional, Ranch (early examples), Millennium Mansion, New Traditional
slight eave overhang, boxed with modillions, dentils, or other classical moldings		Colonial Revival, Neoclassical, Beaux Arts, Federal, Georgian, French Eclectic, Early Classical Revival, Chateauesque, Italian Renaissance, Styled Ranch: Colonial Revival, Millennium Mansion, New Traditional
slight eave overhang, open, not boxed		Stick, Gothic Revival, Ranch, Millennium Mansion, New Traditional
slight eave overhang with brackets		Second Empire, Folk Victorian, Italianate, Millennium Mansion, New Traditional
slight eave overhang with wide band of trim below		Greek Revival, Millennium Mansion, New Traditional
wide eave overhang, boxed without brackets		Prairie, Ranch, New Traditional
wide eave overhang, boxed with brackets		Italianate, Italian Renaissance, Prairie, occasionally Mission, New Traditional

wide eave overhang, open, not boxed	IF YOU SEE	TRY THESE FIRST
	rafters exposed	Stick, Craftsman, Mission, Ranch, Contemporary, American Vernacular, New Traditional
	rafters covered	Contemporary, Prairie, Ranch
	roof openings between rafters	Contemporary

Chimneys	IF YOU SEE	TRY THESE FIRST
dominant decorated chimney		Tudor, Queen Anne, Postmedieval English, French Eclectic (towered), Millennium Mansion, New Traditional
low broad chimney		Ranch, Contemporary, Prairie, New Traditional, American Vernacular
wood-clad chimney		Shed, early Millennium Mansion, early New Traditional, and early Contemporary built ca. 1960–1990

Railings (around porch, along roofline, on rooftop)	IF YOU SEE	TRY THESE FIRST
balusters	slender turned spindles	Georgian, Federal, Colonial Revival, Neoclassical, Queen Anne, Folk Victorian, Beaux Arts, Spanish Revival, Early Classical Revival, French Eclectic, New Traditional

classical balusters historical spacing as below (or a bit farther apart) sleeve — belly —	Italian Renaissance, Federal, Early Classical Revival, Neoclassical, Richardsonian Romanesque, Beaux Arts, New Traditional	
	spaced very closely to meet modern building codes (no opening over 4" wide)	Millennium Mansion, New Traditional
	spaced very sparsely to save cost (placed where code does not require close spacing)	Millennium Mansion, New Traditional
geometric patterns	Chinese Chippendale (many variations)	Colonial Revival, Neoclassical, Federal, Georgian, Early Classical Revival, Greek Revival, Queen Anne
	simple masonry design	Richardsonian Romanesque, Contemporary
solid (used for porch only)		Richardsonian Romanesque, Shingle, Craftsman, Mission, Prairie, New Traditional
simple squared		American Vernacular, Folk Victorian, Greek Revival, Colonial Revival, Neoclassical, Craftsman, Prairie, New Traditional
horizontal		Modernistic, Monterey, Contemporary, American Vernacular

Porches	IF YOU SEE	TRY THESE FIRST
entry		Can occur on most styles
full-height entry (commonly with pediment)		Early Classical Revival, Greek Revival, Neoclassical, Folk Victorian (two-tier), Styled Ranch: Neoclassical, Millennium Mansion, New Traditional
full-facade		Greek Revival, Neoclassical, Folk Victorian (two-tier), Styled Ranch: Neoclassical, New Traditional, American Vernacular
full-width, one-story		Prairie, Craftsman, Colonial Revival, Folk Victorian, Italianate, Gothic Revival, Dutch Colonial, Italian Renaissance, Queen Anne, Shingle, Stick, French Colonial, Second Empire, Octagon, Greek Revival, Mission, New Traditional, American Vernacular
partial		Gothic Revival, Italianate, Second Empire, Stick, Queen Anne, Richardsonian Romanesque, Folk Victorian, Monterey (if on second story), Craftsman, New Traditional, American Vernacular
wrap		Queen Anne, New Traditional, American Vernacular, occasionally others
three or more sides		Greek Revival, French Colonial, Folk Victorian, American Vernacular
very shallow porch (3'–5')		Millennium Mansion, New Traditional

Porch Supports	IF YOU SEE	TRY THESE FIRST
classical columns	two-story (colossal)	Neoclassical, Greek Revival, Early Classical Revival, Beaux Arts, Millennium Mansion, New Traditional
	one-story (may be simplified, squared versions)	Italianate, Greek Revival, Early Classical Revival, Neoclassical, Beaux Arts, Federal, Colonial Revival, Queen Anne (Free Classic), Italian Renaissance, Millennium Mansion, New Traditional
columns with cushion capital		Richardsonian Romanesque
chamfered (corners shaved off at 45° angles)		Italianate, Gothic Revival, Second Empire, Stick, American Vernacular, Folk Victorian
unelaborated square columns		Pre-Railroad Folk, National Folk, Greek Revival, Folk Victorian, Ranch, Contemporary, American Vernacular
twisted spiral (often a colonette attached to wall behind)		Spanish Revival, New Traditional, Millennium Mansion
turned spindles		Queen Anne, Folk Victorian, New Traditional
heavy square piers		Prairie, Mission, Craftsman, Millennium Mansion, New Traditional
piers with inward sloping sides (battered)		Craftsman, Prairie, Mission, New Traditional
rough hewn		Pueblo, Pre-Railroad Folk
pipe (thin, round pillar or pilotis)		International, Contemporary, 21st-Century Modern

Arched Doors, Windows, Porch Openings	IF YOU SEE	TRY THESE FIRST
segmental		French Eclectic, Georgian, Federal, Colonial Revival, Italianate, Mansard, Styled Ranch: French, Millennium Mansion, New Traditional
round		Italian Renaissance, Italianate, Richardsonian Romanesque, Spanish Revival, occasionally in Federal, Colonial Revival, Beaux Arts, Mission, Tudor, Other 20th-Century Modern: Formalistic, Mansard, New Traditional
Syrian		Richardsonian Romanesque, Shingle, New Traditional
pointed (Gothic)		Gothic Revival, New Traditional
Tudor (flattened Gothic)		Tudor, Gothic Revival, New Traditional
basket-handle (elliptical)		Chateauesque, Beaux Arts, Italianate, Millennium Mansion, New Traditional
ogee		Exotic Revivals, Chateauesque
multiple stylized arches		Other 20th-Century Modern: Formalistic

Doors	IF YOU SEE	TRY THESE FIRST
transom lights		Georgian, Colonial Revival, Pre-Railroad Folk, New Traditional, American Vernacular
round fanlight or elliptical fanlight with sidelights		Federal, Colonial Revival, Early Classical Revival, Neoclassical, Millennium Mansion, New Traditional
rectangular transom and sidelights		Greek Revival, Neoclassical, New Traditional, American Vernacular

	IF YOU SEE	TRY THESE FIRST				
six- to eight-panel door		Federal, Georgian, Colonial Revival, Early Classical Revival, New Traditional	Palladian			Federal, Queen Anne, Shingle, Colonial Revival, Neoclassical, Millennium Mansion, New Traditional
curved panels on door (often called "French Provincial")		Mansard, Styled Ranch: French, French Eclectic, Ranch, New Traditional French, Millennium Mansion	pediment			Colonial Revival, Georgian, Neoclassical, Federal, Italianate, Greek Revival (triangular only), Beaux Arts, Italian Renaissance, Styled Ranch (Colonial Revival and Neoclassical), Millennium Mansion, New Traditional, occasionally Queen Anne
board-and-batten door		Postmedieval English, Spanish Colonial, Tudor, Spanish Revival, Pueblo Revival				
pilasters to sides of door (may have pediment)		Georgian, Federal, Early Classical Revival, Greek Revival, Italianate, Second Empire, Colonial Revival, Neoclassical, Chateauesque, Beaux Arts, Italian Renaissance, French Eclectic, New Traditional	oriel			Gothic Revival, Tudor, Chateauesque, French Eclectic
			drip mold			Gothic Revival, Chateauesque, occasionally Tudor, French Eclectic, New Traditional
pediment		Colonial Revival, Georgian, Neoclassical, Italian Renaissance, Beaux Arts, Italianate, Styled Ranch (Colonial Revival and Neoclassical), Millennium Mansion, New Traditional	hood mold			Italianate, Second Empire
two-story entry composition		Millennium Mansion, Mansard, New Traditional, Shed	ribbon (three or more matching contiguous windows)	double-hung		Shingle, Prairie, Craftsman, Modernistic, International, New Traditional; occurs on most post-1900 Eclectic styles, but usually on side wings not main house block
large glass doors covered with "wrought-iron" pattern		Millennium Mansion, New Traditional		arched		Shingle, Richardsonian Romanesque, New Traditional
entry door location is not obvious from street		International, Contemporary, Prairie		casement		Tudor, Prairie, New Traditional; occurs on most post-1900 Eclectic styles, but usually on side wings not main house block
Windows	**IF YOU SEE**	**TRY THESE FIRST**		short windows in wall		Ranch, Contemporary
casement		Prairie, Tudor, Spanish Revival, Postmedieval English, Dutch Colonial, Modernistic, International (metal only), Ranch, Styled Ranch, Contemporary, Millennium Mansion, New Traditional, American Vernacular		short windows along ridge of gable roof (clerestory)		Shed

Windows	IF YOU SEE	TRY THESE FIRST
"special front" window, also called "cottage" window (large lower pane with decorative transom above)		Neoclassical, Queen Anne, Craftsman, most Eclectic styles (particularly houses built 1900–1920)
large pane surrounded by smaller panes		Queen Anne, occasionally other Victorian styles
blank lower pane with patterned pane above		Queen Anne, Craftsman, Prairie, most Eclectic styles (particularly houses built 1900–1920), New Traditional
paired windows		Italianate, most post-1860s styles
attic story		Greek Revival, Beaux Arts, Italian Renaissance, New Traditional
bracketed tops		Italianate, Second Empire, Gothic Revival, Stick
horizontal panes		Ranch, Contemporary
square window		Postmodern (introduced early 1960s, see Figure 2, page 669), Other 20th-Century Modern
picture window		Ranch, sometimes Styled Ranch
windows fill gable end		Contemporary, Other 20th-Century Modern: A-Frame
round window	in pediment (also elliptical or half-circle)	Georgian, Federal, Early Classical Revival, Colonial Revival, Neoclassical, New Traditional
	on wall surface (also hexagonal or elliptical window set vertically)	Second Empire, Shingle, Queen Anne, Colonial Revival, Minimal Traditional, Ranch, Styled Ranch, New Traditional, Millennium Mansion

corner window	mitered glass corner	International, Contemporary, Other 20th-Century Modern and 21st-Century Modern
	with corner support	International, Minimal Traditional, Ranch, Prairie, Contemporary, Other 20th-Century Modern and 21st-Century Modern
window wall		International, Contemporary, all post-1950s styles (generally on rear or private facades)

Walls	IF YOU SEE	TRY THESE FIRST
logs		Pre-Railroad Folk
adobe		Pueblo Revival, Spanish Colonial
rough-faced stone		Richardsonian Romanesque, Shingle (first story only), as a veneer in Millennium Mansion, New Traditional
smooth stone		Beaux Arts, Chateauesque, Italian Renaissance, as a veneer in Millennium Mansion, New Traditional
rusticated stone (joints exaggerated)		Beaux Arts, Italian Renaissance, Millennium Mansion, New Traditional
plywood siding (Exterior plywood siding was introduced in the mid-1930s and became popular in the 1950s.)	smooth finish	Modernistic, International, Contemporary
	wood siding emulated in plywood (also called T1-11)	Contemporary, Ranch, Styled Ranch

stucco (cracks, if present, typically random)		Tudor, Mission, Spanish Revival, Prairie, Modernistic, Italian Renaissance, French Colonial, International (white-colored stucco was preferred for International) Occurs occasionally in other pre-1945 styles	board and batten		Gothic Revival, Post-Railroad Folk, Ranch; as either wood or imitation wood product in New Traditional, American Vernacular
stucco boards (popularized as exterior material ca. 1990)	commonly 4 x 8 fiber cement boards with stucco finish joints sealed (cracks, if present, may reveal rectangular board pattern)	Millennium Mansion, New Traditional, American Vernacular	clapboard (weatherboard, bevel siding or lap siding)		Craftsman, Colonial Revival, Postmedieval English, Ranch, Styled Ranch, Split-Level; as either wood or imitation wood product in Millennium Mansion, New Traditional, American Vernacular
	joints covered by battens or half-timbering	Millennium Mansion, New Traditional	metal, finished to look like metal, either new or rusted (These types of metal finishes began to be used in residences ca. 1980; often zinc, steel, or rusty-looking Corten steel. The metal claddings occasionally used right after World War II were typically finished to *not* look like raw metal.)	corrugated	Other 20th-Century Modern (Deconstructivist), 21st-Century Modern
	joints left open (applied as rain screen with open joints that allow air circulation)	21st-Century Modern		other (standing seam, panel, ribbed)	Other 20th-Century Modern, 21st-Century Modern
wood shingles	patterned	Queen Anne, Shingle, Folk Victorian; as either wood or imitation wood product in Millennium Mansion, New Traditional	wood strips with natural finish (smooth tongue-and-groove, open wood screen, unusual wood species)		Other 20th-Century Modern (Deconstructivist), 21st-Century Modern
	rectangular	Shingle, Craftsman, Colonial Revival, Postmedieval English, Ranch, Styled Ranch, Split-Level; as either wood or imitation wood product in Millennium Mansion, New Traditional, American Vernacular	masonry wall cladding applied like wallpaper (on single surface such as front of gable)		Millennium Mansion, New Traditional

Walls	IF YOU SEE	TRY THESE FIRST
multiple wall materials	on flat walls (commonly stone, brick, stucco, and painted or imitation wood)	Tudor, Ranch, Styled Ranch, Contemporary, Millennium Mansion, New Traditional
	on 3-D walls (often includes metal or unpainted wood)	Other 20th-Century Modern: Deconstructivist, 21st-Century Modern: Decoupage
broad surface with pattern	geometric masonry pattern	Contemporary
	concrete screen grille	Contemporary, Other 20th-Century Modern: Formalistic
	board form concrete (wood patterns remain visible)	Other 20th-Century Modern (Brutalist), 21st-Century Modern
broad front facade without windows		Contemporary, Other 20th-Century Modern, 21st-Century Modern
wall surface material extends up into gable without break		Gothic Revival, Tudor, Spanish Revival, Postmedieval English, Contemporary, New Traditional, Millennium Mansion
second-story overhang		Colonial Revival, Tudor, Postmedieval English, Queen Anne, New Traditional
half-timbering		Tudor, Craftsman, Queen Anne, French Eclectic, Prairie, New Traditional
patterned stick work		Stick, Queen Anne, Exotic Revival

Other Decorative Elements	IF YOU SEE	TRY THESE FIRST
quoins		Georgian, Federal, Italianate, Colonial Revival, French Eclectic, Beaux Arts, Italian Renaissance, Second Empire, Styled Ranch, Millennium Mansion, New Traditional
belt course		Georgian, Federal, Italianate, Colonial Revival, French Eclectic, Beaux Arts, Italian Renaissance, Second Empire, Millennium Mansion, New Traditional
garlands, floral ornament		Beaux Arts, Federal, Queen Anne (Free Classic), Colonial Revival, Millennium Mansion, New Traditional
pilasters		Georgian, Federal, Italianate, Colonial Revival, French Eclectic, Beaux Arts, Italian Renaissance, Greek Revival, Neoclassical, Millennium Mansion, New Traditional
traditional details used in different ways (out of scale, oddly placed, flat cut-outs)		Other 20th-Century Modern (Postmodern), occasionally New Traditional
slanting or angled walls, roof lines, overhangs (house is not all rectangular)		Other 20th-Century Modern (Deconstructivist), 21st-Century Modern (Slightly Askew), occasionally Contemporary

Foundation	IF YOU SEE	TRY THESE FIRST
low to ground		Postmedieval English, Georgian (New England), American Vernacular, New Traditional

high		Georgian (southern colonies), Federal, Gothic, Italianate, Second Empire, Stick, Queen Anne, Shingle, Chateauesque, Beaux Arts, Richardsonian Romanesque, American Vernacular, New Traditional
raised first floor		French Colonial, Folk Victorian, International, Contemporary, New Traditional, American Vernacular, most any style if built in flood-prone area
raised platform (podium)		International, Other 20th-Century Modern: Formalistic
slab (very low, even at ground level)		International, Ranch, Contemporary; can be found on all post-1950 house styles (common clue that a traditional styled house is New Traditional rather than a pre–World War II original)
several levels of foundation		Split-Level, Contemporary, Shed

House Shapes	IF YOU SEE	TRY THESE FIRST
broad, low one-story		Ranch, Styled Ranch, Contemporary
tri-level split		Ranch, Styled Ranch, Contemporary, Split-Level
bi-level split		Ranch, Styled Ranch, Contemporary, Split-Level
American four-square		Prairie, Colonial Revival, Neoclassical, Craftsman, Italian Renaissance
very different house—unusual geometries, sweeping curves, "never seen anything like it"		Other 20th-Century Modern (Organic), Other 20th-Century Modern (Brutalist), 21st-Century Modern (Singular Statement)

Date-related Clues	IF YOU SEE	TRY THESE FIRST
paired windows		First found in Italianate beginning around 1850. Used in this and most later styles
brick laid in running bond (all stretchers, no headers)		Began to be used commonly ca. 1915. Indicates house is brick veneer rather than solid masonry. Found on Eclectic and Modern styles, Millennium Mansion, New Traditional, American Vernacular
brick laid in stacked bond		Used after ca. 1945. Indicates masonry is used decoratively. Found on Contemporary, Ranch, some Other 20th-Century Modern
grouped windows (also called "ganged")		Common ca. 1900–1920
very low slab foundation		Indicates house built after ca. 1945
attached garage		Ranch and other styles built after ca. 1945, rarely occurs in houses before ca. 1920, size gradually increases from one-car ca. 1950 to three-car ca. 2000
carport		Contemporary and later styles, found most often in homes built ca. 1935–1975
metal windows		Steel casement first used in Tudor and other early 20th-Century styles (Modern and Traditional); aluminum windows first used in Ranch and other styles built after ca. 1950
shallow porch (4' and less)		New Traditional, Millennium Mansion, occasionally found in Ranch and other houses built after ca. 1950
wood-clad chimney		Shed, early Millennium Mansion, early New Traditional, early Contemporary built ca. 1960–1990.

Pictorial Glossary

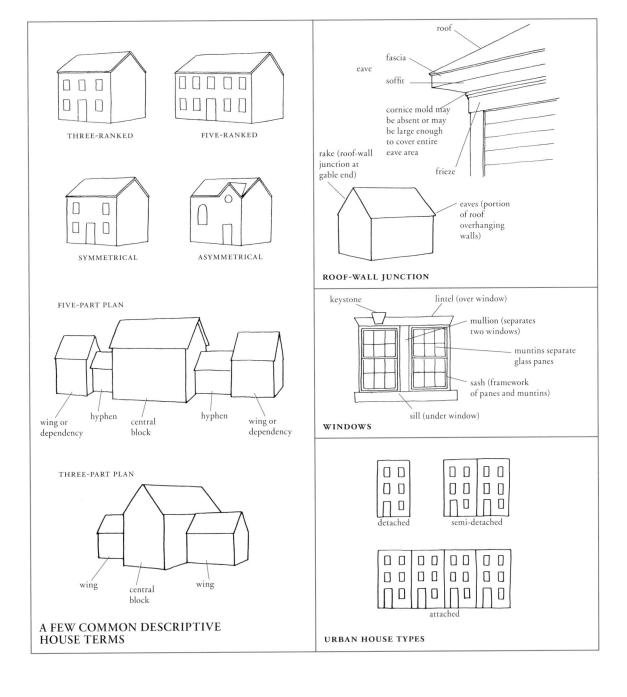

THREE-RANKED

FIVE-RANKED

SYMMETRICAL

ASYMMETRICAL

FIVE-PART PLAN

wing or dependency | hyphen | central block | hyphen | wing or dependency

THREE-PART PLAN

wing | central block | wing

A FEW COMMON DESCRIPTIVE HOUSE TERMS

roof

fascia

eave

soffit

cornice mold may be absent or may be large enough to cover entire eave area

rake (roof-wall junction at gable end)

frieze

eaves (portion of roof overhanging walls)

ROOF-WALL JUNCTION

keystone | lintel (over window)

mullion (separates two windows)

muntins separate glass panes

sash (framework of panes and muntins)

sill (under window)

WINDOWS

detached | semi-detached

attached

URBAN HOUSE TYPES

PARTS OF THE CLASSICAL ORDERS
APPLIED TO HOUSES

ANCIENT CLASSICAL MODELS & HOUSE PORCHES

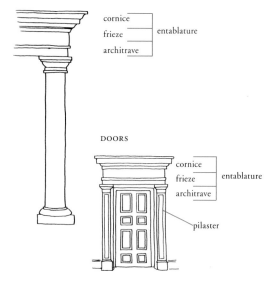

cornice
frieze
architrave
} entablature

DOORS

cornice
frieze
architrave
} entablature

pilaster

WINDOWS

cornice
frieze
architrave
} entablature

WINDOW OR DOOR

architrave trim

ROOF-WALL JUNCTIONS

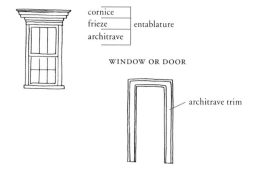

roof

fascia

cornice
frieze
architrave
} entablature

soffit

wall

**USE OF ENTABLATURES:
CORNICES, FRIEZES, & ARCHITRAVES**

FULL-FACADE PORCH

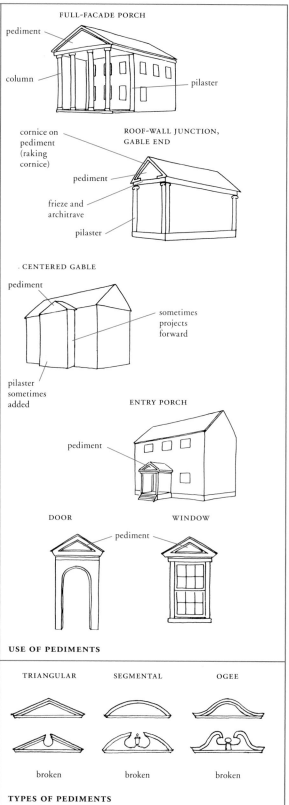

pediment

column

pilaster

ROOF-WALL JUNCTION, GABLE END

cornice on pediment (raking cornice)

pediment

frieze and architrave

pilaster

CENTERED GABLE

pediment

sometimes projects forward

pilaster sometimes added

ENTRY PORCH

pediment

DOOR   WINDOW

pediment

USE OF PEDIMENTS

TRIANGULAR	SEGMENTAL	OGEE
broken	broken	broken

TYPES OF PEDIMENTS
Ogee and segmental are only common over doors and windows

A Field Guide to American Houses

Looking at American Houses

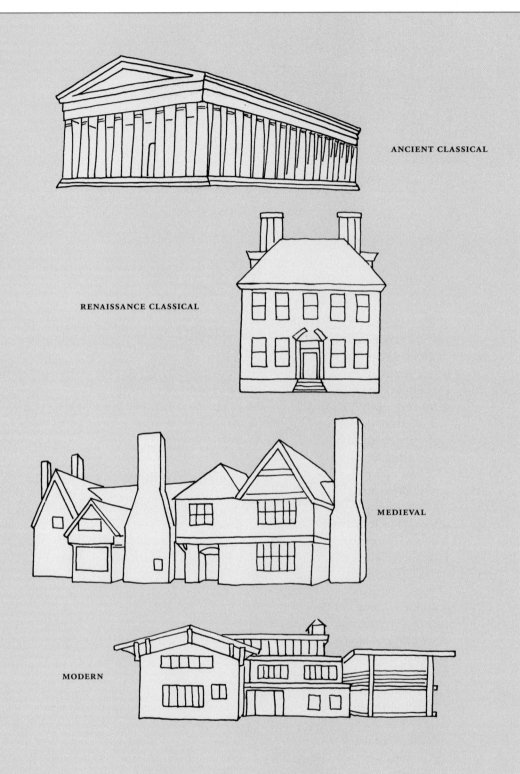

ANCIENT CLASSICAL

RENAISSANCE CLASSICAL

MEDIEVAL

MODERN

OTHER TRADITIONS MIXTURES

Style

The Fashions of American Houses

Domestic buildings are of two principal sorts: folk houses and styled houses. Folk houses are those designed without a conscious attempt to mimic current fashion. Many are built by their occupants or by non-professional builders, and all are relatively simple houses meant to provide basic shelter, with little concern for presenting a stylish face to the world. Most surviving American houses are not folk houses but are styled; that is, they were built with at least some attempt at being fashionable. As such, they show the influence of shapes, materials, detailing, or other features that make up an architectural style that was currently in vogue. The bulk of this book is organized by the changing chronology of these American architectural fashions or styles, for they provide the most effective framework for identifying and understanding American houses.

The majority of styled American houses are loosely modeled on one of four principal architectural traditions: Ancient Classical, Renaissance Classical, Medieval, or Modern. The earliest, the Ancient Classical tradition, is based upon the monuments of early Greece and Rome. The closely related Renaissance Classical tradition stems from a revival of interest in classicism during the Renaissance, which began in Italy in the 15th century. The two classical traditions, Ancient and Renaissance, share many of the same architectural details.

The third tradition, the Medieval, separated the Ancient Classical and the Renaissance Classical in time. The Medieval tradition includes architecture based on the formal Gothic style used for church buildings during the Middle Ages, as well as that based upon the simpler domestic buildings of the same era. Most of the Medieval architecture that has influenced American houses originated in England and France.

The fourth tradition, the Modern movement, began in the late 19th century and continues to the present. It is based primarily on the lack of applied historically influenced ornamentation and a resulting external simplicity or "honesty," as well as on spatial variation and manipulation made possible by new materials and construction techniques.

Other traditions that have influenced American houses are mostly of Spanish origin. Both the simple structures built during the Spanish Colonial era in the United States and the more elaborate architecture of Spain and Latin America have inspired American domestic buildings. In addition, Oriental and Egyptian models have occasionally provided patterns for American house design.

As we shall see in the following pages, each of these traditions has produced several different styles of American houses as they have been interpreted and re-interpreted during different building eras. Stylistic mixtures are also common in American domestic architecture. These have been created both by those who knowingly sought the unusual, as well as by those who unwittingly combined historical precedents.

The following short summary of styles is illustrated with houses found in the U.S. before 1935. In the seventy-five years since, a forty-year interlude (1935–1975) dominated by Modernism, both Bankers and Mainstream (pages 587–683) has been followed by almost five decades (1965–2010) during which the broadest variety of styles ever built during a half century have been constructed. Almost every style illustrated here—whether Ancient Classical, Renaissance Classical, Medieval, Modern, or Other—has been revived in one or more forms. At the same time new approaches to modernism have been explored, although by a small percentage of the population.

Ancient Classical Styles

The monumental architecture of Greece from about the 9th to the 4th century B.C., and that of Rome from the 1st century B.C. to the 5th century A.D., provide the models for those styles based upon Ancient Classical traditions. An entry or full-facade porch supported by large columns, frequently two-story, or "colossal," columns, is the feature most commonly associated with American houses patterned after Ancient Classical buildings. The columns are frequently in one of the classical orders, but simple squared and octagonal interpretations are also found. The houses usually have symmetrical facades and, most commonly, a low-pitched roof.

Three styles of American houses are based on Ancient Classical precedents. The first is the Early Classical Revival style (1780–1830). These are loosely based upon Roman models and are simple side-gabled or hipped roof houses with full-height entry porches, usually with a classical pediment above.

The next Ancient Classical style is the Greek Revival (1820–1860). Greek Revival houses normally have a very wide band of trim beneath the eaves, mimicking the entablature of Greek temples. Many have full-facade or full-height entry porches with large columns, but some have only a small entry porch and others have no porch or columns—although in this case there are usually pilasters. Both side-gabled and hipped roofs are common. In some regions, many of the houses built in this style are oriented so that the gable end becomes the front facade; these most closely resemble their prototype Greek temples.

The third Ancient Classical style is the Neoclassical (1895–1955). These are normally two-story houses with prominent full-height columns. In early examples, the columns usually have very elaborate capitals of either Roman or Greek inspiration; later examples often have slender squared columns reminiscent of those on Mount Vernon's facade facing the Potomac River. The forms of Neoclassical houses are varied, and secondary details characteristic of the later Renaissance Classical movement are often used.

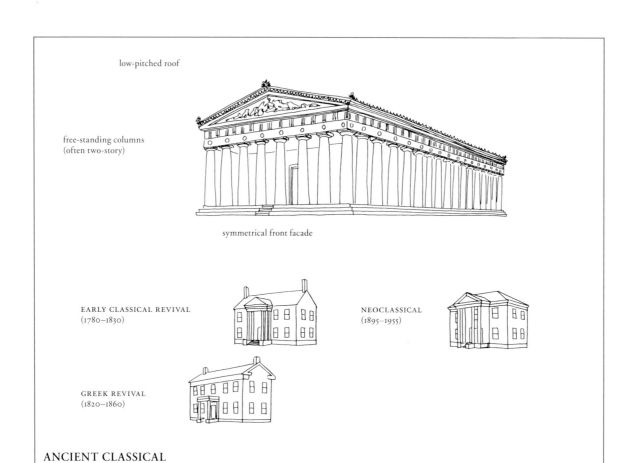

low-pitched roof

free-standing columns
(often two-story)

symmetrical front facade

EARLY CLASSICAL REVIVAL
(1780–1830)

NEOCLASSICAL
(1895–1955)

GREEK REVIVAL
(1820–1860)

ANCIENT CLASSICAL

ITALIAN
Arch emphasis

FRENCH
Roof emphasis

ENGLISH
Door emphasis

symmetrical front facade

dentils, pediments, pilasters, and quoins

ITALIAN

ITALIANATE
(1840–1885)

ITALIAN RENAISSANCE
(1890–1935)

RENAISSANCE CLASSICAL

Renaissance Classical Styles

The Renaissance Classical styles are based upon buildings built during the revival of interest in Ancient Classical models which began in Italy in the early 15th century and gradually worked its way northward to France, where it arrived in the mid-16th century, and to England, where it had little influence until the early 17th century. From England the Renaissance traveled still later to America, where it profoundly influenced 18th-century building in the English colonies. Each country developed somewhat different interpretations of Renaissance Classical ideals and each of these has inspired several later American styles. All, however, share certain features: they usually have balanced, symmetrical facades and typically have such decorative details as pedimented (crowned) doors and windows, dentils, quoins, and pilasters. Two-story columns are rare in American interpretations, although colonnaded, one-story entrance porches are frequent.

In America, the Italian version of the Renaissance tradition inspired both the Italianate (1840–1885) and Italian Renaissance (1890–1935) styles. Round arches (widely used by the early Romans) and cornice-line brackets are the two elements that most consistently mark American houses as having Italian Renaissance roots.

The French Renaissance tradition inspired the Second Empire (1855–1885) and the Beaux Arts (1885–1930) styles as well as some subtypes of the French Eclectic (1915–1945) style. A steeply pitched hipped roof, or dual-pitched mansard roof, is a characteristic feature of many of these French Renaissance-inspired houses.

The English version of the Renaissance tradition was exported to the American colonies as the Georgian (1700–1780) and Federal (1780–1820) styles. Note that these are original Renaissance buildings directly inspired by the earlier Italian Renaissance. Other American houses based on Renaissance traditions are later revivals of these same influences. These are included in the long-lived Colonial Revival style (1880–1955), which draws heavily on American Georgian and Federal precedents. All of these English-inspired Renaissance houses are united by an emphasis on elaborated front door surrounds. These frequently have side pilasters supporting an entablature or pediment (Georgian) or a fanlight above the door (Federal).

Medieval Styles

Medieval architecture is that built during the Middle Ages, the era from the end of the Ancient Classical period until the beginning of the Renaissance (roughly encompassing the 6th to the 15th centuries A.D.). Throughout most of this period, the primary focus of European, styled architecture was on ecclesiastical buildings—churches, cathedrals, and abbeys. The dominant style for these was Romanesque from the end of the 9th century until the 12th century and Gothic from the mid-12th century until the beginning of the Renaissance. The Romanesque, modified from the Roman Ancient Classical tradition, is characterized by the extensive use of rounded arches. It has inspired only one American domestic style, the Richardsonian Romanesque (1880–1900). Gothic buildings are easily identified by their characteristic pointed arches, used over doors and windows and in interior vaulting. These inspired the Gothic Revival style (1840–1880) and, in addition, influenced the Stick style (1860–ca. 1890).

Large-scale domestic architecture during most of the Middle Ages took the form of fortified castles. These have inspired relatively few American houses, although castel-

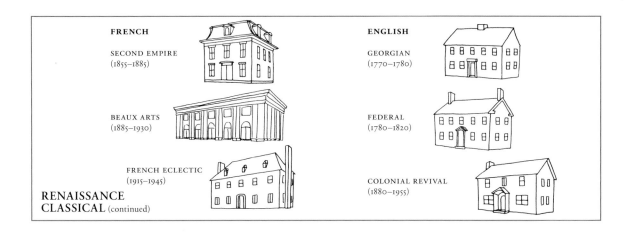

FRENCH

SECOND EMPIRE
(1855–1885)

BEAUX ARTS
(1885–1930)

FRENCH ECLECTIC
(1915–1945)

ENGLISH

GEORGIAN
(1770–1780)

FEDERAL
(1780–1820)

COLONIAL REVIVAL
(1880–1955)

RENAISSANCE
CLASSICAL (continued)

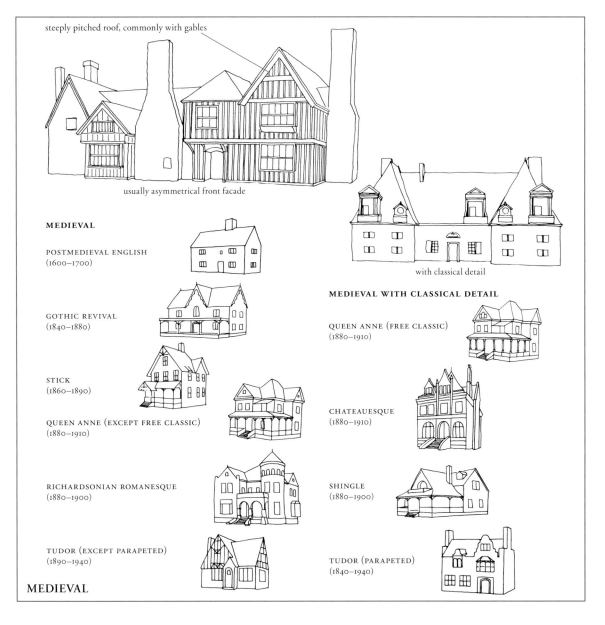

steeply pitched roof, commonly with gables

usually asymmetrical front facade

with classical detail

MEDIEVAL

POSTMEDIEVAL ENGLISH
(1600–1700)

GOTHIC REVIVAL
(1840–1880)

STICK
(1860–1890)

QUEEN ANNE (EXCEPT FREE CLASSIC)
(1880–1910)

RICHARDSONIAN ROMANESQUE
(1880–1900)

TUDOR (EXCEPT PARAPETED)
(1890–1940)

MEDIEVAL WITH CLASSICAL DETAIL

QUEEN ANNE (FREE CLASSIC)
(1880–1910)

CHATEAUESQUE
(1880–1910)

SHINGLE
(1880–1900)

TUDOR (PARAPETED)
(1840–1940)

MEDIEVAL

lated parapets are sometimes used on Gothic Revival and Tudor houses. More modest European domestic buildings from Medieval times usually had roofs covered with thatch; such roofs had to be very steeply pitched in order to shed water properly. During much of the Middle Ages, chimneys were not yet in common use; attics under the steep roofs were left open so that smoke could escape through small openings in the roof. The chimney was a crucial invention, for it allowed second stories and attics to be floored to provide additional living space. Postmedieval houses with prominent chimneys typically have steeply pitched roofs, asymmetrical facades, and, frequently, wall surfaces elaborated either by exposed half-timbered construction or by protective clay tiles hung upon such construction. They also frequently have an overhanging second story that added structural stability to the original heavy timber framing. Such houses were imported directly to the New World as the Postmedieval English style (1600–1700) built by the earliest English colonists. They also provided the inspiration for many informal examples of the later Tudor style (1890–1940).

When Renaissance influence began to spread to France and England from Italy, it first took the form of classical detailing being applied to houses of Medieval form. In France, this era produced many of the great chateaux that provided the inspiration for the American Chateauesque style (1880–1910). In England, such mixed Medieval-Renaissance buildings inspired the more formal examples of the American Tudor style, as well as some examples of the Queen Anne style.

English architects during the latter half of the 19th century, tiring of two hundred years of buildings dominated by classical influences, began to turn back to their Medieval heritage for inspiration. The result, the English Queen Anne movement, was quickly followed by the related American Queen Anne style (1880–1910), which used Medieval forms both with and without the addition of classical detailing. The Shingle style (1880–1900), which was also inspired by the English Queen Anne movement, introduced simplified exterior surfaces and open interior planning, and thus foreshadowed the Modern phase of architectural styling.

Modern Styles

The Modern movement in domestic architecture developed in two stages during the years from 1900 to 1940. The first phase, the Arts and Crafts (or Early Modern) movement, deliberately turned its back on the use of historical precedent for decoration and design. Ornamentation was not eliminated but merely "modernized" to remove most traces of its historic origins. Low-pitched roofs with wide eave overhangs were favored. Although there were many variations within the movement, it led to two distinctive styles of American houses. The first was the Prairie style (1900–1920), which began in Chicago under the leadership of Frank Lloyd Wright, who designed many houses in the style during the period from 1900 to 1913. These elegantly simplified buildings by Wright and his followers were to have a profound influence on the beginnings of Modernism both here and in Europe. The second style inspired by the Arts and Crafts movement is the Craftsman style (1905–1930), begun in southern California in about 1903 by the Greene brothers and others. It emphasizes exposed structural members and wood joinery and, like the Prairie style, eschews formal historic precedents.

A second phase of the Modern movement began after World War I as a full-scale reaction against all previous architectural tradition. The emphasis in this phase was on

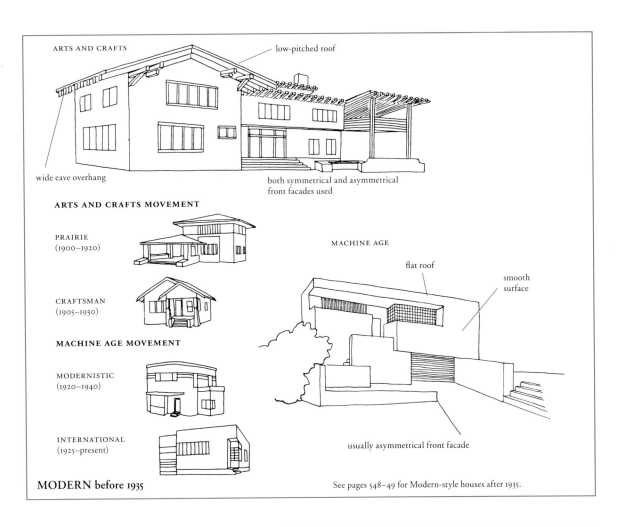

ARTS AND CRAFTS

low-pitched roof

wide eave overhang

both symmetrical and asymmetrical
front facades used

ARTS AND CRAFTS MOVEMENT

PRAIRIE
(1900–1920)

CRAFTSMAN
(1905–1930)

MACHINE AGE MOVEMENT

MODERNISTIC
(1920–1940)

INTERNATIONAL
(1925–present)

MACHINE AGE

flat roof

smooth
surface

usually asymmetrical front facade

MODERN before 1935

See pages 548–49 for Modern-style houses after 1935.

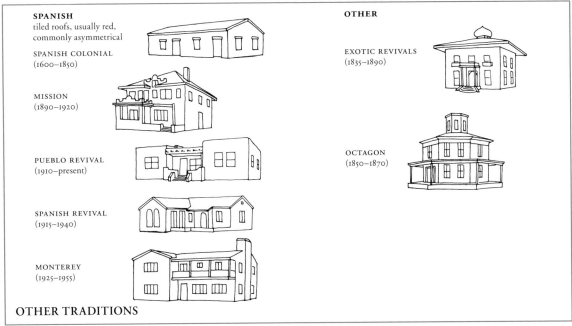

SPANISH
tiled roofs, usually red,
commonly asymmetrical

SPANISH COLONIAL
(1600–1850)

MISSION
(1890–1920)

PUEBLO REVIVAL
(1910–present)

SPANISH REVIVAL
(1915–1940)

MONTEREY
(1925–1955)

OTHER

EXOTIC REVIVALS
(1835–1890)

OCTAGON
(1850–1870)

OTHER TRADITIONS

design that was clearly of the Machine Age, with standardization of parts, absence of all non-functional decoration, and structural "honesty" as hallmarks. Houses were to become "machines for living." Flat roofs and smooth wall surfaces were favored. Both the Modernistic style (1920–1940) and the International style (1925–present) are products of this more austere modernism that marked the beginning of Mainstream Modern.

The Mainstream Modern movement continued to evolve in the decades following 1940 as new stylistic outgrowths of the Arts and Crafts and the Machine Age movements arose. It was joined by a third phase, Banker's Modern, after 1935 in response to FHA's lending preferences (see page 587). These were to dominate American domestic building during the 1950s and 1960s before beginning to be largely replaced, in the 1970s, by a return to stylistic adaptations loosely based on Classical or Medieval prototypes. Today, Modern movement houses are still being built but constitute a relatively small portion of new home construction.

Other Stylistic Traditions

Many of the other traditions that have influenced American domestic architecture are of Spanish or Spanish Colonial origin. In the New World, Spanish colonists blended the adobe building traditions of the Native Americans with similar Spanish housing traditions originally brought to Spain from North Africa. Both the Spanish Colonial style (1600–1850) and the Pueblo Revival style (1910–present) use adobe construction techniques which show this mixing of Spanish and Native American precedents. Spanish Colonial ecclesiastical buildings of the American Southwest provided the inspiration for the Mission style (1890–1920). This was followed by the Spanish Revival style (1915–1940), which broadened the precedents to include the entire spectrum of Spanish and Spanish-American architecture, thus making it an unusually varied style. Some Spanish Revival houses have elaborate decorative detailing patterned after formal Spanish Renaissance buildings. Others show Moorish and Islamic influences, while still others are based upon rural Spanish folk houses with little or no decorative detailing. The most recent style in the Spanish tradition is the Monterey style (1925–1955), which is loosely based on certain houses of the American Southwest that show a mixing of Spanish and English Colonial influences.

Other architectural traditions have influenced several minor styles of American houses. Oriental, Egyptian, and Swiss Chalet prototypes inspired the Exotic Revivals (1835–ca. 1890), while the Octagon style (1850–1870) developed from one man's enthusiastic sponsorship of houses designed with unorthodox ground plans of octagonal shape.

Stylistic Mixtures

Most American houses have been built in one of the many architectural styles outlined in the preceding sections. Some, however, do not fit neatly into one of these stylistic categories but, instead, have characteristics of two or more styles. Such houses may have been originally built as stylistic mixtures or may have resulted from later attempts to alter the style through remodeling.

Prior to about 1840, American architectural styles were rather widely separated by time or by location; that is, only one fashion usually prevailed in a region over a long interval of time. Most early stylistic mixtures occurred during the transitional peri-

MIXTURES: ROMANTIC AND VICTORIAN

1. Cleveland, Ohio; mid-19th century. Otis House. A mixture of Gothic and Italianate design. The shape of the house with its low-pitched hipped roof, symmetrical facade, and centered gable is Italianate, as is the bracketed cornice. The pointed arches over upper-story windows and the flattened arches of the front porch and lower-story windows are Gothic.

2. Canton, Mississippi; mid-19th century. A mixture of Greek Revival, Gothic, and Italianate influences. The doors and porch with classical columns are borrowed from Greek Revival. The bracketed cornice is Italianate, and the flattened arch and jigsaw-cut wood detailing of the upstairs porch show Gothic Revival influences.

3. New Albany, Indiana; 1866. McCord House. This mixture of Gothic and Italianate design is a reversal of Figure 1. The house form with its gabled roof and steeply pitched, front-facing gables shows Gothic influence. The bracketed cornice and the windows with heavy rounded crowns are Italianate.

4. Rolla, Missouri; late 19th century. Romanesque and Shingle elements combined with square Prairie-style porch supports.

5. Richmond, Virginia; late 19th century. A mixture of Queen Anne (patterned masonry subtype), Romanesque, and Exotic influences.

1

3

2

5

4

ods when these persistent fashions were changing. Thus, some transitional houses in the English colonies share Georgian and Federal features, while others blend Federal with Greek Revival detailing. Similarly, Dutch, French, and Spanish Colonial buildings began to show Federal or Greek Revival detailing as Anglo influence increased with the expansion of the country. These originally built combinations of styles increased after about 1840 when pattern books, particularly A. J. Downing's influential *Cottage Residences, Rural Architecture and Landscape Gardening,* published in 1842, presented several choices of fashionable building styles. Downing, for example, advocated both Gothic and Italianate modes of design. As might be expected, some readers and builders avoided the choice by combining features of both. Another popular mixture of the romantic era added Italianate detailing to the previously dominant Greek Revival form.

Houses of the Victorian era seldom show such dramatically obvious mixtures of style. Most Victorian styles are closely interrelated and draw heavily on Medieval precedents for inspiration. Thus they naturally tend to blend into one another. Steeply pitched roofs and textured wall surfaces are common to most. Stick-style structural members are found on many Queen Anne houses; Richardsonian arches occur on Shingle-style houses, wood-shingled walls may dominate on either Queen Anne or Shingle houses, and so on. Thus the separation of the Victorian styles sometimes becomes a matter of degree, whereas the dominant Greek-Gothic-Italianate modes of the preceding romantic era were unmistakably different.

During the early years of the Eclectic era, experimental combinations of styles were common. From about 1890 to 1915, styles as different as the Colonial Revival, Neoclassical, Prairie, Tudor, Mission, and Craftsman were being built simultaneously. Many architects and builders experimented with fanciful combinations of these styles, sometimes adding a touch of Victorian detailing as well. Some early eclectic neighborhoods contain whole streets of such marvelously experimental stylistic combinations. These innovative houses were, however, far less common than more correct stylistic interpretations, even in the early eclectic years, and by 1915 they had all but disappeared. Thus began the era of the Period House, an interval in which stylistic combinations became rare. This lasted until the late 1930s, when architects and builders began to experiment with restrained mixtures of Tudor, Colonial Revival, and Mediterranean influences.

A second and far more common category of stylistic mixture results not from original design, but from later alteration of an existing house. Most houses more than a few years old have had at least some exterior alterations, and it is important to be able to recognize these changes in order to identify a house's original style and appearance.

Most exterior alterations are undertaken for one or more of the following purposes:

- To update the appearance of the house (stylish updates)
- To add additional living space to the house
- To minimize exterior maintenance of the house
- To take advantage of code exemptions[1]

Each of these changes tends to produce somewhat different exterior appearances.

The most common means of updating the appearance or style of a house is to add, remove, or alter a porch. The most frequent porch alteration, because it is the simplest, is to replace the original porch roof supports. For example, many a Queen Anne house had its spindlework supports replaced by heavy masonry piers during the early years of

MIXTURES: ECLECTIC

1. Emporia, Kansas; early 20th century. A mixture showing a Prairie-influenced wide roof-overhang combined with a Shingle-style front gambrel and a rusticated stone arch borrowed from the Richardsonian Romanesque.

2. Dallas, Texas; 1928. Wade House. Here a Tudor front-facing gable with half-timbering is mixed with Italian Renaissance roof tiles and arched windows.

3. Cleveland, Ohio; 1910. Mather House; Charles Schweinfurth, architect. A mixture of Tudor (windows, lintels, and chimneys) and Colonial Revival details (cornice-line balustrade, low-pitched hipped roof).

4. Louisville, Kentucky; 1922. This example combines the side-gabled Craftsman form with Italian Renaissance tiled roofing and arched entries.

5. Louisville, Kentucky; early 20th century. This house combines elements of several stylistic traditions (Prairie, Craftsman, and Germanic).

this century when the Prairie style was in vogue. The massive piers of Prairie and Craftsman houses, in turn, have often been replaced by narrow wooden or metal posts which dramatically alter the appearance of the house. Entire new porches are also commonly added to houses that originally had none, or as replacements for porches of quite different character. Many Queen Anne houses, for example, now sport elaborate Neoclassical porches added in the early 1900s. Equally startling are those houses which have had the original porches removed without replacement.

Following porches, the most commonly altered facade elements are doors, windows, and wall materials, changed in an attempt to mimic current fashion. Most of these updating changes in facade details, including porches, are easily recognized with a little practice, for the new additions appear out of context with the overall shape, form, and materials of the remainder of the house.

Still more fundamental changes occur when a smaller earlier house is incorporated into a larger later house of a different style. All housewatchers have had the experience of visiting, for example, an Italianate museum house that the guide insists was built in 1798. Upon close questioning it transpires that a log house was built on the site in 1798 and that in 1855 the original owner's granddaughter's husband came into some money, leading to a remodeling (we would say "rebuilding"). For purposes of identification, such houses can be considered to have been built in 1855; the fact that an earlier house is buried within is of historical significance but does not affect the exterior appearance. When the rebuilding is less complete, however, traces of the earlier house may be revealed by a careful look at roof, walls, and—especially—the roof-wall junctions, which quite often provide the best clues to large-scale stylistic updating.

The second principal reason for exterior alteration is to add living space to an existing house. This is usually accomplished in one of two ways: either by adding an entire extension or wing to the existing house or, at less expense, by converting a house's underutilized areas (attic, basement, porch, or garage) into living space. In the first instance, extensive additions can be undertaken in the style of the original house and, depending on the skill of the architect involved, leave the original lines of the house undiminished or, occasionally, enhanced. Lyndhurst in Tarrytown, New York, is an outstanding example of this (page 278). Carefully done additions and alterations that use the same materials and style as the existing house can be very difficult to detect. More commonly, additions differ in some fundamental way—form, materials, or details—from the original house and are easily recognized.

Converting existing spaces to living areas does not usually affect the exterior appearance of the house when it involves only a basement or attached garage (although the method of handling the garage door opening is important). An attic remodeling usually involves the addition of dormers or skylights but otherwise leaves the facade intact. The decision to gain space by enclosing all or part of a front or side porch, on the other hand, can drastically change the character of a house. Rarely can such alterations be done in a manner which maintains the stylistic integrity of the facade.

The third principal reason for altering house exteriors is to minimize maintenance. The need regularly to paint wooden walls, caulk drafty windows, and repair leaky roofs can cause a house owner to make drastic changes that are designed to decrease this routine maintenance. Some of these maintenance-minimizing alterations even promise to do away with these problems "forever." Owners tired of painting wooden walls frequently add a layer of pre-finished siding (aluminum, asbestos, etc.). In addition to

ALTERATIONS: STYLISH UPDATES

1. Cooperstown, New York; 1804 (roof, late 19th century). Lakeland; John M. Bowers. A Federal house with a Victorian roof added (the porch is likely an intermediate addition). Cover the roof to see the symmetrical house; uncover it to see how completely the roof form changes the feel of the house.

2. Granbury, Texas; late 19th century (porch, early 20th century). A Queen Anne house (note hipped roof with cross gable and tower) behind an added Neoclassical porch. This was a common update.

3. Cooperstown, New York; mid-19th century (addition, late 19th century). Holt House. A Second Empire house (on the right) has had a major half-timbered Queen Anne addition to the left.

4. Dallas, Texas; 1914. Arrington House. A relatively unaltered Prairie-style example. Both Figures 5 and 6 below originally resembled this house, although without the porte cochere to the side.

5. Dallas, Texas; early 20th century (remodeling ca. 1975). This remodeling of a house similar to Figure 4 removed the porch and added a small broken pediment to the door, which is poorly scaled and out of character with the form and roof of the house.

6. Dallas, Texas; early 20th century (remodeling 1982; Teddy Taylor, designer). This remodeling of a house similar to Figure 4, although obscuring the earlier Prairie character, picks up on the Mediterranean tiled roof by adding a Palladian entry motif. The changed brick pattern shows the line of the original porch roof. When painted, the brickwork will appear uniform and only very careful observation would reveal the modifications.

1

2

3

4

5

6

1

4

5

8

ALTERATIONS: MAINTENANCE

St. Genevieve, Missouri; ca. 1920. In a development of several dozen almost identical Craftsman houses built in the 1920s, only the example shown in Figure 1 remains essentially unaltered. The photographs show a series of modifications typical of those that obscure the original stylistic details of many older American houses. 1. In the unaltered example, note the wood shingles in the gable, narrow bands of wood siding, triangular knee braces at the cornice, original porch supports, and original window surrounds, sash, and vertical light pattern. 2. This example is original except for the addition of asbestos shingles covering the wood shingles and siding. 3. Another type of added siding, this time with metal awnings. 4. In addition to new siding and awnings, the original wood porch supports and railing have been replaced by iron, the triangular knee braces sheathed, and shutters added. 5. These alterations are similar to those in Figure 4, but without the shutters and awnings. 6. Here the windows have been changed, two types of siding added, the triangular knee braces removed, the porch supports changed, and a rear side porch added. 7. In this example, siding has been added and the front porch screened. 8. The entire porch area has been enclosed and a new window shape and two types of siding added. 9. Here most of the front porch has been enclosed for additional interior space, the triple window on the right has been reduced to one, and siding has been added.

2

3

7

6

9

hiding the texture of the original walls, such siding usually obscures such details as window and door surrounds, cornices, and moldings and thus quite dramatically changes a house's appearance. It also may hasten the deterioration of the wooden walls it covers; fortunately it can often be removed without serious damage. For those tired of caulking, patching, and painting older wooden windows, replacing them with pre-finished metal windows can be tempting. Such changes generally alter the house's appearance significantly. Original slate, tile, tin, or wood-shingle roofs are commonly replaced with composition roofing materials. Sometimes these materials closely resemble the original roof but more often, like changes of wall materials or windows, they fundamentally alter the nature of the facade.

Most maintenance-minimizing alterations do not completely obscure a house's stylistic origins but are apparent as inappropriate changes in external appearance through the loss of wood molding profiles and the pattern of window lights. If the changes are extensive, however—for example, siding added and windows and roofs replaced—the original character of the house may be undiscernible.

The fourth principal reason for major house alterations is to take advantage of the original house's exemptions from new and more strict building codes. In some cases, maintaining the footprint of an existing structure allows exemptions from stringent new construction standards. Among these are wetlands regulations along the East Coast, earthquake standards along the West Coast, and more stringent lot coverage or setback requirements added with changes in zoning codes. Any of these can cause a house to be radically redesigned—even creating a new house for all practical purposes.

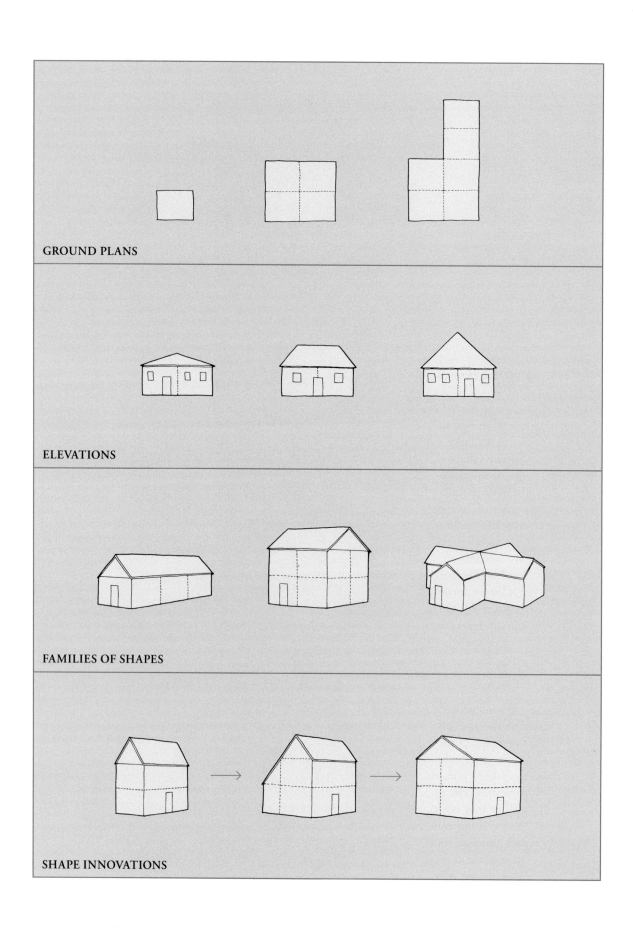

GROUND PLANS

ELEVATIONS

FAMILIES OF SHAPES

SHAPE INNOVATIONS

Form

The Shapes of American Houses

The chronology of changing architectural fashions or styles provides the fundamental framework for identifying American houses. A second basic feature of houses is form or shape. House form is not endlessly varied. Instead, a few fundamental shapes, and relatively minor variations on them, tend to be used again and again through a range of changing architectural styles.

House shape is best analyzed by dividing the three-dimensional house into two separate two-dimensional components. The first is the ground plan, the pattern made by the exterior walls when viewed from directly above. The second two-dimensional component is elevation, the pattern made by wall, roof, and details when viewed, as they normally are, from ground level. In theory, ground plans and elevations can be varied to form an infinite number of house shapes. In practice, there are only a relatively few common variants of both plan and elevation. These combine to make several fundamental families of house shapes that dominate American domestic architecture.

Certain uncomplicated house shapes have been continuously used since the first colonists arrived. On the other hand, technological changes over the past three hundred years have permitted greater flexibility and freedom of design and have led to important innovations in house shape.

Ground Plans

A ground plan shows the shape of a house as if one were viewing it from directly above with the roof and the upper floors (if any) removed to leave only the ground-floor walls. The shape of the ground plan can usually be broken down into a pattern of smaller, room-sized modules or structural units. The simplest folk houses have only a single such room-sized unit. As larger houses were required, folk builders developed techniques for combining two or more units into multi-unit plans. These room-sized structural units may or may not correspond exactly to the placement of interior walls to form actual rooms. In general, the earlier and more modest the house, the more likely it is that each principal room will correspond to a structural unit (although even in the simplest houses, one or more units are commonly partitioned into smaller rooms). Since in this book we are concerned with the external appearance of houses, these differences in internal room arrangement can be discounted. The important point is that ground plans are almost always made up of rather simple combinations of room-sized units. The basic house sizes and shapes defined by these combinations have persisted in all but the largest and most pretentious houses from early colonial times to the present day.

In the simplest case, square or rectangular room-sized units are combined into larger squares or rectangles known as simple plans. These are of two principal types: (1) linear plans, made up of units aligned into single rows one unit wide or deep, and (2) massed plans, which have both a width and depth of more than one unit. The rectangles and squares of simple plans can, in turn, be combined to make compound plans, the most frequent of which resemble in shape the letters L, T, or U. Many other compound arrangements are also possible; some of the most frequent are shown in the illustrations. Note that simple plans with minor wall projections may resemble compound plans but can usually be distinguished by whether or not the projections from the principal mass of the house are room-sized or smaller. Such minor wall projections were impractical with heavy timber construction, but became relatively simple and inexpensive with later balloon and platform framing. Starting about 1990 even greater use was made of compound plans and also more complex roof forms, such as hip-on-hip, which created additional shallow wall projections. See illustration page 33.

Elevations

Elevations show the shapes of houses as viewed normally from the ground at eye level. Elevations are generally straight-on views that show the appearance of a single wall with its overlying roof and architectural details. Four such elevation views—one each of the front, the sides, and the rear walls—are required to describe fully all details of shape. On the other hand, the general form of a house can sometimes be understood from just the

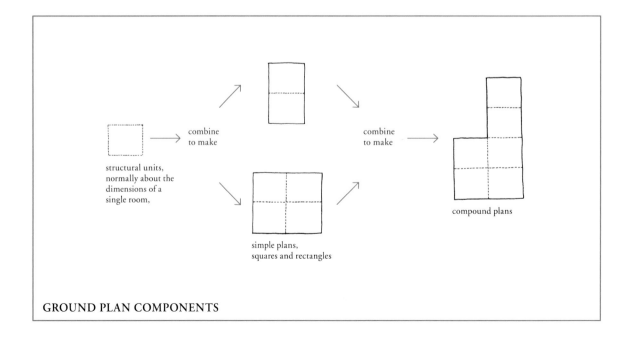

combine
to make

combine
to make

structural units,
normally about the
dimensions of a
single room,

simple plans,
squares and rectangles

compound plans

GROUND PLAN COMPONENTS

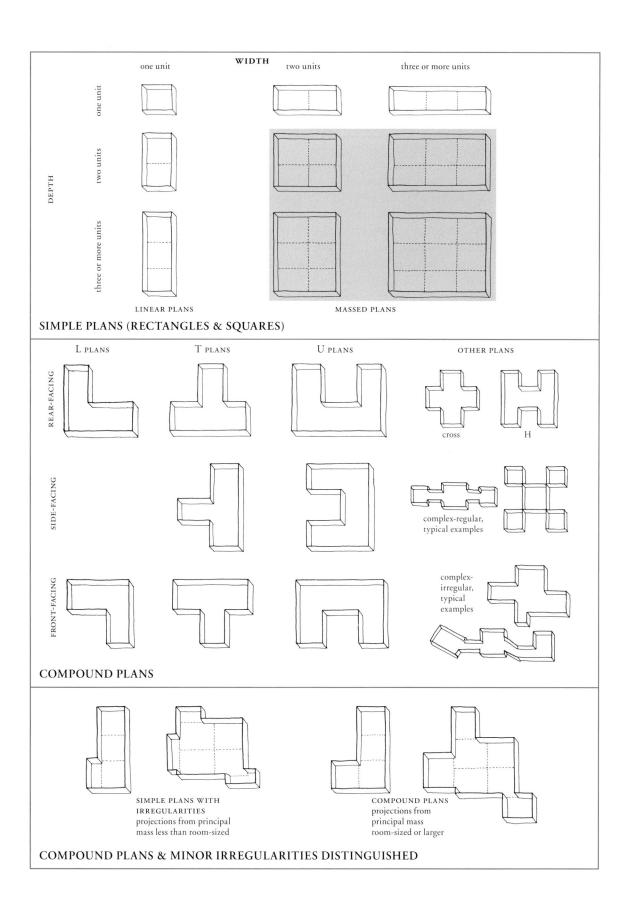

WIDTH

one unit · two units · three or more units

DEPTH

one unit

two units

three or more units

LINEAR PLANS

MASSED PLANS

SIMPLE PLANS (RECTANGLES & SQUARES)

L PLANS · T PLANS · U PLANS · OTHER PLANS

REAR-FACING

cross · H

SIDE-FACING

complex-regular,
typical examples

FRONT-FACING

complex-
irregular,
typical
examples

COMPOUND PLANS

SIMPLE PLANS WITH
IRREGULARITIES
projections from principal
mass less than room-sized

COMPOUND PLANS
projections from
principal mass
room-sized or larger

COMPOUND PLANS & MINOR IRREGULARITIES DISTINGUISHED

front elevation (also called the principal elevation or facade) and the ground plan which, together, define the basic three-dimensional shape of the house.

The most fundamental factor in analyzing elevations is wall height. American houses are normally either one or two stories high. Less common are heights of one and one-half, two and one-half, and three stories (a half-story has less than full-height external walls; the remaining headroom is developed from attic space beneath the roof line). Houses more than three stories high are rare except in densely populated urban settings where narrow town houses sometimes have four or more stories.

Most simple-plan houses have facades either one, two, or three structural units in width. Each width normally has a characteristic pattern of symmetry in the arrangement of door and window details. These patterns frequently allow identification of the width of the underlying ground plan. Two asymmetrical ranks of window and door openings normally occur on one-unit widths; three symmetrical or four asymmetrical ranks on two-unit widths; and five symmetrical ranks on three-unit widths. In symmetrical three-ranked facades the two principal front rooms behind the facade are normally of unequal size, the entrance door opening into the larger of the two. Less commonly the door opens into a narrow entrance hallway or vestibule. The middle unit of three-unit widths is normally a central hallway and may also be somewhat narrower than the two flanking units. The presence of five, rather than three, ranks of window openings normally distinguishes this plan from symmetrical two-unit plans. In urban houses, a one-and-one-half-unit width is typical, with a hallway occupying the half unit and the principal rooms lined up in the full unit.

Elevations reveal not only wall height, width, and symmetry, but also the varying relative proportions of roof and wall. If the roof is flat or of low pitch, the wall will dominate the facade. Conversely, steeply pitched roofs dramatically dominate their underlying walls. Roofs of normal pitch show about equal dominance of roof and wall.

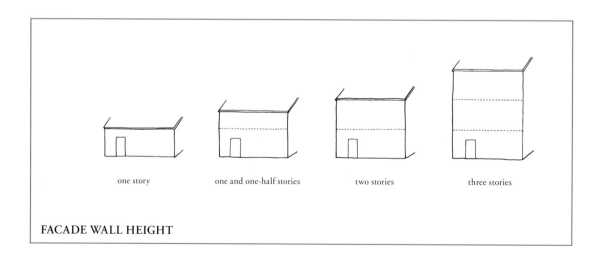

one story   one and one-half stories   two stories   three stories

FACADE WALL HEIGHT

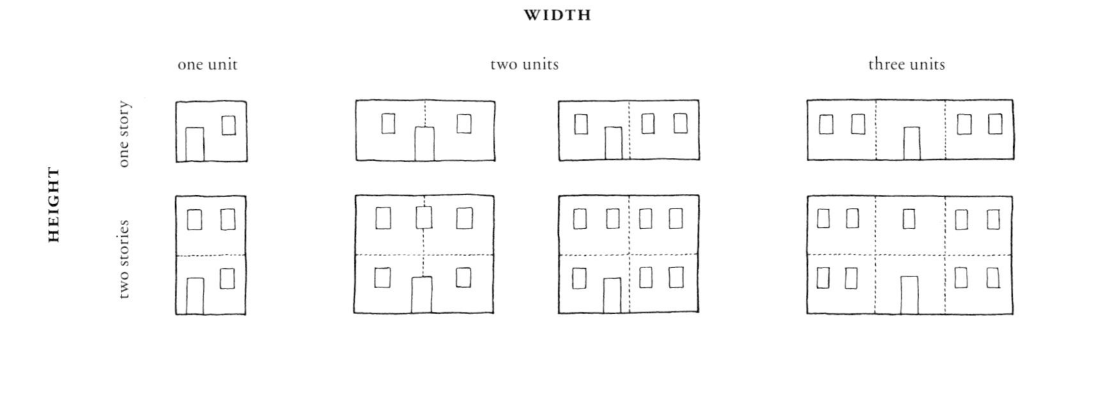

WIDTH

HEIGHT

one unit | two units | three units

one story

two stories

FACADE WIDTH & SYMMETRY

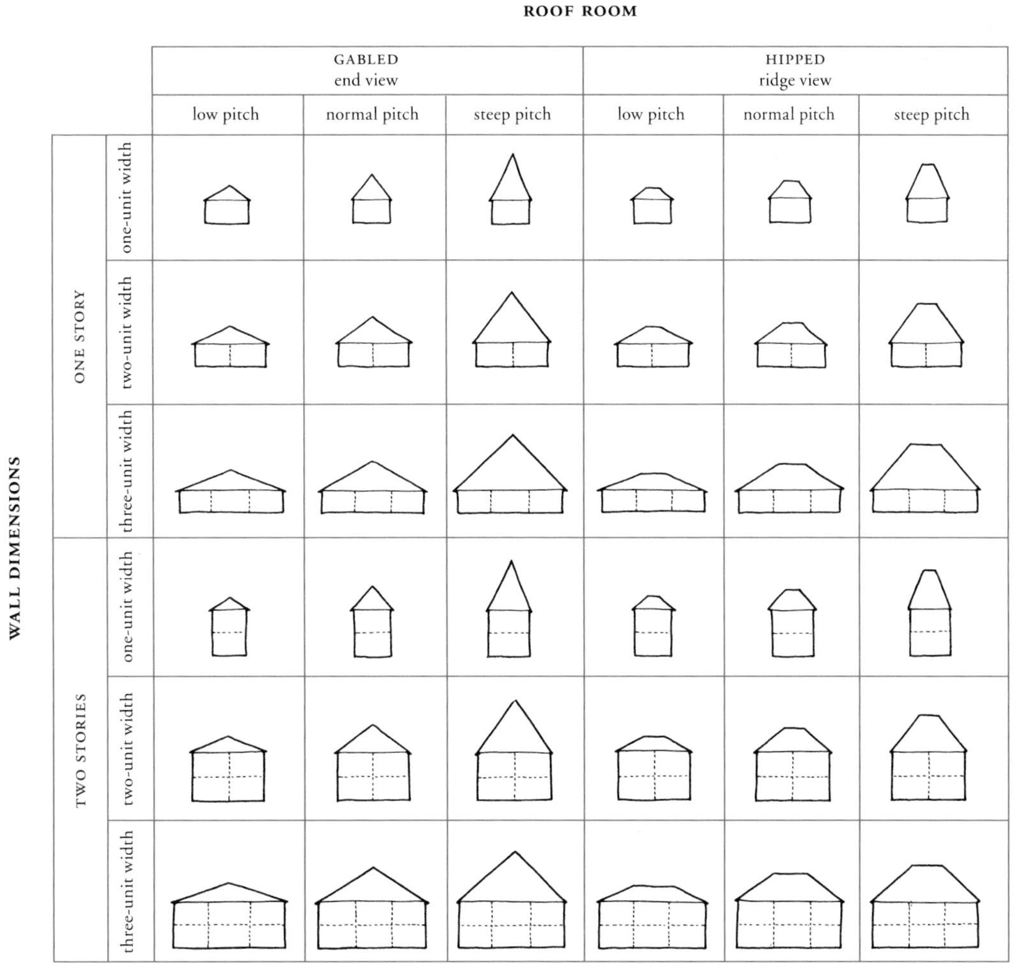

ROOF ROOM

		GABLED end view			HIPPED ridge view		
		low pitch	normal pitch	steep pitch	low pitch	normal pitch	steep pitch

WALL DIMENSIONS

ONE STORY — one-unit width, two-unit width, three-unit width

TWO STORIES — one-unit width, two-unit width, three-unit width

ROOF-WALL PROPORTIONS

Families of Shapes

Ground plan and elevation combine to make several persistent and recurring patterns or families of shapes that are characteristic of most American houses. Much of the history of American domestic architecture involves the varying patterns of details—roofs, doors, windows, chimneys, porches, and decoration—applied to these relatively few basic shapes. Note that several simple-plan families have such distinctive shapes that they have familiar names (saltbox, shotgun, town house, etc.). Others have less common names (I-house, massed side-gable, etc.) but all are easily recognized with a little practice. The principal compound-plan families are also easily recognized, but they show more variation in details of shape. Wings of varying ground plan and elevation can be combined to form many variants of the basic L, T, and U plans.

Most of the fundamental styles of American houses display several of these shape patterns. In a few styles, however, a single family tends to dominate. Thus, Georgian houses are principally box-house or saltbox shapes, Federal mostly box-house, the Prairie often four-square, and so on. In many styles, shape families provide useful criteria for defining one or more of the principal subtypes within the style. The distinctive town-house shape, in particular, makes up a characteristic urban subtype in several styles.

The principal use of shape families in house identification applies not to styled houses but to folk houses. Such houses generally lack the architectural detailing that characterizes and differentiates styled buildings. In these, shape becomes a principal criterion for distinguishing types.

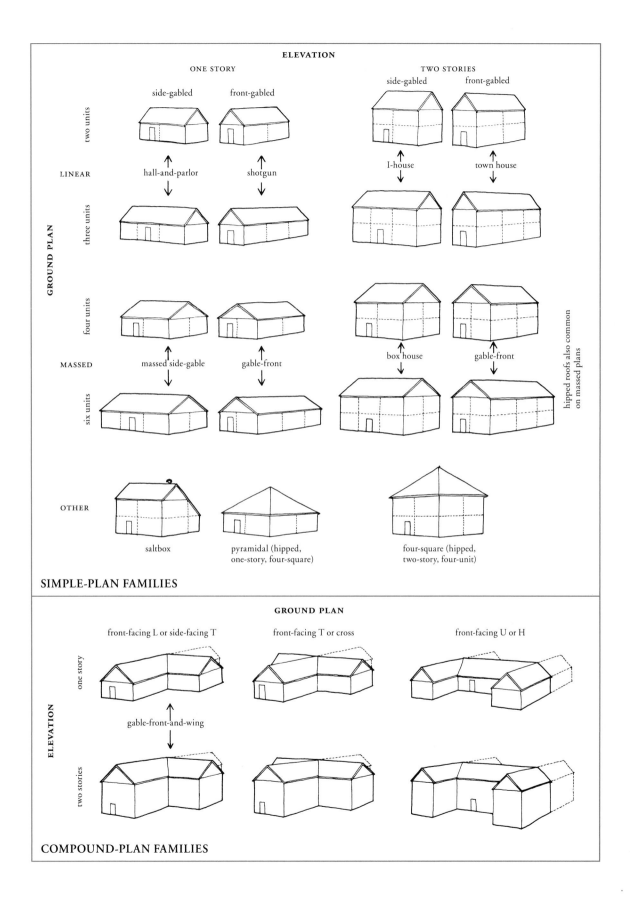

ELEVATION

ONE STORY   TWO STORIES

side-gabled   front-gabled   side-gabled   front-gabled

GROUND PLAN

two units

LINEAR   hall-and-parlor   shotgun   I-house   town house

three units

four units

MASSED   massed side-gable   gable-front   box house   gable-front

six units

hipped roofs also common on massed plans

OTHER

saltbox   pyramidal (hipped, one-story, four-square)   four-square (hipped, two-story, four-unit)

SIMPLE-PLAN FAMILIES

GROUND PLAN

front-facing L or side-facing T   front-facing T or cross   front-facing U or H

ELEVATION

one story

gable-front-and-wing

two stories

COMPOUND-PLAN FAMILIES

Shape Innovations

Several important technological advances have influenced the shapes of American houses over the three and a half centuries that have passed since the earliest European colonization.

MASSED PLANS—The first advance was the introduction of massed plans into the English colonies during the 18th century. All but a rare handful of 17th-century English colonial houses were of linear plan (one room deep) with high, steeply pitched roofs. These traditional roofs were of ancient origin and were designed to be covered with thatch, which sheds water only if the surface to which it is applied slopes very steeply. Such steep roofs became impossibly high when applied to large massed plans; as a result, most modest English dwellings were of linear plan. The rigors of the New World climate soon led to the abandonment of thatch as a roof covering in favor of more durable wooden planks or shingles. At the same time, the long severe winters of the northern colonies made additional interior space desirable. During the period from about 1700 to 1750, many houses were built, or were expanded, to a one-and-one-half-unit depth. The roofs on these, although now usually shingled, retained the steep framing of Medieval origin. The increased depth was accommodated either by a lower-pitched shed roof over the half-unit extension (most common in one-story houses) or by a rearward continuation of the main roof slope to give a saltbox shape (most common in two-story houses). This shape limited the rearward extension to the relatively shallow depth covered by the downward projection of the steeply pitched roof line. It also truncated the rearward extension at the second-floor level, which could be used only for storage rather than as living space. These disadvantages were overcome through the development of lower-pitched roof framing, which could span a full two-unit depth without excessive height. This transition was virtually completed by 1750; since that time, massed-plan houses have been a dominant feature of American architecture. Note, however, that linear plans, descended from the earlier tradition, have also persisted, particularly in rural and folk building.

HEATING—Two separate technological innovations during the 19th century had profound effects on house shape. The first relates to improvements in heating. Massive fireplaces for burning wood or coal were the principal heating devices until the 1830s, when the first practical cast-iron stoves were introduced. These were vented to the exterior either through metal stovepipes or through small masonry flues. Both of these were far easier to install than massive fireplaces and thus permitted the wider use of larger—and less regular—house plans. Compound plans, in particular, now became more common. Still further improvement came with the introduction of central furnaces that burned wood or coal. These came into common use in the colder northern sections of the country after about 1880. In this system, heat is transferred from the furnace to individual rooms by means of heated water, steam, or air; only a single masonry flue is required to serve the furnace. This development further accelerated the trend toward compound and irregular plans. Yet with each of these heating innovations, the earlier systems were not completely abandoned. Many 19th- and 20th-century houses retain one or more fireplaces, along with stoves or coal-burning furnaces, as a sort of nostalgic interior ornament without essential function. In addition, stoves (now most commonly burning

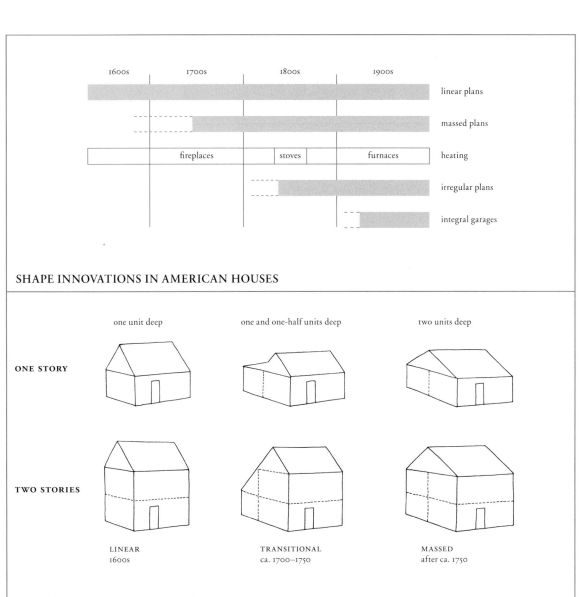

SHAPE INNOVATIONS IN AMERICAN HOUSES

one unit deep   one and one-half units deep   two units deep

ONE STORY

TWO STORIES

LINEAR
1600s

TRANSITIONAL
ca. 1700–1750

MASSED
after ca. 1750

LINEAR TO MASSED PLANS 18th century

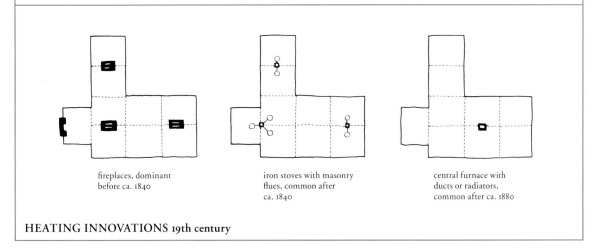

fireplaces, dominant
before ca. 1840

iron stoves with masonry
flues, common after
ca. 1840

central furnace with
ducts or radiators,
common after ca. 1880

HEATING INNOVATIONS 19th century

natural gas rather than wood or coal) and fireplaces have continuously remained the principal means of heating many modest houses, particularly in the milder southern part of the country.

IRREGULAR PLANS—A second 19th-century innovation affecting house shape was balloon-frame construction (see pages 38–40). This relatively rapid and inexpensive method of wooden framing was developed in the Chicago area during the 1830s. In earlier wooden framing systems (post-and-girt; braced-frame), as well as in solid masonry construction, outside corners are particularly difficult to fashion. Masonry is especially susceptible to erosion and failure at corner junctions and usually requires carefully shaped stones—or strengthened brick-bonding patterns—to make secure and permanent corners. Similarly, the heavy timbers of post-and-girt or braced frames require complex, hand-hewn corner joints and braces to give them rigidity. For these reasons, unnecessary outside corners were traditionally avoided in all but the most pretentious houses built with these wall systems. In contrast, corners in balloon (and, later, platform) framing are readily constructed with only a few two-inch boards and wire nails. Balloon framing thus freed house shapes from their traditional plane-walled patterns by allowing for easily constructed irregular plans with many extensions and re-entrants. Since the mid-19th century, such irregular wall forms have been commonly superimposed upon both simple and compound plans as balloon framing became the standard construction technique. Beginning in the late 1980s a new fashion for complex roof forms in some house styles was often accompanied by small extensions added to already irregular ground plans. An added squared bay, for example, could have a small secondary roof above it (also see illustration on page 709).

INTEGRAL GARAGES—One other technological innovation that affected house shape relates not to building techniques but to transportation: the rise of the automobile as the principal means of personal travel in the 20th century. When automobiles first became common in the decade between 1910 and 1920 they were universally housed, as had been carriages and horses before, in detached garages. Such garages have persisted to the present day, but since the 1920s there has been an accelerating trend to house automobiles in extensions to, or within portions of, the main house. This trend has dramatically affected the overall size and shape of some houses constructed between 1920 and 1950, and of almost all constructed since 1950. The illustration shows graphically the changing average amount of space devoted to automobile storage during the period from 1930 to 1960 (in comparison with a standard six-unit plan of 1,000-square-foot area). Whether placed within the principal mass of the house, as shown, or added as attached units, these automobile shelters have affected the style and form of many 20th-century house facades. By the turn of the millennium three- and four-car garages were not uncommon and automobile access and storage had become an important factor in new home design and subdivision planning. See illustration page 33. A three-car garage built in 2010 can be 750 square feet, a space three-quarters as large as many homes built in 1950.

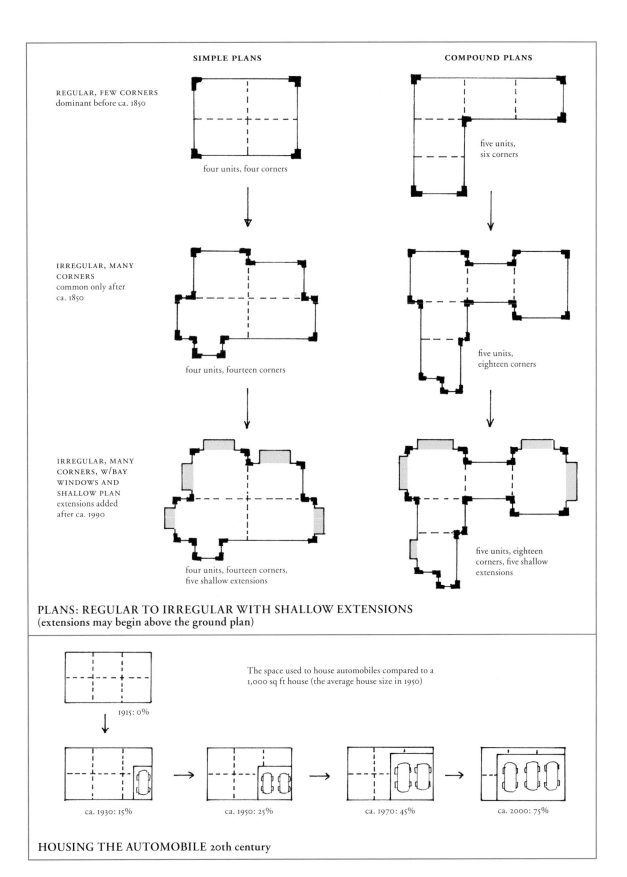

SIMPLE PLANS

COMPOUND PLANS

REGULAR, FEW CORNERS
dominant before ca. 1850

four units, four corners

five units,
six corners

IRREGULAR, MANY
CORNERS
common only after
ca. 1850

four units, fourteen corners

five units,
eighteen corners

IRREGULAR, MANY
CORNERS, W/BAY
WINDOWS AND
SHALLOW PLAN
extensions added
after ca. 1990

four units, fourteen corners,
five shallow extensions

five units, eighteen
corners, five shallow
extensions

PLANS: REGULAR TO IRREGULAR WITH SHALLOW EXTENSIONS
(extensions may begin above the ground plan)

The space used to house automobiles compared to a
1,000 sq ft house (the average house size in 1950)

1915: 0%

ca. 1930: 15%

ca. 1950: 25%

ca. 1970: 45%

ca. 2000: 75%

HOUSING THE AUTOMOBILE 20th century

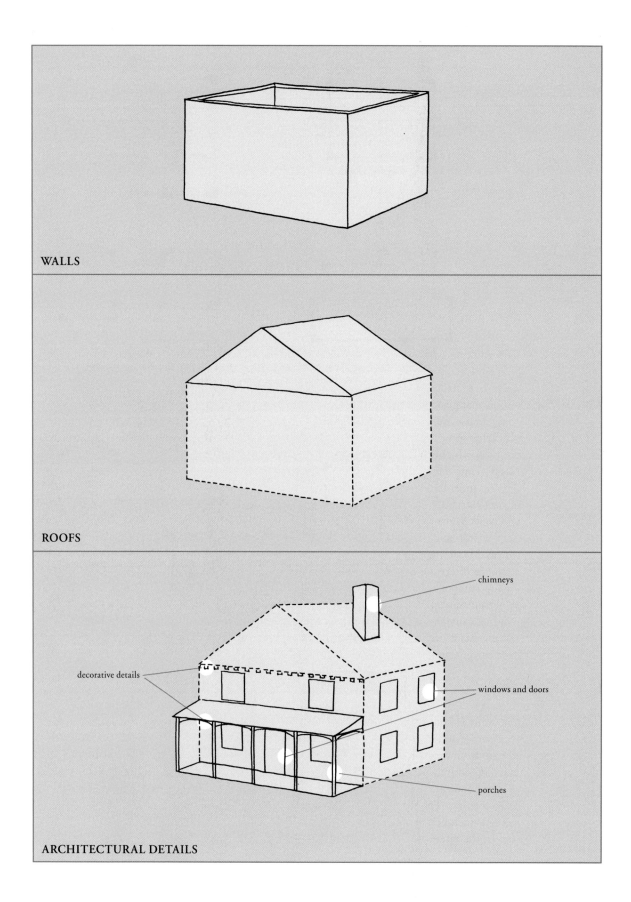

WALLS

ROOFS

ARCHITECTURAL DETAILS

chimneys

decorative details

windows and doors

porches

Structure

The Anatomy of American Houses

In addition to style (fashion) and form (shape), there is a third and somewhat more technical element that is useful for identifying and understanding American houses. This is structure, which can be defined as the several individual components of houses that give them their characteristic forms and styles.

All houses are composed of three basic structural units. First come walls, the vertical units that serve both to screen the interior spaces and to support the second basic unit, the roof, which shields the interior spaces from weather and completes the enclosure. In very simple houses—for example, tipis or modern A-frames—roof and wall may be a single unit. Far more commonly, each is made of different materials combined into separate structural systems. The most important materials and systems used for walls and roofs in American houses are described in the pages that follow. A house made up only of walls and a roof, with an entrance opening in the walls, can be a fully functional shelter. Many simple folk houses have little more. Most American houses, however, have added architectural details to the basic walls and roof, including some or all of the following components: windows, to provide light and ventilation to the interior; doors, to permit the entranceway to be closed against the weather; chimneys, to confine and eliminate smoke from interior fires; porches, partially exposed areas having roofs but lacking one or more walls; and, finally, decorative details, which function to enrich the external appearance of the house.

Walls

The walls of houses have two separate and distinct functions; first, they provide support for the roof and for any upper floors that may be present; second, they screen the house interior from weather and intrusion. In some types of wall structure—for example, those made up entirely of stone or brick—the same materials serve both functions. In others the functions are separated: one material provides the structural support and another the screening. The most familiar example is the wood-frame house, in which vertical wooden members provide structural support while an exterior covering, or cladding, screens the interior. This first section describes the principal structural support systems used for walls of American houses. The principal cladding materials used with these wall structures are treated below.

WALL FOUNDATIONS—Walls of very modest houses are sometimes built directly on the ground with little or no underlying foundation. Such walls rest on the surface soil, which makes a very poor base for most types of construction. Wooden walls tend to rot when in direct contact with damp earth, while masonry tends to be undercut by rainwater erosion of the soil beneath. For these reasons, most house walls are set upon foundations designed to protect them by raising them above the underlying soil. Simplest are wooden walls set upon wooden posts of some rot-resistant variety such as oak, cedar, or bois d'arc. (Sometimes the posts are, themselves, set directly on the ground surface, but more commonly with this and all other foundation systems, the soil is removed to a depth ranging from several inches to several feet and the base of the foundation is "buried" to provide firmer support.) Columns of brick or stone masonry known as masonry piers provide a similar supporting system for wooden walls, without the danger of rotting. On the other hand, failure of mortar joints can lead to equally serious problems that can be avoided by the use of monolithic piers, sometimes of metal but usually of concrete reinforced by steel rods.

The strong basal timbers of wooden walls can be supported by separated posts or piers; masonry walls, on the other hand, require continuous underlying support. In earlier masonry houses, soil has typically been excavated beneath the proposed wall and the first courses of stone or brick laid on the firm base of the trench. For additional stability, this underlying masonry wall is usually wider and of heavier materials than is the masonry of the overlying walls. When a basement is desired, some or all of the space between the exterior walls is excavated and the foundation walls constructed around the margins of the pit. Similar masonry wall foundations are also common beneath wooden walls, particularly in larger houses or in smaller houses requiring a basement. Foundation walls of masonry, like masonry piers, are subject to erosion and failure of the mortar joints and thus require periodic repair. This problem is avoided by monolithic concrete walls made of concrete beams poured in place and reinforced with internal steel rods. Such foundations first became common in the late 19th century; by the mid-20th century they had generally replaced wooden and masonry foundations beneath all types of wall construction. Note that in all the foundation systems mentioned so far, the internal floors and walls are supported by piers of wood, masonry, concrete, or metal even when the external walls have a continuous masonry or concrete foundation. One additional foundation system, developed in this century, eliminates these internal piers. In such concrete slab foundations, a relatively thin sheet of monolithic poured concrete underlies the entire house. This system completely eliminates floor framing and support at the first-floor level, and has become increasingly common since the 1950s.

WOODEN STRUCTURAL SYSTEMS—Most American houses (probably well over 90 percent) use pieces of wood to support the upper floors and roof. Simplest are walls of horizontal logs, either left round or hewn square, which serve to provide both structural support and, when the cracks between the logs are filled with clay or other materials, weather screening as well. The principal structural support of a log wall is provided by the notched corners, where adjacent logs are in close contact. Several systems of log corner notching have been developed to strengthen this crucial junction. Simplest to con-

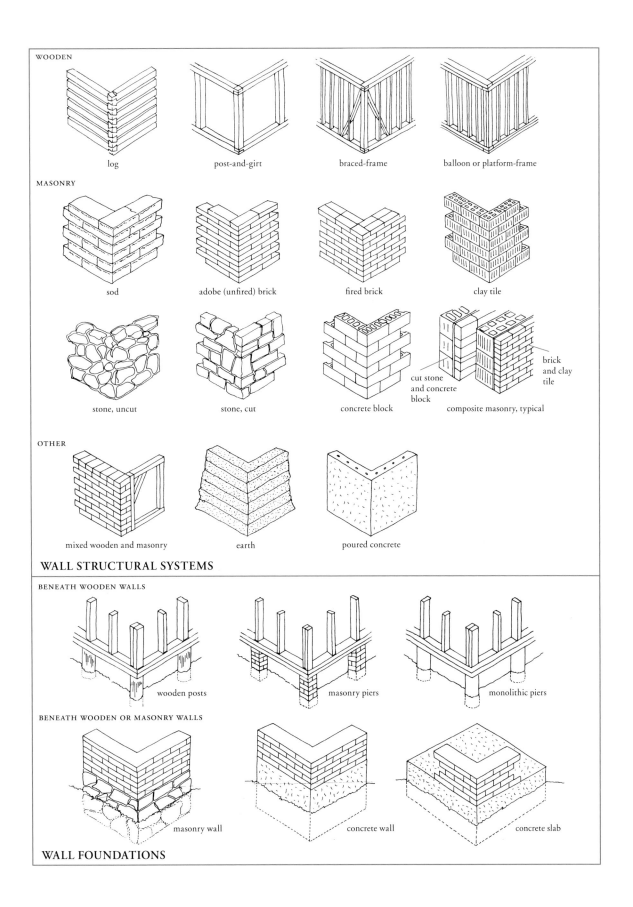

WOODEN

log   post-and-girt   braced-frame   balloon or platform-frame

MASONRY

sod   adobe (unfired) brick   fired brick   clay tile

stone, uncut   stone, cut   concrete block   cut stone and concrete block   brick and clay tile   composite masonry, typical

OTHER

mixed wooden and masonry   earth   poured concrete

WALL STRUCTURAL SYSTEMS

BENEATH WOODEN WALLS

wooden posts   masonry piers   monolithic piers

BENEATH WOODEN OR MASONRY WALLS

masonry wall   concrete wall   concrete slab

WALL FOUNDATIONS

struct but least rigid is the saddle joint; progressively more rigid are square, V-notched, and half-dovetail joints; while complex full-dovetail joints provide the strongest structure of all (see also the treatment of log houses on pages 126–32).

Far more common than horizontal log walls are those in which spaced vertical members provide structural support. Earliest is the Medieval post-and-girt system, imported from England and France by the first colonists. In this system, upper loads are borne by heavy corner posts and widely spaced intervening posts; heavy cross timbers carry upper floors which are unsupported by the thin internal walls below. Typically, all structural joints in post-and-girt houses are laboriously hewn into interlocking shapes and held fast by wooden pegs. Post-and-girt houses dominated the English and French colonies and persisted until well after the American Revolution. In the early 19th century, however, the increasing abundance of commercially sawed lumber, together with the development of relatively inexpensive wire nails, led to a modification of the traditional post-and-girt system known as braced-frame construction. This system still employs heavy corner posts connected by heavy horizontal timbers, generally with hewn joints. But within this heavy skeleton, loads are carried not by widely spaced and equally massive intervening posts and cross members, but by light, closely spaced vertical studs nailed between the horizontal timbers. Internal walls constructed entirely of light studs also now become strong bearing walls which help support the floors and roof above. This system takes its name from diagonal corner braces used to give lateral stability to the wooden framework. Note, however, that such braces are by no means unique to the system, but are common in all types of wooden framing.

By the early 19th century, braced frames were replacing post-and-girt construction throughout the former English colonies of the Atlantic seaboard; in this region braced-frame houses persisted well into the 20th century. Westward migration from these states also made this a common mode of construction throughout the country during the 19th century. By the time of the Civil War, however, another still more simplified method of frame construction was coming to dominance in the rapidly developing midwestern states. This was the balloon-frame system, begun in Chicago in the 1830s. This system

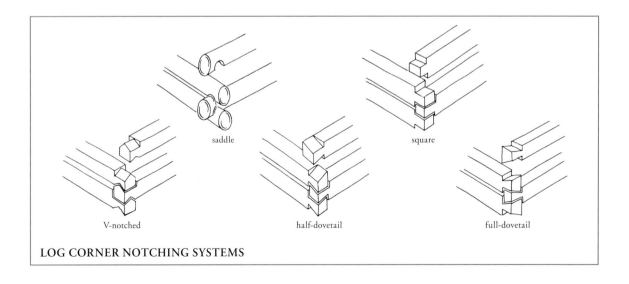

saddle

square

V-notched

half-dovetail

full-dovetail

LOG CORNER NOTCHING SYSTEMS

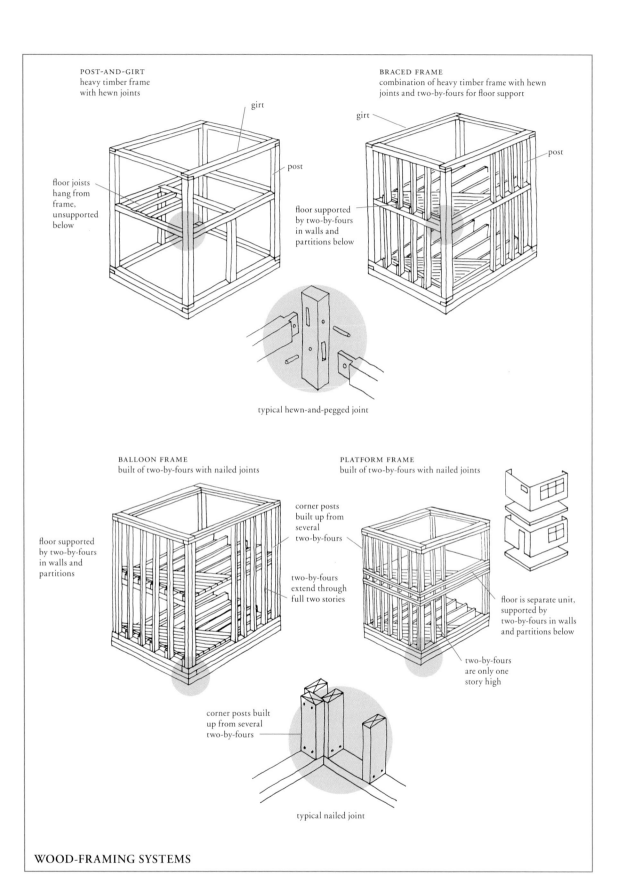

POST-AND-GIRT
heavy timber frame
with hewn joints

girt

post

floor joists
hang from
frame,
unsupported
below

BRACED FRAME
combination of heavy timber frame with hewn
joints and two-by-fours for floor support

girt

post

floor supported
by two-by-fours
in walls and
partitions below

typical hewn-and-pegged joint

BALLOON FRAME
built of two-by-fours with nailed joints

corner posts
built up from
several
two-by-fours

two-by-fours
extend through
full two stories

floor supported
by two-by-fours
in walls and
partitions

PLATFORM FRAME
built of two-by-fours with nailed joints

floor is separate unit,
supported by
two-by-fours in walls
and partitions below

two-by-fours
are only one
story high

corner posts built
up from several
two-by-fours

typical nailed joint

WOOD-FRAMING SYSTEMS

eliminated altogether the tedious hewn joints and massive timbers of braced-frame and post-and-girt construction, for balloon-frame houses are supported entirely by closely spaced two-inch boards of varying widths (two-by-two, two-by-four, two-by-six, two-by-twelve, etc.) joined only by nails. Corner posts and principal horizontal members are made of two or more two-inch boards nailed together. As in braced-frame houses, the principal supporting members are the closely spaced two-by-four or two-by-six vertical studs of both the exterior and key interior walls. This system allowed both cheaper and more rapid construction by eliminating the need for skilled hand-hewing of the principal wall timbers. With slight modification it remains the dominant method of American house construction today. The most common modification, known as platform framing, relates primarily to the wall studs and flooring. In balloon-frame construction, the studs are continuous from foundation to roof and the floors are hung upon the studs. In platform framing the floors are constructed as independent units, like thin, flat platforms; the shorter wall studs are then erected upon these platforms to support the overlying platform or roof. This system is both simpler and more rigid than balloon framing, which it had largely replaced by World War II.

MASONRY STRUCTURAL SYSTEMS—Although wooden framing has always dominated American house construction, European immigrants to the New World brought with them an intimate knowledge of masonry techniques as well. Indeed, in colonial times, just as today, masonry houses far outnumbered those made of wood throughout most of western Europe. (For this reason first-time visitors from Europe are always surprised to find the United States to be a land of wooden houses.) Although making up only a few percent of American houses, those with masonry walls show almost all variations of masonry building technique. Spanish colonists brought traditions of building in uncut stone and unfired adobe brick. The English, French, and Dutch had elaborate techniques of building with harder, fired brick and cut stone, as well as more modest folk traditions of building with sod (blocks of earth held together by grass roots) and uncut stone. These traditions tended to dominate certain regions during the colonial period; most persisted through the 19th century and a few survive even today. Beginning in the early 20th century, technology has added two more masonry materials to the traditional repertoire: hollow, fired clay tiles and hollow concrete blocks. These new materials are as strong as fired brick or stone, but are both lighter and cheaper. They have thus come to dominate 20th-century masonry construction, either alone or combined with an exterior layer of brick or stone to make composite masonry walls.

OTHER STRUCTURAL SYSTEMS—Only a very small fraction of one percent of American houses rely on structural systems other than wood or masonry. A few houses, mostly built in colonial times, used both wood and masonry in combination for structural walls.* Typically, end-chimney bearing walls were of masonry, the other walls of post-and-girt frames. In another variation, favored in the French colonies, the first-floor walls were of masonry and the overlying floor was post-and-girt.

Wooden and masonry walls are both composite, that is, they are made up of many small units linked together to make a wall system. Walls can also be of massive or monolithic construction, where only one or, at most, a very few units make up the entire wall.

---

* Note that many houses have exterior wall *claddings* of both wood and masonry. Houses with true structural walls of both materials are, however, rare.

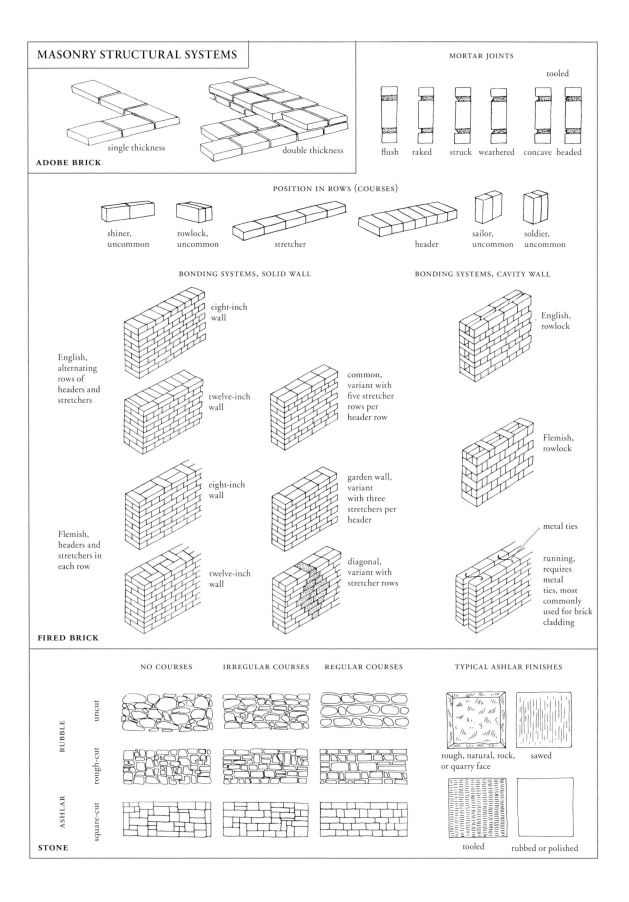

MASONRY STRUCTURAL SYSTEMS

ADOBE BRICK

single thickness

double thickness

MORTAR JOINTS

tooled

flush   raked   struck   weathered   concave beaded

POSITION IN ROWS (COURSES)

shiner, uncommon

rowlock, uncommon

stretcher

header

sailor, uncommon

soldier, uncommon

BONDING SYSTEMS, SOLID WALL

BONDING SYSTEMS, CAVITY WALL

English, alternating rows of headers and stretchers

eight-inch wall

twelve-inch wall

common, variant with five stretcher rows per header row

English, rowlock

Flemish, headers and stretchers in each row

eight-inch wall

twelve-inch wall

garden wall, variant with three stretchers per header

diagonal, variant with stretcher rows

Flemish, rowlock

metal ties

running, requires metal ties, most commonly used for brick cladding

FIRED BRICK

NO COURSES   IRREGULAR COURSES   REGULAR COURSES

TYPICAL ASHLAR FINISHES

RUBBLE — uncut

ASHLAR — rough-cut

square-cut

rough, natural, rock, or quarry face

sawed

tooled

rubbed or polished

STONE

The simplest such walls are made of earth, either mixed with water to make mud and then built up in layers, or pressed into layers while only slightly damp (rammed earth). Such walls are found in both European and Native American folk houses, but are rare in post-colonial America. Somewhat more common are monolithic walls of poured concrete, usually reinforced with iron or steel rods. Such walls can either be poured in place or pre-cast and then transported to the building site. They are common in 20th-century commercial buildings but are only rarely found in houses, most of which date from the late 19th and early 20th centuries.

WALL CLADDING—Relatively few systems of wall structure are immediately evident from looking at the exteriors of houses. In masonry walls the structural units of stone or brick *may* be exposed, but they also may be covered with a protective and decorative layer of stucco which masks the underlying structure. As a further complication, wood-frame buildings are often covered with an external layer of brick or stone, which gives them a superficial resemblance to masonry construction. These cladding materials can, however, provide clues to the underlying structure, which is almost always evident on close examination of foundations, basements, and attics.

All wood-frame houses *must* have external cladding. Traditionally the cladding is also of wood, either boards or shingles; since these materials are rarely applied to masonry walls, they indicate an underlying wooden frame. It is usually difficult to tell the exact system of wood framing unless some of the cladding is removed (although, again, a careful examination of wall openings, foundations, and attics may reveal the underlying framing). Such modern cladding materials as plywood or fiberboard panels, metal or plastic strips, or asbestos, asphalt, metal, or shingles are also seldom applied to masonry walls, and thus indicate an underlying wood frame. Brick and stone veneers were introduced in the early 20th century. By 1920, brick veneering in particular was in general use. These veneers may be difficult to distinguish from solid masonry, except that veneers are far more common; thus the first suspicion should be that *any* house showing external masonry—particularly if constructed within the last century—has a veneered wooden frame. An additional clue is that most brick veneers use only a running (stretcher) bond, since no headers are necessary to lock together the multiple rows required in a solid brick wall. By the turn of the millennium even thinner masonry veneers were in use—half-thickness bricks, thin stones, and lightweight "manufactured" stone. Stucco walls can

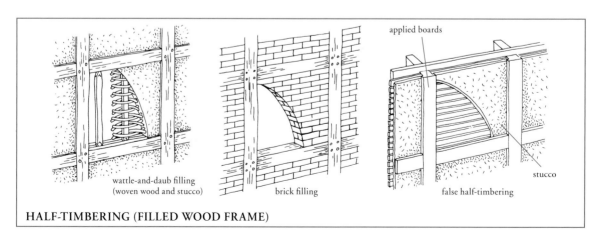

wattle-and-daub filling
(woven wood and stucco)

brick filling

applied boards

stucco

false half-timbering

HALF-TIMBERING (FILLED WOOD FRAME)

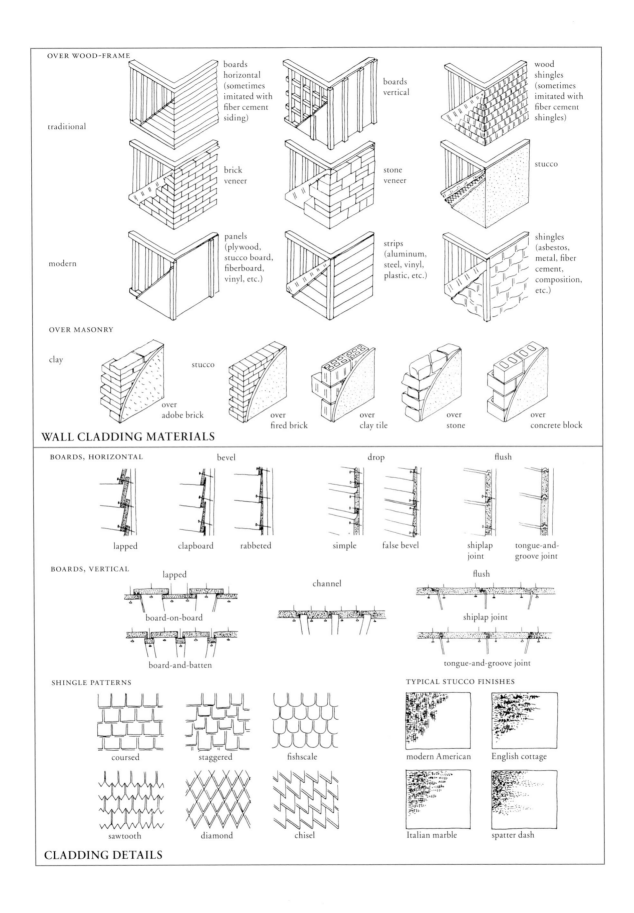

OVER WOOD-FRAME

boards horizontal (sometimes imitated with fiber cement siding)

boards vertical

wood shingles (sometimes imitated with fiber cement shingles)

traditional

brick veneer

stone veneer

stucco

modern

panels (plywood, stucco board, fiberboard, vinyl, etc.)

strips (aluminum, steel, vinyl, plastic, etc.)

shingles (asbestos, metal, fiber cement, composition, etc.)

OVER MASONRY

clay

stucco

over adobe brick

over fired brick

over clay tile

over stone

over concrete block

WALL CLADDING MATERIALS

BOARDS, HORIZONTAL

bevel

drop

flush

lapped

clapboard

rabbeted

simple

false bevel

shiplap joint

tongue-and-groove joint

BOARDS, VERTICAL

lapped

channel

flush

board-on-board

shiplap joint

board-and-batten

tongue-and-groove joint

SHINGLE PATTERNS

coursed

staggered

fishscale

sawtooth

diamond

chisel

TYPICAL STUCCO FINISHES

modern American

English cottage

Italian marble

spatter dash

CLADDING DETAILS

be the most enigmatic of all, for stucco finishes are commonly applied to both wood-frame and masonry buildings. Simple tapping to see if the walls sound hollow will sometimes distinguish between underlying wood or masonry. Likewise, areas of thin or failing stucco may reveal the structure beneath.

HALF-TIMBERING (FILLED WOOD FRAMES)—American wood-frame houses normally have cladding added to the exterior of the frame as a continuous covering that conceals the underlying structure. European framed houses of post-and-girt construction have, since Medieval times, commonly used another system of wall enclosure in which the spaces between the heavy supporting timbers are *filled* rather than covered. Such fillings normally leave the sides of the supporting timbers exposed and are known as half-timbered construction. The most frequent filling material is clay (daub), which is usually applied over a lath of short wooden sticks or woven basketwork (wattle). Brick or stone are also commonly used as filling materials; these are generally covered with stucco and thus closely resemble wattle-and-daub fillings. Early colonists in America first built half-timbered houses, but the rigorous New World climate made it difficult to keep the exposed fillings uncracked and weather-tight. As a result, half-timbering was generally abandoned for wooden claddings or full stuccoing, both of which completely covered the underlying frame. Some surviving English and French colonial houses of post-and-girt construction retain the filled frames of Medieval tradition; in most, the filled frame was either originally—or very early in the house's history—covered by continuous external cladding of wood or stucco. (Some of these have, in this century, been overzealously restored to an exposed, half-timbered exterior.) The half-timbered tradition, although unsuited to the American climate, has persisted as an applied surface decoration (false half-timbering) on 19th- and 20th-century houses that mimic the earlier technique.

Roofs

Roofs, the second principal structural component of houses, occur in three fundamental shapes: the first is gabled—that is, with two sloping planes supported at their ends by triangular, upward extensions of two walls known as gables. In gabled roofs, the junction of roof and wall occurs as a single horizontal plane, only on two facades; on the other two facades the wall plane continues up to the roof line, generally forming a triangular shape. In the other two roof shapes, hipped and flat, the roof meets the walls in a single horizontal plane. In hipped roofs, four sloping surfaces form the roof, while only a single horizontal or slightly sloping surface occurs in flat roofs. Each of these three principal shapes has several subtypes. These patterns of roof shape are among the most dominant features in determining the external appearances of houses. Thus they provide the basis for many of the stylistic subtypes defined throughout this book. After shape, the most apparent roof feature is pitch—the angle the sloping roof planes make with the horizontal. Both gabled and hipped roofs show marked changes in character as they pass from low pitches (under 30°) through "normal" pitches (30°–45°) to steep pitches (over 45°).

ROOF FRAMING—Roofs in all but a very small number of American houses are supported by wooden frameworks, for wood combines suitable strength and relatively light weight (as does metal, which is rarely used for this purpose in houses), thus making

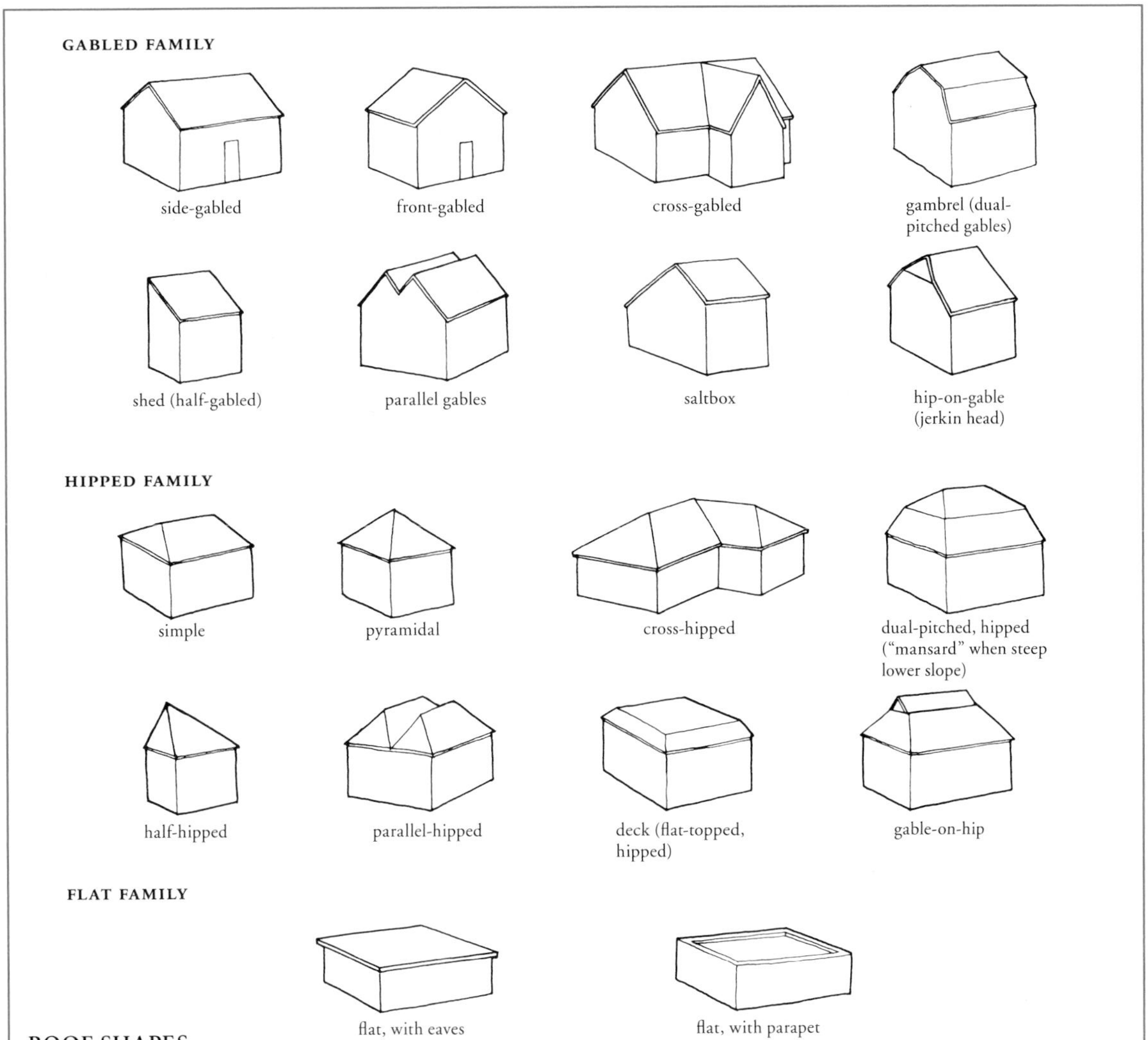

GABLED FAMILY

side-gabled

front-gabled

cross-gabled

gambrel (dual-pitched gables)

shed (half-gabled)

parallel gables

saltbox

hip-on-gable (jerkin head)

HIPPED FAMILY

simple

pyramidal

cross-hipped

dual-pitched, hipped ("mansard" when steep lower slope)

half-hipped

parallel-hipped

deck (flat-topped, hipped)

gable-on-hip

FLAT FAMILY

flat, with eaves

flat, with parapet

ROOF SHAPES

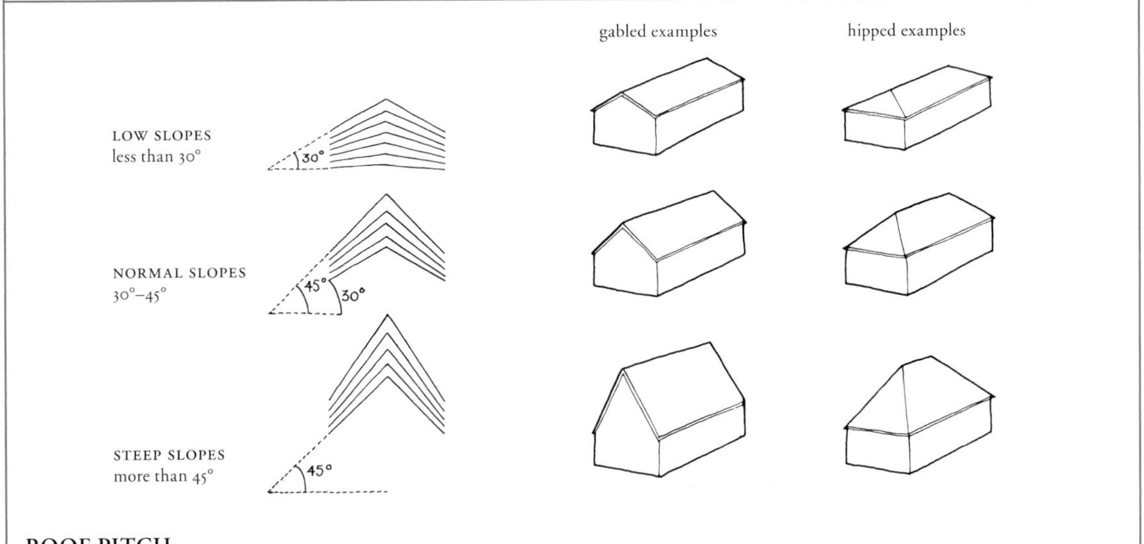

gabled examples

hipped examples

LOW SLOPES
less than 30°

30°

NORMAL SLOPES
30°–45°

45° 30°

STEEP SLOPES
more than 45°

45°

ROOF PITCH

possible the long spanning members required for roof support. Two principal roof-framing systems have been used in American houses.* The earlier employed heavy principal rafters with hewn joints as the principal supporting members. Lighter members (either common rafters or common purlins) were placed between the principal rafters to provide a base for attaching the roofing material. This system is analogous to post-and-girt wall framing and, indeed, is found on most early post-and-girt—as well as masonry—houses. With the rise of lighter braced, balloon, and platform wall framing it was discovered that light, closely spaced common rafters, joined by nails, provided adequate roof support without the need for intervening heavy timbers. Such common rafter roof-framing systems are almost universal in American houses built after the mid-19th century.

Principal rafters of heavy timber require little additional bracing to support the weight of the overlying roof, particularly if the roof is steeply pitched and spans a relatively narrow space below. Rafters of lighter weight, lower pitch, or longer span require underlying supporting systems of joists or trusses.

Simple gabled roofs always require the least complex underlying framing; the additional roof planes of gambreled or hipped roofs demand additional framing members.

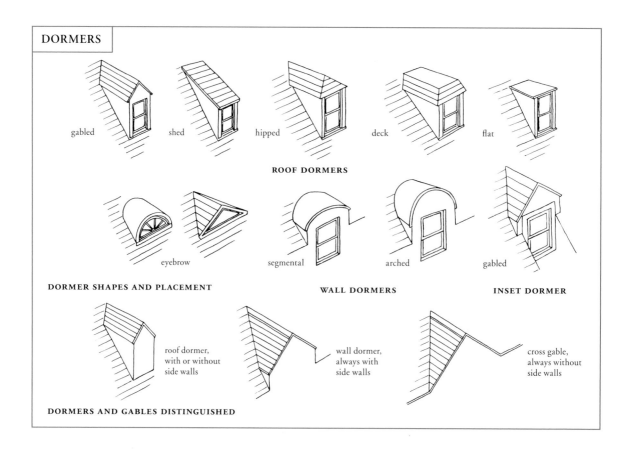

DORMERS

gabled   shed   hipped   deck   flat

ROOF DORMERS

eyebrow   segmental   arched   gabled

DORMER SHAPES AND PLACEMENT   **WALL DORMERS**   **INSET DORMER**

roof dormer, with or without side walls

wall dormer, always with side walls

cross gable, always without side walls

DORMERS AND GABLES DISTINGUISHED

* A third system uses horizontal logs rather than a wooden framework and is employed in many Spanish Colonial houses; see page 191.

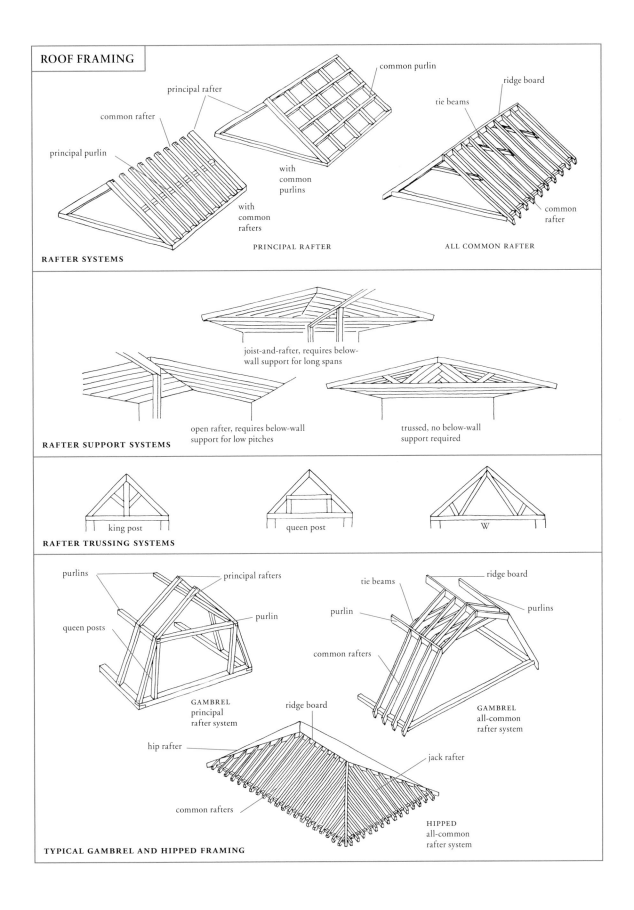

ROOF FRAMING

RAFTER SYSTEMS

principal rafter
common rafter
principal purlin

with common rafters

common purlin

with common purlins

PRINCIPAL RAFTER

ridge board
tie beams

common rafter

ALL COMMON RAFTER

RAFTER SUPPORT SYSTEMS

joist-and-rafter, requires below-wall support for long spans

open rafter, requires below-wall support for low pitches

trussed, no below-wall support required

RAFTER TRUSSING SYSTEMS

king post

queen post

W

TYPICAL GAMBREL AND HIPPED FRAMING

purlins
principal rafters
queen posts
purlin

GAMBREL principal rafter system

tie beams
ridge board
purlin
purlins
common rafters

GAMBREL all-common rafter system

ridge board
hip rafter
jack rafter
common rafters

HIPPED all-common rafter system

ROOF-WALL JUNCTIONS—The lines of junction between roof and wall are crucial features of house design, both esthetically and structurally, for they join differing roof and wall materials in a junction that must be watertight to protect the underlying structure from damaging moisture. There are various systems of attaching roof to wall (and for enclosing this important junction).

DORMERS—Finally, roof slopes may be interrupted by dormers, subunits resembling miniature houses with their own walls, roofs, and windows. These are added to provide space, light, and ventilation to the attic, thus making it a functional part of the house. Dormers are most easily characterized by their roof shapes.

ROOFING MATERIALS—Resting upon the wooden framework is the watertight covering, which adds texture and color to the sloping roof planes and thus has a dominant effect on the external appearance of a house. Four principal kinds of materials are used for roofing.

The first are organic coverings. Of these, thatch, closely packed bundles of reeds or straw, is the most common roofing for folk houses throughout the world. Although thatch is commonly used on modest European dwellings, it was quickly abandoned by American colonists because it was particularly vulnerable to the high winds, driving rains, and severe winters of the New World. Long boards of split wood were sometimes substituted for thatch in early colonial houses but these, too, were rather quickly abandoned for roofs of wooden shingles—thin wedge-shaped rectangles that were either rough-split or sawed from oak, cedar, or other durable woods. Shingles could be closely aligned and generously overlapped to give an impervious and weather-resistant roof;

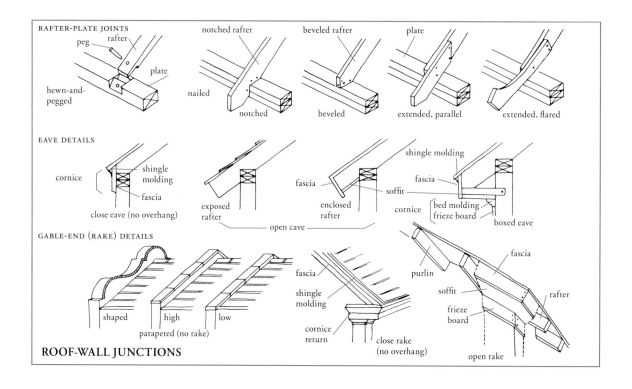

ROOF-WALL JUNCTIONS

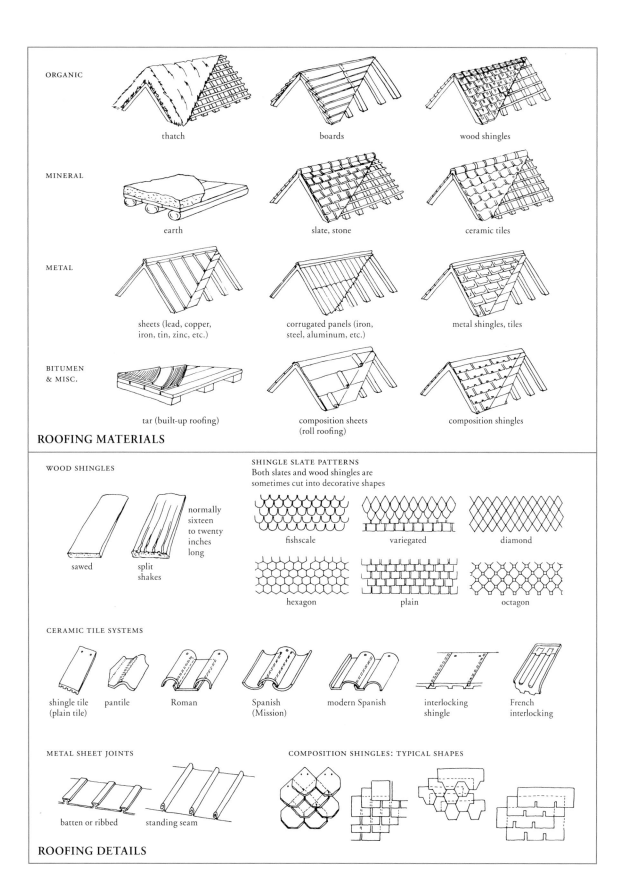

ORGANIC

thatch · boards · wood shingles

MINERAL

earth · slate, stone · ceramic tiles

METAL

sheets (lead, copper, iron, tin, zinc, etc.) · corrugated panels (iron, steel, aluminum, etc.) · metal shingles, tiles

BITUMEN & MISC.

tar (built-up roofing) · composition sheets (roll roofing) · composition shingles

ROOFING MATERIALS

WOOD SHINGLES

sawed · split shakes

normally sixteen to twenty inches long

SHINGLE SLATE PATTERNS
Both slates and wood shingles are sometimes cut into decorative shapes

fishscale · variegated · diamond

hexagon · plain · octagon

CERAMIC TILE SYSTEMS

shingle tile (plain tile) · pantile · Roman · Spanish (Mission) · modern Spanish · interlocking shingle · French interlocking

METAL SHEET JOINTS

batten or ribbed · standing seam

COMPOSITION SHINGLES: TYPICAL SHAPES

ROOFING DETAILS

since colonial times, wooden shingles have remained a dominant roofing material of American houses.

Roofs of mineral materials also have a long history. Simplest are roofs of earth, or of earth bound by grass roots to make sod; both are common on folk dwellings everywhere. Both the earliest New World colonists and 19th-century settlers in the treeless western half of the country commonly used earth or sod roofs on temporary dwellings. They are also used for the roofs of permanent Spanish-influenced dwellings in the American Southwest. Roofs of thin, flat pieces of natural stone, tightly overlapped as with wooden shingles, were common in the larger dwellings of Medieval and Postmedieval Europe. An abundance of wood for making shingles—and a relative scarcity of quality slate, the most easily split and durable type of stone—made such roofs uncommon in this country until the late 19th century, when they began to be used in houses that simulated earlier European traditions. A third type of mineral roof, composed of thin, shaped units of baked clay tiles, was developed in classical times and has since remained a continuous feature in European architecture. Several systems of interlocking tile units have been developed through this long history. Most of these systems have been employed on monumental New World houses since colonial times but, like slate roofs, they have been common only since the late 19th century. In the 20th century, tiles made from concrete and other composite ceramic materials have been developed which simulate clay tile. (Note also that metal and composition roofs are often shaped and colored to resemble ceramic tile.)

Metal roofs also have a long history, for sheets of lead or copper have been used as roofing since classical times. A few landmark colonial houses of the New World used such roofs, but metal became a common roofing material only in the early 19th century when sheet iron (usually coated with zinc, tin, or lead to prevent rust) first became relatively inexpensive and plentiful. Usually metal roofs are applied as large sheets joined with standing seams, which help prevent leaks. Later in the 19th century, stronger corrugated panels of iron became common for roofing of commercial and modest domestic buildings. Their rigidity gives such panels the advantage of requiring less underlying support than do most roofing materials. In the 20th century, panels of corrugated aluminum are sometimes used for the same reason. Other metal roofs are made up of smaller units shaped to resemble shingles or ceramic tiles.

The fourth type of roofing is based on bitumen, natural semi-solid petroleum residues such as tar and asphalt. Since colonial times natural tar deposits have been used—along with tar-impregnated sheets of cloth, felt, or paper—to make built-up roofs. Unlike roofs made up of smaller units, which must be pitched upward to prevent water from entering the joints between units, monolithic roofs of tar (or earth) can remain impervious when almost flat (many flat-roofed Spanish Colonial houses of the Los Angeles area had built-up tar roofs, the material coming from nearby natural tar pits). Although most common on commercial buildings, built-up roofs have also been a standard technique of house roofing since the mid-19th century. Tar normally has to be heated to make it liquid enough to spread on built-up roofs. It also must be protected from the sun's rays, which make it hard and brittle, by gravel or other material. By the late 19th century, techniques had been developed to convert tar or asphalt into "cold" roofing by impregnating sheets or shingles of felt, paper, or cloth with bitumen. Such composition roofs had the advantage of being easy to apply, relatively inexpensive, and fire-resistant. They have become the dominant roofing (or re-roofing) material for American houses in the

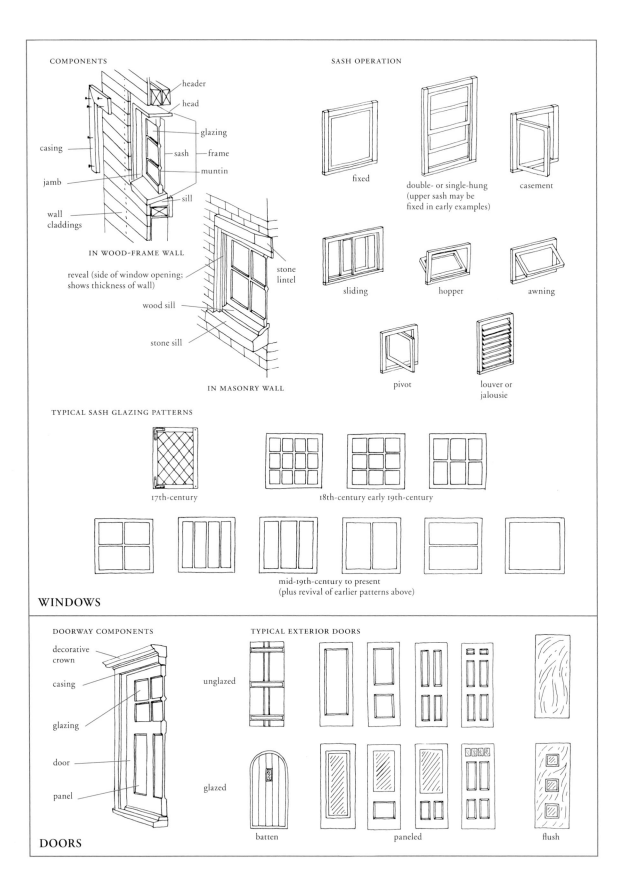

COMPONENTS

header
head
glazing
sash
frame
muntin
casing
jamb
sill
wall claddings

IN WOOD-FRAME WALL

reveal (side of window opening; shows thickness of wall)

stone lintel
wood sill
stone sill

IN MASONRY WALL

SASH OPERATION

fixed

double- or single-hung (upper sash may be fixed in early examples)

casement

sliding

hopper

awning

pivot

louver or jalousie

TYPICAL SASH GLAZING PATTERNS

17th-century

18th-century   early 19th-century

mid-19th-century to present
(plus revival of earlier patterns above)

WINDOWS

DOORWAY COMPONENTS

decorative crown
casing
glazing
door
panel

unglazed

glazed

batten

paneled

flush

TYPICAL EXTERIOR DOORS

DOORS

20th century. Other materials, in addition to petroleum-based bitumen, have also been used for making composition shingles. In particular, shingles of asbestos fibers bound together by concrete were widely used in the early decades of the 20th century.

Architectural Details

In addition to walls and roofs, many kinds of architectural details contribute to the external appearance of houses. The most important of these are windows and doors; chimneys; porches; and decorative details.

WINDOWS AND DOORS—Windows are wall openings that provide light and ventilation for the house interior. The word itself derives from "wind-holes," early openings that served principally to supply draft, and emit smoke, from internal fires. Early windows were without glass, which was a rare and expensive luxury until the 17th century. When ventilation wasn't required, the openings were covered with fabric or skins or by solid wooden sashes or shutters. Many schemes have been devised for opening and closing such shutters, and later glazed sashes; most have been in continuous use since at least Medieval times.

To admit light through the closed window, frames covered with translucent oiled cloth or paper came to be used instead of solid shutters in prosperous Medieval houses. Many such windows were used in colonial America, but glass glazing was also becoming widespread in England, Holland, and France at about the time of the first New World colonization. These 17th-century window sashes were glazed with many small panes of glass, usually either square or diamond-shaped, held in a wooden or metal frame by narrow strips of soft lead. Throughout the 18th and early 19th centuries, window sashes came to be glazed with panes of increasing size, as glass-making techniques improved and costs decreased. By the mid-19th century, panes large enough to glaze sashes in only one or, at the most, two units became widely available. Since then, multi-paned sashes have been used only because of historical precedent rather than technological necessity.

Although some 17th-century window frames and sashes were of iron, windows with wooden frames, sashes, and glazing bars (muntins) became almost universal in the 18th and early 19th centuries. Beginning in the mid-19th century, industrialization made available mass-produced metal windows. These remained relatively rare until the 1930s; since then they have progressively increased in use and are now the dominant type of window in American houses.

Windows are an architectural luxury lacking in some modest folk houses. At least one exterior doorway is essential, however, to permit entrance and exit of the occupants. Originally the doorway served also as the principal "wind-hole" for regulating light and ventilation (hence the phrase: "Never again darken my doorway"). Doors for closing off the doorway are almost universally made of wood in American houses. Because single pieces of wood are never large enough to cover a full door opening, doors are always composite—that is, made up of many small pieces of wood. In the earliest and simplest form of the door, vertical planks are held together with horizontal strips called battens, which are nailed or screwed to the surface of the larger planks.

By the 18th century, more elaborate doors were becoming common. These paneled doors consisted of an exterior framework of relatively thick planks, carefully joined and interlocked, which supported thinner internal planks (or panels). Such doors combine

EXTERIOR

gable wall

eave wall

wood and clay

stone

INTERIOR

end

slope

ridge

brick

brick

stone

composite masonry

CHIMNEYS

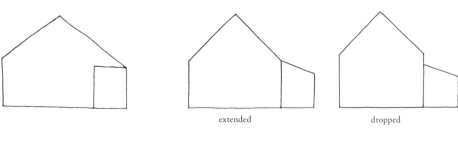

PRINCIPAL ROOF

SECONDARY ROOF

extended

dropped

PORCH ROOF CONSTRUCTION

the virtues of strength, light weight, and decorative appearance; they remain the most common type of door in American houses, although they were increasingly replaced in the mid-20th century by the flush door. Flush doors appear to be single, flat pieces of wood but are, in fact, of veneered construction. They are made up of large, thin sheets of wood that are first peeled from a log with a razor-sharp knife, then glued together to make a strong, composite unit (this same process also produces plywood panels, which have replaced wooden planks for many construction uses since the late 20th century). In more modest flush doors, single thin sheets of veneer are applied to the exterior of a solid or hollow framework of joined planks to make a sort of sandwich structure.

It is usually desirable for external doorways, when closed, to admit light into entrance rooms or hallways. Thus many doors are partially glazed with fixed glass panes, which are found in all the principal types—batten, paneled, and flush. Note also that additional glazing is often provided around the door in the form of side or overhead lights.

CHIMNEYS—Chimneys are hollow columns of masonry that provide a restricted exit for the smoke and fumes of internal cooking and heating fires. Houses have sheltered fires since the dawn of human civilization, yet chimneys are a relatively recent innovation, having only become widespread in modest English houses at about the time of the first American colonization. This innovation was brought to the New World, where chimneys became a standard feature of American houses. The simplest chimneys are constructed of wooden frameworks covered with a hardened coating of clay. Such chimneys require constant repair and become a serious fire hazard if the coating fails. Thus they are usually replaced by solid masonry chimneys as quickly as circumstances permit. Both brick and stone masonry are widely used in chimney construction, but brick is the preferred material since the regular shape decreases the chance of joint failures, and thus hidden chimney fires.

Although internal fires for heating and cooking are all but universal in American houses, chimneys are not. The first cause of their decline was the development of practical iron stoves and ranges. Stoves made of iron plates were known in Medieval Europe and were introduced in the United States by Benjamin Franklin in the 18th century. These sheet-iron stoves were, however, leaky and inefficient; the widespread adoption of iron stoves and ranges did not begin until the 1830s, when relatively cheap and airtight units of cast iron were introduced. These required only a metal pipe to vent smoke and fumes to the outside and led to widespread abandonment of large masonry chimneys. In modest houses the stoves were often vented only by metal pipes extended through roof or wall. More commonly, massive fireplaces were replaced with narrow masonry flues, to which the metal stovepipes were connected. These led to small chimneys and provided a safer, fireproof escape for the hot concentrated fumes of stove and range.

A second cause of the decline of external chimneys was the widespread adoption of gas, oil, and electricity for heating and cooking in the 20th century. These, too, require only metal pipes for external venting and thus the once essential chimney and fireplace have become only nostalgic luxuries in most 20th-century houses.

PORCHES—In British usage the word "porch" means sheltered entranceway, either partially open or enclosed on all sides to make a small room. Porches in the American sense—that is, roofed but incompletely walled living areas—are rare in Europe, where such spaces are known by other names: *verandah* or *piazza* (Britain), *galerie* (France), *portale* (Spain), or *loggia* (Italy). The origin and inspiration of the far more common *porch* of American houses has been much debated. It was clearly adopted because of the oppressive heat and frequent thundershower deluges of the New World summers, but its exact sources remain uncertain.

Porches are normally constructed in either of two ways: one or more external walls can be omitted under the principal house roof to give an inset porch; or, an additional roof can be added onto the principal roof to give a smaller porch roof which is relatively independent of the main roof. Both types are common in American houses. Roofs are normally supported by the external house walls; when some of these are deleted to make a porch, columns or other roof-supporting devices are required. In addition, when porches occur much above ground level, a railing or low wall, usually with an open framework to admit breezes, is required for safety. These supporting members and enclosures can be of wood, masonry, or metal and provide rich opportunities for decorative embellishment of the house facade.

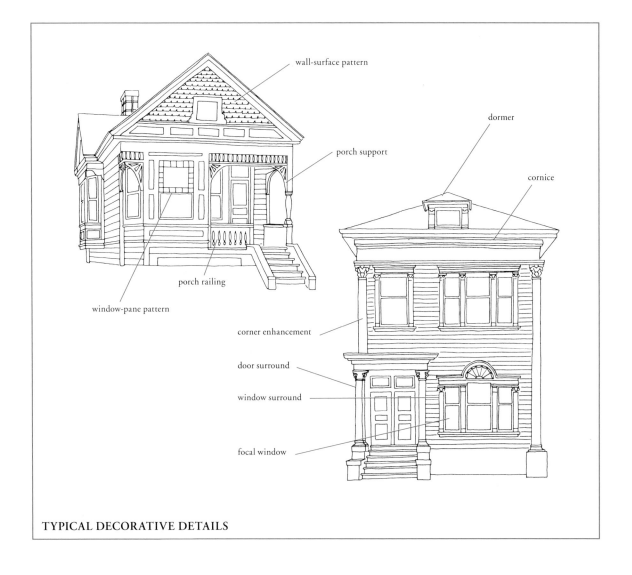

TYPICAL DECORATIVE DETAILS

Even in colonial times, porches were becoming common in the New World: both French and English colonists in the warmer, southern colonies commonly added verandahs or galleries to their houses. The use of large porches expanded until, by the late 19th and early 20th centuries, they had become an almost universal, and quite distinctive, feature of American domestic architecture. These showed an enormous variety of size, shape, and placement; many houses had several porches, or extended porches covering several walls. By the mid-20th century, this trend was completely reversed. Changing fashions—and the development of air-conditioning for summer cooling—all but eliminated this once dominant feature of the American house facade until the late 1980s, when it was re-introduced in traditional neighborhood developments (TNDs).

DECORATIVE DETAILS—Architectural details such as windows, doors, chimneys, and porches all serve important practical functions. One other category of detail has no such obvious use but is, instead, added principally to enhance the beauty of the house exterior. Such decorative details are of two main types: in the first, the principal coverings of the house exterior—the wall cladding or roofing—are decoratively elaborated. Shaped shingles or patterned masonry are examples of this kind of decorative detail. Still more common is the second type of decorative elaboration, in which neither the roof nor walls but rather some smaller functional detail is elaborated with decorative trim. Door and window openings are commonly embellished in this way; door surrounds are particularly favored since they are closely observed by all who enter the house. Indeed, certain eras of American house building are largely characterized by their distinctive elaborated door surrounds. Windows are commonly embellished by decorative surrounds or crowns, by shaped window openings, or, most commonly, by differing shapes and sizes of glass panes. Roof-wall junctions are another favored site for the addition of decorative detail: elaborate moldings or trim, commonly matched to those of doors and windows, are frequently added beneath eaves and rakes. Chimneys, too, provide decorative opportunities; decorative shapes and patterns in brick, stone, or stucco are common. Finally, as noted above, porches provide a wealth of decorative opportunity; roof-support columns and protective railings have been elaborated in a nearly endless variety of decorative patterns.

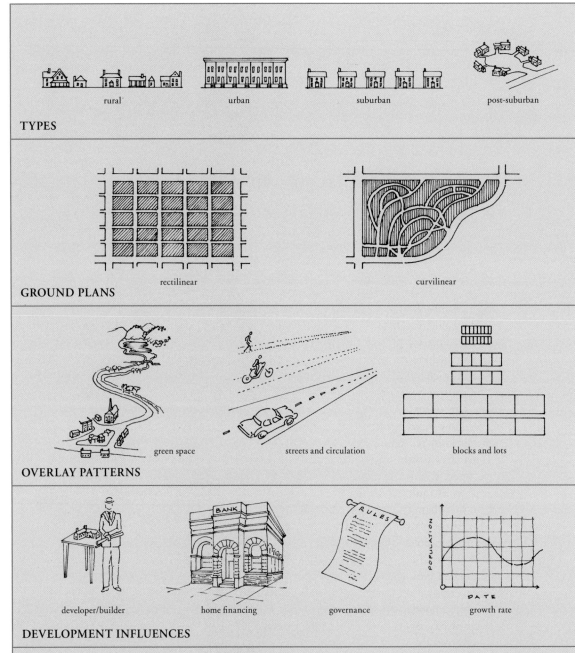

rural   urban   suburban   post-suburban

TYPES

rectilinear   curvilinear

GROUND PLANS

green space   streets and circulation   blocks and lots

OVERLAY PATTERNS

developer/builder   home financing   governance   growth rate

DEVELOPMENT INFLUENCES

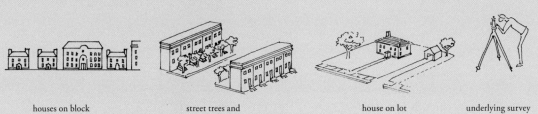

houses on block   street trees and street enclosures   house on lot   underlying survey

READING STREETSCAPES

Neighborhoods

The Groupings of American Houses

*N*eighborhood is a word used in many different ways. For the purposes of this guide, it refers to a geographic area of a town or city that was developed as a whole and/or is generally filled with similar types of houses.[2] Neighborhoods may also include additional housing types and other compatible uses or distinctive community characteristics. In the United States, neighborhoods rarely have a public administrative function but may have private responsibilities, such as enforcing deed restrictions or maintaining shared open space. The boundaries of neighborhoods sometimes follow those of one or more original subdivisions, but frequently boundaries are determined by residents.

This chapter is written for those simply looking at a neighborhood and trying to understand it. A neighborhood develops its distinct visual appearance from the cumulative effect of multiple factors, beginning with the general neighborhood type—rural, urban, suburban, post-suburban, or a subcategory of one of these. Next it considers the kind of street plan utilized, whether rectilinear or curvilinear, and some of the overlay patterns that mold this plan—green space, circulation, and block and lot size. There is an overview of the role that development influences—developer/builder, financing, governance, and growth rate—played in producing individual houses and neighborhoods. These factors all blend together to create understandable streetscapes.

Neighborhoods are the building blocks of cities. One can appreciate the history of a town or city by understanding its neighborhoods and how they interacted with or resulted from the growth and development of commercial, office, civic, and industrial uses.

Types

Neighborhood groupings of houses fall into four general types: rural, urban, suburban, and post-suburban. Just as transportation played a major role in the location of American cities, it has similarly helped govern the location and configuration of American neighborhoods. Only rural and urban neighborhood types were found in the United States in 1800. At that time walking was the primary means of transportation, and according to the census only 5 percent of the population lived in "urban" areas—the thirty-three cities and towns that then had a population over 2,500.[3]

RURAL NEIGHBORHOODS (1750–1940)—A rural *neighborhood* (with a grouping of homes near a congregation of stores and sometimes small-scale industry) must be clearly distinguished from a widespread and less concentrated rural *area*. Except for New England (where a village settlement pattern was typical), prior to the Civil War a majority of the United States was settled with a pattern of widely spaced individual farmsteads that created rural areas. Farmers estimated their "neighborhoods" to include fifty square miles.[4] Trading centers, sometimes as small as a single general store, might serve an early rural area.[5]

The majority of early rural *neighborhoods* were the result of the slow expansion of trading centers for this very low-density agricultural economy.[6] These neighborhoods are characterized by a relatively random mixture of lot sizes as well as varied placement of the houses and outbuildings on the lot. This was made possible by a general absence of regulation (zoning, subdivision, or deed restrictions), by slow-growing economies (rarely producing large subdivisions), by the gradual sale of parcels of original large lots, and by many individual builders and self-built homes. Because everyone walked within the center, generally there was a relatively compact arrangement of free-standing houses. The edges of town usually quickly transitioned to fields and open space. Rural neighborhoods, particularly those built before railroads, often have a distinct regional character.[7]

In 1840 only 131 U.S. towns (commonly ports or on other waterways) had a population exceeding 2,500. By 1880, hundreds of new small towns had been formed and older villages had grown; 872 towns had more than 2,500 inhabitants. This was the result of forty years of intense railroad expansion, including the first transcontinental rail line in 1869. By 1910 a fast-paced golden age of electric trolley transportation had quickly and inexpensively connected still more small towns, and 1,801 towns had passed the 2,500-population mark.[8]

It was the ready supply of rail-delivered goods, products of the expanding industrial revolution, arriving to stock many Main Street stores that created numerous small American rural neighborhoods. Not only did existing villages grow, but the companies themselves laid out hundreds of new small towns in the lands they had been granted along their tracks.[9] It was not until after World War II that the relatively compact and almost organic rural neighborhood pattern began to be altered by the adoption of big-city standards for regulating subdivisions, street width, lot size, and house placement.[10]

URBAN NEIGHBORHOODS (1750–1920)—Urban groupings are found where the economic base required high population density, historically related to water transportation routes and later water-powered industry. In 1800, the size of an urban settlement was limited by the distance one could comfortably walk and generally did not exceed a one-mile radius. Within an older urban area, a high percentage of the land is covered with structures that housed a variety of income levels and accommodated a mixture of land uses, since a lot could be developed for any purpose.

Urban neighborhoods are characterized by narrow houses (attached or closely spaced) sited close to the street, with little or no front yard. This form allowed the construction of as many homes as possible within a short walking radius. Owners lived close to or above their businesses, and dense neighborhoods of small houses for workers could

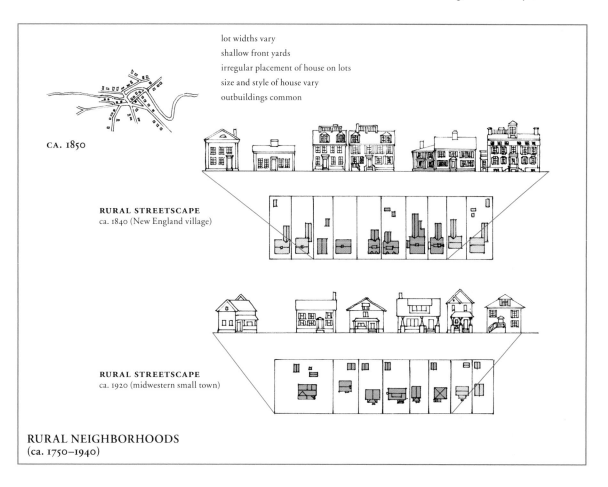

lot widths vary
shallow front yards
irregular placement of house on lots
size and style of house vary
outbuildings common

CA. 1850

RURAL STREETSCAPE
ca. 1840 (New England village)

RURAL STREETSCAPE
ca. 1920 (midwestern small town)

RURAL NEIGHBORHOODS
(ca. 1750–1940)

grow quickly in close proximity to a dock, mill, or factory. In areas where generous rear yards had been originally platted, houses facing onto alleys were sometimes added as demand for housing grew. Even within this diverse mix, areas somewhat differentiated by employment or socioeconomic level often evolved.

Daily lives were tied to a small walkable area.[11] In order to oversee any aspect of a business or factory, one had to walk there. Nothing allowed supervision from afar. No telephone allowed one to consult or even set up a meeting time with a partner or foreman. Furthermore, workers could not escape for a weekend away. They could only walk to a small diversion and then walk back home. Only the very wealthy could afford a horse or carriage in a city.

The 1829 introduction of omnibuses—twelve- to twenty-seat horse-drawn carriages utilized for regularly scheduled public transportation along fixed routes—allowed for small expansions of the tightly packed urban fabric.[12] In addition, the omnibus encouraged more detached houses located just beyond a city's urbanized edge in the "borderlands," where free-standing single-family houses were sited on large tracts of land— a precursor to the preferred *form* of suburbs.[13] A second transportation advance, the steam ferry, allowed the development of neighborhoods remote from a city center, separated by a river or other body of water. Brooklyn, across the East River from Manhattan, was

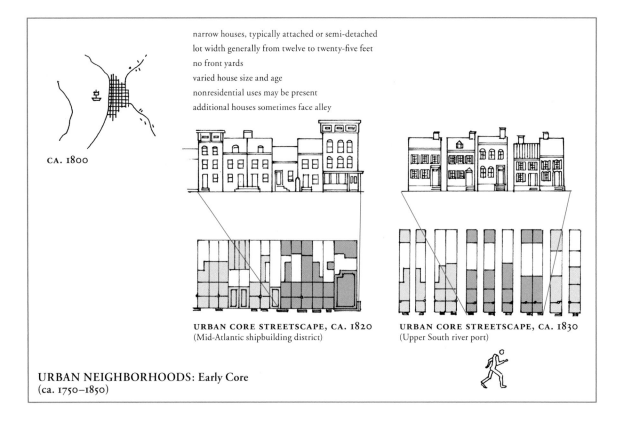

narrow houses, typically attached or semi-detached

lot width generally from twelve to twenty-five feet

no front yards

varied house size and age

nonresidential uses may be present

additional houses sometimes face alley

CA. 1800

URBAN CORE STREETSCAPE, CA. 1820
(Mid-Atlantic shipbuilding district)

URBAN CORE STREETSCAPE, CA. 1830
(Upper South river port)

URBAN NEIGHBORHOODS: Early Core
(ca. 1750–1850)

a rural area until regular ferry service made the development of Brooklyn Heights possible. First advertised in 1823, this early real estate development was built at a distance from the urbanized core—a precursor to the preferred *location* of suburbs. Despite its separation from Manhattan, Brooklyn Heights was primarily developed with the urban form of attached houses on narrow lots—because, after the ferry ride, homes were still accessed primarily on foot.[14]

HORSE-DRAWN STREETCARS—Made possible by the 1852 invention of a method for sinking a track into the street that left a level street surface, horse-drawn streetcars (horsecars) were a huge improvement over the earlier "trackless" omnibuses. The wheel moving over a flat track allowed faster speeds (six to eight miles per hour), smoother rides, and larger-capacity cars (thirty to forty passengers). These provided the first true urban transit system and facilitated the exponential expansion of new urban neighborhoods outward from the center of the city. By 1860, horsecars were in use in New York, Baltimore, Philadelphia, Pittsburgh, Chicago, Cincinnati, and Boston.[15] Coinciding with the rapid industrialization of the U.S.—accompanied by massive immigration from 1850 to 1890, exploding growth in cities—the urban population of the United States rose from 3.5 million in 1850 to 22 million in 1890.[16]

Horsecars facilitated three kinds of development in cities. First and foremost, they allowed extensions of the existing urban fabric. New urban neighborhoods of row houses could be conveniently built farther away from other uses. As larger buildings and more industrial uses were built in the original mixed-use urban cores, many of

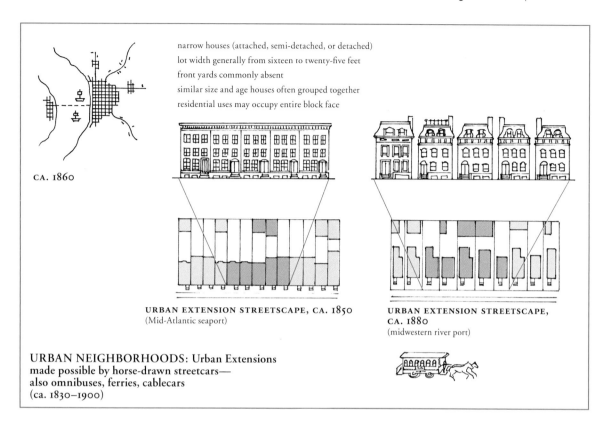

narrow houses (attached, semi-detached, or detached)
lot width generally from sixteen to twenty-five feet
front yards commonly absent
similar size and age houses often grouped together
residential uses may occupy entire block face

CA. 1860

URBAN EXTENSION STREETSCAPE, CA. 1850
(Mid-Atlantic seaport)

URBAN EXTENSION STREETSCAPE,
CA. 1880
(midwestern river port)

URBAN NEIGHBORHOODS: Urban Extensions
made possible by horse-drawn streetcars—
also omnibuses, ferries, cablecars
(ca. 1830–1900)

those who could afford it preferred to move to these quieter residential, yet still urban, settings.[17]

Secondly, horsecars created some very early streetcar suburbs, groupings of detached houses that became widespread with faster electric streetcars. Third, toward the end of a line, they allowed access to the "borderlands."[18] Not confined to cities, a horse- or mule-car line in a small town could make it convenient to live on large-lot mini farms away from the village center—the *rural* equivalent of borderlands.[19]

By the mid-1880s there were almost six thousand miles of horsecar track and the cars were carrying about 188 million passengers a year.[20] In a city, however, horses were finicky, expensive, and, most of all, messy. They required tons of hay, left urine and excrement on the streets, required multi-level stables in large cities, could only work a four-hour shift, were hard to pair evenly into teams, and when they died—not infrequently on the job—the disposal of their bodies presented a challenge. Small wonder that the introduction of electricity to power streetcars was so quickly adopted.[21]

SUBURBAN NEIGHBORHOODS—Suburban neighborhoods are a varied type of house grouping. Rather than resulting from economic necessity, suburbs grew from the utopian vision of living in a pastoral setting close enough to a city to enjoy its jobs and pleasures but removed from the unpleasant aspects of urban life. New transportation methods made a daily commute feasible and were absolutely necessary in the creation of suburbs. In addition, three other innovations made suburban living practical: the rapid spread of light wood balloon-frame construction (making it fast and affordable to build free-standing houses, 1840–1870); the proliferation of gas and electric utility systems (producing inexpensive heat for free-standing houses, 1880–1920); and the expansion of telephone service (allowing remote two-way communication, 1880–1910). [22]

The strong desire to move to the suburbs resulted from both a *push* and a *pull*. A city's older urban neighborhoods could be unpleasant for reasons that included open sewage, shared privies, disease, fire, garbage left to be eaten by pigs or dogs rather than collected, horse and industrial odors, and later the sound pollution from trains and trolleys, and the growing size of post-industrial building types. These conditions helped push those who could afford it out of urban neighborhoods. At the same time a flood of popular mid-19th-century magazines and books extolled the morality and healthfulness of living in the country and the joy of connecting to nature and your own piece of land.[23] The desire for this lifestyle helped pull those who could afford it out of the city as soon as new kinds of transportation made it feasible.

Suburban neighborhoods typically consist of free-standing houses on lots large enough to provide a desirable landscaped setting. These are divided into categories based upon the transportation innovation that connected the suburb to the city, each of which produced a somewhat different scale and look. North America has some of the world's largest and most diverse suburban groupings. It is important to understand that what was first developed as a distinct early suburb has today frequently been encircled by the city it was built to serve. Thus many cities, particularly those that expanded rapidly in the 20th century by annexing additional land, have former suburbs located in what is today a central part of the city.

RAILROAD SUBURBS (1850–1930)—The steam railroad was the first form of transportation that made it possible to escape the city center and live in a rural setting while still commuting to work in the city. After the first U.S. steam locomotive train was introduced in Baltimore in 1830, the expansion of rail lines was very rapid. The miles of laid track grew from about 2,750 in 1849 to 87,800 in 1880.[24] Railroads fueled the growth of new cities in the Midwest and West, and expanded older East Coast cities. The earliest tracks were laid to expand the trade areas of established ports, but soon longer lines were introduced to traverse long distances, crossing the continent in 1869 and opening vast new areas for settlement.[25] As this system was built, it became obvious that increasing daily commuters around urban areas would bring additional income on a regular daily basis.

There were two distinct kinds of railroad towns near large cities. The most well known and publicized were new railroad suburbs planned specifically for commuters—bedroom communities for men who went into the city to work each day. Far more common, however, were fully functional nearby towns with rail stops. These self-contained rail-stop towns provided the city with a rich array of needed services—and also housed the workers that supported them. Among these were farming towns, suburban industrial towns, recreational destinations, and towns based around institutions such as universities. These communities had populations that generally lived and worked in the same place and utilized their rail stops in different ways—for the daily transport of agricultural or industrial products into the city and as transportation for city dwellers out to enjoy a recreational weekend.[26]

The primarily residential railroad suburbs, however, garnered most of the press.

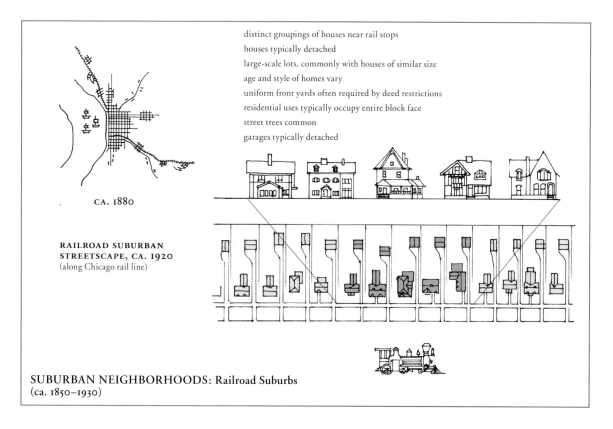

distinct groupings of houses near rail stops

houses typically detached

large-scale lots, commonly with houses of similar size

age and style of homes vary

uniform front yards often required by deed restrictions

residential uses typically occupy entire block face

street trees common

garages typically detached

CA. 1880

RAILROAD SUBURBAN
STREETSCAPE, CA. 1920
(along Chicago rail line)

SUBURBAN NEIGHBORHOODS: Railroad Suburbs
(ca. 1850–1930)

Often renowned for their creative land use and other innovations, planned railroad suburbs bragged of their existence, while their working-class rail-stop brethren served in the background. The cost of a daily suburban commute was steep and tended to make planned railroad suburbs bastions of the well-to-do. But not all residents of classic railroad suburbs were wealthy. Approximately one-third of inhabitants were servants whose families often lived in nearby neighborhoods of small houses.[27]

Llewellyn Park, New Jersey (1857–1859), twelve miles west of New York City, was one of the first and more influential of the planned railroad suburbs. It had a large communal green space in its center, the Ramble, a remarkable innovation in the days before public parks. It featured curved roads that followed the topography of its hillside site, something uncommon in new developments. There were many other well-known railroad suburbs—chief among them Chicago's 1869 Riverside (see pages 78–80).[28]

Railroad suburbs were usually built several miles from the cities they were designed to serve. Since trains were slow to gather speed as well as come to a stop, the space between suburban stations was generally a mile or more, forming railroad towns in the 1800s into individual communities rather than the continuous development that would characterize later suburb types.[29] This led to strings of railroad suburbs, such as the Main Line along the Pennsylvania Railroad's route west of Philadelphia. Prior to the automobile, railroad suburbs had remained small in area due to the walking distance to the station.[30]

ELECTRIC STREETCAR SUBURBS (CA. 1890–1930)—After their introduction in 1887, streetcars powered by electricity rapidly revolutionized transit in U.S. cities. Track originally built for horse-drawn cars was converted to use by electric streetcars. The length of streetcar track in the United States skyrocketed from 5,783 miles in 1890 to 34,404 in 1907, as the country's urban population increased by 50 percent.[31] Electric streetcars were much faster than horsecars and thus allowed large tracts of open land well beyond the edge of the city to be developed.[32]

Trolley and *streetcar* are terms often used interchangeably today. However, from 1890 to 1920, they were considered streetcars when they operated in an urban area and ran down city streets. Outside a city, they were more often called trolleys.[33] In addition to allowing suburban expansion, their speed in open countryside (twenty to thirty miles per hour and up) allowed them to efficiently connect many small towns to each other as well as to cities. In this role, electric cars were sometimes heavier duty and the line was called an interurban.[34]

The speed of electric cars facilitated a new real estate development process. A typical pattern was to build a trolley line into vacant countryside, often terminating at a recreational destination—a park, a fairground, an amusement park, or a large cemetery (which, in the 19th century, functioned as tranquil open space). This planning helped attract riders immediately. House lots were platted adjacent to the line, subdivision improvements were added (sidewalks, utility connections, etc.), and the vacant lots placed on the market. Signs advertising "Home Sites for Sale" greeted passengers traveling along the line. As lots were sold and homes built, the new residents increased the number of daily commuters. The streetcar line added value to the vacant land, and the development of the land brought value to the streetcar.[35] Often the owner of a trolley line and its adjacent property was either the same or connected in some way. By 1900 trolley lines and streetcar suburbs had become the primary factor in the development of new urban neighborhoods throughout the country.[36]

Houses built in streetcar suburbs were typically free-standing. City dwellers wanted houses in neighborhoods with lots large enough to allow for front lawns and a green suburban feeling. The spacing of houses was governed by the fact that one walked home from the streetcar stop, thus side yards were shallow and houses tended to have a narrow facade on the street. Entire neighborhoods of new, detached structures were built, filled with various styles of American four-square houses, bungalows, and front-gabled houses, each with its narrow front turned toward the street.[37] With the exception of a few large older metropolitan areas, new attached houses became relatively rare after about 1900.

Streetcars created long narrow neighborhoods along their tracks. Because these neighborhoods depended on homes having easy pedestrian access to the streetcar line, they extended only a few blocks to each side. By 1920 these straight narrow corridors of development expanding out from the urban center resembled the spokes of a wheel, with vacant land in between.[38]

The introduction of electric trolleys, with their five-cent fare, had opened up a world to middle-class Americans where they not only dreamed of buying a house but also easily escaped the small walking radius in which they had previously lived and worked. For the first time, the electric trolley allowed day trips to a beach or a park, and citizens could see their town as they traveled. It introduced an entirely new kind of freedom and leisure that would soon be multiplied by the automobile.[39]

EARLY AUTOMOBILE SUBURBS (1915–1940)—At first, automobiles were only an avocation for the wealthy, stored in central places and delivered to the door for an afternoon drive, much as a carriage horse would be delivered by the livery. They were expensive, and when kept at home they were stored in a detached garage so gasoline fumes and the threat of fire were well removed. It was not until 1910 that automobile ownership became affordable to the middle class, due to Henry Ford's revolutionary mass production of his Model T. The result was extraordinary. In 1918, only one in thirteen families owned a car. Sales skyrocketed, and by 1929 four out of five families owned one. By 1920 it was feasible to design a new type of suburban neighborhood—one dependent on automobiles for access. This made the vacant land between the spokes formed by streetcar suburbs accessible for new development. These new early automobile suburbs were not only accessed by automobiles, they were planned to accommodate them. They spread rapidly, and by 1941 there were 2,100 communities in the country with populations between 2,500 and 50,000 that did not have any public transportation.[40]

The automobile initiated a number of changes in neighborhoods. Streets were paved.[41] Blocks were often planned longer than in streetcar suburbs. The longer blocks were tolerable because one did not have to walk them. Long blocks were doubly profitable—less street paving to pay for and more land available for lots to build upon. Sidewalks could

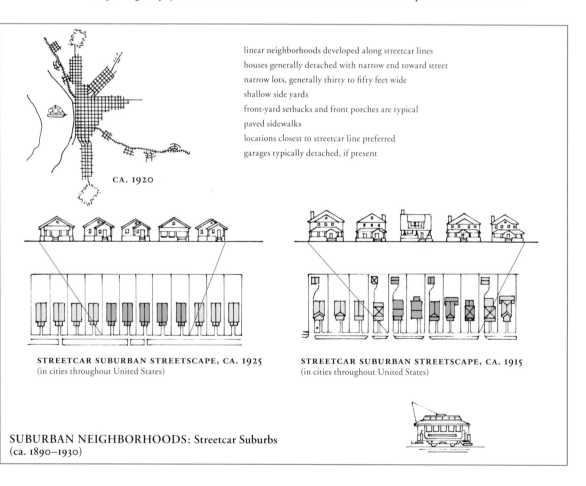

CA. 1920

linear neighborhoods developed along streetcar lines

houses generally detached with narrow end toward street

narrow lots, generally thirty to fifty feet wide

shallow side yards

front-yard setbacks and front porches are typical

paved sidewalks

locations closest to streetcar line preferred

garages typically detached, if present

STREETCAR SUBURBAN STREETSCAPE, CA. 1925
(in cities throughout United States)

STREETCAR SUBURBAN STREETSCAPE, CA. 1915
(in cities throughout United States)

SUBURBAN NEIGHBORHOODS: Streetcar Suburbs
(ca. 1890–1930)

be narrower because they were now optional. Curb cuts were added for driveways leading to a garage that was generally detached. It was feasible for individual lots to be wider than those in streetcar suburbs because walking home was no longer the norm. Setbacks from the street often became deeper.

Early automobile suburbs did not view the automobile as an enemy to be kept out. The plans for many upscale neighborhoods utilized a warped street grid—a grid pattern with subtle curves—sometimes with a handsome central avenue or boulevard adding interest to the interior of the neighborhood (see pages 79 and 80),[42] which was considered a desirable location for the largest homes. However, by 1940 traffic in the interior of a neighborhood plan was considered undesirable.

Early automobile suburban development flourished all across the United States during the 1920s. There was so much land platted that in some places numerous vacant lots remained when the housing industry virtually shut down in the early 1930s.[43]

POST–WORLD WAR II SUBURBS (1940–1980)—The federal legislative changes that fueled the development of post–World War II suburbs began in 1934 with the creation of the Federal Housing Administration (FHA), which initiated strict subdivision planning guidelines (see page 80).[44] However, due to the sluggish economy of the 1930s,

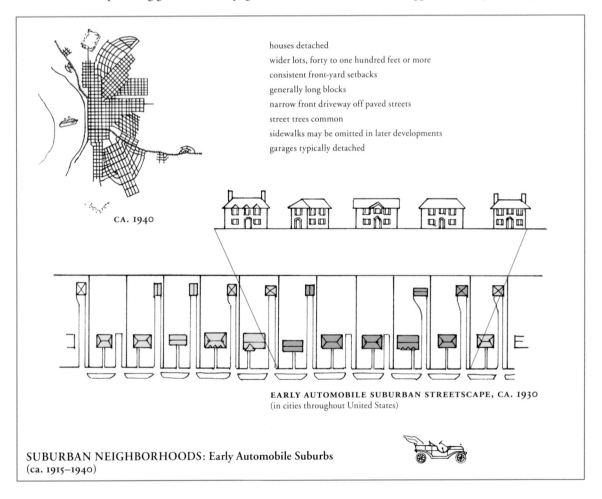

houses detached

wider lots, forty to one hundred feet or more

consistent front-yard setbacks

generally long blocks

narrow front driveway off paved streets

street trees common

sidewalks may be omitted in later developments

garages typically detached

CA. 1940

EARLY AUTOMOBILE SUBURBAN STREETSCAPE, CA. 1930
(in cities throughout United States)

SUBURBAN NEIGHBORHOODS: Early Automobile Suburbs
(ca. 1915–1940)

along with the prohibition of nonessential construction during World War II, these guidelines did not widely influence the form of suburbs until after the war ended. In 1945, after sixteen years with little residential construction, there was a massive pent-up demand for new homes and FHA guidelines began to exert a staggering force on the creation of new neighborhoods.[45] In 1940 the FHA published a bulletin titled *Successful Subdivisions* that in twenty-eight pages explained and illustrated what was expected in developments utilizing their new mortgage insurance. In addition to well-located, dry land with a strong market, the agency required a competent professional plan and suggested it include good streets of prescribed width, well-shaped building lots with driveways, protection of the neighborhood from through traffic, and the use of protective covenants.[46] The desire to avoid direct through traffic produced profound changes in neighborhood design. The FHA exploited the leverage of their mortgage insurance to implement completely new approaches to neighborhood street patterns that eliminated easy automobile access. (See "FHA-guided Subdivisions," page 80, and discussion of arterials in Primary Roads, pages 83–86.)

Most post–World War II neighborhoods were located beyond the developed edges of cities where many municipalities were planning or beginning to build an expandable

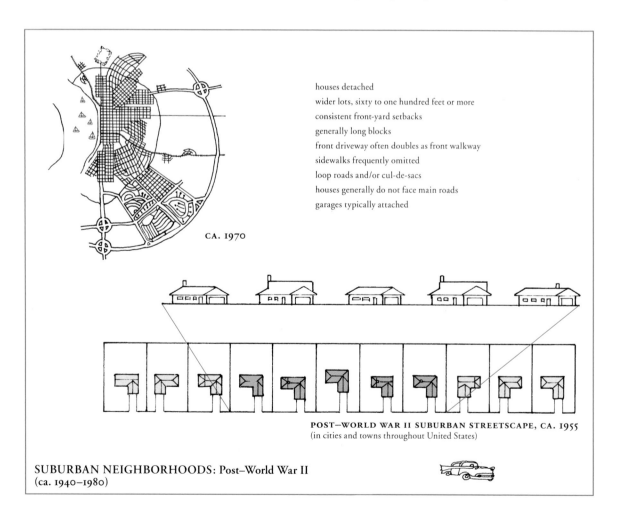

CA. 1970

houses detached
wider lots, sixty to one hundred feet or more
consistent front-yard setbacks
generally long blocks
front driveway often doubles as front walkway
sidewalks frequently omitted
loop roads and/or cul-de-sacs
houses generally do not face main roads
garages typically attached

POST–WORLD WAR II SUBURBAN STREETSCAPE, CA. 1955
(in cities and towns throughout United States)

SUBURBAN NEIGHBORHOODS: Post–World War II
(ca. 1940–1980)

network of federally subsidized highways that fed into a system of arterials—new broad city streets designed to carry substantial traffic.[47] The FHA guidelines encouraged post–World War II subdivisions both to take advantage of and to protect themselves from this new system of major streets and thoroughfares. It was recommended that new subdivisions nestle beside an arterial for easy access but with few entrances from this major road into the neighborhood. Street patterns inside the neighborhood were carefully designed to prevent use of neighborhood streets as short cuts, utilizing devices such as loop roads and cul-de-sacs. A second defining feature of post–World War II suburbs is the widespread use of curvilinear planning and long blocks.

Within the plan, lots sometimes became wider in order to accommodate new Ranch or Split-Level houses with their long facade facing the street. Sidewalks became less relevant and were often omitted, as were front walks leading from the sidewalk to the front door. Wide driveways that led to an attached front-facing garage or carport often served as the front walk. Later upscale subdivisions might feature side-entry or alley-entry garages to avoid garage doors on the front facade.

Mass-construction techniques, perfected during the war years, were utilized for both economy of scale and rapid construction. In some cases, entire neighborhoods were built from only a few home plans with similar size and layout.[48] The FHA encouraged small home size by limiting the maximum loan amount they would insure. This gave more people the ability to purchase a home and helped fulfill a national goal of providing homeownership for the sixteen million servicemen who had served in World War II (see Home Financing, page 88).

Today the popular belief is that post–World War II suburbs were isolated residential areas, but the model they were encouraged to follow—and seen in postwar suburbs from the late 1940s into the 1970s—was a more integrated approach that included schools, churches, nearby retail, parks, and community facilities based in large part on Clarence Perry's suggestions for a "Neighborhood Unit."[49] The elements were perhaps farther apart than in the streetcar and early automobile suburbs, but requirements for a day-to-day family life were generally nearby. Specific FHA suggestions for subdivisions included school and church sites, commercial sites where needed, and parks as an asset.[50]

POST-SUBURBAN (1970–PRESENT)—Suburban neighborhoods were built to serve as residential areas connected to and serving a downtown. By contrast, many developments after about 1970 are post-suburban, built to serve "edge nodes" located beyond the ring of post–World War II suburbs and interacting primarily with other post-suburbs and suburbs. Three types of neighborhoods being built today are easy to identify.

SLUGS: The most prevalent post-suburban neighborhood type is the SLUG (an area of spread-out, low-density, unguided growth). These may be small subdivisions or individual home sites scattered amid forest or farmland far from the kinds of amenities typical of postwar suburbs. Planning for less through traffic has frequently escalated into the formation of gated communities. The FHA's effort to "protect lots from adjacent non-conforming uses" has morphed into huge tracts of residential or apartment use without the parks or community uses found in most postwar neighborhoods. Local shopping has been swept aside by distant big-box retailers that require a huge market area to reach them by automobile.[51]

Governmental policies enabled and continue to encourage out-migration from older

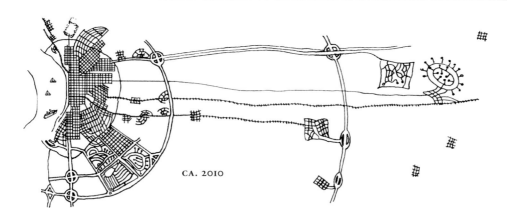

CA. 2010

"PEDVILLE," POP. 12,500

walking distance of rapid transit

one-quarter- to half-mile radius of higher-density development

high residential density supports varied retail

requires green space and community amenities

walking and biking connections common

"SALUTATION," POP. 1,250

re-creates visual qualities of rural, urban, and pre-1940 suburban streetscapes

walking and biking connections common

emphasis on green space and sense of community

daily shopping needs hopefully nearby

"WAYOUT ACRES," POP. 125

small developments, often gated

shopping at a distance

community amenities may not exist (large house accommodates private amenities for each household)

car essential

may be interspersed with agriculture

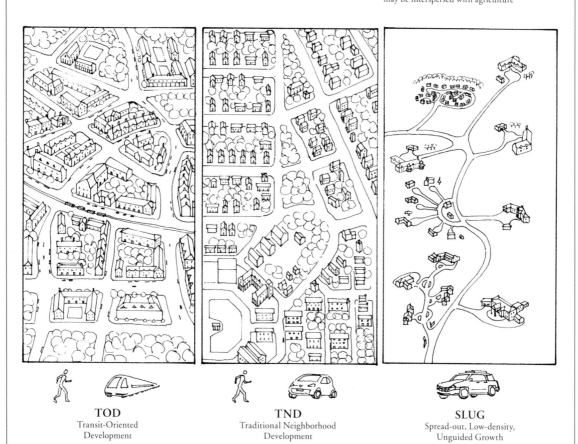

TOD
Transit-Oriented Development

TND
Traditional Neighborhood Development

SLUG
Spread-out, Low-density, Unguided Growth

POST-SUBURBAN NEIGHBORHOODS
(ca. 1970–present)

areas. After the first ring of post–World War II suburbs were built, we entered an era of post-suburban sprawl, including the last two decades of far-flung SLUGs. The 1956 Federal-Aid Highway Act created a dedicated gas-tax funding stream for the accelerated construction of more than 41,000 miles of interstate highways. This was supplemented with both earlier and later federal subsidies for well over a million miles of local highways, farm-to-market roads, inner loops, outer loops, and city-wide networks of arterials—providing the vast roadway network that has enabled sprawl and SLUGs.[52] In addition, federal tax policy has favored new commercial construction—including incentivizing construction of big-box stores at the lucrative nodes where the federally funded roads intersect. In 1970 the Federal National Mortgage Association ("Fannie Mae") was listed on the New York Stock Exchange and removed from the FHA's decades-long oversight of residential construction—involving home size, quality, location, and subdivision amenities.[53]

TODs: Today's forward-thinking national efforts are focused on directing new growth into creating a second post-suburban type, the resource-efficient TODs (transit-oriented developments) of compact neighborhoods within walking distance of rapid transit. TODs often include re-creating new walkable urban and early suburban streetscapes, as well as denser mid- to high-rise condominiums and apartments. Unfortunately, some TODs do not yet include essential pedestrian and bicycle connections and amenities.[54]

TNDs: The third prevalent post-suburban type is the visually inviting TND (traditional neighborhood development) that salutes the form and scale of earlier urban, rural, streetcar, and early automobile suburban types with its more compact scale and pedestrian-friendly streetscapes along with an enlightened emphasis on connectivity and green space. In the best of all worlds, traditional neighborhood developments are served by rapid transit (making them also TODs) and include the amenities needed for a complete neighborhood, along with carefully placed higher-density housing choices.[55]

Neighborhood Plan Types and Density

There is great variety in the plans used for groupings of each neighborhood type. The illustration opposite shows a common plan type that occurs in each of six neighborhood types. Upper left is a rural neighborhood with unplanned roads. Next clockwise is an urban neighborhood with a grid plan of small blocks, an early automobile suburb with a warped grid, a post-suburban SLUG with one house per acre, a post–World War II suburb with an internal loop road, and a streetcar suburb with a rectilinear grid. The factors contributing to these plan types are explored in the following section.

This illustration clearly shows the wide variety of population density (often expressed as the number of persons or dwelling units on an acre of land) that can make up a neighborhood of single-family houses. Approximately two hundred acres of land are covered by each plan, with two hundred dwelling units shown placed on each. Comparing plans, it is easy to see vast differences in the amount of land utilized for the same number of dwelling units.[56]

EXISTING NEIGHBORHOODS—More than one-third of the total U.S. economic asset is invested in our built environment.[57] The preservation of existing neighborhoods—

RURAL

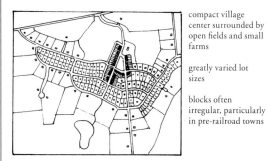

compact village center surrounded by open fields and small farms

greatly varied lot sizes

blocks often irregular, particularly in pre-railroad towns

daily shopping typically in small grouping of Main Street storefronts

URBAN
EARLY CORE

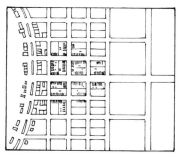

located near waterfront or early manufacturing

mixture of house sizes and of use within a block face

rectilinear plans are most common

short blocks typical

daily shopping typically in large market building or grouping of small storefronts, often with nearby area for open stalls

SUBURBAN
STREETCAR

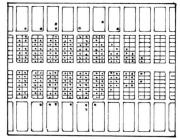

located along streetcar lines forming narrow linear "spokes" out from center city

rectilinear plans are most common

short blocks typical

uniform lot and house sizes often found in a block face

blocks with different house sizes generallly located in close proximity

daily shopping typically located at trolley stops; major shopping in center city

SUBURBAN
EARLY AUTOMOBILE

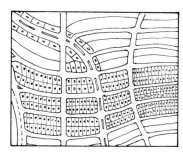

located between (and beyond) "spokes" formed by streetcar lines

curvilinear or rectilinear plans, may combine into warped grid

longer blocks typical

focal street may be part of development

blocks restricted to large houses; blocks intended for smaller houses generally located in close proximity and frequently in same development

daily shopping typically in early small-scale shopping centers; major shopping in center city

SUBURBAN
POST—WORLD WAR II

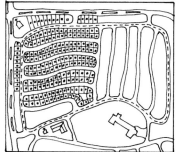

subdivisions often on large tracts located near arterial streets or freeways

curvilinear plans with longer block lengths are typical

through traffic kept outside neighborhood

loop roads common within neighborhood

houses of similar size in each block face

many adjacent blocks typically with similar house sizes (entire development may be for one size of house)

daily shopping in neighborhood shopping centers typically located on nearby arterial streets; major shopping downtown at first and then moves to suburban locations and malls

POST-SUBURBAN
SLUG

small subdivisions may be scattered among rural areas

zoning may require very large lot sizes or very large homes

curvilinear plans with long block lengths

cul-de-sacs, large lots, gated communities all common

daily shopping often not nearby and may be in big-box store; major shopping often in malls or big-box "power centers"

each subdivision typically has similar house sizes and price

NEIGHBORHOOD TYPES sample plans (approximately two hundred acres and two hundred dwelling units per plan)

rural, urban, and suburban, whether or not "historic"—is the most economic, green, and conservation-minded action.

This fact was not understood in the 1950s and early 1960s, when it was believed that the old parts of towns could be effectively wiped clean and rebuilt. There were three major assaults. First, the Housing Act of 1954 provided two-thirds of the money needed to buy up and tear down large areas of inner cities for "urban renewal"—sadly, efficiently removing large areas of existing fabric. Second, the 1956 Federal-Aid Highway Act provided 90 percent of the funds, but gave states and municipalities almost complete control over the routes of interstates, many of which plowed through the hearts of neighborhoods and cities. Third, the FHA's financial guidelines withheld home loans from older neighborhoods through a practice called redlining. These three powerful forces left older neighborhoods in grave shape. For example, about one-third of the old part of Boston was demolished for an interstate and urban renewal—a massive project so destructive that billions of dollars have been spent burying the interstate portion during the last ten years and restoring the street grid.[58] Other cities barely escaped. New Orleans became the first city in the nation to stop an interstate highway for environmental reasons, one that would have plowed through the Vieux Carré right by Jackson Square in the manner that the Boston freeway had impacted the Faneuil Hall Marketplace.[59] At the same time that demolitions were taking place for freeways, large areas of cities were being cleared for urban-renewal projects. In the midst of these controversies Jane Jacobs's pivotal *The Death and Life of Great American Cites* was published, beautifully describing and defending mixed-use urban neighborhoods.[60]

As the high cost of this widespread devastation of existing neighborhoods became obvious, the Historic Preservation Act of 1966 was enacted to survey and protect historic resources; it no longer allowed federal funds to be used to demolish valuable older areas without a thorough professional review. It was another eleven years before lending policies caught up (through the Community Reinvestment Act of 1977) and older neighborhoods had mortgage and home-improvement funds easily available to them.[61]

New high-density areas today can be carefully developed in a way that does not negatively impact or attempt to replace two centuries of public and private investment—and use of natural resources—thus avoiding the urban fabric disruptions that marked the 1950s and 1960s.[62]

Ground Plans

Ground plans for neighborhoods can be divided into two general groups—rectilinear and curvilinear. Towns with rectilinear plans have been common for thousands of years and were joined by curvilinear plans in the 19th century. Both had interconnected streets. There was an abrupt change about 1940, following the rising popularity of automobiles. For the first time, neighborhoods were planned with streets designed specifically *not* to interconnect. Their plans were generally curvilinear and included looping interior streets, cul-de-sacs, and few entries into the neighborhood interior.[63] This is an approach not favored by planners today.

RECTILINEAR PLANS—Until 1940 the vast majority of the United States was developed with a rectilinear street-grid pattern, as rectilinear grids are a quick, efficient way to survey land and subdivide it for sale.

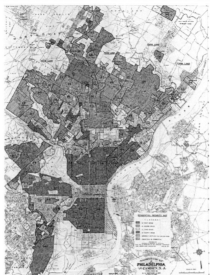

EXAMPLE OF REDLINED MAP
showing downtown Philadelpia with inner-city neighborhoods redlined
to indicate where federal programs would not insure loans

MUNGER PLACE, DALLAS, TEXAS
Before and after from Fannie Mae's 1976 Munger Place project. This demonstrated
that loans could be successfully made in older, dilapidated neighborhoods. This
pilot project helped lead to the Community Reinvestment Act of 1977 that opened
up lending in older neighborhoods that had previously been redlined.

REDLINING
federal loan funds were witheld from many older neighborhoods, a practice that ended in 1977

Multiple blocks of urban fabric cleared for "urban renewal" with use
of federal funds authorized by the Housing Act of 1954

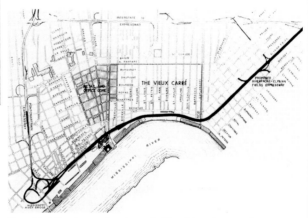

View of historic Jackson Square and the St. Louis
Cathedral from the Mississippi River—had the
elevated New Orleans interstate not been stopped

Heavy black line shows projected route for New Orleans interstate, hugging
river, and elevated—cutting Vieux Carré and Jackson Square off from river. First
interstate highway to be stopped for environmental reasons. Led to the Historic
Preservation Act of 1966 and the Section 106 review process for use of federal
funds that would have an adverse impact on historic buildings

DESTRUCTIVE USE OF FEDERAL FUNDS
in many cities led to 106 review process for impact of federal dollars on important resources

The grid system has been used in planning towns for more than four thousand years.[64] However, when the United States passed the Land Ordinance of 1785, undertaking to divide much of North America with a strict north-south/east-west one-mile-square grid system of "sections," it was by far the most massive project of a rigid rectangular grid survey in history (see page 100). Public roads were planned to run along the one-mile boundaries. The Homestead Act of 1862 reinforced this pattern when it distributed square homesteads cut from this grid to qualifying individuals.[65] This national grid system was also used to grant land to railroad companies as an incentive to build cross-country rail lines. As the railroads platted new towns and sold lots along their tracks, they created hundreds of additional small towns with a north-south grid-system plan.[66]

EARLY TOWN PLANS—A great many American towns were built upon an early plan, often drawn up by the original person or group promoting the settlement. The majority of these were grid plans. The plan often aligned with the waterway the town was built adjacent to or, later, followed the north-south land ordinance grid or a rail line. Squared open spaces were typically included. In the case of towns colonized by the Spanish, the Laws of the Indies prescribed a grid system with a central plaza to be laid out from southwest to northeast.[67]

GRIDIRON PLAT EXTENSIONS—Taking a piece of land and placing a rectangular grid on it was the simplest and most cost-effective way to ready smaller lots for sale. It little mattered if the larger piece of land was a squared section of the western states or an irregular metes-and-bounds survey from an early settlement—a grid was almost always the fastest way to divide it. Generally roads were extended from adjacent developments or from the edge of an early town plan. Where a new survey introduced an angle, roads changed direction. Where roads did not completely align, small jogs were left in place. These gridiron extensions were utilized in creating a majority of neighborhoods prior to 1940.

PLANNED RECTILINEAR SUBURBS—Beginning in 1887, the popularity of the electric trolley spurred the major expansion of trolley lines. Tracks were most efficiently built in a straight line, making it easy for developers to plat their streetcar suburbs in a grid pattern. These fast-moving trolleys, however, also made it economical to purchase large vacant areas beyond the city's built-up edge, where it was feasible to create more highly designed grid plans.

These frequently incorporated City Beautiful elaborations (see page 78). Long, straight, landscaped central medians (often called boulevards, avenues, or parkways) were favorites, and sometimes the trolley tracks were placed within this linear space. Broad, elongated medians were also easily inserted into the prevalent grid street systems of the western states and thus provided a relatively affordable way to add drama and green space into pre–World War II plans for suburban expansion.[68]

Streets featuring broad, landscaped park-like medians were also included in Olmsted's influential plan for Riverside (see illustration on page 79) and remained popular in curvilinear suburbs, particularly those planned for early automobiles. Less commonly, a communal green space was located in the center of a block.

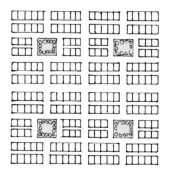

Savannah, Georgia, town plan

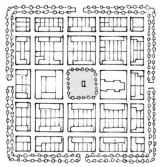

plan based on Laws of the Indies
(would be laid out at 45-degree angle)

EARLY TOWN PLANS

generally prepared by a town's colonizer or promoter

regular grid plans with short blocks most typical

commonly centered around a central plaza or square

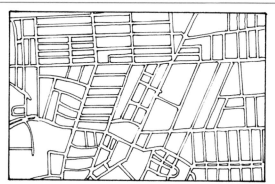

Rochester, New York

GRIDIRON PLAT EXTENSIONS

multiple angles of street grids

old survey lines can be intuited where street grids change

many streets end at T intersection

many streets have slight jogs

PLANNED RECTILINEAR SUBURBS

planned street pattern throughout

straight linear green spaces occur

longer rectilinear blocks are common

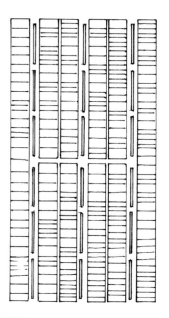

CITY BEAUTIFUL ELABORATIONS

Woodruff Place, Indianapolis, Indiana (above and left)

fountains

decorative lights

landscaped median

public art

formal street trees

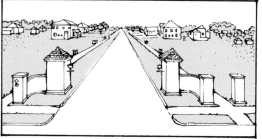

entry features

gates

Munger Place, Dallas, Texas

RECTILINEAR PLANS (most common until ca. 1940)

CITY BEAUTIFUL ELABORATIONS—The 1893 World's Columbian Exposition in Chicago spurred a nationwide interest in creating the City Beautiful. The dramatic axial Beaux Arts plan of this world's fair, followed by later expositions in cities throughout the U.S., stimulated a national interest in planning that transformed parts of cities with a grand plan. Planning elements of civic design—such as a street terminating at a focal point (monument, church, or civic building) and streets divided by a landscaped median park (see page 77)—became desirable for both rectilinear and curvilinear plans. And civic art might be added (elaborate piers, pylons, or gates marking a neighborhood entrance; decorative light fixtures, a fountain, or a statue, etc.). Each of these elements had historical roots, and their use in the U.S. pre-dated—but generally received a huge impetus from—the influential expositions of the era.[69]

CURVILINEAR PLANS—Although some towns have early curvilinear streets laid out as dictated by topography, neighborhoods with designed curvilinear street plans were not developed in the United States until the mid-19th century. Two disparate factors—one aesthetic and one practical—helped introduce the use of curvilinear plans. On the aesthetic side, Andrew Jackson Downing's widely read books promoted the ideal of curvilinear planning for both large and small properties. This theme began in 1841 with his first book, *A Treatise on the Theory and Practice of Landscape Gardening,* and continued throughout his publishing career. His *Treatise,* for example, visually contrasts an angular "Common Farm" with an "improved"—and curvilinear—"Country Seat."[70] Beginning in the 1850s, the principles for residential landscape espoused in Downing's books (based on English influences) were incorporated first into the designs for cemeteries and later into neighborhood plans.[71]

On the practical side, the application of these principles to suburbs required large vacant tracts of land, and it was the rapid spread of a railroad network in the mid-19th century that allowed access to undeveloped tracts well beyond the city center. Curvilinear plans were favored for affluent suburbs throughout the late 19th and early 20th centuries, but they were not commonly used for affordable neighborhoods until the advent of the FHA and its guidelines.

There are two typical places that curved streets appear without being part of a plan. First, some early settlements had neither a plan nor a grid survey. Sometimes roads in these were reported to have followed animal trails or Native American paths, typically along ridges of high ground. Although curving, the street patterns in these places do not have a planned appearance. Second, early development was generally limited to flat or rolling terrain, as steep hillsides and canyons were not easily accessible. The widespread use of private automobiles by about 1920 made it possible to build homes on steep and previously inaccessible sites reached by irregularly curving streets dictated by the contours of the steep topography. These challenging locations did not allow the smooth curves favored by Frederick Law Olmsted.[72]

OLMSTEDIAN PLANS—Although there were earlier planned railroad suburbs such as Llewellyn Park (see page 65), it was Olmsted's well-publicized 1869 plan for Riverside, Illinois, that provided a complete model for subdivision design and introduced curvilinear planning to a broad audience. Olmsted intended the design of his roads to "suggest and imply leisure, contemplativeness, and happy tranquility" rather than the "eagerness to press forward" he felt was inherent in rectilinear plans. He believed Riverside's

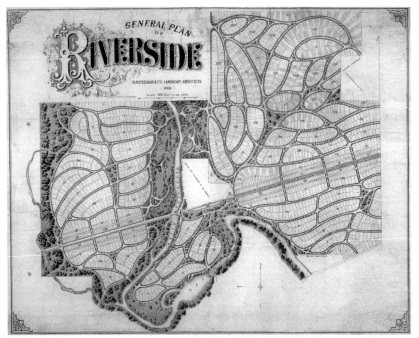

OLMSTEDIAN PLANS (1869–1940)

public green space, often along waterways

smoothly curving streets

few right-angle intersections

street trees

minimum setback of house from road

each block face has similar lot size

broad range of lot size within development

maintains natural drainage system

houses at higher grade than street

utility systems preceded building

deed restrictions

General Plan of Riverside, Illinois; Olmsted and Vaux; 1869

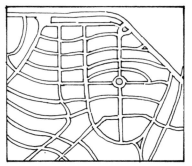

WARPED GRIDS (CA. 1915–1940)

common in early automobile suburbs

street-grid pattern modified with gentle curves

small triangular landscaped islands at angled intersections

broad street sometimes used as central planning feature

St. Francis Wood, San Francisco, CA;
Olmstead Brothers; 1912

FHA-GUIDED SUBDIVISIONS (CA. 1940–1980)

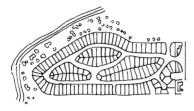

loop road

minimal access to main streets

cul-de-sacs

lots face into subdivision

BEFORE:
SUBDIVISION GRID PLAN SUBMITTED TO THE FHA, CA. 1940

AFTER:
FHA REVISION INTO A CURVILINEAR PLAN

CURVILINEAR PLANS (more common after 1940)

curves had "a controlled sweep and continuity of their own, unlike any precedent."[73] This iconic plan—with smoothly curving streets, generous street width, lack of corners, and ribbons of parkland—served as a prototype for curvilinear neighborhood planning through the early 20th century. Naturalistic Olmstedian plans required relatively large tracts of land to achieve their rural atmosphere with curving streets.

WARPED GRIDS—In many early automobile suburbs the streets are effectively laid out in a grid pattern, but one that is warped into gentle arcs. The grid was an efficient way to carry automobile traffic, but developers and the public alike had come to appreciate the visual effect of a curving street. A grid modified to gently curve provided both. Sometimes a somewhat wider street, either an arterial or a collector, was introduced into this plan and flowed through the neighborhood to gather the traffic from local streets. These often were planned as focal streets.[74]

FHA-GUIDED SUBDIVISIONS—The FHA changed the plan of affordable American neighborhoods from typically rectilinear to generally curvilinear. Prior to 1940, curvilinear plans were more often used in upscale neighborhoods, but under the aegis of the FHA they were introduced into neighborhoods for all income levels. The agency accomplished this first by establishing a set of guidelines for planning new subdivisions, and secondly by their review and approval of plans for neighborhoods where they insured home mortgages. *Successful Subdivisions* (1940), the FHA's first land-planning bulletin, was heavily illustrated with curvilinear plans to achieve many of the agency's planning objectives—such as "natural features preserved for improved appearance" and "streets should fit the contours of irregular land." This publication encouraged the use of long blocks as more economical than short blocks and advised against placing residential streets along tract boundaries. The bulletin featured three pairs of submitted plans along with the revisions advised. The pair illustrated here has a loop road and a cul-de-sac in the revised plan—both favored by the agency as ways to discourage heavy through traffic. This guideline was very specific: "Minor streets should be so arranged as to make fast through traffic impossible."[75] Developers gradually became adept at providing few entrances into a subdivision and designing an almost completely internal street system that made it difficult for a nonresident to locate a specific house, much less find his way back out to a main street.

GOLF COURSE NEIGHBORHOODS—Developments overlooking golf courses gained popularity in the post–World War II period, in part because they provided a scenic overlook for the "rooms with a view" that were integral to Mid-century Modern houses. The course offered a large privately maintained green space that raised the value of the land surrounding it while providing a quiet recreation and exercise opportunity. In the past few decades, golf-course communities, often with gated entrance, have been widely used in post-suburban neighborhoods.[76]

COMBINED PLANS—Rectilinear and curvilinear plans have been combined in a number of ways. Symmetrical geometric shapes were used for subdivisions by a few developers, particularly during the 1910s and 1920s. These combine straight and curved streets within one plan and often have a distinctive bull's-eye appearance. More common were side-by-side combinations, where a developer planned a curvilinear area of

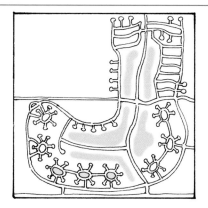

GOLF COURSE DEVELOPMENTS
new way of providing shared green space
golf course creates broad green view for Mid-century Modern's rooms with views
cul-de-sacs very common
frequently private gated communities

CURVILINEAR PLANS (cont.)

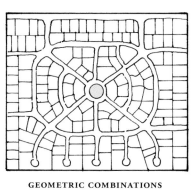

often in bulls'-eye
form

"signature" curvilinear
area with later, often
more affordable,
rectilinear areas

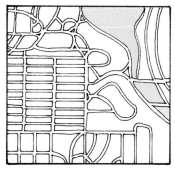

GEOMETRIC COMBINATIONS

SIDE-BY-SIDE COMBINATIONS

COMBINED PLANS rectilinear with curvilinear

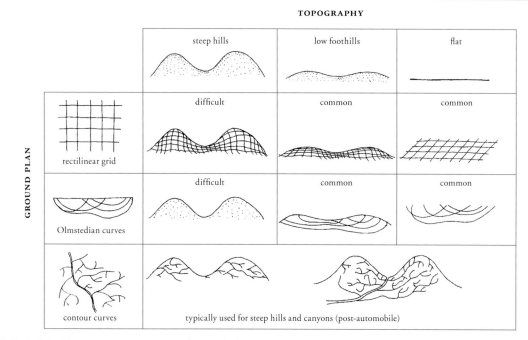

TOPOGRAPHY

GROUND PLAN	steep hills	low foothills	flat
rectilinear grid	difficult	common	common
Olmstedian curves	difficult	common	common
contour curves	typically used for steep hills and canyons (post-automobile)		

BENEATH THE PLAN interaction of ground plans with topography

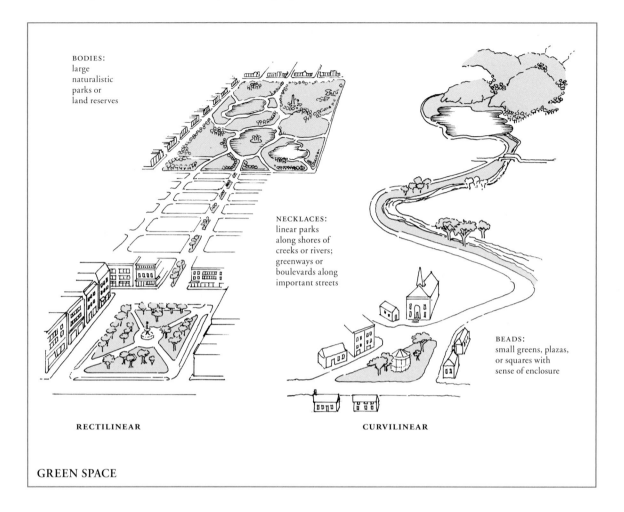

BODIES:
large
naturalistic
parks or
land reserves

NECKLACES:
linear parks
along shores of
creeks or rivers;
greenways or
boulevards along
important streets

BEADS:
small greens, plazas,
or squares with
sense of enclosure

RECTILINEAR

CURVILINEAR

GREEN SPACE

more expensive homes that transitioned to a more economical rectilinear street and lot plan of more modest homes.

BENEATH THE PLAN—A primary factor in the character of a neighborhood is the topography and original vegetation upon which it is built. Cities and towns occupy only a fraction of the vast and varied land area of the United States. Normally their founders chose relatively level sites near dependable water supplies.[77] On sites that were not completely flat, neighborhood street plans interacted with surface relief to add three-dimensional variety to the town's neighborhoods. Much diversity results from the interaction of street patterns and topography. In general, simple-grid streets are appropriate on both flat areas and low foothills, while Olmstedian curved streets are most natural on low foothills, but can be used on flatlands. Contour curves were historically the only affordable solution to development on steep hills and in canyons.

Neighborhoods that have preserved their original ecology, vegetation, and natural drainage are unusual and to be treasured. Retention of native plants not only conserves resources such as water and nutrients, it can also make a neighborhood more distinctive than one where original vegetation was scraped during development and the site then "landscaped" with commonly cultivated and widely available plants. Utilizing an area's natural drainage, rather than burying storm drains, costs less and facilitates native landscape.

Overlay Patterns

Looking at a large map of a city or town, one rectilinear neighborhood appears almost identical to the next. When driving the streets, however, there is great diversity added by the patterns formed by green space, street profile, block size, and lot width. These same overlays add equal diversity to curvilinear plans.

GREEN SPACE—Green space provides a highly visible and attractive organizing element for neighborhoods of every type. In urban neighborhoods, small open spaces are essential to provide relief from the built environment. Hence a square, green, or plaza was incorporated into the original plan for many American towns.[78] In the late 19th century elongated stretches of green space (either curvilinear alongside streams or long rectangular medians or spines) began to be used and were frequently part of well-planned early suburban expansions and park systems. New York's huge Central Park (1857–1873) spurred many cities to develop large reserves of more natural green space or acquire preserves of wilderness land on their periphery as an antidote to rapidly increasing urban population growth.

Green space can be in a curvilinear or rectangular shape, often influenced by the overall neighborhood plan, varying widely in size, location, and detail. Inspired by Olmsted's Emerald Necklace chain of parks in Boston (1878–1900), small compact green spaces can be thought of as "beads" (spaces small enough that surrounding buildings read as an enclosure surrounding the green space), elongated linear parks as "necklaces" (discernable strands of green running through a neighborhood or part of a city), and quite large green spaces as "bodies" (generally with a naturalistic interior design, where one feels completely surrounded by green rather than a small "clearing" in the built environment).[79]

STREETS AND CIRCULATION—Access into and through a neighborhood is a critical function that has evolved with neighborhood types and related transportation. The overview is to determine the types of circulation systems present in a neighborhood (pedestrian, automobile, bicycle, streetcar, or mass transit), how each is designed to flow within the neighborhood, how the different systems relate and connect to one another, and how these systems within a neighborhood connect to exterior circulation systems and plans. Discrete elements of these systems—such as street width, vehicular lanes, and curb and sidewalk patterns—are easy to observe. They are each important contributors to neighborhood character. Understanding how these relate to larger area plans requires research.

PRIMARY ROADS—There have been dramatic changes in how streets providing main transportation routes have been viewed, used, planned, and built along. The role of primary roads evolved from a favored location for homes in early urban and rural neighborhoods to a shunned location for homes in postwar suburbs.

In early urban and rural neighborhoods there were few main roads. Generally unpaved, they only carried light traffic. In both urban and rural areas, a home located close to a road was desirable. This preference continued during the early streetcar era, when a location on the streetcar line meant convenience. Many cities had at least one major street lined with late 19th- or early 20th-century mansions whose occupants were easily able to walk out their door and step onto a nearby streetcar. In modest neighborhoods the finest homes were often right on the streetcar line.

By about 1915 there were enough automobiles on city streets that planners knew additional provisions had to be made for them. An early step in accommodating cars was to convert the wider streets that had contained streetcar lines into arterials for automobiles.[80] Due to higher traffic volumes, the desirability for residential uses fell and their attraction for commercial uses increased. The net effect was that many of the finest rows of late 19th-century and very early 20th-century American homes were either converted to commercial uses or demolished. A common early automobile suburb answer was to simply embrace the automobile and introduce an arterial or collector running *through* the neighborhood to gather the traffic from the local streets. Such a street might be curved, have a green median or other City Beautiful feature, and create something of an automobile promenade for Sunday afternoon drives. The overall neighborhood plan

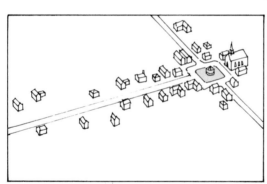

EARLY "PIKES" OR "HIGHWAYS" (PRE-1850)
desirable location for farmsteads in early rural areas, road necessary to access trade centers or cities

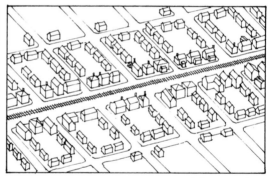

HORSECAR AND STREETCAR SUBURBS (1850–1920)
convenient location on streetcar line preferred, larger homes often closest to line

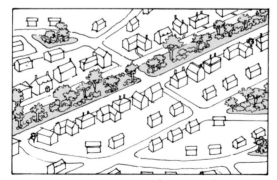

EARLY AUTOMOBILE SUBURBS (1920–1940)
enhanced road often used as focal planning element, largest home sites often face enhanced road

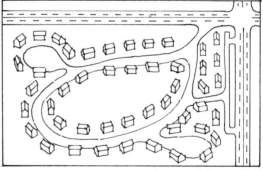

POST–WORLD WAR II SUBURBS (1940–1980)
primary arterials exterior to neighborhood, homes rarely face primary road, smaller slip street used when necessary

DEVELOPMENT PATTERNS ALONG PRIMARY ROADS

was generally still a grid, perhaps warped. As the number of automobiles increased in the 1920s, adding a showy street through the middle of a neighborhood was quickly abandoned—and replaced by planning both regional road systems and individual subdivisions to keep traffic outside a neighborhood. This new approach to subdivision design was encouraged by the widely publicized 1929 model community of Radburn, New Jersey, called "A Town for the Motor Age." A project of the Regional Planning Association of America, Radburn separated pedestrian and automobile traffic by utilizing changes in grade and introducing large "superblocks"—a planning term for huge blocks in both directions—and cul-de-sacs. Implementation of complete separation was not feasible on a widespread basis, but planners and home buyers eagerly embraced the concept of minimizing traffic within neighborhoods.

As an affordable solution, the FHA planners strongly encouraged a new way to relate neighborhoods to primary roads like arterials that carried heavy traffic. They encouraged less traffic by nestling new neighborhoods *next to* arterials (whether major or minor), with few entrances into the neighborhood. Where the edge of the neighborhood abutted a major street, two solutions were suggested. Preferably, lots on the outer edge faced inward with an arterial-screening wall behind. If this was not possible, it was suggested that a small secondary access road (or slip street) be added for edge houses to

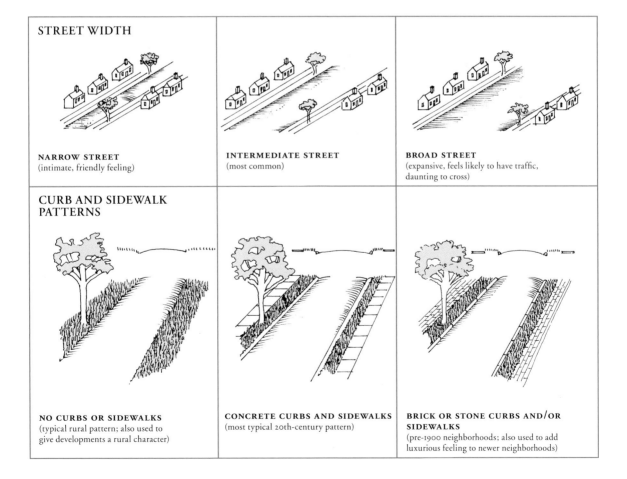

STREET WIDTH

NARROW STREET
(intimate, friendly feeling)

INTERMEDIATE STREET
(most common)

BROAD STREET
(expansive, feels likely to have traffic, daunting to cross)

CURB AND SIDEWALK PATTERNS

NO CURBS OR SIDEWALKS
(typical rural pattern; also used to give developments a rural character)

CONCRETE CURBS AND SIDEWALKS
(most typical 20th-century pattern)

BRICK OR STONE CURBS AND/OR SIDEWALKS
(pre-1900 neighborhoods; also used to add luxurious feeling to newer neighborhoods)

BLOCK SHAPE

LOT SIZE
extra-wide
lots (rural
areas or luxury
neighborhoods)

SQUARE   RECTANGULAR   ELONGATE

intermediate-width
lots (most suburban
neighborhoods)

narrow lots (urban
neighborhoods
or working-class
neighborhoods)

LOT SIZE AND BLOCK SHAPE

VARIETY WITHIN GRIDIRON PLANS

200-FOOT BLOCK LENGTH PRODUCES:
higher connectivity in neighborhood
fewer lots to sell (5,000 front feet)
more paving (200,000 square feet extra)
perceived as more walkable

1,200-FOOT BLOCK LENGTH PRODUCES:
lower connectivity in neighborhood
more lots to sell (6,200 front feet)
less paving
perceived as less walkable

EFFECT OF INCREASING BLOCK LENGTH
(shown in forty-acre parcel with dimensions in feet)

face onto or for neighborhood streets to end in. Beginning around 1980, the more definitive solution of a gated neighborhood with single entrances began to be used.

CURBS AND SIDEWALKS—Curbs, or lack thereof, contribute to the character of a
neighborhood. Streets without curbs seem more rural and like a small town. Streets with
curbs seem more urban and suburban. Although concrete curbs of varied profiles are the
norm today, before about 1900 local stone was often used.

Sidewalks are similar in their effect. Their absence feels rural and their presence
urban. Post–World War II neighborhoods frequently do not have sidewalks, presum-
ing that almost everyone would arrive via automobile. Although curbs and sidewalks
are generally found together, some moderate-income streetcar suburbs had sidewalks
installed but not curbs. Sidewalks were considered essential for the many people walking, while curbs were a luxury.

There are many fine early automobile suburbs, however, where the omission of both
curbs and gutters was more a neighborhood-character decision than an economic one.
Such areas typically have large lots and a rolling pastoral quality. Tiny bridges over
grassy drainage channels create interest, and curbs would negatively impact the neighborhood's appearance.[81]

BLOCKS AND LOTS—A surprising amount of diversity is possible within a simple
grid street pattern, despite the fact that in plans they may look identical. The size and
shape of the individual blocks is the first place variety is introduced. Rectangular blocks
are the most common, and the houses built on these often face out in only two directions. The length and depth of rectangular blocks can differ significantly, with the most
distinct alternative being unusually long blocks. Square blocks may have deep lots with

houses facing only two directions, or they may have houses facing all four directions, the least common pattern.[82]

Blocks of identical size and shape may be platted with different-size lots, creating a varied visual interest from block to block or neighborhood to neighborhood. Lots can be narrow, such as the 13- to 30-foot-wide lots found in urban environments and some working-class neighborhoods; or of medium width, such as the 40- to 60-foot-wide lots found in many late 19th- and early 20th-century streetcar suburbs; or very wide, such as the 65- to more than 150-foot-wide lots found in many upper-income and postwar neighborhoods. An advantage of elongated rectangular blocks is that there is far less area to be paved and, at the same time, more land area available to be divided into salable lots. These same kinds of block and lot differentials can be found in curvilinear plans, where there are even more ways of introducing variety into the plan through design.

People generally prefer to walk shorter blocks. In addition, narrower streets invite a stroll and give a friendlier neighborhood feeling. The neighborhood-savvy planners designing new TNDs and TODs frequently recommend both of these elements.

Development Influences

A broad range of economic and governmental factors have had a powerful effect on neighborhoods through the evolution of government regulation, financial control, and publicly funded infrastructure. These have influenced, and in some cases controlled, the type of neighborhood built, who builds them, where they are located, and if they can survive.

DEVELOPER/BUILDER—A subdivision—the basic landscape unit of residential development—is created when a large parcel of undeveloped land such as a farm is cut into smaller lots suitable for building a home. When subdivision occurs, improvements such as streets, storm drainage, utilities, and sewers may be added.[83] Each lot is sold either as vacant or with a house already built. A neighborhood generally contains one or more subdivisions.

The entity that subdivides and improves land today is usually the developer. Until about 1850, however, vacant land was simply subdivided into lots by "sub-dividers" with few, if any, improvements. A builder—generally different from the subdivider—constructed the house or building. Every lot sold could be employed for any use or structure—the genesis of the old-fashioned, mixed-use city.

Beginning in the mid-19th century a few early prototypes of today's developers purchased large tracts of land outside cities and subdivided them into lots intended exclusively for expensive residences and necessary support uses. Improvements such as landscaping, roads, and utility systems were frequently added. Private deed restrictions (see page 90) often governed what could be built. Houses were most often constructed by individual builders—some for a specific family and others on speculation that a buyer would be found. The majority of them constructed only a few houses each year.[84] Even in these controlled neighborhoods, there was no guarantee the neighborhood would develop as intended. Far more lots were platted for sale than there was a demand for. Nonetheless, the pattern of a developer subdividing land, adding restrictions, and selling vacant lots continued to grow until the beginning of the Depression. The development of these restricted neighborhoods spread throughout the United States and reached maturity in the 1920s, when they effectively governed the design and regulation of a great many *high*-end residential neighborhoods.[85]

The national trauma of the Great Depression initiated changes at the *moderate* end.[86] By 1933 housing construction had come to a virtual standstill. The National Housing Act of 1934, adopted to revive home building, also dramatically changed how American neighborhoods were developed. It created the FHA, with the broad charge to "improve nationwide housing standards, provide employment and stimulate industry, improve conditions with respect to mortgage financing, and realize a greater degree of stability in residential construction."[87] The FHA did not lend mortgage money. Instead, it insured the home loans banks made against losses. The FHA adopted strict standards for the loans it would insure and demanded both lower-priced homes and a broad set of development practices designed to ensure long-term neighborhood stability. For economic efficiency the agency encouraged the same developer to build houses on all lots of a subdivision so that an entire neighborhood would be constructed at once, lending both economy of scale and predictability. The earlier practice of separating land subdivision from home building became far less common and one development profession emerged, sometimes called "community building."[88] Now large-scale neighborhoods, rather than individual homes, were built. No longer did one purchase a vacant lot in an area with an uncertain future. Instead, one purchased a home within a completed neighborhood.

HOME FINANCING—The revolutionary shift affected in neighborhood development by the FHA was accompanied by a major change in how one purchased a home. Earlier, potential home buyers commonly had to save the entire cost of a residential site and purchase it before contracting with a builder to construct the house. Local banks made short-term mortgage loans to pay for construction costs. They required periodic interest payments, with the entire principal amount falling due at some future date, generally about five years later.

By the early 20th century, a few large home-building enterprises had begun to offer custom-designed homes that could be purchased with the lot along with a long-term, installment-payment mortgage that included both interest and principal reductions.[89] Americans now take for granted this method of home financing—an amortizing loan paid over a period of up to thirty years—but it is barely a century old, a revolutionary innovation that spurred the development of countless 20th-century neighborhoods.

As a result of the financial crisis of the early 1930s, many Americans were unable to make payments on their homes, no matter which financing method was used. Banks repossessing the houses could not resell them at a reasonable price due to the depressed economy. Soon the banks themselves were suffering. An entire industry ground to a halt.

The FHA renewed private mortgage lending by insuring banks and other lenders against losses from the new long-term amortizing mortgage loans. In return, the FHA required the houses so insured to meet their subdivision design and construction standards.

The FHA's programs were a great success in stimulating new-house construction and homeownership. During World War II (1941–1945), only housing necessary to the war effort was permitted built. After the war, however, the pent-up demand for housing—along with the GI Bill of 1944, which financed the down payment of a new

UNIFIED STREETSCAPES
open front lawns and uniform setback of houses result from original deed restrictions; note level changes from house on terrace to street level, broad sidewalk, tree-planting strip, and green median

DEED RESTRICTIONS

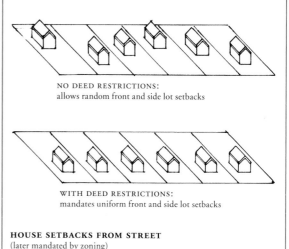

NO DEED RESTRICTIONS:
allows random front and side lot setbacks

WITH DEED RESTRICTIONS:
mandates uniform front and side lot setbacks

HOUSE SETBACKS FROM STREET
(later mandated by zoning)

home for all veterans—set the stage for an enormous housing boom when the war ended.[90] For decades the agency's policies guided neighborhood development across the United States.

It was through its requirements for insuring loans for both builders and home purchase that the FHA exerted a strong influence on the development of American neighborhoods. The agency encouraged professional plans for subdivisions and then reviewed these plans, pushing the nation toward curvilinear plans and new street circulation patterns (see pages 83–86). In addition, their mortgage-insurance guidelines (in effect the maximum amount they would insure any given year) encouraged smaller and more standardized house designs, making it less expensive to buy a house than to rent it.[91]

Unfortunately, the FHA's focus on new construction left the country's older neighborhoods without mortgage sources, resulting in a devastating effect throughout the 1950s, 1960s, and 1970s. The FHA's policies went even further and actively redlined some areas as "undesirable for lending."[92] The FHA (through their arm Fannie Mae, the Federal National Mortgage Association) participated in its first inner-city lending project in 1976 in Munger Place, a streetcar suburb of Dallas, Texas, that had previously been redlined, meaning it had been deemed not secure for home lending.[93] In 1977 Congress passed the Community Reinvestment Act, requiring lending institutions to reinvest in older neighborhoods and thus enabling the widespread reclamation of the nation's historic neighborhoods.[94]

GOVERNANCE—There are three primary ways to control how a neighborhood looks: deed restrictions, zoning, and subdivision-platting regulations. The first two are most relevant to the house built on a lot, while the third governs the design of the lots themselves. None of these were generally used prior to about 1870, when deed restrictions began to be utilized.

Deed Restrictions—In the 19th century municipalities rarely regulated construction, and only private protections were available. These private protective covenants (often called deed restrictions) could govern a broad variety of things. First used in early upscale suburbs, they typically might require houses to be built with uniform setbacks from the street, generous side yards, open front lawns, and street trees—all intended to create a pleasing visual unity. An unfortunate additional provision often excluded minorities from ownership. Additional requirements might include a restriction to residential use, and a minimum building cost ensured that the most expensive homes were grouped on certain blocks. A broad range of housing prices might be incorporated into a single development on a block-by-block or street-by-street basis. For example, a development of eighteen square blocks, laid out along six parallel streets, might require houses on the most prime street to cost a minimum of $10,000 to build, with the minimum dropping to $8,000 on the next street, then $5,000, then $3,500, and to $2,500 on the last two streets.[95]

Planned neighborhoods where developers put protective covenants in their deeds were widespread by the early 1900s. Early sets of deed restrictions expired after a certain number of years and were often difficult to renew. By the early 20th century J. C. Nichols had produced refined wording so deed restrictions would renew automatically.

Zoning—Deed restrictions proved so successful that some began to wonder if municipalities could successfully legislate protection for all their neighborhoods, not just those with deed restrictions. The idea evolved quickly. Protective covenants had commonly relied on homeowners for enforcement, and implementing them could be difficult. Lower-income neighborhoods were often not protected by such covenants. If zoning was adopted by municipal law, the burden of enforcing compliance would fall to the city and, in theory, the same protections would be provided to all. Two initial steps were taken when Boston imposed height restrictions during 1904–1905, and Los Angeles followed by dividing itself into residential and industrial sections in 1909.

Then, in 1914, the New York state legislature adopted a statute allowing towns to provide more comprehensive restrictions on development. In 1916 New York City became the first city in the country to adopt a zoning code. The idea of zoning legislation spread quickly. The U.S. Department of Commerce prepared a draft of the Standard State Zoning Enabling Act (SZEA) in 1922, and by the end of that year twenty states had adopted statutes allowing their cities to make and enforce zoning restrictions, and fifty cities had already taken advantage of this right. By 1926 twenty-three more state legislatures had passed zoning statutes, and cities and towns across the country were rushing to adopt zoning codes. That same year the U.S. Supreme Court upheld the legality of such efforts in a landmark decision.[96]

Today, zoning laws are almost ubiquitous in American cities, and few people realize how recent they are. While some rhapsodize about the wonderful years when everyone agreed what a city should look like, that was before the industrial revolution rapidly changed the scale of buildings as well as the kinds of transportation that made up a city. The requirements of railroads carved the downtowns of many cities into sections. New structural systems and elevators allowed large factories and high-rise buildings. The advent of automobiles brought road widening, freeways, and parking lots. These dramatic changes began to evolve rapidly in about 1850 and were hastened by the proliferation of automobiles during the 1920s.

The old agreement of how cities should look was swept aside during these seventy-five years of massive change. No wonder the ability to regulate the location of these new uses through zoning ordinances swept the country in the ten short years between 1920 and 1930. In the mid-20th century a new kind of zoning code began to be written that allowed older neighborhoods to become historic districts with zoning to protect the original historic buildings and their features. In addition, new zoning laws were written that allowed the creation of conservation districts where design elements such as scale or architectural style were protected—rather than the historic homes themselves.

But the location of uses and the height of a building were only a small part of planning a quality built environment for a city. Because SZEA came first (it was finally published in 1924) and its governance of uses was so specific and desired at the time, zoning is sometimes thought of as planning. In actuality zoning is only a small part of planning. It was two years later, in 1926, that the Standard City Planning Enabling Act (SCPEA) was published by the Department of Commerce, making it easy for states to undertake more broad-based land-use planning. Although the Act covered farsighted topics like master plans and regional planning, at the neighborhood level the effects are most specifically seen in subdivision regulations.

Subdivision Regulations—Because there had been an oversupply of lots platted, often with no improvements, many towns began to limit the supply of lots to be built upon through new subdivision regulations. Historically simply a way of tracking land ownership and street continuation, the Standard City Planning Enabling Act made subdivision design an important part of directing the growth of cities. It ensured coordination with overall plans (such as highways and parks), required developers to build good roads and infrastructure at their expense, and controlled the amount of land available for development at any one time to avoid oversupply of vacant lots. Subdivision regulations generally control the size of lots, the width of streets, and the location of utilities. These controls govern a subtle but large part of the streetscape.[97]

The enforcement of zoning laws and platting restrictions has proved almost as challenging for neighborhoods as enforcing deed restrictions. A more far-reaching effect is that both subdivision and zoning regulations have today evolved in ways that can legislate urban sprawl. New urbanist planners emphasize the need to rewrite these codes as an important step in preventing future sprawl. In order to avoid an unintended consequence of harming intact older residential neighborhoods, a recommended approach is to lasso new densification, keeping it compact and concentrating it on the nation's large supply of underutilized commercial and industrial land.[98]

Growth Rate—The economic origins of an area—and the income level and rate of population growth these produced through time—are a major factor in shaping neighborhoods and their streetscapes. The fluctuations of the resident population determined the size of homes that could be supported and how large new neighborhoods could be. Fast and steady growth typically produced large areas of similar houses. A new industry with many workers might produce a nearby neighborhood of small homes. In fast-growing cities, middle-class streetcar suburbs could be built by the mile, but they extended only a few blocks in slower-growth areas. An area that experienced a single boom has houses almost solely from that period, sometimes widely spaced, in the belief that intervening lots would soon sell. Because small towns typically grew slowly, they often have neighborhoods with a mixture of house sizes and styles reflecting different eras. However, this was not always the case, and a small mining town in Colorado, for example, might be built seemingly overnight and then continue to exist almost as a time capsule. Neighborhoods and their homes can often be tied directly to an area's economy and the varied factors that influenced its growth.[99]

Reading Streetscapes

The streetscapes that have been created over time reveal much about a neighborhood's history. They give you an idea about the period of time during which houses were originally built, the care the original developer took, and the current condition of the homes—thus recording how economic conditions changed.

HOUSES ON THE BLOCK—The interaction of growth rate, governance, and method of development with the age and styles of individual houses establishes a rhythm on the street. One can have a smooth rhythm of uniform lots with similar houses or a syncopated rhythm of varied lot sizes with dissimilar houses.

The smooth rhythm of a unified streetscape was produced by uniform lot sizes, deed restrictions mandating similarities (lot placement, two-story houses, etc.), and rapid growth. Where a neighborhood developed quickly, the houses are more likely to be

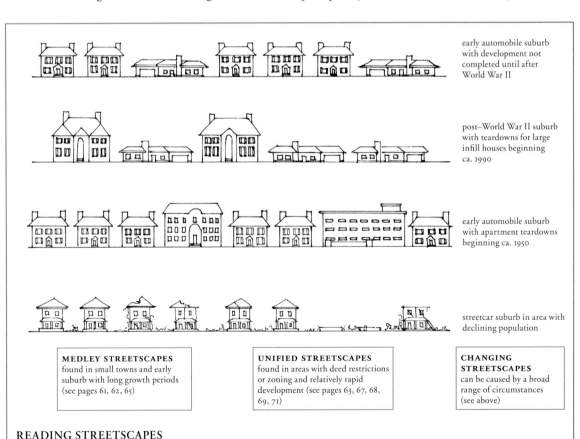

early automobile suburb with development not completed until after World War II

post–World War II suburb with teardowns for large infill houses beginning ca. 1990

early automobile suburb with apartment teardowns beginning ca. 1950

streetcar suburb in area with declining population

MEDLEY STREETSCAPES
found in small towns and early suburb with long growth periods (see pages 61, 62, 65)

UNIFIED STREETSCAPES
found in areas with deed restrictions or zoning and relatively rapid development (see pages 63, 67, 68, 69, 71)

CHANGING STREETSCAPES
can be caused by a broad range of circumstances (see above)

READING STREETSCAPES

of similar age and form (urban extension, streetcar, and post–World War II suburbs). Where development was spread over a long period, as in many smaller towns that never had a major growth period, the streetscape is more of a medley (rural neighborhoods and some early railroad suburbs). Many planners and even the FHA recommend slight differences in spacing and placement to create variety.

Interesting rhythmic changes can be seen in early automobile suburbs that began developing with two-story period houses before World War II and then did not fill up. After the war, one-story Ranch houses are likely to have been constructed on the remaining lots. Beginning in the 1990s many desirable older neighborhoods experienced rapid change in their previously unified streetscape by the introduction of houses far larger than those that make up the original neighborhood. Placing a few massive houses into a smaller-scale neighborhood can make the remaining houses seem like potential teardowns—with "smaller-scale" applying to what would generally be considered spacious houses. A street's rhythm is greatly changed by the addition of just one or two intrusive out-of-scale houses, and these are even more overwhelming if two lots have been combined into one.

Areas with zoning changes or expired deed restrictions may have newer apartment buildings that greatly change the neighborhood rhythm with their greater lot coverage and/or height. Historic neighborhoods in less desirable areas, or those with shrinking populations, may have their street rhythm interrupted by vacant lots created by fire (or code-enforcement efforts without any restoration funds or incentives attached), producing devastating changes.

Some early homes are widely spaced because they were built originally as large-lot mini farms and gradually unneeded land was sold off for new construction. Or they might have been built in a large subdivision that was designed and platted with the belief that a building boom would continue unabated.

STREET TREES AND STREET ENCLOSURE—Of the many amenities that add character to a neighborhood, street trees are perhaps the most important. Nothing makes a stronger impression when looking at a streetscape than the absence or presence of street trees. Jefferson understood this when he lined Pennsylvania Avenue with poplar trees in the early 19th century. It was not until the late 19th century that residential neighborhoods began to receive the same attention.[100] Many early developers worked with landscape architects to lay out their subdivisions, fully understanding the importance of landscape on neighborhood character. Frequently advertised as important neighborhood amenities, street trees were planted at regular intervals along a planting strip between the sidewalk and the street. Typically a single species of tree was planted. While the downside of single-species planting is that the trees will be more vulnerable to disease (as in the case of Dutch elm disease), a single species can have dramatic effects depending on the appearance and growth habits. Broad, spreading trees planted along mid- to narrow-width streets will eventually form an attractive tree tunnel. Columnar trees create a more formal allée. Palm trees give a tropical flair. Beverly Hills strikes a balance between monoculture and allées by planting each individual street with its own species of tree. Intermixing multiple tree species along a single street produces a soft and varied look.[101]

A second street-enhancing device—changing the grade between the house and street—was used by Olmsted at Riverside and is sometimes found in suburbs developed

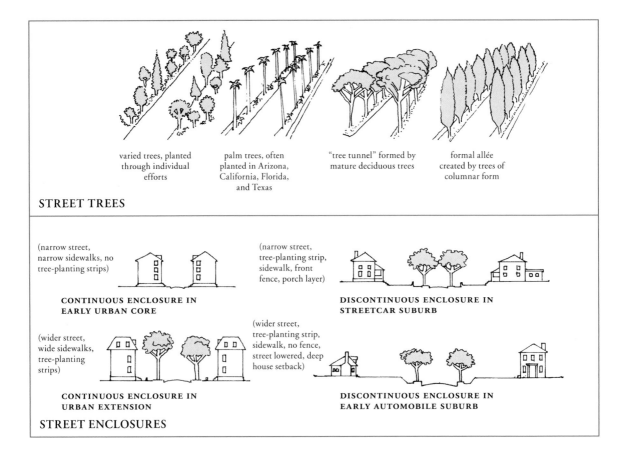

varied trees, planted
through individual
efforts

palm trees, often
planted in Arizona,
California, Florida,
and Texas

"tree tunnel" formed by
mature deciduous trees

formal allée
created by trees of
columnar form

STREET TREES

(narrow street,
narrow sidewalks, no
tree-planting strips)

(narrow street,
tree-planting strip,
sidewalk, front
fence, porch layer)

**CONTINUOUS ENCLOSURE IN
EARLY URBAN CORE**

**DISCONTINUOUS ENCLOSURE IN
STREETCAR SUBURB**

(wider street,
wide sidewalks,
tree-planting
strips)

(wider street,
tree-planting strip,
sidewalk, no fence,
street lowered, deep
house setback)

**CONTINUOUS ENCLOSURE IN
URBAN EXTENSION**

**DISCONTINUOUS ENCLOSURE IN
EARLY AUTOMOBILE SUBURB**

STREET ENCLOSURES

between about 1870 and 1940. The house was built on a flat site one to four feet higher than street level, and the transition between the two grades was most commonly accomplished by a short section of lawn that sloped up at an angle from the sidewalk.

Street enclosure refers to the effect created by the structures that line a street. Historically this was the wall created by the front facades of attached buildings in an urban neighborhood. The height of the wall (i.e., the building height) and the width of the space it encloses visually (i.e., street, sidewalk, and setbacks) are important elements of a streetscape, forming a room-like space. Varying the ratios of width to height creates different effects in urban neighborhoods.

In suburban neighborhoods the street enclosure is discontinuous, but the setback of the houses can create a somewhat room-like feeling (or lack thereof, in some post–World War II suburbs). The quality of enclosure can be modified by other continuous or semi-continuous elements, such as front fences, porches, or steps.[102]

HOUSE ON THE LOT—Landscape patterns around homes add character to many neighborhoods. These patterns result from the public streetscape, from legislated private responsibilities and regulations, and from individual private practices. While some patterns have evolved over time, there are many variations, including those related to climate, native landscape, regional practices, legislation, ethnic origin, and economic requirements.[103]

Prior to the mid-19th century, American gardens, whether herb, flower, or vegetable, tended to be laid out in geometric patterns. There was more than enough wild countryside offering a completely naturalistic effect. It was not until 1841, with the publication of Andrew Jackson Downing's *A Treatise on the Theory and Practice of Landscape Gardening* (see page 78), that more naturalistic landscape design was first advocated for larger house grounds.[104]

Victorian-era neighborhoods often had low or open fences at the sidewalk line to keep out wandering chickens, pigs, and other farm animals. Victorian houses rarely had original plantings placed along their foundations because these plantings were thought to inhibit crawl space ventilation, thus creating mold or harboring germs. Instead, beds of blooming plants were set in the middle of the yard. The ground plane was the most dominant part of the garden, and plants might be placed in an elaborate design. Individual elements of the landscape were visually separated from each other and from the house, which stood alone in splendid isolation.[105] Outdoor living was on the front and side porches, and rear yards were typically used as service areas. In less populated areas much food was still grown at home and, in a small town, one who could afford it might purchase a quarter of a block or more for a small farm with chickens, a cow, a fruit orchard, and a vegetable garden.

In the early 20th century broad expanses of front lawn became favored; they were an expensive status symbol that demonstrated that an area was more civilized, having no

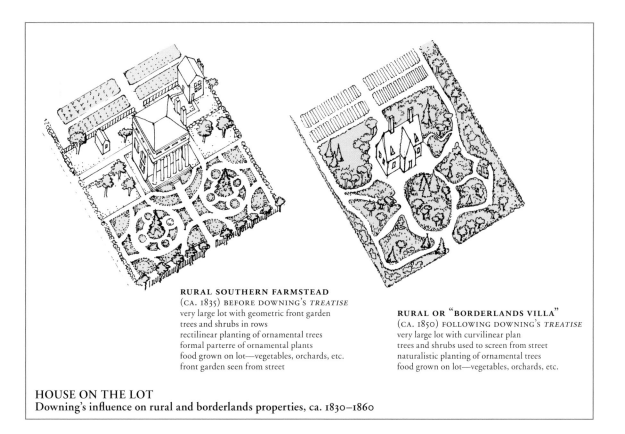

RURAL SOUTHERN FARMSTEAD
(CA. 1835) BEFORE DOWNING'S *TREATISE*
very large lot with geometric front garden
trees and shrubs in rows
rectilinear planting of ornamental trees
formal parterre of ornamental plants
food grown on lot—vegetables, orchards, etc.
front garden seen from street

RURAL OR "BORDERLANDS VILLA"
(CA. 1850) FOLLOWING DOWNING'S *TREATISE*
very large lot with curvilinear plan
trees and shrubs used to screen from street
naturalistic planting of ornamental trees
food grown on lot—vegetables, orchards, etc.

HOUSE ON THE LOT
Downing's influence on rural and borderlands properties, ca. 1830–1860

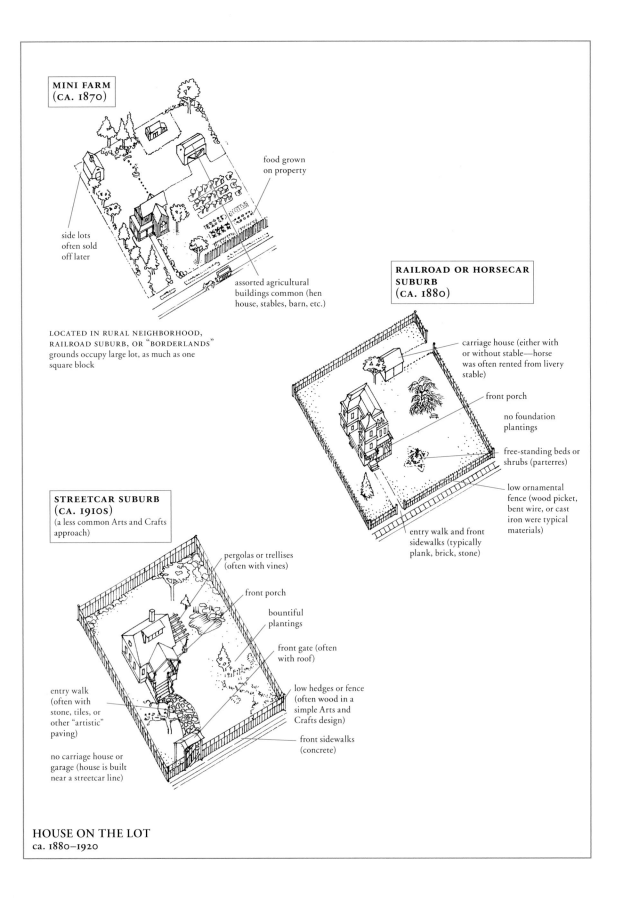

MINI FARM
(CA. 1870)

food grown
on property

side lots
often sold
off later

assorted agricultural
buildings common (hen
house, stables, barn, etc.)

LOCATED IN RURAL NEIGHBORHOOD,
RAILROAD SUBURB, OR "BORDERLANDS"
grounds occupy large lot, as much as one
square block

RAILROAD OR HORSECAR
SUBURB
(CA. 1880)

carriage house (either with
or without stable—horse
was often rented from livery
stable)

front porch

no foundation
plantings

free-standing beds or
shrubs (parterres)

low ornamental
fence (wood picket,
bent wire, or cast
iron were typical
materials)

entry walk and front
sidewalks (typically
plank, brick, stone)

STREETCAR SUBURB
(CA. 1910S)
(a less common Arts and Crafts
approach)

pergolas or trellises
(often with vines)

front porch

bountiful
plantings

front gate (often
with roof)

low hedges or fence
(often wood in a
simple Arts and
Crafts design)

front sidewalks
(concrete)

entry walk
(often with
stone, tiles, or
other "artistic"
paving)

no carriage house or
garage (house is built
near a streetcar line)

HOUSE ON THE LOT
ca. 1880–1920

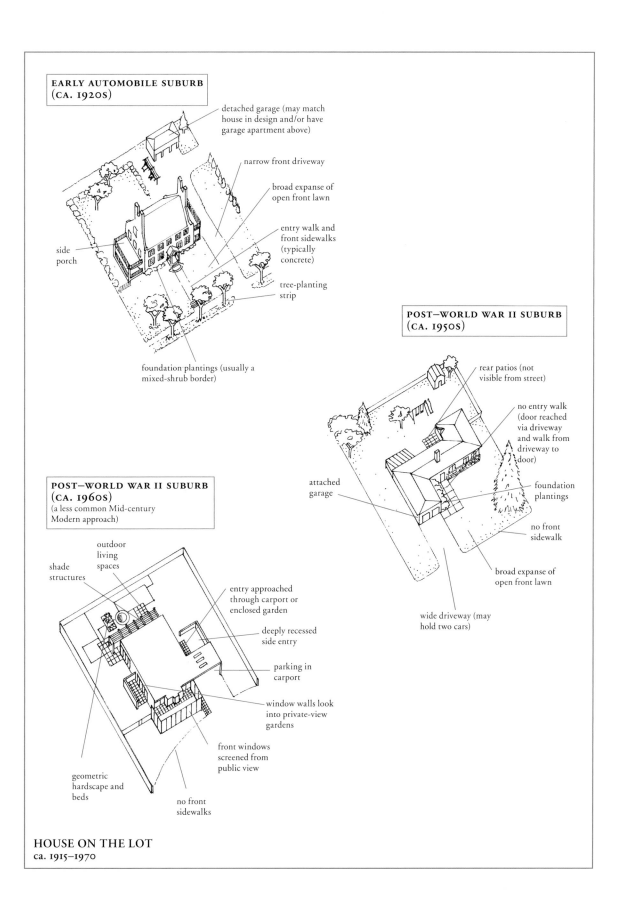

EARLY AUTOMOBILE SUBURB
(CA. 1920S)

detached garage (may match house in design and/or have garage apartment above)

narrow front driveway

broad expanse of open front lawn

entry walk and front sidewalks (typically concrete)

side porch

tree-planting strip

foundation plantings (usually a mixed-shrub border)

POST–WORLD WAR II SUBURB
(CA. 1950S)

rear patios (not visible from street)

no entry walk (door reached via driveway and walk from driveway to door)

attached garage

foundation plantings

no front sidewalk

broad expanse of open front lawn

wide driveway (may hold two cars)

POST–WORLD WAR II SUBURB
(CA. 1960S)
(a less common Mid-century Modern approach)

outdoor living spaces

shade structures

entry approached through carport or enclosed garden

deeply recessed side entry

parking in carport

window walls look into private-view gardens

front windows screened from public view

geometric hardscape and beds

no front sidewalks

HOUSE ON THE LOT
ca. 1915–1970

need to fence out livestock, and presented a lavish park-like space for passersby. Foundation plantings around houses often consisted of a mixed-shrub border, designed to visually connect the house to its site and to hide the raised foundation.[106] Porches that were generally in front of the house in streetcar suburbs might be located to one side in early automobile suburbs. Garages were typically detached and backyards still functioned as service areas. Some neighborhoods followed the advice of *Craftsman Magazine,* which promoted hedges or low fences at the sidewalk, distinctive front garden gates, and bountifully planted front and side yards.[107]

Postwar suburbs continued the practice of front lawns and foundation plants, but garages were now generally attached to the house, often opening to the front, with porches moved to the rear. With the advent of electric appliances (particularly washers and dryers) and supermarkets, backyards could be converted from service yards to private outdoor living areas. Architect-designed postwar homes sometimes went further in their use of outdoor space. A house might have a relatively blank facade facing the street yet incorporate views of side and rear gardens. In some examples, small gardens were tucked behind front walls, providing views for rooms across the front of the house. In addition, the entry to the house might be deeply recessed, creating a side-entry courtyard and eliminating the need for much interior hall space.[108]

Underlying Survey

This continent's initial occupants, the many tribes of Native Americans, had a very different concept of land and land ownership than the European colonists. The Indians did not believe that individuals owned the land, rather that humans shared the land with all other living things, both plant and animal. Although tribes fought over the right to hunt or gather in certain localities, these disputes were not over ownership.

In contrast to Native Americans, the early colonists brought with them the European tradition of individual ownership of land. The United States and its neighborhoods bear traces of the original land-survey practices, not only of our own government but also of England, Spain, France, and Holland. Many settlers received land grants from those sovereign entities.

Each colonial power surveyed portions of land, establishing a system of boundaries to accurately trace the ownership of parcels as they changed hands. These initial surveys provide the basis upon which the lands of today's United States were first granted to individuals and offered accurate physical descriptions that allowed them to later be sold. These surveys are often reflected today in the street patterns visible on maps, still shaping towns and neighborhoods.[109]

METES-AND-BOUNDS SURVEY—The earliest surveys used landscape features to establish the boundaries of landownership. The use of natural landmarks—such as mountain ridges, the ocean, rivers, or even rocks, large trees, or river bends—was typical of some early land grants. Using major landmarks was appropriate for large grants of what were then low-value lands, but in more settled areas like New England the distances between landscape features were measured in more formalized metes-and-bounds (measurements-and-boundaries) surveys. This type of survey was used in the original thirteen colonies, and spread to Tennessee, Kentucky, and Texas.[110]

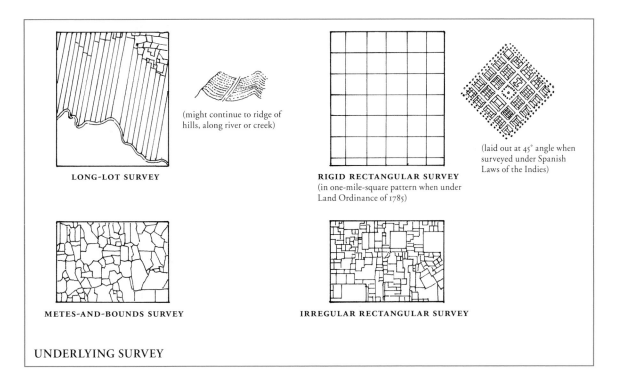

(might continue to ridge of
hills, along river or creek)

LONG-LOT SURVEY

RIGID RECTANGULAR SURVEY
(in one-mile-square pattern when under
Land Ordinance of 1785)

(laid out at 45° angle when
surveyed under Spanish
Laws of the Indies)

METES-AND-BOUNDS SURVEY

IRREGULAR RECTANGULAR SURVEY

UNDERLYING SURVEY

LONG-LOT SURVEYS—The Spanish, French, and Dutch employed a second and closely related method, the long-lot survey, for apportioning relatively small tracts along waterways such as the Mississippi, Rio Grande, and Hudson rivers. Governed by the colonists' need for reliable water in order to survive, long-lot surveys had a short and carefully measured dimension along the valuable waterway, while the longer and less valuable dimension at right angles to the waterway might be less carefully defined. This longer stretch commonly terminated at the crest of the hills that defined the valley of the waterway, creating a long narrow shape that included water from the river as well as woodlands on the hillside. Crops could be located waterside to allow for irrigation, and sheep could graze the areas in the hills. In prairie states, valuable woodlands were in the river floodplain. Long lots were also laid out along Spanish *acequias* (irrigation canals).[111]

IRREGULAR RECTANGULAR SURVEYS—In many parts of the country, settlers arriving in advance of the land's becoming U.S. territory simply surveyed town sites and neighborhoods in a grid pattern, but their grids rarely conformed to the U.S. government's prescribed north-south/east-west orientation. Texas, in particular, has many areas initially divided into what cultural geographer Terry Jordan describes as "irregular rectangular surveys"—places where "the individual land holdings are roughly rectangular or square, as in the rigid rectangular system, but they vary greatly in size and lack an orderly grid pattern."[112]

These irregular surveys evolved in many different ways. Where adjacent to a river or port, the early grids usually aligned with the waterfront. Others align with early railroads or important wagon roads. Still others are relatively arbitrary choices by individual entrepreneurs.

RIGID RECTANGULAR SURVEYS—In 1785, the Continental Congress of the United States passed the farsighted Northwest Ordinance, also known as the Land Ordinance. Today the system it created is called the Public Land Survey System (PLSS).[113] Drafted by Thomas Jefferson, it defined a systematic way of surveying new lands, inspired by the need to sell land in Ohio to raise money for the new government. The Land Ordinance prescribed a system of continuous square-mile sections, each containing 640 acres. These were surveyed on a strict north-south/east-west grid system and organized into thirty-six-square-mile townships. Public roads were to be established at one-mile intervals along the section lines, and smaller private roads were encouraged at the half-mile and half-section markers. Beginning with Ohio, federal land managers efficiently surveyed, identified, and mapped most newly acquired territory before it was opened for settlement. As U.S. government surveys were completed, newly available lands were granted or sold in north-south square-mile sections or fractions thereof. Some of these newly surveyed lands were made available to early settlers under various homestead acts beginning in 1862. Others were assigned to entrepreneurs to encourage the building of railroads across the West. No matter who first owned the land, the mark of the federal survey system has been indelibly stamped across the western states. Today many parts

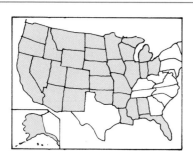

STATES WITH RIGID RECTANGULAR SURVEYS

states with one-mile grids surveyed under Land Ordinance of 1785 (parts of Texas followed this practice later; some other states also have parts with earlier surveys)

original survey pattern of Land Ordinance of 1785 reflected in agricultural fields viewed from air

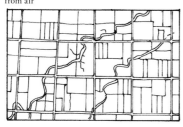

original survey pattern of Land Ordinance of 1785 platted into "Planned Rectilinear" plan

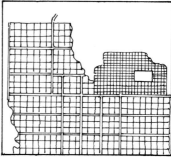

Salt Lake City, Utah

RIGID RECTANGULAR SURVEYS
A Visible Legacy

of the United States have roads running due north-south and due east-west at one-mile intervals—a visible legacy of these early U.S. surveys. The north-south/east-west grid remains even where the original one-mile pattern has been lost.[114]

In California, New Mexico, and Texas—all under Spanish rule prior to being annexed by the United States—another grid orientation was required by Spanish law. The Laws of the Indies prescribed a 45° southwest-by-northeast angle for laying out streets. It was believed that this was the most desirable orientation for maximum light and ventilation. A plaza (small public square) was prescribed at the center of a Spanish grid town. This orientation is seen today in the downtown area of older cities in these states.[115]

THE MODERN LEGACY OF EARLY SURVEYS—The differing patterns of early land surveys are often obvious on modern city and town maps. This is particularly noticeable where lands assigned by different surveys collide. The original survey method can still contribute to today's neighborhood identity and character. Every city and town is unique, and the following examples are intended only to give a hint of the history revealed by analyzing the quilt pattern formed by a town's neighborhoods.

Dallas, Texas, has three easily distinguishable street angles. One is from a land grant based on the 45° angle prescribed by the Laws of the Indies. In a grid related to the bank of the Trinity River, another angle was surveyed by the Dallas founder, who simply laid out his own grid and began selling lots. The third is a huge area of north-south/east-west

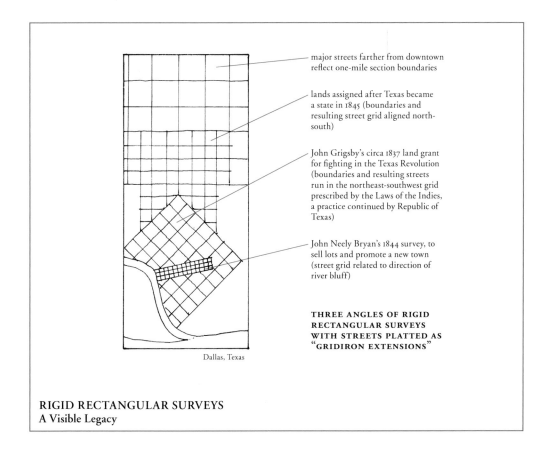

major streets farther from downtown reflect one-mile section boundaries

lands assigned after Texas became a state in 1845 (boundaries and resulting street grid aligned north-south)

John Grigsby's circa 1837 land grant for fighting in the Texas Revolution (boundaries and resulting streets run in the northeast-southwest grid prescribed by the Laws of the Indies, a practice continued by Republic of Texas)

John Neely Bryan's 1844 survey, to sell lots and promote a new town (street grid related to direction of river bluff)

THREE ANGLES OF RIGID RECTANGULAR SURVEYS WITH STREETS PLATTED AS "GRIDIRON EXTENSIONS"

Dallas, Texas

RIGID RECTANGULAR SURVEYS
A Visible Legacy

original metes-and-bounds survey pattern
reflected in agricultural fields viewed from air

original metes-and-bounds surveys platted as "gridiron extensions"

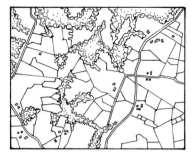

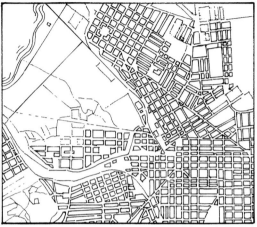

Schenectady, New York

METES-AND-BOUNDS SURVEYS
A Visible Legacy

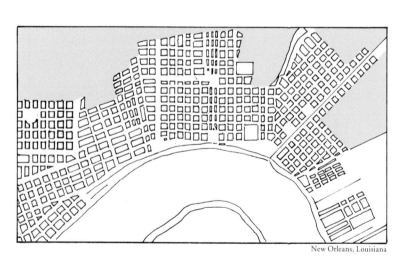

original long-lot surveys along
Mississippi; later platted as
"gridiron extensions"

New Orleans, Louisiana

LONG-LOT SURVEYS
A Visible Legacy

streets surveyed at this orientation after Texas became a U.S. state. In the post–World War II northern suburbs of Dallas, freeway entrances are located at one-mile intervals feeding broad arterial streets built along the original section-line boundaries, as prescribed in 1785.[116]

Schenectady, New York, shows a grid pattern imposed on an early metes-and-bounds survey, with a resulting web of grid extensions as small land holdings were platted and joined to the existing grid. In contrast, Salt Lake City, Utah, has a very regular gridiron plan placed onto land surveyed by the Northwest Ordinance.

New Orleans, Louisiana, was originally divided by the French into long-lot holdings called *faubourgs* that extended north from the Mississippi River. Different *faubourgs* formed fan and pie shapes as they followed the meandering river. These were eventually platted with grids at differing angles, thus maintaining the legacy of the original land division.[117]

Most American houses are built in one of the many architectural fashions, or styles, that have been popular during our country's long history. These changing fashions, which are the subject of the succeeding sections of this book, either incorporate earlier architectural images (for example, Classical porch columns or Medieval half-timbering) or consciously eschew the past to create modern styles with their own fashionable images. There is, however, another and less familiar type of dwelling that lacks this concern for architectural taste. These folk houses are built to provide basic shelter with little regard for changing fashion.

Early folk houses were constructed of materials found near the building site—rock, clay, logs, and timbers—and prepared by the builders themselves, rather than in distant mills, kilns, or factories. Usually the future occupants of the house, these builders were often aided by part-time local craftsmen. Unlike fashionable styles, folk building traditions, handed down from generation to generation, show relatively little change with time; they are, however, more strongly influenced by *geography* than are architectural styles. The local availability of building materials, as well as the building traditions of the earliest settlers in an area, can lead to strong contrasts in the structure and form of folk houses from region to region.

Our country's first folk dwellings were, of course, those built by the Native American inhabitants. Early European explorers found them using a remarkable variety of complex building techniques that had developed over many millennia. The European colonists, in turn, imported their own folk building techniques but adapted these to the same local materials used by the indigenous dwellers: wood in the heavily forested eastern half of the country and stone or clay in the more arid West. These European folk traditions persisted, with minor modifications, from the earliest colonies of the 17th century until the spread of the railroads in the mid-19th century. Rail transportation made inexpensive building

Folk Houses

materials—principally lumber from large mills located in timber-rich areas—readily available over much of the nation. This in turn led to a change in folk building traditions, as local materials, such as logs, heavy timbers, and crude masonry, were replaced by light and inexpensive sawn lumber in most folk dwellings. In spite of this change in building materials, many traditional Folk *shapes* persisted into the 20th century, when they were joined, and eventually replaced, by still other forms of National Folk housing.

A relatively high percentage of houses built before 1890 are vernacular folk houses. Daniel Reiff's survey of Fredonia, New York, showed that 40 percent of houses built before 1840 were vernacular houses "without even the 'tiniest elusive gesture' to high-style movements."[1]

After World War II, few folk houses were built. Mobile homes and Manufactured houses fulfilled the need for basic housing beginning soon after World War II.

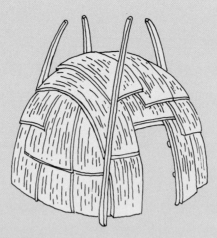

ROUND-PLAN, WOOD-FRAME FAMILY

RECTANGULAR-PLAN, WOOD-FRAME FAMILY

EARTH-WALL FAMILY

Native American

to ca. 1900

The most truly American folk houses are those that were built by the native inhabitants before Europeans discovered and occupied the North American continent. Native peoples have occupied North America for thousands of years, and during that long interval many diverse building traditions arose and evolved. The first Europeans thus found cultures with widely differing patterns of dwelling construction. These are known primarily from written descriptions, drawings, and early photographs, for most tribes have long abandoned their traditional dwellings in favor of European-influenced houses. Modern reconstructions with varying degrees of authenticity are, however, found in museum villages scattered throughout the country, and these provide a glimpse of the complex building traditions of our native forebears. In addition, a few traditional dwellings survive in isolated areas of the American West, where a handful of native cultures have persisted relatively intact to the present day.

The first Europeans found native buildings constructed with both wood-frame and masonry techniques. The wood-frame structures were particularly remarkable since they were fashioned not with the Europeans' iron axes, saws, and other implements but only with simple stone tools. These wood-frame houses were of two general sorts. Round-plan houses, such as the familiar tipi, were relatively small and partially or fully portable. These tended to be associated with nomadic or semi-nomadic hunting cultures. Rectangular-plan houses, on the other hand, tended to be larger, permanent dwellings built by sedentary, usually agricultural, societies. Masonry houses, usually with earth-wall construction, were common in the more arid regions of the American West. These ranged from simple dugouts to the familiar multi-storied pueblos of some southwestern tribes.

Round-Plan, Wood-Frame Family

Wood-frame houses with rounded ground plans were generally constructed with a framework of relatively light poles or branches fastened together with leather cords. Various materials were then used to cover the framework and make it weatherproof. Among the most frequent were tanned animal skins, sheets of bark, which were sometimes sewn together to make larger mats, thatch (tied bundles of straw), and woven mats of veg-

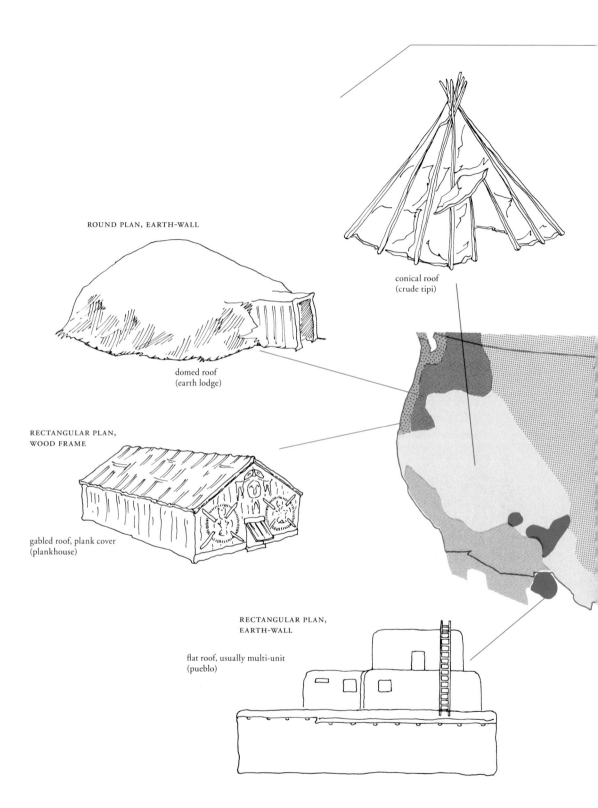

ROUND PLAN, EARTH-WALL

domed roof
(earth lodge)

conical roof
(crude tipi)

RECTANGULAR PLAN,
WOOD FRAME

gabled roof, plank cover
(plankhouse)

RECTANGULAR PLAN,
EARTH-WALL

flat roof, usually multi-unit
(pueblo)

DOMINANT NATIVE AMERICAN HOUSE TYPES
(adapted from Driver and Massey, 1957)

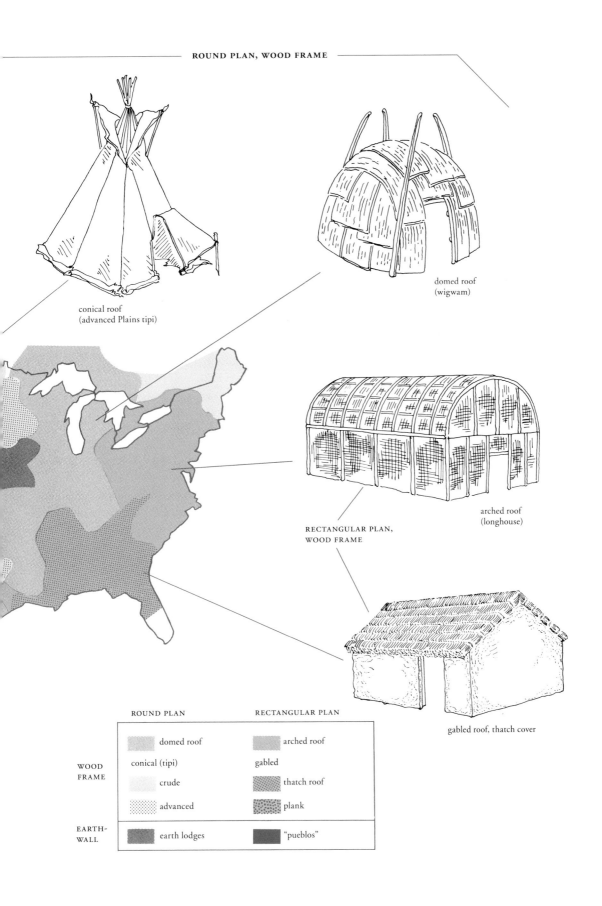

conical roof
(advanced Plains tipi)

domed roof
(wigwam)

arched roof
(longhouse)

RECTANGULAR PLAN,
WOOD FRAME

gabled roof, thatch cover

	ROUND PLAN	RECTANGULAR PLAN	
WOOD FRAME	domed roof	arched roof	
	conical (tipi)	gabled	
	crude	thatch roof	
	advanced	plank	
EARTH-WALL	earth lodges	"pueblos"	

etable fiber. The houses were built in two principal shapes: some were dome-shaped with rounded tops; others were conical with pointed tops. The dome shape dominated in the midwestern transition zone between woodlands and plains and tended to be larger and more permanent than dwellings of conical shape. Crude conical shelters of sticks and brush were commonly built on hunting expeditions, and these were the principal shelters of some nomadic tribes. Such shelters were generally abandoned and rebuilt elsewhere as needed. From them probably evolved the tipi, a conical shelter that could be transported from place to place by being dragged behind domestic dogs or, after the beginning of European colonization, by captured wild horses. Simple tipis were the principal dwellings of many hunting tribes of the northern woodlands and arid Great Basin regions. These consisted of a number of straight poles joined at the top to form a cone and covered with many separate hides, mats, or pieces of bark, which were generally held down by having additional poles laid upon them. From this simple tipi evolved a still more efficient portable dwelling, the Plains tipi. This was covered not by separate units of hide, bark, or fiber, but by a tailored covering made by sewing together many carefully tanned buffalo hides. As a further improvement, two flaps, or ears, extending outward from the top of the cover, could be adjusted by attached poles to make a sort of controlled chimney that eliminated smoke from the interior (most round-plan dwellings have only a simple smoke hole at the top). Before the introduction of the horse, such tipis were probably used only during short seasons when the buffalo herds could be easily followed for hunting on foot. Most plains tribes then returned to villages where they practiced agriculture and lived in permanent wood-frame or earth-wall dwellings. This pattern changed after the introduction of the horse, which escaped from 16th-century Spanish expeditions to become wild on the vast grasslands of the American West. The plains tribes domesticated some of these wild horses and evolved a new culture based on year-round nomadic hunting of the buffalo, which was easily killed from horseback. Horses could also drag heavy tipi poles and covers from place to place. As a result, both the size and refinements of the Plains tipi increased during the centuries between the introduction of the horse and the first extensive European contacts with the Plains tribes in the 19th century.

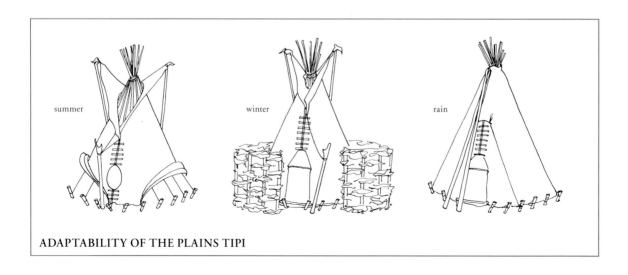

summer   winter   rain

ADAPTABILITY OF THE PLAINS TIPI

ROUND-PLAN, WOOD-FRAME FAMILY

1. Wisconsin(?); photo ca. 1890. Winnebago Tribe. Bark-covered, dome-shaped dwelling.

2. Uintah Valley, Utah; photo ca. 1875. Ute Tribe. Crude conical shelter.

3. Oklahoma(?); photo 1898. Wichita Tribe. Thatch-covered, dome-shaped dwelling. Note the wooden framework exposed at the top.

4. Idaho(?); photo ca. 1900. Umatilla Tribe. Tipi covered by woven mats and canvas cloth introduced by Europeans. Note the pole holding down the mats at right. Such tipis normally had many of these surface poles.

5. Kansas(?); photo ca. 1870. Kiowa Tribe. Plains tipi with fitted cover of tanned buffalo hides. Note the adjustable flaps at the top for controlling drafts to eliminate smoke from interior fires. The ends of the hide covering are joined by the horizontal wood pins above and below the entrance.

Rectangular-Plan, Wood-Frame Family

Wood-frame houses of rectangular ground plan were generally large, permanent dwellings housing several related families. These were the first native houses encountered by European colonists along the Atlantic coast, for they were the principal dwelling type of the many woodlands tribes of the eastern United States. Regrettably, they are also among the most poorly known because the natives of that region were the first to be displaced and their villages and traditional cultures destroyed by European colonization. Two principal types of houses appear to have been present in the eastern woodlands. To the north occurred large arched-roof dwellings (longhouses) made of light wooden frames. These were usually covered with bark; woven mats, thatch, and hides were less common coverings. In construction, these houses resembled larger and more refined versions of the round-plan, domed dwellings found farther west. In the southern woodlands these arched-roof forms were replaced by gabled (or, less commonly, hipped) roofs covered with thatch. Unlike the northern longhouses, where the same material was generally used for both roof and walls, these southern rectangular houses had varying wall materials beneath the thatched roofs. Woven mats and hides were sometimes used, as was a sort of half-timbering in which a light wooden framework was laced with basketry and covered with clay. In the warmer regions thatched summer houses without enclosing walls were also common. All of these rectangular houses of the eastern woodlands were associated with agricultural traditions based on the cultivation of corn. Some anthropologists believe that the house form spread northward from Middle America where corn was first domesticated and where somewhat similar houses are found.

An entirely different tradition of rectangular, wood-frame building was found along the humid Pacific Coast from northernmost California to southern Alaska. There the natives built large dwellings with heavy timber frames having carefully fitted joints. The frames were covered with large softwood planks split with stone tools from the abundant local timber. These houses most commonly had gabled roofs, although shed roofs were used in the Puget Sound area. The more pretentious houses were sometimes adorned with decorative and ceremonial carvings, particularly the familiar totem pole. This building tradition is believed to be a relatively recent introduction from northeastern Asia, where similar native dwellings occur.

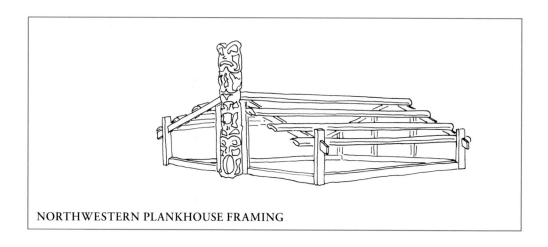

NORTHWESTERN PLANKHOUSE FRAMING

RECTANGULAR-PLAN, WOOD-FRAME FAMILY

1. Washington, District of Columbia (reconstruction); photo 1899. Abnaki-Passamaquoddy Tribe; northern New England. Bark-covered, arched-roof longhouse.

2. Fort Sill, Oklahoma, vicinity; photo ca. 1875. Caddo Tribe; displaced from Louisiana and eastern Texas. Thatch- and bark-roofed dwellings. Note the half-timbered walls on the enclosed buildings.

3. Fort Lauderdale, Florida; photo ca. 1917. Seminole Tribe. Thatch-roofed, open-sided dwellings.

4. Albert Bay, British Columbia, Canada; photo ca. 1889. Kwakiutl Tribe. Gabled, plank-walled houses. The siding behind the totem pole and the small building in the foreground were introduced by Europeans.

1

2

3

4

Earth-Wall Family

The third basic type of Native American dwelling used earth, rather than organic materials (hides, bark, straw), for covering the walls and roof. These earth-wall buildings ranged from crude dugouts to the magnificent multi-unit pueblos of the American Southwest. All use some system of wooden support for their earth-covered roofs—most commonly, heavy timbers spanned by smaller timbers and then covered with sticks, straw, or sod. The earth-covered walls were also sometimes supported by such a wooden framework. Alternatively, the walls were excavated below ground level or, as in the massive pueblos, built of sun-dried mud applied in successive layers (this is called puddled adobe; sun-dried adobe bricks were introduced by the Spaniards, although there is some archeological evidence for their use much earlier, along with complex stone masonry, by native peoples of the American Southwest). The most typical earth-wall dwelling was the round, partially excavated earth lodge, which generally housed several related families. These dwellings were usually supported by a carefully constructed wooden framework. An opening at the top permitted light to enter and smoke to escape. Sometimes the top opening was the only entrance, with descent inside by means of a log ladder; other earth lodges were entered by ground-level openings or tunnels. In the 18th and early 19th centuries these earth lodges were the dominant dwellings over much of the east-central plains and Columbia Plateau regions. They are also common among the native peoples of northeastern Asia and are thought to be among the earliest New World dwellings. There is some suggestion they were far more widespread before the introduction of the horse made possible year-round nomadic buffalo hunting over much of the West.

The most familiar of all Native American dwellings are the monumental pueblos of the Southwest, which are believed to have evolved from simple earth lodges (many incorporate round ceremonial chambers similar to lodges in shape and arrangement). The pueblos are multi-storied, communal structures made up of many rectangular rooms; exterior rooms are used for living quarters and interior rooms for food storage. The earthen roofs are supported by massive horizontal timbers placed on top of the thick adobe walls. Because of the difficulty of cutting the roof timbers to precise lengths with

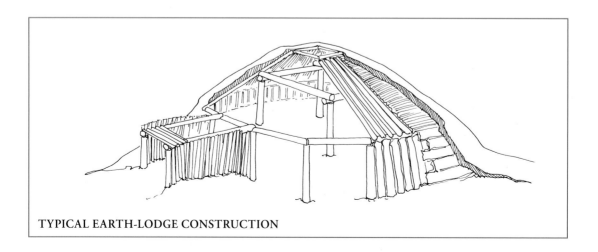

TYPICAL EARTH-LODGE CONSTRUCTION

EARTH-WALL FAMILY

1. Loup Fork, Nebraska; photo 1871. Pawnee Tribe. Village made up of several earth lodges. Note the timber frame visible in the entrance tunnel and the bundles of tipi poles used on hunting expeditions.

2. Zuni Pueblo, New Mexico; photo 1879. Zuni Tribe. Close-up view of upper stories. Note roof-support timbers and access ladders.

3. Arizona?; photo ca. 1895. Navaho Tribe. Earth-walled dugout supported by conical frame of timbers (such Navaho dwellings are called hogans).

4. Acoma Pueblo, New Mexico; photo 1899. Acoma Tribe. General view showing earth roofs in foreground.

stone tools, the ends were normally allowed to project somewhat beyond the wall surface. This is the principal difference between these native buildings and related Spanish Colonial buildings built of adobe, which have otherwise similar roof-support systems (see page 191). Several of the New Mexico pueblos have been continuously occupied since pre-Columbian times and thus have the distinction of being the most authentic surviving Native American dwellings.

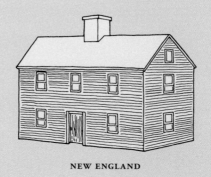

NEW ENGLAND

TIDEWATER SOUTH

FRAME TRADITIONS

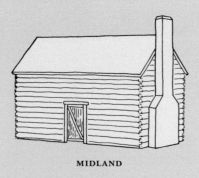

MIDLAND

LOG TRADITION

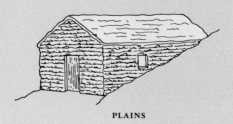

PLAINS

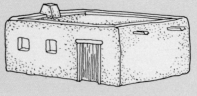

HISPANIC SOUTHWEST

MASONRY TRADITIONS

Pre-Railroad

before ca. 1850–1890; locally to ca. 1920

The first period of American folk architecture built by European colonists spanned the long interval between the earliest permanent settlements of the 17th century and the growth of the railroads as an efficient national transportation network in the last half of the 19th century. Throughout these two hundred years many modest dwellings were, of necessity, constructed of local materials without stylistic embellishment. Before the railroads, the only means of efficiently transporting bulky goods of relatively low value, such as lumber, brick, and quarried stone, was by water. Coastal towns and villages thus had access to a variety of domestic or imported construction materials, as did those inland farms and villages located near canals or the few dependably navigable rivers. Even modest houses in these areas tended to follow current architectural fashion and thus were generally styled, rather than folk, houses. Elsewhere the costs and difficulties of horse-and-wagon transport—the only alternative to boats and barges—restricted all but the most affluent to folk dwellings built with materials found on, or very near, the construction site. The eastern half of the country was covered with a seemingly endless supply of virgin forests; there, wooden folk building became the rule. The early English and French colonists were familiar with wooden building principally in the form of massive frameworks of hewn timber (post-and-girt construction) which, in the New World, were generally covered by thinner strips of wood to make a watertight exterior. These traditions dominated early folk building both in New England, where frame, massed-plan (more than one room deep) houses became the norm, and in the early settlements of the Tidewater South, where frame houses of linear plan (one room deep) dominated, probably because of the shorter and less confining southern winters. As settlement expanded to the West, a more distinctive tradition of wooden folk building evolved from a blending of the linear plans of the Tidewater South with techniques of construction using horizontal log walls brought to the middle colonies by immigrants from the heavily timbered areas of central and northern Europe. This Midland tradition of log building is the most familiar and well-studied aspect of American folk architecture. Still farther west, the vast woodlands gave way to grassy plains where timber was scarce. Large-scale settlement did not reach this area until well into the 19th century, but in the relatively brief interval before the arrival of the railroads a new folk tradition developed in this region: as a result of the shortage of wood, folk houses were

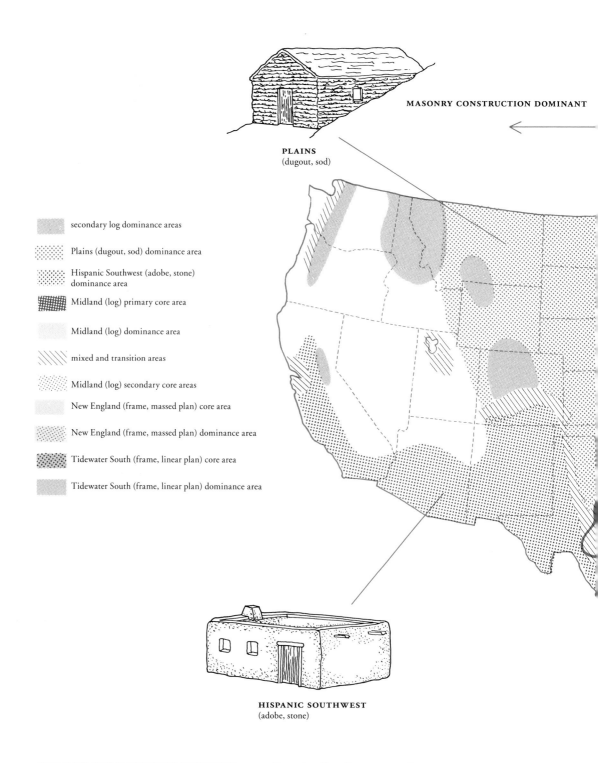

MASONRY CONSTRUCTION DOMINANT

PLAINS
(dugout, sod)

secondary log dominance areas

Plains (dugout, sod) dominance area

Hispanic Southwest (adobe, stone)
dominance area

Midland (log) primary core area

Midland (log) dominance area

mixed and transition areas

Midland (log) secondary core areas

New England (frame, massed plan) core area

New England (frame, massed plan) dominance area

Tidewater South (frame, linear plan) core area

Tidewater South (frame, linear plan) dominance area

HISPANIC SOUTHWEST
(adobe, stone)

PRE-RAILROAD FOLK TRADITIONS to ca. 1850–1890 (locally to ca. 1920)

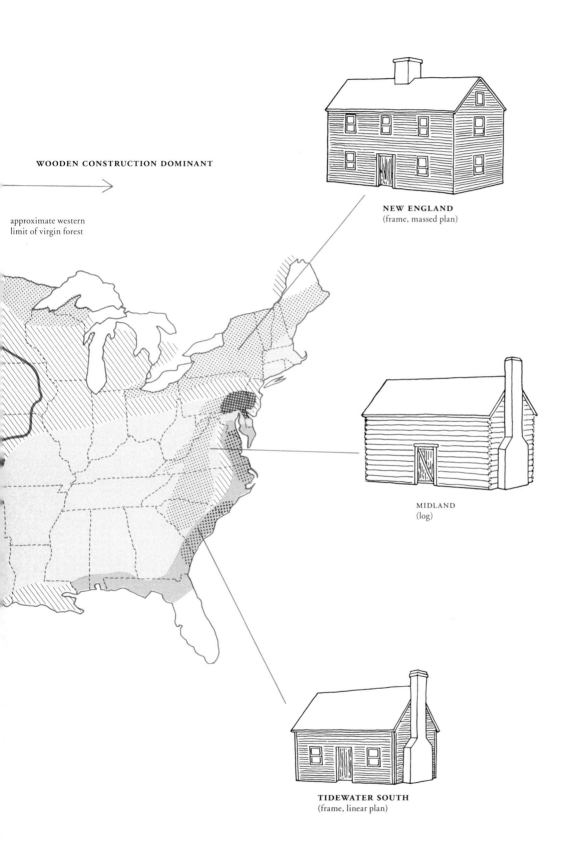

WOODEN CONSTRUCTION DOMINANT

approximate western
limit of virgin forest

NEW ENGLAND
(frame, massed plan)

MIDLAND
(log)

TIDEWATER SOUTH
(frame, linear plan)

constructed of primitive masonry. In a few areas the skills and materials were available to construct rough stone dwellings. More commonly, houses were made of sod—earth held together by fibrous grass roots. Still other masonry traditions developed in the southwestern United States, which was part of Spain or Mexico throughout most of the pre-railroad era. In this Hispanic Southwest, Spanish folk traditions of building with sun-dried adobe bricks or with rough stonework were dominant.

New England Tradition

The first New England colonists of the 17th century built primarily linear-plan houses having heavy timber frames covered with boards or shingles. These were commonly of the two-story, I-house form, although single-story, hall-and-parlor houses were also built. Both were among the commonest folk forms in 17th-century England. In the early 18th century, these plans were expanded to the rear to give increased interior space; this resulted in the one-and-one-half-room-deep saltbox and Cape Cod forms, which were better adapted to the severe and confining New England winters. From these evolved, by the mid-18th century, massed-plan houses that were to dominate New England building throughout the following century. These houses at first had two-room widths and central chimneys, as had their saltbox and I-house precursors. By the time of the Revolution, center-hall plans with paired end chimneys were common. One more change came in the early 19th century when the Greek Revival style made accentuated front gables

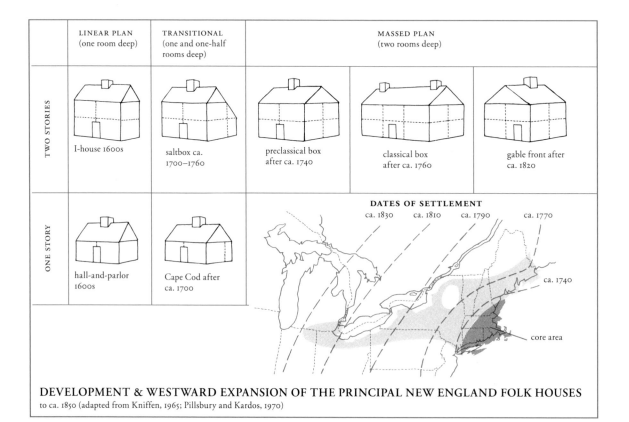

DEVELOPMENT & WESTWARD EXPANSION OF THE PRINCIPAL NEW ENGLAND FOLK HOUSES
to ca. 1850 (adapted from Kniffen, 1965; Pillsbury and Kardos, 1970)

NEW ENGLAND TRADITION

1. Newbury, Massachusetts; 1696. Jackman House (restoration). Rare northern hall-and-parlor without stylistic detailing.

2. Melrose, Massachusetts; 1703. Upham House (restoration). Early saltbox without stylistic detailing.

3. Truro, Massachusetts; late 18th century. Isaac Small House. A well-preserved original Cape Cod house. This house form has continued to be built for two centuries. See pages 427 and 592–93 for similar forms with additional details.

4. Meriden, Connecticut; late 18th century. Redfield House. Preclassical box house (note central chimney) with modest Georgian doorway.

5. New Harmony, Indiana; 1815 (photo, 1903). Schnee House. Gable front without stylistic detailing. This example was built by German immigrants; similar forms were spread throughout the Midwest by settlers from New England.

3

1

5

2

4

fashionable. This trend ultimately led to simple gable-front folk houses, which became increasingly common after about 1825.

This full sequence of change in building traditions took place only in those parts of New England that were settled first—coastal Massachusetts, Connecticut, and Rhode Island. There, most surviving examples reflect the early affluence of the region in the predominance of Postmedieval, Georgian, or Federal stylistic detailing. As New Englanders spread northward and westward from this core area in the late 18th and 19th centuries, they tended to build less pretentious folk houses in the same forms as the more fashionable houses then being built farther east. Saltboxes and I-houses thus occur only in the coastal region; box houses occur farther afield; and gable-front houses are the most widespread of all. An exception was the 19th-century revival of one-story forms having both the linear-plan, hall-and-parlor shape as well as the deeper Cape Cod plan. These smaller houses were well suited for initial settlement in remote areas; they were replaced or adjoined by two-story forms as prosperity increased.

Settlers from New England first moved westward along the Mohawk corridor of central New York. From there they dominated the Western Reserve area around Lake Erie and spread beyond into the upper Midwest, where their building traditions became diluted by others from farther south. New England folk houses are scattered today

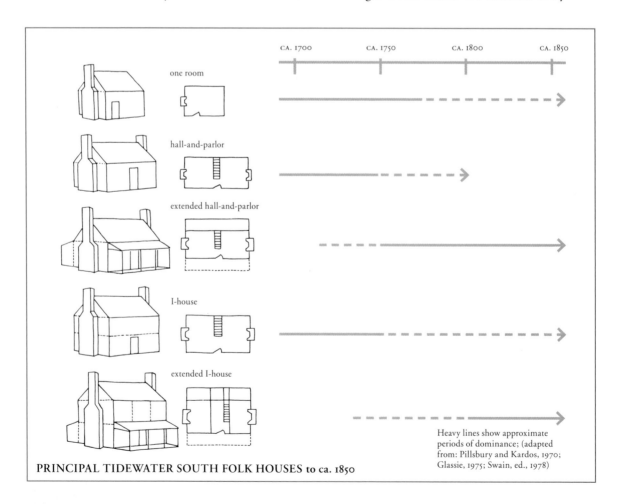

one room

hall-and-parlor

extended hall-and-parlor

I-house

extended I-house

CA. 1700   CA. 1750   CA. 1800   CA. 1850

PRINCIPAL TIDEWATER SOUTH FOLK HOUSES to ca. 1850

Heavy lines show approximate periods of dominance; (adapted from: Pillsbury and Kardos, 1970; Glassie, 1975; Swain, ed., 1978)

TIDEWATER SOUTH TRADITION

1. Rocky Mount, North Carolina, vicinity; late 18th century(?). Wilkins House. Rare surviving example of early single-room frame house.

2. Guilford, Virginia; ca. 1820. Clayton House. A late example of the traditional British hall-and-parlor plan, without a porch. The hipped roof of a later rear wing is barely visible; the dormer windows are probably also a later addition.

3. Perquimans County, North Carolina; ca. 1825. Winslow House. Typical extended hall-and-parlor plan. The rear flue and decorative shutters are later additions.

4. Newlin, North Carolina; ca. 1830. Allen House. Hall-and-parlor plan, with added shed porch. The metal roofing and door are also later modifications; the original chimney has been removed.

5. Wrendale vicinity, North Carolina; 1789. Early I-house with added shed porch and rearward extension and later metal roof.

6. Ingold, North Carolina, vicinity; 1840. Johnson House. Typical extended I-house; note the additional shed extension at the rear.

throughout this large area, but intact survivors are quite rare. Because they were relatively large and substantially built, many of these houses had original stylistic details that took them beyond the folk threshold. Even when built as pure folk forms, they have usually been modified beyond recognition by later stylistic alterations. The New England tradition is, however, reflected in large gable-front-and-wing folk houses that became common throughout the Northeast after the expansion of the railroads.

Tidewater South Tradition

Like their countrymen to the north, the earliest English colonists of the coastal South built primarily linear-plan, hall-and-parlor houses or I-houses. In contrast to the northern colonies, however, a tradition of building with brick masonry was established early in the South. The exact reason for this is unclear, although an abundance of brick clay in the region and differing English backgrounds of many of the southern colonists are probably responsible. Because of the expense of masonry construction, most of these brick houses were built with Postmedieval, Georgian, or Federal stylistic detailing and thus were not folk houses. Massive timber-frame construction, like that in the northern colonies, was also used in the South, and these early wood-frame houses were more commonly modest folk dwellings; unfortunately very few 17th- or 18th-century examples survive intact. Instead, these early southern folk houses are known primarily from their modified descendants built in the first half of the 19th century, many of which survive.

Because of the milder winters of the southern colonies, there was less emphasis on enlarging the early linear plans to create more interior space. One-story houses are far more common than in the North and true massed plans (more than one room deep) are rare. Instead, one-story shed extensions were typically added to the rear of both one- and two-story, linear-plan houses as more space was needed. By the late 18th century, another innovation was becoming universal in the southern folk house. This was the full-width, shed-roofed front porch, which provided a cool shelter in summer from the scorching sun and frequent sudden thunderstorms. Tidewater hall-and-parlor and I-house forms were the prototypes for similar pre-railroad shapes executed with log walls; these became far more widely distributed as a part of the Midland folk tradition. These Tidewater forms also persisted into the railroad era and were the dominant folk architecture throughout the rural South until well into the 20th century.

Midland Tradition

This third principal folk building tradition, like those of New England and the Tidewater South, originated with early colonization along the Atlantic seaboard. It began in the middle colonies (Pennsylvania, New Jersey, Delaware, and Maryland), where Germanic immigrants from heavily wooded areas of central and northern Europe introduced techniques of building with logs hewn square and then placed horizontally, one on top of the other, to make a solid wooden wall. This massive structure was held together by various systems of carefully interlocking or notching the squared timbers where they joined at the corners of the buildings (see page 38). Such construction contrasted sharply with the frame buildings of the adjacent English colonies to the north and south, where open frameworks of hewn timbers were covered by lighter planks or shingles to make them weatherproof. This framing technique used far less wood than did solid log walls and

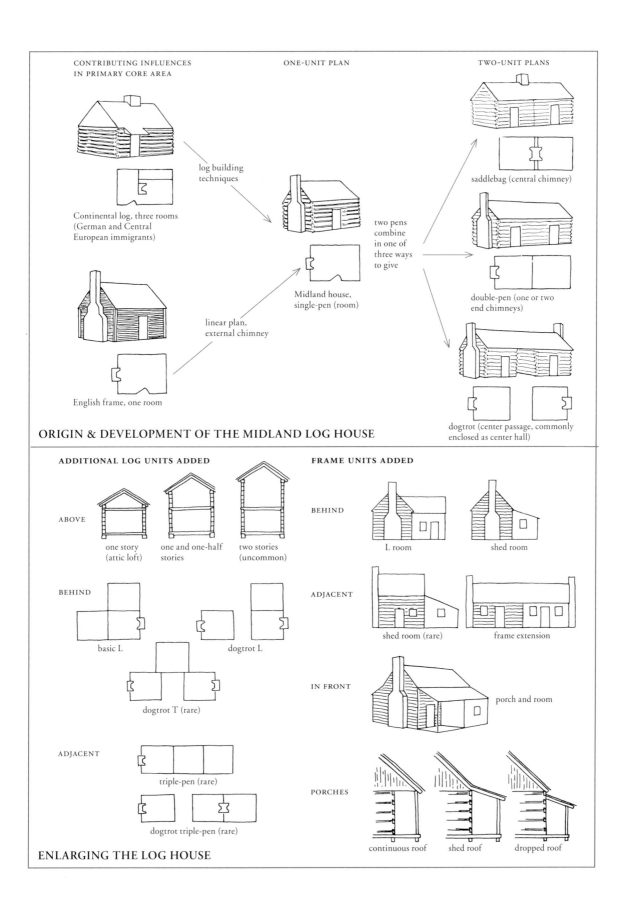

CONTRIBUTING INFLUENCES
IN PRIMARY CORE AREA

ONE-UNIT PLAN

TWO-UNIT PLANS

log building
techniques

Continental log, three rooms
(German and Central
European immigrants)

Midland house,
single-pen (room)

two pens
combine
in one of
three ways
to give

linear plan,
external chimney

English frame, one room

saddlebag (central chimney)

double-pen (one or two
end chimneys)

dogtrot (center passage, commonly
enclosed as center hall)

ORIGIN & DEVELOPMENT OF THE MIDLAND LOG HOUSE

ADDITIONAL LOG UNITS ADDED

FRAME UNITS ADDED

ABOVE

one story
(attic loft)

one and one-half
stories

two stories
(uncommon)

BEHIND

L room

shed room

BEHIND

basic L

dogtrot L

ADJACENT

shed room (rare)

frame extension

dogtrot T (rare)

IN FRONT

porch and room

ADJACENT

triple-pen (rare)

dogtrot triple-pen (rare)

PORCHES

continuous roof

shed roof

dropped roof

ENLARGING THE LOG HOUSE

was originally inspired by the relative scarcity of timber in westernmost Europe, where the virgin forests had largely been cleared by the late Middle Ages.

The early Germanic settlers in the core area of Pennsylvania and adjacent colonies built large log houses with an almost square, three-room plan and a central chimney (the Continental log house). This pattern persisted as settlement spread westward from the core area to central Pennsylvania and then southward along the forelands and valleys in front of the Appalachian Mountain barrier which loomed to the west. In this secondary core area (see map on page 122) the Germanic settlers were joined by Scotch-Irish and English pioneers who quickly adopted the log-building techniques, which were much simpler than constructing complex hewn frameworks to be covered with laboriously split planks or shingles. These settlers from the British Isles, however, modified the shape of the three-room Continental house into the familiar one-room-deep linear plan with external chimney that dominated in the Tidewater South. Thus was born the Midland log house, a tradition that was carried across the Appalachians by frontiersmen to become the dominant Pre-Railroad Folk housing over much of the heavily wooded eastern half of the country. Because of their strong, massive walls, many early log houses survive relatively intact, particularly in out-of-the-way rural areas. For this reason, Midland log houses are the most familiar and thoroughly studied Pre-Railroad Folk dwellings.

A principal problem of log-wall houses is the difficulty of expanding them as additional space is required. Because the strength of the structure depends on the four corner joints, log houses are generally made up of room-sized square or rectangular units called "pens." The simplest log houses have only a single unit, usually with a loft area above

3

4

7

8

MIDLAND TRADITION

1. Summers, Missouri, vicinity; photo 1880. Typical single-pen (one room). Note the absence of windows and the stick chimney, which is lined on the inside with clay. Ladders were usually kept handy so that chimney fires could be easily reached. A later frame extension is visible to the rear.

2. Springfield, West Virginia; photo ca. 1947. Urban single-pen (one room) with upper half-story and window openings fitted with early, small-paned sashes. The original roof was probably shingled.

3. Duchesne County, Utah. Primitive log cabin (rounded logs and saddle notching) typical of those built in wooded areas of the western mountains.

4. Hale County, Alabama. Dogtrot (note central passage) with later roof and rough-sawn siding added over log walls.

5. Mercer County, Kentucky; photo ca. 1895. Typical saddlebag. Note the difference in corner notching on the two units. The right-hand pen was probably added later, around the chimney of the pen to the left.

6. Versailles, Kentucky, vicinity; 1783. Crittenden House. Early double-pen with primitive corner notching. The original roof would have been shingled.

7. Boundary County, Idaho. Typical log house of the western mountains.

8. Jessamine County, Kentucky; 1796. Peyton House. Dogtrot with upper half-story. Note the recessed doorway added to the central passage.

9. Warrensville, North Carolina, vicinity. Gentry House. Double-pen with upper half-story and typical Tidewater porch.

10. Louisiana, Missouri; ca. 1830. Stark House. Restored example of unusual double-pen with units of differing size.

used for sleeping. Two-unit plans, joined in various ways, are very common; three-unit and two-story forms were also developed. Framed additions and porches were commonly added to log houses as local sawmills provided nearby sources of cut lumber. Similarly, many log houses were later covered with weatherboards, both to provide an additional seal and to make them appear more up-to-date. The tradition of building with horizontal log walls persisted in many areas long after cut lumber was locally available. Usually a framework of roughly squared and notched logs was constructed to be originally covered with either shingles or weatherboard. These second-generation log houses can sometimes be distinguished from those originally built with exposed log walls by imprecise squaring of the logs, which resulted in relatively large, irregular gaps between timbers.

A distinction is usually made between log *houses,* such as those discussed so far, which have walls of square-hewn logs joined by carefully hewn corner notching, and log *cabins,* in which the timbers are left round and are joined at the corners by overlapping saddle notches. Such walls are difficult to chink—that is, to fill the spaces between the rounded logs with clay or other material to make them weatherproof. For this reason they were generally used only for temporary shelters in the woodlands of the eastern United States. In wooded areas of the western mountains, however, folk traditions of building with rounded logs became established in the 19th century and persist to the present day in isolated areas.

Plains Tradition

Folk building traditions based on wood-frame or log construction dominated the pre-railroad era in the heavily timbered eastern half of the country. As settlement spread into the treeless plains of the West in the mid-19th century, new building techniques had to be developed (see map on pages 120–21). Only the most arid western regions lacked wood altogether. Over much of the plains, rivers and streams were bordered by at least small trees that provided short timbers for roof support and other essential construction details. Walls and roofs made entirely of wood were, however, rare and expensive luxuries on the plains before the expansion of the western railroad network in the late 19th century. Like their Native American predecessors, early settlers on the plains generally solved the shortage of wood by building with crude masonry. Many of these settlers were undoubtedly familiar with brick construction but, although suitable brick clays were widely distributed in the West, the fuel required to fire the bricks was not. Brick buildings were thus confined to areas near rail or water transport. In some regions local stone could be gathered or quarried without elaborate equipment; in these areas crude stone dwellings were common. Much of the best agricultural land of the plains was covered with thick soils that prevented access to the underlying rock for use as building stone. In these regions, which included most of Kansas, Nebraska, and the Dakotas as well as eastern Colorado, Wyoming, and Montana, pioneer settlers developed techniques of building with sod. In sod construction the uppermost few inches of soil, along with the interlocking roots of the tough plains grasses, were cut into brick-like units with a special plow. These were then laid like bricks to make thick earthen walls that provided excellent insulation from both summer heat and winter cold. The exact origins of this building tradition are obscure. Some writers suggest that the earliest settlers borrowed it from the somewhat similar earth lodges of local native tribes. Others point out that

PLAINS TRADITION

1. Custer County, Montana. Typical plains half-dugout. Partial walls of rounded logs with primitive notching were commonly used when nearby stream valleys provided sufficient timber. Note the earth roof.

2. Jackson County, Oklahoma; 1888. Perryman House. Partly restored plains half-dugout with partial walls of primitive stonework laid without mortar. Such stonework was common in the eastern and southern plains where exposures of bedrock are frequent.

3. Custer County, Nebraska; photo 1887. Barnes House. Plains half-dugout with partial walls of sod blocks. Note the sod roof.

4. Pennington County, South Dakota. Sod house with improved roof and framed rear addition. The house was still in use in 1936 when the photo was made.

5. Custer County, Nebraska; photo 1886. Reeder House. Typical plains sod house with sod roof. Timbers support the sod blocks above the windows.

6. Custer County, Nebraska; 1884. Haumont House. Elaborate two-story sod house which survived into the 1970s.

1

2

3

4

5

6

similar construction is used for simple folk dwellings in some treeless parts of Britain. Whatever their sources, folk houses made of sod quickly became the standard plains dwelling and were built at all levels of refinement, from simple dugouts to elaborate two-story mansions.

A principal difficulty with early sod dwellings was the roof. Lacking wood shingles as a roof covering, roofs were typically also made of sod blocks set on a framework of wooden poles, sticks, and brush. Such roofs were notoriously unpleasant in wet weather, as they normally leaked and dripped muddy water into the interior for several days after a rain. A high priority for plains dwellers thus became watertight roofing. Roofs were supported by wooden planks, when available, on which sod was placed for insulation. As affluence increased, fully framed roofs covered with shingles were sometimes added. Most sod houses of the plains have long disappeared, but a few with these improved roofs are still in use as comfortable, energy-efficient dwellings.

Hispanic Southwest Tradition

The houses of the Hispanic Southwest are treated in the chapter on the Spanish Colonial style, which also outlines Hispanic building techniques of the region.

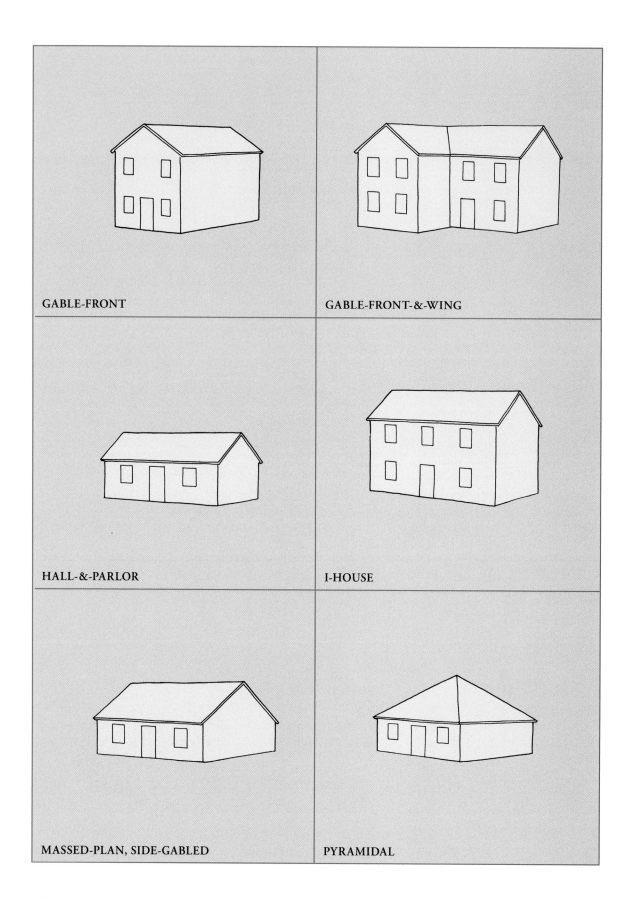

GABLE-FRONT

GABLE-FRONT-&-WING

HALL-&-PARLOR

I-HOUSE

MASSED-PLAN, SIDE-GABLED

PYRAMIDAL

National

after ca. 1850–ca. 1930

The nature of American folk housing changed dramatically as railroads mush-roomed across the continent in the decades from 1850 to 1890. Modest dwell-ings built far from water transport were no longer restricted to local materials. Instead, bulky items used for construction, particularly lumber from distant sawmills in heavily forested areas, could now be moved rapidly and cheaply over long distances. As a result, large lumberyards quickly became standard fixtures in the thousands of new towns which sprouted as trade centers along the railroad routes. Soon folk houses built with logs, sod, or heavy hewn frames were being abandoned for wooden dwell-ings constructed with light balloon or braced framing covered by wood sheathing. The railroads thus changed the traditional building materials and construction techniques of folk dwellings over much of the nation. By the turn of the century, pre-railroad building traditions survived only in isolated areas, far from the nearest rail service.

The railroad-inspired era of national folk housing did not completely erase the earlier traditions, however, for many of the previous folk shapes persisted even though now built by different techniques. These, along with some new shape innovations, make up six distinctive families of house shapes that dominated American folk building through

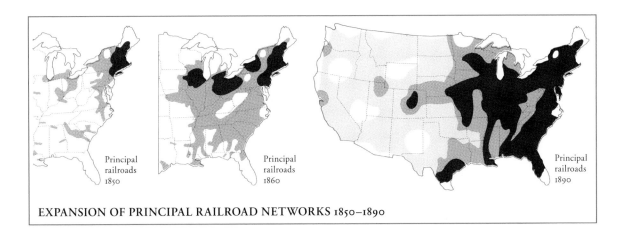

Principal
railroads
1850

Principal
railroads
1860

Principal
railroads
1890

EXPANSION OF PRINCIPAL RAILROAD NETWORKS 1850–1890

the first half of the 20th century. Only recently have these generally been abandoned for still other forms of folk dwellings (see pages 149–55).

After the expansion of the railroads, gable-front houses remained common in the northeastern region formerly dominated by the New England folk tradition, as did similar massed plans with an added extension known as gable-front-and-wing houses. In much of the remaining eastern half of the country, hall-and-parlor and I-house shapes, both descended from the Tidewater South tradition by way of the Midland log adaptations, remained the dominant folk dwellings. All of these later folk forms, however, tend to show much less geographic restriction than did their pre-railroad predecessors, for as transportation and communication improved, each shape became distributed beyond its area of traditional dominance. Light framing techniques also led to new folk forms which grew in popularity through the early decades of this century. These were generally massed-plan houses that were now relatively simple to construct because light wooden roof framing could easily be adapted to span two-room depths. Such houses, when of rectangular shape, normally had side-gabled roofs and are called massed-plan, side-gabled folk houses. More nearly square plans typically had pyramidal (equilateral hipped) roofs.

Gable-Front Family

The Greek Revival movement, which dominated American styled houses during the period from 1830 to 1850, commonly used the front-gabled shape to echo the pedimented facade of typical Greek temples. This form was particularly common in New England and the adjacent northeast region where simple gable-front folk houses also became popular during the pre-railroad era. This shape persisted with the expansion of the eastern railroad network in the 1850s and became a dominant folk form until well into the 20th century. Gable-front houses were particularly suited for narrow urban lots in the rapidly expanding cities of the Northeast. There, many late 19th- and early 20th-century neighborhoods are dominated by both styled and simple folk examples built in this form. Most are narrow, two-story houses with relatively steep roof pitches. A related one-story urban form first became common in expanding southern cities in the late 19th century. This is the shotgun house, narrow gable-front dwellings one room wide that dominated many modest southern neighborhoods built from about 1880 to 1930.

5

6

GABLE-FRONT FAMILY

1. Cuba, New York; late 19th century. Typical urban two-story example. The spindlework porch detailing and patterned shingles in the gable are borrowed from the contemporary Queen Anne style.

2. Buffalo, New York; ca. 1907. An urban one-and-one-half-story example with modest Queen Anne detailing. The door and windows are later additions.

3. Cleveland, Ohio; late 19th century. Urban example executed in masonry.

4. Carteret County, North Carolina; 1864. Thomas House. Early example showing Greek Revival influence in the pedimented gable and double porch, which was common in the coastal Carolinas. Metal doors and storm windows are later additions.

5. Biloxi, Mississippi; ca. 1905. Typical shotgun house of the urban South. This example has integral porch and modest Queen Anne detailing.

6. Louisville, Kentucky; ca. 1910. Shotgun with Greek Revival–like entry porch.

7. Gibson County, Indiana; ca. 1935. Late example inspired by the Cape Cod shape of the Colonial Revival movement.

8. Thomaston, Louisiana; ca. 1938. Typical example inspired by similarly shaped Craftsman houses.

1

2

3

4

7

8

Some are elaborately styled but most are simple folk houses. The origin of these south-ern shotgun houses has been much debated. Some scholars note that similar forms are common in the West Indies and trace them from Africa to early Haitian influences in New Orleans, whence they became popular with Black freedmen migrating to southern urban centers following the Civil War. A less complex theory is that they are simply the familiar one-room-deep, hall-and-parlor plan of the rural South turned sideways to accommodate narrow urban lots.[2]

An additional wave of interest in the gable-front shape grew from styled houses of the early 20th-century Craftsman movement, which were typically built in this form. Many modest folk houses without stylistic detailing were inspired by such Craftsman houses in the decades from 1910 to 1930. These are usually one-story, double-width forms with low-pitched roofs; they are most common in rural areas and occur throughout the country.

Gable-Front-and-Wing Family

While two-story gable-front houses dominated urban folk building in the Northeast, a related shape, also descended from styled Greek Revival houses, became common in rural areas. In this form, an additional side-gabled wing was added at right angles to the gable-front plan to give a compound, gable-front-and-wing shape. A shed-roofed porch was typically placed within the L made by the two wings. Because these were relatively large and complex houses, most built in the pre-railroad era had Greek Revival detailing and were not folk houses. With the coming of the railroads, however, abundant lumber and balloon framing led to an expansion of unstyled folk houses with this form. Some grew in stages as two-story, front-gabled wings were added to simple hall-and-parlor and I-house plans. These were typically stepped in shape—that is, the roof ridge of the gable-front portion was higher than the adjacent wing. More commonly, the entire structure was built as a unit with a roof ridge of uniform height.

Two-story houses of gable-front-and-wing plan became common only in the north-eastern and midwestern states. In the South, however, traditional one-story, hall-and-parlor plans were frequently built with an added one-story, gable-front wing. These

5

6

GABLE-FRONT-AND-WING FAMILY

1. Hartwick, New York; late 19th century, photo 1914. Gardner House. Stepped example. Note the small attic windows, common on Greek Revival houses, on the right-hand wing, which was probably built first, with the gable-front portion added later.

2. North Collins, New York; late 19th century. Stepped example.

3. Seaford, Delaware; ca. 1947. Temple House. Late example inspired by the Minimal Traditional style of the 1940s.

4. Lawtons, New York, vicinity; late 19th century.

5. Belmont, New York; ca. 1900.

6. Fayetteville, Arkansas; ca. 1910.

7. Dallas, Texas; 1916. This variation has a hipped rear wing that extends to each side, rather than a gable extending in one direction.

one-story, gable-front-and-wing houses had more flexible interior spaces than the typical southern hall-and-parlor plan, which they steadily replaced during the early decades of this century. These one-story forms also became common, along with larger two-story examples, in adjacent areas of the expanding Midwest and are the most widely distributed of the gable-front-and-wing family of shapes.

Hall-and-Parlor Family

Simple side-gabled, hall-and-parlor houses (two rooms wide and one room deep) are a traditional British folk form which, when expanded by a front porch and rearward addition, became the dominant Pre-Railroad Folk housing over much of the southeastern United States. Hall-and-parlor houses were first executed with heavy timber framing in the Tidewater South and then with hewn log walls over the vast Midland region. After the expansion of the railroad network, this form, now executed with light framed walls, remained the dominant folk housing over much of the rural Southeast until well into the 20th century. This folk form is thus a persistent survivor which has shown relatively little change since colonial times. The principal variations in extended hall-and-parlor houses involve differing chimney placements, porch sizes, porch roof shapes, and differing patterns of rearward extensions for enlarging the interior space.

3

4

6

7

HALL-AND-PARLOR FAMILY

1. Gadsden County, Florida; late 19th century. Note the open shuttered window without a glass sash and the discontinuous siding on the rearward extension, added after the main house was built. Early hall-and-parlor houses had separate front doors leading to the two principal rooms, a pattern that survives in this example and those in Figures 4, 6, and 7.

2. Smithfield, North Carolina; ca. 1910.

3. Carteret County, North Carolina; ca. 1898. The gabled entry porch is probably a later addition.

4. McAlester, Oklahoma; ca. 1890. Note the vertical, board-and-batten siding, which is less expensive than horizontal weatherboarding and is commonly seen on modest folk houses.

5. Salisbury, North Carolina; ca. 1900. Note the central chimney and double rearward extension.

6. Smithfield, North Carolina; ca. 1910. Note the central chimney and ornamental front gable. A full rear wing replaced the traditional shed-roofed rearward extension on many later examples.

7. New Roads, Louisiana, vicinity; late 19th century. Early example expanded by adding a room to the right of the original house. The metal roof, now covering both, is a later addition.

8. Crocketville, South Carolina; ca. 1890. Front-porch rooms were often added to increase interior space.

9. Lexington, Kentucky; ca. 1870. Dolan House. A one-and-one-half-story example on its way to becoming an I-house.

I-House Family

Like the one-story, hall-and-parlor plan, two-story I-houses (two rooms wide and one room deep) are traditional British folk forms that were common in pre-railroad America, particularly in the Tidewater South. Similar forms occurred in the Midland area of log construction but were uncommon, probably because of the difficulty of constructing two-story walls made of solid, hewn logs. With the arrival of the railroads, however, I-houses again became a popular folk form over much of the eastern half of the country. They were particularly favored as modest folk dwellings in the midwestern states where the relatively long and confining winters made large houses more of a necessity than farther south. Post-railroad southern examples are also common, but these were usually the more pretentious houses of affluent local gentry. For this reason, many of these later southern I-houses have added stylistic detailing to make them appear fashionable. Like their hall-and-parlor relatives, post-railroad I-houses were elaborated with varying patterns of porches, chimneys, and rearward extensions.

I-HOUSE FAMILY

1. Beaumont, Texas; 1845. John Jay French House. The basic I-house form is extended with original one-story shed-roofed extension on the rear and one-story full-width porch across the front (there are simplified Greek Revival doors).

2. Mason County, West Virginia; ca. 1860. Porchless central chimney examples, such as this, are most frequent in the midwestern states.

3. Clintonville, Kentucky; mid-19th century. Sidener House. An early post-railroad example. The windows and porch are later additions. Note the inside end chimneys and absence of side windows.

4. Helton, North Carolina, vicinity; ca. 1890. Blevins House. This example was expanded from a small log house, the walls of which are barely visible beneath the porch roof.

5. Salisbury, North Carolina; ca. 1898. Cannon Mill House.

6. Cabarrus County, North Carolina; ca. 1900.

7. Perquimans County, North Carolina; mid-19th century. Skinner House. An early example with Greek Revival detailing and large rear wing.

I

3

4

7

Massed-Plan, Side-Gabled Family

Massed-plan (more than one room deep) folk houses were common in the pre-railroad era only in parts of the Northeast where the early New England building tradition developed roof-framing techniques for spanning large, two-room depths. With the expansion of the railroad this tradition evolved into the massed-plan versions of the gable-front and gable-front-and-wing families previously discussed. Lightweight lumber made widely available by the railroads permitted still simpler methods of light roof framing, and these, in turn, led to other types of modest folk dwellings with two-room depths. These massed-plan houses, normally constructed with either side-gabled or pyramidal hipped roofs (see next section), had relatively large and flexible interior plans and thus slowly replaced the traditional one-room-deep hall-and-parlor and I-house forms.

Side-gabled folk houses with massed plans are usually one-story forms that vary principally in roof pitch and in the size and placement of porches. Earlier examples, particularly in the South, commonly had full-width, shed-roofed porches. From the front, these resemble their extended hall-and-parlor predecessors, but lack the latter's rearward extensions and resultant broken rear roof line. Examples from the 1930s and later commonly have only small entry porches, or no porch at all, probably in imitation of the then popular Cape Cod shape of the Colonial Revival style. These were recommended by the FHA in its *Principles for Planning Small Houses* and widely built in the years 1935 to 1950. They are included on pages 592–93 of the Minimal Traditional section of this revision.

I

4

MASSED-PLAN, SIDE-GABLED FAMILY

1. Yanceyville, North Carolina, vicinity; ca. 1930.

2. Abbeville, Louisiana, vicinity; late 19th century. The larger house to the right illustrates an early tradition of massed-plan, side-gabled folk building brought to Louisiana by French Canadian (Acadian) immigrants with a knowledge of long-span roof-framing techniques. Such Louisiana houses are known as Creole Cottages; they normally have the front wall moved back to make an integral porch under the steep roof line. Note how it dwarfs the traditional linear-plan hall-and-parlor to the left.

3. New Madrid County, Missouri; 1940. The roof pitch of this example is lower than is typical of closely related Minimal Traditional houses. The hint of exposed roof rafters is a holdover from building practice during the preceding Craftsman era.

4. Rolla, Missouri; ca. 1920. Example inspired by the contemporary Craftsman movement.

5. Key West, Florida; 1829. "The Oldest House in South Florida"; Richard W. Cussans, builder. It was moved to its current location in about 1836. The dormer on the far left was enlarged in 1936. Note raised foundation.

6. Irwinville, Georgia, vicinity; ca. 1920. Board-and-batten example similar to traditional hall-and-parlor plan, but with full, two-room depth. Note the lack of a broken rear roof line to cover a rearward extension.

2

3

5

6

Pyramidal Family

Massed-plan folk houses of rectangular shape are normally covered by side-gabled roofs. Those with more nearly square plans, in contrast, are commonly built with pyramidal (equilateral hipped) roofs, which require more complex roof framing but need fewer long-spanning rafters, and thus are less expensive to build. Such roofs appeared on modest folk houses earlier in the post-railroad era than did the side-gabled form. In the South, one-story, pyramidal houses became a popular replacement for the less spacious southern-type hall-and-parlor house during the early decades of the 20th century. One-story pyramidals are less common in the northern and midwestern states but are joined there by two-story examples, which similarly began to replace the traditional but less spacious rural I-houses of the region in the years from about 1905 to 1930. During the same period these two-story, pyramidal houses also became a popular urban house form throughout the country. Most urban examples were called American four-square houses (page 555) and were enhanced with Colonial Revival, Neoclassical, Folk Victorian, Prairie, or Craftsman stylistic detailing; but many also remained simple folk forms which lacked such fashionable details.

Like their side-gabled relatives, pyramidal folk houses differ principally in roof pitch and in the size and placement of porches.

2

4

5

PYRAMIDAL FAMILY

1. Greene County, Georgia; ca. 1900. Note the very steeply pitched roof. Such roofs are common on early southern examples; they may have been influenced by earlier roofs of similar shape built by French descendants in the Gulf Coast region.

2. Stillwater, Oklahoma; ca. 1935.

3. Coffee County, Alabama; ca. 1905.

4. Gwinnett County, Georgia; ca. 1920. Many one-story pyramidals have full or partial integral porches included under the principal roof.

5. Emporia, Kansas; ca. 1915. Such two-story pyramidals were a dominant urban form in the early decades of the century. Most urban examples had stylistic detailing but some, like this one, were unadorned folk houses. The metal storm windows are a later addition.

6. Cabarrus County, North Carolina; ca. 1900. An unusually large two-story example.

I

3

6

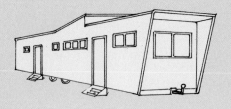

BEFORE WORLD WAR II

AFTER WORLD WAR II, CA. 1960S

MOBILE HOME—PRE-1980

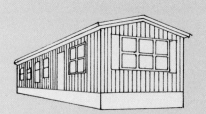

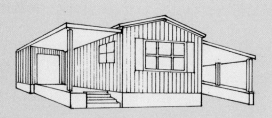

SINGLE-WIDE WITH EXTENSIONS

MANUFACTURED HOUSING—SINGLE-WIDE

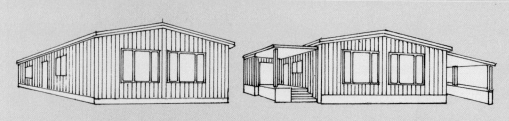

DOUBLE-WIDE WITH EXTENSIONS

MANUFACTURED HOUSING—DOUBLE-WIDE

Manufactured

ca. 1930–present

The years since 1930 have witnessed an extraordinary change in the nature of American folk housing as the production of relatively inexpensive prefabricated, factory-built dwellings has largely replaced new construction of traditionally built wood-frame folk houses. Manufactured housing is now the dominant folk house of contemporary America. These are loosely grouped into mobile homes (their original use, and name, prior to 1980); manufactured housing: single-wide (one unit wide and the most common shape); and manufactured housing: double-wide (two units wide and gaining popularity). Today around 10 percent of all new homes in the United States are manufactured—in 2009, one manufactured home was produced for every nine standard housing starts. The map shows areas where more than 20 percent of existing dwellings were manufactured housing in 1990.

Manufactured houses are dispersed throughout rural areas and grouped in parks that are as varied as neighborhoods of conventional houses. And just as neighborhoods often cluster houses by size, some entire parks are limited to single-wides or double-wides exclusively. These parks are generally located near cities and towns nationwide; there are also concentrations in resort and retirement communities and near worker-intensive rural industries.[3]

Because manufactured housing is factory built, with all appliances and sometimes even the furnishings included, it is now the cheapest and simplest means of acquiring basic shelter, as its wide popularity attests.

Manufactured homes differ from closely related "modular homes" in two ways. A manufactured house is exempt from local building codes, while modular houses must meet local codes. In addition, a manufactured house must maintain the steel chassis that makes it technically movable. Newer models of manufactured houses often appear identical to modular houses, may be produced in the same factories and, except for code requirements, are pretty much interchangeable.

Mobile Homes

The earliest examples, designed for use as campers and travel trailers, appeared in the 1930s. These early mobile homes were eight feet wide and could easily be pulled behind ordinary automobiles. During World War II these were utilized as semi-permanent housing for large influxes of workers relocating near wartime industries. Although these provided small rudimentary dwellings, the concept of a complete home that could be moved onto a site was appealing, and after the war designs more suitable for permanent housing were introduced.

In 1954 the first ten-foot-wide model was produced; in 1969, this grew to twelve feet wide, and today fourteen to sixteen feet wide is more typical. Widths over eight feet allow a narrow side hall for privacy (rather than walking through a middle room to reach the rear). Lengths grew as well, and the new size allowed bathrooms, absent in most early campers, to be included. As these larger designs, more suitable for longer periods of habitation, became popular, the units lost most of their mobility and are now moved by special trucks with warning vehicles ahead and behind. In the early years, the mobile home industry was largely unregulated. Many small manufacturers built homes of varying quality and safety.

Manufactured Housing

SINGLE-WIDES—In 1974, Congress demanded that safety standards be adopted for the popular mobile homes. In 1976, the U.S. Department of Housing and Urban Development (HUD) completed a set of uniform national standards for their construction that has since been strengthened. HUD's 1980 Housing Act mandated that the term *mobile home* henceforth be replaced by *manufactured housing.* By the 1990 census, manufactured homes made up one-fifth of the housing stock in rural areas.

Single-wides are by far the most prevalent manufactured home. They typically come in widths up to sixteen feet and their length can now reach seventy feet or more. Single-wides are transported to a site essentially complete and are placed on foundations constructed onsite. They can be customized by adding decks, porches, carports, garages, and even room extensions. These are infrequently moved once sited, and about 90 percent remain permanently in place.

Like many earlier folk forms, the prevalent single-wide manufactured house is of linear plan—that is, made up of a single file of rooms. This shape allows them to be placed either long side to the road, as in the traditional hall-and-parlor plan—or, where land is more expensive, on narrow lots with the short end to the road, as in the traditional shotgun plan. About 75 percent of manufactured housing is placed on private property and more likely to be sited in the hall-and-parlor configuration, lining rural roads and often interspersed among conventional houses. The remaining 25 percent of manufactured housing is placed on rented sites, often sited in a shotgun configuration. Manufacturers typically offer many different designs for units that will be placed broad side to the road, generally adding shallow gables or changes in cladding often designed to mimic a small Ranch house.

DOUBLE-WIDES—In the 1970s, double-wides (two linear units, each without one side wall and designed to be joined together, see illustration page 148) began to be produced. Like single-wides, these are placed on built-in-place foundations, but they have to join their two open-side walls together to create a single broad structure. These are unlikely to be moved once sited. Double-wides are growing in popularity; they have increased from about 20 percent of units sold in 2000 to about 50 percent in 2010. They may have exterior style elements that can make them harder to differentiate from other new homes.

Today, as manufactured housing is trending toward these larger double-wide models, there is a nascent movement to create small basic housing from widely available used shipping containers.

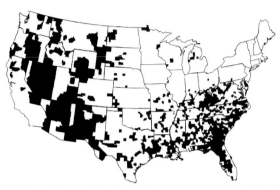

Areas of United States where manufactured housing and mobile homes constituted more than 20 percent of all housing units in 1990

LOCATIONS WITH HIGH PERCENTAGE OF MANUFACTURED HOMES

RURAL SITING
long side faces the road
(similar to a rural hall-and-parlor house)

URBAN PARK SITING
narrow and faces the road
(similar to a row of urban shot-gun houses; this early configuration for single-wides has a slight slant so units can be moved in and out of park with ease)

URBAN PARK SITING
narrow end faces the road; newer park is limited to double-wides, not intended to be moved and sited without the slant.

TYPICAL SITING OF
MANUFACTURED HOMES

MOBILE AND SINGLE-WIDE

1. Los Angles (hillside), California; ca. 1960s. A mobile home on a steep rural hillside is sited on a sturdy deck and has a picturesque roof added.

2. Athens, Texas; ca. 2012. A very basic single-wide configured to face the road.

3. Athens, Texas; ca. 2010. Nested gables on both the side and front facade, and a change of color enhancing the door, give this single-wide a more stylish look.

4. Key West, Florida; 1970s. This single-wide is in an urban trailer park. The covered trailer mount for the required chassis is visible in front.

5. Boulder City, Nevada; ca. 1969. Located in a neighborhood filled with manufactured houses, this has a carport added on one side and porch on the other.

6. Anywhere, U.S.A.; ca. 2010. The narrow end faces the road and is enhanced by a paired window with a small roof, windowbox, and shutters.

7. Anywhere, U.S.A. A pre-1984 single-wide.

8. New Orleans, Lousiana; ca. 2010. The Barrone. A single-wide styled like a Folk Victorian and configured with the entrance in the narrow end like the shotgun folk houses of the south.

1

4

5

7

2

3

6

8

**FOLK HOUSES—MANUFACTURED
HOUSING: DOUBLE-WIDE**

1. Las Vegas, Nevada; 1981. A double-wide without additions.

2. Carlsbad, California; 1985. An added side porch and carport help give this double-wide a Contemporary feel.

3. Athens, Texas; ca. 2012. The accented entry on the long side is favored when a double-wide is placed sideways to the road in rural areas.

4. Las Vegas, Nevada; 1970. A double-wide with a Craftsman-style front.

5. Anywhere, U.S.A.; ca. 2010. The Picasso. Note how the roof overhang accents the nested front facing gables above the entry. Compared to similar Figure 3 without the overhang.

6. Key West, Florida (vicinity); ca. 1980s. A manufactured house in an idyllic setting.

7. Dallas, Texas; ca. 2010. A triple-wide with its three units placed running from front to back. Note the pleasant living porch.

8. Dallas, Texas; ca 2010. A triple-wide with its three units placed running from side-to-side.

I

4

6

2

3

5

7

8

The early colonists arriving in the New World from Europe brought with them the prevailing architectural styles and building practices of their native countries. At first these were of late Medieval inspiration, for the new classicism of the Renaissance had not yet spread beneath the grandest palaces and mansions of their homelands. Indeed, most Colonial dwellings built during the 1600s lacked all Medieval decorative detailing and might be classified as folk houses if they did not so strongly reflect—in form and structure rather than stylistic detail—the distinctive building traditions of their countries of origin.

High-style Dutch, French, and Spanish dwellings remained rare in our area of the New World, for the Netherlands soon lost their colonies to England, and the centers of French and Spanish colonization were concentrated elsewhere. By contrast, the prospering English colonies of the eastern seaboard began in the early 1700s to import Renaissance-inspired Georgian fashion, which was to dominate these colonies for almost a century before being replaced by the closely related English Adam style (called Federal in the United States) just as the American Revolution brought an end to British rule.

It should be noted that Old World building practices persisted in each of these colonial empires well beyond the end of European rule. The Dutch continued to settle and build traditional dwellings in the Hudson River area for more than a hundred years after the formal loss of their colony to England. Likewise, French and Spanish influence lasted for many decades after their former territories became a part of the United States. Finally, the Federal style and a general taste for English fashion persisted in the English colonies for many decades after the Revolution.

Books on architecture and architectural detail, of the type that were to have a major influence on later periods of home building, were rarely a factor in Colonial houses. Only the two English styles, Georgian and Federal, evidence the use of books in their design. Before 1740 less than a handful of architecture books were even available in the English colonies, but their numbers increased rapidly; by 1776, approximately one hundred titles had been published or imported and were in wide use by carpenters and builders. Another one hundred or more books were published during the Federal era and played the major role in bringing the work of the Adam brothers, the latest British architectural fashion, to the New World.[1]

Colonial Houses

Extant Colonial houses are relatively rare and generally owe their continued existence to active preservation efforts. These homes have an irreplaceable character that visibly demonstrates the colonial and immigrant history of the United States. Today most of those that remain have some sort of legal protection without which their survival would be in jeopardy.

While original examples of Colonial houses are relatively rare, the forms and detailing are abundantly familiar because, beginning with the Centennial celebrations of 1876, they have been repeatedly copied during various stylistic revivals. When faithfully followed, the copies may be difficult to distinguish from originals. Two principal clues are of help here.

First, each original style was built in a rather limited area of the country, while revival copies are widespread. For this reason, maps of the areas of original occurrence are provided for each Colonial style; outside these areas, *any* example is almost certain to be a later copy. Secondly, Colonial houses were built before the era of industrialization, and unaltered examples thus have, on close inspection, a characteristic handmade quality in such details as doors, windows, brickwork, or siding that is always lacking on revival examples.

1600–1820

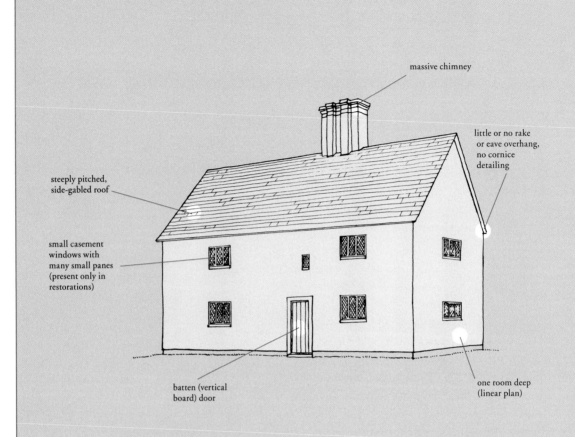

massive chimney

little or no rake or eave overhang, no cornice detailing

steeply pitched, side-gabled roof

small casement windows with many small panes (present only in restorations)

batten (vertical board) door

one room deep (linear plan)

NORTHERN TRADITION
wood, usually two stories, central chimney

SOUTHERN TRADITION
brick, usually one story, end chimneys

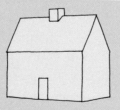

pages 162–63

pages 164–65

PRINCIPAL SUBTYPES

Postmedieval English

1600–1700; locally to ca. 1740

Identifying Features

Steeply pitched, side-gabled roof with little or no rake or eave overhang and no cornice detailing; massive central or end chimneys of brick or stone, often formed into decorative shapes; small windows, originally with narrow surrounds and fixed or casement sashes having many diamond-shaped panes (these were universally replaced by larger double-hung sashes during the 18th and 19th centuries; when the earlier-type windows are present today, they are modern restorations); most were originally one room deep (linear plan) with batten (vertical board) doors.

Principal Subtypes

Two distinct traditions became established in the 17th-century English colonies:

NORTHERN TRADITION—In the northern colonies wood-frame walls covered with weatherboard or wood shingles were the dominant mode of construction. These houses most commonly had two stories and a single large central chimney.

SOUTHERN TRADITION—Separated from the northern colonies by the Dutch in New York and New Jersey, the southern English colonies emphasized one-story forms with paired end chimneys. Most surviving examples have brick walls.

Variants and Details

In Massachusetts and Connecticut a characteristic second-floor wall overhang is commonly present on the front facade; this is sometimes ornamented with decorative brackets or pendants. Similar wall overhangs at attic level are common beneath the end gables. Full-height cross gables were frequently used on the steeply pitched roofs to add space and light to the tall attic (few of these have escaped later roof modifications). In Rhode Island, stone end walls and chimneys were common on timber-frame houses; few of these stone-enders survive. In one-story southern examples, small dormers were sometimes used to provide attic light (many seen today are later additions).

Originally most Postmedieval houses were one room deep and symmetrical from front to back; later, lean-to rear projections were added to increase first-floor space. By around 1700 these rear additions were usually included under a single main roof in new construction, or under reframed and lowered roofs on earlier houses, to give the familiar saltbox roof form (see pages 29 and 31). In all colonies, both timber-frame and masonry examples sometimes showed small, projecting wings or towers centered on the front or rear facades. In front, these typically served as entry areas, with a bedroom above; in the rear, they housed the stairway. When both were present, they gave the house a characteristic cross-shaped plan; few of these projections survive except in restorations.

Occurrence

This was the only style in the English colonies from their founding (1607–1620) to about 1700, when their population had grown to 220,000 and occupied the areas shown on the map. Only a few hundred houses remain of the many thousands built in this period. Most are in Massachusetts and Connecticut, where about a hundred are preserved as museum houses and at least that many more are in private hands. Fewer examples survive in Maryland, Virginia, and the middle colonies. After 1700, early Georgian houses with less steep roof slopes, smaller chimneys, large double-hung windows having one fixed and one movable sash, and classical door surrounds rapidly replaced this style throughout the English colonies. Postmedieval houses survived longest in the South, where scattered examples with Postmedieval details were built throughout the 18th century.

Comments

These earliest English Colonial houses are New World adaptations of modest English domestic buildings which, in the decades immediately preceding colonization, had begun to undergo a transition from Medieval to Renaissance structural details. The steeply pitched roofs were a surviving Medieval development for thatch covering, which must be steep to shed water. In America the earliest roofs were also of thatch, but the ice, snow, thunderstorms, and high winds of the more severe New World climate soon made wooden shingles the preferred roofing material. The high pitch, now without function for relatively impervious shingle roofs, persisted for nearly a century. The roof pitch has been lowered in later alterations of most examples, including many restorations.

The chimney stack, replacing the open fire of Medieval vernacular houses, was the crucial Postmedieval improvement. Attic space, formerly unenclosed so that smoke could escape through roof openings, could be floored over to provide sleeping rooms. In the New World, large chimneys were used on all but the most modest 17th-century houses. In the northern colonies, central chimney placement was preferred, probably to conserve heat during the severe winters. In the southern colonies, the end chimneys allowed a central hall to improve cross-ventilation and may have helped to dissipate the heat of cooking fires during the oppressively hot summers.

Although only a few Postmedieval timber-frame houses survive in the southern colonies, they were probably far more common originally. With the growth of the southern

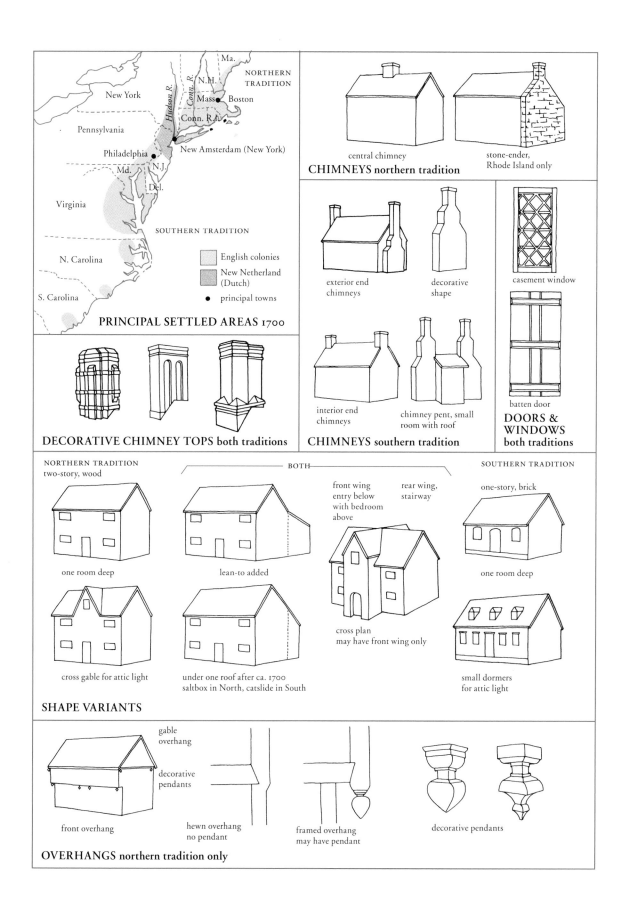

PRINCIPAL SETTLED AREAS 1700

NORTHERN TRADITION

SOUTHERN TRADITION

New York

Pennsylvania

Philadelphia

Md.

N.J.

Del.

Virginia

N. Carolina

S. Carolina

New Amsterdam (New York)

Hudson R.

Conn. R.

Ma.

N.H.

Mass.

Boston

Conn. R.I.

English colonies

New Netherland (Dutch)

principal towns

CHIMNEYS northern tradition

central chimney

stone-ender, Rhode Island only

exterior end chimneys

decorative shape

interior end chimneys

chimney pent, small room with roof

CHIMNEYS southern tradition

casement window

batten door

DOORS & WINDOWS both traditions

DECORATIVE CHIMNEY TOPS both traditions

SHAPE VARIANTS

NORTHERN TRADITION two-story, wood

BOTH

SOUTHERN TRADITION one-story, brick

one room deep

lean-to added

front wing entry below with bedroom above

rear wing, stairway

one room deep

cross gable for attic light

under one roof after ca. 1700 saltbox in North, catslide in South

cross plan may have front wing only

small dormers for attic light

OVERHANGS northern tradition only

gable overhang

decorative pendants

front overhang

hewn overhang no pendant

framed overhang may have pendant

decorative pendants

NORTHERN TRADITION

1. Medfield, Massachusetts; 1680. Peak House (restoration). One of the few surviving northern one-story examples.

2. Watertown, Massachusetts; 1694–1701. Browne House (restoration).

3. Topsfield, Massachusetts; 1683. Parson Capen House (restoration). The original windows were probably smaller casements.

4. Lincoln, Rhode Island; ca. 1687. Arnold House (restoration). A typical Rhode Island stone-ender.

5. Saugus, Massachusetts; ca. 1686. Boardman House. The saltbox rearward extension was added before 1696; the double-hung sash windows were probably added in the 18th century.

6. Salem, Massachusetts; ca. 1668. Turner House (House of the Seven Gables, restoration). The original windows were probably smaller casements.

7., 8. Saugus, Massachusetts; ca. 1680. Appleton House (Ironworks House, restoration). Figure 7, taken about 1900, shows the house after two hundred years of modifications. Figure 8 shows a later restoration to its probable 17th-century cross-plan form.

9. Salem, Massachusetts, ca. 1698. Hunt House. An early photo; the house was demolished in 1863. The double-hung sash windows are probably an 18th-century addition.

1

4

7

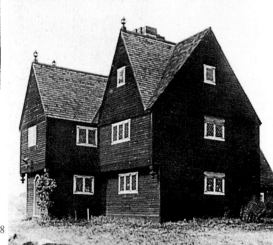

8

SOUTHERN TRADITION

1. Virginia Beach, Virginia, vicinity; mid-18th century. Hudgins House. A rare survivor of the once common wood-frame hall-and-parlor folk houses in the tidewater South. This example has high-style Postmedieval chimneys, which may remain from a partially destroyed earlier brick house.

2. Norfolk, Virginia, vicinity; mid-17th century. Thoroughgood House. Note the decorative shape of the exterior end chimney.

3. Hollywood, Maryland, vicinity; ca. 1660 (left two-thirds only). Resurrection Manor. The double-hung sash windows were probably added when the house was expanded from two or three rooms in the 18th century.

4. Virginia Beach, Virginia; 1680. Keeling House. The windows and cornice-line dentils are probably 18th-century additions.

5. Salisbury, North Carolina, vicinity; chimney late 18th century. Long House. A late example of a composite Postmedieval chimney (the house is a much modified restoration). Most such chimneys date from the late 17th and early 18th centuries when houses two rooms deep first replaced the earlier southern linear plans. The space between the two principal chimneys was commonly enclosed and covered by a shed roof to make a small interior room or closet.

6. Newport News, Virginia, vicinity; early 18th century (as modified). Jones House. An earlier one-story house (note the trace of the original steep roof) altered to a two-story cross plan in the 18th century. The windows are modern.

7., 8. Surry County, Virginia; mid-17th century. Bacon's Castle. Although somewhat altered, this is the only high-style house surviving from the 17th century. Note the cross form, shaped parapets, and multiple chimney stacks. Figure 7 shows the front facade and Figure 8 the rear.

1

3

5

6

4

2

7

8

plantation economy in the 18th century, many early wooden houses were converted to slave quarters or storage; most were ultimately abandoned and razed. As a result, the houses that survived were primarily early masonry examples. Most of these have also been lost due to indifference and neglect, some in only the past few decades.

The few surviving Postmedieval houses have generally been in continuous use for almost three hundred years. During this long period they have been modified, improved, remodeled, and rebuilt, with the result that few reached this century in anything approaching their original form. Beginning about 1900, concern for our earliest colonial heritage led to modern restoration of many examples. When based on precise architectural and historical research, these restored houses closely approach the appearance of the 17th-century originals. When less carefully done, such restoration has produced bastard buildings with combinations of features that never existed.

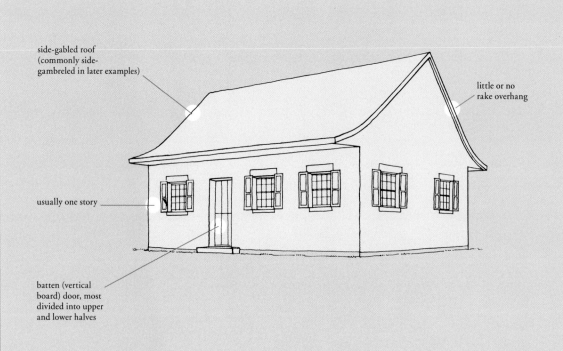

side-gabled roof (commonly side-gambreled in later examples)

little or no rake overhang

usually one story

batten (vertical board) door, most divided into upper and lower halves

URBAN TRADITION
brick walls; steeply pitched, parapeted roof with paired end chimneys

page 173

RURAL TRADITION, UNFLARED EAVES
stone walls (rarely wooden); eaves with little or no overhang

page 174

RURAL TRADITION, FLARED EAVES
stone walls (rarely wooden); flared (slightly flattened) eave overhang

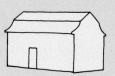

page 175

PRINCIPAL SUBTYPES

Dutch Colonial

1625–ca. 1840

Identifying Features

One story (less commonly one and one-half stories, rarely two stories) with side-gabled or side-gambreled roof having little or no rake (side) overhang; most originally with entrance doors divided into separately opening upper and lower halves (in about half the surviving examples, these have been replaced by later single-unit doors).

Principal Subtypes

New World colonists from the Netherlands constructed three distinctive types of houses:

URBAN TRADITION—Among the earliest were brick urban houses of Medieval inspiration having steeply pitched and parapeted gable roofs and paired end chimneys. This type dominated the 17th-century Dutch trading settlements that grew at each end of the region's principal navigation route, the Hudson River: New Amsterdam (later New York) to the south and several outposts in the Albany area to the north. These towns became increasingly Anglicized in the 18th century with the result that few Dutch urban houses were built after about 1730.[2]

RURAL TRADITION, UNFLARED EAVES—Dutch building traditions persisted far longer in rural areas. Brick, the preferred Dutch building material, was replaced by coursed stone in most rural houses. The shaping and finish of the stonework became increasingly refined as colonial inhabitants grew more affluent during the 18th century. Early rural examples had side-gabled roofs and little or no eave overhang. After about 1750 gambrel roofs became common in this type.

RURAL TRADITION, FLARED EAVES—This tradition is similar to the rural subtype described just above, but has flared, overhanging eaves, which became common on both gable- and gambrel-roofed examples after about 1750 in the southern Hudson River area (see maps on page 171).

Variants and Details

As in the adjacent English colonies, the pitch of rural Dutch roofs decreased during the early 18th century as wood shingles replaced thatch, tile, and slate as the preferred roofing material. Steeply pitched, Medieval-style roofs survive on only a few rural Dutch houses, all built before about 1720. (The dating of roofs and architectural details in rural Dutch houses is unusually difficult because early stone walls were typically incorporated into expansions and modifications throughout the 18th and 19th centuries. For this reason, most houses of supposed early date show later features, particularly roof, door, and window details.) In many rural examples the stone walls do not extend into the side gables, which are instead constructed of either brick or, more commonly, shingle- or weatherboard-covered wooden framing. After about 1750, distinctively shaped gambrel roofs with short, flattened upper slopes became common, along with gable roofs of normal pitch which continued to be built. In the southernmost areas of Dutch influence, around present-day New York City and adjacent New Jersey, distinctive flared eaves were usual on both gable and gambrel roofs after about 1750. Where the Dutch colonists were in close contact with English building traditions, particularly on western Long Island, timber-frame rural houses with weatherboard or shingle siding replaced the more usual stone construction. Most existing Dutch Colonial houses have double-hung sash windows which may be original or replacements of earlier types. Like their English counterparts, 17th-century Dutch houses apparently had leaded casement windows. In the English colonies these were supplanted by wooden, double-hung windows with one movable sash early in the 18th century. The Dutch, however, apparently used outward-swinging wooden casements, sometimes hung in side-by-side pairs, during an early 18th-century transitional period between leaded casements and wooden double-hung sashes. Few of these early casement windows, either leaded or wooden, survive. The Dutch double door was probably developed to keep out livestock (with the bottom section closed) while allowing in light and air through the open top. This style of door is found in about half of the surviving houses. From the early 18th century, the treatment of the door surround commonly reflected the Georgian and subsequent Federal styles of the English colonies. It had previously been thought that porches were likely later additions to rural Dutch Colonial houses. However, recent research has demonstrated that porches were found in the Low Countries (today's Netherlands and Belgium) from the 16th to the 18th centuries. Further, written evidence establishes that porches were part of original Dutch Colonial houses in the Hudson River Valley, making them some of the earliest examples in America.[3]

Occurrence

Formal control by the Dutch of their New World colonies was remarkably brief. Dutch fur traders founded settlements near Albany in 1614 and at New Amsterdam (New York) in 1626. Centered in these areas, and along the Hudson River which connected them, Dutch colonization proceeded for only fifty years before expanding English colonies on either side led to English control in 1664. Thus New Netherland became New York and Dutch influence began to fade in the principal towns of the colony. All Dutch urban buildings have long vanished from New Amsterdam (the tip of Manhattan Island in what is now New York City) but a very few—probably less than a half-dozen—

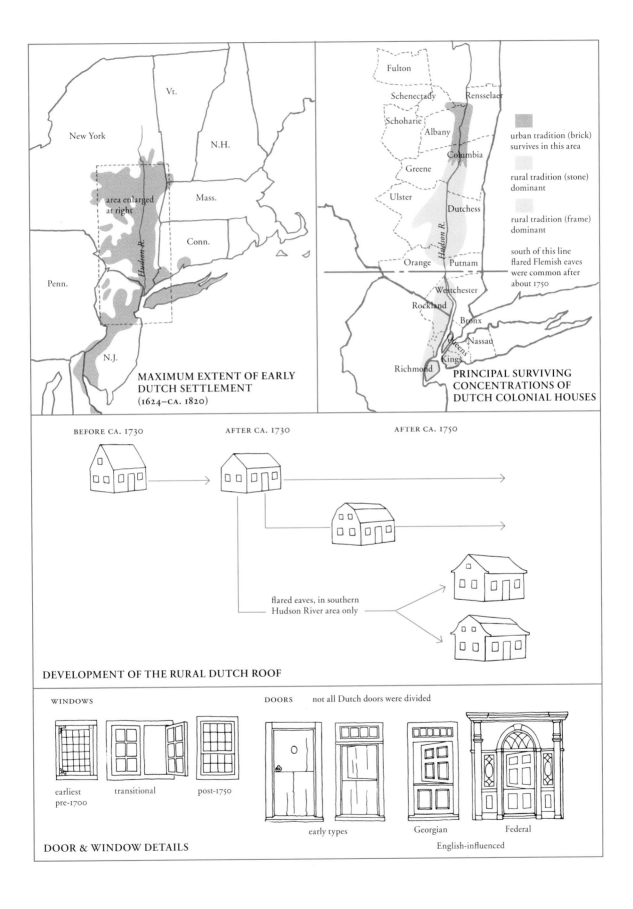

MAXIMUM EXTENT OF EARLY
DUTCH SETTLEMENT
(1624–CA. 1820)

PRINCIPAL SURVIVING
CONCENTRATIONS OF
DUTCH COLONIAL HOUSES

New York

Vt.

N.H.

Mass.

Conn.

Penn.

N.J.

area enlarged
at right

Hudson R.

Fulton

Schenectady   Rensselaer

Schoharie

Albany

Columbia

Greene

Ulster

Dutchess

Hudson R.

Orange   Putnam

Westchester

Rockland

Bronx

Queens   Nassau

Richmond   Kings

urban tradition (brick)
survives in this area

rural tradition (stone)
dominant

rural tradition (frame)
dominant

south of this line
flared Flemish eaves
were common after
about 1750

DEVELOPMENT OF THE RURAL DUTCH ROOF

BEFORE CA. 1730   AFTER CA. 1730   AFTER CA. 1750

flared eaves, in southern
Hudson River area only

DOOR & WINDOW DETAILS

WINDOWS

earliest
pre-1700

transitional

post-1750

DOORS   not all Dutch doors were divided

early types

Georgian

Federal

English-influenced

urban houses still survive in the Albany region. These are among the rarest of American domestic buildings; regrettably, several of the finest remaining examples have been lost during only the last few decades. In contrast, several hundred Dutch rural houses survive in various states of preservation and modification throughout the area of former Dutch influence. The English permitted feudal Dutch landholders, some of whom controlled enormous tracts along the Hudson, to retain their property. These landlords, in turn, continued to encourage rural immigration from Holland during the 18th century. As a result, most Dutch Colonial rural houses post-date by many years the era of Dutch ownership of the colony.

The building traditions brought by these Dutch immigrants survived, in isolated examples, into the early decades of the 19th century. Today, concentrations of Dutch rural houses are found principally in Bergen County (New Jersey), adjacent Rockland County (New York), and farther up the Hudson, in Ulster and Dutchess counties (New York). A handful of formerly rural houses are preserved within the bounds of present New York City, particularly in Queens County and Staten Island. Scattered examples are found throughout the area of former Dutch influence (see maps on page 171).

Comments

Dutch Colonial houses of the urban type are quite similar to their Old World counterparts built in the prosperous mercantile cities of 17th-century Holland. In sharp contrast, the origins of the American Dutch rural house are uncertain and have attracted much speculation. The earliest were simple stone-walled, gable-roofed folk houses. Similar houses are found in the rural building traditions of Flanders (which includes the coastal regions of modern Belgium and immediately adjacent France) but are rare in the Netherlands, which generally lacks both stone and abundant timber for building (hence the Dutch emphasis on brick construction). Most rural Dutch immigrants, however, were persecuted Protestants from Flanders, France, and elsewhere who sought refuge first in Holland and then in her New World colony. With them most probably came the tradition of stone folk building. The principal controversy thus centers not on the stone walls of the rural Dutch Colonial house, but on its distinctive roof features: the unusual gambrel and, especially, the flared eaves, both of which became common after about 1750. The gambrel is perhaps the easiest to explain, since gambrels of somewhat different shape were also becoming common, as a means of increasing both roof span and useful attic space, throughout the English colonies at the same time. More difficulty attaches to the origin of the flared eaves. These have been considered to be: (1) a distinctive New World innovation, or (2) an adaptation of a French-Flemish tradition of protecting plastered walls under steeply sloping, thatched roofs by adding a more gently sloping extension of tiles at the eaves. Pending actual research on the question, the latter explanation appears more likely, particularly since many French-influenced Colonial buildings show similar eaves (see the next chapter, on French Colonial houses, pages 179–86).

Dutch rural houses, with their substantial stone walls, were less easily expanded than were their wooden English counterparts. Although there are many examples of early Dutch stone walls being incorporated into later, and larger, houses, these thrifty colonists generally favored another method of house expansion. When a house became too

URBAN TRADITION

1. Schenectady, New York; early 18th century. Yates House. The only surviving example in an urban setting with the entrance in the narrow gable end. Note the dagger-shaped wrought-iron anchors for roof and wall beams, a characteristic feature of urban Dutch houses. This example has wood-frame side walls. The windows and Classical doorway are later additions.

2. East Greenbush, New York; 1723. Bries House. Typical urban house built in rural setting, with entrance on long, non-gabled wall. The windows and porch are later additions.

3. Kinderhook, New York; 1737. Van Alen House (restoration). Urban house in rural setting expanded by adding an adjacent unit in typical Dutch fashion.

4. Cohoes, New York; mid-18th century. Van Schaick House. A transitional example with urban-style brickwork and newly fashionable gambrel roof. The porch is a late 19th-century addition.

RURAL TRADITION, UNFLARED EAVES

1. Rotterdam, New York; early 18th century. Mabie House. One of the few surviving rural Dutch houses that preserve the steep Medieval roof pitch. The walls are of whitewashed stone; the frame extension to the right is a later addition.

2. Hurley, New York; 1725. Restoration.

3. New Paltz, New York; ca. 1692. Bevier House. The original house (left-hand portion) was expanded by early additions. The gable-end entrance is unusual.

4. Coeymans, New York; ca. 1761 (altered ca. 1790). Coeymans House. An early example expanded and altered by the early addition of a fashionable gambrel roof.

5. Ulster County, New York; mid-18th century. Ten Broeck House. Note the expansion by adding two units to the portion to the left with casement windows, which is the earliest. The middle unit was added in 1751 and the right-hand unit in 1765.

1

3

2

5

4

RURAL TRADITION, FLARED EAVES

1. Old Tappan, New Jersey; ca. 1751. Haring House. Note the more carefully finished stonework on the front facade.

2. Dumont, New Jersey; ca. 1760 (smaller portion in foreground), ca. 1810 (larger portion). Zabriskie House. Note the absence of flared eaves on the small early portion. The wide-end overhang of the gambrel roof is a 19th-century development.

3. Brooklyn, New York; ca. 1676. Schenck House. A very early wood-frame example preserving the steep Medieval roof pitch. The dormers, porch, and flared eaves are 18th-century modifications.

4. Mahwah vicinity, New Jersey; late 18th century. Van Horn House.

5. Closter, New Jersey; ca. 1800. Durie House. The dormers and porch supports are later additions, as is the smaller frame wing added in 1854.

1

3

2

4

5

small, a larger version was built immediately beside the smaller, which then became a kitchen or bedroom wing of the new dwelling. Dutch Colonial houses thus often show a linear sequence of two or three (rarely more) units built at different times. Although the smallest unit is normally the oldest, this is not invariably the case, for small kitchen or bedroom wings were also added to larger houses long after they were built.

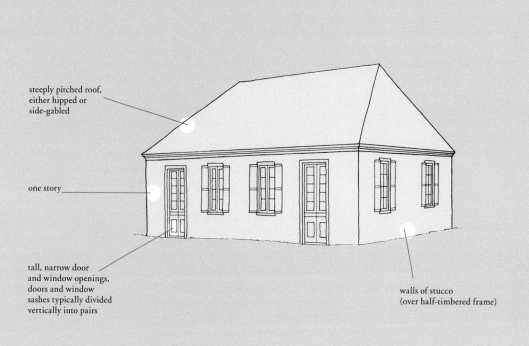

steeply pitched roof,
either hipped or
side-gabled

one story

tall, narrow door
and window openings,
doors and window
sashes typically divided
vertically into pairs

walls of stucco
(over half-timbered frame)

URBAN TRADITION
side-gabled roof
(less commonly hipped)
with flared overhanging
eaves, no porch

RURAL TRADITION
hipped (less commonly
side-gabled) with integral
porch, usually on raised
foundation

page 183

pages 184–85

PRINCIPAL SUBTYPES

French Colonial

1700–1830; to ca. 1860 in New Orleans

Identifying Features

One story with many narrow door and window openings having paired shutters (these openings originally had paired French doors and paired casement windows which have commonly been altered to single doors and double-hung sash windows); steeply pitched roof, either hipped or side-gabled; walls of stucco, usually over a half-timbered frame.

Principal Subtypes

French Colonial houses are of two basic types:

URBAN TRADITION—In New Orleans there remain many French urban cottages which lack porches and are built right up to the adjacent sidewalk. These normally have side-gabled (sometimes hipped) roofs and flared eaves that overhang the front facade.

RURAL TRADITION—More familiar than the urban cottages of New Orleans are French rural houses with extensive porches supported by slender wooden columns under the main roof line. These usually have steeply pitched, hipped roofs and are commonly raised on high masonry foundations, the porch area above being supported by massive masonry columns. They may be raised a full story above grade, allowing the main living level of the house to escape seasonal floods.

Variants and Details

As in their 17th-century English and Dutch counterparts, early French Colonial houses had very high, steeply pitched roofs, following the Medieval tradition of constructing thatched roofs at a very steep pitch in order to shed water. Early French examples usually had a characteristic pavilion roof form, which is steeply hipped with the side roof planes sloping even more steeply than the front and back planes. Very few of these survive. The addition of wide porches around such houses, a mild-climate tradition that probably originated in the West Indies, was accomplished by extending the hipped roof out over the porch but at a gentler pitch, giving it a distinctive, dual-pitched form. As this tradition developed, such roofs were even used occasionally on urban houses without porches. Somewhat later, simple hipped roofs, lower and with uniform slopes on all sides, came to dominate. Original side-gabled roofs are uncommon in rural houses, although many early hipped forms have been modified to this shape. In New Orleans, side-gabled roofs were dominant on urban cottages built after about 1830, probably to reduce roof drainage to narrow passageways between the closely spaced cottages of the expanding city. These later urban cottages also typically have extended and flared eaves, a characteristic that they share with Flemish-inspired Dutch Colonial houses of New York and New Jersey. In all roof forms, tall and narrow gabled dormers were sometimes used to provide attic light.

Most French Colonial houses originally had paired French doors, with small glass panes set above wooden panels. The doors sometimes had a line of transom lights above; in later examples these were often supplanted by a Federal fanlight. Originally the doors were framed by a simple, narrow surround. Vertical board shutters hung on strap hinges covered the doors and transom (but not the fanlight, if present). The interior surface of the shutter was sometimes paneled; the shutters usually swung outward and the doors inward. In later examples, Federal or Greek Revival door surrounds are common. Early French windows were paired wooden casements which swung inward. These were generally glazed with small panes of glass and were covered by vertical board shutters which had horizontal battens on the interior and swung outward on iron strap hinges. The window surround was narrow and simple. In later examples these French-style casements were supplanted by English double-hung sashes.

Occurrence

In the 18th century, France occupied much of eastern North America by means of military outposts and settlements scattered along the principal waterways, particularly the St. Lawrence, Great Lakes, and Mississippi valleys (see map on page 181). After Jefferson's purchase of Louisiana in 1803, French building traditions began to fade, although they persisted in New Orleans for half a century more and survive today in French Canada. In the United States, only a few concentrations of French-influenced buildings remain from this vast empire. All of these are in Louisiana and adjacent Mississippi save one, the little-known French Colonial houses of St. Genevieve, Missouri (see map on page 181). Several hundred houses, all of the rural type, survive in these areas; a handful of others are scattered elsewhere. Most date from the late 18th and early 19th centuries. The early outskirts of New Orleans had many similar rural houses but only a few survived the later growth of the city. Until at least the 1860s, however, French-style urban cottages were built in the Creole suburbs of New Orleans, to the north and east of the original town, or Vieux Carré.

More than half of the country's surviving French Colonial houses are found in these New Orleans neighborhoods, but are seldom seen by visitors to that city. Only a handful remain in the Vieux Carré, which was all but destroyed by fires in 1788 and 1791. As the commercial center of town, the Vieux Carré was rebuilt during the early 19th century largely with mixed-use structures having shops on the first floor and living quarters above. Many of these survive and show strong French influences, especially in the door and window treatments, but most were altered as the city grew during the later

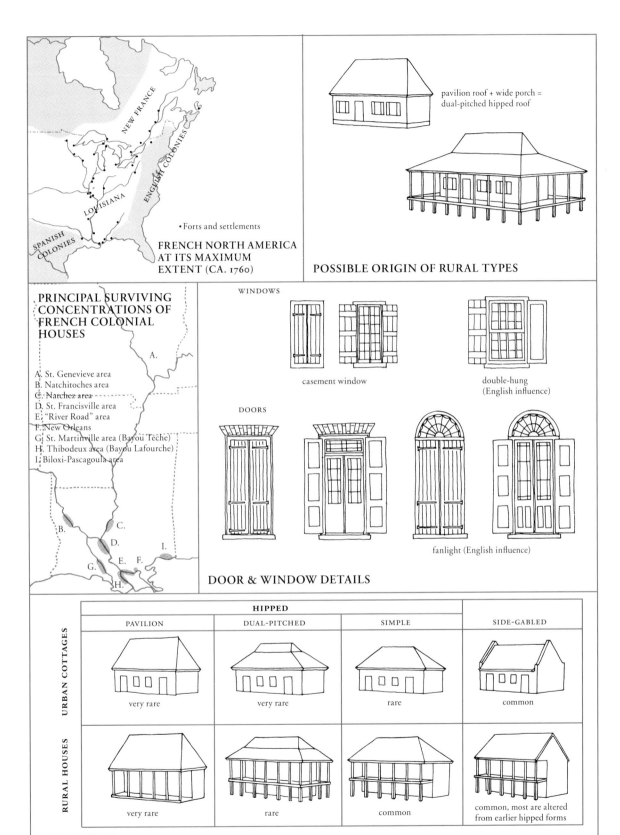

FRENCH NORTH AMERICA AT ITS MAXIMUM EXTENT (CA. 1760)

NEW FRANCE

ENGLISH COLONIES

LOUISIANA

SPANISH COLONIES

• Forts and settlements

POSSIBLE ORIGIN OF RURAL TYPES

pavilion roof + wide porch = dual-pitched hipped roof

PRINCIPAL SURVIVING CONCENTRATIONS OF FRENCH COLONIAL HOUSES

A. St. Genevieve area
B. Natchitoches area
C. Natchez area
D. St. Francisville area
E. "River Road" area
F. New Orleans
G. St. Martinville area (Bayou Teche)
H. Thibodeux area (Bayou Lafourche)
I. Biloxi-Pascagoula area

WINDOWS

casement window

double-hung (English influence)

DOORS

fanlight (English influence)

DOOR & WINDOW DETAILS

	HIPPED			
	PAVILION	DUAL-PITCHED	SIMPLE	SIDE-GABLED
URBAN COTTAGES	very rare	very rare	rare	common
RURAL HOUSES	very rare	rare	common	common, most are altered from earlier hipped forms

ROOF FORMS

19th century. For example, small and delicate wrought-iron balconies were originally common under full-length upper windows (Figure 5, below). The expansion of cast-iron technology in the mid-1800s led to the replacement of many by elaborate systems of iron porches extending over the sidewalks and around the building at each upper level (Figure 6, below). These provided outdoor living areas for residents of the upper floors, but they also dramatically altered the facades. Paradoxically, it is these American-made additions, almost unknown in France, that have come to characterize French New Orleans.

With the growth of the city as a principal United States seaport after the Louisiana Purchase, a flood of American immigrants built principally upriver (southwest) of the Vieux Carré. At the same time, the more slowly expanding French population built new suburbs in the opposite or downriver direction. Most of the city's surviving French houses are urban cottages built in these neighborhoods from 1810 to about 1860.

Comments

English houses are usually directed inward; they have few external entrances and emphasize internal halls and stairways for access to the rooms. French houses, on the other hand, typically look outward; each room is likely to have its own exterior doorway and the stairways are commonly on exterior porches, rather than within the main body of the house. Hallways are also normally absent, the interior rooms opening instead directly into each other. These traditions are reflected in the many exterior doors and in the external stairways of French Colonial houses. Even small urban cottages, usually built in a square four-room plan, have at least four external doors, two of which lead from the two front rooms directly onto the adjacent sidewalk.

Most French Colonial houses were constructed, at least in part, with half-timbered walls. Earliest, and most primitive, was post-in-ground construction, with closely spaced vertical timbers buried in the ground and filled in between with clay mixed with such

6

5

URBAN TRADITION

1. New Orleans, Louisiana; 1820. Dolliole House. Hipped-roof example of unusual shape. The roof is covered with the original flat tiles; note the projecting tiles at the eaves and the four doorways.

2. New Orleans, Louisiana; mid-19th century. Late hipped-roof example with wood-frame walls and modest Italianate detailing.

3. New Orleans, Louisiana; ca. 1850. Mansion House. Late wood-frame example with Greek Revival doorway. The three-ranked facade is unusual.

4. New Orleans, Louisiana; 1824. Gaillard House.

5. New Orleans, Louisiana; ca. 1806. Font-Juncadella Building. A well-preserved example of a typical early 19th-century French shop-residence of the Vieux Carré. Note the delicate wrought-iron balcony railing.

6. New Orleans, Louisiana; 1836. Gardette House. Large Vieux Carré town house with elaborate cast-iron porches added in the mid-19th century.

7. New Orleans, Louisiana; ca. 1828. Boutin House. Early parapeted example with Federal doorway and pilasters. The Victorian eave brackets and trim are later additions.

1

2

3

4

7

RURAL TRADITION

1., 2. St. Genevieve, Missouri; late 18th century. Bolduc House (restoration). Figure 1 shows the side and rear of the house before restoration. Figure 2 shows the rear of the house as restored with a dual-pitched hipped roof and exposed wall timbers.

3. Hahnville, Louisiana, vicinity; early 19th century. Lehman House. A modest example built without the usual Louisiana high basement. The dormer and metal roof are later additions.

4. New Orleans, Louisiana; 1820. Olivier House. Large example with dual-pitched hipped roof. Note the brick columns supporting the wood porch above and the outside stairway. Originally a plantation house beyond the city, this example survived the urban growth around it until 1950, when it was demolished.

5. St. Genevieve, Missouri; late 18th century. Amoureaux House. This example has been much modified over the years. The roof framing suggests that the original roof was of pavilion-shaped hipped form without porches.

6. Hahnville, Louisiana, vicinity; early 19th century. Fortier House (Homeplace Plantation). The front stairway replaces an earlier one beneath the right corner of the porch. The metal roof is a later addition.

7. New Roads, Louisiana, vicinity; early 19th century. Riche House. The elaborate stairway probably replaces an earlier one beneath the porch, like that in Figure 4. Note the partial side porches. In low flood-prone areas the main living levels were raised a full story above grade level. Storage and workshops were at grade. This produced the raised house form seen in Figures 4–8.

8. St. Martinville, Louisiana, vicinity; 1765. D'Autrive Chevalier de St. Louis. Houssaye House (Acadian House, restoration). An early example, probably built originally with side-gabled roof as shown.

1

3

6

2

5

4

7

8

binding materials as hair or straw. Later, typical timber framing, using a sill set on a foundation, was adopted; often such walls had soft brick infilling. Both the post-in-ground and framed types were originally covered with stucco or, in later examples, weatherboarding, to protect the timbers and infilling. In raised rural houses the foundation is commonly of stuccoed brick, which supports the half-timbered walls of the main floor above.

The several hundred surviving French Colonial houses are among the rarest and least appreciated American buildings. While comparable English houses of the eastern seaboard have long been revered landmarks, only a few French examples are similarly esteemed. Recent preservation efforts in New Orleans have renewed interest in its urban cottages, but unique rural houses are still being lost through indifference and neglect.

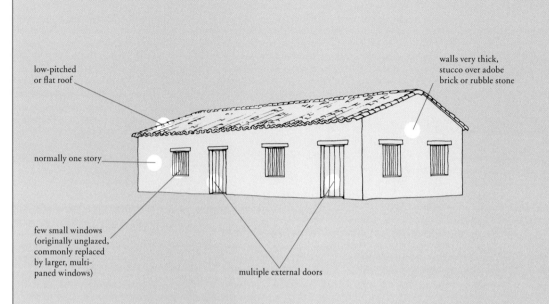

low-pitched
or flat roof

walls very thick,
stucco over adobe
brick or rubble stone

normally one story

few small windows
(originally unglazed,
commonly replaced
by larger, multi-
paned windows)

multiple external doors

PITCHED ROOF

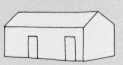

pages 194–95

FLAT ROOF WITH PARAPET

pages 196–97

PRINCIPAL SUBTYPES

Spanish Colonial

1600–1850; locally to ca. 1900

Identifying Features

One story (less commonly two stories) with low-pitched or flat roof; thick masonry walls of adobe brick or rubble stone (usually covered with protective stucco); originally with multiple external doorways and few small window openings lacking glass (bars or grilles of wood or wrought iron covered the exterior openings, which were closed from the interior by solid wooden shutters; except in reconstructions, most such early windows have been altered to accommodate double-hung, glazed sashes and trim).

Principal Subtypes

Spanish Colonial houses are of solid masonry construction[4] but show two fundamentally different roof types which are found both in Spain and in her New World colonies:

PITCHED ROOF—The first basic type includes pitched-roof houses with traditional European roof framing. These, in turn, are of three kinds: The first consists of steeply pitched, usually side-gabled forms in which the wooden framing supports a covering of thatch; in the United States, this tradition survives principally in Hispanic folk houses with steeply pitched, shingled roofs. In the second and most familiar type, the roofs are low-pitched with a covering of half-cylindrical tiles. These tile roofs are usually of shed- or side-gabled form, less commonly hipped. A third variant, originally found in the Los Angeles area but now very rare, consists of an almost flat, tar-covered shed roof with overhanging eaves.

FLAT ROOF WITH PARAPET—The second basic type consists of flat-roofed houses without traditional European roof framing. Instead, massive horizontal timbers are embedded in parapeted masonry walls to support an extremely heavy roof of earth or mortar. Cylindrical rainspouts of wood, tin, or tile project through the parapet along one or more walls to provide drainage. This type, introduced into Spain from North Africa by the Moors, was also developed independently by several groups of Native

Americans, and was well established in Mexico and the southwestern United States when the Spaniards arrived.

From early Spanish Colonial times, each of the two basic roof types has tended to dominate in different parts of Mexico and adjacent Hispanic areas of the United States (see map on page 191). The reasons for this pattern are uncertain; the flat, earthen roof would appear to be more suitable for very hot and dry regions, yet each type dominates through a range of climates. Most probably the building traditions of the original colonial settlers, interacting with those of the local natives, determined the patterns.

Variants and Details

The earliest houses in areas of the United States that were formerly Spanish territories showed few decorative or stylistic details when compared with more imposing Spanish or Mexican prototypes. Built in remote and impoverished colonial outposts, these houses were simple by necessity. Only with the opening of trade with the United States in the 1830s did increased prosperity come to these regions; along with the new wealth came Anglo immigrants with their own building traditions. First came wooden decorative details, principally in the Greek Revival style, and glazed, double-hung sash windows. In areas with the pitched-roof tradition, shingled roofs were introduced. In other areas, flat-roofed houses became modified by the addition of framed, shingled roofs above the parapeted walls. These innovations quickly became fashionable with both Anglo and Hispanic residents, who superimposed them upon the traditional adobe construction. Such Anglo-Spanish–Greek Revival houses, in two-story variants with cantilevered second-floor porches, have come to be called Monterey style, after the colonial capital of California where many survive (Figures 5, 6, 7, pages 194–95).[5] In New Mexico, western Texas, and Arizona, related flat-roofed, single-story forms, usually with a protective topping of fired brick crowning the roof parapet, are known as Territorial style houses (Figures 5, 6, page 196). The spread of the western railroads in the 1880s provided ready access to quantities of milled lumber and led to the final decline of Hispanic building styles as adobe construction was abandoned for wood-frame houses in all but a few remote pockets of surviving tradition.

PORCHES—Spanish domestic buildings commonly have long, narrow porches (the *corredor* or *portale*) that open onto internal courtyards and function as sheltered passageways between rooms, which usually lacked internal connecting doorways. In more pretentious Spanish and Mexican prototypes, the porches often took the form of colonnaded arcades with elaborate masonry arches supporting the roof. In more modest examples, which include all that survive in the United States, porch roofs were supported by hewn logs, usually capped by distinctive carved brackets. In pitched-roof houses these columns supported either extensions of the main roof or separate shed roofs abutting the main walls. In flat-roofed houses, porches were normally recessed into the main structure, with the principal adobe walls supporting the ends of the porch-roof timbers. Upon these were built a lower and somewhat thinner version of the main earthen roof. Because they faced internal courtyards, traditional porches are seldom evident on the external facades. With the arrival of Anglo influence, however, front-facade porches became fashionable. Particularly characteristic were cantilevered second-floor porches on two-story houses. These usually show delicate wooden balustrades and were probably

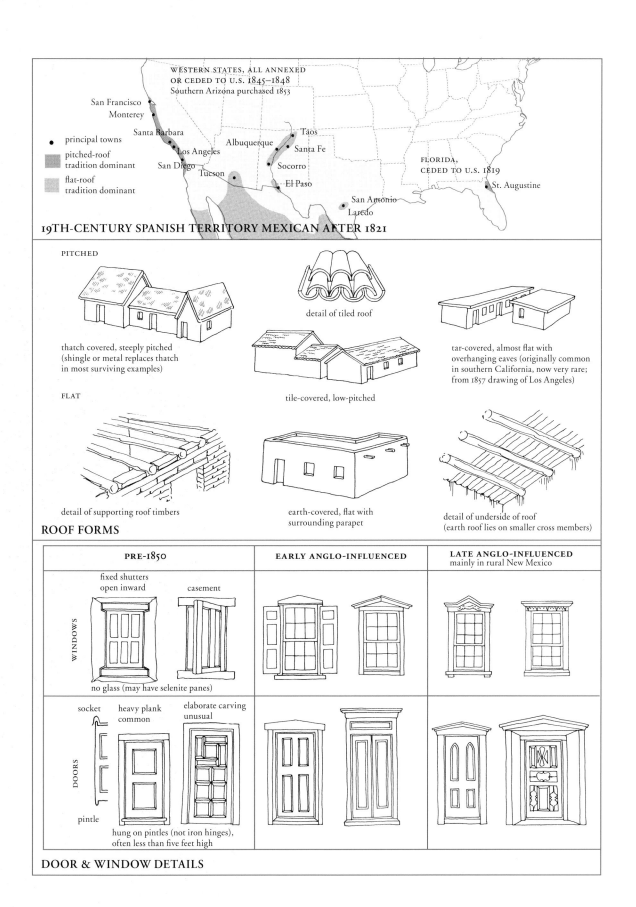

WESTERN STATES, ALL ANNEXED
OR CEDED TO U.S. 1845–1848
Southern Arizona purchased 1853

San Francisco
Monterey
Santa Barbara
• principal towns
Los Angeles
pitched-roof
tradition dominant
San Diego
flat-roof
Tucson
tradition dominant

Albuquerque
Taos
Santa Fe
Socorro
El Paso

FLORIDA,
CEDED TO U.S. 1819

St. Augustine

San Antonio
Laredo

19TH-CENTURY SPANISH TERRITORY MEXICAN AFTER 1821

PITCHED

detail of tiled roof

thatch covered, steeply pitched
(shingle or metal replaces thatch
in most surviving examples)

tar-covered, almost flat with
overhanging eaves (originally common
in southern California, now very rare;
from 1857 drawing of Los Angeles)

FLAT

tile-covered, low-pitched

detail of supporting roof timbers

earth-covered, flat with
surrounding parapet

detail of underside of roof
(earth roof lies on smaller cross members)

ROOF FORMS

	PRE-1850	EARLY ANGLO-INFLUENCED	LATE ANGLO-INFLUENCED mainly in rural New Mexico
WINDOWS	fixed shutters open inward casement no glass (may have selenite panes)		
DOORS	socket heavy plank common elaborate carving unusual pintle hung on pintles (not iron hinges), often less than five feet high		

DOOR & WINDOW DETAILS

inspired, at least in part, by the cantilevered balconies common on the upper floors of traditional Spanish town houses. Alpheus B. Thompson and Thomas O. Larkin, builders of early examples with full-width porches, were familiar with this form from travels in the southeastern United States and Caribbean (Figures 3 and 7, page 195).[6] Anglo influence also led to the traditional massive roof supports being abandoned for more delicate wooden columns of vernacular Greek Revival inspiration.

Occurrence

Most of what is now the southwestern United States was Spanish from the 17th century until 1821, when Mexico gained its independence; it remained part of Mexico until it was ceded to the United States in the late 1840s following the Mexican War. Spanish Texas gained independence from Mexico in 1836 and was a separate country until it was annexed to the United States in 1845. Florida was Spanish from 1565 until it was ceded to the United States in 1821, with a brief interruption of British rule from 1763 to 1783. (A similarly brief interval of Spanish control of French Louisiana, from 1762 until 1800, resulted in a few Spanish public buildings but little change in the local French housing traditions.) This vast territory was a sparsely settled frontier region during the Spanish and Mexican periods. Forts and missions to convert the Native Americans were established at many places, but few led to permanent settlements with substantial domestic architecture: St. Augustine in Florida; around San Antonio, Texas; scattered along the length of the Rio Grande from southern Texas to northern New Mexico; around Tucson, Arizona; and along the California coast from San Diego northward to around San Francisco (see map on page 191). Today significant concentrations remain only in St. Augustine, Tuscon, Santa Fe, Taos, Mesilla, San Diego, Santa Barbara, Monterey, and a few rural communities in Texas and New Mexico. Almost all surviving examples show Anglo-influenced modifications from the mid- and late 19th century. Many have also suffered from 20th-century renovation and overly zealous restoration, this particularly for those in modern urban centers; relatively unaltered examples from the 19th century survive principally in rural areas, from which they are fast disappearing through neglect and decay.

Comments

Unlike their English counterparts, larger Spanish Colonial domestic buildings were not usually conceived as multi-roomed wholes but grew, instead, as series of independent rooms. Modest households had but a single room. As affluence increased, one-room units were added to make extended dwellings whose size was limited only by the wealth of the builder. Typically, the first two or three rooms were joined end-to-end to make a linear row; units were then added single file but at right angles to make an L or U. In the largest houses, the rooms made rectangular masses, enclosing an inner courtyard (the *patio* or *placita*). In smaller houses, masonry walls, rather than rooms, usually completed the enclosure of similar courtyards. Traditionally, few internal openings existed between rooms; each was entered through its own door opening onto the courtyard. Long, narrow porches commonly provided sheltered passageways between rooms. The external facades of extended houses were usually austere, revealing only small windows and a single entrance door or gateway.

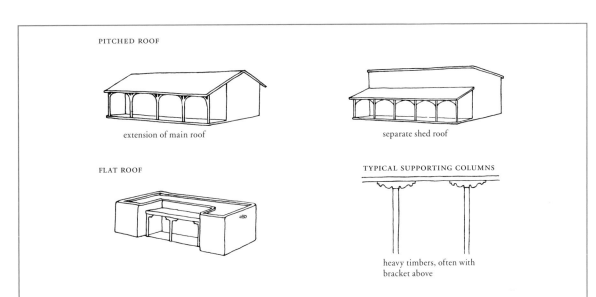

PITCHED ROOF

extension of main roof

separate shed roof

FLAT ROOF

TYPICAL SUPPORTING COLUMNS

heavy timbers, often with
bracket above

ORIGINAL PORCHES Rarely on front facade

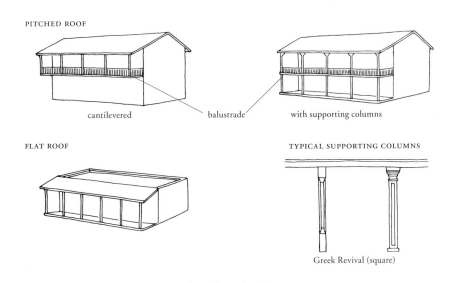

PITCHED ROOF

cantilevered

balustrade

with supporting columns

FLAT ROOF

TYPICAL SUPPORTING COLUMNS

Greek Revival (square)

ANGLO-INFLUENCED PORCHES Commonly on front facade

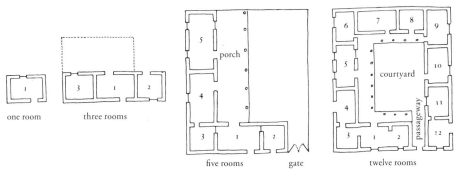

one room

three rooms

porch

five rooms

gate

courtyard

passageway

twelve rooms

PLAN OF THE SPANISH HOUSE

1

2

4

6

PITCHED ROOF

1. Salinas vicinity, California; early 19th century. Sherwood House. Courtyard view of a little-altered rural survivor of modest scale. The wide rake overhang of the gable is unusual.

2. San Diego, California; 1829. Estudillo House (restoration). Exterior view of a part of an extended, U-shaped example that survives relatively intact. Note the intersecting shed roofs.

3. Sonoma County, California; 1836. Petaluma Adobe; Alpheus B. Thompson, designer/builder. Large adobe house included ranch headquarters. Note extensive dual-level porches and semi-enclosed courtyard.

4. Templeton vicinity, California; early 19th century. Blackburn House. Courtyard view of a little-altered rural survivor. Note the intersecting roof planes.

5. Rio Grande City vicinity, Texas; 19th century. A modest rural two-story example with a Monterey-style cantilevered porch. Note the absence of windows.

6. San Juan Bautista, California; 1841. Castro House. A very large example of the Monterey style. Note the adobe bricks exposed beneath the falling stucco. The house has been restored since the photograph was taken.

7. Monterey, California; 1835. Larkin House; Thomas Oliver Larkin, owner/builder. The first of the California adobes with Anglicized details and broad two-level sheltering porches.

FLAT ROOF WITH PARAPET

1. Tucson, Arizona; ca. 1875. Verdugo House. In this example the original flat roof, revealed by the rainspouts, has been covered by a later pitched roof. The doors and windows are probably also later additions.

2. Ranchos de Taos, New Mexico; early 19th century. Courtyard view; note the recessed porch with simple, bracketed roof supports. The Anglo door and windows are probably later additions.

3. San Ygnacio, Texas; ca. 1851 (later additions). Trevino House. Extended example built from right to left in three progressively larger units (defined by the doors and rainspouts). Note the stone walls and adjacent *"jacal"* folk house with crude half-timbering and thatch roof.

4. San Pablo, Colorado; mid-19th century. An extended example with Anglo doors and windows.

5. Santa Fe, New Mexico; 1851. Tully House. A Territorial example with the exterior surviving as originally built.

6. Santa Fe, New Mexico; early 19th century (later additions). Borrego House (restoration). A Territorial example modified from an earlier house by the addition of front porch, brick coping along the parapet, and Anglo window crowns.

7. San Antonio, Texas; ca. 1772. Spanish Governor's Palace.

1

3

5

6

2

4

7

Spanish Colonial buildings are unusually durable when executed in stone. Although the wooden roof framing quickly decays if neglected, walls often survive many decades, even centuries, of abandonment. Spanish mission buildings in Texas, Arizona, and California, some constructed in the 17th and early 18th centuries, have mostly been reconstructed in this century upon such remaining wall segments. In sharp contrast, adobe walls are unusually susceptible to deterioration; if the roofs are not continually repaired, rainwater literally melts them into a formless mass of mud. As a general rule, adobe buildings abandoned for more than twenty-five years are beyond repair. Because most Spanish Colonial houses had adobe walls, the only survivors are those that have had continuous care. Regrettably, many of the most authentic examples were abandoned just during the past thirty years in favor of frame dwellings. This is particularly true in rural New Mexico, where irreplaceable examples have been, and are being, lost.

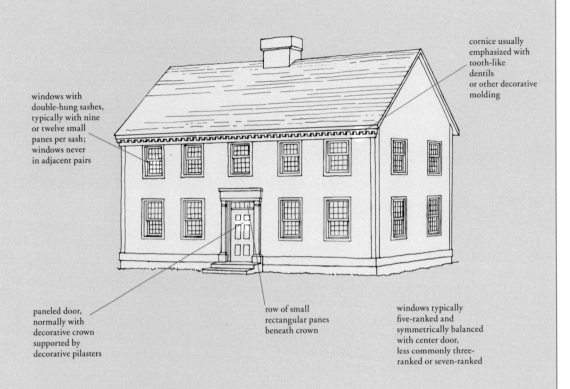

cornice usually
emphasized with
tooth-like
dentils
or other decorative
molding

windows with
double-hung sashes,
typically with nine
or twelve small
panes per sash;
windows never
in adjacent pairs

paneled door,
normally with
decorative crown
supported by
decorative pilasters

row of small
rectangular panes
beneath crown

windows typically
five-ranked and
symmetrically balanced
with center door,
less commonly three-
ranked or seven-ranked

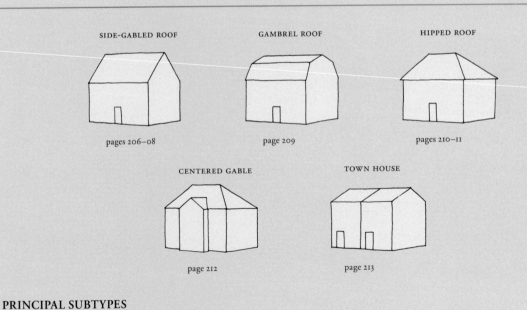

SIDE-GABLED ROOF

GAMBREL ROOF

HIPPED ROOF

pages 206–08

page 209

pages 210–11

CENTERED GABLE

TOWN HOUSE

page 212

page 213

PRINCIPAL SUBTYPES

Georgian

1700–1780; locally to ca. 1830

Identifying Features

Paneled front door, usually centered and capped by an elaborate decorative crown (entablature) supported by decorative pilasters (flattened columns); usually with a row of small rectangular panes of glass beneath the crown, either within the door or in a transom just above; cornice usually emphasized by decorative moldings, most commonly with tooth-like dentils; windows with double-hung sashes having many small panes (most commonly nine or twelve panes per sash) separated by thick wooden muntins; windows aligned horizontally and vertically in symmetrical rows, never in adjacent pairs, usually five-ranked on front facade, less commonly three- or seven-ranked.

Principal Subtypes

The Georgian house is usually a simple one- or two-story box, two rooms deep, with doors and windows in strict symmetry. Five principal subtypes can be distinguished:

SIDE-GABLED ROOF—About 40 percent of surviving Georgian houses are of this type, which is the most common in the northern and middle colonies, but also occurs in the southern colonies.

GAMBREL ROOF—This roof form is found primarily in the northern colonies where it is characteristic of about 25 percent of surviving Georgian houses. Few gambrels survive in the middle or southern colonies, although restoration research in Williamsburg indicates they may have formerly been common on one-story southern examples. The shape is an adaptation of the gable form, which provides more attic space for storage or sleeping.

HIPPED ROOF—About 25 percent of surviving Georgian houses have hipped roofs (some are dual-pitched hipped). This is the most common type in the southern colonies, but is not unusual in the middle and northern colonies, where it occurs principally on high-style landmark examples.

CENTERED GABLE—Less than 10 percent of surviving Georgian houses have a gable (pediment) centered on the front facade. The facade beneath the gable may either remain in the same plane as the rest of the wall or be extended slightly forward for emphasis as a pavilion. This subtype became common only after 1750, and is found in high-style examples in all the former colonies.

TOWN HOUSE—The earliest surviving urban houses with narrow front facades and linear plans date from the Georgian period. These were originally built in all the pre-Revolutionary urban centers of the Atlantic Coast (see map on page 205), but only a few examples remain today, principally in Philadelphia and Boston, and in Alexandria, Virginia.

Variants and Details

The structure and detailing of Georgian houses show distinct regional variations:

NORTHERN COLONIES—Wood-frame construction with shingle or clapboard walls and central chimneys dominated, as in the preceding Postmedieval English houses of the region.

MIDDLE COLONIES—Brick or stone construction dominated here. Some examples have details not found elsewhere, notably the pent roof separating the first and second floors, and the hooded front door, in which elements of the decorative crown project forward to form a small roof over the entryway.

SOUTHERN COLONIES—Brick was the dominant building material in surviving southern examples; red brick was most common. End chimneys continued to be common, as in Postmedieval English houses. Shapes were more varied in the South than elsewhere; dependencies were sometimes in separate connecting wings or detached from the main house in separate buildings. Some southern examples are raised off the ground on high foundations. On southern brick examples doors were sometimes accentuated only by changes in the surrounding brick pattern, rather than by an enframement of wooden pilasters and crown.

POST-1750, ALL COLONIES—After 1750, a few well-documented examples have the entire door enframement extended forward to form an entrance porch. Most such porches are, however, post-Georgian innovations. Dormers and decorative quoins became common after 1750 in all colonies. In later brick examples the separation between floors is usually marked by a change in the masonry pattern (belt course). Still more elaborate detailing appears in some high-style examples after 1750. Among these are two-story pilasters, centered gables, and roof balustrades. A cupola projecting above the roof, while common on Georgian public buildings, is found on only a handful of surviving houses. Door and window detailing is discussed in the following chapter, on the closely related Federal style.[7]

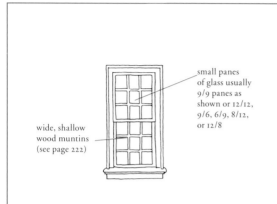

small panes
of glass usually
9/9 panes as
shown or 12/12,
9/6, 6/9, 8/12,
or 12/8

wide, shallow
wood muntins
(see page 222)

TYPICAL WINDOW (see pages 222–23)

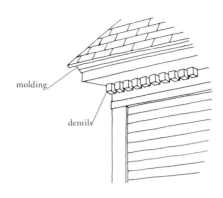

molding

dentils

TYPICAL CORNICE (see page 223)

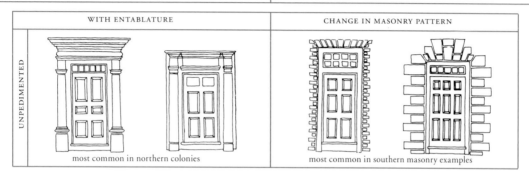

WITH ENTABLATURE	CHANGE IN MASONRY PATTERN

UNPEDIMENTED

most common in northern colonies

most common in southern masonry examples

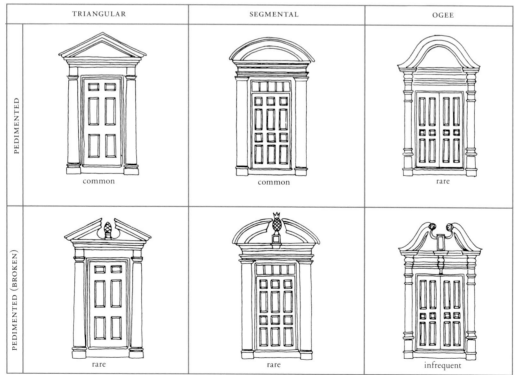

TRIANGULAR	SEGMENTAL	OGEE

PEDIMENTED

common

common

rare

PEDIMENTED (BROKEN)

rare

rare

infrequent

DOOR SURROUND VARIANTS Similar entablatures, pediments, and broken pediments may be found atop Georgian windows (see pages 222–23) and on Colonial Revival houses, both as door surrounds and window crowns

Occurrence

Georgian was the dominant style of the English colonies from 1700 to about 1780, when the population had grown to almost three million and covered the area shown on the map. In this area many thousands of Georgian houses survive today. Most have been lost from those colonial cities, such as Boston, New York, and Philadelphia, that grew rapidly in the 19th and 20th centuries. In sharp contrast are other colonial seaports (all the larger 18th-century towns had direct water communication with England; only villages occurred inland) that declined sharply in importance with the expansion of railroads in the 19th century. Examples are Portsmouth, New Hampshire; Newport, Rhode Island; New Castle, Delaware; Annapolis, Maryland; New Bern, North Carolina; and Charleston, South Carolina. Having had relatively little population growth since colonial times,

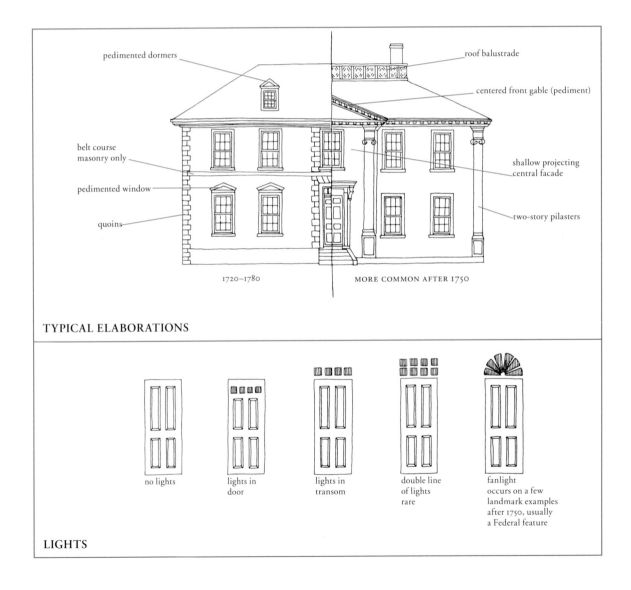

pedimented dormers

roof balustrade

centered front gable (pediment)

belt course
masonry only

shallow projecting
central facade

pedimented window

quoins

two-story pilasters

1720–1780

MORE COMMON AFTER 1750

TYPICAL ELABORATIONS

no lights

lights in
door

lights in
transom

double line
of lights
rare

fanlight
occurs on a few
landmark examples
after 1750, usually
a Federal feature

LIGHTS

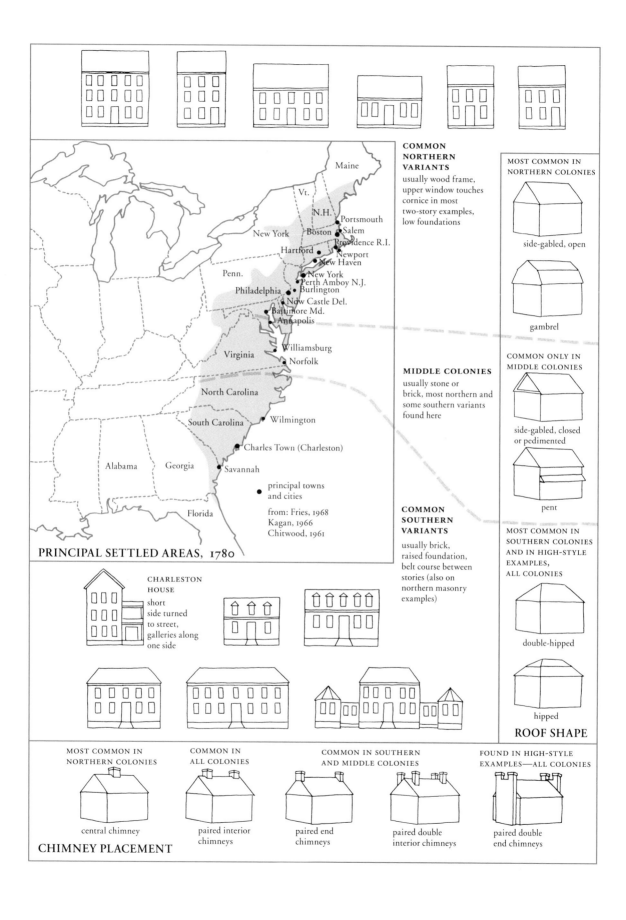

COMMON NORTHERN VARIANTS

usually wood frame, upper window touches cornice in most two-story examples, low foundations

MIDDLE COLONIES

usually stone or brick, most northern and some southern variants found here

COMMON SOUTHERN VARIANTS

usually brick, raised foundation, belt course between stories (also on northern masonry examples)

MOST COMMON IN NORTHERN COLONIES

side-gabled, open

gambrel

COMMON ONLY IN MIDDLE COLONIES

side-gabled, closed or pedimented

pent

MOST COMMON IN SOUTHERN COLONIES AND IN HIGH-STYLE EXAMPLES, ALL COLONIES

double-hipped

hipped

ROOF SHAPE

Maine

Vt.

N.H.

New York

Portsmouth
Boston
Salem
Providence R.I.
Hartford
Newport
New Haven

Penn.

New York
Perth Amboy N.J.
Philadelphia
Burlington
New Castle Del.
Baltimore Md.
Annapolis

Williamsburg

Virginia
Norfolk

North Carolina

South Carolina
Wilmington

Alabama
Georgia
Charles Town (Charleston)

Savannah

Florida

● principal towns and cities

from: Fries, 1968
Kagan, 1966
Chitwood, 1961

PRINCIPAL SETTLED AREAS, 1780

CHARLESTON HOUSE

short side turned to street, galleries along one side

MOST COMMON IN NORTHERN COLONIES

central chimney

COMMON IN ALL COLONIES

paired interior chimneys

COMMON IN SOUTHERN AND MIDDLE COLONIES

paired end chimneys

paired double interior chimneys

FOUND IN HIGH-STYLE EXAMPLES—ALL COLONIES

paired double end chimneys

CHIMNEY PLACEMENT

SIDE-GABLED ROOF

1. Deerfield, Massachusetts; 1749. Barnard House. Note the wide-board cladding and double door. The window screens are a later addition.

2. Providence, Rhode Island; ca. 1743. Hopkins House. Part of this house was built in 1707, with an expansion in ca. 1743; the door was added still later. Four-ranked examples such as this are sometimes called three-quarters houses.

3. Southport, Connecticut; late 18th century. Osborn House. A simple five-ranked, saltbox form with a central chimney.

4. Deerfield, Massachusetts; 1760. Williams House. Note the broken pediment over the door and the triangular pediments above the windows. The 6/6 window sashes are probably later additions.

5. Medford, Massachusetts; 1737. Royall House. Enlarged from a 17th-century brick house; an equally elaborate rear facade was added in 1747. Note the chimney stacks connected by a parapet and the unadorned side, the detailing being concentrated on the front facade.

6. Portsmouth, New Hampshire; 1718–1723. MacPheadris-Warner House. This fine high-style example is built of brick, unusual in early New England. It has a segmental pediment over the entry, a belt course, and dormers with alternating gabled and segmental pediments. Note the cupola, roof-line balustrade, twelve-panel door, and 9/6 windows.

7. Surry County, Virginia; 1652, rebuilt early 18th century. Warren House. This simple one-story example is a Georgian remodeling of a Postmedieval house. As is commonly the case in southern masonry examples, there is not an elaborated door surround but only a segmental arch in the brickwork above the paneled door.

8. Annapolis, Maryland; 1773. Brice House. A fine example of the five-part plan with "hyphens" connecting the main house and dependencies.

1

4

6

7

2

3

5

8

SIDE-GABLED ROOF (cont.)

9. Philadelphia, Pennsylvania; 1772. Deshler House. Note the arched dormer windows.

10. Philadelphia, Pennsylvania; 1768. Johnson House. Note the rubblestone side walls and the more regular ashlar facade. The pent roof above the first floor is a common middle-colonies feature.

11. Philadelphia, Pennsylvania; ca. 1715. The hood over the front door and the cornice carried beneath the side gable are features found primarily in the middle colonies.

9

10

11

GAMBREL ROOF

1. Salem, Massachusetts; mid-18th century. Nathaniel Hawthorne Birthplace. This example was built around a smaller 17th-century house, a common practice. The 2/2 windows are later additions.

2. Newport, Rhode Island; ca. 1748. Nichols House (restoration).

3. Deerfield, Massachusetts; ca. 1725. Dwight House. Moved from Springfield, Massachusetts, this house has a fine door pediment and pedimented windows.

4. Woodbury, Connecticut; 1760. Bacon House. Note the slight overhang of the second story, a holdover from Postmedieval building practices.

5. Alexandria, Virginia; ca. 1780. Robert Townshend Hooe House. An unusual high-style urban example with stone belt courses and delightful lintels with winged keystones.

1

3

2

4

5

HIPPED ROOF

1. Rutland, Massachusetts; ca. 1750. Putnam House.

2. Portsmouth, New Hampshire; 1760. Wentworth-Gardner House. Note the rusticated wall cladding (wood cut to look like stonework), wood quoins (also wood imitating stone), and the variety of pediment shapes used on door, windows, and dormers.

3. Charles City, Virginia, vicinity; 1734. Westover. An early high-style example with steeply pitched roof, double-paired interior end chimneys, belt course, and broken pediment door surround. This photo was taken before the modern addition of adjacent wings.

4. Richmond, Virginia, vicinity; ca. 1753. Wilton. This finely detailed example was moved in 1933.

5. Philadelphia, Pennsylvania; 1734. Stenton House. Note the segmental arches in the brickwork over the door and windows, used in lieu of more elaborate wood crowns.

6. Clarksville, Virginia, vicinity; ca. 1765. Prestwould. Built of coursed stone ashlar with a seven-ranked facade. Both the front and side porches are later additions.

7. Lancaster County, Virginia; ca. 1754. Belle Isle. A three-ranked central block with lower wings forming a three-part plan. Two detached dependencies are not visible in the photo.

1

3

6

2

4

5

7

CENTERED GABLE

1. Cambridge, Massachusetts; 1759. Longfellow House. The side porches were added in 1793, as likely were the 6/6 windows with slender muntins. Note that the centered gable crowns a shallow projection set nine inches forward from the front facade of the house. Two-story pilasters are added for decorative effect.

2. Charleston vicinity, South Carolina; 1738–1742. Drayton Hall. An unusually sophisticated early Georgian design that survives without alteration. The two-story recessed portico was inspired by the designs of Palladio; most American Georgian houses simply simulate such porticos with centered gables, as in the other photos on this page. See the Early Classical Revival style for similar but much later buildings inspired by Palladio.[8]

3. Philadelphia, Pennsylvania; 1763–1767. Cliveden. The front facade is of coursed ashlar; the stone urns on the roof are original.

4. Annapolis, Maryland; ca. 1774. Hammond House; William Buckland, architect. A high-style example in the Palladian five-part plan. The fanlight over the entrance was a feature found only occasionally in very late high-style Georgian houses; it became almost universal in the subsequent Federal style. Buckland owned James Gibbs's *Book of Architecture* and Robert Morris's *Select Architecture,* and both served as sources of house form and detail for this house.[9]

1

2

3

4

TOWN HOUSE

1. Alexandria, Virginia; ca. 1830s. Edward Sheehy, builder. Simple examples such as this continued to be built locally long after Federal style had become common.

2. Alexandria, Virginia; 1786–1810. Gentry Row. An exceptional grouping of late Georgian town houses.

3. Baltimore, Maryland; 1765. Robert Long House. Note the pent roof, a typical middle-colonies feature.

4. Philadelphia, Pennsylvania; 1765. Powell House. A high-style late Georgian town house. Note the stone belt courses, keystone lintels, and door surround with fanlight.

5. Philadelphia, Pennsylvania; mid-18th to early 19th centuries. Elfreth's Alley. These twenty-nine adjoining brick houses have been continuously occupied and have had relatively little exterior alteration. They make up one of our few urban streetscapes surviving from the 18th century.

1

3

2

4

5

these towns today preserve much of their Georgian heritage. In addition to the Georgian houses preserved in such coastal towns, many village and rural residences survive, particularly in New England. Landmark plantation houses are the principal southern survivors. With the end of the Revolution and independence (1781–83), the country began to develop new building styles (Federal and Early Classical Revival) based on changing European fashions. Although scattered Georgian houses were built for many decades after independence, even these usually showed some details of the newer styles.

Comments

Georgian is among the most long-lived styles of American building, having dominated the English colonies for most of the 18th century. The style grew from the Italian Renaissance, which emphasized classical details and reached remote England only in the mid-16th century. There, Renaissance classicism first flourished during the period 1650–1750 under such master architects as Inigo Jones, Christopher Wren, and James Gibbs. The style did not, however, begin to replace Postmedieval traditions in the American colonies until about 1700, when an expanding and increasingly prosperous population began to seek more fashionable buildings. The Georgian style was first brought to the New World by those interested in architecture, particularly carpenters and builders. They were well trained, and the forms they built relatively standardized, so the minimal amounts of added architectural detail were fairly simple to vary. Since only five architecture titles were available in this country before 1740, early Georgian style resulted in large part from the collective knowledge of its builders. After 1740, the number of architecture books increased rapidly and reached approximately one hundred titles by 1776. There was a similar rise in the documented instances of details and house forms copied from books. These influential volumes ranged from treatises stressing Italian models—the same books from which fashionable British architects such as Inigo Jones (1573–1652), Christopher Wren (1632–1723), Colin Campbell (1676–1729), and William Kent (1685–1748) had received much of their inspiration—to carpenter manuals showing how to construct fashionable doorways, cornices, windows, and mantels.[10]

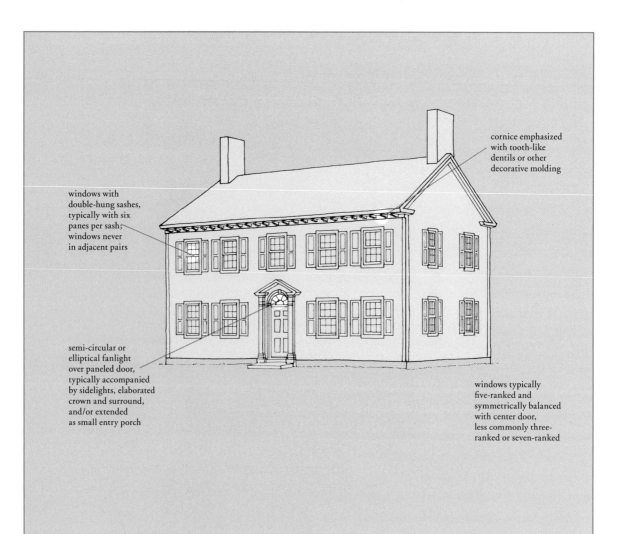

cornice emphasized with tooth-like dentils or other decorative molding

windows with double-hung sashes, typically with six panes per sash; windows never in adjacent pairs

semi-circular or elliptical fanlight over paneled door, typically accompanied by sidelights, elaborated crown and surround, and/or extended as small entry porch

windows typically five-ranked and symmetrically balanced with center door, less commonly three-ranked or seven-ranked

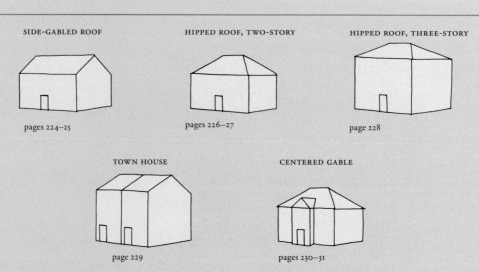

SIDE-GABLED ROOF

pages 224–25

HIPPED ROOF, TWO-STORY

pages 226–27

HIPPED ROOF, THREE-STORY

page 228

TOWN HOUSE

page 229

CENTERED GABLE

pages 230–31

PRINCIPAL SUBTYPES

Federal

1780–1820; locally to ca. 1840

Identifying Features

Semi-circular or elliptical fanlight[11] over front door (with or without sidelights); fanlight often incorporated into more elaborate door surround, which may include a decorative crown or small entry porch; cornice usually emphasized by decorative moldings, most commonly with tooth-like dentils; windows with double-hung sashes usually having six panes per sash and separated by thin wooden supports (muntins); windows aligned horizontally and vertically in symmetrical rows, usually five-ranked on front facade, less commonly three-ranked or seven-ranked; windows never in adjacent pairs, although three-part Palladian-style windows are common.

Principal Subtypes

The Federal house, like the preceding Georgian, is most commonly a simple box, two or more rooms deep, with doors and windows arranged in strict symmetry. More frequently than in Georgian houses, however, the box may be modified by projecting wings or attached dependencies; indeed, the style is perhaps best known for elaborate, but rather atypical, high-style examples having curved or polygonal projections to the side or rear. Five principal subtypes can be distinguished:

SIDE-GABLED ROOF—This is the most common Federal roof form, occurring in over 40 percent of surviving examples from all regions.

HIPPED ROOF, TWO-STORY—Hipped roofs of moderate to very low pitch (the latter may appear to be almost flat) are particularly common in New England, where they slightly outnumber side-gabled examples.

HIPPED ROOF, THREE-STORY—The three-story hipped-roof Federal house is usually large and of landmark quality; it survives primarily in New England, with an unusually important concentration in the town of Salem, Massachusetts.

CENTERED GABLE—Less than 10 percent of surviving Federal houses have gables (pediments) centered on the front facade. The facade beneath the gable may either remain in the same plane as the rest of the wall or be extended slightly forward for emphasis as a pavilion.

TOWN HOUSE—Many Federal town houses survive; these include both attached row houses and narrow detached urban houses. Important concentrations remain in Boston; Philadelphia; Georgetown, District of Columbia; and Alexandria, Virginia. A few projects were built that treated individual houses as part of a larger unit, thus rendering the entire facade as a total composition rather than a collection of individual elements. Regrettably, only a few parts and pieces of these ambitious schemes survive.

Variants and Details

As with the Georgian and Postmedieval English styles, northern house builders continued to show a preference for frame construction with clapboard siding, and southern for brick construction. Stucco and stone occur infrequently in all regions. Smooth wooden siding was sometimes used for the front facade with weatherboards, or even bricks, used for the less conspicuous walls. Chimney placement is less predictable than in Georgian houses, probably as a result of interiors with more complex room arrangements. Nevertheless, central or interior chimneys still tend to dominate in the North, while end chimneys are most common in the South.

The exteriors of most Federal houses have few elaborations other than the fanlight and accentuated front door (which often includes an entry porch). Among the elaborations that sometimes occur are roof-line balustrades, particularly favored in the North; the use of a Palladian-style window in the second story over the main entrance; the use of flat or keystone lintels above the windows with prominent sills below. Elliptical, half-circular, or Palladian windows are sometimes used in side or front gables; dormers typically have arched windows; in brick examples, windows may be slightly recessed into arches built into the facade. A number of decorative details from the Georgian period continue to be found occasionally: quoins, two-story pilasters (which disappeared about 1800), belt courses (now sometimes in stone), and dentils. Typical Georgian dentils are usually supplanted by less blocky, more refined versions called modillions.

Houses of the Federal style are often characterized as having a lightness and delicacy in comparison with their close Georgian relatives. This generalization needs to be interpreted with care, however, for while the scale is smaller in many Federal *details* (moldings, columns, etc.), the scale of many *structural parts* (windows, ceiling heights, etc.) is enlarged.

In attached Federal town houses (row houses) such typical features as roof-line balustrades, Palladian windows, and entry porches are rare. Although the doorway remains the most important identifying feature, fanlights are a less consistent guide than in detached houses. Not only do fanlights occur in both late Georgian and early Greek Revival row houses, but they are often omitted in the simpler and earlier Federal examples. Front stair rails of iron were usual; iron balconies and curved front bays were particularly common in Boston.

The interiors of many Federal houses contain graceful decorative ornament, either

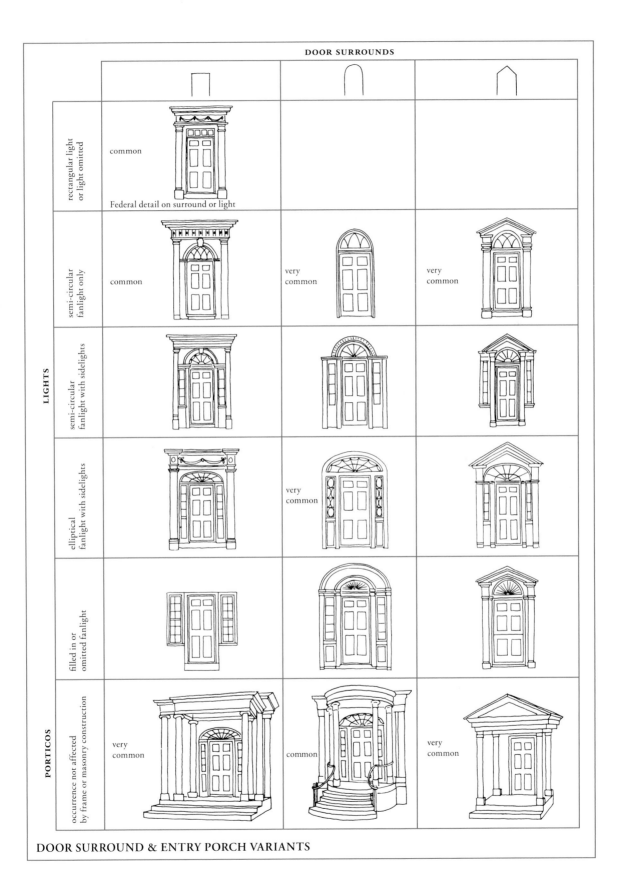

DOOR SURROUND & ENTRY PORCH VARIANTS

DOOR SURROUNDS

LIGHTS

rectangular light or light omitted

common

Federal detail on surround or light

semi-circular fanlight only

common

very common

very common

semi-circular fanlight with sidelights

elliptical fanlight with sidelights

very common

filled in or omitted fanlight

PORTICOS

occurrence not affected by frame or masonry construction

very common

common

very common

carved in wood or cast in plaster, applied to mantels, walls, ceilings, and elsewhere. Less commonly, the external facade shows similar decorative detailing on door surrounds or entry porches, over windows, along the cornice, or in paneled wall insets. Typical decorative motifs include swags, garlands, urns, and classic geometric patterns (most commonly elliptical, circular, or fan-like shapes formed by fluted radiating lines).

FEDERAL AND GEORGIAN WINDOWS—Both Federal and Georgian houses have double-hung sash windows placed singly but in symmetrical rows. These windows have fixed upper sashes and movable lower sashes, the latter held open by metal pins (the familiar system of counterbalancing with weights had not yet been invented). Such windows first began to be used in the English colonies in about 1700, and by 1720 had almost completely supplanted the earlier casement-style window (see page 161). Facilitating this transition was an increasing availability of larger panes of glass. Prior to the Revolution, the standard size of these panes was approximately 6 inches by 8 inches; afterward, the size increased to approximately 8 inches by 12 inches. Georgian houses thus generally have smaller windowpanes than do Federal houses. In Georgian houses these are most frequently arranged with 12 panes in each sash (12/12) in the northern colonies and 9 panes (9/9) in the southern colonies; 9/6, 6/9, 8/12, and other combinations are also found occasionally. Federal houses, with their larger panes, most commonly have 6/6 windows, although the earlier types also persist.

The wooden supporting moldings (or muntins) which hold the individual panes in place also differ in Georgian and Federal houses. In early Georgian houses these tend to be 1¼ inches wide and quite shallow; in later Georgian houses they remain shallow but are usually 1 inch wide; by Federal time they are more likely to be quite deep and narrower than 1 inch.

Both windowpanes and muntins are easily modified and thus many early houses now have 6/6, 1/1, 2/2, or other patterns of glazing. Occasionally the earlier windows will be left on rear or side walls where they reveal the original pattern. As a further complication, some houses were originally built with up-to-date windows on the front facades and with older, less fashionable (and probably less expensive) types on the rear.

Windows in Georgian and Federal wooden houses sometimes have elaborate decorative crowns placed above them. In Georgian houses these might be either a formal pediment, usually in one of the same patterns seen over front doors, or a decorative molding similar to those found on Georgian cornices. Federal windows more commonly have an elaborately decorated frieze above the window. These are sometimes topped by a cornice mold, but full-scale pediments are uncommon (pedimented or otherwise elaborated windows are most common on later, Colonial Revival houses).

Decorative window crowns are far less usual on masonry houses. Such Georgian houses often have changed brick patterns, or simple arches, above the windows. Federal masonry houses commonly have a flat lintel, keystone lintel, or keystone without a lintel set over the windows. These are usually of stone; stone sills are also sometimes used beneath the windows of Federal houses. Both Georgian and early Federal windows set in masonry are generally surrounded by a wooden frame (or architrave); these are usually omitted from Federal houses built after about 1800.

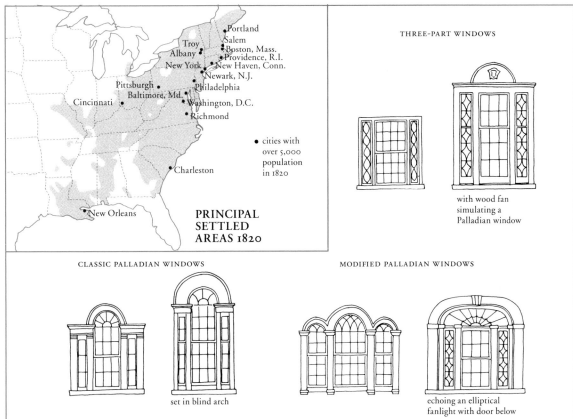

PRINCIPAL
SETTLED
AREAS 1820

• cities with
over 5,000
population
in 1820

THREE-PART WINDOWS

with wood fan
simulating a
Palladian window

CLASSIC PALLADIAN WINDOWS

set in blind arch

MODIFIED PALLADIAN WINDOWS

echoing an elliptical
fanlight with door below

PALLADIAN WINDOW VARIANTS commonly located above the front door,
occasionally in the gable end of a side-gabled roof

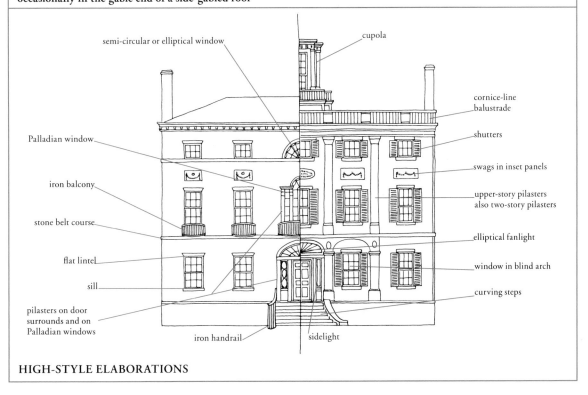

semi-circular or elliptical window

cupola

Palladian window

iron balcony

stone belt course

flat lintel

sill

pilasters on door
surrounds and on
Palladian windows

iron handrail

sidelight

cornice-line
balustrade

shutters

swags in inset panels

upper-story pilasters
also two-story pilasters

elliptical fanlight

window in blind arch

curving steps

HIGH-STYLE ELABORATIONS

Occurrence

Federal was the dominant style of the new United States from about 1780 to 1820, a period in which the population grew from 3 million to about 10 million and expanded to cover the area shown on the map. The style reached its zenith in the prosperous port cities of the eastern seaboard, particularly Boston, Salem, Newburyport, and Marblehead in Massachusetts; Newport, Providence, Warren, and Bristol in Rhode Island; Portland and Wiscasset in Maine; New Castle, Delaware; Portsmouth, New Hampshire; Philadelphia, Pennsylvania; New York, New York; Charleston, South Carolina; and Savannah, Georgia. Alexandria, Virginia, and Georgetown, District of Columbia, both near the newly developing national capital, also prospered during this period. High-style Federal houses are mostly concentrated in these areas, although scattered examples occur elsewhere. Thousands of vernacular examples survive throughout the settled areas; they are least common at the westward edges of expansion, where vernacular Georgian houses persisted throughout the period (occasional Georgian hangovers, some of landmark quality, occur in all regions). By the 1820s a more strictly classical style, the Greek Revival, was supplanting the Federal style. Still earlier, by about 1800, the related Early Classical Revival style was replacing Federal houses in the South.

Comments

The Federal style was a development and refinement of the preceding Georgian style. Established first by wealthy merchants along the New England seaboard, it drew on contemporary European trends, particularly the work of the Adam brothers who, at that time, had the largest architectural practice in Britain. The eldest, Robert, had traveled to Italy and the Mediterranean to study classical buildings for himself. These studies, as well as those of others who reported on first-hand viewing, introduced a new interest in

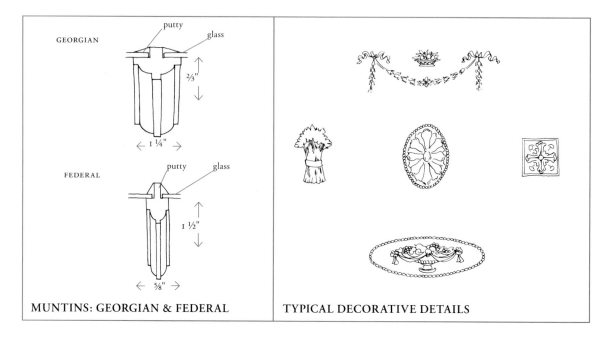

MUNTINS: GEORGIAN & FEDERAL

TYPICAL DECORATIVE DETAILS

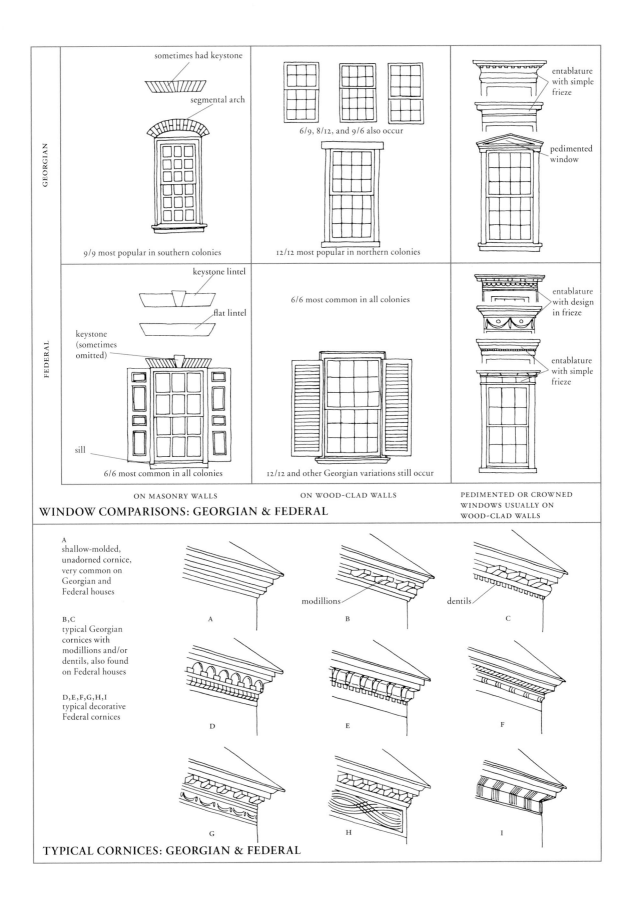

GEORGIAN

sometimes had keystone

segmental arch

9/9 most popular in southern colonies

6/9, 8/12, and 9/6 also occur

12/12 most popular in northern colonies

entablature with simple frieze

pedimented window

FEDERAL

keystone lintel

flat lintel

keystone (sometimes omitted)

sill

6/6 most common in all colonies

6/6 most common in all colonies

12/12 and other Georgian variations still occur

entablature with design in frieze

entablature with simple frieze

ON MASONRY WALLS

ON WOOD-CLAD WALLS

PEDIMENTED OR CROWNED WINDOWS USUALLY ON WOOD-CLAD WALLS

WINDOW COMPARISONS: GEORGIAN & FEDERAL

A
shallow-molded, unadorned cornice, very common on Georgian and Federal houses

B,C
typical Georgian cornices with modillions and/or dentils, also found on Federal houses

D,E,F,G,H,I
typical decorative Federal cornices

modillions

dentils

A

B

C

D

E

F

G

H

I

TYPICAL CORNICES: GEORGIAN & FEDERAL

SIDE-GABLED ROOF

1. Providence, Rhode Island; ca. 1830. Seamans House.

2. Savannah, Georgia; 1808. William House. Note the exterior chimney, a common feature in the South.

3. Powhatan County, Virginia; early 19th century. Keswick. The simple three-ranked facade masks an elaborate H-shaped plan behind.

4. Somerset, Massachusetts; ca. 1800. Pettis House. This five-ranked wooden example has been elaborated with corner quoins. The slight overhang of the gable end is a holdover from Postmedieval building practice.

5. Longmeadow, Massachusetts; 1796. Colton House; attributed to Asher Benjamin, architect. Note the elaborate cornice-line railing and Palladian window.

6. Alexandria, Virginia; ca. 1798. Lloyd House. An elaborate brick example with paired end chimneys, keystone lintels, and arched dormer windows.

7. New Castle, Delaware; 1801. Read House. A high-style example with roof balustrade, cornice-line modillions and dentils, keystone lintels, and elaborate Palladian window and door surround.

1

4

6

2

3

5

7

3

1

4

6

7

HIPPED ROOF, TWO-STORY

1. Auburn, Massachusetts; late 18th century. Chapin House. A simple wood-frame example. The 2/2 windows are later additions.

2. Columbia Falls, Maine; ca. 1818. Ruggles House; Aaron Sherman, architect. Note the flush, horizontal boards on the front facade and the swagged window heads.

3. Mappsville, Virginia, vicinity; ca. 1800. Wharton Place. The interior chimneys are separated by a flat roof deck with balustrade.

4. Providence, Rhode Island; ca. 1815. Burroughs House. Note the quoins. There are two balustrades on the roof.

5. Providence, Rhode Island; ca. 1801. Halsey House. The curved bays were added ca. 1825.

6. Damariscotta Mills, Maine; 1803. Kavanaugh House; Nicholas Codd, architect. This example has flush wood sheathing, a semi-circular entry porch, and a large octagonal cupola.

7. Greenfield, Massachusetts; 1796. Coleman House; Asher Benjamin, architect. Note the elaborate pilasters, Palladian window, and inset panels with swags.

8. Washington, District of Columbia; 1815. Tudor Place; William Thornton, architect. The garden front (shown) has a domed portico and full-length three-part windows in blind arches. The portico forms a circular space extending half inside and half outside the plane of the front facade. Thornton, like most architects at that time, gained design inspiration from books. This circular space was no exception; it appeared six times in George Richardson's *The New Vitruvius,* volumes I and II, both in Thornton's library.[12]

2

5

8

HIPPED ROOF, THREE-STORY

1. Portsmouth, New Hampshire; early 19th century. Barnes House. A wood-frame example with a minimum of exterior elaboration.

2. Washington, District of Columbia; 1819. Decatur House; Benjamin Latrobe, architect. A three-ranked brick example with flat lintels over the windows. The window height varies in the three stories.

3. Boston, Massachusetts; 1797. Otis House; attributed to Charles Bulfinch, architect. A high-style brick example with belt courses and keystone lintels. The Palladian and semi-circular windows align above the elaborate doorway.

4. Salem, Massachusetts; 1821. Phillips House. Note the quoins, Palladian window, and elaborated window crowns.

5. Providence, Rhode Island; 1806. Ives House; Caleb Ormsbee, architect. This example has roof-line and entry porch balustrades; there are matching fanlights on the first and second stories.

TOWN HOUSE

1. Easton, Maryland; 1820–1821. Attached urban houses.

2. Savannah, Georgia; ca. 1820. Clark Houses. The paired doors on the left entrance are a later addition (note the glass panels).

3. Frederick, Maryland; 1799. Taney House. Note the side walls without windows to increase privacy in an urban setting. The 6/6 windows with lintels above and the curved patterning in the rectangular light over the door mark this example as a Federal house.

4. Libertytown, Maryland; ca. 1800. Jones House. Note the parapeted gables with double interior end chimneys.

5. Charleston, South Carolina; ca. 1809. Russell House. An unusual high-style example of compact town house form. Note the polygonal projection visible to the left of the house, the roof-line balustrade of alternating panels and balusters, and the full-width iron balcony and blind arches at second-floor level.

CENTERED GABLE

1. Baltimore, Maryland; ca. 1782. D'Annemours House. A three-ranked masonry example of a simple I-house plan (one room deep) with a rear wing.

2. Canterbury, Connecticut; ca. 1805. Payne House. This wood-frame example has notable pilasters set on pedestals at the corners and beside the slightly projecting center gable.

3. Frankfort, Kentucky; 1800. Liberty Hall. The centered gable covers three ranks of windows; gables of this width are frequent in high-style Federal houses but unusual in the preceding Georgian style.

4. Savannah, Georgia; 1819. Richardson House; William Jay, architect. Note the undulating entry porch roof and curved entry steps. The front door is also recessed into a curved niche.

5. Charleston, South Carolina; ca. 1822. Bennett House. Built in the typical Charleston-house form with the narrow end turned to the street. The principal facade, with a full-length porch, faces a side garden. Entry from the street is through a doorway leading to the porch.

6. Cazenovia, New York; 1807. Lorenzo House. The facade is elaborated by pilasters supporting decorative arches.

7. Clarkson, New York; ca. 1825. Palmer House. Full front-gabled Federal houses like this are uncommon; they are transitional to the Greek Revival style, which popularized the front-gabled form. Most Federal examples occur in western New York and in Ohio.

8. Mount Vernon, Virginia, vicinity; 1805. Woodlawn; William Thornton, architect. In this five-part compound plan, a large central house block is connected to two side dependencies by hyphens. This house has no projection or elaboration below the centered gable.

1

6

7

2

4

5

8

the early Greek and Roman monuments themselves, rather than as interpreted through the buildings of the Italian Renaissance.[13] Adam popularized a number of design elements (swags, garlands, urns, and various stylized geometric designs) that he had seen in his travels. He also incorporated into his interiors a diversity of spatial planning found in some classical ruins. Because of the breadth of his influence the Federal style is considered the Adam style by some American architectural historians. Among the many architectural books that helped spread the Federal style was the Adam brothers' *Works in Architecture of Robert and James Adam* (1779) and Asher Benjamin's *American Builder's Companion* (Boston, 1806), which was so popular it was reprinted five times.[14]

It was during this era that the first true architects appeared on the American scene. Among the most notable of these, with their principal areas of work, were: Charles Bulfinch (Boston); William Jay (Savannah, Georgia); Benjamin H. Latrobe (his early work in Philadelphia and Virginia); Gabriel Manigault (Charleston, South Carolina); John McComb (New York); Samuel McIntire (Salem, Massachusetts); and Alexander Parris (Maine).

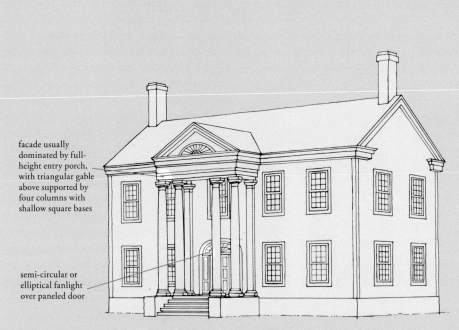

facade usually dominated by full-height entry porch, with triangular gable above supported by four columns with shallow square bases

semi-circular or elliptical fanlight over paneled door

windows typically five-ranked and symmetrically balanced with center door, less commonly three-ranked or seven-ranked

TWO-STORY

ONE-STORY

GABLE FRONT AND WINGS

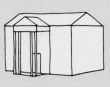

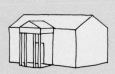

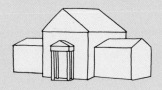

pages 238–39

page 240

page 241

PRINCIPAL SUBTYPES

Early Classical Revival

1770–1830; locally to ca. 1850

Identifying Features

Entry porch (portico) dominating the front facade and normally equaling it in height; porch roof usually supported by four simple columns (Roman Doric or Tuscan types) each with a shallow square base (plinth); the columns support a prominent centered gable; a semi-circular or elliptical fanlight normally occurs above the paneled front door; windows aligned horizontally and vertically in symmetrical rows, usually five-ranked on front facade, less commonly three-ranked or seven-ranked.

Principal Subtypes

Early Classical Revival houses are of three principal types:

TWO-STORY—Similar to one-story type, but with more imposing, two-story facades and entry porches.

ONE-STORY—These are simple, rectilinear houses with side-gabled or low-pitched hipped roofs having the characteristic full-height entry porch. They are commonly built several feet off the ground on tall foundations, which exaggerates the height of the front facade.

GABLE FRONT AND WINGS—Most Early Classical Revival houses are of the first two types with side-gabled or hipped roofs. In this less common variant, a two-story, front-gabled central block dominates the facade; this two-story unit is flanked by one-story wings on either side, making a three-part composition. This plan was introduced by Palladio in his 16th-century Italian pattern book and is called the Palladian three-part plan. In this subtype the dominant central block may have either a full-height, two-story entry porch or a smaller one-story entry porch.

Variants and Details

Early Classical Revival houses closely resemble those of the succeeding Greek Revival period; the doorway, cornice line, and type of column are the three principal distinguishing features. In Early Classical Revival houses, the columns were generally of the Roman type (see pages 237 and 253), although later transitional examples may have columns with Greek details. The Early Classical Revival house also usually lacks the wide band of trim at the cornice line seen on most Greek Revival houses; frequently a narrow line of dentils or modillions adorns the cornice. Like their Federal-style contemporaries, most Early Classical Revival examples have a prominent fanlight over the front door, a feature that became very rare during the subsequent Greek Revival. In addition, Early Classical Revival houses are likely to have Federal interior detailing.

The characteristic Early Classical entry porch shows considerable variation in detail. The porches may differ in: (1) the number of columns: four is most common, two is frequent, and five, six, eight, and ten occur less often; (2) the spacing of columns: even spacing is most common, but a frequent variation has a wider space between the two central columns framing the front entrance; (3) the treatment of columns and second-story porches on two-story examples: four variations occur in about equal overall abundance. The porches are most commonly placed only on the front facade as entry porches but may also appear both on the front and the back, or on any combination of front, back, and side. Occasionally the entry porch is recessed inward (called a portico *in antis*). In all variants the centered gable (pediment) may be embellished with a semicircular window (lunette); occasionally a round or oval window replaces the lunette or is found elsewhere on the facade. The entablature, or horizontal band above the columns and below the centered gable, is most often plain. If elaborated, it is with triglyphs, three closely spaced vertical lines repeated at intervals.

Wall materials may be either wood, brick, stucco, or stone, in order of decreasing frequency. Wall projections, which are only occasionally present, are never curved as in some contemporaneous Federal houses. Roof balustrades are rare, as are original dormers; when present, these are usually later additions. In most other details, Early Classical Revival houses resemble those of the contemporaneous Federal style (see Federal doors and windows, pages 219–23). Many Georgian and early Federal houses, as well as simple folk houses, were updated during the early 19th century by the addition of a full-height Early Classical Revival entry porch. These modified examples may be difficult to distinguish from homes originally built in this configuration.

Occurrence

This is a relatively uncommon style found in isolated examples throughout the areas settled by 1820 (see map, page 221). It is rare north of Pennsylvania; most examples occur in the southern states, particularly Virginia, where it had its most vocal champion in Thomas Jefferson. A handful of houses in the style were built in Virginia just before the Revolution, but most examples were constructed between 1790 and 1830. By 1830 the subsequent and more universally popular phase of classical revivalism, the Greek Revival, had replaced Early Classical models even in Virginia.

no upper porch

upper porch supported
by house only

upper porch supported
by house and columns

two-tiered columns
support upper porch

COMMON PORTICO VARIATIONS

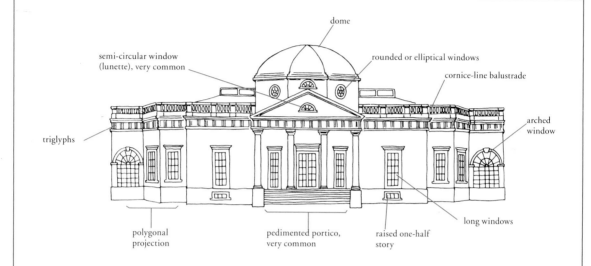

dome

semi-circular window
(lunette), very common

rounded or elliptical windows

cornice-line balustrade

triglyphs

arched
window

polygonal
projection

pedimented portico,
very common

raised one-half
story

long windows

HIGH-STYLE ELABORATIONS

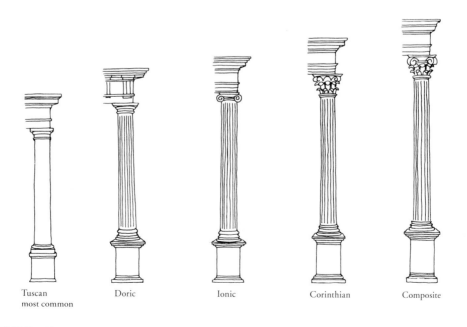

Tuscan
most common

Doric

Ionic

Corinthian

Composite

ROMAN COLUMNS (see also page 253)

Comments

Following the Revolution there was an immediate need for public buildings to house the newly organized government at both the state and national levels. It was natural to have taken Rome as a model, with its Republican ideas and monumental architecture, a choice that symbolized the mood and politics of the new country. Roman Revival architecture thus became fashionable. This was further emphasized by a concurrent neoclassical movement in France, the new country's principal ally in its fight for independence. The United States was not a mere follower in this movement, but led the way by erecting the first large public building in the new style, the Bank of Pennsylvania, completed in 1800 at Philadelphia. Among the prominent architects working in the style were William Jay (Savannah, Georgia); Benjamin H. Latrobe (Philadelphia, Baltimore, and Washington); Robert Mills (Charleston, South Carolina, and elsewhere); and William Thornton (Washington). Most influential of all, however, was Thomas Jefferson, who not only designed Roman Revival buildings himself, but used the influence of his

TWO-STORY

1. Beaufort, South Carolina; 1786. Tabby Manse. Built of tabby, a concrete-like mixture of oyster shell and lime mortar, covered with stucco. Note the delicate two-tiered entry porch with more slender columns above.

2. Berryville, Virginia; 1790. Annefield. Built of stone, this house has a two-tiered entry porch with a fanlight in the pediment. Note the upper balustrade formed in a Chinese Chippendale pattern.

3. Milledgeville, Georgia, vicinity; 1830. Boykin Hall; Daniel Pratt, architect. The relatively simple exterior contrasts with elaborate Federal detailing in the interior. The spindlework balustrade is probably a later addition.

4. Conetoe, North Carolina, vicinity; ca. 1820. Wilkinson House. A simple three-ranked wood-frame example with the exterior chimneys typical of the South. Note the lunette in the pediment; the porch balustrades are probably later additions.

5. Natchez, Mississippi, vicinity; 1812. Auburn; Levi Weeks, architect. Weeks built this impressive home for Lyman Harding and described it as "the first house in the territory on which was ever attempted any of the orders of [classical] architecture." The twin side wings were added after 1827.

6. Charleston, South Carolina; ca. 1816. Nicholson House; attributed to William Jay, architect. A unique example on a high, rusticated foundation. Note the unusual Gothic (pointed-arch) windows in the pediment, which contrast with the round-arch windows of the second story.

7. Warsaw, Virginia; ca. 1730 (entry porch ca. 1830). Sabine Hall. A well-documented case of a full-height entry porch with colossal columns added to an earlier (1730) house in an extensive exterior remodeling, which included lowering the roof.

1

4

6

7

ONE-STORY

1. Strasburg, Virginia; 1794. Belle Grove. Built of coursed ashlar limestone on a high basement.

2. Baltimore, Maryland; 1803. Homewood. Note the five-part compound plan with a large central block connected to distant wings by lower "hyphens." Decorative detailing in the gable is atypical.

3. Staunton, Virginia, vicinity; ca. 1818. Folly. Note the matching entry porch on the side facade.

4. Charlottesville, Virginia, 1770–1809. Monticello; Thomas Jefferson, architect. This view is of the garden facade and is dominated by an octagonal dome. There are two different styles of railing on the roof: a Chinese Chippendale railing is around the higher roof deck, and a cornice-line balustrade surrounds the main roof.

5. Bremo Bluff, Virginia, vicinity; ca. 1819. Bremo. A unique house with entry porches on each facade and dependencies connected by raised terraces.

GABLE FRONT AND WINGS

1. Halifax County, North Carolina; early 19th century. A small example, with careful detailing, built in the typical three-part plan.

2. Williamsburg, Virginia; ca. 1775. Semple House; attributed to Thomas Jefferson, architect. One of the earliest examples of the three-part plan, this house survives essentially as originally built.

3. Fayette, Missouri; 1833. Morrison House. Note the Palladian window and keystone lintels.

4. Lexington, Virginia; 1818. Stono. Note the front-gabled roof extended into a temple-form porch.

5. Louisville, Kentucky; ca. 1805–1808. Spring Station; Norborne Beale, builder and original owner. The porch on the right and porte cochere on the left are later additions. The columns on the porch have also been changed; the originals would have been thinner and more delicate.

political office, and his considerable powers of personal persuasion, to push the United States toward his classical ideal. Jefferson thus shaped early Washington, D.C., the Virginia capitol at Richmond, and, almost single-handedly, the University of Virginia at Charlottesville. Because of his influence, the style is sometimes referred to as Jeffersonian Classicism.

Apart from Jefferson's influence on public architecture, his home, Monticello, his summer home, Poplar Forest, and other houses he designed for friends set the stage for Early Classical domestic architecture. These high-style examples probably sprang from Jefferson's familiarity with the writings of the Italian Renaissance architect Palladio (1508–1580). Inspired by such high-style landmarks, typical Palladian entry porches were soon being built throughout the South, some at the time of original construction, but many also as additions to earlier houses.

A national sympathy for the Greek War of Independence (1821–1830) and an increasing archeological understanding of the Greek roots of Roman architecture and culture made the years 1820–1830 a transition to the succeeding Greek Revival style. Although relatively uncommon and primarily southern, the Early Classical Revival movement provided the background for this more pervasive classicism which dominated the new country for the next thirty years.

During the preceding Colonial era, a single architectural style tended to dominate in each colony for long periods of time; Georgian houses, for example, were the fashion in the English colonies through most of the 18th century. Likewise, the first popular Romantic style, Greek Revival, dominated the newly independent United States through much of the first half of the 19th century. Architectural models evocative of Greek democracy were thought to be especially appropriate in the new republic, as it rejected traditional ties to England in the decades following the War of 1812.

By the 1840s, a new trend toward competition among *several* acceptable architectural fashions was taking shape. The harbinger of this movement was the publication in 1842 of the first popular pattern book of house styles with full-facade drawings—Andrew Jackson Downing's *Cottage Residences.* Downing illustrated several new fashions he considered suitable alternatives to the prevailing Greek classicism. Medieval precedents were recommended in models that were to lead to the Gothic Revival style. Likewise, Italian Renaissance traditions were freely adapted in Downing's Italianate cottages. Now, for the first time, builders and home buyers had a choice. Soon, neighborhoods of alternately Greek, Gothic, and Italianate houses became commonplace. Still more exotic fashions, based on Egyptian and Oriental precedents and on Swiss Chalets or octagonal shapes, also came to be advocated by Downing and others, but these never achieved wide acceptance. The simultaneous popularity of several architectural styles with differing antecedents was to persist as a dominant theme throughout the later history of American housing.

Architecture books were the primary means by which a carpenter increased his knowledge sufficiently to become a designer or architect. The architects who produced homes in the Romantic styles were almost all self-trained. Among them were Alexander Parris, Ithiel Town, Minard Lafever, Henry Austin, Samuel Sloan, Richard Upjohn, Thomas U. Walter, A. J. Davis, and Alexander Downing—several

Romantic Houses

of whom wrote the pattern books that broadly influenced Greek Revival, Gothic Revival, and Italianate homes. Indeed, Benjamin Henry Latrobe was the only formally trained architect in the United States in 1840.[1]

All the Romantic styles originated and grew to popularity in the decades before 1860. The Greek Revival was dominant from about 1830 to 1850 (to 1860 in the South) and the Italianate from about 1850 until 1875. Gothic Revival houses were more complex to construct and were always less common than their Greek and Italian contemporaries. The Civil War marked the end of Greek Classicism, but both Gothic and Italianate houses remained popular into the 1880s, sometimes in more elaborate versions than had appeared before the war. These later examples have been separated as High Victorian Gothic or High Victorian Italianate styles, but this distinction is difficult to recognize in field identification, particularly in houses. Highly detailed early examples are not uncommon, nor are late survivors of the earlier, less elaborate interpretations.

1820–1880

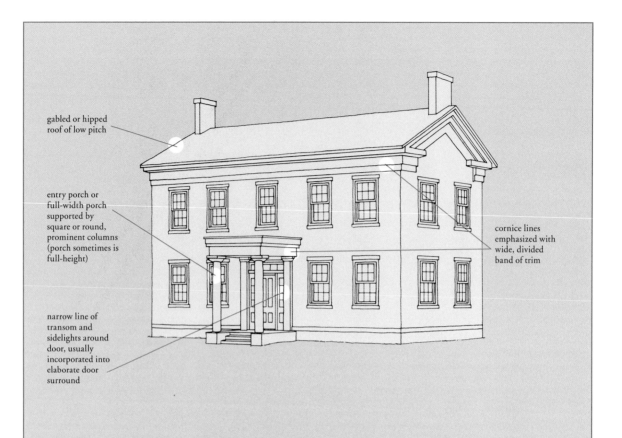

gabled or hipped roof of low pitch

entry porch or full-width porch supported by square or round, prominent columns (porch sometimes is full-height)

cornice lines emphasized with wide, divided band of trim

narrow line of transom and sidelights around door, usually incorporated into elaborate door surround

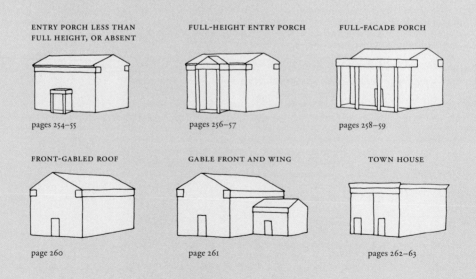

ENTRY PORCH LESS THAN FULL HEIGHT, OR ABSENT

pages 254–55

FULL-HEIGHT ENTRY PORCH

pages 256–57

FULL-FACADE PORCH

pages 258–59

FRONT-GABLED ROOF

page 260

GABLE FRONT AND WING

page 261

TOWN HOUSE

pages 262–63

PRINCIPAL SUBTYPES

Greek Revival

1825–1860

Identifying Features

Gabled or hipped roof of low pitch; cornice line of main roof and porch roofs emphasized with wide band of trim (this represents the classical entablature and is usually divided into two parts: the frieze above and architrave below); most have porches (either entry or full-width) supported by prominent square or rounded columns, typically of Doric style; front door surrounded by narrow sidelights and a rectangular line of transom lights above, door and lights usually incorporated into more elaborate door surround.

Principal Subtypes

Six principal subtypes can be distinguished on the basis of porch and roof configurations:

ENTRY PORCH LESS THAN FULL HEIGHT, OR ABSENT—About 20 percent of Greek Revival houses have small entry porches which do not extend the full height of the facade. In some examples the entry porch is recessed *into* the facade. About 5 percent lack porches altogether.

FULL-HEIGHT ENTRY PORCH—This subtype has a dominant central porch extending the full *height,* but less than the full *width,* of the facade; it thus resembles the Early Classical Revival style from which the Greek Revival sprang. The Greek Revival version can usually be distinguished from its predecessor by the typical band of cornice trim and the rectangular lights, rather than a curving fanlight, over the entrance. As in the earlier style, many Greek Revival examples have a traditional classical pediment above the entry porch. In contrast to the earlier style, however, many Greek examples have flat-roofed entry porches. As in the entry porch less than full height, this type of entry porch also occurs recessed *into* the facade. About one-fourth of Greek Revival houses are of this subtype; like Early Classical Revival houses, these are most common in the southern states.

FULL-FACADE PORCH—In this configuration, the colonnaded porch occupies the full width and height of the facade. No pediment occurs above the porch, which is covered either by the main roof or, less commonly, by a flat or shed-style extension from it. In a few examples, the full-facade porch also extends around one or both sides of the house. This subtype makes up about one-fourth of Greek Revival houses. Like the preceding type, it is most common in the southern states.

FRONT-GABLED ROOF—All of the preceding subtypes have side-gabled or hipped roofs. In this subtype the gable end is turned 90 degrees to make the principal facade. In some high-style examples a full-width, colonnaded porch is present beneath the front gable, giving the house the appearance of a miniature Greek temple with its traditional classical pediment, a variation sometimes called temple-form. Smaller entry porches are common on vernacular examples. This subtype is more common in the northeastern and midwestern states.

GABLE FRONT AND WING—In this subtype a front-gabled roof, as in the type just described, has a side wing (less commonly two wings) added; these are typically lower than the dominant front-gabled portion. This subtype rarely occurs outside of the northeastern states and is particularly common in western New York and Ohio.

TOWN HOUSE—A sixth subtype consists of narrow urban houses with Greek Revival detailing. These occur both with and without porches. They are most common in those port cities of the Atlantic and Gulf coasts that were expanding in the decades from 1830 to 1860. These include Boston; New York; Philadelphia; Washington; Richmond, Virginia; Savannah, Georgia; Mobile, Alabama; New Orleans, Louisiana; and Galveston, Texas.

Variants and Details

The principal areas of elaboration in Greek Revival houses are cornice lines, doorways, porch-support columns, and windows:

CORNICE LINES—The wide band of trim beneath the cornice of both the main roof and the porch roofs is an almost universal feature of Greek Revival houses. Commonly the band is made up of undecorated boards, but complex incised decorations also occur. In gabled houses the trim band may be variously treated along the gabled walls. Post-1850 examples, particularly in the South, often have Italianate brackets added at the cornice line.

DOORWAYS—As in the preceding Georgian, Federal, and Early Classical Revival styles, elaborated door surrounds are a dominant feature of Greek Revival houses. The door itself is either single or paired and is most frequently divided into one, two, or four panels. The door is usually surrounded on sides and top by a narrow band of rectangular panes of glass held in a delicate, decorative frame. Door and glazed surround, in turn, are usually encased in a larger decorative enframement of wood or masonry. Not uncommonly door and glass are recessed behind the front wall, thus creating complex

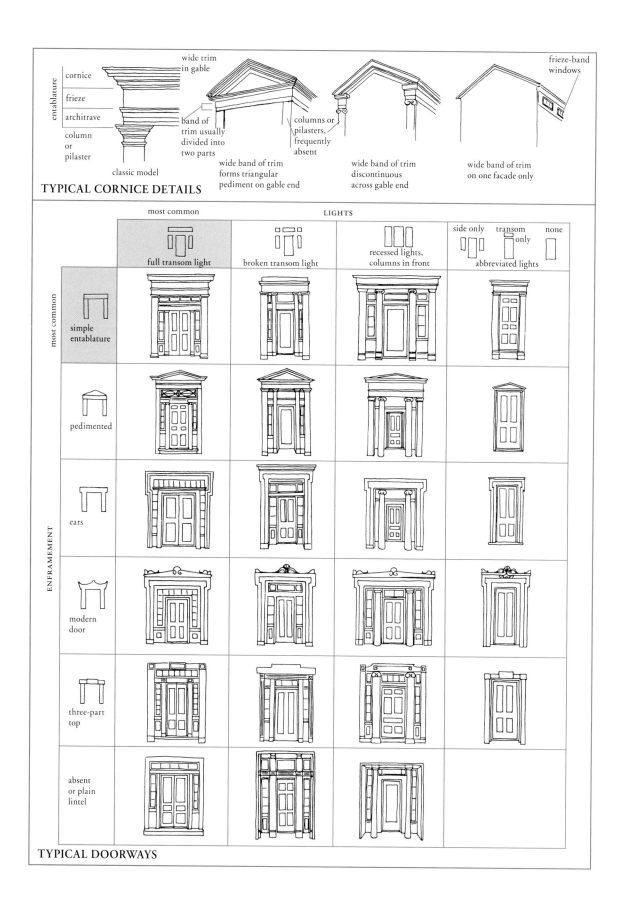

TYPICAL CORNICE DETAILS

entablature
- cornice
- frieze
- architrave

column or pilaster

classic model

wide trim in gable

band of trim usually divided into two parts

wide band of trim forms triangular pediment on gable end

columns or pilasters, frequently absent

wide band of trim discontinuous across gable end

frieze-band windows

wide band of trim on one facade only

LIGHTS

most common

full transom light

broken transom light

recessed lights, columns in front

side only

transom only

abbreviated lights

ENFRAMEMENT

most common

simple entablature

pedimented

ears

modern door

three-part top

absent or plain lintel

TYPICAL DOORWAYS

three-dimensional effects; free-standing columns are sometimes added to the inset portion.

COLUMNS—Classical columns for the support of porch roofs are a prominent feature of most Greek Revival houses. In some examples they dominate the entire facade; others retain only smaller entry porch columns. Although many Greek Revival houses have "correct" Greek columns, many also have Roman details; still more have vernacular adaptations with *no* clear classical precedent. The following guide to Classical Column Identification must therefore be used in combination with other typical features when identifying Greek Revival houses:

Classical columns are distinguished principally by their capitals (tops) and bases. Both Greek and Roman columns share three principal types of capitals which define the three familiar orders of classical architecture: Doric (plain capitals), Ionic (capitals with scroll-like spirals called volutes), and Corinthian (capitals shaped like inverted bells decorated with leaves). All three types are found in Greek Revival houses, as well as in most other classically influenced American styles. Greek and Roman examples of these three orders are distinguished by subtle differences in either the capitals or the bases.

All columns of classical antiquity were round, as are many Greek Revival columns. Vernacular Greek Revival houses, on the other hand, commonly have *square* (and occasionally octagonal) columns, which were simple and inexpensive to construct from boards and moldings. Such columns generally lack classical capitals. About 40 percent of columns found on Greek Revival houses are square; the remaining 60 percent include about 40 percent Doric, 15 percent Ionic, and 5 percent Corinthian. Note that the Greek Doric column has no base, while the Roman version does. This distinction frequently will distinguish Greek Revival Doric columns from the Roman Doric columns of the Early Classical Revival. Note, however, that many Greek Revival houses retained Roman columns, particularly in the southern states, so that column type alone is seldom sufficient to identify the style. Round columns were most commonly constructed of wood staves; occasionally bricks formed in the shape of a slice of pie and covered with stucco were used.

Pilasters are also frequent Greek Revival features. They are most commonly used on the corners of frame houses but are occasionally found across the entire facade in lieu of free-standing columns.

WINDOWS—As in the preceding Federal style, Greek Revival window sashes most commonly had six-pane glazing. The rounded, three-part Palladian windows of Federal houses disappeared, to be replaced only occasionally by rectangular, tripartite examples. Small frieze-band windows, set into the wide trim beneath the cornice, are frequent. These are often covered with an iron or wooden grate fashioned into a decorative Greek pattern. Window surrounds were generally far less elaborate than doorways.

Occurrence

Greek Revival was the dominant style of American domestic architecture during the interval from about 1830 to 1850 (to 1860 in the Gulf Coast states), during which its popularity led it to be called the National Style. It occurs in all areas settled by 1860, as noted on the map, and especially flourished in those regions that were being rapidly

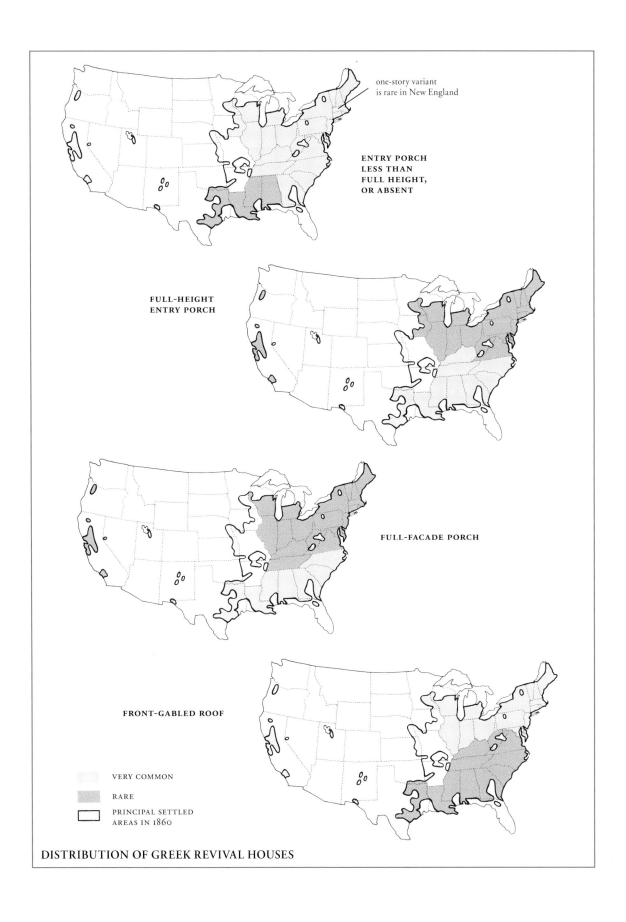

one-story variant
is rare in New England

**ENTRY PORCH
LESS THAN
FULL HEIGHT,
OR ABSENT**

**FULL-HEIGHT
ENTRY PORCH**

FULL-FACADE PORCH

FRONT-GABLED ROOF

VERY COMMON

RARE

PRINCIPAL SETTLED
AREAS IN 1860

DISTRIBUTION OF GREEK REVIVAL HOUSES

settled in the decades of the 1830s, '40s, and '50s. The style moved with the settlers from the older states as they crossed into Kentucky, Tennessee, and the Old Northwest Territory (today's Midwest). It enhanced towns built along the route of the Erie Canal. It followed the southern planters as they moved westward from the Old South into Alabama, Mississippi, and Louisiana. It even arrived on the west coast, sometimes disassembled into packages and shipped by way of Cape Horn! Each of the principal subtypes of the style shows geographic differences in frequency of occurrence, as noted above and in the maps.

Not surprisingly, the largest surviving concentrations of Greek Revival houses are found today in those states with the largest population growth during the period from 1820 to 1860. These are, in descending order of growth: New York, Pennsylvania, Ohio, Illinois, Virginia, Massachusetts, Indiana, Missouri, Tennessee, Alabama, Wisconsin, Georgia, Mississippi, Michigan, Texas, Kentucky, and Louisiana. New York gained about 2½ million persons during the interval, while Louisiana gained about ½ million.

Comments

The final years of the 18th century brought an increasing interest in classical buildings to both the United States and western Europe. This was first based on Roman models (see the Early Classical Revival chapter), but archeological investigation in the early 19th century emphasized Greece as the Mother of Rome, which, in turn, shifted interest to Grecian models. Two additional factors enhanced Greek influence in this country. Greece's involvement in a war for independence (1821–1832) aroused much sympathy in the newly independent United States; at the same time, the War of 1812 diminished American affection for British influence, including the still dominant Federal style in domestic architecture.

The Greek Revival began and ended in this country with public buildings built in Philadelphia. Among the first examples was the Bank of the United States (1818, William Strickland), and one of the last monuments was the Ridgeway Branch of the Philadelphia Library (1870, Addison and Hutton). Most domestic examples date from the period from 1830 to 1860. Among the earliest was a Greek remodeling of the Custis-Lee House in Arlington, Virginia, completed in 1820. The style was spread by carpenter's guides and pattern books, the most influential of which were written by Asher Benjamin (*The Practical House Carpenter; The Builder's Guide*) and Minard Lafever (*The Modern Builder's Guide; The Beauties of Modern Architecture*). These illustrated building details rather than views of overall houses.

In addition to these guides for local carpenter-builders, there were a growing number of trained architects in America, some educated abroad, who designed high-style buildings in the fashionable Grecian mode. Among the most prominent were Benjamin H. Latrobe and his pupils Robert Mills and William Strickland; Strickland's own pupils Thomas U. Walter and Gideon Shryock; Ithiel Town, Alexander Jackson Davis (early work), John Haviland, Alexander Parris, and Isaiah Rogers.

One of the most familiar stereotypes in American architecture is the full-colonnaded Greek Revival mansion of the southern states. In this century these are sometimes called Southern Colonial houses, a historical inaccuracy since most were built long after American independence. This particular Greek Revival subtype does, however, have a little recognized colonial background, for it sprang, at least in part, from French colonial

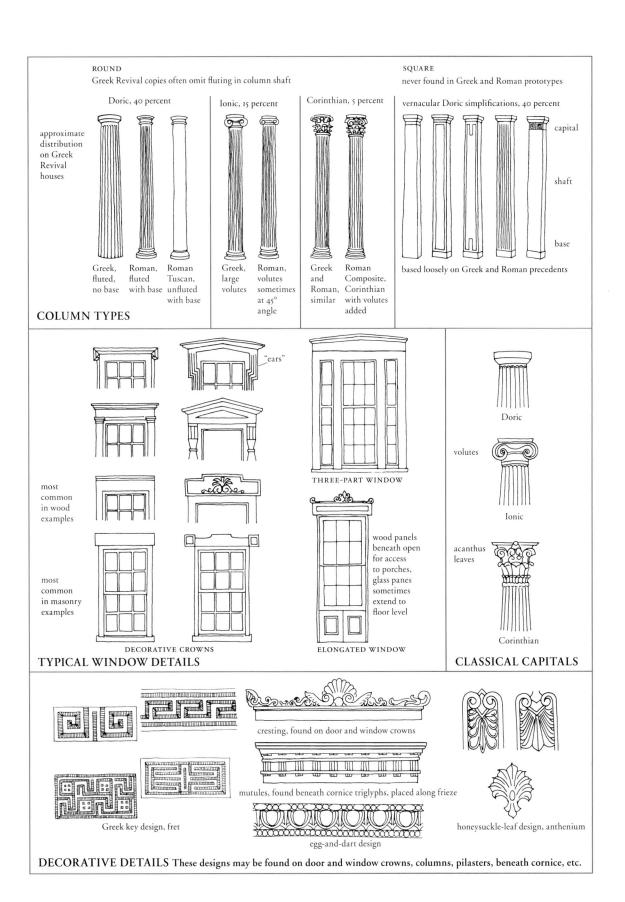

ROUND
Greek Revival copies often omit fluting in column shaft

SQUARE
never found in Greek and Roman prototypes

approximate distribution on Greek Revival houses

Doric, 40 percent

Greek, fluted, no base

Roman, fluted with base

Roman Tuscan, unfluted with base

Ionic, 15 percent

Greek, large volutes

Roman, volutes sometimes at 45° angle

Corinthian, 5 percent

Greek and Roman, similar

Roman Composite, Corinthian with volutes added

vernacular Doric simplifications, 40 percent

capital

shaft

base

based loosely on Greek and Roman precedents

COLUMN TYPES

"ears"

THREE-PART WINDOW

most common in wood examples

most common in masonry examples

wood panels beneath open for access to porches, glass panes sometimes extend to floor level

DECORATIVE CROWNS

ELONGATED WINDOW

TYPICAL WINDOW DETAILS

Doric

volutes

Ionic

acanthus leaves

Corinthian

CLASSICAL CAPITALS

cresting, found on door and window crowns

mutules, found beneath cornice triglyphs, placed along frieze

Greek key design, fret

egg-and-dart design

honeysuckle-leaf design, anthenium

DECORATIVE DETAILS These designs may be found on door and window crowns, columns, pilasters, beneath cornice, etc.

ENTRY PORCH LESS THAN FULL HEIGHT, OR ABSENT

1. Stafford, New York; 1835. Harmon House. A small wood-clad example with nicely detailed tripartite and frieze-band windows.

2. Beaufort, North Carolina; 1866. Croft House.

3. Marshall, Michigan; 1850. Montgomery House. This transitional example combines Italianate brackets under a wide eave overhang with Greek Revival door and window detailing.

4. San Augustine, Texas; 1839. Cartwright House; August Phelps, architect. Note how the very deep band of trim forms a pediment on the gable end.

5. Ashville, New York; 1835. Smith-Bly House. This lavishly detailed house has four Ionic two-story pilasters across the front facade, carved window lintels, and an architrave at the entrance. The door is recessed with two small columns in front.

6. New London, Connecticut; mid-19th century. Note the small windows in the frieze band and the unusual Corinthian capitals on the pilasters and columns.

7. Rochester, New York; 1838–41. Woodside; Alfred M. Badger, architect-builder. This large five-ranked masonry example has a square cupola, topped by a round turret, which lights an interior stairway. Note the matching balusters at four different levels and the tripartite window lintels.

8. New Castle, Indiana; 1847. Murphy House. A simplified but nicely proportioned masonry example. Note the square columns on the entry porch and the absence of capitals on both columns and pilasters.

1

4

7

FULL-HEIGHT ENTRY PORCH

1. San Felipe, Texas; ca. 1838. Lambart House. A very simple one-story example. Note the very slender columns and pilasters. Such simplified details were usual in houses built far from centers of population.

2. Bastrop, Texas; ca. 1860. Reding House. A simple wood-clad two-story example.

3. Meriwether County, Georgia; 1852. Dr. James Stinson House, Mark Hall. This house, similar to Figure 1, has heavier moldings and more substantial columns and pilasters.

4. Pittsford, New York; 1840. Kirby House. The entry porch without a pediment or hipped roof above is unusual. Note the Doric columns without bases.

5. Scott County, Kentucky; 1842. Glencrest. Note the exaggerated depth of the frieze and architrave over the entry porch.

6. Milledgeville, Georgia; 1838. Executive Mansion; Charles B. Clusky, architect-designer.

7. Natchez, Mississippi, vicinity; ca. 1855. Homewood Plantation.

8. Belfast, Maine; 1840. White House; Calvin A. Ryder, architect. This full-height entry porch is a complex and subtle variation of the usual type. Note the elaborate cupola.

1

3

6

2

4

5

7

8

FULL-FACADE PORCH

1. Madison, Georgia; ca. 1859. Massey House. A simple one-story, wood-clad example.

2. Mobile, Alabama; 1851. Lowary House. This one-story cottage is more elaborated than Figure 1. Note the pedimented dormers and full-length windows with transoms.

3. Columbus, Mississippi; ca. 1836. Homewood.

4. Sparta vicinity, Georgia; ca. 1853. Smith House (Glen Mary). The main part is raised above a high masonry basement story, a pattern borrowed from earlier French Colonial houses of the rural South.

5. Geismar, Louisiana; 1841. Ashland; James Gallier, Sr., architect. The columns of this plantation house are four feet square and thirty feet high. The massive entablature hides a low-hipped roof.

6. New Iberia, Louisiana; 1834. Shadows-on-the-Teche. This handsome plantation house has a stairway exterior to the house and no interior halls, reflecting earlier French Colonial influences.

7. Selma, Alabama; 1853. Sturdivant Hall; Thomas Helm Lee, architect.

8. Nashville, Tennessee; 1853. Belle Meade. Note the parapet with cresting crowning the full-facade porch. The cresting on the top of the roof parapet is modeled on a honeysuckle leaf and called an anthemion. More typically found over windows and doors, it was illustrated in Villa No. III in *The Architectural Instructor* by Minard Lafever.

2

5

8

FRONT-GABLED ROOF

1. Breckinridge, Colorado; mid-19th century. A very simple house with just a hint of Greek Revival influence in its front-gabled form and pedimented door and windows.

2. Marietta, Georgia; ca. 1851. Brumbly House.

3. Providence, Rhode Island; mid-19th century. Front-gabled examples commonly lack colonnaded porches but usually have pilasters and elaborate door and cornice details as in this example.

4. Middletown, Connecticut; 1828. Russell House; Ithiel Town, architect. This house is built of masonry covered with stucco scored to look like stone. Note the elaborate Corinthian capitals.

5. Andalusia, Pennsylvania; 1836 (porch and pediment). Andalusia. An earlier house to which a three-sided porch was added.

2

3

4

5

GABLE FRONT AND WING

1. Monroeville, Ohio; mid-19th century. This example, although quite small, has a colonnaded gable front and elaborate frieze-band windows.

2. Wellington vicinity, Ohio; mid-19th century. Here the frieze band is discontinuous across the gable front.

3. Buffalo, New York; mid-19th century. This imposing example has pilasters across the gable front and a two-story wing.

4. Jessamine County, Kentucky; mid-19th century. Bryant House. This brick example has a colonnaded gable front and two wings. Note that the wings have pilasters rather than the more common porch with columns as seen in the other examples.

TOWN HOUSE

1. New Orleans, Louisiana; mid-19th century. Note the exceptionally wide frieze band with windows.

2. Savannah, Georgia; 1845. Constantine House. A wood-clad example with simplified details.

3. Madison, Indiana; 1851. Costigan House. A small, two-ranked example with strong porch and window detailing.

4. St. Louis, Missouri; 1850. Sherrick House. Town houses with full-facade porches like this example were common along the Gulf Coast, particularly in New Orleans (this one slipped upriver). They may also have two tiers of one-story columns rather than the colossal ones illustrated.

5. Richmond, Virginia; 1847 and 1853. Lindon Row. A series of attached town houses.

6. Brooklyn, New York; ca. 1830. Tillary House. Note the tripartite windows and door lintels, and elaborated frieze band. The curved top dormer windows are holdovers from the Federal style.

7. Charleston, South Carolina; 1838. Roper House; attributed to E. B. White, architect. An outstanding example of the Charleston house, with narrow end turned to the street and wide porch along the side. An upper-story porch (omitted in this example) is commonly present.

8. New York, New York; 1833. Colonnade Row; attributed to Robert Higham, architect. A highly unusual row of town houses unified by freestanding columns; this example shows Renaissance influence in the placement of the columns above a rusticated lower story.

1

4

6

7

2

3

5

8

building practices. Early in their colonial expansions both the French and the English appended broad living porches, a rarity in Europe, to houses built in tropical regions. The origins of these large *galeries* or verandahs are obscure, yet they appear wherever British or French colonists encountered warm climates, including the West Indies, Africa, India, and Australia. In the United States, most were built by the French in sub-tropical Louisiana. With the waning of French influence after the Louisiana Purchase in 1803, these forms slowly evolved in the Gulf Coast states into the full colonnaded Greek Revival form now sometimes known as Southern Colonial.

The decline of Greek Revival influence was gradual. In the more fashion-conscious urban centers of the Atlantic seaboard it began to be replaced by the Gothic Revival and Italianate movements in the 1840s. In the interior states, and in rural areas everywhere, it remained a dominant style for domestic buildings until the early 1860s.

An important and enduring legacy of the Greek Revival to American domestic architecture is the front-gabled house. Popularized during the ascendance of the Greek Revival style in the early 19th century, this became the predominant form for detached urban houses in cities of the Northeast and Midwest until well into the 20th century. There it occurs in unadorned folk versions, as well as in styled Gothic, Italianate, Queen Anne, and Shingle houses. In rural areas, the form of Greek Revival known as gable front and wing likewise remained a popular form for folk houses until the 1930s.

steeply pitched roof, usually with steep cross gables

gables commonly with decorated vergeboards

wall surface extending into gable without break

windows extending into gables, with pointed arch (Gothic) shape

one-story entry or full-width porch, commonly with flattened, pointed (Gothic) arches

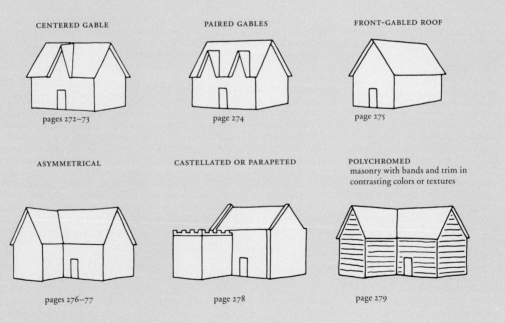

CENTERED GABLE

pages 272–73

PAIRED GABLES

page 274

FRONT-GABLED ROOF

page 275

ASYMMETRICAL

pages 276–77

CASTELLATED OR PARAPETED

page 278

POLYCHROMED
masonry with bands and trim in contrasting colors or textures

page 279

PRINCIPAL SUBTYPES

Gothic Revival

1840–1880

Identifying Features

Steeply pitched roof, usually with steep cross gables (roof normally side-gabled, less commonly front-gabled or hipped; rarely flat with castellated parapet); gables commonly have decorated vergeboards; wall surface extending into gable without break (eave or trim normally lacking beneath gable); windows commonly extend into gables, frequently having pointed-arch (Gothic) shape; one-story porch (either entry or full-width) usually present, commonly supported by flattened Gothic arches.

Principal Subtypes

Six principal subtypes can be distinguished on the basis of roof form, ground plan, or detailing:

CENTERED GABLE—These are symmetrical houses with side-gabled or hipped roofs having a prominent central cross gable. The plane of the cross gable may be either the same as the front wall or projected forward to make a small central wing. Smaller cross gables, or gable dormers, sometimes occur on either side of the dominant central gable. In some examples these are enlarged to give three identical cross gables. This subtype makes up over one-third of Gothic Revival houses.

PAIRED GABLES—Similar to the preceding subtype but with two, rather than one or three, cross gables. The two gables are sometimes extended forward into projecting wings. About 5 percent of Gothic Revival houses are of this type.

FRONT-GABLED ROOF—About 10 percent of Gothic Revival houses are simple gabled rectangles rotated so that the narrower gable end makes up the front facade. Some have additional cross gables added to the roof slope over the *side* walls, but many lack such cross gables.

ASYMMETRICAL—About one-third of Gothic Revival houses are of compound asymmetrical plan. L-shaped plans with cross-gabled roofs are the most common form, but there are many less regular variations. Small secondary cross gables, or gable dormers, were commonly added to one or more wings. After 1860, square towers were occasionally used.

CASTELLATED OR PARAPETED—The four preceding subtypes all have normal roof-wall junctions in which the eaves project outward beyond the wall. A fifth subtype, more closely based on English Medieval models, has either flat roofs with scalloped (castellated) parapets, or gabled roofs ending in high parapeted walls rather than overhanging eaves. Frequently both of these roof types occur on different parts of a single house. About 5 percent of Gothic Revival houses are of this type. These features are far more common on Gothic Revival churches and public buildings; most surviving houses are high-style landmarks, typically constructed of masonry.

POLYCHROMED—A final 5 percent of surviving Gothic Revival houses show distinctive linear patterns in masonry wall surfaces. These decorative polychrome patterns are produced by bands of contrasting color or texture in the brick or stonework, and occur principally around windows and as horizontal bands on wall surfaces. This feature is particularly characteristic of the last phase of the Gothic Revival, from about 1865 to 1880. It is sometimes treated as a separate style called High Victorian Gothic. Like the castellated or parapeted form, it is most common on churches and public buildings. The complex masonry construction was suitable only for high-style, landmark houses. These were once far more common in the prosperous industrial cities of the northeastern and midwestern states, but most have been destroyed.

Variants and Details

Fanciful decorative ornamentation, cut from wood by the newly perfected scroll saw, is a dominant feature in most Gothic Revival houses. Windows, roof-wall junctions, porches, and doors were the principal sites for such decorations.

WINDOWS—Most Gothic Revival houses have at least one window with Gothic detailing. When only a single window is elaborated in this manner, it usually occurs in the most prominent gable. Such windows might have a pointed-arch shape or might consist of two or three such arches clustered together, or might even be designed as small projecting bay windows (oriels). Full-scale bay windows are also common on the first-floor level. In less elaborate houses, cut-out patterns were frequently used on or above rectangular windows to give a pointed-arch effect. A characteristic window crown called a drip-mold is found above many Gothic windows, both arched and square. Originally designed to protect windows from water running down the face of the building, this molding covers the top of the window and continues downward along the side before turning outward so that water will be deflected away from the window frame.

ROOF-WALL JUNCTIONS—Decorative vergeboards, making an inverted V beneath the eaves of the steep gables, are a distinctive feature of most wooden Gothic houses and came in almost as many designs as there were Gothic carpenter-builders. After about

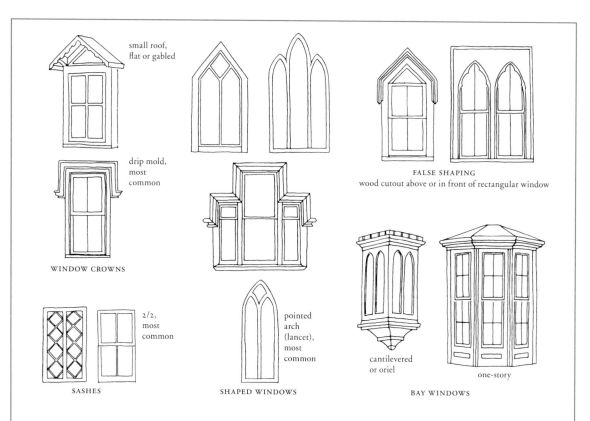

small roof, flat or gabled

drip mold, most common

WINDOW CROWNS

2/2, most common

SASHES

pointed arch (lancet), most common

SHAPED WINDOWS

FALSE SHAPING
wood cutout above or in front of rectangular window

cantilevered or oriel

one-story

BAY WINDOWS

TYPICAL WINDOW ELABORATIONS

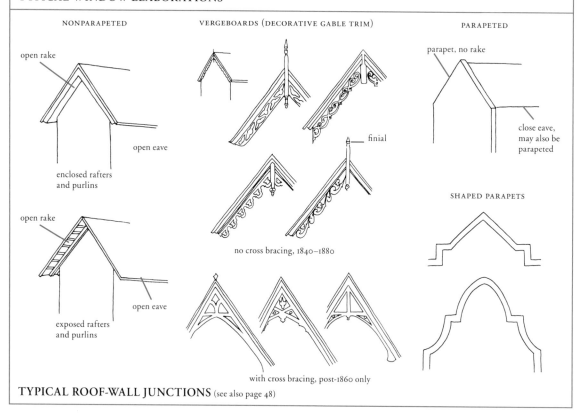

NONPARAPETED

VERGEBOARDS (DECORATIVE GABLE TRIM)

PARAPETED

open rake

open eave

enclosed rafters and purlins

open rake

open eave

exposed rafters and purlins

finial

no cross bracing, 1840–1880

with cross bracing, post-1860 only

parapet, no rake

close eave, may also be parapeted

SHAPED PARAPETS

TYPICAL ROOF-WALL JUNCTIONS (see also page 48)

1865 this feature became less popular and was generally replaced by decorative trusses at the apex of the gables. Gothic cornice detailing showed fundamental changes from the preceding classical styles (Georgian, Federal, Greek Revival, etc.). The latter usually have boxed cornices with the rafters enclosed, while most Gothic Revival houses have open cornices with the rafters either exposed or sheathed parallel to the overlying roof.

PORCHES—One-story porches are found on about 80 percent of Gothic Revival houses.

DOORS—Doors commonly show pointed arches or other Gothic motifs as well as decorative crowns similar to those found on windows. Elaborate paneled doors are common but simple batten doors, mimicking modest Medieval prototypes, also occur.

WALL CLADDING AND DECORATIVE DETAILING—Gothic Revival houses are of both wooden and masonry construction but wood-frame Carpenter Gothic examples predominate. These were usually covered with horizontal cladding, but vertical board-and-batten siding was also common. The latter material was widely advocated by contemporary pattern books for its verticality, which was considered suitably Gothic.

Occurrence

Most Gothic Revival houses were constructed between 1840 and 1870; examples from the 1870s are less frequent. The style was never as popular as were houses in the competing Greek Revival or Italianate styles, yet scattered examples can still be found in most areas of the country settled before 1880. Surviving Gothic Revival houses are most abundant in the northeastern states, where fashionable architects originally popularized the style. They are less common in the South, particularly in the New South states along the Gulf Coast. In this region Greek Revival houses dominated the expansions of the 1840s and 1850s, while the Civil War and Reconstruction all but halted building until the waning days of Gothic influence.

Comments

The Gothic Revival began in England in 1749 when Sir Horace Walpole, a wealthy dilettante, began remodeling his country house in the Medieval style, complete with battlements and multiple pointed-arch windows. Over the next century, others followed his lead and such Picturesque country houses became common in England. Although a handful of earlier houses with Gothic detailing were built, the first documented, fully developed domestic example in America (Glen Ellen in Baltimore, Maryland) was designed by Alexander Jackson Davis in 1832. Davis was the first American architect to champion Gothic domestic buildings; his 1837 book, *Rural Residences,* was dominated by Gothic examples. This was also the first house plan book published in this country. Previous publications had shown details, parts, pieces, and occasional elevations of houses, but Davis's was the first to show three-dimensional views complete with floor plans. Davis's book had only a small circulation but his ideas were picked up by his friend Andrew Jackson Downing, who expanded them in pattern books published in 1842 (*Cottage Residences*) and 1850 (*The Architecture of Country Houses*). Downing's writ-

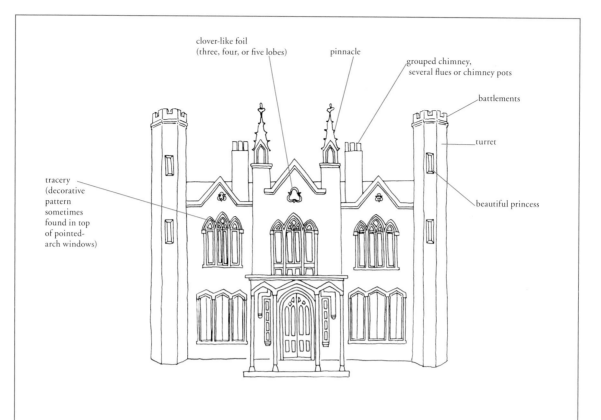

clover-like foil
(three, four, or five lobes)

pinnacle

grouped chimney,
several flues or chimney pots

battlements

turret

beautiful princess

tracery
(decorative
pattern
sometimes
found in top
of pointed-
arch windows)

HIGH-STYLE ELABORATIONS

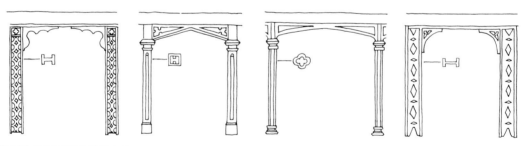

TYPICAL PORCH DETAILS
Space between porch supports most commonly has a flattened arch or side brackets that mimic such an arch

TYPICAL DOORS

CENTERED GABLE

1. Santa Clara, California; 1875. Landrum House. A small wood-clad example; the triangular pediments over the first-story windows are out of character.

2. Denison, Texas; ca. 1883. Eisenhower Birthplace. A small and simplified example. The centered gable has a matching gable on each side.

3. Jackson, Mississippi; 1857. Manship House. Note how the centered gable is extended forward from the main plane of the front facade to form a covered entrance.

4. Brownwood, Texas; ca. 1875. Adams House. This sandstone example has windows with flattened Tudor arches and drip-molds. The porch may have been modified.

5. Woodstock, Connecticut; 1846. Roseland. A landmark example with board-and-batten wood cladding, elaborate porch supports, oriel windows, and two facades elaborated with gables or gable dormers.

6. Salem, Massachusetts; 1851. Brooks House. An elaborately detailed house with foil windows, diamond-shape window panes, drip-molds, and castellations above the porch.

7. Wernersville, Pennsylvania; mid-19th century. A combination of the Gothic Revival form with Italianate cornice brackets and arched windows.

8. Rushford, Minnesota; ca. 1875. Note the decorative trusses at the apex of the gable and gable dormers (see also Figure 1); these are common on post-1865 examples.

2

4

5

8

PAIRED GABLES

1. Ashe County, North Carolina; ca. 1880. McGuire House. This very simple example has wood cladding that dramatically follows the lines of the paired gables. The porch shows later modifications.

2. Demopolis, Alabama; 1858. Ashe House. Both this house and Figure 3 have very delicate lace-like porches and vergeboard details.

3. Columbus, Mississippi; 1880. Episcopal Rectory.

4. Brunswick, Maine; 1849. Boody House; Gervase Wheeler, architect. This house has some applied stickwork (not visible in the photo) and is transitional from the Gothic Revival to the Stick style. A very similar design by Wheeler was published in Downing's 1850 book, *The Architecture of Country Houses,* figure 130.[2]

1

2

3

4

FRONT-GABLED ROOF

1. Georgetown, Colorado; mid-19th century. A very modest example complete with pointed arch window and drip-molds on all front windows and door.

2. Cleveland, Ohio; mid-19th century.

3. New Orleans, Louisiana; ca. 1869. Rountree House. An unusual example with a two-tiered porch and the full-length windows often found in Gulf Coast houses. The Tudor arches between the lower-story porch supports are carefully detailed.

4. Cuba, New York; mid-19th century. Note the wraparound porch and matching side gable. The elaborate window crown shape featured on the gable windows was rarely used prior to ca. 1860.

1

2

3

4

ASYMMETRICAL

1. Hartford, Connecticut; mid-19th century. Although the Gothic decorated gable clearly dominates, a hodgepodge of secondary influences is evident—Italianate brackets, Second Empire tower, Queen Anne porch supports, and pedimented windows.

2. Southport, Connecticut; mid-19th century. Bulkley House. Although similar to Figure 1, the details here are mostly of Gothic inspiration.

3. Selma, Alabama; mid-19th century. A carefully detailed board-and-batten example.

4. Brown's Valley, Minnesota, vicinity; ca. 1885. Similar in form to Figure 3, the ornate trussed gables identify it as a later example.

5. Iowa City, Iowa; 1877. Jackson House.

6. Rochester, New York; 1878. This house shows clearly the transition from the Gothic to the Stick style. Note the Gothic windows and door shapes with stickwork in the main gable and as supports under the upstairs bay windows. Also note the wide roof overhang with open eaves, visible on the right.

7. Newport, Rhode Island; 1841. Kingscote; Richard Upjohn, architect (rear addition by Stanford White). A handsomely detailed house with entrance canopy, castellations over the bay window, drip-molds, and diamond-pane windows.

8. New Castle, Delaware; 1852. Lesley Home; Thomas and James Dixon, architects.

1

4

7

CASTELLATED OR PARAPETED

1. Aberdeen, Mississippi; ca. 1884. The Castle. A relatively modest wood-clad example, unusual for this subtype.

2. Fayette County, Kentucky; 1852. Ingelside; John McMurtry, architect.

3. Brookneal, Virginia, vicinity; 1848. Staunton Hill; John E. Johnson, designer. Note the symmetrical facade with its almost classical feeling.

4. Tarrytown, New York; 1838, major addition 1865. Lyndhurst; Alexander Jackson Davis, architect for both. This marble example is the finest Gothic Revival house surviving in this country—the result of a major 1865 addition to an earlier 1838 structure. Note the multiple parapets, castellations, pinnacles, foil windows, grouped chimneys, window tracery, and castellated tower. The interiors are equally elaborate.

POLYCHROMED

1. Philadelphia, Pennsylvania; 1894. Moore House; Wilson Eyre, architect. A late example with strong early Eclectic influences.

2. Detroit, Michigan; 1876. Gillis House; Brush and Mason, architects. Note the banded surround above the pointed arch window to the right. This was a favorite polychrome motif (see also Figure 5).

3. Cleveland, Ohio; ca. 1878. Winslow House. This example combines the towered Second Empire form with elaborate polychromed Gothic detailing.

4. Brooklyn, New York; 1848. The Gothic influence is seen in the door surround and drip-mold over the windows of these town houses. This example is not polychromed and is included to show a rare early Gothic town house. A roof addition and cornice modifications are evident in the house to the right.

5. New York, New York; 1874. Governor Tilden House; Calvert Vaux, architect. This town house example has elaborate polychromed detailing.

ings were far more successful, because the author promoted them with tireless public speaking and personal energy. Downing thus became the popularizer of the style.

This style was seldom applied to urban houses for two reasons. First, the writings of Davis and Downing stressed its suitability as a *rural* style, compatible with the natural landscape; it was not promoted as appropriate for urban dwellings. Secondly, its emphasis on high, multiple gables and wide porches did not physically lend itself to narrow urban lots. A few urban examples with Gothic door, window, or cornice detailing survive (Figures 4, 5, page 279), but most urban houses of the era are in the contemporaneous Greek Revival or Italianate styles.

Gothic Revival was in declining favor for American domestic buildings after 1865, although a small rebirth of interest during the 1870s was stimulated by the writings of the English critic John Ruskin, who emphasized continental rather than English examples as models. This High Victorian Gothic phase was principally applied to public and religious buildings, although a few surviving landmark houses reflect its influence (see the paragraph on the polychromed subtype, page 268).

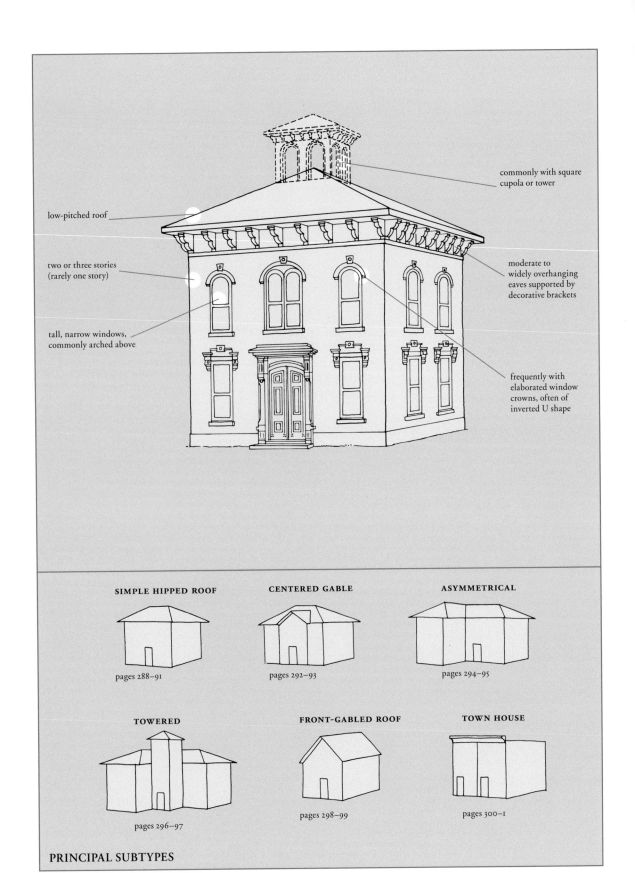

commonly with square cupola or tower

low-pitched roof

two or three stories (rarely one story)

tall, narrow windows, commonly arched above

moderate to widely overhanging eaves supported by decorative brackets

frequently with elaborated window crowns, often of inverted U shape

SIMPLE HIPPED ROOF

pages 288–91

CENTERED GABLE

pages 292–93

ASYMMETRICAL

pages 294–95

TOWERED

pages 296–97

FRONT-GABLED ROOF

pages 298–99

TOWN HOUSE

pages 300–1

PRINCIPAL SUBTYPES

Italianate

1840–1885

Identifying Features

Two or three stories (rarely one story); low-pitched roof with moderate to widely over-hanging eaves having decorative brackets beneath; tall, narrow windows, commonly arched or curved above; windows frequently with elaborated crowns, often of inverted U shape; many examples with square cupola or tower.

Principal Subtypes

Six principal subtypes can be distinguished:

SIMPLE HIPPED ROOF—These are square or rectangular box-shaped houses with hipped roofs that are uninterrupted except, in about half of the surviving examples, by a central cupola (these have been called cube and cupola houses). Facade openings are typically three-ranked, less commonly five-ranked, rarely two- or four-ranked. This is the most common subtype, making up about one-third of Italianate houses.

CENTERED GABLE—These are houses of both simple and compound plan having a front-facing centered gable. The usually rather small gable projects from a low-pitched hipped or side-gabled roof. Frequently the front wall beneath the gable extends forward as a prominent central extension. About 15 percent are of this type.

ASYMMETRICAL—These are compound-plan houses, usually L-shaped, without tow-ers. Roofs are cross-hipped or cross-gabled. In a few examples the addition of a second forward-facing wing makes a U-shaped plan. About 20 percent of Italianate houses are of this type.

TOWERED—Only about 15 percent of Italianate houses have the square tower that is often considered to be characteristic of the Italian Villa. The tower is sometimes cen-tered on the front facade or placed alongside it; more commonly, it occupies the position where the wing joins the principal section of an L-plan house. Typically, such towers have narrow paired windows with arched tops. Tower roofs are most commonly low-pitched and hipped; occasionally, steep mansard roofs are used instead.

FRONT-GABLED ROOF—In this subtype, Italianate detailing is added to the simple front-gabled rectangular box popularized by the Greek Revival style. This subtype, about 10 percent of surviving examples, is common on narrow lots in large cities.

TOWN HOUSE—Italianate styling, along with the related Second Empire style, dominated urban housing in the decades between 1860 and 1880. Italianate town houses are characterized by wide, projecting cornices with typical brackets; the cornice conceals a flat or low-pitched roof behind. Typical Italianate windows further distinguish these examples.

Variants and Details

The principal areas of elaboration in Italianate houses are windows, cornices, porches (including porch-support columns), and doorways. Most American examples show a free intermixing of details derived from both informal rural models as well as formal Renaissance town houses.

WINDOWS—Italianate window sashes most commonly have one- or two-pane glazing. For the first time, arched and curved (segmentally arched) window tops became common, along with the traditional rectangular top. Window enframements show exuberant variation: U-shaped crowns, often with brackets, are most common; simple or pedimented crowns and complete decorated surrounds also occur and appear to be more common in the western states. Paired and triple windows are frequent, as are one- and two-story bay windows.

CORNICES—Large eave brackets dominate the cornice line of Italianate houses. These show an almost infinite variety of shapes and spacings. They are usually arranged either singly or in pairs, and are commonly placed on a deep trim band that is, itself, frequently elaborated with panels or moldings.

PORCHES AND PORCH-SUPPORT COLUMNS—Porches, although almost universally present, are relatively restrained in elaboration and are of single-story height. Small entry porches are most common; full-width porches are also frequent, although many of those seen today are later expansions or additions. The most common type of porch support is a square post with the corners beveled.

DOORWAYS—Paired as well as single doors are common. Large-pane glazing in the door itself, rather than small panes in a frame surrounding the door, first became common in Italianate houses. Doors occur in the same shapes as windows (rectangular, arched, segmentally arched); elaborate enframements above doors are similar to those over windows.

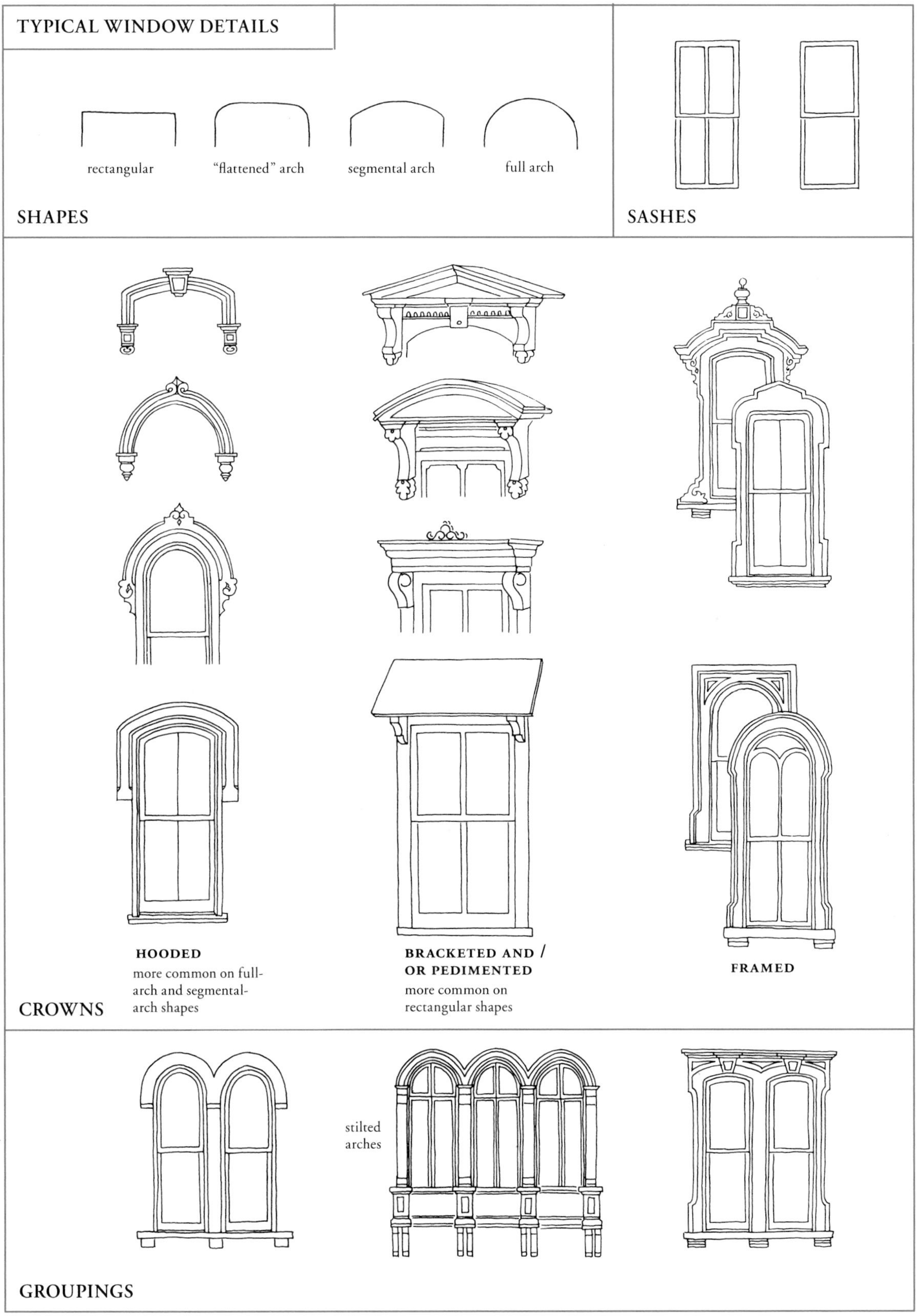
TYPICAL WINDOW DETAILS
rectangular
"flattened" arch
segmental arch
full arch
SHAPES
SASHES
HOODED
more common on full-arch and segmental-arch shapes
BRACKETED AND / OR PEDIMENTED
more common on rectangular shapes
FRAMED
CROWNS
stilted arches
GROUPINGS

Occurrence

The Italianate style dominated American houses constructed between 1850 and 1880. It was particularly common in the expanding towns and cities of the Midwest as well as in many older but still growing cities of the northeastern seaboard. In these decades San Francisco grew from a village to a principal American port; most of its earliest town houses were constructed of wood in this style (see Figure 5, page 300). Many of these escaped the 1906 earthquake and fire to survive today. Italianate houses are least common in the southern states, where the Civil War, Reconstruction, and the 1870s depression led to little new building until after the style had passed from fashion.

Comments

The Italianate style, along with the Gothic Revival, began in England as part of the Picturesque movement, a reaction to the formal classical ideals in art and architecture that had been fashionable for about two hundred years. The movement emphasized rambling, informal Italian farmhouses, with their characteristic square towers, as models for Italian-style villa architecture. Note that other, more formal, Italian models from the Renaissance or ancient Rome had led to the previous era of classicism. Italy, rather paradoxically, thus remained a principal source of artistic nurture during the reaction against the earlier ideals it had inspired.

Italianate houses built in the United States generally followed the informal rural models of the Picturesque movement. In America these Old World prototypes were variously modified, adapted, and embellished into a truly indigenous style with only hints

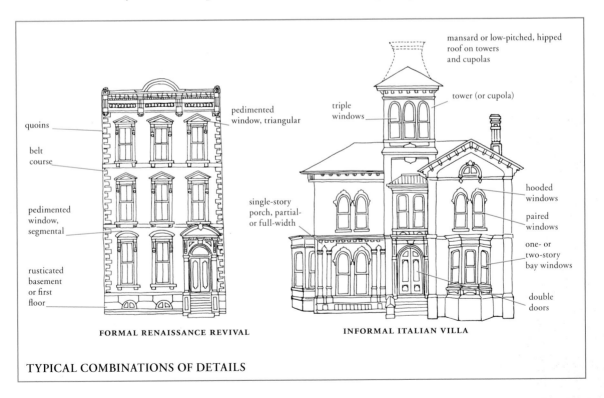

quoins

belt course

pedimented window, segmental

rusticated basement or first floor

pedimented window, triangular

single-story porch, partial- or full-width

mansard or low-pitched, hipped roof on towers and cupolas

triple windows

tower (or cupola)

hooded windows

paired windows

one- or two-story bay windows

double doors

FORMAL RENAISSANCE REVIVAL

INFORMAL ITALIAN VILLA

TYPICAL COMBINATIONS OF DETAILS

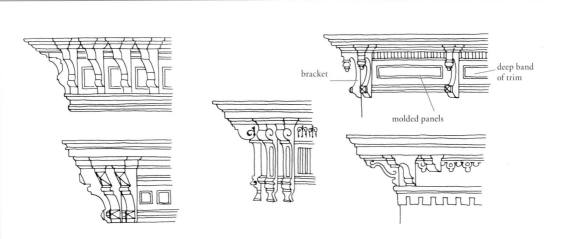

bracket

deep band of trim

molded panels

TYPICAL BRACKETED CORNICES

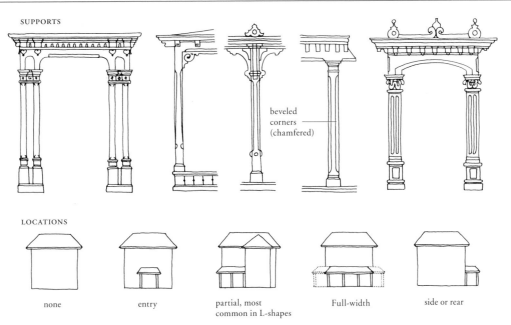

SUPPORTS

beveled corners (chamfered)

LOCATIONS

none   entry   partial, most common in L-shapes   Full-width   side or rear

TYPICAL PORCH DETAILS

TYPICAL DOORS Similar single doors are also found

1

2

4

5

7

8

SIMPLE HIPPED ROOF

1. Salisbury, North Carolina; mid-19th century. A simple masonry two-ranked example.

2. Hartford, Connecticut; mid-19th century.

3. San Jose, California; ca. 1858. Fallon House.

4. Austin, Texas; 1877. Tips House.

5. Cape May County, New Jersey; 1863. George Allen House; Samuel Sloan, architect. A cube and cupola Italianate form with a full-width porch and deep-bracketed cornice that incorporated attic-story windows.

6. Providence, Rhode Island; 1853. Bowen House; Thomas Tefft, architect. This and Figure 9 reflect the more formal Renaissance town house tradition; note the cubic form, pedimented window, quoins, and restrained entry porch.

7. Savannah, Georgia; 1860. Mercer House; John S. Norris, architect. A lavishly detailed example with iron balconies, paired windows with elaborately bracketed hoods, and cornice brackets with double drops.

8. Cleveland, Ohio; 1862. Sanford House. Rear bay windows, seen here, and rear wings, one window wide (as in Figure 4), were common methods of bringing extra light and ventilation to narrow examples built on small city lots. Note the heavy arched window hoods.

9. St. Louis, Missouri; mid-19th century. Frost House. Note the rusticated first story (see additional comments under Figure 6).

3

6

9

SIMPLE HIPPED ROOF (con't)

10. Benicia, California; ca. 1880. A very simple, one-story, wood-clad example.

11. Austin, Texas; mid-19th century. A more elaborate one-story masonry example with quoins accenting the door, windows, and corners.

12. Louisville, Kentucky; mid-19th century. Note the use of segmentally arched windows on the first story with fully arched windows above.

13. Bloomington, Wisconsin; 1877. Ballantine House. The matching pair of bay windows on the front facade is unusual outside of northern California.

14. Salisbury, North Carolina; 1868. Murdock-Wiley House. Occasionally the side-gabled roof form was substituted for the more typical Italianate hipped roof as in this example. Note the unusual use of paired brackets placed on top of pilasters.

15. Fort Smith, Arkansas; 1868. Bonneville House; David McKibben, builder and original owner. Note the handsome paired brackets and windows in the elaborated frieze band.

16. Macon, Georgia; 1855. Johnston House; James B. Ayres, architect. A large and elaborate three-story example raised on a full basement. An octagonal cupola and small round windows light the third story. Note the unusually heavy bracketed pediments above second-story windows on the front facade.

10

12

14

15

11

13

16

CENTERED GABLE

1. Selma, Alabama; mid-19th century. White House. A simple wood-clad example.

2. Oxford, Mississippi; 1878. Howry House. The two-story porches are unusual, as is their recessed position under the main roof of the house.

3. Columbus, Indiana; 1864. Storey House; James Perkenson, architect. This three-ranked masonry example has simplified, but refined, detailing.

4. Richmond, Virginia; 1858. Haxall House. Contrast the ornate detailing here with the restrained detailing of Figure 3. Note the curved centered "gable," the cupola, and the pattern of paired and single windows.

5. Raleigh, North Carolina; 1873. Andrews House; G. S. H. Appleget, architect. The small room on the left is a later addition.

6. Oakland, California; 1868. Pardee House; John J. Newsom and William C. Hoagland, architects.

7. Richmond, Kentucky; 1864. Whitehall; Lewinski and McMurtry, architects. Note the unusual three-part design—a front-gabled central section is flanked by two wings, each with a centered gable; note also the full-height pilasters used across the entire facade.

8. Tarboro, North Carolina, vicinity; 1859. Coolmore Plantation. Rather than the more common centered gable, this unusual example has paired side gables. Note the cupola with centered gable here and in Figure 6.

9. Louisville, Kentucky; ca. 1870, porch ca. 1885. Field House. Bracketed and pedimented windows as well as quoins are used on both the main facade and the gabled central projection.

1

3

6

7

2

4

5

8

9

ASYMMETRICAL

1. Selma, Alabama; mid-19th century. The simple gable front and wing is a common Italianate form. Figures 2 and 3 are also examples of this type.

2. Clintonville, Kentucky; 1881. Crim House.

3. Salisbury, North Carolina; late 19th century.

4. Fort Smith, Arkansas; late 19th century. An unusual example showing Italianate detailing superimposed on a steeply pitched roof with a dominant front gable and dormer borrowed from the Gothic Revival.

5. Salem, Oregon; 1880. Port House. This narrow, deep house form was designed for a narrow urban lot.

6. Raleigh, North Carolina; ca. 1872. Merrimon House. This example has a second, more shallow wing and porch (left) added to the basic gable front and wing form.

7. Oakland, California; 1876. Camron House. Many asymmetrical Italianate examples are formed by the addition of a single large bay window to the basic cubic shape as in this example and Figure 8.

8. Penfield, New York; 1878. Hill and Hollow. A smaller version of Figure 7, this time executed in masonry with a cupola.

1

5

4

7

2

3

6

8

TOWERED

1. South Stockton, New York; mid-19th century. Figures 1, 4, and 7 illustrate progressively more elaborate versions of a tower embraced by the wings of a gable-front-and-wing plan, a favorite Italianate arrangement.

2. Cherry Creek, New York; mid-19th century. Frost House. An unusual composition which builds from a one-story wing (in shadow at left) to the two-story central block to a three-story tower.

3. Hartford, Connecticut; mid-19th century.

4. Lexington, Kentucky; mid-19th century.

5. Marshalltown, Iowa; 1875. Although classical columns are frequently used as porch supports on Italianate houses (see Figures 7 and 8), this large porch is probably a later addition (paired columns and columns raised on pedestals were uncommon before the 1890s).

6. Raleigh, North Carolina; ca. 1880. Centered towers are common in Second Empire houses, but Italianate examples, such as this, are unusual. Note how this placement produces a balanced, classical appearance even with the asymmetrical porch.

7. Portland, Maine; 1859; Morse-Libby House; Henry Austin, architect. An exceptional landmark example with numerous formal details. Note the segmental and the pedimented window crowns with brackets, as well as the quoins, classical columns, and balustrade.

8. San Antonio, Texas; ca. 1876, 1882, 1890. Norton House. In its final form this is a most unusual Italianate house based on formal Renaissance models.

1

4

7

2

3

5

6

8

FRONT-GABLED ROOF

1. Chicago, Illinois; mid-19th century.

2. Buffalo, New York; 1870–78. Tifft Houses. These examples show how the front-gabled form is well adapted to narrow urban lots.

3. New Orleans, Louisiana; mid-19th century. The bracketed wooden canopy over the second-story porch is a common New Orleans innovation on both one- and two-story houses. The full-length windows hark back to the earlier French Colonial building traditions of the region.

4. Union Springs, Alabama; mid-19th century.

5. New London, Connecticut; mid-19th century.

6. Washington, District of Columbia; mid-19th century. Although full-width porches are found throughout the country, they are most common in areas with hot summers.

7. Meriden, Connecticut; ca. 1868. Smith House. Cross gables extending outward the width of a single window or door are often added for light and ventilation toward the rear of front-gabled examples (see also Figure 8).

8. Iowa City, Iowa; 1882. Koza House. Note the unusually robust detailing of the bracketed cornice, flattened-arch window crowns, and door hood.

1

3

6

7

2

4

5

8

TOWN HOUSE

1. Benicia, California; ca. 1880. The cornice and parapet form a false front on this small, wood-clad example (see also Figure 5). In California flat-fronted Italianate town houses like this generally predated those with bay windows like Figure 5.

2. Savannah, Georgia; 1877.

3. Philadelphia, Pennsylvania; ca. 1865; Weightman House. An example inspired by formal Renaissance models.

4. Richmond, Virginia; mid-19th century.

5. San Francisco, California; ca. 1880. Stadtmuller House; P. R. Schmidt, architect. Most early Italianate California town houses have flat fronts, as in Figure 1. Later examples more often have elaborate ornamentation and large bay windows, as in this example.

6. Richmond, Virginia; 1861 and 1859. Putney Houses. Note how these detached town houses are closely spaced with full windowless walls.

7. Pittsburgh, Pennsylvania; mid-19th century. Note the incised Eastlake detailing in the door surround and window crowns.

8. New York, New York; mid-19th century. Residential New York City was once dominated by blocks of attached Italianate brownstone town houses such as these; some neighborhoods still have many surviving examples.

1

3

4

5

2

6

7

8

of its Latin origin. Far less commonly, the formal Italian Renaissance town house, rather than the rural folk house, served as model; these were sometimes imported relatively intact. In purest form such Renaissance Revival houses are austere square or rectangular boxes with little decorative detailing save for formal window crowns (most typically a triangular pediment) and restrained cornice moldings. They are always of masonry (typically stone ashlar or stucco) and typically have horizontal belt courses and corner quoins. As in the originals, most American examples were town houses. Relatively few were built and only a handful survive. More commonly, one or more characteristics of the Renaissance town house were mixed with the general Italianate vernacular.

The first Italianate houses in the United States were built in the late 1830s; the style was popularized by the influential pattern books of Andrew Jackson Downing published in the 1840s and 1850s (see the preceding chapter on Gothic Revival). Other books published plans for Italianate houses, with the most widely used being the two volumes of Samuel Sloan's *The Model Architect* that introduced the cube-and-cupola house. By the 1860s the style had completely overshadowed its earlier companion, the Gothic Revival. Most surviving examples date from the period 1855–1880; earlier examples are rare. The decline of the Italianate style, along with that of the closely related Second Empire style, began with the financial panic of 1873 and the subsequent depression. When prosperity returned late in the decade, new housing fashions—particularly the Queen Anne style—rose quickly to dominance.

Some East Coast writers have distinguished two chronological phases of Italianate styling: an earlier phase from the 1840s and 1850s with relatively simple detailing and a later, more highly decorated phase from the 1860s and 1870s (High Victorian Italianate). For domestic buildings, at least, this seems a rather artificial division. While the few surviving examples from the 1840s do have rather simple detailing, a survey of pattern book models and surviving examples shows a wide variation in decorative exuberance nationwide, with highly elaborated examples found from at least the early 1850s and simpler examples persisting through the 1870s. Local practices can produce a clearly discernible evolution. For example, town houses in San Francisco and northern California have clear differences between those built in ca. 1860–1870 and those from ca. 1870–1880 (see pages 300 and 337).

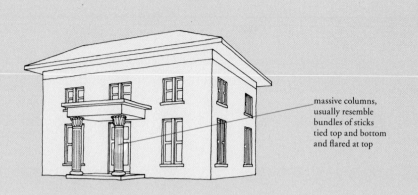

massive columns,
usually resemble
bundles of sticks
tied top and bottom
and flared at top

EGYPTIAN

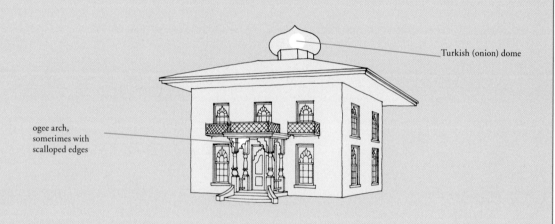

Turkish (onion) dome

ogee arch,
sometimes with
scalloped edges

ORIENTAL

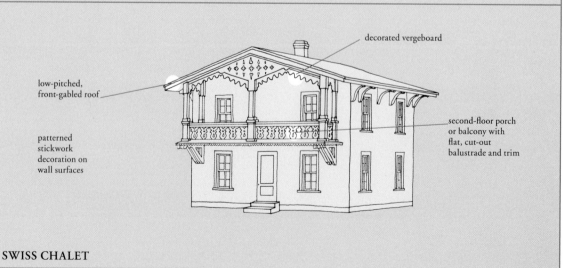

decorated vergeboard

low-pitched,
front-gabled roof

second-floor porch
or balcony with
flat, cut-out
balustrade and trim

patterned
stickwork
decoration on
wall surfaces

SWISS CHALET

Exotic Revivals

1835–ca. 1915

Three principal types of exotic decorative ornament were occasionally used on romantic era houses: Egyptian, Oriental, and Swiss Chalet. These define three very rare styles, which, for convenience, will be treated here as subunits of a single Exotic Revival movement. The Egyptian and Oriental revivals were patterned after similar movements taking place in 19th-century Europe. The Swiss Chalet style, in contrast, was a romantic borrowing from contemporary Swiss domestic practice.

Egyptian

The handful (probably fewer than a dozen) surviving domestic examples superimpose Egyptian columns on otherwise Greek Revival or Italianate forms. These columns resemble massive bundles of sticks tied together at the top and bottom and flared at the top.

The European Egyptian Revival sprang from Napoleon's Egyptian campaign (1798–99), coupled with a subsequent scholarly interest in Egypt as a source for the more familiar architecture of classical Greece and Rome. In Europe, as in this country, Egyptian motifs were most often applied to public buildings.

Oriental

The several dozen surviving examples are mostly hipped-roof Italianate cubes with ogee arches (sometimes with scalloped edges added) and Oriental trim. Another favored feature was the Turkish (onion) dome; few of these survive on domestic buildings.

The Oriental Revival was inspired by increasing exploration and trade in the Far East during the late 18th and early 19th centuries. Numerous detailed accounts of travels in India and China led to a new appreciation of the complexities of Oriental architecture. The resulting use of Far Eastern motifs in Europe and America was long-lived; occasional examples were built into the early 20th century.

EGYPTIAN

ORIENTAL

SWISS CHALET

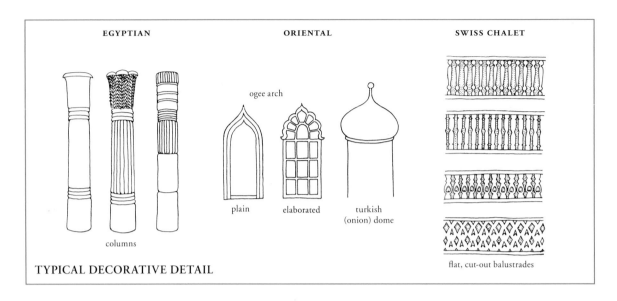

ogee arch

plain

elaborated

turkish
(onion) dome

columns

flat, cut-out balustrades

TYPICAL DECORATIVE DETAIL

3

4

5

EGYPTIAN

1. New Haven, Connecticut; 1837. Apthorp House; Alexander J. Davis, architect. Later additions surround the original cube house. The porch with its Egyptian columns is diminished by the additions above it.

2. Richmond, Virginia; 1847. Cabell House. The original house lacked both the bay windows and the porch balcony, making the two-story Egyptian columns still more prominent.

ORIENTAL

3. Rochester, New York; 1849. Brewster-Burke House. Oriental porch motif and window details on a cube-house form typical of the Italianate (see Figure 1 for an Egyptian counterpart).

4. Louisville, Kentucky; 1901. Biscoe House. A very late example.

5. Church Hill, New York; 1874. Olana; Frederic E. Church, designer, Calvert Vaux, architect. An individualistic interpretation of the Exotic Revival by landscape painter Church.

SWISS CHALET

6. Chautauqua; New York, 1875; Miller House. Reported to have been precut in Akron, Ohio, and assembled on site. The applied stickwork seen here (diagonals in rectangular frames) clearly shows the close connection that could exist between the Stick style and the Swiss Chalet.

7. Hartford, Connecticut; late 19th century.

8. Barrytown, New York, vicinity; 1867. Montgomery Place; Alexander Jackson Davis, architect.

9. Pasadena, California; ca. 1910.

1

2

6

7

8

9

Swiss Chalet

Most of the few dozen surviving examples have low-pitched front-gabled roofs with wide eave overhangs. A second-story porch or balcony with flat, cut-out patterned balustrade and vergeboard trim is characteristic, as is patterned stickwork decoration on exterior walls; the latter is virtually identical to that found on closely related and contemporaneous Stick houses. Some examples superimpose Swiss porches and trim on Greek or Gothic Revival forms; a few late examples were superimposed on Craftsman forms.

The style was introduced into the United States by the romantic popularizer Andrew Jackson Downing, whose pattern book, *The Architecture of Country Houses* (1850), showed several Swiss models suitable for "bold and mountainous" sites. It experienced a revival of interest in the early 20th century.[3]

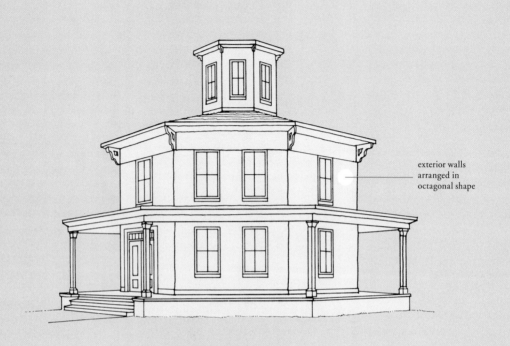

exterior walls
arranged in
octagonal shape

Octagon

1850–1870

The Octagon house is easily recognized by the eight-sided shape of the exterior walls. Most are two-story with low-pitched hipped roofs and wide eave overhangs; eave brackets are common. Occasional examples show six-, ten-, twelve-, or sixteen-sided forms; a few are round. About half have an octagonal cupola and most have porches. Many show Greek Revival, Gothic Revival, or Italianate decorative details; others lack detailing.

This is a very rare style; approximately two thousand of these survive, mostly in New York, Massachusetts, and the Midwest.[4] Most were built in the decades of the 1850s and 1860s.

The style owed its popularity to Orson S. Fowler, a lecturer and writer from Fishkill, New York, who in 1849 published an elaborate defense of its virtues entitled *The Octagon House: A Home for All.* Following Fowler, at least seven other pattern books of the 1850s also illustrated Octagon houses. Fowler stressed that an octagon encloses more floor space per linear foot of exterior wall than does the usual square or rectangle, thereby "reducing both building costs and heat loss through the walls." He also maintained that Octagons were superior to square houses in "increasing sunlight and ventilation" and in "eliminating dark and useless corners." As can be seen in the two typical plans shown in the accompanying drawings, he conveniently ignored interior room shapes, which were *not* octagonal and therefore still had "useless" corners, including triangular spaces not found in conventional shapes. Furthermore, much of this "increased sunlight and ventilation" went into pantries and closets; most rooms, in fact, have only a single exposure rather than the two commonly found in conventional houses. Such practical problems are undoubtedly responsible for the only modest success of the Octagon movement.

Fowler also advocated other improvements such as indoor plumbing, central heating, "board walls" made of lumber scraps, and "gravel walls" of poured concrete. He was not generally concerned with decorative treatment beyond "the beauty of the octagon form itself," although many Octagons were built with decorative detailing. Fowler claimed his domestic use of the Octagon to be original, but there were scattered earlier examples, including Thomas Jefferson's summer house, Poplar Forest, completed in 1819. Octagonal wings and projections were also common in Federal houses (1780–1820).

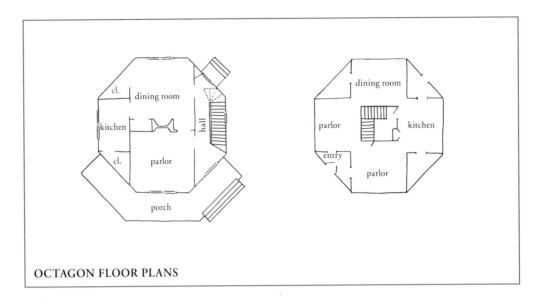

OCTAGON FLOOR PLANS

3

4

6

OCTAGON

1. Eyota, Minnesota; ca. 1865. Mattison House. A small one-story example.

2. Wiscasset, Maine; 1855. Scott House. A two-and-one-half-story brick example with simple entry porch.

3. Williamson, New York; 1850. Sperry House. This house has twenty-inch-thick cobblestone walls that are covered with plaster. The porch is a later addition.

4. Geneva, New York; 1853. Moore House. Entrance steps, porch supports, and first- and second-story railings are all ornamental cast iron. Note the raised basement.

5. Hoosick Falls, New York; 1855. Estabrook House. The balustrade design is repeated in different scales on the roofs of the porch, the cupola, and the main house.

6. Monroe, Wisconsin; 1861. West House. This unusual house is a combination of several smaller octagonal sections rather than the usual large single octagon. Note the octagonal cupola, Italianate cornice detailing, and wraparound porch with cut-out balusters above.

7. Natchez, Mississippi, vicinity; 1862. Longwood; Samuel Sloan, architect. This landmark example shows Exotic Revival influence in the large onion dome and Italianate influence in the porch and the cornice detailing.

1

2

5

7

The long reign of Britain's Queen Victoria lasted from 1837 to 1901 and, in the most precise sense, this span of years makes up the Victorian era. In American architecture, however, it is those styles that were popular during the last decades of her reign—from about 1860 to 1900—that are generally referred to as "Victorian." During this period, rapid industrialization and the growth of the railroads led to dramatic changes in American house design and construction. The balloon frame, made up of light, two-inch boards held together by wire nails, was rapidly replacing heavy-timber framing as the standard building technique. This, in turn, freed houses from their traditional box-like shapes by greatly simplifying the construction of corners, wall extensions, overhangs, and irregular ground plans. In addition, growing industrialization permitted many complex house components—doors, windows, roofing, siding, and decorative detailing—to be mass-produced in large factories and shipped throughout the country at relatively low cost on the expanding railway network. Victorian styles clearly reflect these changes through their extravagant use of complex shapes and elaborate detailing, features previously restricted to expensive, landmark houses.

The way houses were designed underwent a similar transformation. Not only were there now many more pattern books published showing house facades, there was also a new kind of book that began to be published, showing large, easy-to-read drawings of smaller-scale architectural detail for craftsmen to follow. The number of new titles published increased from 88 during the 1850s to 192 during the 1880s.[1] Further, there was a major expansion in design services available, as house plan books began to offer sets of plans for sale by mail. The pattern books published by Bicknell & Comstock; Palliser, Palliser & Company; R. W. Shoppell's Co-operative Building Plan Association, and George F. Barber were particularly successful. All four sold plans to go with their designs.

It was during this era that a formal education in architecture first became possible in the New World. The first architecture program was begun at the Massachusetts Institute of Technology in 1865. Others followed in rapid succession, and by 1898 there were programs at Columbia, Cornell, Syracuse, Illinois, and Pennsylvania Universities, Harvard, and Notre Dame, among others.[2] These formal programs were reinforced by a multitude of architecture journals. The most successful, *American Architect and Building News* (*AABN*), began in 1876. It not only featured illustrations and articles on current buildings designed by architects, it also included frequent features on architecture history, including both America's colonial heritage and its European precedents.

Victorian Houses

Most Victorian styles are loosely based on Medieval prototypes. Multi-textured or multicolored walls, strongly asymmetrical facades, and steeply pitched roofs are common features. Little attempt is made, however, at historically precise detailing. Instead, stylistic details are freely adapted from both Medieval and Classical precedents. These exuberant mixtures of detailing, superimposed on generally Medieval forms, mean that most Victorian styles tend to overlap one another without the clear-cut stylistic distinctions that separate the Greek, Gothic, and Italianate modes of the preceding Romantic era. This architectural experimentation continued beyond Victorian times and reached a climax in the early decades of the 20th century when the first truly modern styles—Craftsman and Prairie—rose to popularity.

A second trend that was to end the Victorian era turned toward more precise copies of earlier styles, especially those of colonial America. This movement began with the Centennial celebration of 1876 and was greatly aided by the architecture history articles and illustrations in the *AABN*. It picked up momentum throughout the 1880s and 1890s and became dominant in the 20th century. Its influence is evident in the borrowed Georgian and Federal details seen in many late Victorian houses built in the Shingle and Queen Anne styles.

1860–1900

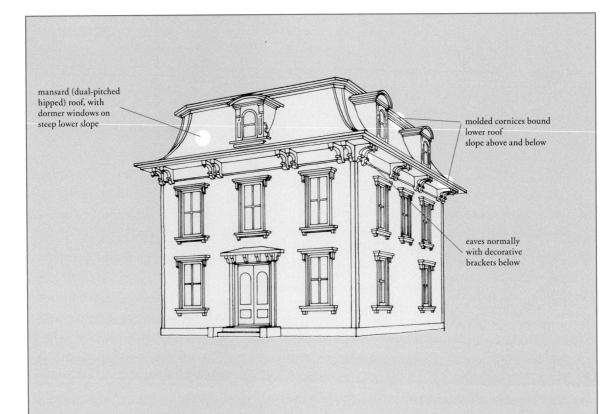

mansard (dual-pitched hipped) roof, with dormer windows on steep lower slope

molded cornices bound lower roof slope above and below

eaves normally with decorative brackets below

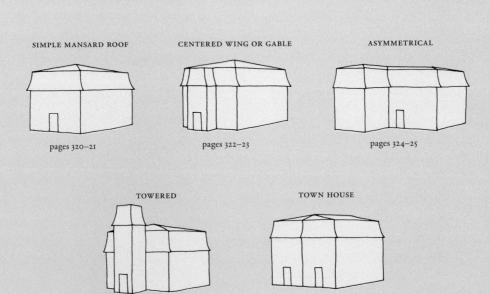

SIMPLE MANSARD ROOF

pages 320–21

CENTERED WING OR GABLE

pages 322–23

ASYMMETRICAL

pages 324–25

TOWERED

pages 326–27

TOWN HOUSE

pages 328–29

PRINCIPAL SUBTYPES

Second Empire

1855–1885

Identifying Features

Mansard (dual-pitched hipped) roof with dormer windows on steep lower slope; molded cornices normally bound the lower roof slope both above and below; decorative brackets usually present beneath eaves.

Principal Subtypes

Five principal subtypes can be distinguished:

SIMPLE MANSARD ROOF—These are symmetrical, either square or rectangular houses with the mansard roof uninterrupted except by dormers. Facade openings are typically three-ranked, less commonly five-ranked, and rarely two- or four-ranked. A few examples have central cupolas. This subtype makes up about 20 percent of Second Empire houses.

CENTERED WING OR GABLE—These are similar to the type just described but have either a centered gable, which usually echoes the mansard silhouette, or a mansard-roofed extension or wing centered on the front wall. About 20 percent of Second Empire houses in America are of this type.

ASYMMETRICAL—These are compound-plan houses, usually L-shaped, which lack towers. The forward-facing portion of the L may be either a full wing or merely a single strongly projecting bay window. About 20 percent of Second Empire houses are of this type.

TOWERED—About 30 percent of Second Empire houses have a rectangular or square tower. Sometimes it occupies the position where the wing joins the principal section of an L-plan house, but it is more commonly centered on the front facade. Occasionally it is placed off-center on the front or side facades. Typically the tower has a mansard roof with small dormer windows in each side.

TOWN HOUSE—Second Empire styling, along with the related Italianate style, dominated urban housing in the decades between 1860 and 1880. The mansard roof was particularly adapted to town houses, for it provided an upper floor behind the steep roof line, and thus made the structure appear less massive than most other styles with comparable interior space.

Variants and Details

The style is characterized principally by its distinctive roof; five principal mansard silhouettes occur. Decorative patterns formed by different colors or shapes of roofing material are common, as is iron cresting above the upper cornice. Slate is a common roofing material. If a tower is present, it may have a roof silhouette different from that of the main house; the convex and ogee (S-curve) shapes, in particular, are more common on towers than on houses. Dormers and dormer windows appear in a great variety of styles. Beneath the distinctive roof line, Second Empire houses commonly have details that are similar to those of the closely related Italianate style. Many show Italianate brackets at the cornice line; note, however, that Second Empire houses normally have less eave overhang than do Italianate examples. Window, door, and porch details are similar to those used in the Italianate style, as are the varied porch locations (see the drawings of those details in the Italianate chapter). Unelaborated windows, usually arched above, are also common on Second Empire houses, but are rare in Italianate examples.

Occurrence

Second Empire was a dominant style for American houses constructed between 1860 and 1880, although the first examples were built in the 1850s and late examples were not uncommon in the 1880s. During the decade of the 1870s it was perhaps the most fashionable and widely built house style.[3] The style was most popular in the northeastern and midwestern states. It is less common on the Pacific Coast and relatively rare in the southern states, although scattered examples survive in all regions settled before 1880.

Comments

The contemporaneous Italianate and Gothic Revival styles were part of a Picturesque movement which looked to the romantic past for inspiration. In contrast, the Second Empire style was considered very modern, for it imitated the latest French building fashions. The distinctive roof was named for the 17th-century French architect François Mansart. Its use was extensively revived in France during the reign of Napoleon III (1852–1870), France's Second Empire, from which the style takes its name. Exhibitions in Paris in 1855 and 1867 helped to popularize the style in England, from whence it spread to the United States. The first American pattern book examples of Second Empire were found in Calvert Vaux's *Villas and Cottages* (1857), which featured three Second Empire designs. Two important public buildings followed, both designs of James Renwick Jr.—Charity Hospital in New York City (begun in 1858) and Corcoran Art Gallery in Washington, D.C. (begun in 1859). For the next twenty years almost every American house pattern book published had at least one or two Second Empire designs.[4] The boxy roof line was considered particularly functional because it permitted a full upper

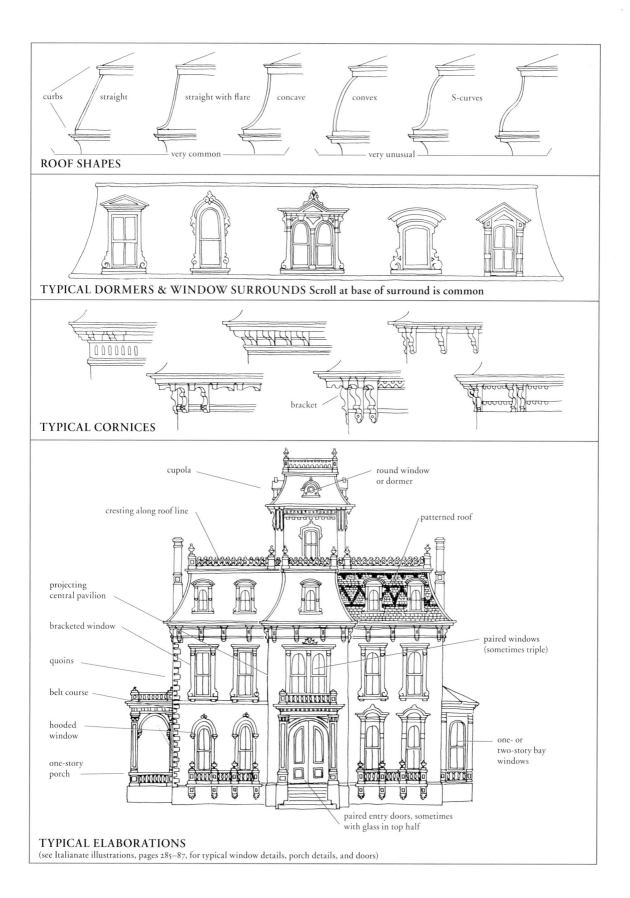

ROOF SHAPES

curbs — straight — straight with flare — concave — convex — S-curves

very common — very unusual

TYPICAL DORMERS & WINDOW SURROUNDS Scroll at base of surround is common

TYPICAL CORNICES

bracket

TYPICAL ELABORATIONS

cupola

round window or dormer

cresting along roof line

patterned roof

projecting central pavilion

bracketed window

paired windows (sometimes triple)

quoins

belt course

hooded window

one-story porch

one- or two-story bay windows

paired entry doors, sometimes with glass in top half

(see Italianate illustrations, pages 285–87, for typical window details, porch details, and doors)

SIMPLE MANSARD ROOF

1. Union Springs, Alabama; mid-19th century. The brackets above the central dormer and under the molded cornice at the roof top are an unusual feature.

2. Peru, Indiana; 1865–1870. Kilgore House. This small example has unusually elaborate detailing. Note the rusticated stone basement facade.

3. Cambridge, Massachusetts; 1860.

4. Cambridge, Massachusetts; 1864. Charles Wellington, builder. This example has paired first-story windows, plus matching entry and side porches.

5. Virginia City, Nevada; ca. 1860s. Savage Mining Company. Often referred to as a "mansion," in fact this large residential-looking building was an office on the first floor with related living quarters on the two upper floors.

6. St. Louis, Missouri; mid-19th century. Kayser House. An unusual stone facade.

7. Baltimore, Maryland; 1845. In 1868 architect Edmund G. Lind updated a three-story brick house with a fourth floor and a fashionable mansard roof.

2

3

5

6

CENTERED WING OR GABLE

1. Hallettsville, Texas; ca. 1880. Lay House. Note the patterned roof shingles and the metal cresting at the roof line.

2. Port Townsend, Washington; 1883. Bartlett House. This example has side wings rather than the more typical centered one.

3. Cambridge, Massachusetts; 1863. Note how the shape of the centered gable echoes the mansard roof line.

4. Fredonia, New York; ca. 1857. Pringle House. A small, earlier porch was replaced in 1929 by the one shown.

5. Savannah, Georgia; 1873. Hamilton House; J. D. Hall, architect. Note the quoins and the slender, paired windows.

6. Southport, Connecticut; mid-19th century. Pomeroy House. The paired windows in the dormers are an unusual feature.

7. St. Paul, Minnesota; 1872. Ramsey House; Monroe Sheire, architect. The hooded windows here and in Figure 4 show the strong Italianate detailing often seen in this style.

1

3

5

2

4

6

7

ASYMMETRICAL

1. Meriden, Connecticut; 1879. Renton House. In this example and in Figure 3, forward-facing wings create the asymmetrical facade.

2. Corning, New York; mid-19th century. In this example, two-story bay windows create an asymmetrical facade.

3. Denver, Colorado; 1885. Knight House.

4. Fort Smith, Arkansas; mid-19th century. Here and in Figure 7 a forward-facing wing is combined with a two-story bay window to create asymmetry.

5. Austin, Texas; 1886. John Bremond House; John Fiegal, architect. The architect's New Orleans background shows in the exquisite decorative ironwork on the wrap-around porches.

6. Cleveland, Ohio; mid-19th century. Roche House. Note the strongly hooded windows borrowed from the contemporary Italianate style.

7. Portland, Oregon; ca. 1870. Failing House. An elaborately detailed example with two principal facades, one with a porte-cochere and the other with a partial porch and two-story bay window.

1

3

6

2

4

5

7

TOWERED

1. Salem, Virginia; 1882. Evans House. Figures 1, 4, and 7 show symmetrical examples with a central tower. Note the contrasting shapes of the tower roof and main roof in this example.

2. Raleigh, North Carolina; ca. 1875. Heck House. Figures 2, 3, 5, and 8 show examples with a tower embraced between two wings of the house. Note the concave tower roof and the convex main roof in this example.

3. Rhinebeck, New York; mid-19th century. Wager House. Note window surrounds similar to one of the typical dormers illustrated. First-story windows are triple-hung.

4. Auburn, Maine; ca. 1880. Jordan House; Charles A. Jordan, architect-builder. Note the arcaded front porch, also seen in Figure 8.

5. Indianapolis, Indiana; 1862. Morris House; Diedrich A. Bohlen, architect. Note the differing window designs in the four-and-one-half-story tower, as well as the absence of the elaborate window surrounds commonly seen in the style.

6. Des Moines, Iowa; 1869. Terrace Hill; William W. Boyington, architect. An extremely large and elaborately detailed example with two towers. This is now the Iowa Governor's Mansion.

7. Omaha, Nebraska; 1886. Cornish House. Note the projecting bays on each side of the centered tower.

8. Woodbury, New Jersey; mid-19th century. Green House. The mansard roof of this house shows the rare S-curve shape. Note the extensive metal cresting on the roof line. Similar cresting, once present in many examples, has usually deteriorated and been removed. Note also the unusual cupola atop the tower.

1

4

7

2

3

5

6

8

1

2

3

5

TOWN HOUSE

1. Richmond, Virginia; mid-19th century. A detached urban example with a full-width porch.

2. St. Louis, Missouri; mid-19th century.

3. St. Louis, Missouri; mid-19th century. A row showing three different interpretations of the Second Empire detached town house. The roof on the center example may have been modified.

4. Washington, District of Columbia; mid-19th century. A row of three attached town houses.

5. Richmond, Virginia; mid-19th century. Note the slightly projecting entrance wing and side-facing bay window, an unusual feature in town houses.

6. New Haven, Connecticut; ca. 1871. A row of four attached town houses. Originally all matching, they have been somewhat modified by later alterations. The doorways, window hoods, and dormers are all heavily carved.

4

6

story of usable living area or attic space. For this reason the style became popular for the remodeling of earlier buildings as well as for new construction. The Second Empire style was used for many public buildings in America during the Grant administration (1869–1877) and has been facetiously called the General Grant style. It rapidly passed from fashion following the panic of 1873 and the subsequent economic depression.

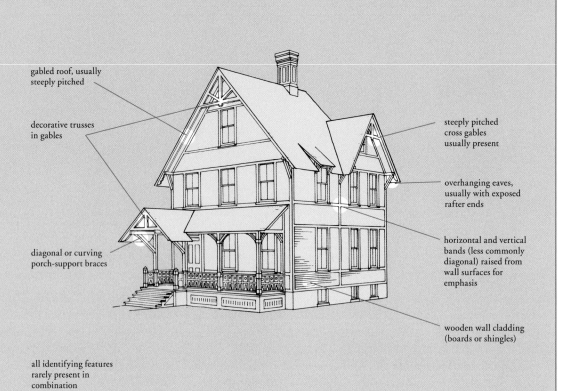

gabled roof, usually
steeply pitched

decorative trusses
in gables

steeply pitched
cross gables
usually present

overhanging eaves,
usually with exposed
rafter ends

diagonal or curving
porch-support braces

horizontal and vertical
bands (less commonly
diagonal) raised from
wall surfaces for
emphasis

wooden wall cladding
(boards or shingles)

all identifying features
rarely present in
combination

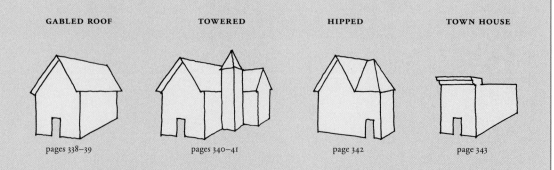

GABLED ROOF	TOWERED	HIPPED	TOWN HOUSE
pages 338–39	pages 340–41	page 342	page 343

PRINCIPAL SUBTYPES

Stick

1860–ca. 1890

Identifying Features

One or more front-facing roof gables on steeply pitched roof; gables commonly show decorative trusses at apex; overhanging eaves, usually with exposed rafter ends (normally replaced by brackets in town houses); wooden wall cladding interrupted by patterns of horizontal, vertical, or diagonal boards (stickwork) raised from wall surface for emphasis; porches commonly show diagonal or curved braces. (Few houses have all of these features in combination.)

Principal Subtypes

Four principal subtypes occur:

GABLED ROOF—This subtype includes the broad range of gabled variations that occur in the Stick: roofs may be either side-, front-, cross-, or multi-gabled; roof pitch varies from high to low; secondary cross gables are common. This subtype is the most common (except in northern California).

TOWERED—Houses in this subtype are generally similar to the gabled-roof subtype above, but with the addition of a square or rectangular tower.

HIPPED—Houses in this subtype have hipped roofs, usually steeply pitched and occasionally even mansard. They are often symmetrical. Late examples may have a hipped roof with asymmetrical lower cross gables, a form that is most characteristic of the succeeding Queen Anne style. In the Pacific Northwest, a hipped-roof house sometimes has a box-bay with vertical stickwork (as seen on San Francisco town houses) as a primary identifying feature.

TOWN HOUSE—This subtype is comprised of flat-roofed urban houses commonly found in San Francisco. Most have box-bay windows with vertical stickwork that terminates in cornice-line brackets. There is sometimes a false-gable roof over the bay, towers also occur. See pages 335 and 337.

Occurrence

Although pattern books of the day show many examples of the Stick style, the contemporaneous Italianate and Second Empire styles are more common. It is likely that deterioration and removal of the characteristic stickwork wall patterns—and loss of other detailing—has obscured many examples. Houses on the East Coast survive principally in the northeastern states and date from the 1860s and 1870s. The style was promoted as being appropriate for suburban locations and for summer cottages; it is frequently found in resort towns and was rarely built in urban locations.

Surviving town houses are concentrated in San Francisco, where rapid growth and an abundance of lumber favored wooden urban houses. The Stick tradition developed its own distinctive urban idiom in San Francisco, where it did not peak until the 1880s, after the style was passing from fashion in the Northeast.

Variants and Details

The style is defined primarily by decorative detailing—the characteristic roof trusses and multi-textured wall surfaces whose stickwork faintly mimics the exposed structural members of Medieval half-timbered houses. Varied patterns of wood siding and shingles were applied in the square and triangular spaces created by the raised stickwork. This fairly simple palette of details was applied to a variety of mid-19th-century house shapes; most show one-story porches, either entry- or full-width. Where dual-level porches occur, they can be visually dramatic. Towers are typically squared or rectangular, not rounded or polygonal as is more typical of Queen Anne, Romanesque, and Shingle houses. Some high-style houses are constructed of brick, and while these may incorporate stickwork infilled with brick, similar picturesque detail was often created by the pattern or color of the brickwork.

West Coast Stick (ca. 1880–ca. 1895)

It is hard to recognize West Coast Stick–style houses simply from knowledge of their eastern counterparts. Stick houses in northern California have their own unique set of identifying features. Most prominent is an almost universal square-sided bay window (box-bay), which was probably simpler to construct than its slant-sided Italianate predecessor.

Decorative cornice-line brackets align with the side framing of the box-bay windows, and these two elements are connected with vertical strips of trim. In addition, cornice-line brackets usually line up with the corners of the house and long vertical strips extend from these down the corner boards.

Commonly, the rectangular areas above and below the windows are also filled with ornament (such as panels), and the box-bay window ensemble thus forms a continuous decorative element from window base to cornice line. A characteristic pattern of short verticals is sometimes found beneath the cornice.

The box-bay window often has a false-gabled roof above it, and upper-story window-

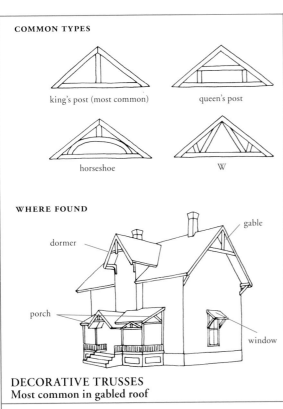

COMMON TYPES

king's post (most common)

queen's post

horseshoe

W

WHERE FOUND

dormer

gable

porch

window

DECORATIVE TRUSSES
Most common in gabled roof

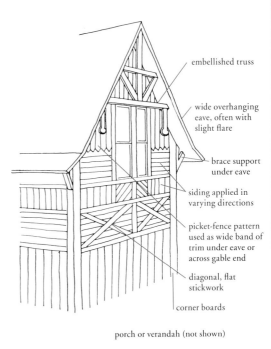

embellished truss

wide overhanging
eave, often with
slight flare

brace support
under eave

siding applied in
varying directions

picket-fence pattern
used as wide band of
trim under eave or
across gable end

diagonal, flat
stickwork

corner boards

porch or verandah (not shown)

GABLED ROOF ELABORATIONS

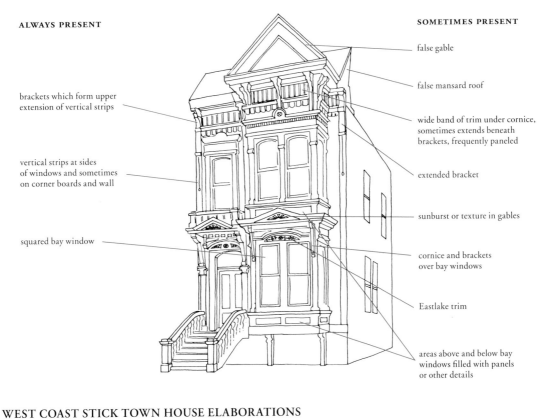

ALWAYS PRESENT

SOMETIMES PRESENT

false gable

false mansard roof

brackets which form upper
extension of vertical strips

wide band of trim under cornice,
sometimes extends beneath
brackets, frequently paneled

extended bracket

vertical strips at sides
of windows and sometimes
on corner boards and wall

sunburst or texture in gables

cornice and brackets
over bay windows

squared bay window

Eastlake trim

areas above and below bay
windows filled with panels
or other details

WEST COAST STICK TOWN HOUSE ELABORATIONS

panes are likely to have flat tops rather than the slight arch often found in Italianate designs.

In contrast to the fairly simple palette of details in the rest of the country, San Francisco examples of Stick town houses offer a plethora of factory-produced decorative architectural detailing. During the 19th century many houses in northern California and the Pacific Coast were built of redwood. This remarkable wood is resistant to rot, termites, and many of the other ills that affect wooden houses—and a ready supply was available in the vast redwood forests of the northern California coast. These qualities have allowed elaborate redwood details to survive relatively unscathed up to the present day. Automatic lathes and milling machines made possible the inexpensive mass production of details such as turned spindles and incised floral designs that previously would have required time-consuming handcrafting. This detailing, often called Eastlake, is also found on furniture. In addition to the dry woods being mechanically shaped, redwood was sometimes soaked, and incised designs were simply stamped into it.[5]

Comments

The Stick is a transitional style that links the preceding Gothic Revival with the subsequent Queen Anne; all three styles are free adaptations of Medieval English building traditions. Unlike early Gothic Revival houses, the Stick style stressed the wall surface *itself* as a decorative element rather than merely as a plane with the principal decorative detailing applied at the doors, windows, or cornices. The emphasis on patterned wood walls seen in the Stick style was developed further still in the succeeding Queen Anne style.

The Stick style grew from the Picturesque Gothic ideals of Andrew Jackson Downing (see Comments, pages 270 and 280) and flourished in house pattern books of the 1860s and 1870s.[6] Downing's earliest pattern book examples were Swiss Chalets. Richard Morris Hunt, the first American architect to design Stick-style houses, had studied extensively in Europe, where the Picturesque movement was inspired by timber-built houses throughout northern Europe—particularly those in France, England, Switzerland, and Germany, where architecture periodicals in the 1850s were promoting these Picturesque models for new houses.[7] Hunt's first fully developed Stick example was the Griswold House in Newport, Rhode Island (1861–1863).

Although its proponents lauded the structural honesty of the style, the visible stickwork (unlike true half-timbering) was merely applied decoration bearing no structural relation to the underlying balloon-frame construction. During the era in which it was built, the term "Stick" was not used.[8]

Differentiating Italianate and Stick Styles in Northern California

In northern California, and occasionally elsewhere along the Pacific Coast, both Italianate and Stick houses have decorative brackets along the cornice line. These brackets, a principal identifying feature for Italianate designs in the rest of the country, are not sufficient to distinguish Italianate from Stick style in this region.

To further complicate matters, the Stick style in northern California (often called West Coast Stick) generally looks quite different from its appearance in the rest of the United States.

Bay windows in two distinctive shapes become a primary distinguishing feature between Italianate and Stick designs. Elaborate box-bay windows are a principal identifying feature for Stick-style houses, while slanted-side bay windows are a principal identifying feature for Italianate houses. In addition, in West Coast Stick, the brackets commonly have long, vertical extensions down the facade. The illustrations above summarize these differences.

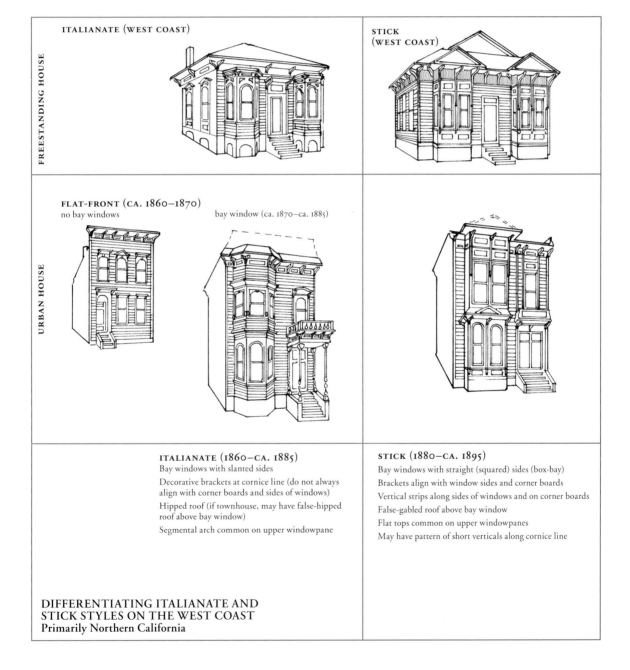

ITALIANATE (WEST COAST)

STICK (WEST COAST)

FREESTANDING HOUSE

FLAT-FRONT (CA. 1860–1870)
no bay windows

bay window (ca. 1870–ca. 1885)

URBAN HOUSE

ITALIANATE (1860–CA. 1885)
Bay windows with slanted sides

Decorative brackets at cornice line (do not always align with corner boards and sides of windows)

Hipped roof (if townhouse, may have false-hipped roof above bay window)

Segmental arch common on upper windowpane

STICK (1880–CA. 1895)
Bay windows with straight (squared) sides (box-bay)

Brackets align with window sides and corner boards

Vertical strips along sides of windows and on corner boards

False-gabled roof above bay window

Flat tops common on upper windowpanes

May have pattern of short verticals along cornice line

DIFFERENTIATING ITALIANATE AND STICK STYLES ON THE WEST COAST
Primarily Northern California

GABLED ROOF

1. New Bedford, Massachusetts; 1870. Smith House. The gable end has vertical, horizontal, and diagonal stickwork.

2. Hartford, Connecticut; late 19th century. A very simple example with stick detailing only in the trussed gables and porch.

3. Salem, Oregon; 1887. Collins House. This West Coast Stick–style house has a deep vertical frieze under the eaves. Note the squared box-bay window and squared porch supports.

4. Honeoye Falls, New York; ca. 1875. Note the trusses supporting small roofs over the first-floor windows and the trussed balcony in the gable.

5. Bismarck, North Dakota; 1884. Former Governor's Mansion.

6. Cambridge, Massachusetts; 1878. The cut-away bay windows are precursors of a popular Queen Anne feature. The stickwork is confined to bands below the windows. Additional stickwork may well have originally been present on this and all other examples; such applied ornamentation is quite susceptible to deterioration and was commonly removed entirely rather than repaired or replaced.

7. Newport, Rhode Island; 1863. Griswold House; Richard Morris Hunt, architect. A well-preserved landmark example; all the style's identifying features are present.

1

4

6

TOWERED

1. Rochester, New York; late 19th century. The picket-fence pattern is used as trim under the eave line and across the gable end.

2. Stony Creek, Connecticut; 1878. Villa Vista; Henry Austin, architect. Note the unusual two-tiered porch and the elaborate curving porch supports and decorative trussing.

3. Fergus Falls, Minnesota; 1882. Clement House. Here the picket-fence pattern is used as frieze below the porch roof and below the tower eave.

4. Richfield Springs, New York; late 19th century. Hinds House. Note the very high pitch of the tower roof. Square towers are typical of Stick houses, whereas round towers are most common in the related Queen Anne style.

5. San Diego, California; 1887. Sherman House; Comstock and Trotsche, architects.

6. Hartford, Connecticut; 1873. Mark Twain House; Edward Tuckerman Potter, architect. This is a high-style brick example where the pattern and colors of the brickwork are substituted for applied Stick ornament.

7. Oakland, California; 1884. Cohen-Bray House. The cutaway bay window is transitional to the Queen Anne style.

1

4

6

2

3

5

7

HIPPED ROOF

1. Portland, Oregon; late 19th century. Welty House.
   An example with vertical wood cladding in the gable,
   horizontal cladding on the main wall surfaces, and
   diagonal cladding below the first-story windows.

2. Columbus, Texas; 1860 and 1890s. Seftenberg-Brandon
   House. A one-story Greek Revival house completely
   updated with a second story and full-width Stick-style
   porches that wrap around one side.

3. Wichita, Kansas; ca. 1878. Miller House. An example
   that is transitional from the Stick to the Queen Anne.
   The hipped roof has cross gables and the diagonal porch
   supports are turned spindles.

4. Yankton, South Dakota; 1886. Cramer-Kenyon Heritage
   Home.

5. Benicia, California; ca. 1890. This California house has
   low roof pitch and dominantly vertical stickwork.

TOWN HOUSE

1. San Francisco, California; late 19th century. A double house (two identical attached houses).

2. San Francisco, California; late 19th century. Westerfeld House. An unusual example of a narrow town house with a massive tower.

3. San Francisco, California; late 19th century.

1

3

2

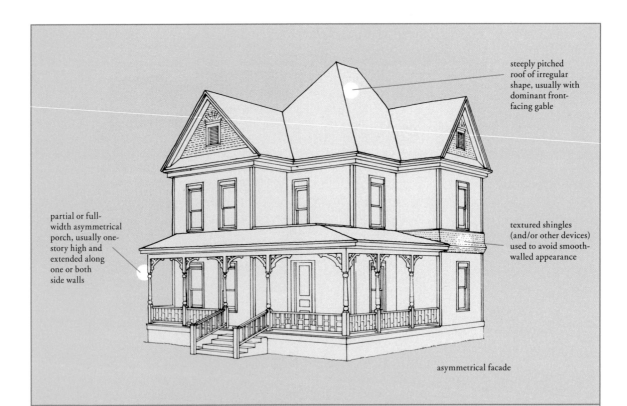

steeply pitched
roof of irregular
shape, usually with
dominant front-
facing gable

partial or full-
width asymmetrical
porch, usually one-
story high and
extended along
one or both
side walls

textured shingles
(and/or other devices)
used to avoid smooth-
walled appearance

asymmetrical facade

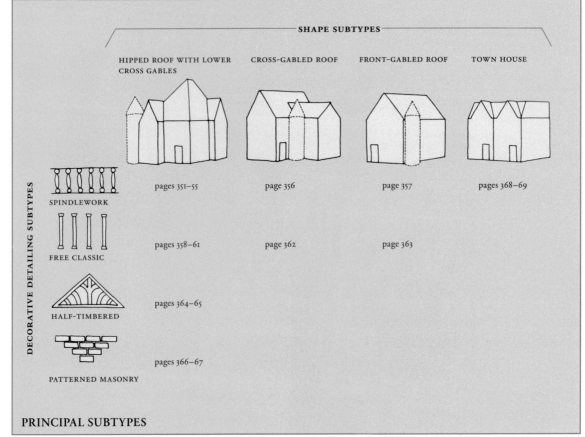

SHAPE SUBTYPES

HIPPED ROOF WITH LOWER
CROSS GABLES

CROSS-GABLED ROOF

FRONT-GABLED ROOF

TOWN HOUSE

DECORATIVE DETAILING SUBTYPES

SPINDLEWORK

FREE CLASSIC

HALF-TIMBERED

PATTERNED MASONRY

pages 351–55

page 356

page 357

pages 368–69

pages 358–61

page 362

page 363

pages 364–65

pages 366–67

PRINCIPAL SUBTYPES

Queen Anne

1880–1910

Identifying Features

Steeply pitched roof of irregular shape, usually with a dominant front-facing gable; patterned shingles, cutaway bay windows, and other devices used to avoid a smooth-walled appearance; asymmetrical facade with partial or full-width porch which is usually one story high and extended along one or both side walls.

Principal Subtypes

Queen Anne houses are most conveniently subdivided into two sets of overlapping subtypes. The first is based on characteristic variations in *shape;* the second on distinctive patterns of *decorative detailing.*

Shape Subtypes

Four principal shape subtypes can be distinguished:

HIPPED ROOF WITH LOWER CROSS GABLES—Over half of all Queen Anne houses have a steeply hipped roof with one or more lower cross gables. Most commonly there are two cross gables, one front-facing and one side-facing, both asymmetrically placed on their respective facades. Unlike most hipped roofs, in which the ridge runs parallel to the front facade, Queen Anne hipped ridges sometimes run front-to-back, parallel to the side of the house. Others have pyramidal roofs with no ridge or merely a small flat deck crowning the hip. The hipped portion of the roof may have a gable-on-hip added; dormers and additional gables are common. A tower, when present, is most commonly placed at one corner of the front facade. The roof form of this subtype is among the most distinctive Queen Anne characteristics and occurs in examples ranging from modest cottages to high-style landmarks.

CROSS-GABLED ROOF—About 20 percent of Queen Anne houses have simple cross-gabled roofs without a central, hipped unit. These are normally of L-shaped plan; a tower, when present, is usually embraced within the L.

FRONT-GABLED ROOF—About 20 percent of Queen Anne houses have a full-width front gable which dominates the front facade. This form occurs most frequently in detached urban houses. A tower, when present, is usually placed at one corner of the front facade.

TOWN HOUSE—Detached Queen Anne urban houses usually have front-gabled roofs (as in the type just described). Attached row houses are uncommon but occur in both gabled and flat-roofed forms. Each attached unit may be individually distinguishable on the facade or may be part of a larger facade design.

Decorative Detailing Subtypes

Four principal subtypes can be distinguished on the basis of decorative detailing:

SPINDLEWORK—About 50 percent of Queen Anne houses have delicate turned porch supports and spindlework ornamentation made possible by machine lathes. This most commonly occurs in porch balustrades or as a frieze suspended from the porch ceiling. Spindlework detailing is also used in gables and under the wall overhangs left by cutaway bay windows. Lacy, decorative spandrels and knob-like beads are also common ornamental elements in this subtype as is incised decorative detail. Spindlework detailing is sometimes referred to as gingerbread ornamentation, or as Eastlake detailing (after Charles Eastlake, an English furniture designer who advocated somewhat similar design elements).

FREE CLASSIC—About 35 percent of Queen Anne houses use classical columns, rather than delicate turned posts with spindlework detailing, as porch supports. These columns may be either the full height of the porch or raised on a pedestal to the level of the porch railing; the railings normally lack the delicate, turned balusters of the spindlework type of Queen Anne house. Porch-support columns are commonly grouped together in units of two or three. Palladian windows, cornice-line dentils, swags and garlands and other classical details are frequent. This subtype became common after 1890 and has much in common with some early (asymmetrical) Colonial Revival houses (see pages 414–15).

HALF-TIMBERED—About 5 percent of Queen Anne houses have decorative half-timbering in gables or upper-story walls. Porch supports in this subtype are usually heavy turned posts with solid spandrels. Groupings of three or more windows are a common characteristic. This subtype occurs principally in the northeastern states and shares certain features with the early Tudor house (see pages 450–52; 456–59).

PATTERNED MASONRY—About 5 percent of Queen Anne houses have masonry walls with patterned brickwork or stonework and relatively little wooden detailing. Terracotta and stone decorative panels are frequently inset into the walls. Gable dormers, sometimes parapeted and shaped, are frequent. Examples of this subtype are usually

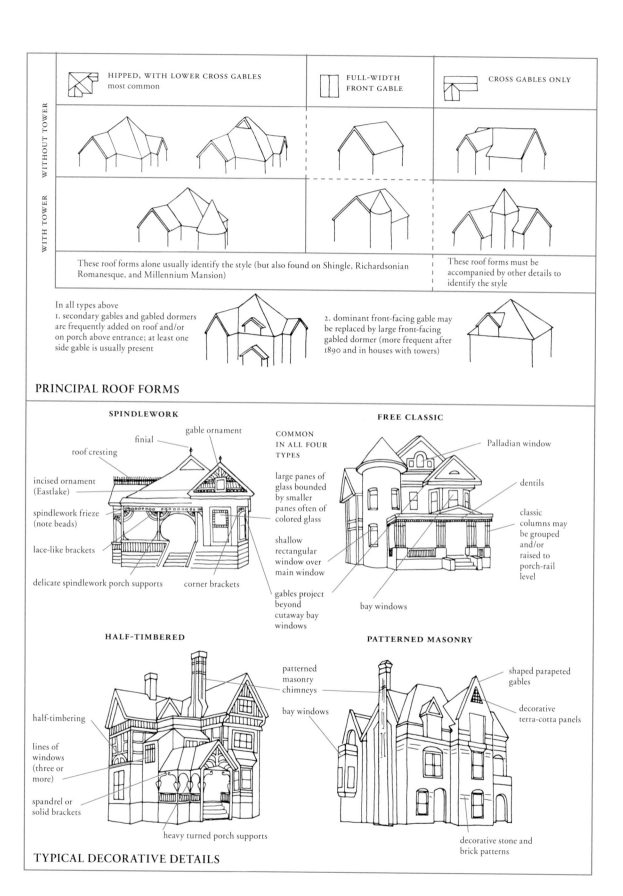

	HIPPED, WITH LOWER CROSS GABLES most common	FULL-WIDTH FRONT GABLE	CROSS GABLES ONLY
WITHOUT TOWER			
WITH TOWER			

These roof forms alone usually identify the style (but also found on Shingle, Richardsonian Romanesque, and Millennium Mansion)

These roof forms must be accompanied by other details to identify the style

In all types above
1. secondary gables and gabled dormers are frequently added on roof and/or on porch above entrance; at least one side gable is usually present

2. dominant front-facing gable may be replaced by large front-facing gabled dormer (more frequent after 1890 and in houses with towers)

PRINCIPAL ROOF FORMS

SPINDLEWORK

- finial
- gable ornament
- roof cresting
- incised ornament (Eastlake)
- spindlework frieze (note beads)
- lace-like brackets
- delicate spindlework porch supports
- corner brackets

COMMON IN ALL FOUR TYPES

large panes of glass bounded by smaller panes often of colored glass

shallow rectangular window over main window

gables project beyond cutaway bay windows

FREE CLASSIC

- Palladian window
- dentils
- classic columns may be grouped and/or raised to porch-rail level
- bay windows

HALF-TIMBERED

- half-timbering
- lines of windows (three or more)
- spandrel or solid brackets
- heavy turned porch supports
- patterned masonry chimneys
- bay windows

PATTERNED MASONRY

- shaped parapeted gables
- decorative terra-cotta panels
- decorative stone and brick patterns

TYPICAL DECORATIVE DETAILS

high-style architect-designed houses which exhibit a wide variation in shape and detail or are attached row houses. Most were built in large cities, particularly New York, Chicago, and Washington, D.C.; few have escaped subsequent demolition.

Variants and Details

The Queen Anne, like the Stick style, uses wall surfaces as primary decorative elements. This is accomplished in two ways: (1) by avoiding plain flat walls through such devices as bays, towers, overhangs, and wall projections, and (2) by using several wall materials of differing textures wherever expanses of planar wall do occur.

DEVICES FOR AVOIDING FLAT WALL SURFACES—Irregularities in ground plan were facilitated by the widespread adoption of balloon framing techniques in the late 19th century (see pages 38–40). Queen Anne houses make full use of this freedom by incorporating frequent bay windows and towers, as well as through the use of wall insets or projections which provide random changes in the horizontal continuity of the wall plane. Other devices are used to avoid planar walls in *elevation*—that is, to provide a similar discontinuity of the wall plane *vertically;* these devices usually mimic the Medieval use of overhanging gables and upper stories. Particularly characteristic features are roof gables that overhang bay windows shaped into the wall below (cutaway bay windows). These occur in over half of all Queen Anne houses. In high-style examples entire gables or second stories are sometimes cantilevered out beyond the plane of the walls below. Many modest examples have less elaborate false overhangs; these are formed from moldings or pent roofs applied directly to the flat wall surfaces.

WALL TEXTURE VARIATIONS—Differing wall textures are a hallmark of Queen Anne houses. These are most commonly achieved with patterned wood shingles shaped into varying designs (note that this original shinglework patterning has been replaced by other materials on many surviving examples). In masonry houses, texture is obtained by using differing patterns of brick courses or brick of different colors. Other materials also provide texture, including terra-cotta panels molded into a wide variety of low-relief designs. Contrasting materials are also commonly used on the different stories of Queen Anne houses (shingle over clapboard or over brick is most common).

PORCHES—Extensive one-story porches are common and accentuate the asymmetry of the facade. These always include the front entrance area and cover part or all of the front facade; they also commonly extend along one or both sides of the house. Second-story porches may be present; recessed porches sometimes occur in gables, second stories, or towers.

TOWERS—Towers are a common Queen Anne feature and may be round, square, or polygonal (the square form is the least common). These are of varying height and may rise from ground level, be cantilevered out at the second floor, or show other variations in position. In later examples the tower may appear to be less a separate design element than a mere bulge growing from the main mass of the house (see also the Shingle style, page 9). Round or polygonal wooden towers are particularly characteristic of the Queen Anne (round masonry towers may be Richardsonian Romanesque; square towers are

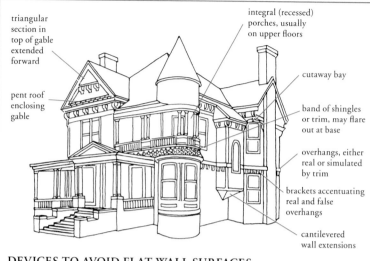

triangular section in top of gable extended forward

pent roof enclosing gable

integral (recessed) porches, usually on upper floors

cutaway bay

band of shingles or trim, may flare out at base

overhangs, either real or simulated by trim

brackets accentuating real and false overhangs

cantilevered wall extensions

DEVICES TO AVOID FLAT WALL SURFACES

PLACEMENT

wrap-around	full	partial	entry only	none
40%	15%	20%	20%	5%

TYPICAL EMBELLISHMENTS

pediment at entry	second-story porch over entry	full double deck	turret on porch	*more common in Gulf Coast and Texas
45%	20%	5%*	5%	

PORCHES

ca. 1885	ca. 1895	post-1905

TYPICAL ROOF-PITCH CHRONOLOGY

WOOD SHINGLES

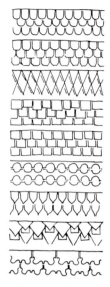

These and numerous other variations may be used either singly or in combination; shingle patterns are most frequent in gables and in horizontal bands between floors, but may occur anywhere.

BRICK

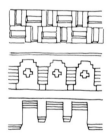

These and other patterns of brick texture and color are found in chimneys and in masonry walls.

TYPICAL WALL-TEXTURE PATTERNS

usually found in spindlework and free classic

wood shingle (most common)

usually found in half-timbered

usually found in patterned masonry

TYPICAL GABLE DETAILING

more common on Stick, Italianate, or Second Empire houses). Towers placed at a front facade corner are most often Queen Anne, whereas those embraced within an L or centered on the front facade are equally common in several other styles.

OTHER DETAILS—Door and window surrounds tend to be simple in Queen Anne houses. Window sashes usually have only a single pane of glass; a frequent elaboration has a single large clear pane surrounded by additional small rectangular panes on one or more sides. These small panes are often of colored glass. Some later examples have curved glass in tower windows. Doors commonly have delicate incised decorative detailing and a single large pane of glass set into the upper portion. Gables are commonly decorated with patterned shingles or more elaborate motifs.

Occurrence

This was the dominant style of domestic building during the period from about 1880 until 1900; it persisted with decreasing popularity through the first decade of this century. In the heavily populated northeastern states the style is somewhat less common than elsewhere. There, except for resort areas, it is usually more restrained in decorative detailing and is more often executed in masonry. Moving southward and westward the style increases steadily in dominance and ebullience; California and the resurgent, cotton-rich states of the New South have some of the most fanciful examples.

Comments

The style was named and popularized by a group of 19th-century English architects led by Richard Norman Shaw. The name is rather inappropriate, for the historical precedents used by Shaw and his followers had little to do with Queen Anne or the formal Renaissance architecture that was dominant during her reign (1702–1714). Instead, they borrowed most heavily from the late Medieval models of the preceding Elizabethan and Jacobean eras. The half-timbered and patterned masonry American subtypes are most closely related to this work of Shaw and his colleagues in England. The spindlework and free classic subtypes are indigenous interpretations.

The half-timbered Watts Sherman House, built at Newport, Rhode Island, in 1874, is generally considered to be the first American example of the style. A few high-style examples followed in the 1870s, and by 1880 the style was being spread throughout the country by a host of pattern books (many selling plans for their illustrated designs) and by the leading architecture magazine, *American Architect and Building News* (through illustrated examples, but with faint textual praise).[9]

Despite having been introduced by architects and illustrated in *AABN,* the Queen Anne style was not widely favored by architects, who preferred the contemporaneous Shingle and experimentation with early Eclectic styles. Instead, the style owed its popularity to the public's enthusiastic embrace and the pattern books and mail-order house plans that allowed them to build a Queen Anne house. The expanding railroad network expedited this process by making pre-cut architectural details conveniently available throughout much of the nation. Hudson Holly's 1878 *Modern Dwellings in Town and Country* was likely the first pattern book specifically to promote Queen Anne style.[10] But

SPINDLEWORK: HIPPED ROOF
WITH LOWER CROSS GABLES

1. Biloxi, Mississippi; ca. 1900. A very simple example. Additional corner-bracket detailing was probably once present above the cutaway bay window, but is now missing (see the corner brackets still present on Figures 2 and 3). The low roof pitch indicates a late construction date.

2. Santa Clara, California; late 19th century. Note the gable-on-hip roof (also present in Figures 1 and 3); these were most common on one- and one-and-one-half-story examples.

3. Cripple Creek, Colorado; 1896. Miller House. This one-and-one-half-story example has unusually fine detailing.

4. Clement, North Carolina, vicinity; ca. 1912. Autry House. The symmetrical placement of the two gables is unusual, as is the steep roof pitch in such a late example.

1

2

3

4

5

6

8

9

11

SPINDLEWORK: HIPPED ROOF WITH LOWER CROSS GABLES (cont.)

5. Atlanta, Georgia; ca. 1893. Martin Luther King birthplace.

6. Greensburg, Indiana; 1885–90. Woodfill House.

7. Meriden, Connecticut; c. 1890. Cahill House. Note the second-story porch over the entrance; the central hipped roof is mostly obscured behind the front gable.

8. San Antonio, Texas; 1886. This masonry example has a two-tiered porch and unusually low-pitched gables, which hide a low-pitched hipped roof behind.

9. Union Springs, Alabama; late 19th century.

10. Waxahachie, Texas; 1893. Williams-Erwin House, based on George F. Barber's Design 56. A fine example of Barber's exuberant spindlework design. Note the four different gable treatments (on house, porch, and two dormers) and the rounded "moon gate."

11. Fleischmanns, New York; 1895. Note the integral upstairs porch beneath the principal roof line and the turreted lower porch roof.

12. Napa, California; ca. 1890. Note the variety of surface textures and elaborate detailing.

7

10

12

13

15

17

SPINDLEWORK: HIPPED ROOF WITH LOWER CROSS GABLES (cont.)

13. Lovelady, Texas; ca. 1895. Nelms House. Note the curved roof on the tower; such roofs are far less common than straight-sided examples.

14. Cambridge, Massachusetts; 1889. Note the absence of the typical front-facing gable; a hipped dormer is used here instead.

15. Santa Cruz, California; 1891. Gray House; LaBaron Oliver, architect. Note how the tower is interrupted at the first-story level by a band of shingles and at the second-story level by a band of roofing. This clearly illustrates the typical Queen Anne aversion to smooth wall surfaces. Figures 16 and 18 also show interrupted towers.

16. Union Springs, Alabama; late 19th century. Note the S-shaped curve of the tower roof.

17. Laurens, South Carolina; ca. 1896. Davis House. Note the porch-roof turret and the delicate beaded spindlework frieze extending around the entire porch.

18. San Francisco, California; 1886. Haas House. The central hipped roof is hidden by gables and tower. Note the unusually elaborate details of the wall surfaces.

19. Waxahachie, Texas; 1890. Dunlap House. Margaret Culberton's *Texas Houses: Built by the Book* documents that this was built from Design 438 in *Shoppell's Modern Houses* 2 (January 1887), 18.

14

16

18

19

SPINDLEWORK: CROSS-GABLED ROOF

1. Biloxi, Mississippi; ca. 1900. Even this small example has an ornamented and textured gable and cutaway bay window to avoid smooth wall surfaces. Compare this with page 400, Figure 1, a Folk Victorian example of similar shape.

2. Hartford, Connecticut; late 19th century.

3. New Haven, Connecticut; late 19th century.

4. Hillsboro, Texas; late 19th century. Note the wide gable overhang. The gable detailing and square tower are transitional to the closely related Stick style.

5. Orange, New Jersey; ca. 1880. Dodd House. Note the roof cresting, patterned chimney, and heavy turned porch supports. This early East Coast example resembles many houses of the half-timbered Queen Anne subtype, but lacks half-timbered detailing.

SPINDLEWORK: FRONT-GABLED ROOF

1. Chicago, Illinois; 1898.

2. New Haven, Connecticut; late 19th century.

3. Rochester, New York; late 19th century. Front-gabled forms may have shallow cross gables extending outward the width of a single door or window, as seen in this example.

4. St. Paul, Minnesota; ca. 1896. Stevens House. This early photograph shows the elaborate wall-texture detailing that was originally present on many modest houses but rarely survives today.

5. Cambridge, Massachusetts; 1886. Parry House. Note the brick first story with wood shingling above. The porch has been modified.

FREE CLASSIC: HIPPED ROOF WITH LOWER CROSS GABLES

1. Salisbury, North Carolina; late 19th century. Brown House.

2. Eutaw, Alabama; late 19th century. Note the Palladian window and recessed arch under the gable.

3. Salisbury, North Carolina; late 19th century. Gaskill House.

4. Dallas, Texas; ca. 1900. Arnold House. The shingled porch-support arches are unusual.

5. Cleveland, Ohio; late 19th century. Note the upper-story window sashes with a single central pane of glass surrounded by smaller panes.

6. Jacksonville, Oregon; 1893. Nunan House. The hipped central roof is hidden by the front gable in this photograph. Note the dominant, elaborately detailed front chimney.

7. Dallas, Texas; ca. 1885. Daron Tapscott, restoration architect. The most typical form of a "hipped roof with lower cross gables" Queen Anne house. No extras added; compare with introductory sample house, page 344. Classical porch supports could be early replacements for spindlework ones.

8. Concord, North Carolina; late 19th century.

9. Warsaw, Indiana; ca. 1894. Wood House. Note the transoms above the windows, a frequent Queen Anne feature that often had decorative beveled or colored glass glazing.

1

5

4

8

2

3

6

7

9

10

12

13

15

16

FREE CLASSIC: HIPPED ROOF WITH LOWER CROSS GABLES (cont.)

10. Union Springs, Alabama; late 19th century.

11. Dallas, Texas; ca. 1899. Wilson House.

12. Santa Clara, California; late 19th century.

13. New Haven, Connecticut; late 19th century.

14. Kirksville, Missouri; 1899. Still House. Note the shingled gable wall curving into the gable window, a motif that is more common in the Shingle style. Although of masonry, this house lacks patterning in the brick-wall surfaces. This and the classical columns differentiate it from the patterned masonry subtype. The porte cochere is a later addition, as is the ribbon of four windows under the front-facing gable. These enclose what was once a small open porch.

15. New London, Connecticut; late 19th century. Note the unusual flared eaves and the decorative frieze beneath the gable.

16. Montgomery, Alabama; late 19th century. Note the dramatically exaggerated S-curved roof of the tower.

17. Concord, North Carolina; late 19th century. Although asymmetrical, this house has a centered entry and a suggestion of classical balance; it is transitional to some early examples of the Colonial Revival style.

11

14

17

FREE CLASSIC: CROSS-GABLED ROOF

1. Cambridge, Massachusetts; 1890. J. Merrill Brown, architect. The siding and shutters are later additions.

2. Marshall, Michigan; 1884. Page House. Note the matching front and side porches with grouped columns set on pedestals. The short, broad tower is less common than more slender versions.

FREE CLASSIC: FRONT-GABLED ROOF

1. New Haven, Connecticut; late 19th century.

2. Hartford, Connecticut; late 19th century. Note the use of board siding on the first story, with shingles above, a common pattern. The two front doors indicate that this is a "two-decker" duplex with separate dwelling units on the first and second floors.

3. Denver, Colorado; 1892. Balcomb and Rice, architects. Note the elaborate Palladian window with decorative swags that recur above the second-story porch.

4. San Francisco, California; late 19th century. Many San Francisco Queen Anne houses combine classical columns with elaborate spindlework detailing used elsewhere on the facade. These closely spaced narrow urban houses are the West Coast version of Queen Anne town houses.

HALF-TIMBERED

1. Buffalo, New York; late 19th century. Note the row of multiple windows in the gable; such window rows are common only in this subtype (see also Figures 2, 4, 6, 7, and 8).

2. Chicago, Illinois; 1888. Miller House; G. A. Garnsey, architect. Shows the close relationship of this subtype to the Tudor style that grew from it. The multiple wall materials (stone, stucco, wood, and wood shingles) and many changes in wall plane mark this house as Queen Anne.

3. Brookline, Massachusetts; late 19th century; E. A. P. Newcomb, architect.

4. Hartford, Connecticut; 1884. Day House; Francis Kimball, architect. Note the light-colored limestone walls banded with brownstone.

5. Brookline, Massachusetts; ca. 1880. Toby House. Note the paneled brick chimney (see also Figures 1, 4, 6, 7, and 8); these are most common on half-timbered and patterned brick examples, although simply decorated chimney *tops* are seen in all subtypes.

6. Newport, Rhode Island; 1876. Watts-Sherman House; H. H. Richardson, architect. This is regarded as the first American Queen Anne house.

7. Newport, Rhode Island; 1878. Baldwin House; Potter and Robinson, architects.

8. Rochester, New York; ca. 1880. Cutler House.

2

3

5

6

8

PATTERNED MASONRY

1. New Haven, Connecticut; 1886. Treat House. It is hard to photograph the textured patterns in the dark red brick, typical of this subtype, in a manner that shows up well in reproduction.

2. Herkimer, New York; late 19th century. Suiter House.

3. New Haven, Connecticut; ca. 1895. Note the cornice patterns formed by the brickwork.

4. Hartford, Connecticut; late 19th century. George Keller, architect. The extensive full-width or wrap-around porches common on the spindlework and free classic subtypes are rare on patterned masonry houses; usually only an entry porch is present, as seen here.

5. Hartford, Connecticut; late 19th century. The one-story wooden projection on the right is a later addition.

6. Cincinnati, Ohio; 1882. Bell House; S. Hannaford, architect. An example with stone, rather than brick, walls. Note the shaped, parapeted gables, a rare but characteristic feature of this subtype.

7. Chicago, Illinois; ca. 1884. Wells House; Wheelock and Clay, architects. Note extensive roof cresting here and in Figure 4.

8. Rochester, New York; ca. 1883. Harvey Ellis, architect. An American copy of a design by the English proponent of the Queen Anne style Richard Norman Shaw.

1

4

7

2

3

5

6

8

TOWN HOUSE

1. Boston, Massachusetts; 1880. Note the false gable with a mansard roof behind. Sculptured terra-cotta tiles add richness to this facade.

2., 3. Savannah, Georgia; 1892. McMillan Houses. A row of attached town houses behind one unified facade. Figure 3 is a close-up detail of the patterned brickwork executed in two colors of brick.

4. Rochester, New York; 1870s. These are half-timbered examples.

5. Hartford, Connecticut; 1888.

6. Camden, New Jersey; 1886. Taylor House; Wilson Eyre, architect. A unique town house of limestone and brick with a large, shaped, parapeted gable.

7. Washington, D.C.; late 19th century. Many miles of these simplified, patterned brick row houses were built in eastern cities. Note the false gable roof; these have deteriorated and been removed from many remaining examples.

8. Cleveland, Ohio; ca. 1890.

I

4

7

2

3

5

6

8

it was soon joined by dozens of others offering Queen Anne plans, among them those of William Comstock, the Palliser brothers, Robert Shoppell, and George Barber.[11]

While the earliest American examples followed Shaw's early half-timbered designs, during the 1880s the inventive American spindlework interpretation became dominant. Throughout the 1880s and 1890s a relatively few high-style urban examples imitated Shaw's later English models, which were executed in masonry. In the decade of the 1890s, encouraged by the Classical theme of Chicago's Columbian Exposition of 1893, the free classic adaptation became widespread.[12] It was but a short step from these to the early asymmetrical Colonial Revival houses and the symmetrical Neoclassical houses, which, along with other competing styles, fully supplanted the Queen Anne style after about 1910.

irregular, steeply pitched roof line, usually with cross gables

wall cladding and roofing of continuous wood shingles

shingled walls without interruption at corners

extensive porches (may be smaller or absent in urban examples)

multi-level eaves

asymmetrical facade

HIPPED ROOF WITH CROSS GABLES

page 376

SIDE-GABLED ROOF

page 377

FRONT-GABLED ROOF

pages 378–79

CROSS-GABLED ROOF

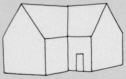

pages 380–81

GAMBREL ROOF

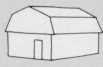

pages 382–83

PRINCIPAL SUBTYPES

Shingle

1880–ca. 1910

Identifying Features

Wall cladding and roofing of continuous wood shingles (shingled walls may occur on second story only; original wooden roofing now replaced by composition shingles on most examples); shingled walls without interruption at corners (no corner boards); asymmetrical facade with irregular, steeply pitched roof line; roofs usually have intersecting cross gables and multi-level eaves; commonly with extensive porches (may be small or absent in urban examples).

Principal Subtypes

Five principal subtypes can be distinguished:

HIPPED ROOF WITH CROSS GABLES—About 15 percent of Shingle houses have hipped roofs with lower cross gables. Asymmetrical gable arrangements, similar to the typical Queen Anne shape, are most common, but Shingle houses may also show paired, symmetrical cross gables.

SIDE-GABLED ROOF—About 20 percent of Shingle houses have side-gabled roofs; many of these have asymmetrically placed towers on the front facade.

FRONT-GABLED ROOF—About 20 percent of Shingle houses have a front gable which dominates the main facade; subordinate cross gables and towers may be added.

CROSS-GABLED ROOF—About 20 percent of Shingle houses have cross-gabled roofs; most are of L or T plan and have secondary cross gables and dormers intersecting the principal roof line. Subordinate hipped sections may also be added.

GAMBREL ROOF—About 25 percent of Shingle houses have gambrel roofs. Normally a full second story is incorporated into the steeper, lower slope of the gambrel, giving a one-story appearance. Gambreled cross gables are usually present.

Variants and Details

Unlike most of the 19th-century styles that preceded it, the Shingle does not emphasize decorative detailing at doors, windows, cornices, porches, or on wall surfaces. Instead it aims for the effect of a complex shape enclosed within a smooth surface (the shingled exterior) which unifies the irregular outline of the house. Most variants and details are designed to enhance either the irregularity of the shape or the uniformity of its surface. Decorative detailing, when present, is used sparingly. It is the first style that begins to emphasize the volumetric spaces within the house more than exterior surface details.

Towers, found in about one-third of Shingle houses, are more likely to appear as partial bulges or as half-towers rather than as fully developed elements. Tower roofs are frequently blended into the main volume of the house by a continuous roof line. Porch supports are most commonly either slender, unadorned wooden posts or massive piers of stone or shingle cladding. Window surrounds are simple; bay windows, multiple windows, and walls curving into windows are common. Massive Romanesque or Syrian arches (see page 389) may be used on porches or entrances. Palladian windows and simple classical columns, both borrowed from the contemporaneous early phases of the Colonial Revival, are the most common decorative details.

Occurrence

Most Shingle houses were built between 1880 and 1900, with a relatively few examples dating from the late 1870s and from the first decade of the 20th century. The style began and reached its highest expression in seaside resorts of the northeastern states. Fashionable summer destinations such as Newport, Cape Cod, eastern Long Island, and coastal Maine had numerous architect-designed cottages in the style, many of which survive today. From this fashionable base, well publicized in contemporary architectural magazines, the style spread throughout the country, and scattered examples can be found today in all regions. It never gained the wide popularity of its contemporary, the Queen Anne style, and thus Shingle houses are relatively uncommon except in coastal New England.

Comments

The Shingle style, like the Stick and spindlework Queen Anne, was a uniquely American adaptation of other traditions. Its roots are threefold: (1) from the Queen Anne it borrowed wide porches, shingled surfaces, and asymmetrical forms; (2) from the Colonial Revival it adapted gambrel roofs, rambling lean-to additions, classical columns, and Palladian windows; (3) from the contemporaneous Richardsonian Romanesque it borrowed an emphasis on irregular, sculpted shapes, Romanesque arches, and, in some examples, stone lower stories (some scholars consider the Shingle to be merely the wooden phase of the masonry Richardsonian Romanesque, but the styles also have many dissimilarities).

The Shingle style was an unusually free-form and variable style; without the ubiquitous shingle cladding it would be difficult to relate many of its different expressions. One reason for this great range of variation is that it remained primarily a high-fashion,

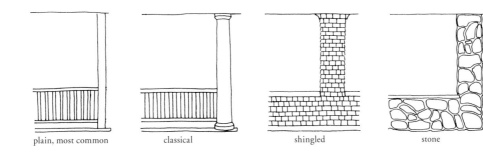

plain, most common   classical   shingled   stone

TYPICAL PORCH SUPPORTS

Less commonly Romanesque arches or spindlework

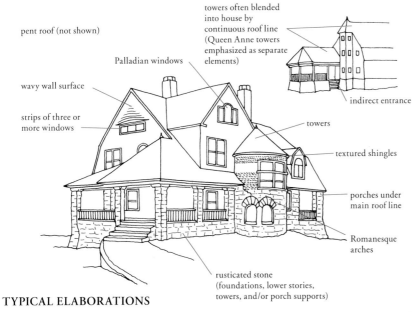

pent roof (not shown)

Palladian windows

wavy wall surface

strips of three or more windows

towers often blended into house by continuous roof line (Queen Anne towers emphasized as separate elements)

indirect entrance

towers

textured shingles

porches under main roof line

Romanesque arches

rusticated stone (foundations, lower stories, towers, and/or porch supports)

TYPICAL ELABORATIONS

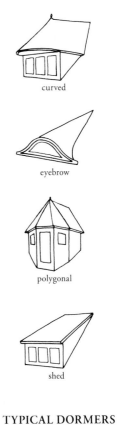

gable most common

hipped

curved

eyebrow

polygonal

shed

TYPICAL DORMERS

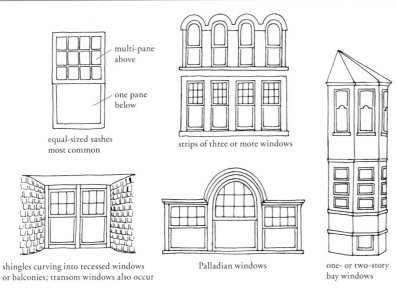

multi-pane above

one pane below

equal-sized sashes most common

strips of three or more windows

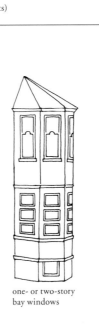

shingles curving into recessed windows or balconies; transom windows also occur

Palladian windows

one- or two-story bay windows

TYPICAL WINDOWS

HIPPED ROOF WITH CROSS GABLES

1. Dallas, Texas; late 19th century. Bookhout House. A transitional house with Queen Anne form, but Shingle porches and porte cochere.

2. New London, Connecticut; late 19th century. Note the varied dormer shapes—hipped, eyebrow, and gabled; the Palladian motif created above the line of gable windows; and the extensive porch with Romanesque arches.

3. Brookline, Massachusetts; late 19th century. E. A. P. Newcomb, architect. Note the rounded bay and oriel windows.

4. Helena, Montana; 1889. Boardman House. Note how the tower roof on the upstairs porch blends into the house with a continuous roof line (rather than being emphasized as a separate conical element, as is typical in Queen Anne towers).

5. Blue Ridge Summit, Pennsylvania; late 19th century. Menz House. A large, symmetrical example.

1

2

3

4

5

SIDE-GABLED ROOF

1. Emporia, Kansas; late 19th century. The wide shingles on this house are probably later additions.

2. Lexington, Kentucky; late 19th century. Note the three different dormer shapes crowded into the front roof.

3. Buffalo, New York; ca. 1885. Note the elaborate detailing of the side gable and the way the enormous tower seems to grow from the roof.

4. Brookline, Massachusetts; late 19th century. This early photograph shows the elaborate original wall detailing that has been lost over the years in most examples.

5. San Francisco, California; ca. 1908. Alto Plaza. This urban version (the left half of a double house) lacks the porches of suburban examples. Note Palladian-type window in the dormer and wide roof overhang. Known locally as the First Bay Tradition, it is the West Coast's version of the Shingle Style.

FRONT-GABLED ROOF

1. Louisville, Kentucky; late 19th century. A modest urban example.

2. Montauk, New York; late 19th century. Benson House. A seaside example with extensive porches.

3. Newport, Rhode Island; late 19th century. Richardson House.

4. New Haven, Connecticut; 1889. A massive front gable that clearly dominates the small, shallow side gable marks this example as the front-gabled, rather than cross-gabled, subtype of the style.

5. Corning, New York; late 19th century. The tower and front facade are united by the extended front wall and the upper band of windows.

6. Corning, New York; late 19th century. Note the paneled chimney and patterned shingles.

7. Dallas, Texas; 1909. Miller House.

8. Bristol, Rhode Island; 1887. Low House; McKim, Mead & White, architects. A now-demolished landmark example of the style.

2

5

6

8

1

2

4

6

CROSS-GABLED ROOF

1. Baltimore, Maryland; late 19th century. The Gothic (pointed arch) windows are unusual in Shingle houses.

2. Meriden, Connecticut; ca. 1890. Hale House. Note the Romanesque arched entry porch.

3. Kansas City, Missouri; late 19th century.

4. Brookline, Massachusetts; late 19th century. The half-timbered detailing seen here and in Figure 7 is unusual in Shingle houses.

5. Cleveland, Ohio; late 19th century. McNairy House. This house, with its colonnaded porch, Palladian window, and overall symmetry shows a strong classical influence.

6. Newport, Rhode Island; 1883. Bell House; McKim, Mead & White, architects.

7. Tuxedo Park, New York; late 19th century. This large house lacks the unified facade seen in most examples of the style.

3

5

7

1

2

4

5

7

GAMBREL ROOF

1. Nebraska City, Nebraska; 1902. Morton House. The off-center doorway and the asymmetrical upper story emphasize the unusual roof form: the left half is gambreled, the right gabled.

2. Cincinnati, Ohio; late 19th century. The walls of these two houses have unusually large shingles.

3. Kansas City, Missouri; 1890. Alderson House. An uncommon three-story example.

4. Salisbury, North Carolina; late 19th century. The cantilevered balcony over the entry is unusual.

5. Wichita, Kansas; 1887.

6. New Haven, Connecticut; late 19th century. Note the dramatic use of windows of varying shape in the dominant front gambrel (see also Figure 5).

7. East Hampton, New York; 1898. Quakenbush House. Cyrus L. W. Eidlitz, architect. Note that both front-facing gambrels have a three-part window (with a blind-arch above to simulate a Palladian window). In the larger slightly asymmetrical gambrel on the left this is grouped with a small triple window above and a small elliptical window to the side. In the smaller gambrel on the right it stands on its own.

8. Gainesville, Texas; late 19th century. Although this house has a side-gabled roof, the dominant front-facing gambrel places it in the gambrel subtype.

3

6

8

architect's style, rather than becoming widely adapted to mass vernacular housing, as did the contemporaneous Queen Anne. Among the innovative designers working in the style were Henry Hobson Richardson and William Ralph Emerson of Boston; John Calvin Stevens of Portland, Maine; McKim, Mead & White, Bruce Price, and Lamb and Rich of New York; Wilson Eyre of Philadelphia; and Willis Polk of San Francisco.

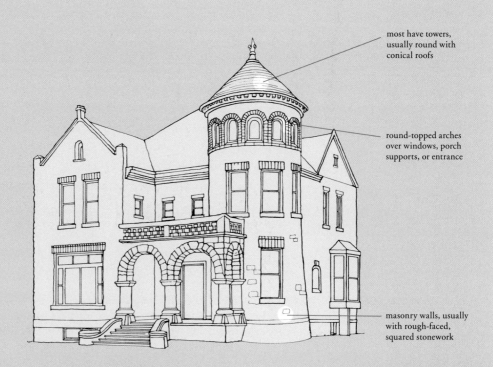

most have towers,
usually round with
conical roofs

round-topped arches
over windows, porch
supports, or entrance

masonry walls, usually
with rough-faced,
squared stonework

facade usually
asymmetrical

**HIPPED ROOF WITH CROSS
GABLES**

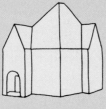

pages 390–91

OTHER ROOF FORMS
page 392

TOWN HOUSE
page 393

PRINCIPAL SUBTYPES

Richardsonian Romanesque

1880–1900

Identifying Features

Round-topped arches occurring over windows, porch supports, or entrance; masonry walls, usually with rough-faced, squared stonework; most have towers which are normally round with conical roofs; facade usually asymmetrical.

Principal Subtypes

Three principal subtypes can be distinguished:

HIPPED ROOF WITH CROSS GABLES—About two-thirds of Richardsonian Romanesque houses have hipped roofs with one or more lower cross gables. Most commonly there are two cross gables, one front-facing and the other side-facing, each asymmetrically placed on its respective facade. This shape is similar to the typical Queen Anne roof form.

OTHER ROOF TYPES—A variety of other roof forms also occur on Richardsonian Romanesque houses. Among the most frequent are side-gabled, cross-gabled, mansard, and simple hipped roofs.

TOWN HOUSE—Richardsonian Romanesque was frequently used for detached urban houses, which typically have front-gabled or mansard roofs; attached row houses in this style are less common.

Variants and Details

Richardsonian Romanesque houses are always of masonry and usually show at least some rough-faced, squared (ashlar) stonework. Frequently two or more colors or textures of stone or brick are combined to create decorative wall patterns. Wide, rounded (Romanesque) arches are a key identifying feature of the style. These may occur above windows or porch supports or over entryways. Most commonly the arches rest on squat columns, but some are supported on massive piers or are incorporated directly into wall surfaces. Column capitals and wall surfaces may be ornamented with floral or other decorative details. Windows are usually deeply recessed into the masonry wall and have only a single pane of glass per sash. The characteristic arched windows sometimes have small decorative columns (colonnettes) on each side. Groupings of three or more arched or rectangular windows occur in over half of the examples.

Towers occur in about 75 percent of free-standing Richardsonian Romanesque houses; these are most commonly round, although polygonal and squared versions are found. A second tower occurs in about 15 percent. Tower roofs are usually conical, but may be convex. Dormers are present in about half of Richardsonian Romanesque houses. Most commonly these are parapeted and gabled wall dormers, but hipped dormers, eyebrow dormers, and other variations occur.

Occurrence

The innovative Boston architect Henry Hobson Richardson (1838–1886) designed houses during the 1860s and 1870s in the then fashionable Second Empire, Queen Anne, or Stick styles; in 1879–1880 he executed the first of his few Romanesque houses, the rectory for his monumental Trinity Church in Boston. Richardson's Romanesque adaptations became very popular for large public buildings during the 1880s but he completed only a few more houses in the style before his premature death in 1886. Other architects, following Richardson's lead, also designed houses in the 1880s, but these were uncommon. In 1888, a sympathetic monograph on Richardson's life and work was published which greatly increased interest in the style. Most domestic examples are an outgrowth of this revival and were built in the 1890s. Because they were always of solid masonry construction (masonry veneering techniques were not yet perfected), Richardsonian Romanesque houses were much more expensive to build than were those Late Victorian styles which could be executed in wood. For this reason, they are mostly architect-designed landmarks and were never common. Scattered examples occur throughout the country but are most frequent in the larger cities of the northeastern states.

Comments

In the middle decades of the 19th century, European Romanesque models were sometimes used for American public and commercial buildings (the Romanesque Revival style), but these precedents reached American *houses* only in a later 19th-century form shaped by the powerful personality and talent of Henry Hobson Richardson. Born in Louisiana, Richardson attended Harvard and then studied architecture at the prestigious École des Beaux-Arts in Paris (he was only the second American to do so). He returned to the United States after the Civil War and opened an office in New York, which he subsequently moved to Boston. During the 1870s he evolved his strongly personal style, which incorporated Romanesque forms and which, like its mid-century predecessor, was applied principally to large public buildings. Unlike the earlier and more correct Romanesque revival, Richardson borrowed from many sources. He incorporated the polychromed walls seen in the contemporary late Gothic Revival (see page 279). His arches are frequently not truly Romanesque but Syrian, an early Christian form which

COMMON ELABORATIONS

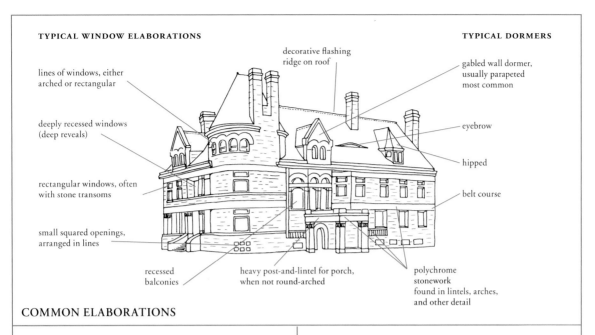

TYPICAL WINDOW ELABORATIONS

lines of windows, either arched or rectangular

deeply recessed windows (deep reveals)

rectangular windows, often with stone transoms

small squared openings, arranged in lines

recessed balconies

heavy post-and-lintel for porch, when not round-arched

decorative flashing ridge on roof

TYPICAL DORMERS

gabled wall dormer, usually parapeted most common

eyebrow

hipped

belt course

polychrome stonework found in lintels, arches, and other detail

ROUND ARCHES

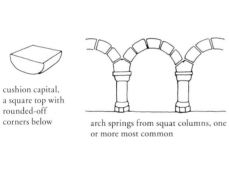

cushion capital, a square top with rounded-off corners below

arch springs from squat columns, one or more most common

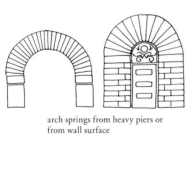

arch springs from heavy piers or from wall surface

Syrian arch springs almost from floor level

TYPICAL DECORATIVE DETAIL
Usually floral and interlacing

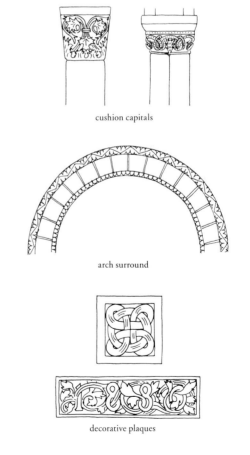

cushion capitals

arch surround

decorative plaques

HIPPED ROOF WITH CROSS GABLES

1. St. Charles, Missouri; 1885. Atkinson House. This example is unusual in lacking rough-faced stonework in the facade above the foundation level.

2. Richmond, Virginia; late 19th century.

3. Lexington, Kentucky; late 19th century. Dark red brick and white stone detailing provide startling contrast in this exuberant example. Note the tiny Romanesque-arched basement window at the left, the inventive open arch of the porch, and the exaggerated width of the stone window arches.

4. Provo, Utah; 1892. Reed House. Note the eyebrow dormer.

5. Richmond, Virginia; late 19th century. The polychromed walls show contrasting light brick and dark stonework.

6. Savannah, Georgia; 1891. Tiedeman House; A. Eichberg, architect. Note the contrasting trim of light colored stone. As in Figure 5, there are wall dormers around the tower roof.

7. Pueblo, Colorado (vicinity); 1890. Orman House; William Lang, architect. There are three towers, each with a different roof form and window type. Note the tall vertically modeled chimney.

8. Louisville, Kentucky; 1893. Conrad House; Clark and Loomis, architects. Two towers with differing roof shapes are used here. Note the floral detailing in the gable and elsewhere on the facade.

I

4

6

2

3

5

7

8

OTHER ROOF TYPES

1. St. Louis, Missouri; 1886. Lionberger House; Henry Hobson Richardson, architect. One of Richardson's fortress-like designs. The towers have very low pitched roofs and barely protrude from the house block.

2. St. Louis, Missouri; 1890. Huse House; Eames and Young, architects. The wide roof overhang is unusual in the style.

3. Chicago, Illinois; 1886. Glessner House; Henry Hobson Richardson, architect. Another of Richardson's few domestic designs, this presents a fortress-like face to the street.

4. Kerrville, Texas; ca. 1895. Shreiner House; Alfred Giles, architect. In this example a full Romanesque facade with a two-tiered porch and end towers has been added to two earlier houses to make a single larger dwelling. Note squared openings in railing design and in basement windows of illustration of 1 and 3.

5. Washington, D.C.; 1880. Heurich House, J. G. Myers, architect. The facade rises a full three stories in this landmark example.

TOWN HOUSE

1. Louisville, Kentucky; 1900. A simple, front-gabled example. It would be hard to miss the Romanesque arches.

2. Louisville, Kentucky; late 19th century. Groups of columns support the Romanesque arches in this front-gabled example.

3. Richmond, Virginia; late 19th century. Here the mansard roof provides a background for the wall dormer and tower.

4. St. Paul, Minnesota; 1887. Riley Row; Wilcox and Johnston, architects. Attached Romanesque town houses are unusual; groups with many uniform units, such as this, are very rare.

springs from ground level rather than from a supporting pedestal. Most importantly, he stressed unusual, sculpted shapes which give his buildings great individuality. His followers were usually less inventive; most houses in this style merely add Romanesque detailing to the typical hipped-with-cross-gables shape of the then dominant Queen Anne style.

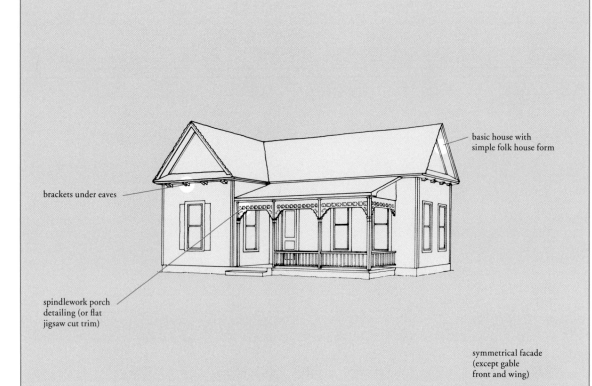

basic house with
simple folk house form

brackets under eaves

spindlework porch
detailing (or flat
jigsaw cut trim)

symmetrical facade
(except gable
front and wing)

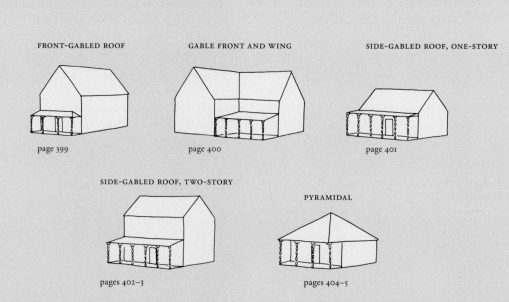

FRONT-GABLED ROOF

page 399

GABLE FRONT AND WING

page 400

SIDE-GABLED ROOF, ONE-STORY

page 401

SIDE-GABLED ROOF, TWO-STORY

pages 402–3

PYRAMIDAL

pages 404–5

PRINCIPAL SUBTYPES

Folk Victorian

ca. 1870–1910

Identifying Features

Porches with spindlework detailing (turned spindles and lace-like spandrels) or flat, jig-saw cut trim appended to National Folk (post-railroad) house forms (see page 134); symmetrical facade (except gable-front-and-wing subtype); cornice-line brackets are common.

Principal Subtypes

Five principal subtypes occur. These are closely related to the subtypes of National Folk (post-railroad) houses.

FRONT-GABLED ROOF—Like their pure folk counterparts, two-story, front-gabled forms with Victorian detailing are most common in the northeastern states, while one-story, narrow shotgun forms are generally found in the urban South.

GABLE FRONT AND WING—Both one- and two-story Victorian versions of this popular folk form are found throughout the country but are particularly common in the southern states.

SIDE-GABLED ROOF, ONE-STORY—This common subtype includes Victorian versions of both the hall-and-parlor (one room deep) and massed, side-gabled (two or more rooms deep) folk forms. It is widely distributed through the country.

SIDE-GABLED-ROOF, TWO-STORY—Most examples of this subtype are I-houses (one room deep) to which Victorian detailing in varying degrees of exuberance was added. They are common in all parts of the country.

PYRAMIDAL—Both one- and two-story versions of this folk form were often given Victorian detailing in the southern states but are less common elsewhere.

Variants and Details

The style is defined by the presence of Victorian decorative detailing on simple folk house forms, which are generally much less elaborated than the Victorian styles that they attempt to mimic. The details are usually of either Italianate or Queen Anne inspiration; occasionally the Gothic Revival provides a source. The primary areas for the application of this detailing are the porch and cornice line. Porch supports are commonly either Queen Anne–type turned spindles or square posts with the corners beveled (chamfered) as in many Italianate porches. In addition, lace-like spandrels are frequent and turned balusters may be used both in porch railings and in friezes suspended from the porch ceiling (see pages 347 and 349). The roof-wall junction may be either boxed or open. When boxed, brackets are commonly found along the cornice. Centered gables are often added to side-gabled and pyramidal examples. Window surrounds are generally simple or may have a simple pediment above. Most Folk Victorian houses have some Queen Anne spindlework detailing but are easily differentiated from true Queen Anne examples by the presence of symmetrical facades and by their lack of the textured and varied wall surfaces characteristic of the Queen Anne.

Occurrence

The style is common throughout the country; the five subtypes show differing patterns of distribution as noted in the descriptions of each above. New Orleans has a particularly rich heritage of Folk Victorian houses. This includes many distinct local forms such as Double Shotguns and Camelbacks (a shotgun house with a two-story section at the rear that resembles the hump on a camel's back).[13]

Comments

Like that of the National Folk forms on which they are based, the spread of Folk Victorian houses was made possible by the railroads. The growth of the railroad system made heavy woodworking machinery widely accessible at local trade centers, where they produced inexpensive Victorian detailing. The railroads also provided local lumber yards with abundant supplies of pre-cut detailing from distant mills. Many builders simply grafted pieces of this newly available trim onto the traditional folk house forms familiar to local carpenters. Fashion-conscious homeowners also updated their older folk houses with new Victorian porches. These dwellings make strong stylistic statements and are therefore treated here as distinctive styled houses, rather than pure folk forms. After about 1910 these Symmetrical Victorian houses, as they are sometimes called, were replaced by the Craftsman, Colonial Revival, and other fashionable eclectic styles.

FRONT-GABLED ROOF

1. New Orleans, Louisiana; late 19th century. A shotgun form, one room wide, with Italianate windows and Queen Anne spindlework porch and gable detailing.

2. New Orleans, Louisiana; late 19th century. A narrow, two-ranked shotgun, with Italianate windows and brackets. Note the hipped front roof that replaces the more usual front gable.

3. Fernandez, Florida; late 19th century. A large two-story front-gabled form with a two-tiered porch. This example has flat jigsaw cut upper balustrade and gable trim.

4. New London, Connecticut; late 19th century. An inventive craftsman's interpretation of spindlework porch detailing.

GABLE FRONT AND WING

1. Bartlett, Texas; late 19th century. This example has modest spindlework porch detailing, with a typical Queen Anne pent roof beneath the gables. The porches in this subtype are usually confined within the L formed by the gable and wing as seen here and in Figures 2 and 3.

2. Hillsboro, Texas; late 19th century. An inventive craftsman's version of a spindlework porch. Note the shingled gable and bracketed window hood to the right. Slight differences in roof pitch and height between the gable front portion and the wing, as well as differing gable and window detailing in the two portions, probably indicate that they were built at different times. Gable-front-and-wing forms were often the result of such melding.

3. Sinclairville, New York, vicinity; late 19th century.

4. Laurens, South Carolina; late 19th century. Huff House. This example has unusually elaborate spindlework detailing and eave brackets. The high-pitched gable is less common than the lower-pitched ones seen in the other examples. Note how the porch roof has been extended upward to simulate a full-scale Victorian tower.

5. Little River, South Carolina; ca. 1910. Ellis House. Note the contrast between the body of the house, a simple two-story folk form with little detailing, and the elaborate spindlework porch with paired gables.

SIDE-GABLED ROOF, ONE-STORY

1. Bastrop, Texas; 1890. Elzner House.

2. Rosin, North Carolina; ca. 1890. McPhail House. Centered front gables are common in this subtype (see also Figures 3 and 5).

3. San Antonio, Texas; ca. 1880. Kuhn House.

4. Galveston, Texas; 1892. Eimar House. Note the typical Queen Anne cutaway corners to the right. First stories raised high above the ground are common along the Gulf Coast.

5. St. Francois County, Missouri; late 19th century. Graves House. The projecting central wing of this carefully detailed example is unusual.

SIDE-GABLED ROOF, TWO-STORY

1. Laurens, South Carolina; late 19th century. Easterby House. Like Figure 7, this I-house also has Italianate brackets and bay windows.

2. Clinton, Missouri, vicinity; ca. 1879. Noble House. An I-house with modified Victorian porch detailing.

3. Canton, Mississippi; late 19th century. Two-tiered, full-facade porches such as this are common in the South (see also Figure 6).

4. Hampton, South Carolina; ca. 1880. Here a full-width, one-story porch is combined with a two-story entry porch.

5. Annapolis, Maryland; late 19th century. A simple side-gabled town house with modest spindlework porch detailing.

6. Waveland, Mississippi, late 19th century. The elaborate jigsaw cut porch detailing of this example shows Gothic influence in the paired gables.

7. Lansing, North Carolina, vicinity; ca. 1890. Howell House. Here a two-tiered, full-height entry porch is added to an I-house form. Full-height entry porches on Folk Victorian houses are always two-tiered; two-story columns would indicate a classically influenced, styled house.

8. Henderson County, North Carolina; 1877. Elliott House. An unusually elaborate I-house. If this transitional example had arched windows or other Italianate detailing in addition to the eave brackets, it would clearly belong to the Italianate, rather than the Folk Victorian, style.

PYRAMIDAL ROOF

1. San Antonio, Texas; 1903. Pancoast House. Note the flat, jig-saw cut porch frieze elaborated with stars, a frequent motif in the Lone Star state.

2. Midway, North Carolina, vicinity; ca. 1880. McLamb House. A five-ranked, hipped-roof I-house with eave brackets and modest spindlework porch detailing.

3. Biloxi, Mississippi, ca. 1900.

4. McPhersonville, South Carolina; late 19th century. Gregorie House. Two-tiered, full facade porches, such as this, are common throughout the South.

5. Brunson, South Carolina; ca. 1875. Brunson House. This example has small eave brackets and flat, jig-saw cut porch decoration.

6. Woodville, Texas; ca. 1880. Shivers House. This example adds centered gables to the low-pitched hipped roof. It is quite large for a Folk Victorian; most houses of this size and detailing more closely followed one of the stylish modes of the day.

1

3

5

2

4

6

The Eclectic movement draws on the full spectrum of Western architectural tradition—Ancient Classical, Medieval, and Renaissance Classical—for stylistic inspiration. Unlike the free stylistic mixtures that had dominated the preceding Victorian era, the Eclectic movement stresses relatively pure copies of domestic architecture as originally built in various European countries and their New World colonies. This movement lasted from the 1880s until 1940 and occurred in two phases. The first, and smaller, arrived at the end of the 19th century and receded around 1900. The second phase arrived around 1920 and spread rapidly across the United States, dominating house styles between the two world wars. Throughout the Eclectic era many different styles engaged in a sort of friendly competition.

The first phase began quietly in the last decades of the 19th century as fashionable, European-trained architects designed landmark houses for wealthy clients in historic styles—mostly Italian Renaissance, Chateauesque, Beaux Arts, Tudor, or Colonial Revival—a trend that gained momentum with the Chicago Columbian Exposition of 1893, which stressed historical styles. In the first two decades of the 20th century this first phase was interrupted and almost overwhelmed by the first wave of architectural modernism presented by Craftsman and Prairie styles with their purely American origins. Many of the Eclectic homes built from 1900 through 1920 incorporated aspects of these two early modern styles—primarily broad overhangs, exposed roof rafters, front porches, and grouped windows.

At the end of World War I, fashions in domestic architecture quickly shifted back toward traditional styles. This was undoubtedly encouraged by the two million American soldiers returning from Europe, where they had observed original historic homes first hand. The homes built in this second phase, sometimes called "period houses," strived to present exteriors with relatively "correct" architectural detail.

Two major changes facilitated widespread and more authentic copies of Euro-

Eclectic Houses

pean styles. First, new inexpensive methods of reproducing photographs allowed architects and clients to peruse illustrated books showing historic houses and their architectural details. Second, by the early 1920s, a technique was perfected for adding a thin veneer of brick or stone to any exterior. The new affordability of "masonry" houses revolutionized the design of small homes. Previously, it had been difficult to copy historic European styles, as these were built of solid masonry, often with decorative stone- or brickwork patterns. Now, masonry veneers allowed modest cottages to mimic Old World dwellings. Traditional homes dominated domestic building during the 1920s and 1930s. Although the Great Depression led to simpler houses with less architectural detail, period fashions remained dominant until the end of World War II, when modernism swept aside historical styles. (Paradoxically, European reactions were exactly the opposite. After World War I, Europeans embraced modernism, while following World War II they embarked on precise restoration and rebuilding of the past.)

1880–1940

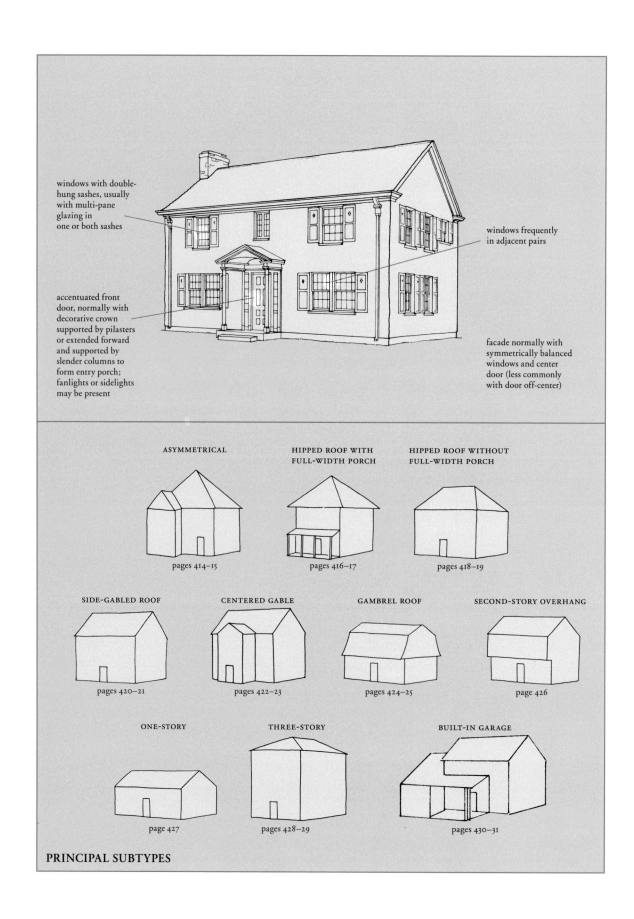

windows with double-hung sashes, usually with multi-pane glazing in one or both sashes

accentuated front door, normally with decorative crown supported by pilasters or extended forward and supported by slender columns to form entry porch; fanlights or sidelights may be present

windows frequently in adjacent pairs

facade normally with symmetrically balanced windows and center door (less commonly with door off-center)

ASYMMETRICAL
pages 414–15

HIPPED ROOF WITH
FULL-WIDTH PORCH
pages 416–17

HIPPED ROOF WITHOUT
FULL-WIDTH PORCH
pages 418–19

SIDE-GABLED ROOF
pages 420–21

CENTERED GABLE
pages 422–23

GAMBREL ROOF
pages 424–25

SECOND-STORY OVERHANG
page 426

ONE-STORY
page 427

THREE-STORY
pages 428–29

BUILT-IN GARAGE
pages 430–31

PRINCIPAL SUBTYPES

Colonial Revival

1880–1955

Identifying Features

Accentuated front door, normally with decorative crown (pediment) supported by pilasters, or extended forward and supported by slender columns to form entry porch; doors commonly have overhead fanlights or sidelights; facade normally shows symmetrically balanced windows and center door (less commonly with door off-center); windows with double-hung sashes, usually with multi-pane glazing in one or both sashes; windows frequently in adjacent pairs.

Principal Subtypes

Nine principal subtypes can be distinguished. Some examples may be almost identical to their colonial (particularly Georgian and Federal) prototypes. Clues for distinguishing Revival copies from early originals are given below under Variants and Details.

ASYMMETRICAL—About 10 percent of Colonial Revival houses have asymmetrical facades, a feature rarely seen on their colonial prototypes. These asymmetrical examples range from rambling, free-form houses resembling the free classic Queen Anne style (see pages 358–63) to simple boxes with asymmetrical window or porch arrangements. Prior to 1900 this subtype accounted for about one-third of all Colonial Revival houses. After 1910 few examples were constructed until the 1930s, when irregular facades reappeared with less elaborate detailing. These were, in part, inspired by the desire for attached garages, which were difficult to incorporate within a balanced facade.

HIPPED ROOF WITH FULL-WIDTH PORCH—About one-third of Colonial Revival houses built before about 1915 are of this subtype, which is sometimes called the Classic Box. These have a one-story, full-width porch with classical columns, which is added to a symmetrical, two-story house of square or rectangular plan. Sometimes these are American Four-Square in form, while others strongly resemble the four-square but have an added central hall. Two-story pilasters are common at the corners; dormers, hipped or gabled, are usually present. Doors may be centered or placed to the side. These houses have both Neoclassical and Colonial Revival influences, but lack the full-height porches of typical Neoclassical houses.

HIPPED ROOF WITHOUT FULL-WIDTH PORCH—About 20 percent of Colonial Revival houses are simple two-story rectangular blocks with hipped roofs; porches are usually absent or, if present, are merely small entry porches covering less than the full facade width. This subtype, built throughout the Colonial Revival era, predominates before about 1915. On early examples, the colonial detailing tended to be highly exaggerated and of awkward proportions; fanciful, pedimented dormers were particularly favored. Eaves often have a broad overhang, and front-facade windows were grouped together. After about 1920 detailing became more "correct" by closely following Georgian or Federal precedents.

SIDE-GABLED ROOF—About 30 percent of Colonial Revival houses are simple, two-story rectangular blocks with side-gabled roofs. As in the type just described, the details tend to be exaggerated prior to 1910 and more "correct" afterward. This subtype was built throughout the Colonial Revival era but predominates after about 1915 and was widely built after 1930.

CENTERED GABLE—Less than 5 percent of Colonial Revival houses have a centered front gable added to either a hipped or side-gabled roof. These uncommon Revival houses mimic high-style Georgian or Federal prototypes. Scattered examples were built throughout the Colonial Revival era.

GAMBREL ROOF—About 10 percent of Colonial Revival houses have gambrel roofs. Most are one story with steeply pitched gambrels containing almost a full second story of floor space; these have either separate dormer windows or a continuous shed dormer with several windows. A full-width porch may be included under the main roof line or added with a separate roof. This subtype is known as Dutch Colonial, but very few examples closely follow early Dutch precedent. From about 1895 to 1915 the most common form has a front-facing gambrel roof, occasionally with a cross gambrel at the rear. These are influenced by the typical gambrels of the earlier Shingle style (see pages 382–83), but their narrower, front gambrel form fit onto narrow streetcar suburb lots. Side gambrels, usually with long shed dormers, became the predominant form in the 1920s and 1930s.

SECOND-STORY OVERHANG—This subtype is loosely based on Postmedieval English prototypes (see page 161), commonly built with the second story extended slightly outward to overhang the wall below. The subtype was relatively rare until the 1930s, when stylized, side-gabled examples (called Garrison Colonial houses) became very popular. These persisted into the 1950s. Unlike their early prototypes, these typically have masonry-veneered first stories with wooden wall claddings above. Georgian- or Federal-inspired doorways are commonly mixed with decorative pendants or other Postmedieval details.

ONE-STORY—The preceding subtypes are all based on familiar two-story prototypes, but one-story Colonial Revival houses are also common. These are generally Cape Cod

ORIGINAL EXAMPLES

Georgian

Federal

Dutch

REVIVAL EXAMPLES

paired, triple, or
bay windows

never found
in originals

prominent entry porch on
original Georgian house is
probably an addition

front-facing
gambrel roof
with cross gambrel

never found
in originals

one-story side
wings, either
open or
enclosed, usually
with flat roof

if found
on original
probably an
addition

steeply pitched
gambrel containing
a nearly full
second story

originals with
moderate- to
low-pitched roofs

broken
pediments

segmental,
triangular,
or ogee

only ogees
found on
originals and
even these
not common

continuous dormer
across front
and/or Federal
or Georgian entry
detail

dormer never
in originals

brick houses
with Georgian
doorways

originals primarily
in Virginia,
Maryland, or
landmark examples

Be certain to check range map, page 17,
for Dutch Colonial houses. Originals
occur *only* within the range shown on this map

DISTINGUISHING THE COLONIAL REVIVAL HOUSE
FROM GEORGIAN, FEDERAL, & DUTCH ORIGINALS

cottages, loosely patterned after early wooden folk houses of eastern Massachusetts, usually with the addition of Georgian- or Federal-inspired doorways. These were built throughout the Colonial Revival era but were particularly common in the 1940s. Cape Cods with added Colonial Revival detailing appear in this chapter. Very modest Cape Cod–shaped houses with little added architectural detail (popular during the 1940s) are treated as side-gabled Minimal Traditionals (see pages 592–93).

THREE-STORY—A small percentage of Colonial Revival houses are three stories high. These include both narrow urban houses and more typical forms modeled after three-story Federal prototypes, common in parts of New England (see page 228). These typically have low-pitched, hipped roofs which appear almost flat; Federal fanlights are usual over entrances. In the early decades of this century, narrow urban houses were becoming less common in all but the largest cities. In those populous cities where urban houses persisted, Colonial Revival detailing remained popular through the 1920s.

BUILT-IN GARAGE—In 1940, an FHA bulletin illustrated two ways to integrate a garage into the main block of a side-gabled Colonial Revival house. Variations of this appeared in house pattern books until ca. 1980, with the house size growing over the decades.[1]

Variants and Details

As in their Georgian and Federal prototypes, the principal areas of elaboration in Colonial Revival houses are entrances, cornices, and windows.

ENTRANCES—The illustrations of Georgian and Federal entrances on pages 203 and 219 include most variants found on colonial prototypes; some common additional variations favored on Colonial Revival houses are illustrated here. Broken pediments, rare on colonial originals, were particularly favored by the Revivalists. Entrance details on careful Colonial Revival copies can be distinguished from originals only by their regular, machine-made finish, which contrasts with the slightly irregular hand finishes of early examples. On less precise Colonial Revival copies, door surrounds are typically flatter than the originals; that is, less wood and fewer and shallower moldings are used to gain a similar frontal effect but less depth and relief are apparent when viewed from the side.

CORNICES—In original Georgian and Federal houses the cornice is an important identifying feature. It is almost always part of a boxed roof-wall junction with little overhang, and is frequently decorated with dentils or modillions (see pages 219 and 222–23). These are also typical of many Colonial Revival examples. Some, however, have open eaves and rake, or even exposed rafters, features never found on original colonial houses.

WINDOWS—As in the originals, most Colonial Revival windows are rectangular in shape with double-hung sashes. In the more accurate copies, windows stand alone as single units (i.e., they are not paired or grouped) and each sash has six, eight, nine, or twelve panes. Equally common are multi-pane upper sashes hung above lower sashes

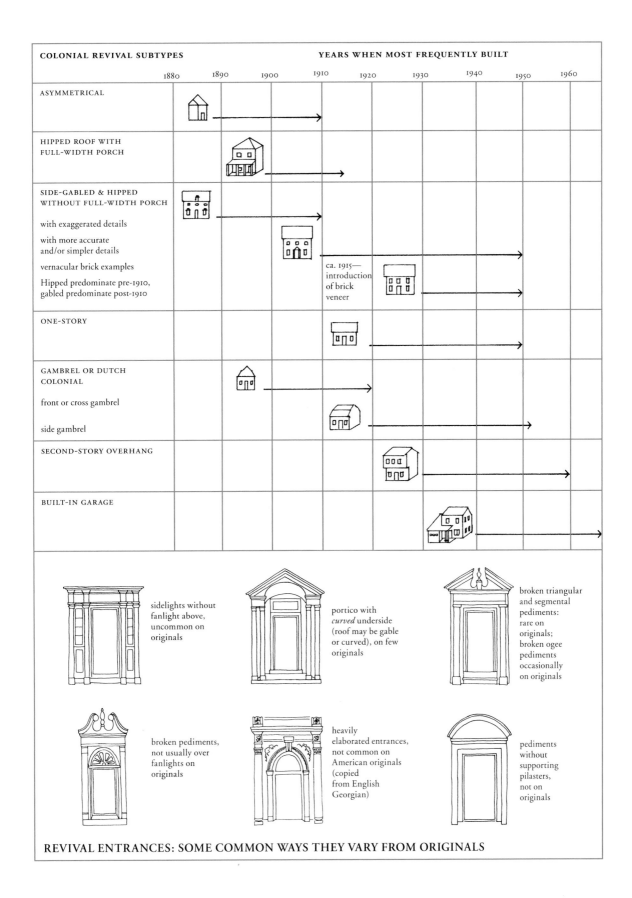

COLONIAL REVIVAL SUBTYPES	YEARS WHEN MOST FREQUENTLY BUILT									
	1880	1890	1900	1910	1920	1930	1940	1950	1960	
ASYMMETRICAL										
HIPPED ROOF WITH FULL-WIDTH PORCH										
SIDE-GABLED & HIPPED WITHOUT FULL-WIDTH PORCH with exaggerated details with more accurate and/or simpler details vernacular brick examples Hipped predominate pre-1910, gabled predominate post-1910				ca. 1915—introduction of brick veneer						
ONE-STORY										
GAMBREL OR DUTCH COLONIAL front or cross gambrel side gambrel										
SECOND-STORY OVERHANG										
BUILT-IN GARAGE										

sidelights without fanlight above, uncommon on originals

portico with *curved* underside (roof may be gable or curved), on few originals

broken triangular and segmental pediments: rare on originals; broken ogee pediments occasionally on originals

broken pediments, not usually over fanlights on originals

heavily elaborated entrances, not common on American originals (copied from English Georgian)

pediments without supporting pilasters, not on originals

REVIVAL ENTRANCES: SOME COMMON WAYS THEY VARY FROM ORIGINALS

that have only a single large pane, a pattern never seen on colonial originals. Where bay, paired, grouped, or triple windows (except the Federal Palladian type) are present, they clearly signify a Colonial Revival house rather than an original.

OTHER DETAILS—All common wall materials were used, but masonry predominates in high-style examples. Brick is typically red—the color most commonly used for Georgian and Federal originals. Vernacular examples were generally of wood before about 1920, with masonry progressively more common as veneering techniques became widespread in the 1920s. High-style elaborations of Georgian and Federal originals may also occur on landmark Colonial Revival copies.

Occurrence

This was *the* dominant style for domestic building throughout the country during the first half of the twentieth century. It was built in relatively small numbers from 1880 until about 1910, years when the Queen Anne was more dominant. During the next two decades (1910–1930) about 40 percent of the houses built were in the Colonial Revival style.[2] Unlike most other Eclectic styles, the Colonial Revival was not completely eclipsed by World War II, but continued to be built, albeit in far less elaborate forms, into the 1950s and early 1960s. The different subtypes were not, however, equally common throughout this long period, but shifted with changing fashion (see each subtype above and chart on page 413). Today the Colonial Revival style is used for many New Traditional houses.

Comments

The term "Colonial Revival," as used here, refers to the entire rebirth of interest in the early English and Dutch houses of the Atlantic seaboard. The Georgian and Federal styles form the backbone of the Revival, with secondary influences from Postmedieval English and Dutch Colonial prototypes. Details from two or more of these precedents are freely combined in many examples so that pure copies of colonial houses are far less common than are eclectic mixtures.

4

5

ASYMMETRICAL

1. Cambridge, Massachusetts; 1897. Note the exaggerated broken pediments on the dormers.

2. Brookline, Massachusetts; ca. 1900. Note the two-story wing set at an angle to the left and the almost centered gable with Palladian window below to the right.

3. Salisbury, North Carolina; 1898. The line between some late free classic Queen Anne houses and some early Colonial Revival examples is not a sharp one: compare this photo with the similar transitional example shown in Figure 17, page 361. The Palladian window and Federal swags link this house more closely with the Colonial Revival movement.

4. Hartford, Connecticut; ca. 1900. This early example shows Craftsman influence in its open eaves with exposed rafters and porch supports.

5. Dallas, Texas; 1937. Hershfelt House. The tall, broad ground floor windows are almost as tall as the front door. Large-scale, double-hung, multi-pane windows like this were popular in the 1930s.

6. Dallas, Texas; 1939. Bowers House. Later asymmetrical examples mostly date from the 1930s and commonly have either gabled roofs with side wings, as in this house, or forward-facing gable-fronted wings as in Figure 5. One-story bay windows, as seen here, were also popular in the 1930s examples.

1

2

3

6

HIPPED ROOF WITH FULL-WIDTH PORCH

1. Galveston, Texas; ca. 1910. Lawrence House. On narrow urban lots a front-gabled roof occasionally replaces the more common hipped roof.

2. Dallas, Texas; ca. 1910. This early, two-ranked house with an off-center entrance is adapted from the simple four-square folk plan with a pyramidal roof. When embellished with a central dormer and front porch as seen here, this form is called American Four-Square. Compare with Figure 4, a narrower and more simply detailed American Four-Square.

3. Ashe County, North Carolina; ca. 1920. Livesy House. This example, like Figures 5, 6, and 7, has a centered entrance and a three-ranked facade, indicating the likelihood of a central-hall plan rather than the simple four-square plan seen in Figures 2 and 4.

4. Buffalo, New York; ca. 1900. Foster House. A simple, early two-ranked example; note the corner pilasters.

5. Union Springs, Alabama; ca. 1910. Note the elaborate pedimented entranceway moved to the front of the porch, rather than around the doorway as in Colonial examples. Less grand pediments are seen in Figures 2 and 3.

6. Winston-Salem, North Carolina; ca. 1910. Note the grouped columns on pedestals. This pattern of porch supports was uncommon before about 1900.

7. Brooklyn, New York; 1900. John J. Petit, architect. Paired windows and a front door with sidelights, but no fanlight, are common Revival details seen clearly in this example.

8. Buffalo, New York; ca. 1900. White House. An unusually elaborate example with roof and upper-porch balustrades, upper-story bay windows, and a heavily detailed cornice with a solid railing above.

1

4

7

2

3

5

6

8

HIPPED ROOF WITHOUT FULL-WIDTH PORCH

1. San Francisco, California; ca. 1900. A fine early example with exaggerated pediments on the dormers, an overwide entablature above the entry-porch columns, an overwide belt course, and grouped windows with decorative transoms on the first story. Such details never appear on more correct, later examples.

2. Dallas, Texas; 1924. Stickle House. This house demonstrates several features common from about 1900 to 1925. Note the broadly overhanging eaves, absence of dentils and modillions, grouped windows, and use of a single pane of glass in the bottom window sashes. These were not found in original Georgian or Federal houses and show the influence of contemporaneous Prairie houses. Compare with Figure 5.

3. Cincinnati, Ohio; ca. 1920s. Such austere examples emphasize the shift to more correct copies of Colonial dwellings.

4. Pittsburgh, Pennsylvania; ca. 1915. Note the exaggerated center dormer, the deep rounded entry porch, and the matching two-story curved window bays.

5. Dallas, Texas; 1927. O'Neil House. This more "correct" example has a shallow roof overhang with modillions below and single windows with 6/9 pane sashes. It is more typical of the "period houses" of the 1920s. Compare with Figure 3.

6. Dallas, Texas; 1938. Varner House. This Regency variation of the Colonial Revival, loosely based on English rather than American precedents, was popular in the 1930s. The octagonal window, simplified door surround, and low-parapeted roof-wall junction are typical of this variant.

7. Brookline, Massachusetts; ca. 1900. E. A. P. Newcombe, architect. Another early example with exaggerated detailing. Note the dormers with Palladian windows and broken pediments, the two colonnaded upstairs balconies, and the very deep entry porch.

8. Atlanta, Georgia; 1922. McDuffie House. Hentz, Adler, and Schutze, architects. A very large and elaborate example. Note the pilasters, roof-line balustrade, and arched windows.

1

4

7

SIDE-GABLED ROOF

1. Baltimore, Maryland; ca. 1910. A very simple, two-ranked example.

2. Louisville, Kentucky; ca. 1920s. Side porches are common on Colonial Revival houses (see Figures 3, 4, and 7).

3. Louisville, Kentucky; ca. 1930s. Another Regency house (see also page 419, Figure 6). This type of metal entry porch, with a canopy roof is a characteristic Regency feature.

4. Kansas City, Missouri; ca. 1910s. Although at first glance this looks like an accurate copy, the roof overhang is too wide and the windows too broad for an original colonial house.

5. Cleveland, Ohio; ca. 1920s. The entry porch with a curved underside is a favored Revival detail.

6. Dallas, Texas; 1941. Young House. Large multi-pane double-hung windows, extending to the first-floor level, and small round windows (above the entry here and in the gable end of Figure 3) were widely used in the 1930s, '40s, and early '50s on Colonial Revival houses. This kind of small round accent window was also found on other styles from ca. 1930 to ca. 1955.

7. Dallas, Texas; 1919. Thomson House. This example was inspired by the Middle Colonies Georgian house. Note the pent roof and the hood over the entry. The side porch to the left has a summer sleeping porch above with windows on three sides. These were especially favored in the South, where they appear in many early 20th-century styles.

8. Cambridge, Massachusetts; 1903. John W. Ames, architect. This house demonstrates that reasonably accurate Colonial copies were being designed in the early years of the Revival; those with exaggerated detailing were, however, far more common.

9. Louisville, Kentucky; ca. 1920s. The garden facade of a very large example. Note the door surround with the pediment extending over the sidelights but lacking a fanlight. Although this combination was never used in colonial houses, the example here faithfully captures the spirit of a Georgian or Federal doorway.

1

4

7

8

2

3

5

6

9

CENTERED GABLE

1. Buffalo, New York; ca. 1900. Harrover House. Centered gables that cover three ranks of window or door openings (here and in Figure 8) are less common than those that are only one or two ranks wide.

2. Buffalo, New York; ca. 1910s. Note the fine detailing: the entrance with a rounded door, the sidelights without fanlight, the wide classical pediment, the Palladian and bay windows, and the carefully executed dormers.

3. Buffalo, New York; ca. 1920s.

4. Des Moines, Iowa; 1905. Witmer House; Liebbe, Nourse and Rasmussen, architects. Note the first-story windows crowned with broken pediments (see also Figure 7). Although common above the main entrance, such pediments became rare on windows and dormers after about 1910.

5. Cleveland, Ohio; ca. 1910s. The open overhanging eaves and the entry porch with trellised roof are borrowed from the Craftsman movement. Note how the door area is recessed into the main body of the house.

6. Dallas, Texas; 1938. Lincoln House. The simplicity of detailing on this house is typical of examples from the 1930s and 1940s.

7. Madison, Wisconsin; 1896. Ely House. Round windows were sometimes found when the triangular roof pediment was closed at the bottom, as here and in Figures 1 and 8.

8. Raleigh, North Carolina; 1935. Tatton Hall; William Lawrence Bottomley, architect. A five-ranked central block is flanked by one-story wings (obscured by trees and shadows in the photograph) in this landmark example. Typically the gabled portion of the house projects slightly out from the front wall plane as is seen here and most other photos in this spread.

1

4

7

2

3

5

6

8

GAMBREL ROOF

1. Louisville, Kentucky; ca. 1920s. Figures 1, 4, and 7 are typical examples of the popular Dutch Colonial house of the 1920s and 1930s. The side-gambrel shape, most often with a full-width shed dormer (see also Figures 7 and 10), is the most common form.

2. Lexington, Kentucky; ca. 1910. This cross-gambrel form, with wood cladding, was a popular pattern-book design during the period from about 1905 to 1915.

3. Kittery, Maine, ca. 1910s. Note the grouped windows in the upper half-story with decorative diamond-pattern muntins in the upper sashes.

4. Cincinnati, Ohio; ca. 1920s.

5. Union, South Carolina; ca. 1910. Figures 5, 8, and 9 are all early gambrel-roof designs showing varying degrees of adventuresomeness. They are clearly descendants of the free-form gambrel designs of the preceding Shingle style.

6. Washington, D.C.; ca. 1900. An early example with a full-front gambrel. Note the swags, often found on Federal houses, on the porch frieze.

7. St. Louis, Missouri; ca. 1920s.

8. Cleveland, Ohio; ca. 1910.

9. New Haven, Connecticut; 1910. Brown and Von Beren, architects.

10. Durham, North Carolina; ca. 1920s. This is a less common cross-gambrel form of the Dutch Colonial. Note the flared eaves, here and in Figures 1, 4, 7, and 8. These mimic the Flemish eaves of many Dutch Colonial originals.

1

4

7

8

2

3

5

6

9

10

SECOND-STORY OVERHANG

1. Cambridge, Massachusetts; 1940. C. Crowell, architect. This Garrison Colonial subtype was especially popular in the latest phases of the Colonial Revival, from about 1935 to 1955. The overhang required a wood-sided second floor since cantilevered brick veneering was very difficult to construct. Here brick is used only on the front facade of the first story.

2. Dallas, Texas; 1953. Wilson House. Unlike their Colonial precedents, most Revival examples have a brick-sided first story.

3. Mission Hills, Kansas; ca. 1930s. This example shows more detailing (door surround, wall dormers, centered gable) than is typical for the subtype.

4. Dallas, Texas; 1951. Voss House. Note the two tall bay windows; these were very popular during the 1950s.

ONE-STORY

1. Greeleyville, South Carolina; ca. 1910. Wilder House. Note modest pediment over door and more exaggerated pediment over dormers.

2. Louisville, Kentucky; ca. 1920s. This is a typical example of the Cape Cod cottage. Figure 1 is an earlier Cape Cod, which lacks the proportions of the Colonial originals (note the lower roof pitch, oversized dormers, and extra width and height of the front facade). The Cape Cod is the most common form of one-story Colonial Revival house. As a form, it originated in the early 18th century and continued with few changes through the 1950s. Note lights in transom over door.

3. Dallas, Texas; 1929. Randall House. This house has a formal, Federal-inspired entry porch and doorway.

4. Dallas, Texas; 1925. This was a common pattern book design in the 1920s. In some versions the entry porch is exaggerated in scale, occupying up to one-third of the front facade.

5. Macon, Georgia; 1912. Stetson House; Hentz and Reid, architects. Note the lower one-story wings; this finely detailed example, like Figure 3, was inspired by more pretentious Colonial antecedents than the typical Cape Cod examples shown in Figures 1 and 2. See pages 592–93 for related side-gabled Minimal Traditionals that do not typically have modest stylistic details added.

1

2

3

4

5

THREE-STORY

1. Cambridge, Massachusetts; 1900. John A. Hasty, architect. Not a single-family house, but a triple-decker (one dwelling unit on each of three floors), this has the exuberant detailing associated with early examples. Note the broken pediments on the roof and over the central second-story window.

2. Cambridge, Massachusetts; 1916. J. W. Ames, architect. Figures 2 and 4 are both modeled after the three-story Federal subtype that was popular in New England (see page 228).

3. Richmond, Virginia; ca. 1910s. A three-story detached urban house with full-width porch.

4. Cambridge, Massachusetts; 1911. President's House, Harvard University; G. Lowell, architect.

5. Washington, D.C.; 1915. Woodrow Wilson House.

6. Buffalo, New York; 1894–ca. 1900. A portion of The Midway block of row houses. On left is the 1894 Bartow House, Marling and Johnson, architects. Note the exaggerated broken pediments on the original dormers and the original window lintels (a refined two-story shopfront window was added in the 1920s). In the center is the ca. 1900 Curtiss House, Marling and Johnson, architects. Note the high-style Federal-era detailing. On the right is the ca. 1900 Birge House, Green and Wicks, architects. It has an elaborate entry porch, blind arches with swags, and a cornice-line parapet.

7. New York, New York; 1909–1926. Pyne, Filley, Sloane, and Davison Houses; McKim, Mead & White, Delano and Aldrich, and Walker and Gillette, architects for various houses. A remarkable surviving row of large attached town houses with detailing drawn from Georgian and Federal precedents.

3

6

BUILT-IN GARAGE

1. Chicago, Illinois; 1949. One of the FHA's three recommendations for built-in garage placement was to put the entrance in a plane in front of that of the house. This approach is used here and in Figures 2, 4, 5, and 6.

2. Minneapolis, Minnesota; 1965. Using a porch to visually connect a front-plane garage with the front door was quite popular (see also Figures 4 and 6). Note how the generally strict ranks of windows and doors of earlier Colonial Revival houses is lost here.

3. Chicago, Illinois; 1960. Here the garage is in the same plane as the house facade and interlocks with the main house block.

4. Bowie, Maryland; ca. 1964. This is the only example on this spread that does not have either a second-story overhang or a change in wall material between the two stories.

5. Chicago, Illinois; 1963. Note the use of two wall-cladding materials on most of the houses on this spread. Brick is used for the lower story—as would have been structurally appropriate in earlier eras—and frame, shingles, or other less expensive cladding material such as vinyl is used in the upper story and garage.

6. Lisle, Illinois; 1979.

7. Alexandria, Virginia; 1965. Here the typical Tri-Level Split spatial pattern is carried out on the level.

8. Seattle, Washington; ca. 1978. This later example places the garage on a third level.

2

4

6

8

In the years between 1880 and 1900 the Colonial Revival movement also influenced two other architectural styles: Queen Anne and Shingle. In the Queen Anne this produced the free classic subtype, which grades into the closely related asymmetrical Colonial Revival house. In the Shingle style, the shingled walls and rambling forms were thought to evoke early New England shingled houses with shed and lean-to additions. Moreover, colonial details such as Palladian windows were used in many examples.

The Philadelphia Centennial of 1876 is credited with first awakening an interest in our colonial architectural heritage.[3] In 1877 the fashionable architects McKim, Mead, White, and Bigelow took a widely publicized tour through New England to study original Georgian and Federal buildings at first hand. By 1886 they had executed two landmark houses in the style—the Appleton House (1883–1884) in Lennox, Massachusetts, and the Taylor House (1885–1886) in Newport, Rhode Island. These important examples typify the two subtypes that were most common before 1910: the asymmetrical form with superimposed colonial details and the more authentic symmetrical hipped roof shape; details in both tended to have exaggerated proportions.

These early examples of Colonial Revival were rarely historically correct copies but were instead free interpretations with details inspired by colonial precedents. During the first decade of this century, Colonial Revival fashion began to shift toward carefully researched copies with more correct proportions and details. This was encouraged by new methods of printing that permitted wide dissemination of photographs in books and periodicals. In 1898 *The American Architect and Building News* began an extensive series called "The Georgian Period: Being photographs and measured drawings of Colonial Work with text." This was joined in 1915 by the *White Pine Series of Architectural Monographs,* which was dominated by photographs of colonial buildings. These and similar ventures led to a wide understanding of the prototypes on which the Revival was based. Colonial Revival houses built in the years between 1915 and 1935 often reflect these influences by more closely resembling early prototypes than did those built earlier or later—with those constructed between 1920 and 1930 often having the most accurate details. The restoration of historic Williamsburg and the writings of Royal Barry Wills helped maintain an interest in building Colonial Revival houses from the 1930s into the 1950s. However, the economic depression of the 1930s, World War II, and changing postwar fashions led to a simplification of the style in the 1940s and 1950s. These later examples are most often of the side-gabled type, with simple stylized door surrounds, cornices, or other details that merely suggest their colonial precedents rather than closely mirroring them. In addition, Colonial Revival Ranch houses were built from the 1940s through the 1960s, many of them inspired by Wills's books and well-publicized designs.[4] Since the Colonial Revival began in the 1880s there has seldom been a time when some version of it was not being built somewhere in the United States. Although new Colonial Revival houses slowed to a trickle in the late 1950s, their production never completely disappeared. The Built-in Garage subtype appeared in pattern books until about 1980, when New Traditional versions of the Colonial Revival were already beginning to appear.

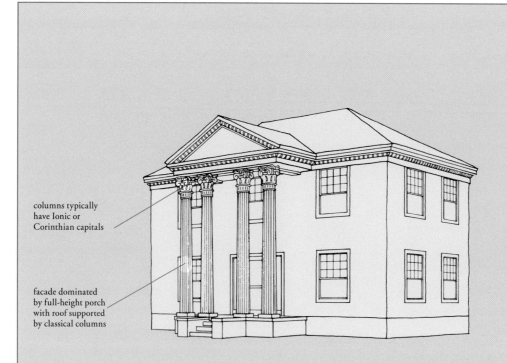

columns typically have Ionic or Corinthian capitals

facade dominated by full-height porch with roof supported by classical columns

facade with symmetrically balanced windows and center door

FULL-HEIGHT ENTRY PORCH

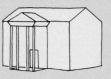

pages 438–39

FULL-HEIGHT ENTRY PORCH WITH LOWER FULL-WIDTH PORCH

page 440

FRONT-GABLED ROOF

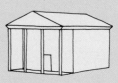

page 441

FULL-FACADE PORCH

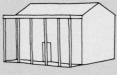

pages 442–43

ONE-STORY

pages 444–45

PRINCIPAL SUBTYPES

Neoclassical

1895–1955

Identifying Features

Facade dominated by full-height porch with roof supported by classical columns; columns typically have Ionic or Corinthian capitals; facade shows symmetrically balanced windows and center door.

Principal Subtypes

Five principal subtypes can be distinguished:

FULL-HEIGHT ENTRY PORCH—This common subtype has a dominant central entry porch extending the full height, but less than the full width, of the facade. It closely resembles certain Early Classical Revival and Greek Revival subtypes. As in both of these earlier styles, the entry porch may have a classical pediment and gabled roof above or, as in the Greek Revival only, the porch roof may be flat. Some Neoclassical examples have curved, semi-circular entry porches with flat roofs, a variation unusual on earlier prototypes.

FULL-HEIGHT ENTRY PORCH WITH LOWER FULL-WIDTH PORCH—In this relatively uncommon subtype, a full-width, one-story porch is added to the full-height entry porch just described. This dual-level entry porch is without precedent in the earlier classical styles. Most examples were built from 1895 to 1915; few, after World War I.

FRONT-GABLED ROOF—In this uncommon subtype, the full-facade, colonnaded porch beneath the front-facing gable gives the house the appearance of a miniature Greek temple. This form was very common in Greek Revival houses, but makes up only a small percentage of Neoclassical examples.

FULL-FACADE PORCH—In this subtype, as in the one just described, a colonnaded porch occupies the full width and height of the facade. Here, however, the porch is not covered by a traditional pedimented gable but instead either by the principal (side-gabled or hipped) roof or by a flat or shed extension from such a roof. This subtype became particularly popular in the period from about 1925 to 1950. These later examples normally have slender columns without elaborate capitals or fluted surfaces.

ONE-STORY—One-story Neoclassical cottages, a common subtype, usually have hipped roofs with prominent central dormers. The colonnaded porch may be either full- or partial-width and may be included under the main roof or have a separate flat or shed roof.

Variants and Details

The principal areas of elaboration in Neoclassical houses are porch-support columns, cornices, doorways, and windows.

PORCH-SUPPORT COLUMNS—In Neoclassical houses built before about 1920, the columns are generally more ornate than those of Early Classical Revival or Greek Revival prototypes. Corinthian or Ionic capitals, or mixtures of the two, are found in about 75 percent of Neoclassical houses but in less than 20 percent of Greek Revival examples. This change was made possible by the introduction of mass-produced capitals prefabricated of molded plaster or composition materials. Fluted column shafts are common in early houses. After about 1925, very slender, unfluted (often square) columns began to be used, primarily on houses with full-facade porches. Those usually lack capitals, and their proportions readily distinguish them from earlier Neoclassical and Greek Revival examples.

DOORWAYS—Doors commonly have elaborate, decorative surrounds based on Greek Revival, Federal, or even Georgian precedents (see pages 203, 219, and 249). Those with Georgian or Federal doorways are easily distinguished, because original examples very rarely had full-height, two-story columns (although some have had such porches added later). Greek Revival–type doorways may be more easily confused with original examples.

CORNICES—Neoclassical houses usually have a boxed eave with a moderate overhang, frequently with dentils or modillions beneath; a wide frieze band is occasionally found beneath the cornice. These are loosely based on Federal or Greek Revival precedents.

WINDOWS—Windows are rectangular with double-hung sashes. Examples following early precedent have six or nine panes to each sash; others have a multi-pane or single-pane upper sash and a single-pane lower sash. The presence of bay windows, paired windows, triple windows (except the Palladian type), transomed windows, or arched windows differentiate Neoclassical from Greek Revival or Early Classical Revival examples.

OTHER DETAILS—Many elaborations found on Early Classical Revival and Greek Revival houses also occur in Neoclassical examples. Roof-line balustrades, in particular, are much more common in Neoclassical houses than in the earlier styles. These are commonly found on top of full-height entry porches with flat roofs (without a pediment

ORIGINAL
EXAMPLES

EARLY CLASSICAL REVIVAL

with
full-
height
entry
porch

GREEK REVIVAL

with
full-
facade
porch

GREEK REVIVAL

NEOCLASSICAL
EXAMPLES
column capitals
are usually ornate,
columns are slender
and simple post-
1920

Corinthian
Composite
in only
5 percent
of originals

Ionic
in only
15 percent
of originals

side extensions
and porticos may
be added, unusual
in originals

window variations
not found in
originals

paired
and
triple
windows

transomed
and bay
windows

arched
windows

atypical portico
and porch
variations

two-story
entry
porch
with one-
story porch
unusual on
originals

curved
portico
in only
2 percent
of originals

cornice-line
balustrade
unusual on
originals

DISTINGUISHING THE NEOCLASSICAL HOUSE FROM EARLY CLASSICAL REVIVAL & GREEK REVIVAL ORIGINALS

cornice-line balustrade

exaggerated broken pediment

side and wing porches

full-width raised
platform porch

low balustrade around
platform porch

TYPICAL ELABORATIONS

Door with more than one line of lights always
post-1890 (it may, however, replace an original)

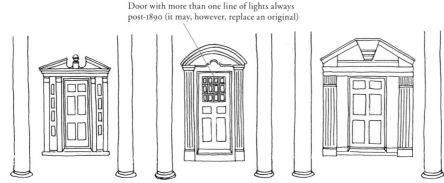

Houses with a broken
pediment at the entrance
or above a window and
two-story columns are
always Neoclassical;
houses with an unbroken
pediment at the entrance
and two-story columns
are usually Neoclassical
(a few Greek Revival
originals have unbroken
triangular pediments)

TYPICAL ENTRANCES

above), above full-facade porches, along the cornice line of the roof, or around the roof deck. Another type of railing, inspired by the detail found on Chinese Chippendale furniture, is also typical. A Chinese Chippendale railing consists of a repetitive geometric line pattern, generally contained in a series of rectangular frames. It is more commonly found in later examples built after ca. 1920 (see caption for photo 4 on page 442).

Occurrence

Neoclassical was a dominant style for domestic building throughout the country during the first half of the 20th century. Never quite as abundant as its closely related Colonial Revival contemporary, it had two principal waves of popularity. The first, from about 1900 to 1920, emphasized hipped roofs and elaborate, correct columns. The later phase, from about 1925 to the 1950s, emphasized side-gabled roofs and simple, slender columns. During the 1920s, the style was overshadowed by other Eclectic fashions.

3

4

7

FULL-HEIGHT ENTRY PORCH

1. Dallas, Texas; 1936. Bell House. A typical later example with side-gabled roof, roof-line balustrade, and simple square columns.

2. Dallas, Texas; 1940. Musgrove House. A late example with a side-gabled roof and slender columns. The somewhat awkward-looking projection of the entry porch results from the omission of an entablature under the pediment.

3. Raleigh, North Carolina; 1903. Goodwin House; William P. Rose, architect. This early example has fluted columns with Roman Ionic capitals. Note the variety of pediments—segmental over the lower-story windows, broken-ogee over the entrance fanlight, and triangular over the arched upper-story window.

4. Montgomery, Alabama; 1906. Governor's Mansion; Moses Sabel, architect. An elaborately detailed early example. Note the composite capitals on the pilasters and columns. These and the arched and double windows are never seen on earlier classical styles.

5. Dallas, Texas; 1933. Lee House. Here the entry porch (or portico) has been recessed into the body of the house; this is known as a portico in antis (see also Figure 6).

6. Kansas City, Missouri; ca. 1930s. Slender columns, side-gabled roof, and simplified Chinese Chippendale railing along the roof-line mark this as a late example.

7. New London, Connecticut; ca. 1910. An unusual gambrel-roof example. The triple windows, broken pediment occurring with full-height columns, and the curved entry porch with balustrade all mark this as a Neoclassical example.

8. Louisville, Kentucky; ca. 1910s. This entry porch is both recessed into the body of the house and extended outward. Note the keystone lintels over the upper-story windows and three-part lintels over the lower-story triple windows and the roof-line balustrade.

1

2

5

6

8

FULL-HEIGHT ENTRY PORCH WITH LOWER FULL-WIDTH PORCH

1. Dallas, Texas; ca. 1900. Harris House. In many examples the full-width lower porch is built independently, passing behind the tall entry porch as here and in Figure 5. In this example the lower porch even has a pediment at the entry.

2. Dallas, Texas; 1905. Baird House. In this example, the lower porch attaches to the tall entry porch; where they meet, both are supported by the same columns.

3. Dallas, Texas; 1911. Squared masonry pillars were sometimes substituted for classical columns.

4. Eufaula, Alabama; ca. 1910. This example is somewhat unusual in that no colossal columns are used for the full-height entry; instead, a second tier of one-story columns occurs above the lower porch.

5. Taylor, Texas; ca. 1910. This brick example has a tiled roof; the flat roof of the full-height porch is less common than the triangular pediments on Figures 1, 2, and 4; the triple columns supporting it are unusual.

FRONT-GABLED ROOF

1. Jamestown, New York; 1906. The fanlight over the front door distinguishes this example and that in Figure 2 from a Greek Revival original.

2. Brooklyn, New York; 1905. George Hitchings, architect. This house has a cross-gabled roof behind the dominant front gable. Note the unusual use of corner quoins next to the pilasters.

3. Little Rock, Arkansas; 1906. Haliburton Houses. Although not front-gabled, the hipped roof with front-to-back ridge gives these houses a similar look. As with most examples of this subtype, they were designed for narrow urban lots.

FULL-FACADE PORCH

1. Buffalo, New York; ca. 1910. Geir House.

2. Buffalo, New York; ca. 1930. The porch is recessed under the main roof of the house. The small entry porch with balustrade is an unusual addition. The simple square columns mark this as a late example.

3. Jackson, Mississippi, ca. 1910. A richly detailed house with tiled roof, paired balconies, and multiple swags.

4. Dallas, Texas; 1919. Warren House; Henry B. Thomson, architect. Note the full-length casement windows opening onto the porch and recessed side wings. The Chinese Chippendale cornice-line railing seen here and on Figure 8 was once used on Mount Vernon's river facade. Inspired by the nation's first museum house, these appeared on many homes (and other structures) from about 1920 to 1950. This eye-catching, and for a time iconic, feature was later discovered to be an addition. Now removed from Mount Vernon, it lives on in miniature tributes throughout the country, where it is an important character-defining feature. See also pages 439 (Figures 1 and 6) and 445 (Figures 3, 6, and 8).

5. Mission Hills, Kansas; ca. 1930. The side-gabled form and slender, simplified columns indicate a late date for this example.

6. Buffalo, New York; 1895. Williams House; Stanford White, architect. A green copper roof accents this landmark house.

7. Salisbury, North Carolina; ca. 1910. The forward extension in the central part of a full-facade porch (seen here and in Figures 3 and 6) is a Neoclassical feature not used during the earlier classical revivals.

8. Union Springs, Alabama; ca. 1920s. Note the one-story side wing to the left with a roof-line balustrade matching that of the main house.

2

4

5

8

ONE-STORY

1. Louisville, Kentucky; ca. 1910. An unusual early example.

2. Louisville, Kentucky; ca. 1910. Kettig House.

3. Dallas, Texas; 1929. Ohrum House. A late example with slender, square porch supports.

4. Smithfield, North Carolina; ca. 1910. Figures 4, 5, and 7 are all variations of the most common early form of the subtype. Note that all have hipped roofs, centered dormers, and full-facade porches. This example has a porch under a separate roof.

5. Selma, Alabama; ca. 1910.

6. Dallas, Texas; 1947. Marsh House. The entry porch is recessed into the house (portico in antis). A cupola has been added to suggest a miniature Mount Vernon.

7. Dallas, Texas; 1914. Gordon House. Note how the porch is under the main roof and the columns are set on pedestals.

8. Dallas, Texas; 1939. Harrison House. A one-story version of the most common late Neoclassical house with side-gabled roof, full-facade porch, and Chinese Chippendale cornice-line railing, inspired by the one once on Mount Vernon's river facade. Similar railings are on Figures 3 and 6.

3

6

8

Comments

This revival of interest in classical models dates from the World's Columbian Exposition, held in Chicago in 1893. The exposition's planners mandated a classical theme, and many of the best-known architects of the day designed dramatic colonnaded buildings arranged around a central court. The exposition was widely photographed, reported, and attended; soon these Neoclassical models became the latest fashion throughout the country.

The central buildings of the exposition were of monumental scale and inspired countless public and commercial buildings in the following decades. The designs of smaller pavilions representing each state of the Union were more nearly domestic in scale and in them can be seen the precedents for most Neoclassical houses. Those of Ohio, Utah, and South Dakota, for example, all had semi-circular, full-height entry porches. Nebraska and Kentucky were represented by more traditional full-height porches with triangular pediments. The Connecticut pavilion had a full-height entry porch with a lower full-width porch. All of these drew heavily on the country's previous interest in the Early Classical Revival and Greek Revival styles. The Virginia pavilion was a copy of Mount Vernon, whose full-facade porch, among the first in the country, had been added in 1777 to an earlier Georgian house. The presence of this replica at the fair, and the original's wide familiarity as the nation's premier museum house, contributed to the incorrect impression that such porches were colonial or perhaps "Southern colonial." Thus did Georgian, Federal, Early Classical Revival, and Greek Revival traditions, which originally spanned a century and a half of the nation's history, become fused into the eclectic Neoclassical style.

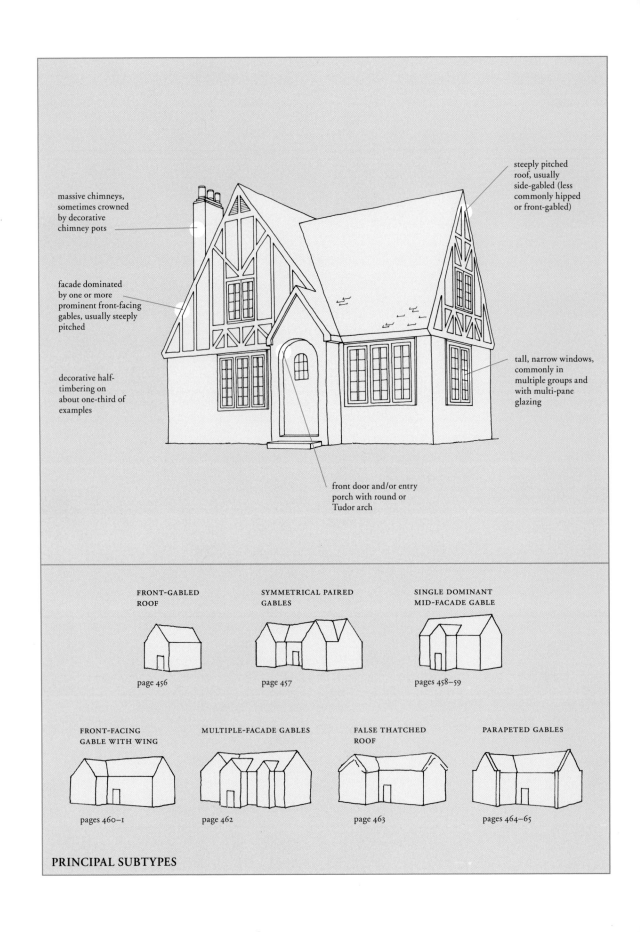

massive chimneys, sometimes crowned by decorative chimney pots

steeply pitched roof, usually side-gabled (less commonly hipped or front-gabled)

facade dominated by one or more prominent front-facing gables, usually steeply pitched

decorative half-timbering on about one-third of examples

tall, narrow windows, commonly in multiple groups and with multi-pane glazing

front door and/or entry porch with round or Tudor arch

FRONT-GABLED ROOF

page 456

SYMMETRICAL PAIRED GABLES

page 457

SINGLE DOMINANT MID-FACADE GABLE

pages 458–59

FRONT-FACING GABLE WITH WING

pages 460–1

MULTIPLE-FACADE GABLES

page 462

FALSE THATCHED ROOF

page 463

PARAPETED GABLES

pages 464–65

PRINCIPAL SUBTYPES

Tudor

1890–1940

Identifying Features

Steeply pitched roof, usually side-gabled (less commonly hipped or front-gabled); facade dominated by one or more prominent front-facing gables, usually steeply pitched; tall, narrow windows, usually in multiple groups, with multi-pane glazing; massive chimneys, sometimes crowned by decorative chimney pots; front door and/or entry porch with round or Tudor arch; decorative (i.e., not structural) half-timbering present on about one-third of examples.

Principal Subtypes

Eight principal subtypes can be distinguished:

FRONT-GABLED ROOF—About 15 percent of Tudor houses have a full-width front gable that dominates the front facade. Pre-1920 examples may include a full-width one-story front porch, and details from the contemporaneous Craftsman style, while later examples often have a massive roof form, sometimes with large side-facing dormers.

SYMMETRICAL PAIRED GABLES—Only about 5 percent of Tudor houses have a pair of symmetrical gables. Early examples sometimes had a lower-pitched roof and details from the contemporaneous Craftsman style.

SINGLE DOMINANT MID-FACADE GABLE—About 20 percent of Tudor homes are side-gabled or hipped form with a single front-facing gable added in the middle as the dominant facade element. This gable is rarely centered and generally includes the entry composition.

FRONT-FACING GABLE WITH WING—About 40 percent of Tudor houses are of this subtype, with a front-facing gable placed on one side of a side-gabled, or occasionally hipped, main house block. The front-facing gable sometimes includes a smaller gable nested inside.

MULTIPLE-FACADE GABLES—This picturesque subtype is found in about 15 percent of Tudor houses. It has two or more dominant cross gables placed randomly on the front facade and often includes gabled wall or roof dormers.

FALSE THATCHED ROOF—This rare but distinctive subtype mimics the picturesque thatched roofs of rural England with modern materials. Typically, composition roofing is rolled or wood shingles steamed around eaves and rakes, suggesting a thick layering of thatch. Originally these materials often had irregular textures, suggesting thatch, but usually these have been replaced with new materials of a more uniform texture. Such roofs were occasionally used on both symmetrical and asymmetrical forms of Tudor houses, from modest to grand.

PARAPETED GABLES—This less common subtype is based on the more formal building traditions of early Renaissance England and generally has masonry walls. The walls of the characteristic front-facing gables rise in a parapet above the roof behind. Elaborate facade detailing of Gothic or Renaissance inspiration is typical and includes windows with transoms and surrounds, and castellated parapets on flat-roofed towers, porches, and bays. Shaped Flemish gables are also found. This subtype was used in architect-designed landmarks built from about 1890 to 1915, particularly in the Northeast. Parapeted gables do not have half-timbering, but occasionally a non-parapeted half-timbered gable is added to a house of this subtype. After World War I, less formal and more picturesque early English models dominated, although scattered parapeted landmarks were built through the 1930s.

Variants and Details

The Tudor style is loosely based on a variety of early English building traditions, ranging from simple folk cottages to early Renaissance palaces. Decorative detailing is varied. In addition to its early English roots, the style may incorporate details from America's contemporaneous Craftsman houses.

GABLES—The composition and roof form of the prominent cross gables are diverse. While Tudor houses are almost always asymmetrical after about 1920, the composition of each individual front-facing gable element is more often symmetrical. The composition within a single-gabled section may include only windows, only the entry, or, more frequently, both. Compositions including a chimney are less common. The most common gable variant is a smaller gable nested within a larger one; these share the same roof pitch, and the smaller gable generally extends forward. Other gable-roof variations include: one eave much shorter than the other; one eave curving or sweeping outward; very steep or exaggerated sloops; clipped gables (a small hipped section replaces the gable peak); and gables that overlap. Gables without parapets are by far the most common and generally have a slight overhang of the gable roof. Plain vergeboards are typical, but decorative verges may have a simple scallop cut into the edge or be embossed with a floral or geometric design.

HALF-TIMBERING—Decorative (i.e., false) half-timbering, mimicking Medieval infilled timber framing, is found on about one-third of Tudor houses. It is generally a

  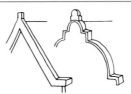

vergeboards, frequently half-timbered most common

plain, occasionally half-timbered

parapeted, never half-timbered

shaped Flemish gable

false thatched, occasionally half-timbered

TYPICAL GABLE DETAILS

smaller gable nested inside larger gable (usually with identical pitch and smaller gable extending outward)

overlapping gables

one eave longer than other

eave with sweeping curve

very steep gable

clipped gable

GABLE ROOF VARIATIONS

door only

window plus door in nested gable (most typical asymmetrical composition)

(windows set into half-timber pattern)

door with porch

windows only

door and porch with window above

chimney plus windows

GABLE COMPOSITION
(individual gable elements are most often symmetrical)

LOCATION

TYPICAL PATTERNS
infill usually stucco, but occasionally brick

in gable (most common)

 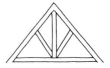

in second story

combination

in first story rare

HALF-TIMBERING

wood layer of two to three inches attached to the material below. Many different designs are found; most have stucco infilling between the timbers, but brick is also used, often laid in decorative patterns.

DOORWAYS AND PORCHES—Simple round-arched doorways with heavy wide-plank or board-and-batten wood doors are most common; small windows are often present in door. Similarly constructed rectangular and Tudor-arched doors are also used. The door surround is a favorite place for added detail. Small tabs of cut stone may project into surrounding brickwork, giving a quoin-like effect, or more informal patterns of stone or brickwork are used. A small entry porch is often present, commonly round or Tudor arched. Some examples have a deep one-story American sitting porch. Before about 1920, these often appear on the front facade, supported by squared piers. Later, sitting porches are generally located to the side, often under the main roof form.[5]

WINDOWS—Tudor homes almost always have one or more groupings of wood or metal casement windows, generally gathered into series of three or more. Small transoms are sometimes present, delineated with cast-stone mullions in high-style examples. Focal groups of casements may have small rectangular or diamond-shaped glass panes held in place by thin grooved lead strips rather than wood muntins. Original English Tudor-era houses had only casement windows (double-hung wood-sash windows had not been invented). American Tudor houses commonly use a combination of casement and double-hung windows, usually with very simple or no surrounds. Windows on half-timbered walls are typically integrated into the half-timbering pattern.

WALL CLADDING—The English precedents for this style were almost always stone, brick, or stucco, and masonry is therefore the preferred cladding for Tudor homes. Wood cladding of shingles or weatherboard was used primarily for less expensive homes.

Before about 1920, stone and brick walls had to be built of expensive solid masonry and were used for landmark examples. More modest early houses might have masonry first floors, but upper walls clad with weatherboard, shingles, or stucco (applied over wood lath), thus avoiding the expense of complete solid-masonry construction. By 1920, brick veneering was perfected and immediately became the preferred wall finish for even the most modest Tudor cottages. Stone walls, inspired by homes in the Cotswold area of England, were also popular and dominated a few stone-rich locales. Stone houses became more widespread as stone cladding was refined.

Before 1920 the least expensive way of achieving a "masonry" house was to apply stucco over a wood frame; stucco over hollow tile cost far more. In addition, stucco was favored by English architect C. F. A. Voysey for cladding his early Tudor homes in the English Arts and Crafts tradition. After 1920, solid stucco remained the choice for those desiring a "modern English home"—eschewing half-timbering and masonry patterns for a smooth-wall appearance.[6]

OTHER DETAILS—Large, elaborate chimneys are commonly placed in prominent locations on the front or side of the house. The lower part of the chimney may be decorated with complex masonry or stone patterns and the chimney may step inward as it rises from the ground. Multiple chimney shafts and ornamental chimney pots are common but often only decorative, rather than expressing the number of flues con-

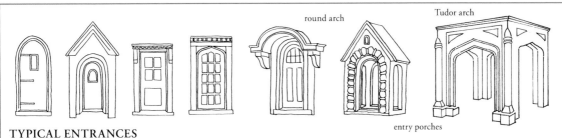

round arch

Tudor arch

entry porches

TYPICAL ENTRANCES

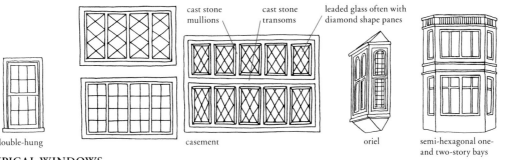

cast stone mullions

cast stone transoms

leaded glass often with diamond shape panes

double-hung

casement

oriel

semi-hexagonal one- and two-story bays

TYPICAL WINDOWS

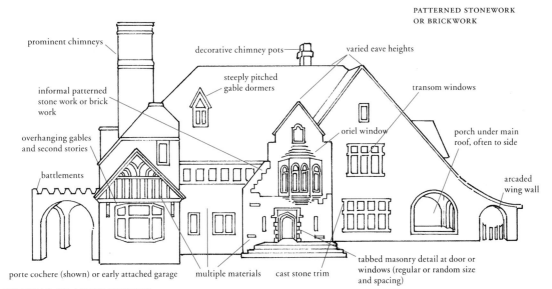

PATTERNED STONEWORK OR BRICKWORK

prominent chimneys

decorative chimney pots

varied eave heights

steeply pitched gable dormers

transom windows

informal patterned stone work or brick work

oriel window

porch under main roof, often to side

overhanging gables and second stories

battlements

arcaded wing wall

porte cochere (shown) or early attached garage

multiple materials

cast stone trim

tabbed masonry detail at door or windows (regular or random size and spacing)

TYPICAL ELABORATIONS

STRAPWORK

tained within, as in English originals. Upper stories and gables may overhang lower stories—a feature that made the heavy-timber structural skeleton stronger in original Tudor homes. Roofs were often of slate—with thick or irregularly shaped slates preferred by many architects.[7]

Both gabled and hipped-roof dormers and wall dormers are typical, as well as shed and eyebrow dormers. These facilitated additional half-stories of living space and are often found under the high-pitched Tudor roofs. It was easy space to construct, made good use of the roof volume, and added both varied eave heights and dormers to the composition. In front-gabled roof examples, broad side-facing shed dormers often add an almost complete second story under the massive roof. In the front-facing gable-with-wing subtype, a two-story front-facing gable often has a one-and-one-half-story side wing lighted either by multiple dormers or by a single large shed dormer.

Occurrence

This dominant style of domestic building was used for a large proportion of early 20th-century suburban houses throughout the country—probably comprising about 25 percent of houses built during the 1920s. Colonial Revival is the only style that surpassed Tudor in popularity between 1900 and the late 1920s. Early landmark examples were built around 1890 and by 1900 were joined by slightly more modest versions. The style was particularly fashionable during the 1920s, when it was sometimes called Stockbroker's Tudor. Tudor houses were simplified by the Depression, and during the 1930s French Eclectic houses began to supplant Tudor in popularity. Both Tudor and French were replaced with more modern styles after World War II.[8]

Comments

The popular name for the style is historically imprecise, since relatively few examples closely mimic the architectural characteristics of Tudor (16th-century) England. Instead, the style is loosely adapted from a variety of late Medieval and early Renaissance English prototypes, ranging from thatch-roofed folk cottages to grand manors. This broad variety provided the basis for a well-publicized English domestic architecture revival that began around 1850 and lasted until 1930. British architects such as Phillip S. Webb (1831–1915), C. F. A. Voysey (1857–1941), M. H. Baillie Scott (1865–1945), and Sir Edwin Lutyens (1869–1944) produced homes that were imitated both in the U.S. and Great Britain. Beginning about 1880, the publisher B. T. Batsford of London advanced this revival by publishing numerous books containing photographs, measured drawings, and drawings of old English homes, which were distributed in the U.S. In 1911 they published *The Domestic Architecture of England During the Tudor Period* by Thomas Garner and Arthur Stratton, perhaps the style's best sourcebook.[9]

Thus, many sources are freely combined in their American revivalist expressions but united by an emphasis on steeply pitched, front-facing gables that, although absent on many original English prototypes, are almost universally present as a dominant facade element in American Tudor houses.

The earliest American houses in the style date from the late 19th century. These tended to be architect-designed landmarks that might closely copy English models.

Many were patterned after late Medieval buildings with Renaissance detailing that were popular during the reigns of Elizabeth I (1558–1603) and James I (1603–1625), the Elizabethan and Jacobean eras of English history. Architecture historians have proposed the contracted term "Jacobethan" for these early Tudor landmarks. Most fall into the parapeted-gable subtype described above.[10]

The Tudor landmarks of the 1890s were joined in the decades from 1900 to 1920 by less pretentious Tudor houses, which superimposed half-timbering and other typical detailing upon symmetrical facades or simple gables-with-wing forms. Still relatively uncommon before World War I, the style exploded in popularity during the 1920s as masonry veneering techniques allowed even the most modest examples to mimic closely the brick and stone exteriors seen on English prototypes. They display endless variations in overall shape and roof forms. It is not uncommon for the character of Tudor-style homes to vary geographically. Wall materials greatly influence the appearance style, and nearby availability of a particular stone or brick can impart a distinct local character.[11] Second, respected local architects and their preferred approach to Tudor design can affect the typical appearance of the style in a neighborhood or an entire town.[12]

In addition to the variety in materials and detailing, the picturesque and asymmetri-

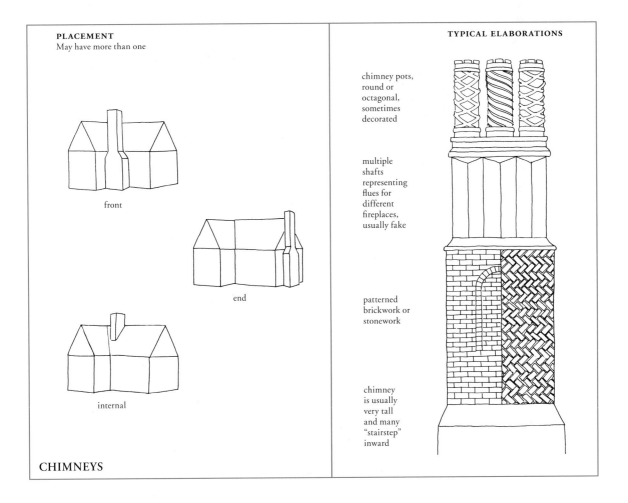

PLACEMENT
May have more than one

front

end

internal

TYPICAL ELABORATIONS

chimney pots, round or octagonal, sometimes decorated

multiple shafts representing flues for different fireplaces, usually fake

patterned brickwork or stonework

chimney is usually very tall and many "stairstep" inward

CHIMNEYS

FRONT-GABLED ROOF

1. Buffalo, New York; ca. 1910s. An early symmetrical example with a full front-gabled roof. Note the open eaves with exposed rafters, borrowed from contemporaneous Craftsman houses.

2. Kansas City, Missouri; ca. 1930s. An unusually tall and steeply pitched front-gabled roof forms the principal facade. Note the pedimented entry; varying interpretations of Classical doorways were added to Tudor house forms beginning in the 1920s.

3. Louisville, Kentucky; ca. 1910s. Such examples, with the dominant front gable capped by a hip, suggest Continental, rather than British, precedents. They were sometimes referred to as Germanic Cottages by Eclectic builders.

SYMMETRICAL PAIRED GABLES

1. Duluth, Minnesota; 1924. The symmetrical form seen here is common in pre-1920s examples, but unusual in later examples like this one.

2. Seattle, Washington; 1911. The overall symmetry almost masks the different window and half-timbering pattern in the second-story gables. Note how the windows fit within the half-timbering.

3. Philadelphia, Pennsylvania; ca. 1920s. Stone was locally available and widely utilized in Philadelphia; it is used here for the first story and for the entry area with small parapeted gable above.

4. Louisville, Kentucky; ca. 1910s. Open eaves with exposed rafters indicate a house with Craftsman influence. These were generally built before about 1915. The early date of this example is confirmed by the symmetrical form. Such elaborate half-timbered effects are also less common on later examples.

5. Hartford, Connecticut; ca. 1910s. A brick lower story with wood-shingled walls above.

SINGLE DOMINANT MID-FACADE GABLE

1. Duluth, Minnesota; 1947. What is basically a side-gabled Minimal Traditional house assumes a Tudor air when a small brick composition of entry with asymmetrical roof, prominent chimney and single casement window is placed asymmetrically in front.

2. Minneapolis, Minnesota; 1940. A simple side-gabled house is easily visible behind a large full-facade front-facing gable with arched door, swooping roof, and prominent chimney. Note use of informal decorative stone work around entrance and on chimney.

3. Lexington, Kentucky; ca. 1930s. One step up from Figure 1. Note how the distinctive form (side-gabled roof with the facade dominated by a prominent, steep cross gable and a massive chimney) marks this as a Tudor house even with little additional detailing.

4. Cleveland, Ohio; ca. 1920s. Note the finely detailed entry gable with very tall leaded glass windows, vergeboard, and decorative paneling. The curved roof line over the bay window is a distinctive but relatively rare Tudor feature.

1

2

3

4

SINGLE DOMINANT MID-FACADE GABLE (cont.)

5. Chicago, Illinois; 1928. The half-timbering pattern is unusual.

6. Salisbury, North Carolina; ca. 1910s. An early symmetrical example with exposed rafters.

7. Mendon, Utah; ca. 1935. Note the high foundation and basement windows on the side.

8. Chicago, Illinois; 1927. Note the one-car attached garage that served even a grand house prior to World War II. The garage wing may be a 1930s addition with a door that appears original and with leaded glass across the top.

9. Cleveland, Ohio; ca. 1920s. This example appears to retain the original roof of rough-cut slate. Note the unusually low eave line and the massive front chimneys.

5

6

7

8

9

FRONT-FACING GABLE WITH WING

1. Portland, Oregon; 1927. This house is similar in size and plan to Figure 3, but has neither entry nor sitting porch.

2. Hartford, Connecticut; ca. 1910s. The Craftsman-influenced front porch indicates the early date.

3. Lexington, Kentucky; ca. 1920s. Note how a small rounded English entry porch is used in conjunction with a broad American sitting porch on the right.

4. Duluth, Minnesota; 1907. Note the Craftsman detailing on the front porch. The porch begins at the ground and slopes inward with exposed wood beams over the entry.

5. Homewood, Alabama; ca. 1920s. Hollywood Historic District. Note the unusual half-timbering pattern.

6. Minneapolis, Minnesota; ca. 1920s. The welcoming entry features a nested gable, decorative stonework and a front door with vertical lights.

7. Seattle, Washington; ca. 1930. Note sweeping curve of the front-facing gable.

8. Dallas, Texas; 1929. Compare this 1920s "period house" example, with a side porch under the main roof, to Figure 4, a 1900s example with a Craftsman-influenced porch.

9. Seattle, Washington; 1931. A two-story front-facing gable was often combined with a one-story wing. Here it has a large shed dormer.

1

3

6

7

MULTIPLE FACADE GABLES

1. Dallas, Texas; ca. 1930s. The trio of front-facing gables has an unusually steep pitch.
2. Homewood, Alabama; ca. 1920s. Hollywood Historic District. Each gable has a different pattern of half-timbering.
3. Toledo, Ohio; ca. 1920s. A landmark example with multiple gables and chimneys and a Renaissance-inspired door surround.
4. Cleveland, Ohio; remodeled 1924. S. Weringen House; Philip L. Small, architect. This landmark example has a three-story bay window with castellations above and an irregular roof shape.

FALSE THATCHED ROOF

1. Portland, Oregon; ca. 1920s. This steeply pitched roof with curved dormer and curved gable roof gives a convincing imitation of thatch.

2. Cleveland, Ohio; ca. 1920s. Note how the windows in the front-facing gable are carefully inserted into the overall half-timbering pattern and the side porch on the left, under the main roof of the house.

3. Columbus, Georgia; 1930.

4. San Francisco, California; 1909. This house has distinctive massing with four easily discernible elements: a rounded sunroom, a wing, an unusual narrow and tall half-timbered central gable, and an unusual broad and long main front-facing gable.

5. Cedarhurst, New York; ca. 1910s. This atypical example lacks the front-facing gable usually found on Tudor houses. The trellised front entry shows some Craftsman influence. The original composition roofing is shown; note the textured pattern, which closely simulates thatch. There are a number of examples of similar side-gabled houses with false thatched roofs, possibly inspired by Anne Hathaway's cottage in Warwickshire, England.

PARAPETED GABLES

1. Cleveland, Ohio; ca. 1910s. An unusual interpretation with flat roof and battlements all around.

2. St. Louis, Missouri; ca. 1910s. Note the shaped Flemish gables and tabbed window and door surrounds.

3. Richmond, Virginia; ca. 1910s. This finely detailed example was designed for a relatively narrow urban lot.

4. Tuxedo Park, New York; ca. 1910s. Mitchell House. Note the flat-roofed tower with battlements, shaped Flemish gables, and the Renaissance-influenced door surround with columns and pediments.

1

2

3

4

PARAPETED GABLES (cont.)

5. Seattle, Washington; 1914. This adds an air of informality by combining a half-timbered gable with a parapet gable.

6. San Francisco, California; ca. 1910s. The narrow end is turned toward the street.

7. Buffalo, New York; 1910s. Albright House. The multiple chimneys with paired flues and the lines of casement windows with stone transoms are features seen in many examples of this subtype.

8. Chicago, Illinois; 1895. Hyde Park.

9. Concord, North Carolina; ca. 1920s. This and Figure 7 are symmetrical interpretations that are relatively common in parapeted examples.

5

6

7

8

9

cal Tudor offered architects great versatility in floor planning. The house plan could rule the design rather than its being dictated by symmetry. This freedom allowed rooms to be oriented in any direction and windows to be placed where needed; it allowed simple inclusion of wings only one room deep; rooms that were two stories high and wings placed at an angle; and it allowed studios, service rooms, and, later, attached garages, to be effortlessly incorporated into the design.

busy roof
line with many
vertical elements (spires,
pinnacles, turrets, gables,
shaped chimneys)

steeply pitched,
hipped roof

multiple dormers,
usually wall dormers
extending through
cornice line

walls of masonry,
usually stone

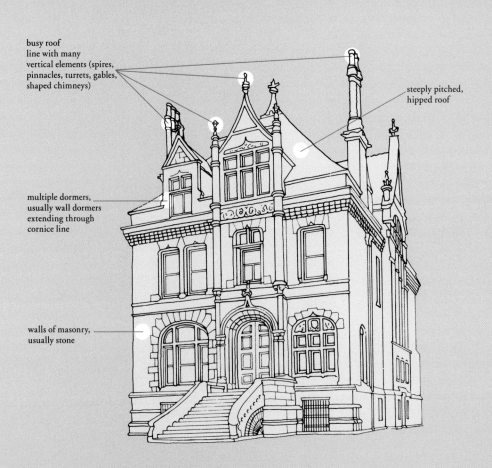

Chateauesque

1880–1910

Identifying Features

Steeply pitched hipped roof; busy roof line with many vertical elements (spires, pinnacles, turrets, gables, and shaped chimneys); multiple dormers, usually wall dormers extending through cornice line; walls of masonry (usually stone).

Variants and Details

The steeply pitched hipped roofs are sometimes truncated above by a flat roof deck; others rise to a high pyramidal apex or hipped ridge. Towers and turrets have steep candle-snuffer roofs. Dormer roofs are usually steep, parapeted gables. Ornamental metal cresting is sometimes used along roof ridges or above cornice lines; the latter generally have elaborate moldings. Gables, doorways, windows, and other facade elements are commonly ornamented with shallow relief carving or Gothic tracing. Windows are usually divided by stone mullions into narrow vertical units with smaller transoms above. Windows and doorways may be arched; the arches often have a characteristic Gothic basket-handle shape.

Occurrence

Chateauesque is a rare style used primarily for architect-designed landmark houses. Scattered examples are found throughout the country but are most frequent in the larger cities of the northeastern states. Most of these date from the late 1880s and 1890s. Elsewhere the fashion persisted through the first decade of this century.

Comments

The Chateauesque is loosely based on monumental 16th-century chateaus of France, which combined earlier Gothic elements with that century's increasingly fashionable trend toward Renaissance detailing. As in the originals, Chateauesque houses show varying mixtures of Gothic and Renaissance detail. The style was popularized in this country by Richard Morris Hunt, the first American architect to study at France's prestigious École des Beaux-Arts. In France, a mid-19th-century revival of buildings in the chateau (or François I) style undoubtedly influenced Hunt, who returned to advocate similar buildings for his wealthy clients. Among these were the Vanderbilts, for whom he designed several Chateauesque houses, culminating in Biltmore, George W. Vander-

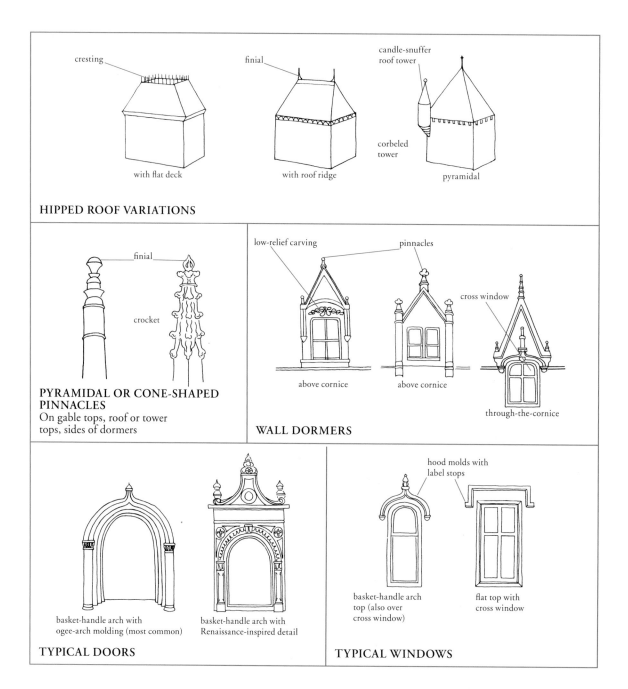

HIPPED ROOF VARIATIONS

cresting — with flat deck

finial — with roof ridge

candle-snuffer roof tower — corbeled tower — pyramidal

PYRAMIDAL OR CONE-SHAPED PINNACLES
On gable tops, roof or tower tops, sides of dormers

finial

crocket

WALL DORMERS

low-relief carving — pinnacles — above cornice

above cornice

cross window — through-the-cornice

TYPICAL DOORS

basket-handle arch with ogee-arch molding (most common)

basket-handle arch with Renaissance-inspired detail

TYPICAL WINDOWS

hood molds with label stops

basket-handle arch top (also over cross window)

flat top with cross window

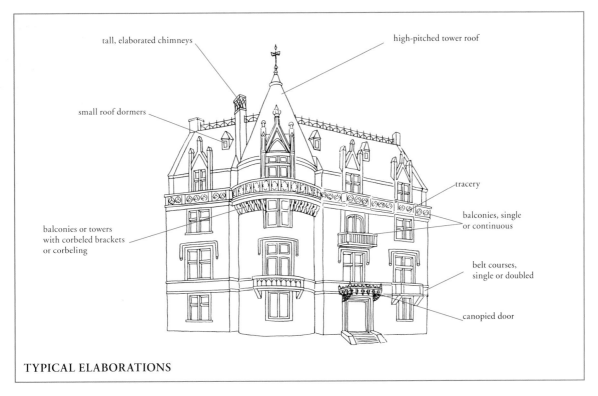

tall, elaborated chimneys

high-pitched tower roof

small roof dormers

tracery

balconies, single
or continuous

balconies or towers
with corbeled brackets
or corbeling

belt courses,
single or doubled

canopied door

TYPICAL ELABORATIONS

CHATEAUESQUE

1. Boston, Massachusetts; 1890s. An attached town house; note the through-the-cornice wall dormer.
2. Louisville, Kentucky; 1890s. The paired wall dormers begin above the cornice in this detached town house.

1

2

CHATEAUESQUE (cont.)

3. Montgomery, Alabama; 1906. Sabel House. The pyramidal hipped roof is also seen in Figures 4 and 7.

4. Chicago, Illinois; ca. 1880. Byram House; Burnham and Root, architects. The entrance door is in a basket-handle arch surrounded by ogee-arch molding.

5. Milwaukee, Wisconsin; ca. 1900. Goldberg House. Note the delicate tracery above the dormers.

6. St. Louis, Missouri; 1892. Bixby House. White paint covers original brick and the colors of the terra-cotta trim. Note the elaborately sculpted dormer detailing.

7. Cincinnati, Ohio; ca. 1890s. The rough-faced stone of this house is more common in Richardsonian Romanesque houses; Chateauesque examples are more often of brick or smooth-faced stone.

8. New Haven, Connecticut; 1896. Joseph W. Northrup, architect.

9. Asheville, North Carolina; 1895. Biltmore; Richard Morris Hunt, architect. This, the ultimate Chateauesque landmark, is located in a setting of gardens worthy of the French originals.

10. Redlands, California; 1897. Kimberly Crest; Dennis and Farwell, architects. Constructed of frame walls with smooth stucco cladding and wood trim, rather than of the stone construction more typical of Chateauesque.

4

7

8

10

bilt's North Carolina country house completed in 1895, which rivaled its early French prototypes in size and splendor. The Chateauesque style required massive masonry construction and elaborate, expensive detailing and was therefore unsuitable for vernacular imitation. It thus remained a relatively rare, architect-designed fashion throughout its brief period of popularity.

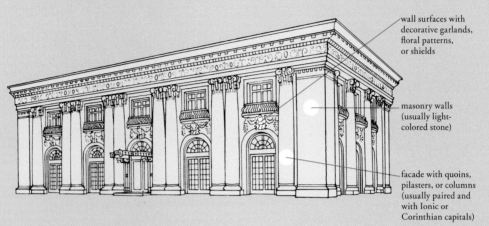

wall surfaces with
decorative garlands,
floral patterns,
or shields

masonry walls
(usually light-
colored stone)

facade with quoins,
pilasters, or columns
(usually paired and
with Ionic or
Corinthian capitals)

facade symmetrical

first story typically
rusticated (stonework
joints exaggerated,
see typical
elaborations, page 479)

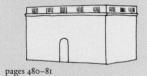

FLAT OR LOW-PITCHED HIPPED ROOF

pages 480–81

MANSARD ROOF

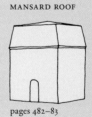

pages 482–83

PRINCIPAL SUBTYPES

Beaux Arts

1885–1930

Identifying Features

Wall surfaces with decorative garlands, floral patterns, or shields; facade with quoins, pilasters, or columns (usually paired and with Ionic or Corinthian capitals); walls of masonry (usually smooth, light-colored stone); first story typically rusticated (stonework joints exaggerated); facade symmetrical.

Principal Subtypes

Two principal subtypes can be distinguished:

FLAT OR LOW-PITCHED HIPPED ROOF—This more common of the two subtypes is based on Italian or northern European Renaissance models. Examples lacking full-height, two-story columns are similar to some landmark Italian Renaissance houses, which, however, lack the elaborate decorative detailing typifying the Beaux Arts. This detailing also generally serves to distinguish colonnaded Beaux Arts houses from closely related Neoclassical examples, which, in addition, seldom have the paired columns typical of the Beaux Arts. In brief, look for paired columns and/or elaborate decorative detailing to most easily help distinguish Beaux Arts houses from similar Italian Renaissance and Neoclassical examples.

MANSARD ROOF—This subtype is loosely based on 17th- and 18th-century French Renaissance models that have distinctive mansard (dual-pitched hipped) roofs with dormer windows on the steep lower slope. These may resemble earlier Second Empire houses with similar roofs, which are, however, generally of smaller scale with walls of wood or brick, rather than stone, and without the distinctive facade decoration of Beaux Arts examples.

Variants and Details

The Beaux Arts is a classical style and has many of the same details found in other styles of Renaissance classical inspiration, which, however, seldom have the exuberant surface ornamentation that characterizes the Beaux Arts. Entry porches with roofs supported by classical columns are common. Cornice lines are accented by elaborate moldings, dentils, and modillions. Roof-line balustrades and balustraded window balconies are common, as are elaborated window crowns and surrounds. Classical quoins, pilasters, and columns are almost universal. Walls are usually smooth stone or brick; decorative details and elaborations are often made from glazed terra cotta or cast stone.[13]

Occurrence

Houses in the Beaux Arts style are usually architect-designed landmarks and were built principally in the prosperous urban centers where turn-of-the-20th century wealth was concentrated. New York, Chicago, Washington, D.C., St. Louis, and San Francisco had many examples, as did Newport, Rhode Island, a favorite summer playground for the affluent. Most domestic examples were built before 1915 but the style persisted until the economic depression of the 1930s. Isolated examples occur throughout the country.

Comments

The term "Beaux Arts" (the approximate French equivalent of "Fine Arts") is used by architectural historians in two different senses. Some use it to describe the entire 1885–1920 period of elaborate eclectic styles because these tended to be advocated by Americans who studied at France's École des Beaux-Arts, the era's premier school of architecture. A more limited meaning, followed here, stresses only one Eclectic tradition among the many that were then popular. This is based on Classical precedents elaborated by lavish decorative detailing, and was perhaps the most typical of the many styles inspired by study at the École. More than any other style (except perhaps the Chateauesque), the Beaux Arts expressed the taste and values of America's industrial barons at the turn of the 20th century. In those pre-income tax days, great fortunes were proudly displayed in increasingly ornate and expensive houses. Many were of such a size that they were impossible to maintain in later eras of economic recession and higher taxes. Most of the grandest have been destroyed, but some are preserved as schools, club houses, or museums. The Preservation Society of Newport County, in particular, has saved several of the most elaborate examples as public museums.

Another concern of the École des Beaux-Arts was for formal planning of the spacial relationships between buildings. This influence provided the impetus for the City Beautiful movement which was prevalent at the turn of the 20th century. The first major example was the planning, supervised by Richard Morris Hunt, for the World's Columbian Exposition in Chicago in 1893. Soon cities such as Cleveland, Philadelphia, and Washington, D.C., implemented monumental planning for their city centers. On a domestic scale this interest in formal design expressed itself in planned suburbs with extensive parks and boulevards lined with landmark houses.

shields (escutcheons)

ornamented keystones, commonly with acanthus leaf

leaf or floral decoration in window crowns

elaborately bordered panels, most commonly round or oval cartouche

swags of draped cloth or flowers

brackets with acanthus leaf or other elaboration

panels with low-relief floral or leaf carving (rinceau)

TYPICAL DECORATIVE DETAILS (often made of glazed terra cotta)

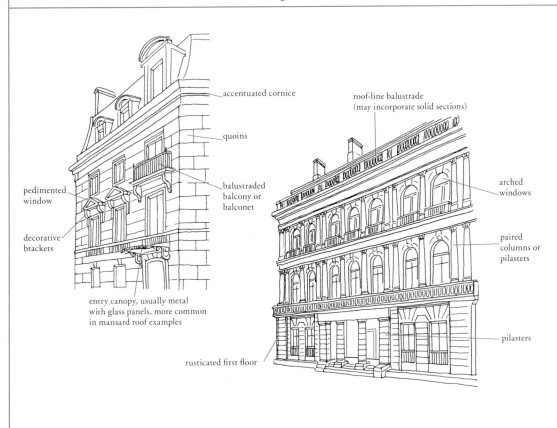

accentuated cornice

quoins

pedimented window

balustraded balcony or balconet

decorative brackets

entry canopy, usually metal with glass panels, more common in mansard roof examples

rusticated first floor

roof-line balustrade (may incorporate solid sections)

arched windows

paired columns or pilasters

pilasters

TYPICAL ELABORATIONS

FLAT OR LOW-PITCHED HIPPED ROOF

1. Louisville, Kentucky; 1901. Ferguson House.

2. Cincinnati, Ohio; ca. 1910. Note the wide frieze with windows and floral swags.

3. Dallas, Texas; 1906. Alexander House. This example lacks the floral ornamentation typical of the style, but the paired columns with bands and flat roof with attic windows indicate a Beaux Arts, rather than Neoclassical, inspiration.

4. Cleveland, Ohio; 1914. Tremaine House; Frederic W. Striebinger, architect. This example, and Figures 6 and 8, reflect a common Renaissance form in which a main block is flanked by symmetrical front-projecting wings. As in Figure 8, an arcaded porch is set here between the wings.

5. Frankfort, Kentucky; 1914. Governor's Mansion.

6. Newport, Rhode Island; 1902. Rosecliff; McKim, Mead & White, architects.

7. St. Louis, Missouri; 1899. Hills House. An example with a low-pitched hipped roof. Note the flat-roof portico on the left, pedimented portico on the front, and semi-circular portico to right.

8. Newport, Rhode Island; 1892. The Breakers; Richard Morris Hunt, architect (seaside facade). Low-pitched hipped roofs, usually covered with tiles as seen here, also occur in Beaux Arts houses. In other details these are similar to flat-roof examples. Unfortunately the photograph cannot show the numerous small floral details in this Beaux Arts landmark.

1

3

5

7

2

4

6

8

MANSARD ROOF

1. Washington, District of Columbia; 1907.
   Bliss House; A. Goenner, architect.
   Attached Beaux Arts town houses such
   as this are found principally in the larger
   cities of the Northeast. The mansard roof
   is particularly favored for urban houses
   because it reduces the apparent height of
   upper-floor living space.

2. Washington, District of Columbia; 1909.
   Fahnestock House; Nathan C. Wyeth,
   architect.

3. Washington, District of Columbia; 1901.
   Walsh House; Henry Andersen, architect.

4. Montgomery, Alabama; ca. 1910. Sabel
   House. A rare example built far from the
   urban centers of the Northeast.

5. San Francisco, California; ca. 1915. James
   F. Dunn, architect. Dunn's distinctive
   Beaux Arts houses have a sinuous Art
   Nouveau influence in their details.

6. Buffalo, New York; ca. 1920s. The curved
   central wing is unusual in this late
   example.

7. Washington, District of Columbia; 1909.
   Moran House; George Oakley Totten, Jr.,
   architect. The entryways of this subtype
   rarely have the colonnaded entry porches
   seen in the flat-roof subtype. Here only
   a simple glass canopy is used over the
   entrance door.

8. New York, New York; 1905. DeLamar
   House; C. P. H. Gilbert, architect. This
   example has the paired side wings that
   are seen more frequently in the flat-roof
   subtype.

1

4

5

6

2

3

7

8

commonly has segmental arch on door, windows, or dormers

tall, steeply pitched, hipped roof (occasionally gabled in towered subtype) without dominant, front-facing cross gable

brick, stone, or stucco wall cladding, sometimes with false half-timbering

eaves commonly flared upward at roof-wall junction

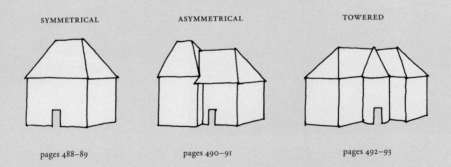

SYMMETRICAL

ASYMMETRICAL

TOWERED

pages 488–89

pages 490–91

pages 492–93

PRINCIPAL SUBTYPES

French Eclectic

1915–1945

Identifying Features

Tall, steeply pitched hipped roof (occasionally gabled in towered subtype) without dominant front-facing cross gable; eaves commonly flared upward at roof-wall junction; commonly has segmental arch on door, windows, or dormers; brick, stone, or stucco wall cladding, sometimes with decorative half-timbering.

Principal Subtypes

Three principal subtypes can be recognized; each shows a great variety of detailing and wall materials:

SYMMETRICAL—In this subtype, the massive hipped roof, normally with the ridge paralleling the front of the house, dominates a symmetrical facade with centered entry. Facade detailing is usually rather formal, inspired by smaller French manor houses rather than grand chateaus or modest farmhouses. Wings are frequently added to the sides of the main block.

ASYMMETRICAL—This is the most common subtype and includes both picturesque examples based on rambling French farmhouses as well as more formal houses similar to the symmetrical subtype, but with off-center doorways and asymmetrical facades.

TOWERED—This common subtype is immediately identifiable by the presence of a prominent round tower with a high, conical roof. The tower generally houses the principal door or stairway. Decorative half-timbering is particularly common in this subtype, which is loosely patterned after similar farmhouses from the province of Normandy in northwestern France; Eclectic builders often called these Norman Cottages.

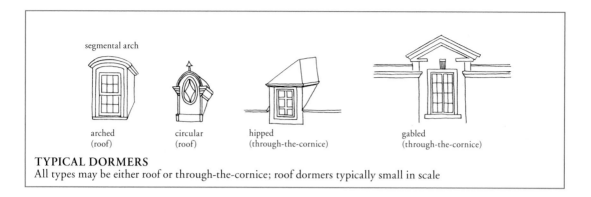

segmental arch

arched
(roof)

circular
(roof)

hipped
(through-the-cornice)

gabled
(through-the-cornice)

TYPICAL DORMERS
All types may be either roof or through-the-cornice; roof dormers typically small in scale

Variants and Details

Based upon precedents provided by many centuries of French domestic architecture, the style shows great variety in form and detailing but is united by the characteristic roof. (Only the Spanish Revival style, similarly based upon a long and complex architectural tradition, approaches it in variety.) Informal domestic building in northwestern France (particularly Normandy and Brittany) shares much with Medieval English tradition. The use of half-timbering with a variety of different wall materials, as well as roofs of flat tile, slate, stone, or thatch, are common to both. As a result, French Eclectic houses often resemble the contemporaneous Tudor style based on related English precedent. French examples, however, normally lack the dominant front-facing cross gables characteristic of the Tudor. In contrast to these generally informal, rural prototypes, many French Eclectic houses show formal Renaissance detailing resembling that of the English Georgian.

Doors in informal examples are usually set in simple arched openings; doors in symmetrical and formal houses may be surrounded by stone quoins or more elaborate Renaissance detailing (pilasters, pediments, etc.). Windows may be either double-hung or casement sashes, the latter sometimes with small leaded panes. Full-length casement windows with shutters (French doors) are sometimes used. The dominant high-pitched roof may be enhanced by one of these distinctive features that indicate a house is likely to be French Eclectic: (1) through-the cornice dormers or windows and (2) roof dormers that are relatively small in scale or that form a high second tier of dormers on a steep roof.

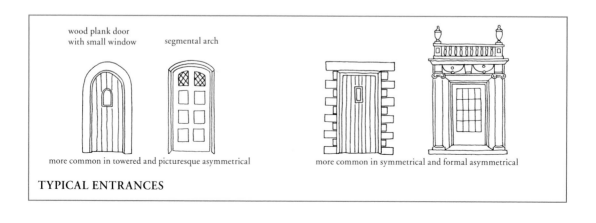

wood plank door
with small window

segmental arch

more common in towered and picturesque asymmetrical

more common in symmetrical and formal asymmetrical

TYPICAL ENTRANCES

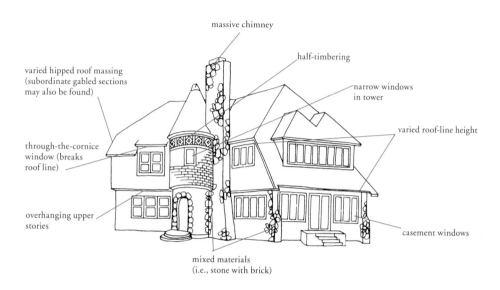

massive chimney

half-timbering

varied hipped roof massing
(subordinate gabled sections
may also be found)

narrow windows
in tower

varied roof-line height

through-the-cornice
window (breaks
roof line)

overhanging upper
stories

casement windows

mixed materials
(i.e., stone with brick)

MORE COMMON IN SYMMETRICAL SUBTYPE

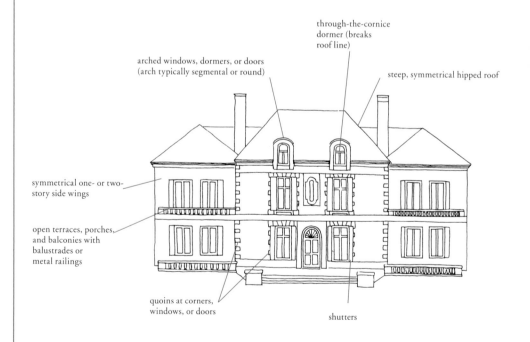

through-the-cornice
dormer (breaks
roof line)

arched windows, dormers, or doors
(arch typically segmental or round)

steep, symmetrical hipped roof

symmetrical one- or two-
story side wings

open terraces, porches,
and balconies with
balustrades or
metal railings

quoins at corners,
windows, or doors

shutters

TYPICAL ELABORATIONS

SYMMETRICAL

1. Buffalo, New York; ca. 1920s. This example has been turned 90° to adapt to a narrow urban lot. What would ordinarily be the side facade faces the street and has been elaborated with shutters and a dormer.

2. Dallas, Texas; 1941. Evans House.

3. Dallas, Texas; 1924. Hall House. Henry B. Thomson, architect. Note small scale of the roof dormers here and in Figure 6.

4. Cleveland, Ohio; ca. 1920s. Although the main block of this house appears symmetrical, a close look will reveal the right side to be narrower than the left. The open eave with exposed rafters is uncommon in French Eclectic houses.

5. Buffalo, New York; ca. 1920s. This house has two identical forward-facing wings; the left one is hidden behind a tree in the photograph. The through-the-cornice wall dormers have windows placed higher in the wing than those in the taller main block.

6. Dallas, Texas; ca. 1917. Lewis-Aldredge House; Henry B. Thomson, architect. This house has Renaissance detailing borrowed from the Beaux Arts movement. Note the columns beside the door and in the side wings, the pediment over the entry at roof level, the balustrades on the porch, over the door, and in the roof section. The pitch of the hipped roof is also lower than in most examples of the style.

7. St. Louis, Missouri; 1914. Mallinckrodt House; James P. Jamieson, architect. A strong Chateauesque influence is evident in the door surround, dormers, and roof ornaments of this early example.

I

4

6

ASYMMETRICAL

1. Louisville, Kentucky; ca. 1920s. Note the irregular quoins around the door and windows.

2. Richmond, Virginia; ca. 1920s. A formal example with a shallow-projecting wing that is difficult to distinguish in the photograph. The house is designed for a narrow urban lot.

3. Cincinnati, Ohio; ca. 1920s. Note the varied eave-line heights, massive chimney, and two types of through-the-cornice wall dormers. Compare this informal, picturesque house with Figure 7, a formal, Renaissance-inspired example.

4. Cleveland, Ohio; ca. 1920s. Examples based on informal French models sometimes affect Medieval half-timbering as here.

5. Dallas, Texas; ca. 1930. Note the five through-the-cornice windows.

6. St. Louis, Missouri; 1891. Meysenburg House; Eames & Young, architects. A very early example with Beaux Arts influence in the decorative detail at the entrance and windows.

7. Washington, District of Columbia; 1904. Graff House; Jules Henri de Sibour, architect. This house has formal Renaissance detailing; note the regular quoins, keystone lintels, cornice-line dentils, and pedimented dormers with a row of smaller dormers above.

8. Dallas, Texas; 1929. Owens House; Greene, LaRoche & Dahl, architect. Note the decorative brick pattern of the entryway and the open front balustrade terrace.

2

5

6

8

TOWERED

1. Raleigh, North Carolina; ca. 1930s. Note the three slightly different dormers.

2. Dallas, Texas; 1937. Gilliland House; Charles S. Dilbeck, architect. This example is unusual in not having the entrance in the tower (see also Figure 8). Note the two chimneys of differing shapes and materials and also that none of the five windows are identical.

3. Mission Hills, Kansas; ca. 1930s.

4. Kansas City, Missouri; ca. 1930s.

5. Buffalo, New York; ca. 1930s. The regular, formal placement of the windows is not typical of this subtype.

6. Kansas City, Missouri; ca. 1930s. Note the multi-colored slate roof, tower overhang, massive chimney, and tiny band of half-timbering on the tower.

7. Cleveland, Ohio; ca. 1930s. Here a stone tower is combined with walls of half-timbered stucco or brick. Note the curving secondary hipped roof, simulating thatch, above the bay windows.

8. Tuxedo Park, New York; ca. 1930s. Kent House. This landmark example has several towers and an unusually tall roof—note the double row of dormers.

3

4

6

7

Occurrence

French Eclectic houses were rarely built before World War I. Those that occur before 1920 are commonly of the symmetrical subtype, and are more formal examples—perhaps inspired by the Chateauesque of Beaux Arts traditions. The style began to be somewhat fashionable in the early 1920s, and in 1925 about 5 percent of the new homes built were French, according to a study of houses published in architectural journals that year. By 1930, French Eclectic houses were overtaking Tudor to become the second most popular Eclectic style during the 1930s (behind the always leading Colonial Revival). As with most other Eclectic styles, the French faded from favor after World War II.[14]

Comments

Many Americans—among them both architects and builders—served in France during World War I, and gained a firsthand familiarity with the broad spectrum of smaller French houses upon which this style is based. During the following decade, the 1920s, Americans were entranced by France, having helped rescue it during the war. Much press was given to the reconstruction of France's historic villages that had been damaged. In addition, a number of photographic studies of modest French houses were published in the 1920s, giving a wide variety of models to draw from.

Arthur Meigs and George Howe were among the architects who served in France and subsequently designed French houses; they designed the well-publicized Arthur Newbold house in Pennsylvania (1923). Another veteran was Walter Davis, who built "The French Village" in Hollywood. Architect Frank Joseph Forster began building award-winning French Eclectic houses in 1920s, and also published articles on the style. By the late 1920s even architects who had long embraced the Tudor, such as Harrie T. Lindeberg, were designing French houses, and continued to do so into the 1930s. The attention and architectural awards given to high-style French Eclectic houses made the style also desirable to local architects and builders during the 1930s.[15]

hipped roof
of low pitch
(occasionally flat)

typically with
tile roof covering

upper-story windows
smaller and less
elaborate than
windows below

widely overhanging
eaves supported by
decorative brackets

entry area usually
accentuated by small
classical columns
or pilasters

commonly with round
arches above door,
first-story windows,
or porches

facade most
commonly symmetrical

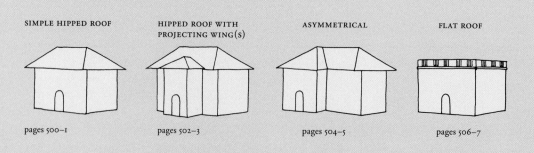

SIMPLE HIPPED ROOF

HIPPED ROOF WITH
PROJECTING WING(S)

ASYMMETRICAL

FLAT ROOF

pages 500–1

pages 502–3

pages 504–5

pages 506–7

PRINCIPAL SUBTYPES

Italian Renaissance

1890–1935

Identifying Features

Low-pitched hipped roof (flat in some examples); widely overhanging eaves supported by decorative brackets; roof typically covered by ceramic tiles; upper-story windows smaller and less elaborate than windows below; commonly with round arches above doors, first-story windows, or porches; entrance area usually accented by small classical columns or pilasters; facade most commonly symmetrical.

Principal Subtypes

Four principal subtypes can be distinguished:

SIMPLE HIPPED ROOF—Over half of Italian Renaissance houses have a simple hipped roof with a flat, symmetrical front facade. Full-width porches, often with massive square piers as porch supports, are frequent in examples built before 1920.

HIPPED ROOF WITH PROJECTING WING(S)—Many Italian Renaissance houses have either a small central wing projecting forward from the front facade, or two small wings at either end of the facade with a recessed central block in between.

ASYMMETRICAL—A relatively small proportion of Italian Renaissance houses have unbalanced, asymmetrical facades. Usually the asymmetry involves only door and window placement on an otherwise symmetrical building of simple square or rectangular plan. Less commonly L plans or more complex shapes are used.

FLAT ROOF—Many high-style Italian Renaissance houses have flat roofs, usually with a prominent, dentiled cornice and roof-line balustrade. Typically the first story is rusticated (finished as exaggerated stonework courses), while the floors above have smooth wall finishes. Facades are symmetrical. These are almost always architect-designed landmarks built of stone; they are closely related to flat-roofed, Beaux Arts–style houses, which are similar but add more elaborate facade detailing.

Variants and Details

Details are borrowed more or less directly from the Italian originals. Among the most characteristic are recessed entry porches and full-length first-story windows with arches above. The roof, except when flat, commonly has broadly overhanging, boxed eaves; normally the eaves have decorative brackets beneath. These features of the roof-wall junction are helpful in distinguishing Italian Renaissance houses from related Mediterranean styles with tiled roofs. Mission houses usually have wide eave overhangs, but these are commonly open rather than boxed-in. Spanish Revival houses normally have little or no eave overhang. Eave brackets are rare on both Mission and Spanish Revival houses. Common decorative details include quoins, roof-line balustrades, pedimented windows, classical door surrounds, molded cornices, and belt courses. Walls are constructed of or clad with stone, stucco, or brick (generally stone-colored); wooden wall claddings are not used. Note that similar details appear in several earlier styles with Renaissance roots, particularly the Georgian, Federal, and Italianate. Because of these similarities, Italian Renaissance houses sometimes resemble Georgian- or Federal-inspired examples of the contemporaneous Colonial Revival.

Occurrence

The Italian Renaissance style is found in early 20th-century houses throughout the country but is considerably less common than the contemporaneous Craftsman, Tudor, or Colonial Revival styles. Primarily a style for architect-designed landmarks in major metropolitan areas prior to World War I, vernacular interpretations spread widely with the perfection of masonry veneering techniques; most of these date from the 1920s. The style steadily declined in popularity through the 1930s, and post-1940 examples are rare.

Comments

The latest revival of interest in Italian Renaissance domestic models began with the landmark Villard Houses in New York (McKim, Mead & White, 1883). Other fashionable architects used the style in the late 1880s and 1890s as a dramatic contrast to

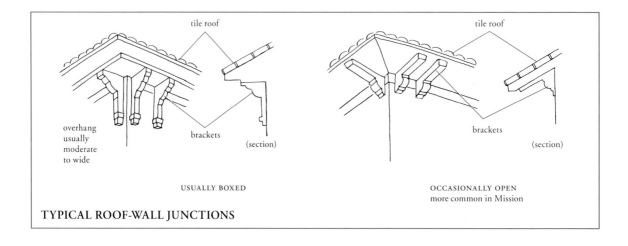

tile roof   tile roof

overhang
usually
moderate   brackets   brackets
to wide   (section)   (section)

USUALLY BOXED   OCCASIONALLY OPEN
                                       more common in Mission

TYPICAL ROOF-WALL JUNCTIONS

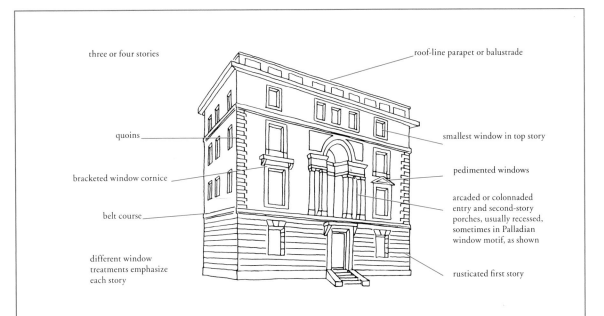

three or four stories

roof-line parapet or balustrade

quoins

smallest window in top story

bracketed window cornice

pedimented windows

belt course

arcaded or colonnaded entry and second-story porches, usually recessed, sometimes in Palladian window motif, as shown

different window treatments emphasize each story

rusticated first story

COMMON HIGH-STYLE ELABORATIONS

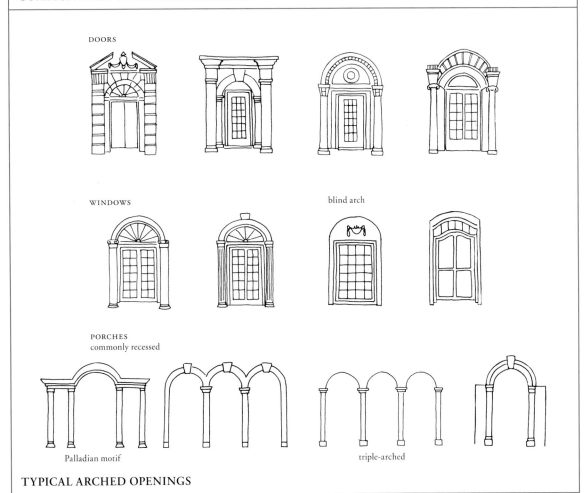

DOORS

WINDOWS

blind arch

PORCHES
commonly recessed

Palladian motif

triple-arched

TYPICAL ARCHED OPENINGS

SIMPLE HIPPED ROOF

1. Kansas City, Missouri; ca. 1910. A simple stucco interpretation with Spanish influence in the door surround.

2. Montgomery, Alabama; ca. 1920s. An unusual one-story example with an elaborate entry porch bounded by paired pilasters.

3. Montgomery, Alabama; ca. 1910s. This example has paired cornice-line brackets and a triple-arched entry porch with balusters above.

4. Shelbyville, Kentucky; ca. 1920. Note the cornice-line brackets and full-length arched windows on the first story.

5. Washington, District of Columbia; 1910. MacVeagh House; Nathan Wyeth, architect. This landmark town house now has a carriage porch added at the entry.

6. New Orleans, Louisiana; ca. 1905. Weis House; MacKenzie and Goldstein, architects. This example shows Prairie influence in its heavy square brick piers and Beaux Arts influence in the paired columns and the elaborated shields ornamenting the brick piers.

7. Cincinnati, Ohio; ca. 1910. Note the attic-story windows, the quoins, and the second-story windows with triangular pediments above and balustraded balconies below.

8. St. Louis, Missouri; 1906. Pendleton Investment Company. This simple four-square example is built of then-innovative concrete blocks. It adds pronounced Italian Renaissance brackets and the suggestion of an attic story to an otherwise Prairie house.

9. Louisville, Kentucky; 1908. Rostrevor; Loomis and Hartman, architects. A large five-ranked stone example with an unusual recessed entry porch. Note that the shape of the porch echoes that of a Palladian window (see also Figure 2).

1

3

6

7

8

2

4

5

9

HIPPED ROOF WITH PROJECTING WING(S)

PROJECTING CENTRAL WING

1. Montgomery, Alabama; ca. 1920. A simple three-ranked brick example. Note the recessed entry with Palladian motif, full-length French doors set in blind arches, and one-story side wings.

2. Buffalo, New York; ca. 1920. This example is unusual in lacking wide overhanging eaves.

3. Los Angeles, California; ca. 1920s. Hancock Park. Red brick is a less typical cladding for Italian Renaissance houses than are stucco, stone, or brick in stone colors.

4. New Orleans, Louisiana; ca. 1910. This elaborate stucco example has quoins and recessed upper and lower porches in the front wing.

PROJECTING SIDE WINGS

5. Wichita, Kansas; ca. 1920. The tall window to the left of the front door probably lights the stairway.

6. Kansas City, Missouri; 1913. Halpin House; John W. McKecknie, architect. Made of concrete clad with cut stone, this house is unusual in having elaborated, arched windows in the upper story rather than the lower.

7. Saratoga, California, vicinity; 1912. Villa Montalvo; William Curlett, architect. This large house has little decorative detailing. The raised terrace with balustrade, a typical feature, is also seen in Figures 2 and 3.

8. Richmond, Virginia; ca. 1920. This unusual example has a three-story central block with two-story wings projecting forward.

9. Dallas, Texas; 1924. Ragland House; Clarence C. Bulger, architect.

1

4

6

8

2

3

5

7

9

ASYMMETRICAL

1. Dallas, Texas; 1922. This one-story example has Craftsman influence in the exposed rafters and in the muntin pattern on the front door and sidelights. But the tall arched windows, and the balustrade along the front terrace, show its Italian Renaissance aspirations.

2. Durham, North Carolina; ca. 1920s. This stucco example is a simpler version of its neighbor shown in Figure 3.

3. Durham, North Carolina; ca. 1920s. A seven-ranked brick example with asymmetrical recessed porch.

4. Louisville, Kentucky; ca. 1920s. This example has Beaux Arts detailing over the door and arched windows.

5. Kansas City, Missouri, ca. 1910s. An unusual feature for this style is the prominent front chimney.

6. Montgomery, Alabama; ca. 1910s. The taller, projecting section recalls the towers of the Italianate style.

7. St. Louis, Missouri; 1926. Tom Barnett, architect. Note the prominent Palladian-motif entry and angled side wings.

8. Montgomery, Alabama, ca. 1910s.

1

4

5

7

2

3

6

8

FLAT ROOF

1. Richmond, Virginia; ca. 1910. A detached, three-ranked town house. There is actually a low-pitched roof behind the roof-line balustrade.

2. Dallas, Texas; 1909. Hill House; C. D. Hill, architect. A Prairie–Italian Renaissance hybrid. Remove the brackets and add a hipped roof with overhanging eaves and you would have a house similar to those on pages 556–57.

3. Pasadena, California; 1905. Fenyes Mansion; Robert D. Farquhar, architect. It is less common to have arched windows in the second story.

4. St. Louis, Missouri; ca. 1910. Note the solid roof parapet, rather than the more usual balustrade, and the recessed Palladian entry.

5. Washington, District of Columbia; ca. 1910.

6. Savannah, Georgia; 1917. Armstrong House; Henrik Wallis, architect. A colonnaded, curved side porch or gallery is visible to the right. Arcaded and colonnaded porches such as these are sometimes called "loggias" (see page 505 for other examples).

7. St. Louis, Missouri; ca. 1910. Note the rusticated first story, the triangular and segmental pediments above the second-story windows, and the upper-story pilasters. An unusual note is the unaccented entry at the left side of this absolutely symmetrical house; a bay window is used where one would expect the entry.

2

3

6

I

4

5

7

the Gothic-inspired Shingle or Queen Anne styles. These Second Renaissance Revival houses tended to mimic more closely their Italian predecessors than did the free interpretations of the preceding Italianate style. There are several reasons for this increased authenticity. By the late 19th century a great many American architects, and their clients, had visited Italy and thus had some first-hand familiarity with the original models. Furthermore, improved printing technology provided ready access to excellent photographic documentation of these models. The earlier Italianate style, in contrast, was usually based on pattern book drawings by professionals with no first-hand knowledge of Italian buildings. In addition, many houses of the earlier Italianate style had wooden wall cladding, whereas later examples invariably mimic the stuccoed or masonry walls of their original Italian prototypes. The perfection of masonry veneering techniques after World War I made this possible in even the most modest examples of the style.

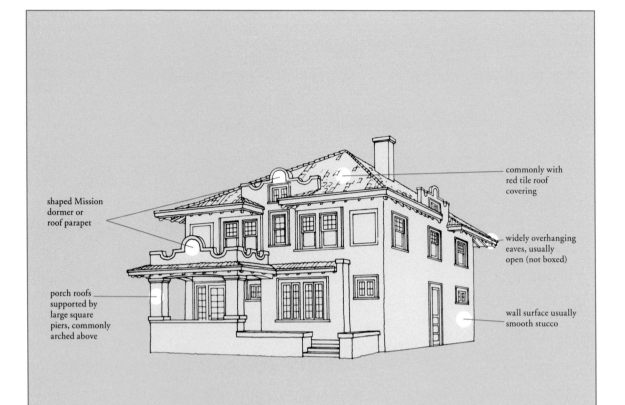

shaped Mission dormer or roof parapet

commonly with red tile roof covering

widely overhanging eaves, usually open (not boxed)

porch roofs supported by large square piers, commonly arched above

wall surface usually smooth stucco

SYMMETRICAL

ASYMMETRICAL

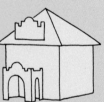

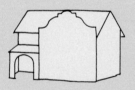

pages 514–15

pages 516–17

PRINCIPAL SUBTYPES

Mission

1890–1920

Identifying Features

Mission-shaped dormer or roof parapet (these may be on either main roof or porch roof); commonly with red tile roof covering; widely overhanging eaves, usually open; porch roofs supported by large, square piers, commonly arched above; wall surface usually smooth stucco.

Principal Subtypes

Two principal subtypes can be distinguished:

SYMMETRICAL—About half of Mission houses have balanced, symmetrical facades. These are most commonly of simple square or rectangular plan with hipped roofs.

ASYMMETRICAL—The remaining half of Mission houses have asymmetrical facades of widely varying form. Most typically the facade asymmetry is superimposed on a simple square or rectangular plan. Elaborate, rambling compound plans are found on some landmark examples.

Variants and Details

A great variety of shaped dormers and roof parapets mimic those found on some Spanish Colonial mission buildings. Few are precise copies of the original models. Most examples have prominent one-story porches either at the entry area or covering the full width of the facade; these sometimes have arched roof supports to simulate the arcades of Hispanic buildings. Mission-like bell towers occur on a few landmark examples. Quatrefoil windows are common; decorative detailing is generally absent, although patterned tiles, carved stonework, or other wall surface ornament is occasionally used. Windows are typically double-hung and are sometimes grouped together. Some examples have unusual visor roofs. These are narrow, tiled roof segments cantilevered out from a smooth wall surface (similar to the pent roofs seen in some Georgian or Colonial Revival houses). They most commonly occur beneath the parapets of flat roofs.

Occurrence

California was the birthplace of the Mission style and many of its landmark examples are concentrated there. The earliest were built in the 1890s; by 1900 houses in this style were spreading eastward under the influence of fashionable architects and national builders' magazines. They also appeared in house plan books such as those of Sears Roebuck and Co. that sold plans for a "Mission type" house called the Alhambra in the late 1910s. Although never common outside of the southwestern states, scattered examples were built in early 20th-century suburbs throughout the country. Most date from the years between 1905 and 1920.

Comments

One scholar has noted that the style "is the Californian counterpart" of the Georgian-inspired Colonial Revival that was then gaining popularity in the northeastern states. Rather than copy the East's revival of its own colonial past, California turned to its Hispanic heritage for inspiration. Several California architects began to advocate the style in the late 1880s and early 1890s. This resulted in the large California Building at the 1893 World's Columbian Exposition being built in a Mission-inspired style that gained attention and admiration. Mission Revival received further impetus when the Santa Fe and Southern Pacific railways adopted the style for stations and resort hotels throughout the

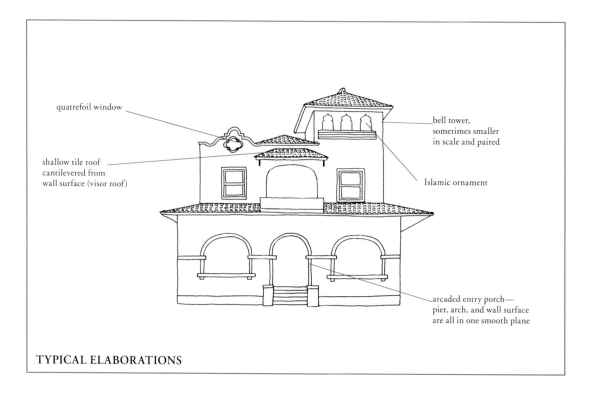

quatrefoil window

shallow tile roof
cantilevered from
wall surface (visor roof)

bell tower,
sometimes smaller
in scale and paired

Islamic ornament

arcaded entry porch—
pier, arch, and wall surface
are all in one smooth plane

TYPICAL ELABORATIONS

coping

TYPICAL REVIVAL DORMERS & PARAPETS

Mission San Diego Alcala

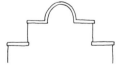

Mission San Luis Rey de Franca

Mission San Antonio de Valero (the Alamo)

Mission San Juan Capistrano

PARAPETS OF ORIGINAL MISSIONS Most are restorations

SYMMETRICAL

1. Dallas, Texas; 1912. Bianchi House; Lang & Witchell, architects.

2. Hammond, Louisiana; ca. 1910. Preston House. The wood wall cladding is unusual. Although open eaves are most common in the style, boxed eaves also occur, usually with brackets below as seen here and in Figure 3.

3. Dallas, Texas; 1917. Harris-Savage House. This house has had the original entry arch with the shaped parapet above restored. The materials used here—brown wirecut brick, Vermont slate roof—are unusual for a Mission house.

4. Kansas City, Missouri; ca. 1910. This house shows the four-square shape that was popular in various styles built from about 1900 to 1915.

5. Oklahoma City, Oklahoma; ca. 1910.

6. Washington, District of Columbia; 1902. Barney House; Waddy B. Wood, architect. A rare example of a Mission town house.

7. Louisville, Kentucky; ca. 1910. Caperton House.

8. Redlands, California; 1901. Burrage House; Charles Bingham, architect. This landmark house is a full-scale copy of a Spanish mission, complete with bell towers and arcaded side wings.

2

6

5

8

1

3

4

6

7

ASYMMETRICAL

1. Fort Smith, Arkansas; ca. 1910. In this example the entire side gable of the main roof is covered by a shaped parapet.

2. Oklahoma City, Oklahoma; ca. 1910. Here a flat roof is surrounded by a parapet with a projecting visor roof beneath; the porch roof repeats this pattern on a smaller scale.

3. Salisbury, North Carolina; ca. 1910. The recessed arcaded porch on the second story creates asymmetry on this otherwise balanced facade.

4. Kansas City, Missouri; ca. 1910. The bell tower is unusual on relatively modest examples such as this.

5. Dallas, Texas; 1915. Green House; Daren Tapscott, restoration architect. This house has a flat roof surrounded by a parapet, with a projecting tiled visor roof beneath. The porch roof repeats this pattern. Note the carefully restored original details—including grouped windows with the original muntin pattern, porch railing, and ornament below the shaped parapets.

6. Fullerton, California; ca. 1915. Note the Exotic influence in the recessed porch over the entry, and in the porch columns. This house looks symmetrical, but the right and left sides of the facade are quite different. Compare it to Figure 7, on page 514, where the house looks asymmetrical because of its wings, but has a symmetrical central block.

7. Kansas City, Missouri; ca. 1910. Few Mission houses are built of stone; brick and stucco are the most common materials.

8. White Plains, New York; ca. 1910. Scholz House.

9. Redlands, California; 1903. Holt House; Frederick Thomas Harris, architect. The decorative detailing is unusually exuberant for the Mission style, which normally stresses smooth, flat wall surfaces.

2

5

8

9

West. Most commonly, typical Hispanic design elements (shaped parapets, arches, qua-trefoil windows, etc.) were borrowed and freely adapted to adorn traditional shapes. It was not uncommon for a typical four-square shape, with massive square porch supports and double-hung windows, to have tile roofs and one or more shaped parapets added to create a simplified Mission house. In a few landmark examples, however, the forms of the early missions, including twin bell towers and elaborate arcades, were faithfully followed in domestic designs. In still other examples, innovative architects designed Mission buildings with many features borrowed from the contemporary Craftsman and Prairie movements; some even anticipate the simplicity of the subsequent International style. The style quickly faded from favor after World War I as architectural fashion shifted from free, simplified adaptations of earlier prototypes to more precise, correct copies. From this concern grew the Spanish Revival style which drew inspiration from a broader spectrum of both Old and New World Spanish buildings.

low-pitched roof

red tile roof covering

eaves usually with little or no overhang

wall surface extends into gable without break

wall surface usually stucco

arches above doors, principal windows, or beneath porch roofs

asymmetrical facade

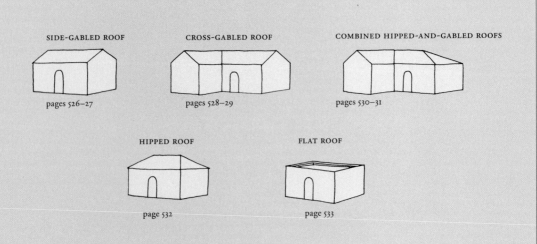

SIDE-GABLED ROOF

pages 526–27

CROSS-GABLED ROOF

pages 528–29

COMBINED HIPPED-AND-GABLED ROOFS

pages 530–31

HIPPED ROOF

page 532

FLAT ROOF

page 533

PRINCIPAL SUBTYPES

Spanish Revival

1915–1940

Identifying Features

Low-pitched roof, usually with little or no eave overhang; red tile roof covering; typically with one or more prominent arches placed above door or principal window, or beneath porch roof; wall surface usually stucco; wall surface extends into gable without break (eave or trim normally lacking beneath gable); facade normally asymmetrical.

Principal Subtypes

Five principal subtypes can be distinguished:

SIDE-GABLED ROOF—About 20 percent of Spanish Revival houses have side-gabled roofs. Many of these are multi-level with taller, side-gabled sections bounded by lower, side-gabled wings.

CROSS-GABLED ROOF—About 50 percent of Spanish Revival houses have cross-gabled roofs with one prominent, front-facing gable. These are usually L-plan houses; one-story and two-story forms are both common, as are examples with wings of differing heights.

COMBINED HIPPED-AND-GABLED ROOFS—Some landmark examples have rambling, compound plans in which different units have separate roof forms of varying heights arranged in an irregular, informal pattern. Typically both hipped and gabled roofs are used in combination, a pattern which mimics the varied roof forms of Spanish villages.

HIPPED ROOF—About 10 percent of Spanish Revival houses have low-pitched hipped roofs. These are generally two-story forms with simple rectangular plans.

FLAT ROOF—About 10 percent of Spanish Revival houses have flat roofs with parapeted walls. These typically show combinations of one- and two-story units. Narrow, tile-covered shed roofs are typically added above entryways or projecting windows. This subtype, loosely based on flat-roofed Spanish prototypes, resembles the Pueblo Revival house.

Variants and Details

The style uses decorative details borrowed from the entire history of Spanish architecture. These may be of Moorish, Byzantine, Gothic, or Renaissance inspiration, an unusually rich and varied series of decorative precedents. The typical roof tiles are of two basic types: Mission tiles, which are shaped like half-cylinders, and Spanish tiles, which have an S-curve shape. Both types occur in many variations depending on the size of the tiles and the patterns in which they are applied. Dramatically carved doors are typical of Spanish architecture; these are more common on high-style Spanish Revival houses but also occur on modest examples. Doors are often emphasized by adjacent spiral columns, pilasters, carved stonework, or patterned tiles. Less elaborate entrance doors of heavy wood panels, sometimes arched above, are also common. Doors leading to exterior gardens, patios, and balconies are usually paired and glazed with multiple panes of rectangular glass. Many examples have at least one large focal window. These are commonly of triple-arched or parabolic shape and may be filled with stained glass of varying design. Decorative window grilles of wood or iron are common, as are similar balustrades on cantilevered balconies, which occur in a variety of shapes and sizes. Stucco walls could be smooth or have various rough or tooled finishes. Other typical details include tile-roofed (and otherwise decorated) chimney tops; brick or tile vents; fountains; arcaded walkways (usually leading to a rear garden); walled entry courtyards; twisted spiral columns (officially Solomonic columns and informally barbershop-pole columns); and round or square towers.

Occurrence

Spanish Revival is most common in the southwestern states, particularly California, Arizona, and Texas, and in Florida, all regions where original Spanish Colonial building occurred and continued into the 19th century. Landmark houses in this style are rare outside of Florida and the Southwest but, as in the related Mission style which preceded it, scattered vernacular examples are found in suburban developments throughout the country. During the 1920s, many new communities in Florida and southern California were planned in the Spanish Revival style, and older towns (such as Santa Barbara, California) also sought to affect a Spanish Colonial image in new construction. Los Angeles, in particular, added large neighborhoods of Spanish Revival homes.

Comments

Before about 1920, houses of Hispanic precedent were based on simple early Spanish missions. It was the Panama-California Exposition held in San Diego in 1915 that introduced the elaborate Spanish prototypes found in other countries. This exposition was designed by Bertram Grosvenor Goodhue (1869–1924), who emphasized the richness of Spanish Colonial precedents seen in the major buildings of other countries.[16] The exhibition was widely publicized and well received. Soon other architects were inspired

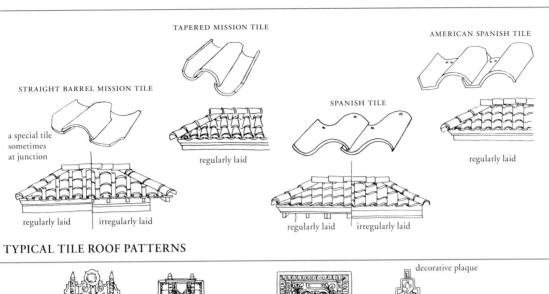

TAPERED MISSION TILE

AMERICAN SPANISH TILE

STRAIGHT BARREL MISSION TILE

SPANISH TILE

a special tile sometimes at junction

regularly laid

regularly laid

regularly laid   irregularly laid

regularly laid   irregularly laid

TYPICAL TILE ROOF PATTERNS

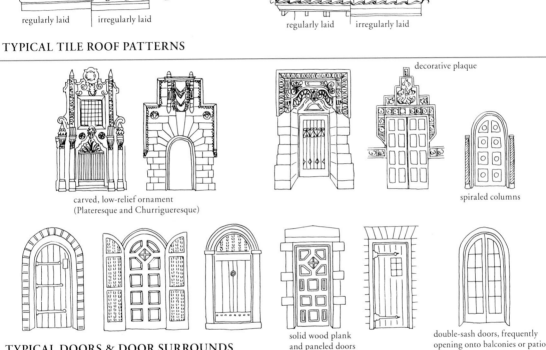

decorative plaque

carved, low-relief ornament
(Plateresque and Churrigueresque)

spiraled columns

TYPICAL DOORS & DOOR SURROUNDS

solid wood plank
and paneled doors

double-sash doors, frequently
opening onto balconies or patios

FOCAL WINDOWS

CASEMENT WINDOWS

WINDOW GRILLES

balconet (full-length window and railing without projecting floor)

metal

wood

parabolic arch

boxed grille to allow
casement windows
to open outward

TYPICAL WINDOWS Double-hung windows also common

towers
(round, square, or polygonal)

elaborated chimney tops,
often with small tiled roof

stucco or tile
decorative vents

arcaded wing wall

walled entry courtyard

balconies, open or roofed,
with wood or iron railings

COMMON ELABORATIONS

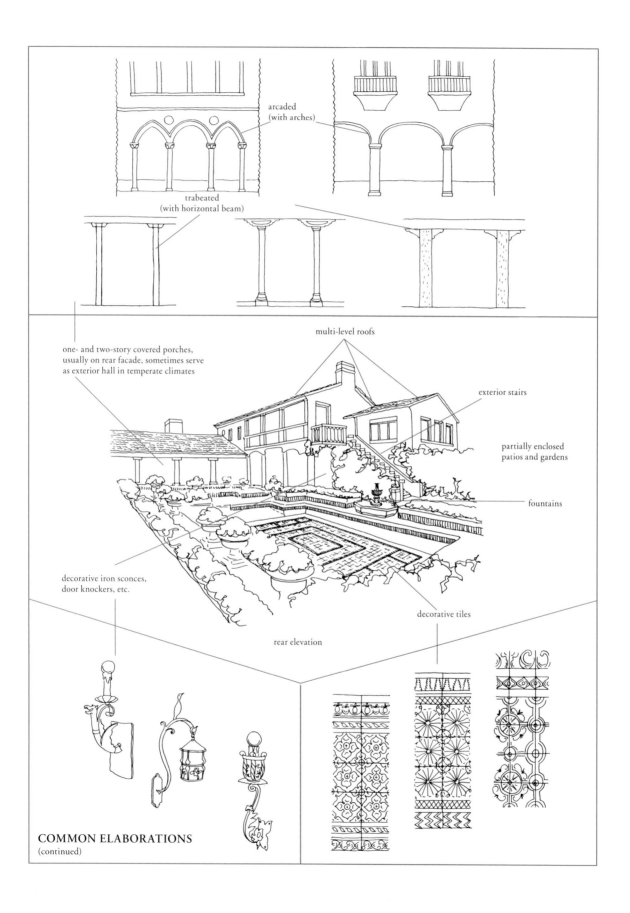

arcaded
(with arches)

trabeated
(with horizontal beam)

multi-level roofs

one- and two-story covered porches, usually on rear facade, sometimes serve as exterior hall in temperate climates

exterior stairs

partially enclosed patios and gardens

fountains

decorative iron sconces, door knockers, etc.

decorative tiles

rear elevation

COMMON ELABORATIONS
(continued)

SIDE-GABLED ROOF

1. Mission Hills, Kansas; ca. 1920s. This house shows symmetrical Renaissance influences in its centered doorway with quoined door surround.

2. Wichita, Kansas; ca. 1930s. The unadorned main block, with its short broad chimney and paucity of windows, resembles a smaller version of Figure 5.

3. New Orleans, Louisiana; ca. 1920s. The doorway is surrounded by low-relief carving of Plateresque inspiration. Note the elaborate window grilles.

4. Dallas, Texas; 1927. Hollywood Heights/Santa Monica Conservation District. Symmetrical examples like this are far less common than asymmetrical ones.

5. Santa Barbara, California; 1916. El Hogar; George Washington Smith, architect. Inspired by the houses of southern Spain, this example presents an austere facade to the world (few windows and little ornamentation) but opens into an elaborate garden behind.

6. Dallas, Texas; ca. 1930s. Note the spiraled columns beside the entry and the lower-story windows.

7. Wichita, Kansas; ca. 1930s. The projecting door surround is atypical.

8. Dallas, Texas; 1926. Green House; Thomson and Swaine, architects. Although similar to Figure 5 in basic form, this example adds numerous double-hung windows to the front facade, giving it a less authentic look. Note the strongly textured stucco walls.

9. Santa Barbara, California; 1925. Casa del Herrera; George Washington Smith, architect. This entry facade shows Smith's ease with picturesque asymmetry. This entry facade suggests the gradual accumulation of informal additions that was typical of Spanish folk dwellings.

1

3

6

7

2

4

5

8

9

CROSS-GABLED ROOF

1. Delano, California; ca. 1930s. Simple one-story examples similar to this dominate many 1930s neighborhoods in Florida and California.

2. Santa Barbara, California; 1923. Burke House; George Washington Smith, architect. Note the restrained facade with large expanses of windowless wall. The small house-shaped chimney capping at the right is a favorite Spanish Revival detail.

3. Louisville, Kentucky; ca. 1930s. Note the strong textured pattern of the stucco walls.

4. Dallas, Texas; 1936. Baty House. This small example is complete with a bell tower, a focal window with stained glass, and a front entry court enclosed by a low stone wall.

5. St. Louis, Missouri; ca. 1930s.

6. Oklahoma City, Oklahoma; ca. 1930s.

7. Los Angeles, California; ca. 1930s. The arched entry is accented with four spiraled columns. Note the large parabolic art glass window.

8. Los Angeles, California; ca. 1920s.

1

4

3

7

2

5

6

8

COMBINED HIPPED-AND-GABLED ROOFS

1. Dallas, Texas; 1938. Turner House. Note the overhanging balcony and enclosed entry court.

2. San Antonio, Texas; ca. 1929. Monte Vista Historic District; Adams & Adams, architects.

3. Montecito, California; 1916. Bliss House; Carleton Winslow, Sr., architect. Note the bell tower and multiple-arched chimney crowns.

4. Santa Barbara, California; ca. 1930. Villa Eseanado. Note the ornate Renaissance-inspired entryway and the differing roof heights of the three wings, which enclose an interior courtyard.

5. Santa Barbara, California; 1925. Dreyfus House; W. Maybury Somervell, architect. This landmark example, with its varying roof forms, resembles an entire block of a Spanish village.

6. Palm Beach, Florida; 1927. Mar-A-Lago; Addison Mizner, architect. A major landmark of the style.

7, 8. Montecito, California; 1930. Dieterich House; Addison Mizner, architect. These photographs illustrate the elaborate courtyards found in most landmark examples. Figure 7 shows an automobile entry court and Figure 8 an interior courtyard. Note the fountain, arcaded gallery, and decorative paving.

1

3

6

2

4

5

7

8

HIPPED ROOF

1. Palo Alto, California; ca. 1930s. Kennedy House.

2. Morgan Hill, California; ca. 1930s. Fountain Oaks.

3. Corning, New York; ca. 1930s.

4. Dallas, Texas; 1942. Luse House; Fooshee & Cheek, architects. Note the elaborate door surround, the two focal window areas, and the corner quoins.

5. Los Angeles, California; ca. 1920s. Hancock Park Historic District.

1

3

4

5

FLAT ROOF

1. Santa Barbara, California; ca. 1930. Figures 1 and 3 are typical of smaller examples built by the thousands in California suburbs during the 1920s and 1930s. The flat roof with decorative tiles along the parapet is typical, as is the arched entryway with either gabled or flat roof.

2. St. Louis, Missouri; ca. 1930s. Figures 2, 4, and 5 combine both one- and two-story sections. Note the small shed roofs over the windows and the shed-roof entryways.

3. Santa Barbara, California; ca. 1920.

4. Independence, Missouri; ca. 1930s.

5. Los Angeles, California (vicinity); ca. 1920s.

to look directly to Spain for source material. World War I (1914–1918) caused architects wishing to study and sketch in Europe to concentrate on Spain.[17] There they found a centuries-long and very rich sequence of architecture traditions that they could meld into the quite varied Spanish Revival.[18]

The range of decorative detail found in Spain was extraordinarily diverse. But of equal interest was the way buildings were composed and massed, a subject studied particularly in rural Andalusian houses. These vernacular dwellings resulted when homes were gradually expanded in a very informal, additive way. Facades generally had little decorative detail and instead emphasized their varied massing. This approach was favored by some high-style Spanish Revival architects such as George Washington Smith (1876–1930) in southern California.

In Florida, Spanish Revival was introduced by industrialist turned developer Henry Flagler to promote tourism. It developed its own Florida flavor, epitomized by the designs of Addison Mizner (1872–1933) and Maurice Fatio (1897–1943).[19] The style reached its apex on both coasts during the 1920s and early 1930s and passed rapidly from favor during the 1940s.

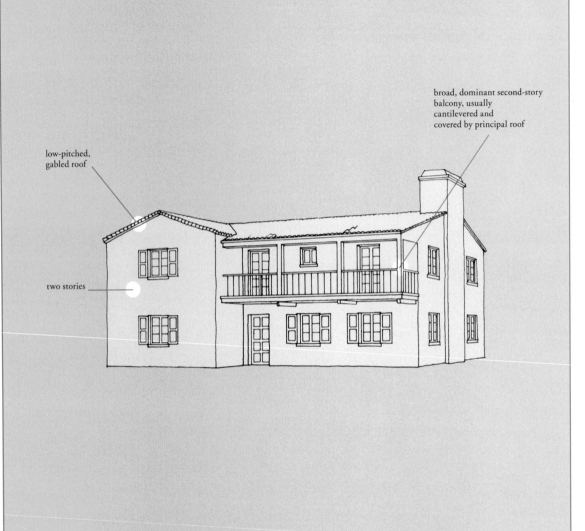

broad, dominant second-story
balcony, usually
cantilevered and
covered by principal roof

low-pitched,
gabled roof

two stories

Monterey

1925–1955

Identifying Features

Two stories, with low-pitched gabled roof (occasionally hipped); broad, dominant second-story balcony, usually cantilevered and covered by principal roof.

Variants and Details

Roofs are usually covered with wooden shingles but are occasionally tiled or standing seam metal in later examples. Wall cladding materials are either stucco, brick, or wood (weatherboard, shingle, or vertical board-and-batten). The first and second stories frequently have different cladding materials, with wood over brick being the most common pattern. Door and window surrounds sometimes mimic the Territorial examples of their Spanish Colonial prototypes; paired windows and false shutters are common. Doors may show Colonial Revival influences. One variant substitutes balcony columns and balustrades of cast iron for the more typical wooden detailing. These are sometimes called Creole French houses. Balconies are also typical in Spanish Revival houses, where they are often narrower and joined by exuberant Hispanic decorative detail on the rest of the house. In Monterey houses the balcony is generally the primary decorative feature on the house and extends the full width of the house—or the full width of the wing in a gabled-front-and-wing form.

Comments

The Monterey is a free interpretation of the Anglo-influenced Spanish Colonial houses of northern California. These blended Spanish adobe construction with pitched-roof, massed-plan English shapes brought to California from New England. However, the key identifying feature of the Monterey—the full-width cantilevered balcony (or occasionally two-story porch)—was derived from house forms built in the southeastern United States, the Caribbean, and the Bahamas. The 1834 Larkin House in Monterey, California, is generally identified as the first of this distinctive form of early pitched-roof Spanish Colonial houses. Thomas Oliver Larkin, the owner-designer of it, had traveled

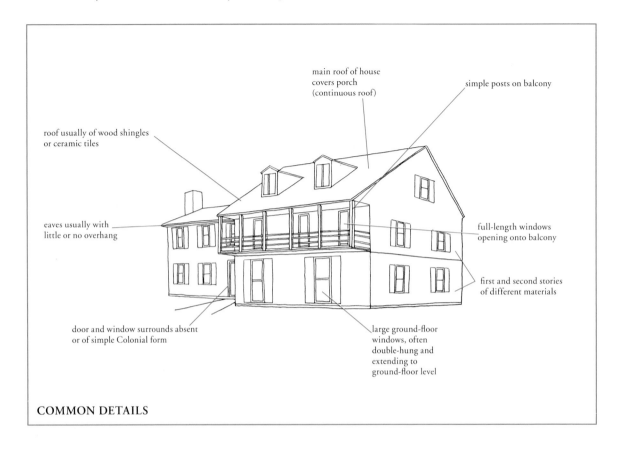

roof usually of wood shingles
or ceramic tiles

main roof of house
covers porch
(continuous roof)

simple posts on balcony

eaves usually with
little or no overhang

full-length windows
opening onto balcony

first and second stories
of different materials

door and window surrounds absent
or of simple Colonial form

large ground-floor
windows, often
double-hung and
extending to
ground-floor level

COMMON DETAILS

4

5

MONTEREY

1. Dallas, Texas; 1937. Braly House. This example, with its tiled roof and parabolic focal window, is transitional to the Spanish Revival style.

2. Montecito, California; 1929. Morphy House; Roland Coate, Sr., architect. Note the asymmetrical placement of doors and windows and the shaped ends of the heavy beams supporting the balcony.

3. Kansas City, Missouri; ca. 1930s. Many examples of the style have three-ranked facades. When a broader facade was desired, a separate parallel wing was added, as here.

4. San Marino, California; ca. 1930s. The full-width balcony wraps around the side.

5. Dallas, Texas; ca. 1930s.

6. Dallas, Texas; 1951. Bywaters House. In the late 1940s and 1950s the simple wood balcony railings and roof supports of the style were commonly replaced by lacy cast iron, leading to a variant called the Creole French style by its builders. These were, of course, inspired by the iron balconies of New Orleans. Asymmetrical interpretations of these Creole French houses, usually with front-facing gable wings, were also popular.

7. Pasadena, California; 1941. Jordan House; Whitney R. Smith, architect. The upper story has board-and-batten cladding.

in South Carolina and Bermuda, where similar houses were found. See Figures 5–7 on pages 194–195 for the Larkin House and other examples of this Anglicized form of Spanish Colonial house.[20]

California architect Roland E. Coate, Sr., played a crucial role in reviving the style. Between 1929 and 1932 he wrote about the early Monterey homes, designed at least two homes in the Monterey, and won a prestigious Better Homes in America Award for an elegant Santa Barbara example.[21] His efforts helped bring the style to the attention of both professionals and the public.

Some early examples from about 1925 to 1940 have Spanish detailing, while those from the 1940s and 1950s generally include only English Colonial details. A third, less common, variation was sometimes called Creole French; these had decorative iron balconies inspired by the upper-level balconies found in the Vieux Carré in New Orleans. Though scattered examples of Monterey houses occur throughout the country in suburbs built during the second quarter of the 20th century, they are perhaps most common in California and Texas.

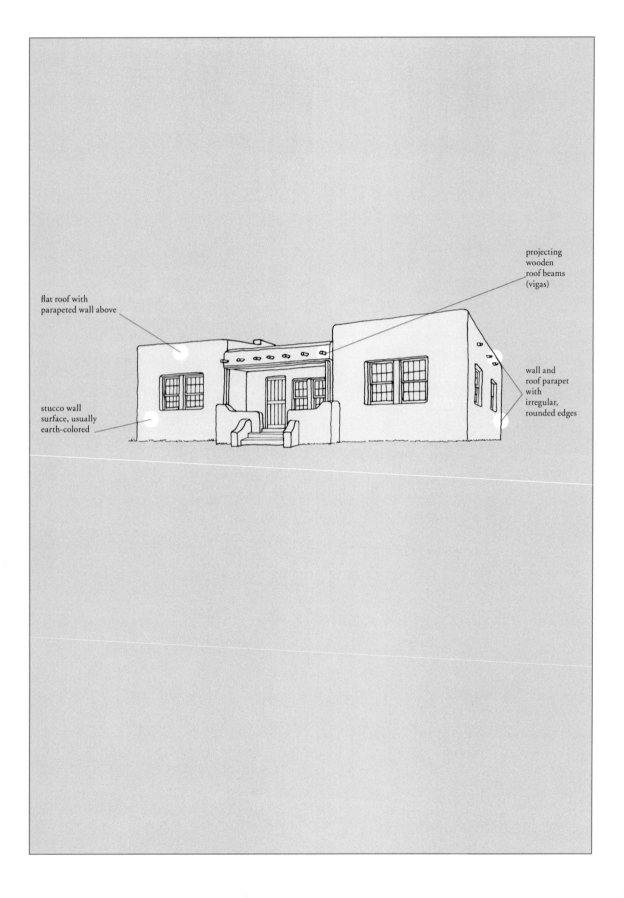

projecting
wooden
roof beams
(vigas)

flat roof with
parapeted wall above

wall and
roof parapet
with
irregular,
rounded edges

stucco wall
surface, usually
earth-colored

Pueblo Revival

1910–present

Identifying Features

Flat roof with parapeted wall above; wall and roof parapet with irregular, rounded edges; projecting wooden roof beams (vigas) extending through walls; stucco wall surface, usually earth-colored.

Variants and Details

Pueblo Revival houses imitate the hand-finishes of their Native American prototypes. Corners are blunted or rounded and wall surfaces are given irregular, stuccoed textures. In addition, rough-hewn vigas (roof beams), window lintels, and porch supports carry out the hand-built theme. The stepped-back roof line of the original pueblos is often used, and larger examples may also feature their picturesque additive massing. This effect is more easily imitated with roof parapets and garden walls that have irregularly rounded, stepped-up tops. The actual structure of the house can vary from stabilized adobe or concrete block to balloon frame. Windows are double-hung or casements of wood or metal.

Comments

Like the contemporary Mission movement, the Pueblo Revival draws on local historical precedents for inspiration. The buildings are a mixture of influences from both flat-roofed Spanish Colonial buildings and Native American pueblos (see pages 115 and 196–97). For this reason some architectural historians have proposed the name "Pueblo–Spanish Revival" for the style. The earliest examples were built in California around the turn of the 20th century. The style became most popular, however, in Arizona and New Mexico, areas where the original prototypes survive. It is particularly common in Tucson, Albuquerque, and Santa Fe, where it persists today, in part because of the requirements of special design control districts. Scattered examples occur throughout

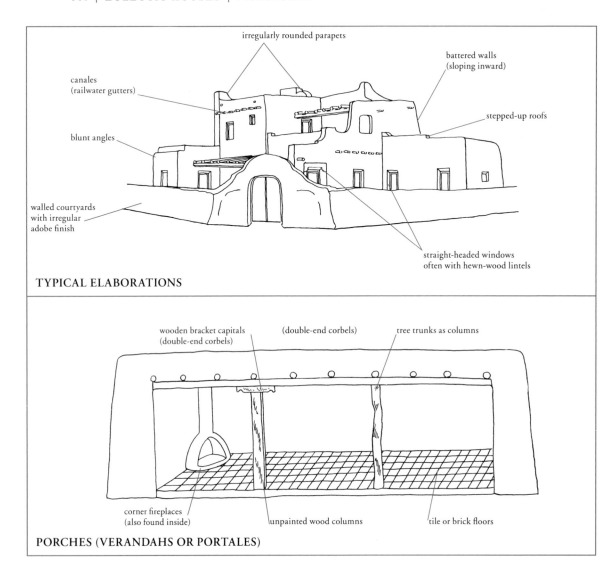

irregularly rounded parapets

battered walls (sloping inward)

canales (railwater gutters)

stepped-up roofs

blunt angles

walled courtyards with irregular adobe finish

straight-headed windows often with hewn-wood lintels

TYPICAL ELABORATIONS

wooden bracket capitals (double-end corbels)

(double-end corbels)

tree trunks as columns

corner fireplaces (also found inside)

unpainted wood columns

tile or brick floors

PORCHES (VERANDAHS OR PORTALES)

4

PUEBLO REVIVAL

1. Sante Fe, New Mexico; ca. 1930s.

2., 5. Santa Fe, New Mexico; ca. 1920s. John Gaw Meem, architect. The closeup shows the irregular rounded edges of the roof parapet and walls, the irregular stucco texture, and the inset window lintels. Note the difference between the two projecting roof beams (vigas) and the rainwater gutter (canale) immediately to the left. In the full view the stepped-up effect (emphasized by the heavy shadows) begins with the garden wall at lower left and continues to the first- and second-story sections. Note the inward curving profile of the walls at right.

3. Sante Fe, New Mexico; ca. 1930s. Note adobe chimney here and in Figures 1, 2, and 4.

4. Santa Fe, New Mexico; 1918. Vierra House; Carlos Vierra, architect. This seminal example has stepped roofs and strongly rounded edges to walls and roofs. Note the ladder, the only stairway of the original Pueblos.

6. Phoenix, Arizona; 1928. El Encanto Historic District.

the southwestern states, most of which date from the 1920s and 1930s. A variation, introduced in New Mexico about 1920, could be more aptly termed the Territorial Revival. Although executed in adobe, it picked up the form and detail of the Anglo-Spanish Colonial Territorial house (page 196, Figures 5 and 6) with roof parapets topped by fired brick and wooden decorative details influenced by the Greek Revival movement.

Innovative American-born architect Frank Lloyd Wright exercised his prodigious talent and powerful personality first in shaping the early Modern movement in the United States and then in disseminating it throughout Europe. In 1893, after working for pioneering modernists Adler & Sullivan, Wright opened his own architecture practice, and by 1902 he had created the first of an entirely new kind of house—the Prairie—with free-flowing interior spaces, new spatial effects, and an innovative vocabulary of ornament that did not mimic historic forms. Wright believed in architectural ornament—as did Greene and Greene, his West Coast counterparts who perfected the Craftsman style. These architects and their followers spread early modernism and its American Arts and Crafts ornamentation throughout the United States in the form of Craftsman and Prairie houses.

But it was Wright alone who carried American modernism abroad. While self-exiled in Europe after a personal scandal, Wright prepared renderings of his early work for publication. Titled the *Wasmuth Portfolio* (1910), it dispersed his concept of organic architecture and modern spatial design to European architects.

His message was eagerly received, but European architects dramatically changed the Modern movement by rejecting ornament and designing instead "machine age" buildings reduced to basic functional forms—the beginning of mainstream modernism. Their new approach was exported back to the United States by pre-1925 émigrés like Rudolf Schindler, Richard Neutra, and William Lescaze. In the 1930s they were joined by the elite of Europe's great Bauhaus School—Walter Gropius, Mies van der Rohe, and Marcel Breuer—all fleeing Hitler. Their more austere modernism, christened the International style, swept the United States during the following two decades (1930s–1950s). Its stark forms, however, proved to be more beloved for skyscrapers than for homes.

Instead, another mainstream Modern style, originally called simply Contemporary, dominated avant-garde domestic architecture at mid-century. Favored by architects into the mid-1960s, Contemporary houses were greatly influenced by Wright's Usonian houses and his prolific writing for shelter magazines and professional journals.

The American banking system, however, through the practices of the Federal Housing Administration's mortgage insurance program, effectively regulated the kind of modern home that could be broadly built in typical neighborhoods at mid-century. The nation had adopted a goal that all returning World War II veterans would be able to own a home, and vast

Modern Houses

single-family suburban neighborhoods were built to accomplish this. The FHA did not believe that neighborhoods of starkly modern houses were a good investment for veterans—or for anyone else— and therefore lenders primarily financed a more conservative branch of modernism: the less daring "Bankers Modern" styles, consisting of basic Minimal Traditionals and casual Ranch houses. Described as "middle-of-the-road modern" and "modern inside, traditional outside," the Ranch style was considered more acceptable to American home buyers than International or Contemporary homes—and thus a safer investment.

By the mid-1960s home finance was no longer a problem. In addition, an entire generation of postwar American architects trained only in modernism were seeking new approaches to home styles. During the last half-century, a broad and ever-expanding array of architect-designed late-modern styles have appeared primarily in high-style homes designed by architects. With the exception of the Shed style, beginning in the 1960s, few examples of other modern styles made their way into typical neighborhoods. In recent decades, even more varied and dramatic modern house designs have had little effect upon typical American homes, which have mostly returned, once again, to historic and vernacular architectural roots.

1900–present

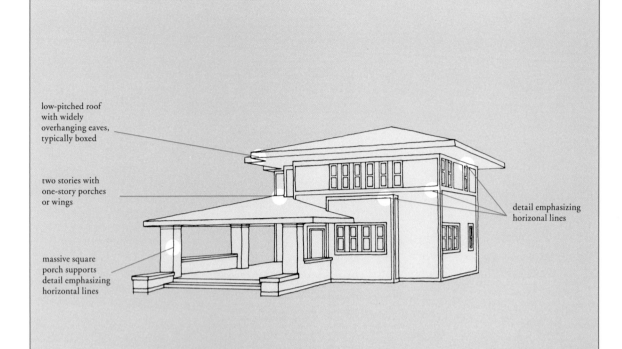

low-pitched roof with widely overhanging eaves, typically boxed

two stories with one-story porches or wings

massive square porch supports detail emphasizing horizontal lines

detail emphasizing horizontal lines

HIPPED ROOF, SYMMETRICAL, WITH FRONT ENTRY

pages 556–57

HIPPED ROOF, SYMMETRICAL, NO FRONT ENTRY

pages 558–59

HIPPED ROOF, ASYMMETRICAL

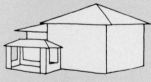

pages 560–61

GABLED ROOF

pages 562–63

PRINCIPAL SUBTYPES

Prairie

1900–1920

Identifying Features

Low-pitched roof, usually hipped, with widely overhanging eaves that typically are boxed; two stories, with one-story wings, porches, and porte cocheres; eaves, cornices, and facade detailing emphasizing horizontal lines; often with massive, square porch supports.

Principal Subtypes

Four principal subtypes can be distinguished:

HIPPED ROOF, SYMMETRICAL, WITH FRONT ENTRY—This subtype, which is sometimes called the Prairie Box or American Foursquare, has a simple square or rectangular plan, low-pitched hipped roof, and symmetrical facade. One-story wings, porches, or carports are clearly subordinate to the principal two-story mass. The entrance, which may be centered or off-center, is a conspicuous focal point of the facade. This was the earliest Prairie form and developed into the most common vernacular version. In vernacular examples, hipped dormers are common, as are full-width, single-story front porches and double-hung sash windows. Many show Mission or Italian Renaissance secondary details, such as tiled roofs or cornice-line brackets.

HIPPED ROOF, SYMMETRICAL, NO FRONT ENTRY—Similar to the type just described but with inconspicuous entrances and facades dominated by horizontal rows of casement windows having sharply defined vertical detailing. This is a favorite form for smaller, architect-designed Prairie houses and also for those built on narrow urban lots.

HIPPED ROOF, ASYMMETRICAL—Most high-style examples are of this form. Typically a single two- or three-story, hipped-roof mass is contrasted with equally dominant, but lower, wings, porches, or carports with hipped roofs. The front entrance is usually inconspicuous, the facade being dominated by horizontal rows of casement windows having sharply defined vertical detailing. Many variations occur, but in all cases the facade is asymmetrical; most have masonry walls.

GABLED ROOF—In this subtype, gables replace the more typical hipped roofs. High-style examples typically have both front-facing and side gables, each with exaggerated eave overhangs. In some, the gables have swept-back profiles with the peaks projecting beyond the lower edges. The pitch of the roof edges may also be flattened to give a pagoda-like effect. Vernacular examples usually have simple front- or side-gabled roofs. Tudor secondary influences are common, particularly false half-timbering in gables.

Variants and Details

Massive square or rectangular piers of masonry used to support porch roofs are an almost universal feature of high-style examples. They remain common in vernacular examples, which also show squared wooden imitations. The characteristic horizontal decorative emphasis is achieved by such devices as: (1) contrasting caps on porch and balcony railings, (2) contrasting wood trim between stories, (3) horizontal board-and-batten siding, (4) contrasting colors on eaves and cornice, and (5) selective recessing of only the horizontal masonry joints. Other common details in both landmark and vernacular examples include window boxes or flattened pedestal urns for flowers; geometric patterns of small-pane window glazing (usually in leaded casement windows in high-style examples and upper sashes of wooden-muntin, double-hung windows in vernacular houses); broad, flat chimneys; contrasting wall materials or trim emphasizing the upper part of the upper story; and decorative friezes or door surrounds consisting of bands of carved geometric or stylized floral (Sullivanesque) ornamentation.

Occurrence

The Prairie style originated in Chicago and landmark examples are concentrated in that city's early 20th-century suburbs, particularly Oak Park and River Forest, and in other large midwestern cities. Vernacular examples were spread widely by pattern books and popular magazines; they are common in early 20th-century suburbs throughout the country. Most were built between 1905 and 1915; the style quickly faded from fashion after World War I.

Comments

This is one of the few indigenous American styles. It was developed by an unusually creative group of Chicago architects that have come to be known as the Prairie School. Frank Lloyd Wright's early work is in this style and he is the acknowledged master of the Prairie house. Wright was unusual in that he early turned his creative genius toward the problems of domestic architecture rather than public buildings. His 1893 Winslow House was perhaps the first Prairie house; it is a symmetrical rectangle (see page 556). It was not until about 1900 that he began to use the asymmetrical hipped form, which he continued to develop until about 1913. As Wright explained, "Democracy needed something basically better than the box." Many of the other Prairie architects worked either with Wright himself or with his earlier employer and teacher, Louis Sullivan. Oth-

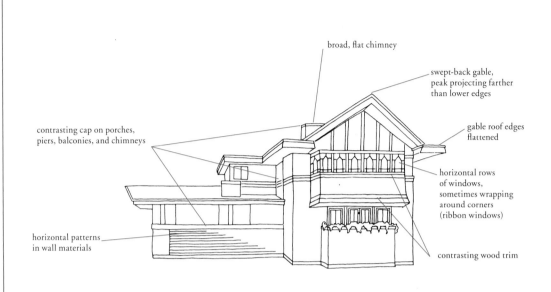

broad, flat chimney

swept-back gable,
peak projecting farther
than lower edges

gable roof edges
flattened

contrasting cap on porches,
piers, balconies, and chimneys

horizontal rows
of windows,
sometimes wrapping
around corners
(ribbon windows)

horizontal patterns
in wall materials

contrasting wood trim

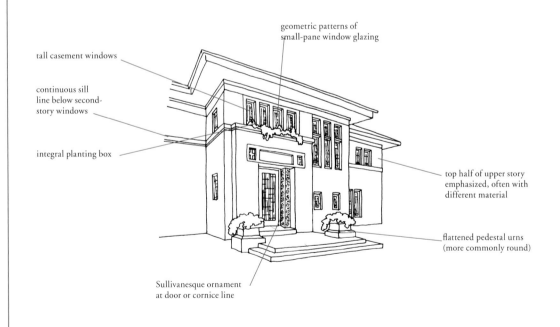

geometric patterns of
small-pane window glazing

tall casement windows

continuous sill
line below second-
story windows

integral planting box

top half of upper story
emphasized, often with
different material

flattened pedestal urns
(more commonly round)

Sullivanesque ornament
at door or cornice line

TYPICAL ELABORATIONS

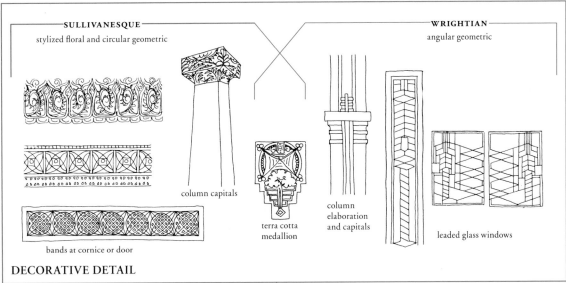

stylized floral and circular geometric

column capitals

terra cotta medallion

angular geometric

column elaboration and capitals

leaded glass windows

bands at cornice or door

DECORATIVE DETAIL

FOUND IN BOTH
CRAFTSMAN & PRAIRIE

"cottage" window decorative transom above broad bottom pane

single pane is common in bottom sash

TYPICAL DOORS

TYPICAL WINDOW GLAZING & SURROUNDS
casement windows common on Prairie high-style examples

hipped (through-
cornice dormer)

gabled
(roof dormer)

Palladian
(roof dormer)

COMMON DORMER VARIANTS

COMMON PORCH VARIANTS

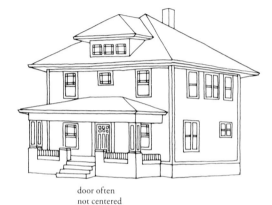

door often
not centered

American Four-Square,
a house shape, has a squared
floor plan with four rooms
upstairs and four rooms down;
central hall is absent; found in
many styles, including Prairie,
Colonial Revival, Neoclassical,
and Craftsman—and as folk houses

AMERICAN FOUR-SQUARE
the most common vernacular form

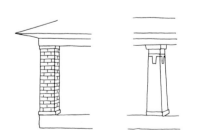

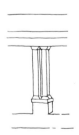

COMMON PORCH SUPPORT VARIANTS

HIPPED ROOF, SYMMETRICAL, WITH FRONT ENTRY

1. Dallas, Texas; ca. 1920. Jones House. Aluminum siding has been added to the walls and porch supports.

2. Dallas, Texas; 1910. Harrison House. This example has a door surround of stylized Sullivanesque floral ornament (not visible in the photograph). Note the Wrightian column capitals.

3. Louisville, Kentucky; ca. 1910. One-story Prairie examples like this are uncommon; one-story houses of the period were usually built in the Craftsman style.

4. Dallas, Texas; ca. 1910. The four-square plan, which was very popular during the period from about 1900 to 1920, is indicated by the two ranks of windows and the off-center entrance.

5. Tulsa, Oklahoma; 1915–1917. O'Rouke House. This house resembles some of the homes designed by Prairie architect George W. Maher and featured in the March 1914 *Western Architect*. The handsome entrance was likely inspired by Maher's Seymour House entry.

6. Gowanda, New York; ca. 1910. Houses of concrete blocks simulating stone, as seen here, were widely advocated by early 20th-century pattern books as a novel new building method. Note the through-the-cornice wall dormer.

7. River Forest, Illinois; 1893. Winslow House; Frank Lloyd Wright, architect. This is Wright's first Prairie house and is much simpler than his later examples, most of which have asymmetrical hipped roofs. This house, and similar examples, provided the model for most later pattern book and builder interpretations of the style. Note how the horizontal effect is emphasized by the thin bricks and trim band above (subtle decorative patterning in the dark upper wall is not visible in the photograph).

8. Lexington, Kentucky; ca. 1910. Note the uncoursed stone used for the lower two-thirds of the house, with stucco walls above.

9. Fort Dodge, Iowa; 1903. Butler House; Nourse and Rasmussen, architects.

1

4

7

8

HIPPED ROOF, SYMMETRICAL, NO FRONT ENTRY

1. Wichita, Kansas; ca. 1910.

2. Buffalo, New York; ca. 1910. Note the flat flower pots at the entrance to the right.

3. St. Louis, Missouri; ca. 1910. The entry is in the right wing; a porte cochere, in the left.

4. Portland, Oregon; 1911. Bennes House; John Virginius Bennes, architect. This house deftly combines Italian Renaissance with Prairie, a fairly common pairing.

5. Oak Park, Illinois; 1904. Mrs. Thomas H. Gale House; Frank Lloyd Wright, architect. This Wright design—with two levels of broad horizontal solid railings—was influential for the next century.

6. Racine, Wisconsin; 1905. Hardy House; Frank Lloyd Wright, architect. Note the wide, low chimney with dark coping at the top. The vertical emphasis here is particularly pronounced.

7. Lake Minnetonka, Minnesota; 1913. Decker House (garden facade); Purcell, Feick and Elmslie, architects. Note the ribbon of leaded casement windows across the second story.

8. Milwaukee, Wisconsin; 1916. Bogk House; Frank Lloyd Wright, architect. This house, done after Wright's principal Prairie years, has the simple box-like shape of some of his earlier houses.

3

6

8

HIPPED ROOF, ASYMMETRICAL

1. Kansas City, Missouri; ca. 1910. One-story examples such as this are very uncommon.

2. Mission Hills, Kansas; ca. 1915. This house has a strong horizontal emphasis in the linear pattern of the lower-story masonry, the dark band above, and the differing wall material of the upper one-third.

3. St. Louis, Missouri; ca. 1910. Note the massive chimney with narrow side toward the street (see also Figure 7).

4. Dallas, Texas; 1910. Parker House. This wood-clad example shows Craftsman influence in the open eaves with exposed rafters and in the stickwork between the porch supports. Note the decorative transom over the first-story windows.

5. Wichita, Kansas; 1917. Allen House; Frank Lloyd Wright, architect. In this late example, Wright includes an interior garden not found in earlier Prairie houses.

6. Lexington, Kentucky; ca. 1915. Note the similarity in form between this example and Figure 4. This one, however, is pure Prairie with boxed eaves and ribbons of casement windows.

7. Minneapolis, Minnesota; 1913. Purcell, Feick and Elmslie, architects. This house has particularly dramatic ribbons of decorative casement windows.

8. Buffalo, New York; 1904. Martin House; Frank Lloyd Wright, architect. Note the variety of hipped roofs and heavy masonry piers on this major Prairie landmark. The copings along low walls provide horizontal emphasis. Greenery overflows from planting boxes and planters placed at several levels.

1

4

6

7

2

3

5

8

GABLED ROOF

1. Kansas City, Missouri; ca. 1910. Figures 1 and 2 are front-gabled examples. This one has a stone lower story, with wooden shingles above. Narrow lot size dictates few extensions.

2. Dallas, Texas; ca. 1920. Jeremiah House. This late example is dominated by a wide front gable, although there is a hipped roof unit hidden behind. The wide lot allows for a one-story porte cochere and porch wings not present in Figure 1.

3. Oak Park, Illinois; 1912. Eastabrook House; Tallmadge and Watson, architects. Figures 3, 8, and 9 are cross-gabled examples; this is the simplest. Note the double-gabled roof on the left wing.

4. Dallas, Texas; 1918. Peck House. This side-gabled example has a band of Sullivanesque trim below the porch eave.

5. El Paso, Texas; 1908. Henry Trost House; Trost and Trost, architects. This clearly shows a wide eave overhang that is open—not boxed—and with the rafters covered, not exposed. Note the band of trim beneath the cornice.

6. Kansas City, Missouri; ca. 1910.

7. Montgomery, Alabama; ca. 1910. Note the four heavy piers ending two-thirds the way up the walls.

8. Pine Bluff, Arkansas; 1903. MacMillan House; Hugh Mackie Gorden Garden, architect. This photo shows clearly the open eave with enclosed rafters that is typical of this subtype (particularly those examples designed by architects). This contrasts with the open eave having exposed rafters that is found in contemporaneous Craftsman houses.

9. Grand Rapids, Michigan; 1910. Amberg House; Marion Mahony and Frank Lloyd Wright, architects.

2

6

7

9

ers absorbed Wright's and Sullivan's influence simply by being in Chicago. Among the most important were George W. Maher, Robert C. Spencer, Jr., Thomas E. Tallmadge, John S. Van Bergen, Vernon S. Watson, Charles E. White, Jr., Eben E. Roberts, Walter Burley Griffin, Marion Mahony Griffin, William Drummond, F. Barry Byrne, George G. Elmslie, and William G. Purcell.

Outside of the Chicago area, numerous local architects produced creditable and sometimes outstanding Prairie houses throughout the midwestern states and, less commonly, in other regions. The style in its vernacular form was spread throughout the country by pattern books published in the Midwest. It is among the more short-lived styles, having grown, flourished, and declined in the years between 1900 and 1920. Wright's ideas about domestic architecture—first explored in Prairie homes—were refined in his Usonian houses (1936–1959) and had an even greater effect on typical American houses through the Contemporary style.

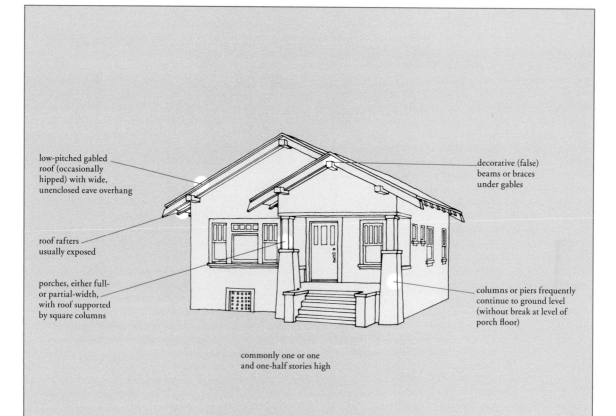

low-pitched gabled
roof (occasionally
hipped) with wide,
unenclosed eave overhang

roof rafters
usually exposed

porches, either full-
or partial-width,
with roof supported
by square columns

decorative (false)
beams or braces
under gables

columns or piers frequently
continue to ground level
(without break at level of
porch floor)

commonly one or one
and one-half stories high

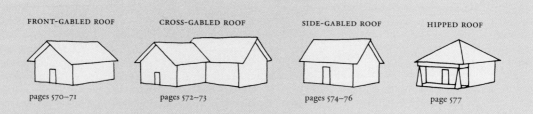

FRONT-GABLED ROOF

pages 570–71

CROSS-GABLED ROOF

pages 572–73

SIDE-GABLED ROOF

pages 574–76

HIPPED ROOF

page 577

PRINCIPAL SUBTYPES

Craftsman

1905–1930

Identifying Features

Low-pitched, gabled roof (occasionally hipped) with wide, unenclosed eave overhang; roof rafters usually exposed; decorative (false) beams or braces commonly added under gables; porches, either full- or partial-width, with roof supported by tapered square columns; columns or piers frequently extend to ground level (without a break at level of porch floor); commonly one or one and one-half stories high, although two-story examples occur in every subtype.

Principal Subtypes

Four principal subtypes can be distinguished:

FRONT-GABLED ROOF—About one-third of Craftsman houses are of this subtype. Porches, which may either be full- or partial-width, are almost evenly divided between those sheltered beneath the main roof and those with separate, extended roofs. Most examples of this subtype are one story, but one-and-a-half- and two-story examples are not uncommon; dormers are found in only about 10 percent of this subtype.

CROSS-GABLED ROOF—Cross-gabled examples make up about one-fourth of Craftsman houses. Of these, three-quarters are one-story examples; dormers occur on about 20 percent. Porches are varied, but by far the most common type is a partial-width, front-gabled porch, its roof forming the cross gable.

SIDE-GABLED ROOF—About one-third of Craftsman houses are of this subtype. Most are one and one-half stories high with centered shed or gable dormers. Porches are generally contained under the main roof, sometimes with a break in slope. Two-story examples commonly have added, full-width porches. This subtype is most common in the northeastern and midwestern states.

HIPPED ROOF—These make up less than 10 percent of Craftsman houses; they are almost equally divided between one- and two-story examples. This subtype is similar to some simple Prairie houses, which normally lack the exposed rafters and other typical Craftsman details.

Variants and Details

PORCH ROOF SUPPORTS—Columns for supporting the porch roofs are a distinctive and variable detail. Typically short, square upper columns rest upon more massive piers, or upon a solid porch balustrade. These columns, piers, or balustrades frequently begin directly at ground level and extend without break to a level well above the porch floor. Commonly the piers or columns have sloping (battered) sides. Materials used for piers, columns, and solid balustrades are varied. Stone, clapboard, shingle, brick, concrete block, or stucco are all common; they frequently occur in combination. Small rounded stones, such as those found in the arroyos of southern California, were particularly favored.

ROOF-WALL JUNCTIONS—Among the most distinctive features of the style are the junctions where the roof joins the wall, which are almost never boxed or enclosed. The roof has a wide eave overhang; along *horizontal* edges the actual rafter ends are exposed, or false rafter ends are added. These are sometimes cut into decorative shapes and rafter tails may extend beyond edge of roof. Along the sloping, or rake, edges, three or more beams (usually false) extend through the wall to the roof edge. These are either plain or embellished by a triangular knee brace.

OTHER DETAILS—Craftsman doors and windows are similar to those used in vernacular Prairie houses (see page 554). Two or more windows are often grouped together in one assembly; a narrow window on each side of a broad center window is common. Dormers are commonly gabled or shed, with exposed rafter ends and braces such as are found at the main roof-wall junction. The most common wall cladding is wood clapboard; wood shingles rank second. Stone, brick, concrete block, and stucco are also used, most frequently in the northern and midwestern states. Secondary influences such as Tudor false half-timbering, Swiss balustrades, or Oriental roof forms are also sometimes seen.

Occurrence

This was the dominant style for smaller houses built throughout the country during the period from about 1905 until the early 1920s. The Craftsman style originated in southern California and most landmark examples are concentrated there. Like vernacular examples of the contemporaneous Prairie style, it was quickly spread throughout the country by pattern books and popular magazines. The style rapidly faded from favor after the mid-1920s; relatively few were built after 1930.

Comments

Craftsman houses were inspired primarily by the work of two California brothers—Charles Sumner Greene and Henry Mather Greene—who practiced together in Pasadena from 1893 to 1914. About 1903 they began to design simple Craftsman-type bungalows;

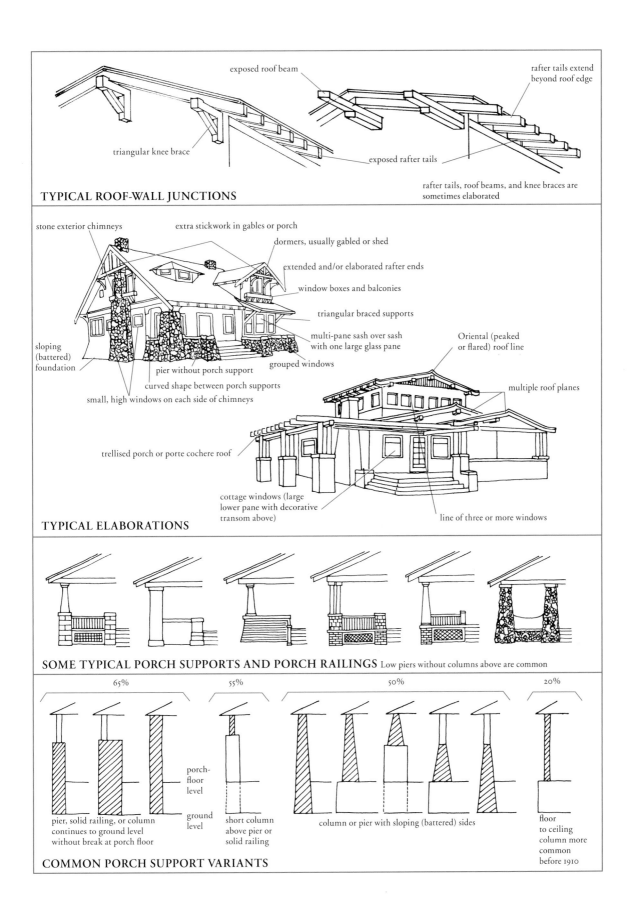

TYPICAL ROOF-WALL JUNCTIONS

exposed roof beam

rafter tails extend beyond roof edge

triangular knee brace

exposed rafter tails

rafter tails, roof beams, and knee braces are sometimes elaborated

TYPICAL ELABORATIONS

stone exterior chimneys

extra stickwork in gables or porch

dormers, usually gabled or shed

extended and/or elaborated rafter ends

window boxes and balconies

triangular braced supports

multi-pane sash over sash with one large glass pane

Oriental (peaked or flared) roof line

multiple roof planes

sloping (battered) foundation

pier without porch support

grouped windows

curved shape between porch supports

small, high windows on each side of chimneys

trellised porch or porte cochere roof

cottage windows (large lower pane with decorative transom above)

line of three or more windows

SOME TYPICAL PORCH SUPPORTS AND PORCH RAILINGS Low piers without columns above are common

COMMON PORCH SUPPORT VARIANTS

65%

55%

50%

20%

porch-floor level

ground level

pier, solid railing, or column continues to ground level without break at porch floor

short column above pier or solid railing

column or pier with sloping (battered) sides

floor to ceiling column more common before 1910

1

3

4

6

7

FRONT-GABLED ROOF

1. Holmes County, Florida; ca. 1910s. Here a Craftsman porch is attached to a simple folk form.

2. Canton, Mississippi; ca. 1910s. The porch roof is a separate gabled element in this very common version of the subtype.

3. Lexington, Kentucky; ca. 1910s. Note the doubled porch supports set on a closed porch railing. There is a section of hipped roof in the front with a gable above.

4. Kansas City, Missouri; ca. 1910s. This stucco example has three front-facing gables, all with half-timbered detailing.

5. Jackson, Mississippi; ca. 1910s. This photograph emphasizes the triangular knee braces commonly used in the gable ends of Craftsman houses. The slightly tapered porch-roof supports, extending from ground level, are of irregular brick masonry. Note how the main roof extends over the porch.

6. Kansas City, Missouri; ca. 1910s. A large two-story example of stone and stucco. The gable encompassing the entire second story is unusual.

7. Emporia, Kansas; ca. 1910s. This is a more typical two-story form than Figure 6. Note the matching roof-support columns and gables over the entry and porte cochere.

8. Santa Monica, California; 1911. Note the striking interlocking porch support detailing and the roof rafters that extend beyond the edge of the roof.

9. Santa Monica, California; 1911. Milbank House. Protruding roof beams (single, paired, and tripled), all with multiple setbacks that read almost like saw teeth.

2

5

8

9

CROSS-GABLED ROOF

1. Abbeville, South Carolina; ca. 1920s. Modest examples with Craftsman detailing, such as this, were common in outlying areas into the early 1930s.

2. San Jose, California; ca. 1910s. The two picture windows in this house are obvious later alterations. Note how the vergeboards here and in Figure 5 extend a bit beyond the roof edge to give a visual effect that the rafter tails extend beyond the edge of the roof.

3. Ardmore, Oklahoma; ca. 1910s. Note the similarity between this and Figure 6. Examples with the single room on the second story were called airplane bungalows, presumably because they afforded a panoramic view.

4. Kansas City, Missouri; ca. 1910s. Note the triple front-facing gables.

5. Louisville, Kentucky; ca. 1910s. Brick Craftsman houses were less common than wood; most occur in the larger cities of the Northeast and the Midwest. Fire codes in some cities—Denver and Chicago, for example—prohibited wooden exteriors.

6. Santa Barbara, California; ca. 1910. Note the intentional omission of center porch supports here and in Figures 2 and 5. This was done to allow an unobstructed view from front rooms.

7. Wichita, Kansas; ca. 1910s. Note the tapered porch supports that rise from ground level and are made of rough-faced stone.

8. Bellingham, Washington; 1908. Roeder House; Alfred Lee, architect. Triangular knee braces are used under the rafters, not just the roof beams, as is typical.

9. Pasadena, California; 1908. Gamble House; Greene and Greene, architects. A garden view of one of the great landmarks of the style. Note the numerous low-pitched gables, open porches, and exposed wooden structural elements. (In this case they *are* structural, not just added decoration as in most Craftsman houses.) Here the rafter tails extend beyond the edge of the roof, a typical high-style elaboration that is also visible in Figure 6.

7

8

SIDE-GABLED ROOF

1. Dallas, Texas; 1915. Lorrimer House. The typical exposed rafter ends show clearly here.

2. Salisbury, North Carolina; 1913. Rock House. Entry porches such as this are less common than full-width porches.

3. Lexington, Kentucky; ca. 1910s.

4. Louisville, Kentucky; ca. 1910s. Side-gabled Craftsman houses frequently have the attic area finished for bedrooms. Light comes from windows in the gable and from large centered dormers (see also Figures 2, 3, 5, and 7).

5. Kansas City, Missouri; ca. 1910s. The elaborate shed dormer with twin gables gives this example a Swiss Chalet feel.

6. Denver, Colorado; ca. 1910s. Note the peaked Oriental influence in the gables.

7. Durham, North Carolina; ca. 1910s. The wide expanse of porch without porch supports allows an unrestricted view from the front windows (see also Figures 3, 4, and 5).

8. Dallas, Texas; 1920. Clem House. Note the half-timbering in the gables and the use of paired, tapering porch supports atop the wide pedestals.

9. Dallas, Texas; 1917. Wheaton House. Large round columns such as this are seen in Craftsman pattern books, but are uncommon in actual examples.

1

4

7

9

SIDE-GABLED ROOF (cont.)

10. Santa Monica, California; ca. 1910s.

11. Dallas, Texas; 1914. Cranfill House.

12. Dallas, Texas; 1911. Defreese House. Note the full-width two-tiered porch. The typical triangular knee braces are clearly visible along the side gable. Derived from *Associated Architects Fifty House Plans* (published in 1910).[1]

13. Wichita, Kansas; ca. 1920. Lewis House.

14. Buffalo, New York; ca. 1910s. Note the contrasting stonework of the first and second stories and the shed dormers with matching shed-roof porch.

10

11

12

13

14

HIPPED ROOF

1. Dallas, Texas; ca. 1910s.

2. Washington, District of Columbia; ca. 1910s. Note the trellised entry porch. Similar porches were also used as side or wing porches in many examples of the style.

3. Dallas, Texas; 1912. Gibbs House. Note the porte cochere with a sleeping porch above. This was a typical addition to the main-house block in early 20th-century houses.

4. Dallas, Texas; 1917. Burgoyne House. This house shows the close relationship of the subtype with simple Prairie houses built in the four-square shape. The unenclosed eaves distinguish this example from similar Prairie forms; the porch supports are clearly Craftsman, but these are also used frequently on Prairie houses.

1

2

3

4

by 1909 they had designed and executed several exceptional landmark examples that have been called the "ultimate bungalows." Several influences—the English Arts and Crafts movement, an interest in Oriental wooden architecture, and their early training in the manual arts—appear to have led the Greenes to design and build these intricately detailed buildings. These and similar residences were given extensive publicity in such magazines as the *Western Architect, The Architect, House Beautiful, Good Housekeeping, Architectural Record, Country Life in America,* and *Ladies' Home Journal,* thus familiarizing the rest of the nation with the style. As a result, a flood of pattern books appeared, offering plans for Craftsman bungalows; some even offered completely pre-cut packages of lumber and detailing to be assembled by local labor. Through these vehicles, the one-story Craftsman house quickly became the most popular and fashionable smaller house in the country. High-style interpretations are rare except in California, where they have been called the Western Stick style. One-story vernacular examples are sometimes called bungalows. However, during the early 20th century, the term "bungalow" could refer to small, one-story examples of other styles—for example, a Spanish or a Tudor bungalow. Craftsman examples were often called California bungalows.

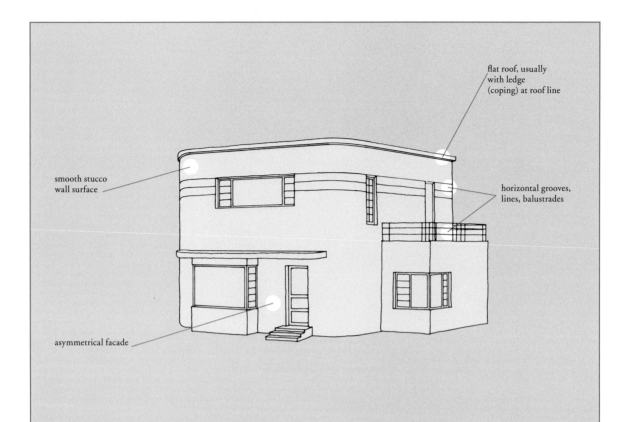

smooth stucco
wall surface

flat roof, usually
with ledge
(coping) at roof line

horizontal grooves,
lines, balustrades

asymmetrical facade

ART MODERNE (streamline modernistic)

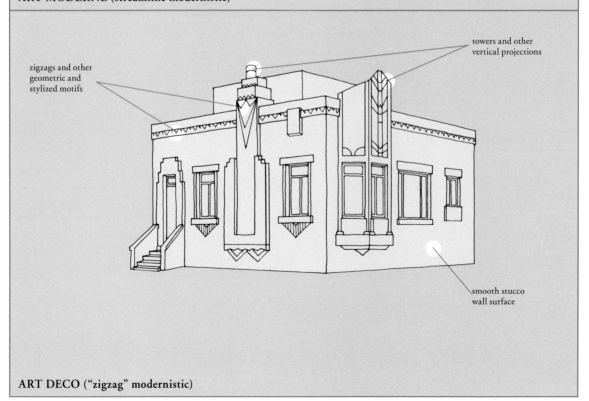

towers and other
vertical projections

zigzags and other
geometric and
stylized motifs

smooth stucco
wall surface

ART DECO ("zigzag" modernistic)

Modernistic

1920–1940

Identifying Features

ART MODERNE—Smooth wall surface, usually of stucco; flat roof, usually with small ledge (coping) at roof line; horizontal grooves or lines in walls and horizontal balustrade elements give a horizontal emphasis; facade usually asymmetrical.

ART DECO—Smooth wall surface, usually of stucco; zigzags, chevrons, and other stylized and geometric motifs occur as decorative elements on facade; towers and other vertical projections above the roof line give a vertical emphasis.

Variants and Details

ART MODERNE—One or more corners of the building may be curved; windows frequently are continuous around corners; glass blocks are often used in windows, or as entire sections of wall; small round windows are common.

Occurrence

The Modernistic styles were built from about 1920 to 1940. The earlier form was the Art Deco, which was common in public and commercial buildings in the 1920s and early 1930s. It was, however, extremely rare in domestic architecture; we know of only a few surviving houses, although it was frequently used for apartment buildings. After about 1930, Art Moderne became the prevalent Modernistic form. Although never common, many houses were built in the style; scattered examples can be found throughout the country.

Comments

The Modernistic styles received their first major impetus in 1922 when the Chicago *Tribune* held a world-wide competition for a headquarters building in Chicago. Although the first prize went to a Gothic design, the second prize went to an Art Deco design by a young Finnish architect, Eliel Saarinen. His design was widely publicized and much of the architectural profession felt that he deserved the first prize; the style quickly became the latest architectural fashion. The style gained its name from the Paris Exhibition of 1925—the Exposition Internationale des Arts Décoratifs et Industriels Modernes. Shortly after 1930 another, more diffuse influence affected the Modernistic style—the beginning of streamlined industrial design for ships, airplanes, and automobiles. The smooth surfaces, curved corners, and horizontal emphasis of the Art Moderne style all give the feeling that airstreams could move smoothly over them; thus, they were streamlined. In most building types, both the horizontal, streamlined Art Moderne and the vertical, zigzagged Art Deco influences occur in combination. In houses, however, the streamline influences predominate. Many examples resemble the contemporaneous International style, in which decorative detailing was reduced to the barest minimum.

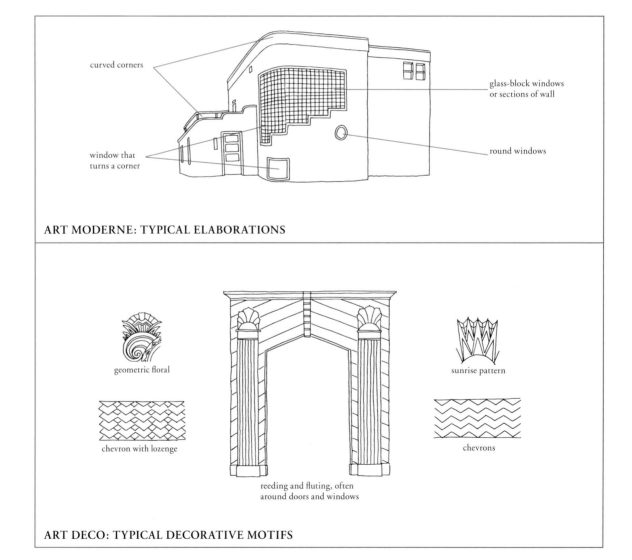

curved corners

glass-block windows
or sections of wall

window that
turns a corner

round windows

ART MODERNE: TYPICAL ELABORATIONS

geometric floral

sunrise pattern

chevron with lozenge

chevrons

reeding and fluting, often
around doors and windows

ART DECO: TYPICAL DECORATIVE MOTIFS

MODERNISTIC: ART DECO

1. San Francisco, California; ca. 1930. A rare
   example of an Art Deco house; note the
   geometric decorative details and vertical roof
   projections.

2. Los Angeles, California; 1930. Smith House;
   J. C. Smale, architect. Note the fluting along
   the parapet and the vertical elements created
   by the windows and deco ornament.

3. Boise, Idaho; ca. 1930s.

1

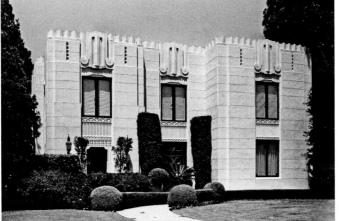

2

3

MODERNISTIC: ART MODERNE

1. San Antonio, Texas; ca. 1930s. Note the entry area with its round window, curved glass-brick window, and curved porch roof with coping above the entry.

2. Fargo, North Dakota; ca. 1930s. Note the curved front with two glass-block windows wrapping around it and the small octagonal window.

3. Toledo, Ohio; ca. 1930s. This popular Art Moderne design is almost symmetrical.

4. Palm Springs, California; 1936. "Ship of the Desert"; Wilson and Webster, architects. Rebuilt from its original plans after a fire.

5. Des Moines, Iowa; 1937. Butler House; Kraetsch and Kraetsch, architects. This landmark example is built of poured-in-place structural concrete with metal windows. It has several curved sections and a dramatic frieze of horizontal grooves. Note also the varied angles and corner windows in the section to the left.

6. Fergus Falls, Minnesota; 1937. Lee House; Foss and Co., architects. The brick wall cladding is atypical of the style. Note the extensive horizontal railings and curved one-story section.

7. Daly City, California; ca. 1950. Westlake District; Henry Doelger, builder. This late example has an atypical overhang added.

8. Denver, Colorado; ca. 1930s. Three horizontal lines in graduated lengths wrap the corners, giving this house a Moderne feeling. They are made of elongate brick embedded into stucco.

1

3

5

6

2

4

7

8

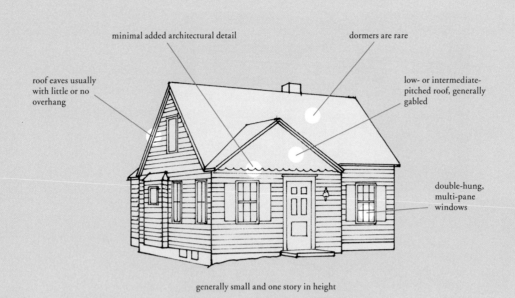

minimal added architectural detail

dormers are rare

roof eaves usually with little or no overhang

low- or intermediate-pitched roof, generally gabled

double-hung, multi-pane windows

generally small and one story in height

GABLE-AND-WING ROOF

pages 590–91

SIDE-GABLED ROOF

pages 592–93

OTHER ROOF

pages 594–95

SUBTYPES

Minimal Traditional

ca. 1935–1950

Identifying Features

Low- or intermediate-pitched roof, more often gabled; small house, generally one-story in height; roof eaves usually have little or no overhang; double-hung windows, typically multi-pane or 1/1; minimal amounts of added architectural detail; rarely has dormers.

Principal Subtypes

GABLE-AND-WING ROOF—This subtype has a low-pitched front-facing gable added on one side of a side-gabled roof. Typically the front-facing gable does not protrude very far in front of the side gable and consists only of a small extension added to one room of the house. Two-story examples are sometimes found.

SIDE-GABLED ROOF (COMMONLY CALLED CAPE COD)—Comprised of simple one-story side-gabled houses, this subtype was widely published in mass-market shelter magazines in the 1930s and 1940s. Besides being a beloved early New England folk-house form and symbol of colonial America, the Cape Cod provides some of the most economical cubic space that can be built.[2]

Although many examples were symmetrical, in keeping with the original folk form, there was much experimentation with asymmetrical variations, including varied window placement and small porches or carports; some had an extra half-story finished under the roof. Two-story side-gabled examples are found, but those would not be called Cape Cod, a term properly confined to the one-story form.

OTHER ROOF—Hipped-roof and front-gabled houses are also found, with hipped-roof versions the more widespread. These variations appear to be less common than other subtypes.

Variants and Details

"Simplicity in exterior design gives the small house the appearance of maximum size." So states the FHA's 1940 version of *Principles for Planning Small Houses,* which uses the word "simple" four times in its first five sentences describing exterior design. The pamphlet recommends a simple composition, simple roof lines, and simple variations and materials (thus avoiding a "restless appearance"). It also suggests the overall appearance can be improved by avoiding unnecessary gables and dormers, breaks in the roof form, and over-elaborate cornices. Indeed, "all nonessential features can profitably be omitted." The recommendation was to concentrate on scale, carefully place the windows and doors, and make the house look larger by cladding it with one material—or, if two materials are used, they should be the same color. Porches, bay windows, and platform steps were the only additions the FHA suggested. However, in practice, Minimal Traditionals commonly had a traditional paneled front door (sometimes with a multi-pane window in the upper half), perhaps accompanied by shutters or a chimney. Occasionally, Minimal Traditionals have other bits of stylistic detailing added—such as elements of Tudor or Colonial Revival.

Occurrence

Minimal Traditional homes can be found throughout the United States. During the early 1940s, concentrations were rapidly built where new sites for World War II production plants created an urgent local need for worker housing. After the war, developers built instant communities—such as Levittown, New York, on Long Island, and Brentwood in Denver, Colorado—filled with Minimal Traditional houses, sometimes using only a few designs in a subdivision. These were sometimes located beyond the city's built-up edge, where large tracts of land were available and new broad highways and arterials were planned for easy automobile access. In postwar subdivisions, the style is found with early Ranch houses (sometimes called Minimal Ranches or Ranchettes).

Further Comments

The Minimal Traditional house was "the little house that could." It was the small house that could be built with FHA-insured loans in the midst of the Great Depression between 1935 and 1940; the house that could be built quickly to accommodate millions of relocating World War II production-plant workers (1941–1945); and the house that could be built rapidly during the late 1940s in large post–World War II developments (1946–1949). These late-1940s developments were necessary to begin to fulfill the wartime GI Bill promise that every returning serviceman would be able to purchase a home.[3]

The Minimal Traditional was a well-studied and thoughtful response to the most challenging conditions ever to affect home construction in the United States. In the early 1930s, the Great Depression virtually shut down the home-building industry. Housing starts fell from 330,000 in 1930 to an unprecedented 93,000 in 1933.[4] Banks were going under, mortgages were past due, and there were no funds for new construction. The urgent first step was the creation of a new method for insuring long-term, low-interest mortgages. This was accomplished in 1934 through the creation of the FHA, whose goal was to produce small homes the average working American could afford (see financing, below). The FHA not only provided insurance that covered the mortgage loan a bank made, it also prepared publications that showed how to most effectively design a small house.

Architects, desperate for work after 1930, had enthusiastically turned their attention to the design of the small house. Large portions of professional journals were devoted to this subject beginning in the mid-1930s. It was of paramount importance to design the most efficient floor plans, kitchens, and baths, since every extra square foot added to the cost. A higher home cost both limited the market and made it harder to qualify for the all-important FHA loan insurance. At that time, the FHA, along with its associated Fannie Mae, limited the maximum sales price of homes they would insure so that the average home size and cost remained within the reach of a broad market. Nonetheless, a little known bonus of FHA loans was that they allowed all major appliances to be included in the home loan amount.[5]

A veritable flood of house plans and pattern books for small houses featuring Minimal Traditionals was published between 1935 and 1950—and the book contents often included careful descriptions of the FHA loan programs available.[6] The most influential publications were the FHA's own bulletins, *Principles of Planning Small Houses*. The original 1936 version had only a few drawings, but the revised and expanded 1940 edition illustrated most of the basic shapes and variations of Minimal Traditional houses.[7] Builders knew that following the guidelines in this bulletin was the quickest way to ensure construction funds and home-purchase mortgages for their projects.

No sooner had the orderly construction of homes gotten under way in the late 1930s than there was an immediate pressing need for small houses to accommodate the unprecedented relocation of workers to ramp up wartime production.[8] Approximately 2.3 million war and defense homes, the vast majority of them Minimal Traditional, were built between 1940 and 1945. The builder-developers who quickly erected these large developments of necessary wartime housing taught themselves, on the job, how to speed up construction through both offsite and onsite prefabrication of needed components and then applying assembly-line techniques to construction.[9]

When the war ended in 1945, there arose the immediate problem of housing ten million returning servicemen and their families, promised the right to purchase a new home with no down payment.[10] There were no new homes available, so these same builder-developers went to work, applying their wartime experience in rapid construction to large subdivisions of homes available for purchase. In an explosion of home building at the war's end, 5.1 million homes were built between 1946 and 1949.[11] Minimal Traditionals made up a significant portion of these.[12] The fact that the FHA had already blessed these designs meant a developer could get speedy approval of loans for building to begin. Those who strived for a more modern look often encountered obstacles and costly time delays. [13]

By 1950 the Minimal Traditional was being replaced by Ranch homes. Postwar prosperity meant that larger homes could be built and financed, and the Ranch was a perfect fit for the tastes of a new decade.

GABLE-AND-WING ROOF

1. Hamptons, New York; ca. 1940s. Note the double-hung windows and overall cladding. Door faces to side.

2. Portland, Oregon; ca. 1930. This early example is unusual in having the entry in the gable.

3. Chicago, Illinois; ca. 1950. This is beginning to transition to the Ranch with the broader form and the beginnings of a picture window.

4. Alexandria, Virginia; 1950.

5. Phoenix, Arizona; 1940.

6. South San Francisco, California; ca. 1940s. Compare to Figure 7 in same area. The second-story gable could be original or an addition. The window in the first-floor gable appears modified.

7. South San Francisco, California; ca. 1940s. As the FHA suggested, in order to make the house look larger the secondary material in the gable is painted the same color as the house. Note the design of the porch rail.

8. Dallas, Texas; 1946. Two-story examples occur.

2

4

5

7

1

3

6

8

SIDE-GABLED ROOF
(CAPE COD)

1. Burbank, California; 1940. Note the paired double-hung windows placed toward the corners of the house.

2. Levittown, New York; ca. 1946. This was one of Levitt's alternative Cape Cod designs and is in the shape of a three-quarter house.

3. Burbank, California; 1941 (renovated 1953). Windows on the main house block are not double-hung and are likely later additions.

4. Levittown, New York; ca. 1947. Reportedly the most intact remaining example of Levittown's early Cape Cod houses. These were 750 square feet and sold for $7,500.

5. Prairie Village, Kansas; 1947. The tall double windows on the left might first have been a garage as in Figure 6.

6. Prairie Village, Kansas; 1947. Note the uncommon built-in garage.

7. Dallas, Texas; 1939. Note the large double-hung windows. This house was financed by the FHA.

8. Seattle, Washington; 1940.

9. Atlanta, Georgia; ca. 1940s. A neighborhood of Minimal Traditional houses.

1

4

7

8

2

3

5

6

9

OTHER ROOF

1. Burbank, California; 1939.

2. Burbank, California; ca. 1940. This and Figures 1 and 4 were built to house employees of the Lockheed Vega aircraft plant and the Burbank airfield. The entire area was camouflaged during World War II to look like a pastoral rural setting rather than a factory and housing for workers.

3. Fairway, Kansas; 1941. Compare to the slightly larger example, Figure 6, in the same neighborhood.

4. Burbank, California; ca. 1940. Note the shingle cladding, and board shutters with cutouts (even on corner windows).

5. Portland, Oregon; ca. 1940s. The corner-window placement was among the FHA's recommended designs.

6. Fairway, Kansas; 1942. Note use of second wall-cladding material and scalloped cornice board on front-hipped wing.

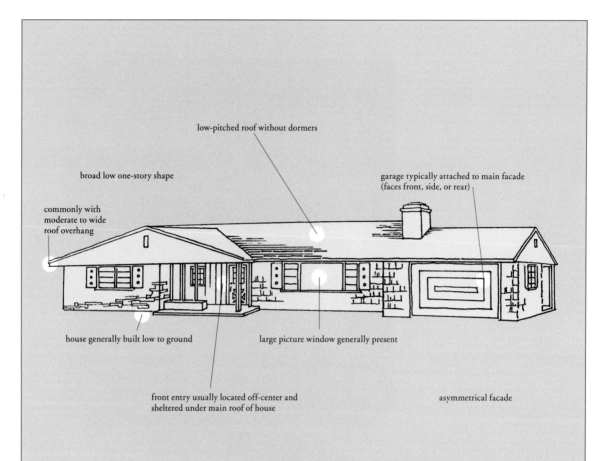

low-pitched roof without dormers

broad low one-story shape

commonly with
moderate to wide
roof overhang

garage typically attached to main facade
(faces front, side, or rear)

house generally built low to ground

large picture window generally present

front entry usually located off-center and
sheltered under main roof of house

asymmetrical facade

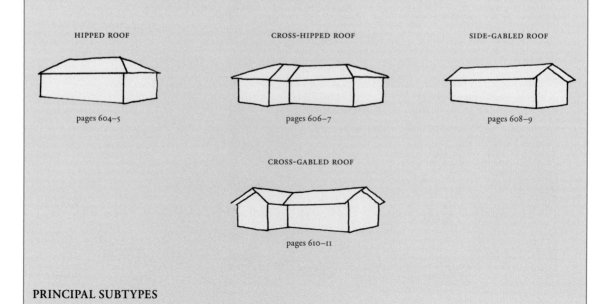

HIPPED ROOF

pages 604–5

CROSS-HIPPED ROOF

pages 606–7

SIDE-GABLED ROOF

pages 608–9

CROSS-GABLED ROOF

pages 610–11

PRINCIPAL SUBTYPES

Ranch

ca. 1935–1975

Identifying Features

Broad one-story shape; usually built low to ground; low-pitched roof without dormers; commonly with moderate-to-wide roof overhang; front entry usually located off-center and sheltered under main roof of house; garage typically attached to main facade (faces front, side, or rear); a large picture window generally present; asymmetrical facade.

Principal Subtypes

Four principal subtypes can be distinguished:

HIPPED ROOF—About 10 percent of one-story Ranch houses have a simple hipped roof with a long roof ridge running parallel to the front facade. These are more common in rural areas and in neighborhoods of smaller houses. Very occasionally, as in the side-gabled subtype, a large example with broadly angled wings occurs.

CROSS-HIPPED ROOF—About 40 percent of one-story Ranch houses have a cross-hipped roof. Typically these are one-story houses with a long roof ridge running parallel to the front facade with a single hipped extension. Occasionally a second hipped front extension is also present.

Sometimes the cross-gabled and cross-hipped types have a combination roof with a front hip on a side-gabled roof or, conversely, a front-facing gable on a hipped roof. Very large examples may feature rather complex roof forms with a combination of roof heights and types.

SIDE-GABLED ROOF—About 10 percent of one-story Ranch houses have side-gabled roofs with a long roof ridge running parallel to the front facade. These are more common in rural areas and in neighborhoods of smaller houses. Some high-style examples have slight angles in the front (or other) facade, giving the appearance of wide-spread welcoming arms.[14]

CROSS-GABLED ROOF—About 40 percent of one-story Ranch houses have a broad side-gabled form, with a long roof ridge parallel to the street, and a single prominent, front-facing gable extension. Occasionally a second such gable is present.

SPLIT-LEVELS—Split-level versions of all Ranch subtypes are common. This variation is discussed on pages 613–14.

Variants and Details

WINDOWS—A remarkable variety of sizes and types of pre-manufactured windows were available to builders during the Ranch era, and most Ranch houses exhibit several different sizes and/or types of windows. After World War II, factories used for war production were quickly adapted to the manufacture of domestic products and a profusion of window types was made possible by applying production methods perfected during the war. These were manufactured in standardized sizes newly regulated by the industry's trade associations. Metal (aluminum, steel, or bronze) and wood versions of double-hung, casement, and sliding windows were manufactured, as were awning styles. Metal sliding windows and jalousie windows (very common in southern Florida) also occurred.

More than 50 percent of Ranch houses have at least one picture window on the front facade, and some examples have more. These large focal windows commonly had sections that could be opened from side or top hinges for ventilation. In later examples, groups of tall fixed vertical panes were often used instead of picture windows.[15] Very short windows were often utilized, sometimes grouped into ribbons and placed high on the facade. This allowed for light and ventilation without loss of interior privacy and accommodated flexibility in furniture arrangement below the high windows.

In the rest of the house, traditional window lengths were typically used—either in a casement or double-hung design. In the latter, horizontal light patterns (2/2 or 3/3) and multi-pane patterns (9/9, 8/8, 6/6, 12/12, or 1/1) were common. Generally, several window sizes or shapes occur on a house, typically made of the same material and in the same design family (meaning that the details and pattern of lights are matched). Corner windows sometimes occurred in early examples, usually with a corner support (in contrast to the mitered glass corners on Mid-century Modern homes).

FRONT ENTRIES—The front entry is almost always sheltered by the main roof of the house. At its simplest, the front entry is only recessed, with extra shelter provided by the overhanging front-facade roof. Alternatively, the door is set into the L formed by the cross-hipped or cross-gabled roof, providing two overhangs for additional shelter. In about half the examples, entry or partial-width porches occur, almost always contained under the main roof of the house, making them relatively inconspicuous. Two porch forms are common. In one, a portion of the front-facing cross gable or hip has inset walls that form a roofed entry area. In the other, a partial-width porch occurs, often in the L created by the cross-hipped or gabled-roof form; occasionally a porch is full-width. It is common for the material cladding the entry area to differ from that of the main body of the house.

Porch supports are most often simple wood posts—sometimes with triangular braces to each side—or wrought iron in a wide variety of designs, from simple modern forms to

TRADITIONAL WINDOWS

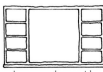

horizontal panes,
2/2 or 3/3

jalousie,
most common
in Florida

horizontal panes,
2/2 or 3/3

horizontal
panes, 8/8

6/6

AWNING   CASEMENT   DOUBLE-HUNG

SHORT WINDOWS

on upper facade, may be grouped

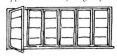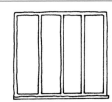

casement (as shown) or sliding

awning or hopper

PICTURE WINDOWS

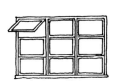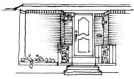

large central pane with
sections of multiple lights

multiple lights

horizontal lights

ribbons of tall vertical panes

SOME PART OF WINDOW MAY OPEN FOR CROSS-VENTILATION,
common in early examples

WINDOW MAY NOT OPEN,
more common in later examples

TYPICAL WINDOWS commonly steel, aluminum, or wood

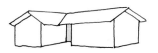

ENTRY ON FLAT FACADE
usually recessed with additional
protection from roof overhang

note distinctive curvilinear door panels

ENTRY SET INTO L
usually recessed with additional protection
from two roof overhangs

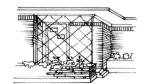

ENTRY PORCH IN CROSS GABLE
OR CROSS HIP
under main roof form

BROAD ENTRY PORCH
usually partial-width and under
main roof form

wrought-iron patterns of vines and leaves

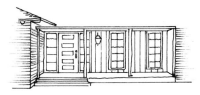

TYPICAL SHELTERED ENTRIES

more traditional patterns that often feature vine and leaf motifs.[16] Occasionally, porch supports are omitted and the roof spans wall to wall.

An unusually wide variety of entry details appear. The front door itself may be single or paired and occurs in many diverse designs. The simplest is a resolutely plain flush door. Some designs are "modern" and may feature multiples of three (three small windows, three raised horizontal panels). Other designs feature panels—either distinctive curvilinear panels or multiple squared panels more typical of Colonial Revival; these often have glass panes above. Doors may have a single sidelight or matched sidelights or side panels. Occasionally the entry door faces to the side rather than toward the street.

ROOF-WALL JUNCTIONS—The overhanging eave was either boxed or open. When boxed, it had either a simple, unadorned cornice board or no cornice at all. When open, the rafter tails were typically either sheathed with plywood or exposed, commonly with smooth-rounded rafter tails that did not extend beyond the roof edge.[17]

OTHER DETAILS—The new emphasis on standardization seen in windows produced the Ranch style's very common eight-foot ceiling height, since sheetrock, gypsum board, and two-by-four lumber were now generally produced at this uniform length. Concrete-slab foundations, used in rapid prefab construction during World War II, became common and allowed the Ranch house to move even closer to the ground as slabs replaced the higher masonry-pier foundations of earlier homes.

Garages were generally attached and could face to the front, rear, or side. The typical one-car attached garage (1930s to early 1950s) soon became a two-car garage, and later even a three-car one. Houses built early in the era, and those squeezed onto older, narrow lots, might have a detached garage or one connected by a covered breezeway. Carports were also sometimes found but were more common in Contemporary houses.

Wood, brick, stone, asbestos and wood shingles, concrete blocks, and stucco wall cladding were all used. Board-and-batten, used in Cliff May's early Ranch designs, was a favored wood-siding pattern. Frequently two or more materials were combined. Cladding might vary on whole sections of a wall (such as the front entry area), in the top of gable ends, or in horizontal sections (such as between the bottom third of a wall, typically below the base of the windows, and the upper two-thirds). The predominant wall cladding material used sometimes varies regionally (such as red brick in Georgia or stucco in Arizona) and can differ from subdivision to subdivision.

Simple, low masonry planters were favorite elaborations and could be small and located near the entry, horizontal and stretched along the front facade of the house, or free-standing and enclosing an entry courtyard.

The FHA discouraged a pronounced modern appearance in the homes they helped finance. Thus builders frequently added modest bits of traditional detailing, usually loosely based on Spanish, French, or English Colonial precedents. Decorative window shutters are the most common of these. Window boxes were often used, and small roof cupolas (sometimes of prefab metal) and pieces of metal decoration at gable ends (such as eagles) are not unusual. It was rare to find a house that featured details from a single style—most of them freely mixed and matched. Ranch houses that exhibit one distinct style are treated under Styled Ranch.

Early, small examples of the Ranch are sometimes called Ranchette, Minimal Ranch, or Transitional Ranch. These generally lack the broader overhang of later examples and

rafters do not extend beyond roof edge, tips often rounded

cornice board is absent, or single unelaborated board

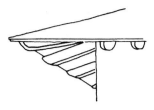 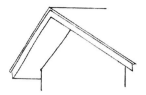 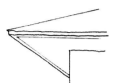

open eave, rafter exposed (very common)   open eave, rafters boxed (less common)   boxed eave (very common)

TYPICAL ROOF-WALL JUNCTIONS

dormers not present

OVERALL

three small windows in door

partial-width porch at entry
(occasionally full-width)

multiple window shapes and sizes

broad low chimney

corner window

INTEGRATED "SLANTS"

gable-roof overhang slants
outward

architectural elements that slant

**DIFFERENT WALL-
CLADDING MATERIALS**

wall cladding changes in
entry area

wall cladding changes at base
of window

wall cladding changes in
gable end (usually wood
boards, applied horizontally
or vertically)

board-and-batten cladding
(for California-rustic look)

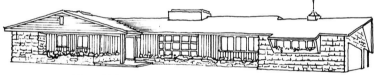

TRADITIONAL ARCHITECTURAL FEATURES

"Colonial" roof cupola

shutters

decorative wrought iron

INTEGRATED PLANTERS

squared masonry planter near entry

long low masonry planters add horizontal emphasis

window-box planters

TYPICAL ELABORATIONS

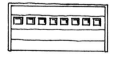    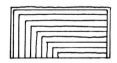

high-style designs, unusual and fast disappearing

TYPICAL GARAGE DOORS single or double most common

many of the elaborations that became common as house size increased. Ranchettes are commonly found in neighborhoods that contain or are located close to Minimal Traditionals. The line between Minimal Traditional and Ranchette is a matter of judgment. However, the intent was likely a Ranch house if a picture window and other Ranch elaboration is present (such as a corner window or wall cladding that differs at the base of the windows). While Ranch houses commonly have a broader profile than Minimal Traditionals, neighborhoods platted with narrow lots before World War II may have Ranch-style houses adapted to these lot sizes.

REAR-YARD ELABORATIONS—Outdoor patios are common features at the rear of the house, often reached through sliding glass doors or a double French door, and sometimes with built-in free-standing masonry grills. These private outdoor living areas are a direct contrast to the large front or side porches of most late 19th- and early 20th-century styles. Large view windows faced, and patios and covered verandahs opened onto, the more private rear of the house. Front porches, when present, were generally shallow and rarely served as the outdoor living spaces of earlier styles.

Occurrence

The Ranch style originated in southern California in the mid-1930s, after a few earlier precursors.[18] During the 1940s, it was only one of the small house types built under FHA financing guidelines. As the financial controls that mandated very small houses were gradually lifted following World War II, the Ranch style began to gain in popularity. During the decades of the 1950s and 1960s it became by far the most popular house style built throughout the country. Often located in large subdivisions, post–World War II Ranch-house suburbs form a dominant part of many American cities—particularly those that grew in the postwar Sunbelt Boom of the 1950s and 1960s, such as Dallas, Houston, Phoenix, Los Angeles, and Atlanta. As well as being nearly ubiquitous across the most southern, southwestern, and western states during those decades, Ranch was also found in the northern half of the nation. The northern states, however, also favored split-level and even two-story houses. This may have been due to relatively more expen-

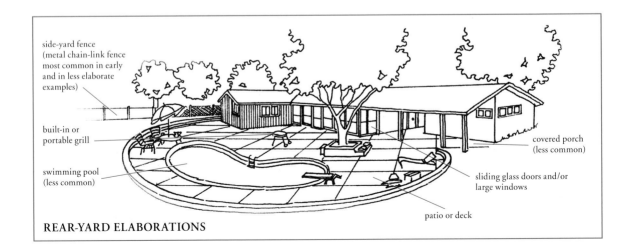

side-yard fence (metal chain-link fence most common in early and in less elaborate examples)

built-in or portable grill

swimming pool (less common)

covered porch (less common)

sliding glass doors and/or large windows

patio or deck

REAR-YARD ELABORATIONS

sive land and the heating savings offered by more compact houses. It is important to understand that FHA financing guidelines similar to those that made construction of houses possible in the 1930s continued to exert a strong influence on new houses built through the 1950s and 1960s.[19] The size of a Ranch was quite small in the late 1940s, but the typical size gradually increased as builders actively lobbied for higher loan limits and FHA guidelines were revised upward. The FHA also encouraged the building of entire neighborhoods at once by a single large developer. A topic of great concern to developers was how to inexpensively vary the appearance of similar house plans in a neighborhood in order to avoid a monotonous appearance.[20]

Comments

The popularity of "rambling" Ranch houses was made possible by the country's increasing use of automobiles. Streetcar suburbs in the early 20th century had relatively compact houses on narrow lots to facilitate walking home from the stop. As the automobile became the principal means of transportation after World War II, houses with narrow fronts could be replaced by sprawling designs on wider lots. Never before had it been possible to be so lavish with land, and the rambling form of the Ranch house emphasizes this by maximizing facade width (often broadened farther by attached garages).[21]

The style is very loosely based on early Spanish Colonial precedents in the American Southwest—primarily the larger pitched-roof homes that featured private courtyards and covered inward-facing porches.

Cliff May, the innovative southern California builder, designer, and promoter, who had joined with California-based *Sunset Magazine* to introduce Ranch houses to a larger audience, was a sixth-generation Californian and intimately familiar with Spanish Colonial houses. In 1946, May and the editorial staff of *Sunset* wrote, and the magazine published, *Western Ranch Houses*. It featured a history of Spanish Colonial houses and a number of plans and drawings on how to build new Ranch houses based on them. Highly successful, it was quickly reprinted for a broader national audience. In 1958, *Sunset* published a second version, mainly featuring photographs of May's work. National shelter magazines like *House Beautiful* and *House and Garden* began publishing Ranch-house articles in the 1950s.

These same magazines also contained numerous articles promoting a casual family-oriented lifestyle for postwar families. In the hands of builders throughout the country, the Ranch became the favored way of experiencing this informality.[22] Described as "middle-of-the-road modern" and "modern inside, traditional outside," the Ranch style was also considered, both by lending institutions and builders, to be more acceptable to the American home-buying public than more dramatic modern designs. While in the 1950s and early 1960s architects occasionally designed Ranch-style homes, most favored Mid-century Modern styles such as the Contemporary.[23] Home buyers, however, embraced Ranch houses and greatly enjoyed their modern amenities and large family rooms that were available for affordable prices.[24]

In the 1970s the pitch of the Ranch-house roof began to rise, and traditional stylistic detailing was added in greater quantity. While deliberately "styled" Ranch houses had been built throughout the Ranch era, these variations became ever more popular. By the 1980s, rising land prices nationwide, and changing tastes, meant an abandonment of the one-story house and a return to two-story houses.

HIPPED ROOF

1. Chicago, Illinois; 1957. One of a row of Ranch houses built on narrow lots with garages behind. Note wide eave overhang, picture window with a different cladding at base, and entry inset under main roof with wrought-iron porch support.

2. San Marino, California; 1948 (renovated 1955).

3. Miami, Florida; 1954. This minimal Ranch (or Ranchette) is part of a small subdivision. The "shutters" are actually tiles laid in the stucco walls, and the windows have the horizontal 2/2 muntin pattern favored in Ranch houses.

4. Duluth, Minnesota; 1950. The roof form appears as a single hip, despite variation in the front-facade plane.

5. Portland, Oregon; 1953. Note the stylish ribbon windows on contrasting wall cladding to the left of the picture window.

6. Atlanta, Georgia; ca. 1950s. Collier Heights Historic District. This Ranch takes advantage of the change in grade with a side-down garage.

7. Los Angeles, California; ca. 1960. The wall cladding has a horizontal pattern.

8. Dallas, Texas; ca. 1960s. Fritch House (demolished). This elegant Ranch house makes clear the relation of many Ranch houses to Prairie style. Note the ribbon window, broad roof overhang, and low wide chimney.

9. Dallas, Texas; 1950. This large Ranch has wings that angle backward. Not visible is a rear-down section that includes the garage.

1

3

5

8

CROSS-HIPPED ROOF

1. St. Petersburg, Florida; ca. 1950. Kenwood Historic District. The entry door faces sideways and is recessed under the right corner of the front hip. In addition a picture window, horizontal window muntins, and low roof pitch with broad overhang make this small house a Ranch. (Compare with Figure 2.)

2. San Francisco, California; ca. 1950s. A front-gabled garage is used with a hipped-roof house block. The metal porch supports are an abstracted vine pattern, with the "vines" escaping to the side at the tops.

3. Seattle, Washington; 1953. This appears to have the same sections as Figure 6, but at a smaller scale. Sleeping section at left, living in the center, and cars on the right.

4. Chicago, Illinois; 1958. This has two corner windows and a row of three small windows near the entry. The long, low masonry planter adds horizontal emphasis to entry area.

5. Pasadena, California; ca. 1950s. Board-and-batten siding and thick wood shake roof are part of the "California Ranch" vocabulary. Note horizontal stonework, the small cupola

above the garage wing, and the exposed rafters with rounded ends.

6. Prairie Village, Kansas; 1959. This Tri-Level Split has a good example of the small cupolas (often prefabricated of metal) that are popular in Ranch-style houses.

7. Dallas, Texas; ca. 1952. A classic Ranch-house arrangement with a sleeping section at the left (marked by high ribbon windows), a living section in the middle (marked by a picture window), and a section for cars on the right (marked by garage doors). It was not uncommon for front-facing garages like this to have a utility room and kitchen area located behind.

8. Carlsbad, California; 1972. Board-and-batten siding, exposed rafters, and a roof clad with thick wood shingles are typical of the "California Ranch" house (found in many parts of the country). Note house in U shape around entry court and low-pitched gable on hip roofs.

9. Baltimore, Maryland; 1962. A carport, as seen here, is less common in Ranch houses than in Contemporary. There is a side-down section on the left.

10. San Marino, California; 1951. Note the ribbon windows and corner windows.

2

5

6

8

10

SIDE-GABLED ROOF

1. Levittown, New York; ca. 1950. This was one of Levitt's Ranch designs, first offered in 1949. It sold for just under $8,000 and featured a sixteen-foot picture window on the rear facade.

2. Los Angeles, California; 1958. Double-hung windows have the diamond-shape window pattern that is common in southern California—as are windows that are grouped, enframed by siding, and slightly project from the wall plane (seen at left).

3. Duluth, Minnesota; 1965. This minimal Ranch has a roof overhang in front and a corner picture window.

4. Pasadena, California; 1961.

5. Phoenix, Arizona; 1938. Edwin G. Smith House. Early for a Ranch and with quite interesting shutters.

6. St. Paul, Minnesota; 1960. Slightly angled wings were often used in larger Ranch houses.

7. Kansas City, Missouri; 1951. The full-width front porch has simple porch supports with diagonal braces.

8. Duluth, Minnesota; 1970. Note the outward slant of the gable roof overhang and the rear-down story.

9. Dallas, Texas; 1950. McNatt House; George Marble, local architect. This is Cliff May's award-winning 1948 design for *House Beautiful*'s Pace Setter House Program.

10. Duluth, Minnesota; 1961. This large Tri-Level Split has a triple diamond pattern on the garage door that is echoed in other doors—but at this scale only the storm doors with a similar theme are visible. Note sunburst ornament on chimney. Window patterns give clue to use of different levels. Short windows indicate bedrooms on upper level. Curved bay indicates some sort of living area on lower level, likely informal and connecting to the garage wing. And full-height windows and fireplace on mid-level indicate this likely is the formal living level.

11. Westlake, Texas; 1938 (restored 1977). Dealey House; Charles Dilbeck, architect, Nancy McCoy, restoration architect. This large and elegant house sprawls across the Texas prairie.

2

4

6

9

II

CROSS-GABLED ROOF

1. Kansas City, Missouri; 1952. A minimal Ranch with a picture window and masonry below the window on the front gable.

2. Phoenix, Arizona; 1959. Built-in planter at entry is accented by a slanting architectural element.

3. University Park, Texas; 1938. Dilbeck Home and Studio; Charles S. Dilbeck, architect. Located on a prominent corner, this advertised the architect's proficiency in the California Ranch to all who passed by.

4. Pasadena, California; 1936. A minimal Ranch similar to Figure 6 but with a partial porch and metal porch supports.

5. Pasadena, California; 1958. Note very long window on the left wing, exposed roof beams on the front-facing gable, and board and batten siding.

6. Wyndmoor, Pennsylvania; 1963. A Tri-Level Split with a stone first story and handsome rounded bay window. Slightly thicker muntins on four bottom panes indicate that these open for circulation. The siding above appears to be newer, perhaps a vinyl overlay.

7. Las Vegas, Nevada; 1973.

8. Washington, D.C.; 1966. Note change in wall cladding around entry area.

9. Kansas City, Missouri; ca. 1950s. The overlapping front-facing gables are unusual in Ranch houses.

10. Los Angeles, California; 1951. A breezeway connects the garage wing on the left to the house. One can guess that a powder room, or perhaps a coat closet, is located behind the single high window to the left of the entry. The door sidelights and the leaded glass in this window make an interesting contrast with the three large picture windows.

1

4

6

8

9

2

3

5

7

10

TRI-LEVEL SPLIT

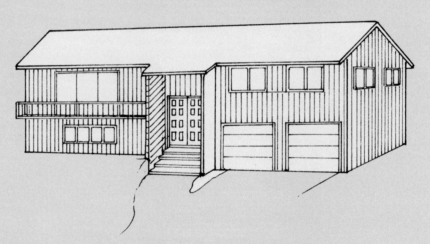

BI-LEVEL SPLIT

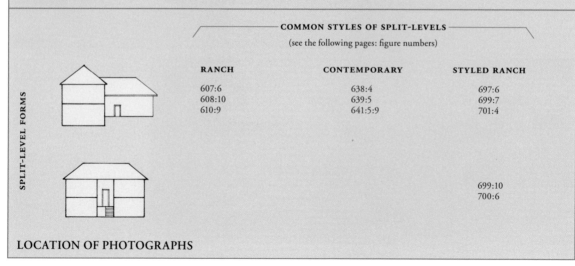

SPLIT-LEVEL FORMS

COMMON STYLES OF SPLIT-LEVELS

(see the following pages: figure numbers)

RANCH	CONTEMPORARY	STYLED RANCH
607:6	638:4	697:6
608:10	639:5	699:7
610:9	641:5:9	701:4
		699:10
		700:6

LOCATION OF PHOTOGRAPHS

Split-Level

ca. 1935–1975

Split-Level is the name of a new and distinctive *form* of house—rather than *style*—that rose to popularity during the 1950s for both practical and aesthetic reasons. The shape is found in many different styles—primarily Ranch, Styled Ranch, and Contemporary—and photographs of Split-Level houses appear on photo spreads for these styles.

A Split-Level house has three or more separate levels that are staggered and separated from each other by a partial flight of stairs rather than a full flight (six to eight steps rather than twelve to sixteen). There are two primary types: the Tri-Level Split, with three distinct living stories each a half-level apart, and the Bi-Level Split, with two distinct living stories and a split-entry level staggered in between.

Studies of how floor plans—particularly those of small houses—could best serve modern living needs were undertaken beginning in the 1930s. The Small Homes Council encouraged such studies, and in 1960 they published a pamphlet on Split-Level homes outlining their advantages and disadvantages.[25] Split-Levels take up less room on a lot, making them ideal where land is more expensive. They also provided some construction economies. The floor plan offers the advantages of privacy, noise control, and good interior circulation. The half-flight of stairs is less daunting than a full flight, but a disadvantage of Split-Levels is that they are not ideal for the elderly or those with disabilities.[26]

Home buyers liked the fact that Split-Levels looked big—more like large two-story homes. Aesthetically, it was a plus that the garage was tucked under part of the house. Splits were particularly suited to sloping ground, where they could accommodate to fit the terrain. The form proved so popular, however, that it was also constructed on level ground, where it was less at home. Split-Level houses were built throughout the country but are less common in the southern and southwestern states.

The Tri-Level Split offered a practical way to incorporate a location for two new family possessions, the automobile and the television, and an elaborate theory of interior spatial planning grew around this form. It was felt that families needed three types of interior spaces: quiet living areas, sleeping areas, and noisy living/service areas. In the Tri-Level Split form, each of these generally occurs on a separate level. The mid-level wing contained the "quiet" traditional living and cooking functions, while the upper level was reserved for private bedrooms. A third and lower level was then added to house "noisy" living—the automobile in a garage and a multipurpose recreation room for the family television, which was rapidly becoming an almost universal possession during the 1950s.[27] The public entry was generally located on the middle, quiet-living level. An additional basement and/or attic level was sometimes added, another half-story up or down, normally used for storage.

Rudimentary Tri-Levels had appeared in the *Sears Honor Bilt Home* catalogue by 1933, but it was not until after World War II that this shape gained broad popularity. By 1954 Split-Levels were outselling one-story Ranch houses four to one on Long Island.[28] It was not uncommon for a large-scale developer to build entire subdivisions of Split-Level homes. (The Tri-Level Split was widely popularized by the ABC sitcom *The Brady Bunch,* which ran from 1969 to 1974.)

Bi-Levels came later and were widely built from the 1960s into the 1980s. The Bi-Level had its entry at an intermediate level, placed between two full living stories, one of which was partially underground. The first appears to have been Carl Koch's "New Kind of Two-Story House"—a 1954 prefab Package House erected in Weston, Massachusetts, by Techbuilt, in just six days. With a highly flexible interior floor plan, it was widely publicized in magazines as well as in a two-part NBC Special funded by the Ford Foundation.[29] The Bi-Level was also called a "raised Ranch" since it resembled a one-story Ranch house elevated half a story above ground. Bi-Levels popularized a new kind of spacious split-entry foyer with high ceilings—typically one and one-half stories high. Some foyers led immediately into a full two-story stair hall. These may have played a role in the widespread use of tall entry halls beginning around 1990.

There are related variations, such as "side-down" (where one side of the house has a lower story, often with the garage) and "rear-down" (where the rear of the house has a lower story)—both of these typically used on sloping sites. Neither, however, is technically a Split-Level, as the added partial story is separated by a full story and flight of steps, but they can have a similar appearance at first glance.

Split-Levels are most commonly found in the Ranch, Styled Ranch, and Contemporary styles. Splits have the same windows, wall cladding, and other details typical of the style they emulate. Roof forms are similar, but the change in height gives a slightly different look. Split-Level houses helped make multiple levels within a house desirable, and partial level changes became a major part of the design of both Contemporary and Shed houses.

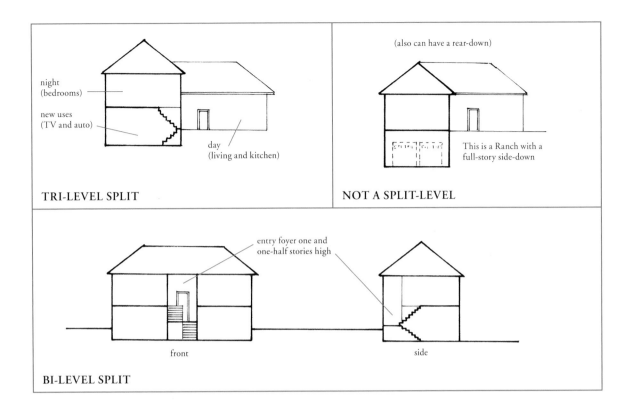

TRI-LEVEL SPLIT

night (bedrooms)

new uses (TV and auto)

day (living and kitchen)

NOT A SPLIT-LEVEL

(also can have a rear-down)

This is a Ranch with a full-story side-down

BI-LEVEL SPLIT

entry foyer one and one-half stories high

front

side

SPLIT-LEVEL:

1. Boston, Massachusetts; ca. 1950. A Tri-Level Split with an extra basement story.

2. Duluth, Minnesota; ca. 1960s. A Bi-Level Split.

1

2

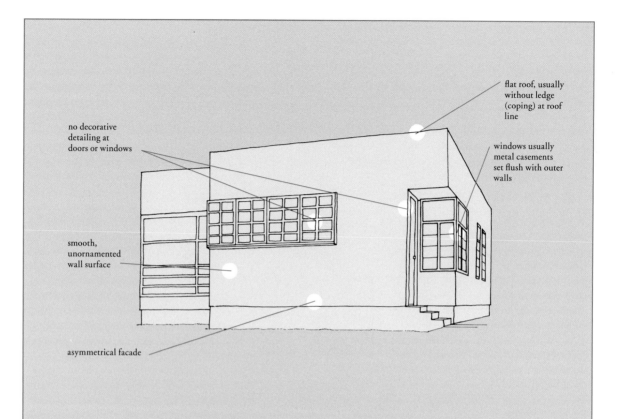

flat roof, usually without ledge (coping) at roof line

no decorative detailing at doors or windows

windows usually metal casements set flush with outer walls

smooth, unornamented wall surface

asymmetrical facade

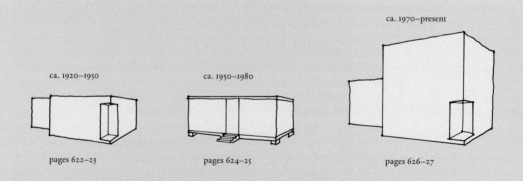

ca. 1970–present

ca. 1920–1950

ca. 1950–1980

pages 622–23

pages 624–25

pages 626–27

International

ca. 1925–Present

Identifying Features

Flat roof, usually without ledge (coping) at roof line; windows set flush with outer walls; smooth, unornamented surfaces with no decorative detailing at doors or windows; facade composition commonly includes large window groupings, often linear, and expanses of windowless wall surface; unified wall cladding, generally white stucco; commonly asymmetrical.

Variants and Details

In 1932, New York's Museum of Modern Art mounted the influential "Modern Architecture: International Exhibition." In the accompanying book, *The International Style,* authors Henry-Russell Hitchcock and Philip Johnson identified three principles common to early International buildings: architecture as volume, regularity, and avoiding the application of ornament.[30]

A fundamental difference between International style structures and earlier buildings was that previously the walls, commonly of solid masonry, had provided structural support. By contrast, International buildings were supported by a lightweight structural skeleton (often metal). Walls were freed simply to enclose a volume or architectural space—and could have more flexible fenestration (windows). House facades could feature a three-dimensional composition rather than consisting primarily of ornament applied to an essentially flat surface, as with earlier styles.

The structural skeleton allowed walls and windows to be arranged asymmetrically to reflect interior needs, but their placement was regulated and given subtle order by the structural system beneath. Asymmetrical facades gained coherence by this visual "regularity." These first two principles applied primarily to the grandest houses, as most homes were too small to make steel-skeleton construction economical; in modest houses, a similar look might be more inexpensively achieved with balloon framing.[31] Other materials also were used for structural support, most commonly concrete—whether poured in place, gunnite, tilt wall, or hollow block.

Freeing exterior walls from structural demands allowed facade treatments not feasible earlier. Now windows could wrap around building corners. Where interior functions did not require windows, or where privacy was needed, solid windowless expanses of exterior wall were used. Cantilevered projections were possible—sections of roof, balcony, or second stories extending outward and dramatizing the non-supporting nature of the walls—and these were more common on the West Coast. Removing walls as the support system also meant that interior walls could become mere partitions that allowed great flexibility in room layout, and floor plans further explored the open free-flowing spaces pioneered by Frank Lloyd Wright.

Simple, underplayed windows—often casements—were preferred. These could be metal or simply detailed wood, generally placed flush with the wall and often grouped into horizontal ribbon windows. In the 1930s this fenestration style was joined by picture windows, and after World War II the affordability of plate glass made floor-to-ceiling window walls possible. The windows were no longer placed in a rigid manner governed by exterior symmetry but related instead to the interior plan or were arranged primarily to create a pleasing facade design.[32]

Added exterior decoration was avoided, maintaining the spirit of the building as a smoothly sheathed volume. Exterior walls were clad with a single surface—commonly white stucco in the 1920s and 1930s—to clearly differentiate them from load-bearing masonry and emphasize the interior volume. By the late 1930s smooth board and plywood cladding were also used—as these could be applied to a more common and less expensive balloon frame—and Marcel Breuer had introduced the concept of adding a picturesque brick or stone wall.

After World War II, International houses entered a new phase. While builders and many architects gravitated to the more "natural" Contemporary style, International houses were not completely abandoned. In 1945, Breuer introduced the bi-nuclear plan, clearly separating quiet, private sleeping spaces from public living spaces with a courtyard or entry hall in between. This inspired a new exploration of symmetrical domestic examples. Courtyards of all types—entry, side, rear, and interior (either enclosed as atria or open)—gained in popularity and provided an excellent way to create private views

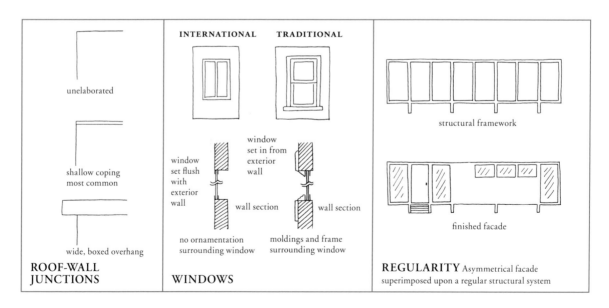

ROOF-WALL JUNCTIONS

unelaborated

shallow coping most common

wide, boxed overhang

WINDOWS

INTERNATIONAL   TRADITIONAL

window set flush with exterior wall

window set in from exterior wall

wall section

wall section

no ornamentation surrounding window

moldings and frame surrounding window

REGULARITY Asymmetrical facade superimposed upon a regular structural system

structural framework

finished facade

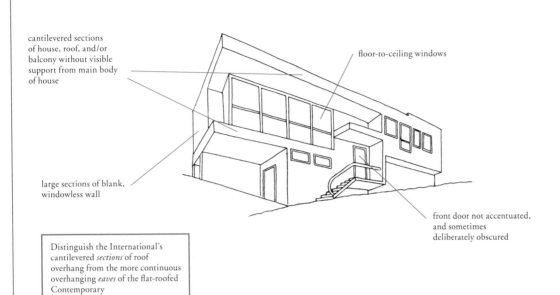

cantilevered sections of house, roof, and/or balcony without visible support from main body of house

floor-to-ceiling windows

large sections of blank, windowless wall

front door not accentuated, and sometimes deliberately obscured

Distinguish the International's cantilevered *sections* of roof overhang from the more continuous overhanging *eaves* of the flat-roofed Contemporary

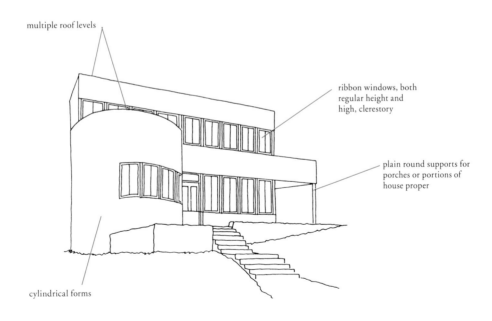

multiple roof levels

ribbon windows, both regular height and high, clerestory

plain round supports for porches or portions of house proper

cylindrical forms

COMMON ELABORATIONS

(see illustrations pages 621, 631).[33] Also in the late 1940s, Mies van der Rohe's glass-clad Farnsworth House—and Philip Johnson's tribute to it, his own Glass House—created a new interest in glass as cladding. This "Miesian" interpretation of the International style achieved its broadest appeal in commercial buildings. From circa 1950 to 1970 symmetrical, or near-symmetrical, versions of the International, often with large areas of glass window wall opening onto private areas or views, were favored by architects. At the same time, wood-clad asymmetrical examples occurred, similar to pre–World War II designs but clad in the natural materials promoted by Wright and used for Contemporary houses.[34]

In the 1970s, a group known as the New York Five (Charles Gwathmey, Michael Graves, John Hejduk, Richard Meier, and Peter Eisenman) began designing new homes based on the early white stucco International house. This sparked a strong revival of "the Whites" that has continued to the present day. These typically have a far greater percentage of glass on their private or view facades than did their early 20th-century predecessors.

Occurrence

This avant-garde and primarily architect-designed style is relatively rare. Landmark examples from the 1930s occur principally in fashionable suburbs in the northeastern states and in California. The early experimental nature of the style is highlighted by how many of the well-publicized early houses were designed for the architect, the architect's mother, or a professor.

During the 1950s and 1960s International houses continued to be built, but Contemporary houses were a far more common modern house style. In the 1970s a revival of interest in the original white stucco-clad houses began. This revival gained momentum as the turn of the millennium spurred publication of many books looking back on a century of modernism. *DWELL* magazine, launched in 2000 with a focus on modern homes, helped further spread this new wave, and the International continues to enjoy a strong resurgence today.

Comments

In the decades separating World War I and World War II—while Americans were building neighborhoods of period houses—European architects were busy creating dramatic new modern homes and buildings. Le Corbusier in France, Oud and Rietveld in Holland, and Walter Gropius and Mies van der Rohe in Germany were all working without historic precedent, trying to exploit the materials and technology of the day. In addition, as these pioneers explained in the first book published by the Bauhaus, they wished to create an International architecture "independent of specific materials, sites or cultural tradition"—thus avoiding the regional differences they felt had led to World War I—and specifically chose white stucco as a uniting material to achieve these ideals.[35] Their designs came to be known as International Style when the 1932 Museum of Modern Art exhibition christened the movement with this name.[36]

The International style was brought to the United States by architects who emigrated from Europe. Three early émigrés were already at work in the 1920s: William Lescaze in New York City and Rudolf Schindler and Richard Neutra in Los Angeles.[37] They were joined in the 1930s by elite Bauhaus architects Walter Gropius, Mies van der Rohe, and Marcel Breuer, all fleeing Hitler. These later arrivals had a profound influence because their theories and concepts were widely disseminated through architectural education. Gropius became the dean at Harvard's Graduate School of Design and Mies the dean of architecture at Illinois Institute of Technology. Their new curricula swept Beaux Arts precepts out—and those of the Bauhaus in—as other schools of architecture quickly followed their lead.

Another theory of the Internationalists—Le Corbusier's view of the house as a "machine for living"—was appealing in a world of rapidly advancing technology. All superfluous ornament could be stripped away, while the latest domestic machinery was installed in kitchens and bathrooms, and true efficiency brought to the home.[38] Functionalism, emphasizing how a building served its inhabitants, was of prime importance; traditional elements of the house that were merely decorative were to be discarded. International houses built today typically dwarf those of the 1920s to 1950s. And while added decoration is avoided, the mantra of functionalism can result in greatly enlarged kitchen, bath, and closet areas designed to the hilt and enjoyed with impunity.[39]

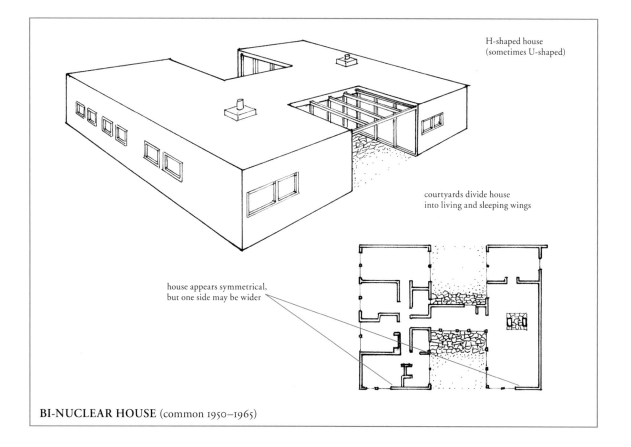

H-shaped house
(sometimes U-shaped)

courtyards divide house
into living and sleeping wings

house appears symmetrical,
but one side may be wider

BI-NUCLEAR HOUSE (common 1950–1965)

1920–1950

1. Los Angeles, California; 1938. Richard Lind, architect. Note the blank expanses of wall in three different planes, the garage incorporated into the facade design, and the cantilevered section of roof.

2. Cambridge, Massachusetts; 1937. Carl Koch and Edward T. Stone, architects. Note the ribbon windows in an otherwise blank expanse of wall and the cutaway section at right with a recessed entry and courtyard screened by a pictorial stone wall.

3. Cohasset, Massachusetts; 1938. Josephine Hagerty House; Walter Gropius, architect. This house clearly shows the simple and boxier quality of many New England homes designed by the European émigrés of the 1930s.

4. Los Angeles, California; 1936. Fitzpatrick House; Rudolf M. Schindler, architect. Note the lack of overhang on the right-side facade coupled with multiple, deep, boxy cantilevered roof sections, and large expanses of glass window walls on the front facade.

5. Cambridge, Massachusetts; 1935. Bowen House; Howard T. Fisher, architect.

6. Lincoln, Massachusetts; 1939. Walter Bogner House. Uncommon natural wood cladding on a pre–World War II example.

7. Los Angeles, California; 1934. Buck House; Rudolf M. Schindler, architect. Schindler and Neutra's West Coast International houses were influenced by their work with Frank Lloyd Wright and by the sunny California climate, making use of broad roof overhangs and cantilevered elements. Their designs here and in Figures 1, 4, and 8 typically are more three-dimensional than those on the East Coast.

8. Palm Springs, California; 1946. Kaufman Desert House; Richard Neutra, architect. One of Neutra's masterpieces recently restored, this is a view from the street.

9. Lincoln, Massachusetts; 1938. Gropius House; Walter Gropius, architect. Gropius related his home to nearby New England houses by using wood-clad walls. His home incorporated many standard elements ordered from catalogues. As with Figure 3, this is a simplified house form, but here an angled glass brick entry element is added.

1

4

7

8

1950–1980

1. Palm Springs, California; 1962. "All-Steel-House"; Alexander and Alexander, builders, Donald Wexler, architect. This is transitional to the Contemporary. It has a carport and deep recessed entry with small garden—but with only a small selective section of roof overhang.

2. Chicago, Illinois; 1951. Farnsworth House; Mies van der Rohe, architect. The Farnsworth House is one of the most significant of Mies van der Rohe's works. Note that the entire house is raised above the ground on a podium; this was intended to protect it from seasonal flooding of the nearby river.

3. Hamptons, New York; 1987.

4. New Canaan, Connecticut; 1949. Glass House; Philip Johnson, architect. This was Philip Johnson's tribute to the Farnsworth House (that had been designed earlier but not yet built).[40] A solid rounded masonry section contains the bathroom and almost bolts the house to the ground—accentuating that Johnson built his house directly on the ground rather than on a podium like Farnsworth House.

5. New Canaan, Connecticut; 1954. Noyes House 2; Eliot Noyes, architect. This is a pure bi-nuclear house with living spaces in the foreground, sleeping spaces at the rear, and a courtyard between. The stone wall faced the road, and each wing had a glass wall facing non-public views.

6. Los Angeles, California; 1949. Hale House; Craig Elwood, architect. This house has a steel structural skeleton that is partially exposed, much in the Miesian manner.[41]

7. Sarasota, Florida; 1952 (Lido Shores). Philip Hiss Studio; Philip Hiss, architect and developer. Here, the living level is raised a story above ground level, allowing movements beneath it, a principle promoted by Corbusier, who also suggested the use of slender columns (piloti), as seen here, to raise the house.

8. La Jolla, California; 1960. Case Study "Triad" House; Killingsworth, Brady & Smith, architects. Marcel Breuer introduced the bi-nuclear house in 1945, and many almost symmetrical examples like this were modeled after it.

9. Duluth, Minnesota; 1955. Starkey House; Marcel Breuer, architect. Originally more of a raised one-level house, space has now been enclosed on the ground level.

10. New Canaan, Connecticut; 1952. The Campbell House; John Johansen, architect. This bi-nuclear house is raised on a low podium.

1

3

6

7

9

2

4

5

8

10

1970–PRESENT

1. Los Angeles, ca. 1970.

2. Dallas, Texas; ca. 1980.

3. Dallas, Texas; ca. 2010. Urban Reserve; Robert Meckfessel, architect. The thin lines visible on the walls allow the rainscreen covering to better circulate air.

4. Los Angeles, California; 1963, remodeled 2000s; Roger Sherman, architect. Note private entry courtyard and the two-story vertical window that highlights the staircase.

5. Deephaven, Minnesota; 1973. Rappaport House; Milo H. Thompson, architect. Note the very long ribbon window.

6. Dallas, Texas; ca. 2010. Lionel Morrison, architect. Urban Reserve.

7. Los Angeles, California; 1992.

8. Darien, Connecticut; 1965–1967. Smith House; Richard Meier, architect. Meier's crisp white box houses helped usher in a new enthusiasm for the International design elements that had dominated prior to World War II, albeit with larger expanses of glass on rear-view facades like this one. The chimney is brick and the house is clad with smooth vertical wood boards—all painted white to resemble stucco.

9. Destin, Florida; 2005. Corbusier's preference of raising the house above ground level is very practical on flood-prone beachfronts like this. The house is placed on the site rather than integrated into it, producing the "house as a piece of sculpture" appearance that Frank Lloyd Wright detested.

10. Venice Beach, California; 1992. International has been used for town-house-type developments in recent decades.

2

5

8

9

1

3

4

6

7

10

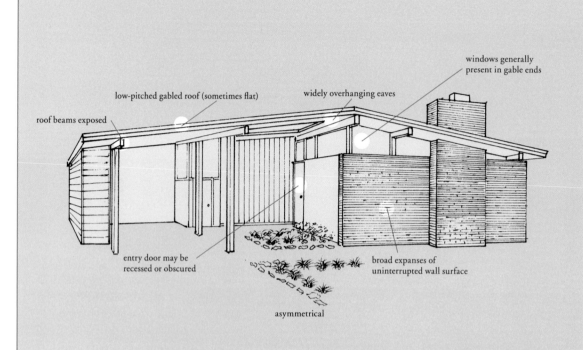

roof beams exposed

low-pitched gabled roof (sometimes flat)

widely overhanging eaves

windows generally present in gable ends

entry door may be recessed or obscured

broad expanses of uninterrupted wall surface

asymmetrical

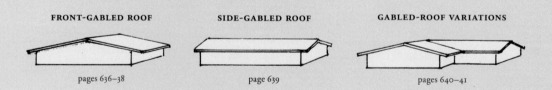

FRONT-GABLED ROOF

pages 636–38

SIDE-GABLED ROOF

page 639

GABLED-ROOF VARIATIONS

pages 640–41

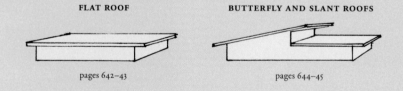

FLAT ROOF

pages 642–43

BUTTERFLY AND SLANT ROOFS

pages 644–45

Contemporary

ca. 1945–1990

Identifying Features

Low-pitched gabled roof (sometimes flat) with widely overhanging eaves; roof beams commonly exposed; windows generally present in gable ends (or just below roof line in non-gabled facades); built with natural materials (wood, stone, brick, or occasionally concrete block); broad expanse of uninterrupted wall surface typically on front facade; entry door may be recessed or obscured; asymmetrical.

Principal Subtypes

Five principal subtypes can be distinguished:[42]

FRONT-GABLED ROOF—This subtype includes a broad range of simple front-gabled forms. These are ideal for showing off triangular gable-end windows that indicate a high "vaulted" ceiling inside. Two variations are common: a broad one-story form with a very low-pitched roof (popularized by California developer Joseph Eichler) and an asymmetrical gable front often found on Split-Level houses (nicknamed the "wounded dove").[43]

SIDE-GABLED ROOF—The least common of the gabled forms, this subtype is more often found in later examples.

GABLED-ROOF VARIATIONS—Most commonly this subtype consists of a front-gabled roof with a side-gabled extension. Other combinations include houses with two wings or two front-facing gables. From the street it is sometimes difficult to discern the roof form of low side wings.

FLAT ROOF—This subtype includes flat-roof variations; these have long, continuous broad roof overhangs, and exposed roof beams that differentiate them from contemporaneous International-style houses. Some have shallow horizontal windows located just below the roof line, sometimes set in the space between roof beams.

BUTTERFLY AND SLANT ROOFS—This subtype of less common roof types includes a slanted roof (with more reliable drainage than a flat roof), an upside-down gable called a butterfly roof (this creates a flat valley prone to leaking), and exaggerated gable roofs that might extend even to the ground. All of these could be combined with flat or gabled roofs, but the eye-catching butterfly- or slant-roof element tends to dominate visually.

Variants and Details

Earlier styles were generally defined by the types of decorative detail applied to their exteriors—on doors, windows, porch supports, wall surfaces, dormers, and roof-wall junctions (see page 55). The Contemporary style rejects this approach and is instead more concerned with the spaces inside the house and the way in which each space relates to the outdoors. Therefore, the design is created from the inside out, with the attention not on details visible as one approaches the house but rather on the functionality of the interior space and the integration of outdoor views. House plans were no longer simply diagrams of room layouts; they now expanded to cover a large portion of the site (for small lots, the entire site) and included the various outdoor spaces—and views—associated with each room. This approach confers a very spacious quality to the house, particularly important because of the small size of houses in the 1940s and 1950s.[44] The indoor-outdoor quality is achieved in two basic ways: by adding varied exterior living spaces or view gardens, and by using courtyards to bring the outside into the house. Enclosed and semi-enclosed interior courts had been used for millennia—most familiarly in the houses of ancient Greece and Rome. View gardens also had a long history, particularly in China and Japan, where for centuries small gardens had been planned specifically to create pleasing views for teahouses and interior spaces. Hundreds of thousands of U.S. military personnel were exposed to this Oriental style during the occupation of Japan (1945–1952). During 1954–1955, New York's Museum of Modern Art built and displayed a carefully constructed Japanese house and garden that clearly demonstrated how Japanese gardens were designed from an interior perspective.[45] The seamless integration of house and landscape was unlike the pristine white International house that often appeared more like a piece of sculpture distinct from the landscape.

Entry facades typically reveal little of the house itself. A large area of uninterrupted wall surface is common and might have a design or pattern within the finish. Screening fences protect private side and front gardens. Grilles, most commonly concrete screen block, in see-through designs forming an overall pattern, might be used for visual screening or as brises-soleil to create shade.[46]

The entrance is downplayed and sometimes deeply recessed. In modest houses it might be tucked deep inside a carport and in others approached through an entry garden or court. Entering the house in the mid-section creates space-saving floor plans by omitting a central hall for circulation. Frank Lloyd Wright advocated carports as a cost-saving device—and low broad masonry chimneys to service large open fireplaces in the heart of the house.[47]

The Contemporary house could be built on steep hillsides where Ranches—and even Split-Levels—are difficult to place.[48] These sites were now easily accessible by the automobile, and architects devised many creative ways the Contemporary could adapt to a challenging site. From the street, houses can look completely different on the downhill side than on the uphill side. Downhill might reveal only a carport or garage and perhaps

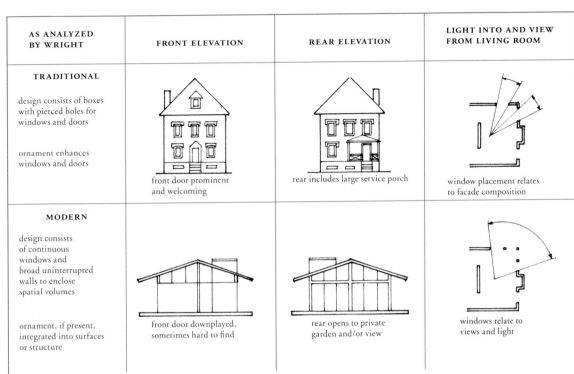

AS ANALYZED BY WRIGHT	FRONT ELEVATION	REAR ELEVATION	LIGHT INTO AND VIEW FROM LIVING ROOM
TRADITIONAL design consists of boxes with pierced holes for windows and doors ornament enhances windows and doors	front door prominent and welcoming	rear includes large service porch	window placement relates to facade composition
MODERN design consists of continuous windows and broad uninterrupted walls to enclose spatial volumes ornament, if present, integrated into surfaces or structure	front door downplayed, sometimes hard to find	rear opens to private garden and/or view	windows relate to views and light

TRADITIONAL DESIGN V. MODERN DESIGN AS ANALYZED BY FRANK LLOYD WRIGHT

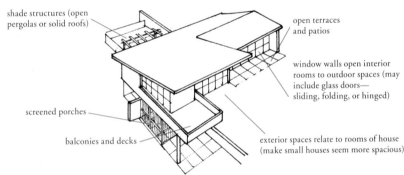

shade structures (open pergolas or solid roofs)

open terraces and patios

window walls open interior rooms to outdoor spaces (may include glass doors—sliding, folding, or hinged)

screened porches

balconies and decks

exterior spaces relate to rooms of house (make small houses seem more spacious)

OUTDOOR SPACES EXPAND THE HOUSE

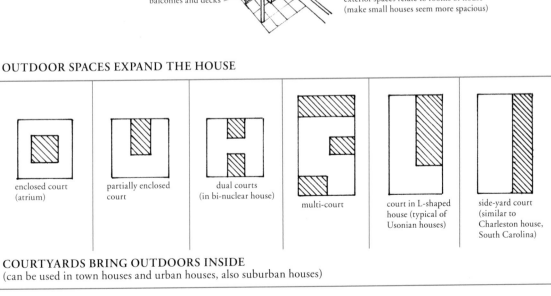

enclosed court (atrium)

partially enclosed court

dual courts (in bi-nuclear house)

multi-court

court in L-shaped house (typical of Usonian houses)

side-yard court (similar to Charleston house, South Carolina)

COURTYARDS BRING OUTDOORS INSIDE
(can be used in town houses and urban houses, also suburban houses)

a small entry area, while uphill might show broad roof overhangs and balcony railings, or the underside of decks facing the view—perhaps with a glimpse of the window walls that embraced it.

Overhangs generally have open eaves (i.e., not boxed). Rafters can be exposed (with their ends covered by a single board) or disappear (smoothly covered, with affordable new exterior-grade plywood). High-style examples might incorporate subtle ornament into the design of the overhang.[49] Openings in the roof are relatively common and allow natural light into carports or provide light and rain to the beds in a covered garden area.

Contemporary house design was aided by three 1930s building innovations: thick plate glass, allowing window walls; exterior-grade plywood, allowing inexpensive wall cladding and sheathed-roof overhangs; and new glues, allowing engineered wood to be used for wood paneling and post-and-beam construction.[50]

Japanese influence was also present in wood construction with exposed timbers and a panelized appearance. Post-and-beam construction was often used and might be topped by a planked roof or enclosed with a variety of solid panels or window units forming the walls. This influence came from the West Coast, where it was sometimes referred to as the Second Bay Tradition—although architects in the Pacific Northwest such as Pietro Belluschi and John Yeon also used the same vocabulary. There, a nearby supply of redwood and a strong tradition of timber construction—seen in the earlier Craftsman joinery of Greene and Greene and timberwork of Bernard Maybeck—inspired mid-century architects to design extraordinary wood detailing that united interior and exterior design.[51]

Window walls appeared in an almost infinite variety and were composed primarily of large single fixed-glass panes, with a few sections that opened, and often some sort of door. The spatial effect of the inside flowing out might be enhanced by allowing the floor material, the roof beam, or the ceiling material to continue from the inside to the outside, making the glass window wall seem to disappear.[52]

By the late 1950s builders had learned that an economical way to build Contemporary houses with brick cladding was to end the masonry at the sides of windows and run a vertical panel of wood cladding from the ground to the roof line. This avoided the expense of laying window headers and bases in the masonry and created an easily recognizable vertical look.

Occurrence

The Contemporary style was favored most by American architects from about 1945 to 1965, when it filled architectural journals and dominated awards. While Ranch-style houses proliferated in most builder subdivisions, a few successful developers built Contemporary subdivisions—among them, Joseph Eichler in California, Charles M. Goodman in suburban Washington, D.C., and Edward Hawkins in Denver. The most prolific was Joseph Eichler (1900–1974), who built close to ten thousand homes in the San Francisco Bay area. A wholesale grocer early in life, Eichler rented a Usonian house in 1942, where he and his wife fell in love with modern architecture. Changing professions, Eichler devoted the remainder of his life to building well-designed Contemporary houses that were affordable to a large segment of the economic spectrum.[53] In the late 1960s the Contemporary style began to lose popularity.

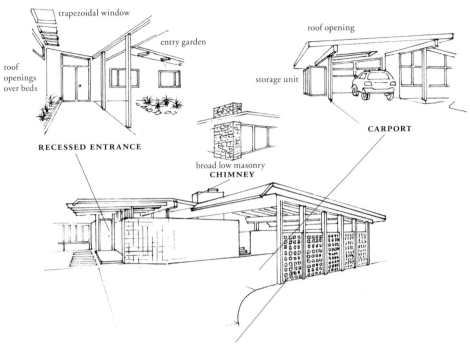

trapezoidal window

entry garden

roof openings over beds

roof opening

storage unit

RECESSED ENTRANCE

CARPORT

broad low masonry
CHIMNEY

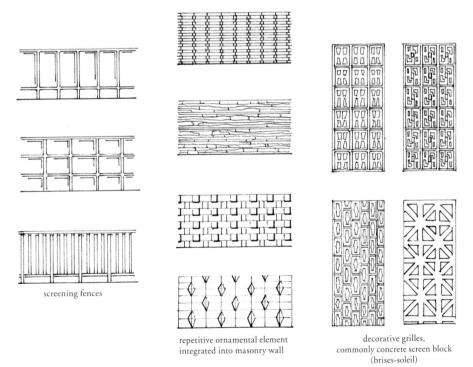

BROAD SURFACES WITH INTEGRAL PATTERN

screening fences

repetitive ornamental element
integrated into masonry wall

decorative grilles,
commonly concrete screen block
(brises-soleil)

ELABORATIONS COMMONLY VISIBLE FROM STREET

Comments

The Contemporary had two practical design advantages over the contemporaneous Ranch. In addition to being adaptable to steep hillsides, the Contemporary was as appropriate for a two-story house as for a one-story house, unlike the Ranch. Thus, a larger house could be built on a smaller footprint with the Contemporary, leaving more exterior green space.

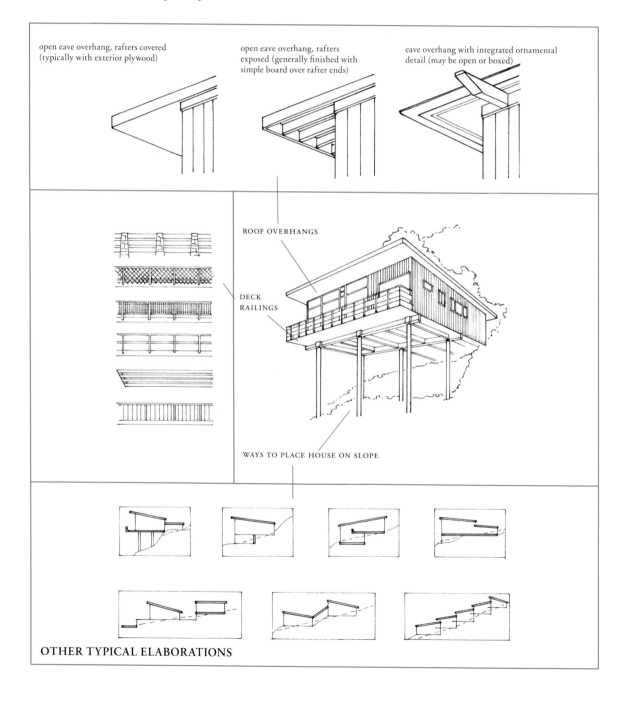

open eave overhang, rafters covered (typically with exterior plywood)

open eave overhang, rafters exposed (generally finished with simple board over rafter ends)

eave overhang with integrated ornamental detail (may be open or boxed)

ROOF OVERHANGS

DECK RAILINGS

WAYS TO PLACE HOUSE ON SLOPE

OTHER TYPICAL ELABORATIONS

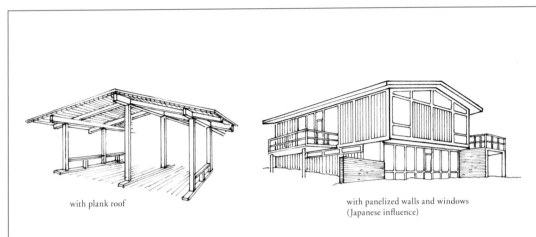

with plank roof

with panelized walls and windows
(Japanese influence)

POST-AND-BEAM CONSTRUCTION (WOOD OR STEEL)

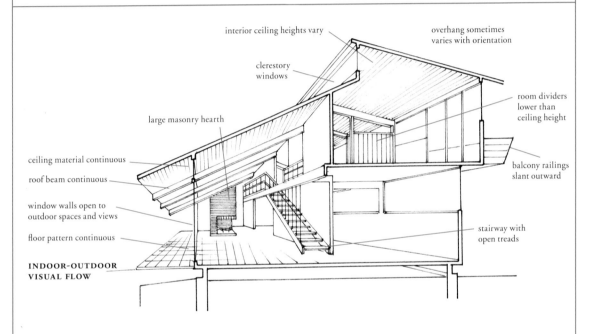

interior ceiling heights vary

overhang sometimes
varies with orientation

clerestory
windows

room dividers
lower than
ceiling height

large masonry hearth

ceiling material continuous

roof beam continuous

balcony railings
slant outward

window walls open to
outdoor spaces and views

floor pattern continuous

stairway with
open treads

**INDOOR-OUTDOOR
VISUAL FLOW**

SOME SPATIAL CONFIGURATIONS

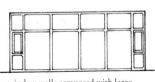

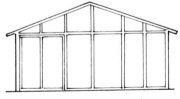

window walls composed with large
single windowpanes (most panes fixed)

doors often included in
composition

windows continue upward
to fill gable ends

WINDOW WALLS

FRONT-GABLED ROOF

1. Palo Alto, California; ca. 1955. Joseph Eichler, developer. This is a variation—a front gable with side wings—that was a favorite design of Eichler but less common elsewhere. Note the windows placed between roof beams on the garage wing and recessed entry under centered gable.

2. Los Angeles, California; 1965. The entry feature soars on three slender piloti and is open to the sky. The relatively symmetrical front-gabled roof makes it hard to discern that this is likely a Tri-Level Split.

3. Silver Spring, Maryland; 1959. The triangular window groupings in the gable here (and in Figures 1, 4, 5, 7, 8, and 10) advertise that there is a vaulted ceiling in the room behind.

4. San Diego, California; 1960. Broad one-story houses with very low-pitch front-gable roofs were the most common builder form (see also Figures 7 and 10).

5. East Hampton, New York (vicinity); ca. 1960. Rear-facade view. A deep gable-roof overhang shelters the deck facing the ocean, while the roof overhang on right side of the house is quite shallow.

6. Baltimore, Maryland; ca. 1959. Here both gable end and sides of roof have broad overhangs.

7. Phoenix, Arizona; 1959. Note the entry placed inside the carport on the right and the roof opening with exposed structure.

8. Baltimore, Maryland; 1956. The free-standing exposed "post-and-beam" structure is uncommon.

9. Daly City, California; ca. 1950s. This has an original diamond-pattern garage door. Note how vertical elements extend up to the roof beams.

10. Las Vegas, Nevada; ca. 1961. Here a fence of concrete screen block is used to create a private front garden.

1

4

7

10

2

3

5

6

8

9

FRONT-GABLED ROOF (cont.)

11. Beverly Hills, California; 1968. This clearly shows the deeply recessed entry with exposed roof structure above.

12. Atlanta, Georgia; 1960. Collier Heights Historic District. The white section at left is likely a later alteration to the original garage. The driveway ends right in front of it.

13. Falcon Heights, Minnesota; 1966. Note how the wall cladding is applied in vertical strips with the windows set into a separate material. This was often a cost-saving device.

14. Seattle, Washington; 1959. Even in the rain, the "wounded-dove" gabled roof is quite distinctive and perfectly adapted to this Tri-Level Splits.

11

12

13

14

SIDE-GABLED ROOF

1, 2. Los Angeles, California; 1963. This hillside adaptation has geometric texture on retaining wall at right, V-shaped supports for the main house level, and view of exposed structural beams.

3. Silver Springs, Maryland; 1951. Note how broad this chimney is. The front door is a later modification and its oval shape is an almost shocking contrast with the rectilinear design of the adjoining windows.

4. Minneapolis, Minnesota; 1951. Niels House; Frank Lloyd Wright, architect. The large chimney is a central anchor with two gable-roof forms extending out from it. Each ends with an outward slant like a ship's prow.

5. Portland, Oregon; 1969. A Tri-Level Split with cladding change between ranks of windows.

GABLED-ROOF VARIATIONS

1. Duluth, Minnesota; 1961. Different shapes of windowpanes are used to create windows in the gables.

2. Dallas, Texas; 1960s. This and Figure 6 are the broad horizontal Ranch form, but with Contemporary detailing.

3. Key West, Florida; ca. 1960s. This house substitutes a second front gable for the wing.

4. St. Paul, Minnesota; 1967. Note the broad, low stone chimney.

5. Seattle, Washington; 1961. This Bi-Level Split has original garage doors.

6. Kansas City, Missouri; 1967. Putting windows in a separate vertical strip of cladding was more cost-efficient than having to build brick headers and footers above and below each window. It also kept trades separate (the bricklayer did not have to be coordinated with the window installer).

7. Dallas, Texas; 1962.

8. Seattle, Washington; 1976. As in Figure 9 on page 637, vertical supports align with the roof beams.

9. Kansas City, Missouri; 1954. A Tri-Level Split needs only vertical elements and a roof overhang with patterned surface beneath to achieve a Contemporary look. Note the slight outward slant of balcony railing.

1

3

6

FLAT ROOF

1. Bernardsville, New Jersey; 1940. Christie House; Frank Lloyd Wright, architect. This large L-shaped Usonian house has a carport on the right and a broadly overhanging flat roof.

2. Los Angeles, California; 1965.

3. Englewood, Colorado; 1955. Arapahoe Acres Historic District. Edward B. Hawkins, developer. Note corner windows, obscured entry, and carport.

4. St. Paul, Minnesota; 1961. Broad shallow windows are set between roof beams.

5. San Francisco, California (vicinity); ca. 1960. This "across the valley" view shows how a Contemporary house could be inserted on a very steep site.

6. Los Angeles, California; 1960. Silver Lake; Richard J. Neutra, architect. Somewhat similar to Wright's 1904 Gale House in Oak Park (Figure 5 on page 558), this symmetrical house has two full-width balconies with solid railings and a deep roof overhang.

7. Palm Springs, California; 1955. Wexler House; Donald Wexler, architect. Wexler described plywood as a treasured new material that made many Contemporary features affordable.

8. Highland Park, Texas; 1967. E. G. Hamilton, architect. This house is surrounded by a brick wall and softened with raised garden beds. This defines several courtyards and allows use of window walls with complete privacy. Note the generous roof overhang.

9. Kansas City, Missouri; 1952. Note the five distinct sections of this house: high windows at left (bedrooms?), broad chimney, window wall, projecting section with high ribbon windows, and a set-back garage.

10. Palo Alto, California; 1954. Joseph Eichler, developer. Some of Eichler's most popular small houses combined a single slanted roof with a flat roof.

1

4

7

9

10

BUTTERFLY AND SLANT ROOFS

1. Palm Springs, California; 1962. "House of Tomorrow" (Vista Las Palmas); Palmer and Krisal, architects. Futuristic design for what was originally a model home built on three levels.

2. Palo Alto, California; 1954. Note how the concrete block wall on the right wing is laid in a regular grid pattern—a 1950s favorite.

3. Los Angeles, California; 1959. Silver Lake. Two railing designs are used on the full-width balcony.

4. Minneapolis, Minnesota; 1958. Paul and Helen Olfelt House; Frank Lloyd Wright, architect. The carport forms an integral part of the design.

5. San Francisco, California; 1948. The carport extension with added slanted elements exaggerates the simple inverted gable-roof form.

6. Palm Springs, California; ca. 1960s. "Swiss Miss" House; Charles Dubois, designer, Alexander Construction, builder.

7. Atlanta, Georgia; ca. 1960. The broad wall surfaces have an integral horizontal pattern incorporated into the brick pattern. Note how the entire roof floats above an almost continuous ribbon of windows that separates the roof from the walls of the house.

1

4

6

A major strike against the Contemporary was that lending institutions preferred to avoid financing more avant-garde designs in favor of the widely popular Ranch style. The FHA in particular did not like houses with unusual roof forms (even slanted) and felt more comfortable with homes sporting "traditional" exterior details such as shutters.[54]

The moving force behind Contemporary houses was Frank Lloyd Wright (1867–1957) and his Usonian houses.[55] Wright had been formulating his ideas about houses for almost fifty years when he designed his first Usonian in 1937. These small and affordable houses were constructed from natural materials, built low to the ground, included open floor plans with a free flow of interior space (only the bedrooms and baths had walls), and had broad sheltering roof overhangs. They also featured a significant spatial and visual interplay of indoor and outdoor spaces. For Wright, glass was a magical super-material, allowing window walls with views of private gardens partially enclosed by an L-shaped house.[56] Wright also favored "continuity" in a house and did not admire the post-and-beam construction used in many Contemporary homes.[57]

Wright tirelessly promoted his theories—to the general public in *House Beautiful* magazine, to architects and builders in *House and Home* magazine, and to all in his many books, most notably *The Natural House* in 1954. By the early 1950s, Wright's philosophy had entered the mainstream of American architectural design and swept the country in the form of Contemporary houses. Contemporary houses are sometimes called simply Mid-century Modern, but, as used here, this is a broader category that includes other modern styles being built at mid-century.[58]

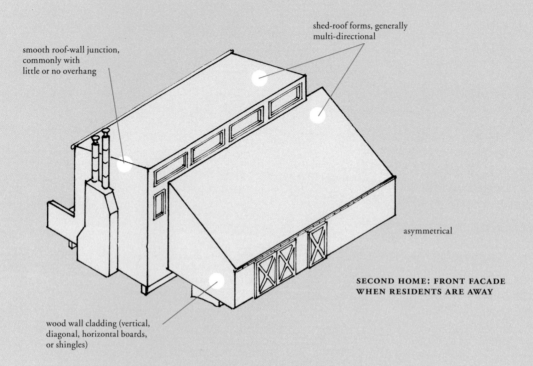

smooth roof-wall junction, commonly with little or no overhang

shed-roof forms, generally multi-directional

asymmetrical

SECOND HOME: FRONT FACADE WHEN RESIDENTS ARE AWAY

wood wall cladding (vertical, diagonal, horizontal boards, or shingles)

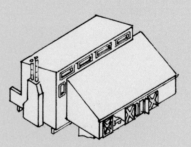
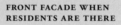

FRONT FACADE WHEN RESIDENTS ARE THERE

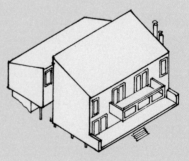

VIEW FACADE TOWARD LAKE

Shed

ca. 1965–1990

Identifying Features

Shed-roof forms, generally multi-directional and occasionally coupled with a gable roof; wood wall cladding (vertical, diagonal, horizontal, or shingles), occasionally with brick veneer; smooth roof-wall junction commonly with little or no overhang; asymmetrical.

Variants and Details

The overall effect of a Shed house is that of bold diagonals, counterpointed shapes, and multiple massing. The form of the house imparts its style, not the smaller elements. The shed roof is often multi-directional and used in ways that give the effect of colliding geometric shapes. The front door and entry area is generally inconspicuous, and may even be obscured.

There is little added exterior detail; elaborations are primarily simple window variations. There are few window openings on walls that face public areas and those that occur are generally quite varied and asymmetrically placed. As in the Contemporary, large fixed panes of plate glass are typically used; these are generally set flush with the exterior wall. Ribbons of clerestory windows are found high on facades or above lower roof forms, often operable for ventilation. Lower windows are often composed of vertical sections with a tall, narrow upper pane above a short lower pane. Window tops are either flat or sloped with the angle of the roof. Elaborations include a "boxed" enframement that partially surrounds a window grouping, and deep box-bay windows (sometimes called saddlebags).

Typically no more than a single board is used as a cornice at the roof-wall junction.[59] The chimney is typically rectangular, unelaborated, and often clad in wood or plywood. Tall metal chimney flues may be exposed and extend above the chimney top.

The architects who originated the style generally preferred wood-shingle wall cladding, but later interpretations of the style often used wood board siding (applied either horizontally, vertically, or diagonally), T1-11 plywood (that imitated wood siding), and/or brick veneer.

Occurrence

While never common, this late-century modern style is the primary one that evolved beyond one-of-a-kind architect-designed homes into the widespread house pattern books used by builders. First presented as appropriate for second homes, Shed-style homes were also built as primary residences in many suburban settings. They can be found throughout the United States.

Comments

Although there were precursors, the Shed style was launched in earnest by the publicity surrounding development of the Sea Ranch, a carefully thought-out second-home community 125 miles north of San Francisco. Sea Ranch introduced innovative ways of designing a dwelling and placing it into native landscapes.[60] The initial projects, the first phases of the Sea Ranch Condominiums and the Hedgerow Houses, were built of vernacular forms clad with unpainted wood materials—inspired by the structures found on old farms and western mines.[61]

Two creative architecture firms were involved: Charles Moore (Moore Lyndon Turnbull Whitaker—MLTW) sited and designed the Sea Ranch Condominiums, and Joseph Esherick (Joseph Esherick and Associates) directed the Hedgerow Houses. Reportedly, the designs were generated separately in 1963, however, the projects appeared strikingly similar in their approach, each featuring shed roofs—the distinctive element adopted throughout the country. Even as the initial Sea Ranch structures were being completed, the Shed style burst upon the architectural scene. It seemed that young architects could hardly wait to move beyond boxy International forms to create more interesting interior spaces. The new Shed houses allowed a dynamic flow of different spatial experiences.[62] In the *Architectural Record* "Record Houses 1967," six houses featured the new Shed style.[63]

The style's rapid spread was undoubtedly aided by Moore's appointment as dean of the Yale School of Architecture from 1965 to 1970.[64] In addition to the spatial qualities, Shed reflected broad societal factors at work from the mid-1960s through the 1970s. Its genesis from useful and simply built structures—such as barns, mining structures, and folk houses—was in sync with a new interest in "architecture without architects."[65] The vertical shed shapes with high clerestory windows could facilitate passive solar cooling, an important tenet of early energy conservation. Finally, Sea Ranch's requirements that houses be placed lightly on the land—leaving natural meadows and forests intact—fit with the emerging environmental movement of the 1970s. By the 1980s, Shed, along with the activism of the 1970s, was fading away and being replaced by traditional styled houses.

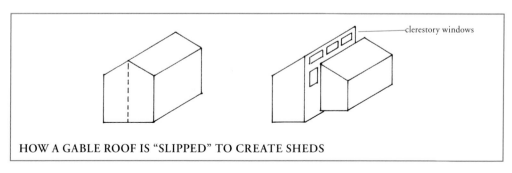

HOW A GABLE ROOF IS "SLIPPED" TO CREATE SHEDS

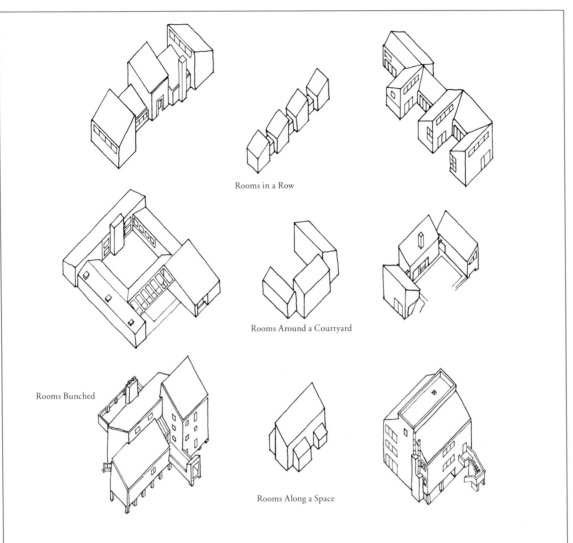

Rooms in a Row

Rooms Around a Courtyard

Rooms Bunched

Rooms Along a Space

SOME WAYS TO ORGANIZE SHED-ROOF ELEMENTS AND ROOMS

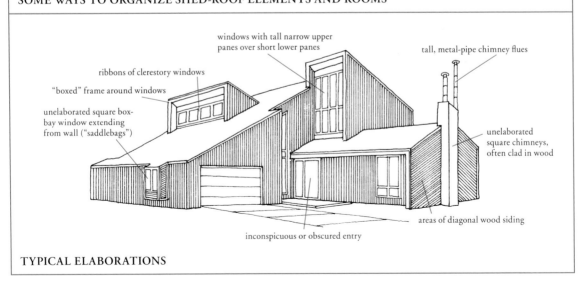

windows with tall narrow upper
panes over short lower panes

tall, metal-pipe chimney flues

ribbons of clerestory windows

"boxed" frame around windows

unelaborated square box-
bay window extending
from wall ("saddlebags")

unelaborated
square chimneys,
often clad in wood

areas of diagonal wood siding

inconspicuous or obscured entry

TYPICAL ELABORATIONS

SHED

1. Amagansett, New York; ca. 1970s. This is uniformly clad with smooth vertical boards.

2. Amagansett, New York; 1982. A single high-pitched shed roof juts upward, forming a dramatic angular shape.

3. Fayetteville, Arkansas; 1999. Coudren House; James Lambeth, architect. A 21st-Century Modern house that incorporates stepped wood sheds.

4. Duluth, Minnesota; 1979. When half of a gable roof is slightly "slipped" upward it forms a line of clerestory windows (as on the left of this house)—excellent for light and passive cooling. Note diagonal siding on front facade.

5. Sea Ranch, California; ca. 1970s. A low roof pitch and a broad house mass allow this house to settle into the landscape.

6. Minneapolis, Minnesota; ca. 1970. This house is composed of three distinct volumes (one is behind). Note how the volume on the right almost seems to float above its dark recessed base.

7. Amagansett, New York; ca. 1970s. Like Figure 5, three main shed forms are visible. Here window placement, a simple but contrasting cornice board, and a very slight overhang, give greater individual definition to each shed form.

8. Dallas, Texas; 1979. Here shed elements are arranged in a formal five-part composition.

2

4

5

7

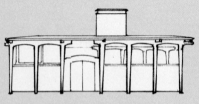

ORGANIC

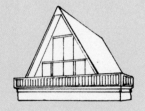

A-FRAME

NEW FORMALISM

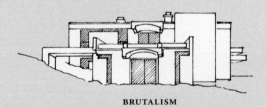

BRUTALISM

POSTMODERN

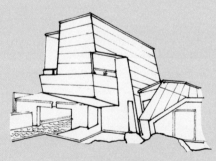

DECONSTRUCTIVISM

Other 20th-Century Modern

Modern houses are divided into early modern houses (the creatively decorated Prairie, Craftsman, and Modernistic styles); banker's modern (generally grouped into developments of Minimal Traditional, Ranch, and Split-Level houses) and mainstream modern (the modern styles favored by architects). This last category of modern styles is called mainstream not because it constitutes the bulk of modern houses built in America (an honor belonging to the banker's modern styles) but rather because it has dominated architectural education, awards, criticism, and even histories of 20th-century houses.

Many histories of 20th-century modernism separate styles built during the mid-20th century—Mid-century Modern—from those being designed towards the end of the twentieth century. Most Mid-century Modern houses were either Contemporary or International style (each covered in a separate chapter). However, a small group of architects rejected the orthogonal nature of these two styles and instead designed Organic houses, an approach to house design united by the use of natural shapes or non-rectilinear geometries that includes an extraordinarily broad range of designs.

Other devices created three other Mid-century styles. Adding a new roof form to an otherwise simple house was discovered to be a good way to create innovative modern designs. High-style variations included airplane, paraboloid, umbrella, and multi-arched roofs—all rarely encountered in real life. However a very simple roof-form, called the A-frame, became widespread in Mid-century, particularly for casual vacation houses. At the opposite end of the spectrum, Formalism could create a more dignified, high-style appearance by adding slender attenuated arches to modern boxes. Brutalism was yet another Mid-century Modern style, where concrete was used to create a more rugged and insular look.

By 1965 even these variations were not enough and, following publication of the critically acclaimed book, *Complexity and Contradiction in Architecture* by Robert Venturi (New York: Museum of Modern Art, 1966), house style moved beyond Mid-century Modern and into other directions. Postmodernism came first, adding historical elements onto houses in new and different ways. Following this the elements of houses were exploded and rearranged in a movement called Deconstructivism.

As the millennium approached, the modern movement gained a new impetus—leading to exploration of both new interpretations of modernism and to revivals of past modern styles. This is treated in a final appendix on 21st-century Modern.

Organic Houses (1950s–present)

Organic architecture is based on the coalescence of the built environment with nature, allowing the design to respond to the natural environment rather than impose on it. While other modern movements more often championed straight lines and orthogonal designs, Organic modernism favored natural shapes and interesting geometries. Designs—conceived as reactive both to the environment and to the building material—were developed "organically" into one harmonious unit. Organic architects utilized new technologies and building materials but rejected them as sources of stylistic inspiration, believing they imposed a design from outside sources. An Organic architect would instead carefully study the exact site for a house and then create a design that grew from within, a careful relationship between all of the parts of a house. This might begin with a geometric shape used for the floor plan and then extend into the design of all parts of the house—fixtures, furnishings, and even window shapes.[66]

According to Frank Lloyd Wright, America's premier Organic architect, form no longer *followed* function; it was one and the same. This principle began its evolution in Wright's Prairie houses and had matured in the mid-1930s when he demonstrated it magnificently on both the high and low ends. In 1936, Wright designed his most famous and intrinsically Organic house, Fallingwater in Pennsylvania. Constructed on a waterfall, the cantilever design complements the surrounding rock formations. The interior incorporates an original ledge rock, a small stream, and expansive windows that reconnect the interior to the exterior. During the same time that he was creating Fallingwater, Wright

ORGANIC

1. North Carolina; ca. 1990s. Mountainside House; James Fox, architect. This house, which includes a path through it to a valley view, incorporates Wrightian rectilinear ornament executed in many materials.

2. North Carolina; ca. 2000s. Water Fall House; James Fox, architect. View from creek. Note pattern created in the concrete on bottom of house.

3. North Carolina; ca. 2000s. Water Fall House; James Fox, architect. Entry facade.

4. Mill Run, Pennsylvania; 1936–1939. Fallingwater; Frank Lloyd Wright, architect.

5. Carmel, California; 1948. Walker House; Frank Lloyd Wright, architect. The only house on the ocean side of Monterey Bay's scenic road, this house follows Wright's Organic design principles. It is stone and looks like part of the cliff it is built into. The low copper roof mirrors the ocean's color. This view shows the wall of windows facing the private courtyard.

ORGANIC (cont.)

6. Pleasantville, New York; 1948. Friedman House; Frank Lloyd Wright, architect. The round carport, resembling a large mushroom, is paired with rounded house and entry roof (in background).

7. Palm Springs, California (vicinity); ca. 1960s. This hexagonal house rotates so view and sunlight can be controlled.

8. North Carolina; ca. 1980s. Steel House; James Fox, architect. Here curvilinear Organic elements are incorporated.

9. Pasadena, California; 1948. A rounded house with organic elements found in a typical post–World War II neighborhood.

10. Dewey, Oklahoma; 1957. C. A. Comer House; Bruce Goff, architect. This house is an angular example.

11. Mountain Lake, Minnesota; 1970. Glen Harder House; Bruce Goff, architect. This combines huge piers growing out of the ground with an almost paper-thin roof above house and chimneys.

7

10

11

12. Minneapolis, Minnesota, vicinity; 1969, John Howe, architect, who became Frank Lloyd Wright's chief draftsman. Curves meet at a point, providing an unusually broad angle of views.

13. Los Angeles, California; 1957. Silvertop: Reiner-Burchill Residence; John Lautner, architect. Sweeping curves with broad overhangs angle and overlap.

6

8

9

12

13

was also preoccupied with creating homes for middle-class America and began to design his Usonian houses. His affordable single-story homes showcased natural construction materials and utilized solar heating and natural cooling. Furniture was often built in and the house plan featured a free-flowing floor plan, specifically arranged to incorporate views of outdoor gardens. Many of Wright's Usonians also incorporated his geometrically based patterns of window design and ornament that is frequently called Wrightian.

Wright's designs had a threefold effect on American houses at mid-century. First, his Usonian houses helped spawn the Contemporary house. Second, Wright's body of work inspired a large diverse group of unique Organic houses by other architects (including Bruce Goff, and Wright's and Goff's students and followers), in effect making Organic a dramatic style of architecture. Finally, and of most lasting importance, Wright—through his publications, his works, and his lectures—instilled American architects with Organic as a way to approach a design. He railed against the International style with its orthogonal structures deliberately designed almost as a piece of white sculpture able to be placed anywhere in the world, and not, like the Organic, designed for a specific location, with local materials, adapted to the conditions of a site.

Organic modernism of the 1960s also appropriately reflected the ideals of the environmentalist movement. Adapting a house specifically to its site allowed full use of passive solar building design. While design was still meant to reflect the natural setting, eco-friendly elements were an ideal addition. This further development of Organic architecture was also characterized by more free-form designs. Some were still inspired by the landscape, others by various organic shapes found in leaves, shells, flowers, and fauna.

A-Frame (1950s–1970s)

The A-frame was a trendy house design that emerged in the 1950s and lasted through the 1970s. Resembling the letter A, the design is comprised of two sloping roofs creating an overall triangular shape.[67] Architects learned that the standard form of a modern house could be visually transformed through simple experimentation with unusual roof shapes.[68] The sloping roof of an A-frame house extends all the way down to the ground, in effect becoming a continuous wall. This bold, yet whimsical, design was seen as an appealing choice for vacation homes because it was suitable for a variety of terrains. Some featured a front deck, which provided a pleasant sitting and viewing area for both mountain and waterfront properties.

The notion of a weekend retreat was new to middle-income Americans. Travel tended to be lengthy and expensive prior to the proliferation of the automobile. But the combination of a new highway interstate system and the opening of shorelines for recreational use by the Bureau of Reclamation in the 1960s made travel to a vacation home more attractive. As a result of increased free time and disposable income, the middle class became the target market for the A-frame house. Advertised as affordable and aesthetically refreshing, the A-frame was presented as an exciting second-home option for those desiring a weekend retreat from city life. Stylistically, it also provided an exotic architectural alternative to traditional primary dwellings. Aside from enjoying this weekend retreat, the consumer was encouraged to take part in its construction as do-it-yourself guidebooks and house kits were made readily available by the 1960s.

As people became more conscious of efficient living, they realized the A-frame had several inherent design problems, including awkward unused space, lack of adequate

A-FRAME

1. Key West, Florida (vicinity); ca. 1960s. Here the A-frame appears to serve as a base camp for boating in the Gulf.

2. Unidentified House; ca. 1960s. Raised, perhaps anticipating high water, and with a deck to enjoy what one assumes is a water view.

3. Hamptons, New York; 1964. Higher ground and a relatively flat site allow placement on the ground.

natural light, and inefficient heating and cooling solutions. Variations of the A-frame attempted to solve some of these structural problems. A gambrel-roof A-frame created more usable space, an A-frame with wings provided a more open floor plan, and a double standard A-frame (two A-frame plans placed perpendicular to each other) allowed more natural light.

Despite its practical flaws, by the mid-1960s the A-frame had become a cultural icon as the style was incorporated into commercial buildings, restaurants, churches, and even backyard playhouses. As the once-distinctive style became rather ubiquitous, its popularity declined, and the form fell out of favor by the 1970s.

New Formalism (1950s–1970s)

In the early 1950s the International style—in the Miesian glass-and-steel aesthetic—was the style of choice for most non-domestic buildings. But when Edward Durrell Stone received the commission to design an American embassy in New Delhi in 1954, International did not seem appropriate for such a symbolic building. Stone's solution was to create a new and more ceremonial modern style based on classical elements but utilizing building materials and technologies of the International style. The embassy celebrated monumental, rather than minimalist, forms. It featured an ornamental concrete screen grille, free-standing slender columns, and an interior courtyard. Other architects then began to use this as a model, while some preferred an even more classical version that omitted the screen.[69]

The style is most commonly characterized by a symmetrical facade with columnar

NEW FORMALISM

1. Dallas, Texas; 1965. This row of slender, outward-slanting porch supports seems almost like seven ballet dancers executing an *arabesque en pointe*—making it easy to see how the name "ballet classicism" came to be used for Philip Johnson's work in this style.

2. Houston, Texas; ca. 1960s.

3. Dallas, Texas; 1971. Harwood K. Smith, architect.

4. Beverly Hills, California; ca. 1960s. Side wings with decorative grille are combined with a classicized modern entry.

5. Dallas, Texas; 1957. Oak Court; Edward Durell Stone, architect; 2007, Russell Buchanan, restoration architect. A screen grille (brise-soleil) of white terrazzo lends privacy to and shades the public, south-facing facade.

6. Dallas, Texas; 1964. Beck House; Philip Johnson, architect. The formalistic arches are not just an exterior feature; they continue into interior spaces. Johnson had used this same attenuated arch profile for the pond pavilion at his Glass House.

1

2

4

6

arched supports. New Formalism concentrated on updating, rather than re-creating, Classical forms, providing a visible and theoretic distinction from the Neoclassical style. An overall massiveness is achieved through a concrete-block-like structure set on an elevation and typically crowned with a flat slab roof. Wall surfaces, commonly made of stone, brick, and marble, are normally smooth and unadorned; columns generally take on a slender and attenuated form.

While New Formalism was readily applied to civic and commercial buildings, it was far less common in residential architecture. Philip Johnson's 1964 Beck House and Stone's 1956 Graf House in Dallas, Texas, are rare high-style examples. The Beck House exterior visibly references Johnson's small Lake Pavilion built at Glass House, while the interior dining area recalls his Guest House. The Graf House seems inspired by the embassy at New Delhi. Most Formalistic houses are a bit more simplified.

Brutalism (1950s–1970s)

Brutalism began as an aesthetic philosophy favoring the exposure of building materials, namely rough concrete and structural supports. The name is derived from the French term for raw concrete, *béton brut,* illustrating its devotion to using materials in a direct and visible way. In opposition to the glass curtain wall, Brutalism favored bulky and angular designs with fewer visible glass surfaces. In a house, a simple juxtaposition of vertical and horizontal blocks might produce an exterior of slits and slabs—broad expanses of solid material with narrow vertical slits of glass surface—for a low ratio of void (glass windows) to solid (wall surface). This style has attracted criticism by those who perceive it as unappealing, but today it is regaining favor as a new generation comes to appreciate its bold design and monumentality.

One of the earliest examples of Brutalist architecture in the United States is the Yale Art and Architecture building designed by the school's dean, Paul Rudolph, in 1963. The deep recessions and sharp projections exemplified the grammar of this style; however, it was these same elements that were later frequently criticized.[70]

This style is more often found in civic buildings than in residential architecture. Houses, however, can retain the main components, which include a bulky angular exterior, unornamented facades, recessed windows, often in vertical slits, exposed ducts, and exposed concrete (although domestic examples may instead use brick, stucco, or, rarely, wood).

Postmodern (late 1960s–present)

Postmodern houses appropriate and imitate elements of traditional styles, while incorporating these with new forms and materials. The result is both familiar and original. It is common to reference several different historical styles within one design, creating an interesting juxtaposition of period and regional elements.

Advocates of this style believed it was more important to absorb and reformulate traditional components than to continue constructing glass boxes void of heritage. Robert Venturi, a leading proponent of Postmodern architecture, believed a reference to traditional designs spawned thought-provoking interpretations. His 1966 book *Complexity and Contradiction in Architecture* illustrated two thousand years of traditional designs and promoted new design that incorporated elements borrowed from buildings of the past. Responding to the modern idiom "Less is more," Venturi rebutted with "Less is a bore." Simplicity in design does not generate complex resolutions, which he believed to be the ultimate aim.

While paying homage to the past, many houses within this stylistic movement feature playful designs and ironic combinations. It is as if a repository of architectural elements existed and the architect could select any combination of forms. The elements selected could additionally be exaggerated, manipulated, and even distorted. This idea is illustrated in Vanna Venturi's house, in which Venturi dissected the proverbial arch, removing the keystone that provides the primary structural function of this architectural element. With a Postmodern style, the result can be a house that suits the desire for historic reference, fresh design, or contradictory interpretations.

A number of Postmodern architects, among them Robert Stern and Albert, Righter, & Tittmann, have now come to design New Traditional houses, often bringing to their designs the ability to slightly modify historic design elements and make them of today.

Deconstructivism (1980s–present)

Deconstructivism is an architectural style that challenges the idea of oneness or unity in a structure and instead embraces the individuality of parts, producing designs that are fragmented. Deconstructivist philosophy regarded the parts of a whole more revealing than the whole itself, generating a multiplicity of interpretations. Applied to residential architecture, the form of a house is commonly divided into separate volumes that appear to have little coherent connection to one another. Each part is visually distinct from the others.

Deconstructivist houses have a wide range of influences but no visible single source or predictability in design, other than unusual geometries. Exteriors can look unfinished, complicating usual boundaries between indoor and outdoor space. The standard 90°-angle wall is no longer the default option. Windows can extend from walls to roof lines, creating an unexpected continuation of space.

The Frank Gehry house in Santa Monica illustrates this fragmentation of form and space, resulting in a visually unsettled design. In 1978 he first wrapped the original Dutch Colonial Revival house with unusual materials, obscuring any semblance of the original design.[71] An uneven and disjointed corrugated-metal wall envelops the facade, while chain-link panels are used near roof lines and glass windows. The house appears unfinished, following Gehry's belief that a "finished building has security, and it's predictable. I want to try something different. I like playing at the edge of disaster."[72]

These unusual designs presented engineering and construction challenges until the spread of CAD (computer-aided design) and CAM (computer-aided manufacturing). Used together, these programs can effectively visualize unusual three-dimensional spaces and electronically tool and manufacture corresponding work pieces needed for the design. Computer programs like these have allowed architects to more efficiently create and control their chaotic designs.

BRUTALISM (SLITS & SLABS)

1. Dallas, Texas; ca. 1970. Narrow slits for windows combined with brick slabs for a neighborhood-friendly interpretation of Brutalism.

2. Palm Springs, California; ca. 1956. Williams House; E. Stewart Williams, architect. Made of the Brutalist material of choice—concrete with small ridges broken off to resemble rough corduroy. Rarely seen in houses.

3. Kenwood, Minnesota; 1970. Horty, Elving and Associates, architects. Note the stepped effect of the massing in this example; similar massing occurs in the Pueblo Revival style. Although clad in wood, narrow vertical windows and large areas of cladding relate it to the Brutalist style.

4. Pasadena, California; 1990. Condos on Grand Avenue combine a heavy Brutalist building with a Craftsman trellis to relate it to the historic side of the street.

5. Pasadena, California; 1988. Buff House; Conrad Buff III of Buff & Hensman & Assoc., architect. Vertical massing—composed of rectilinear living modules—is punctuated by narrow window slits and clad in gunnite stucco.

6. Chicago, Illinois; 1982. Kirsch House ("The Bunker"); Earl Jay Kirsch Architects. A high-style Brutalist residence.

7. Venice, California; 1999. Brutalist concrete slabs are turned sideways for an ocean view. Note vertical window slits on right.

1

3

4

5

2

6

7

POSTMODERN

1. Cambridge, Massachusetts; 1991. "Checkerboard House" (Albert House); Albert, Righter, and Tittmann, architects. Asphalt shingles form a black-and-gray diamond pattern that can be found providing a maintenance alteration in many parts of Boston. With its combination of subtle classical details and a Main Street false front, one might need a second look driving down the street to realize this is a new house, not a much modified one.

2. Philadelphia, Pennsylvania; 1962. Vanna Venturi House; Robert Venturi, architect. One of the early Postmodern houses designed by the author of *Complexity and Contradiction in Architecture* shows how Postmodernism could play with traditional elements. Here the blind arch above the entrance has a void where the keystone would have been historically placed for support. Note the square windows, one of the earliest uses of this distinctive window shape.

3. Carlsbad, California; 1982 (remodeled ca. 2010). A Postmodern remodeling of an earlier stucco town-house row. Each is getting its own front that dominates the appearance.

4. East Quogue, New York; 1979–1981. Lawson House; Robert A. M. Stern, architect. This iconic house combines a compact form with carefully placed historicist details. This entry facade has classical columns and an oversized eyebrow dormer window.

5. Rosemary Beach, Florida; 2003. George Israel, architect. An interesting Postmodern house with shaped parapets that also incorporate Deconstructivist features. The stucco wall on the right is not supported from below, and faux bullet holes add an almost destructive flare.

6. Pasadena, California; ca. 1990s. Stair-stepped gables combined with Postmodern porch supports and entry surrounds.

1

3

5

DECONSTRUCTIVISM

1. Orona, Minnesota (moved from Lake Minnetonka); 1983–1986. Winton Guest House; Frank Gehry, architect. A still life of forms created a small guesthouse.

2. Venice, California; 1981. Hopper House; Brian Murphy, architect. An exterior staircase covered in roof shingles is set into the inset on the right.

3. Venice, California; 1984. (Venice Beach) Norton House; Frank Gehry & Associates, architects. The owner had been a lifeguard in earlier years, and this provided a theme—complete with the lifeguard tower and turquoise-blue pool tile popular in the 1950s.

4. Los Angeles, California; 1982. Petal House; Eric Owen Moss, architect. A Minimal Traditional house has a Deconstructivist remodeling and additions to house and detached garage. The stepped gable at right is a free-standing wall; this stepped motif is echoed by the wall cladding above the upstairs entry to the garage. The two-story gabled addition exposed the wood stud and plywood connection (visible behind the front gable of the house), and stepped windows reveal there is a roof deck to observe the adjacent freeway.

5. Santa Monica, California; 1903 (first renovated 1978, with later changes).Gehry House; Frank Gehry, architect. The shape of the gambrel roof of the original house is barely visible behind the extensive remodeling. To add more space, Gehry formed a secondary exterior skin around the old house using common materials—plywood, corrugated steel, and chain-link fencing—to create an experimental design that he has likened to a jazz riff.[73]

1

2

4

3

5

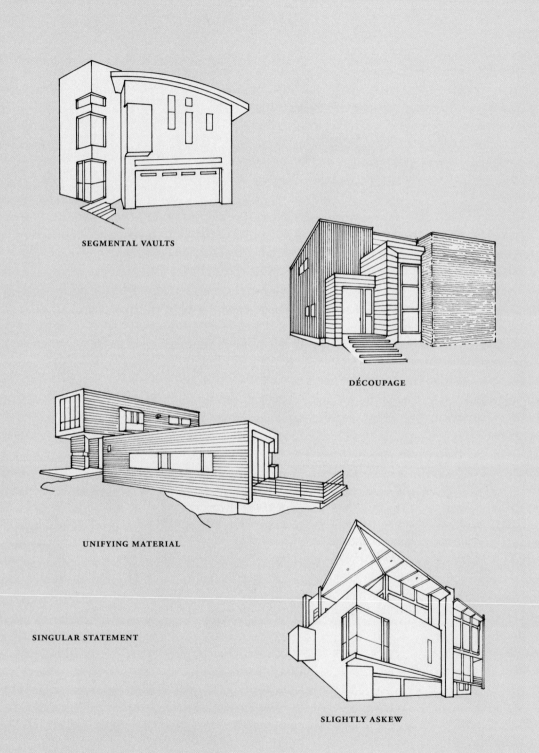

SEGMENTAL VAULTS

DÉCOUPAGE

UNIFYING MATERIAL

SINGULAR STATEMENT

SLIGHTLY ASKEW

21st-Century Modern

As the turn-of-the-millennium drew near, a multitude of books catalogued and examined the modern homes of the previous century, offering a compelling synthesis of the variety and depth of the modern movement. During the 1980s and 1990s the sophistication of CAD (computer-aided design) and CAM (computer-aided manufacturing) programs developed rapidly—giving architects an unprecedented ability to model complex designs, to display how they would look in three dimensions, and to easily make small changes. Thus a generation of young architects was now working on computers and inculcated with the rich possibilities offered by CAD. By 1990, designing new iterations of smooth-surfaced white stucco homes no longer presented a sufficient challenge, and many different approaches to modern house design began to be explored. As a result of this growing interest a new shelter magazine, *DWELL,* launched in 2000, focused on modern home design and further spread this new wave of modernism.

This short appendix on 21st-Century Modern houses does not in any way attempt to be exhaustive. It cannot begin to cover the landmark modern houses that are being built today and are so well treated in monographs, series of books, and architectural periodicals. Instead the examples presented here are based almost solely on modern houses encountered while driving through typical American neighborhoods—built as infill, as replacement houses, or, more recently, in neighborhood groupings limited to modern design. The homes here are loosely gathered into a few visual groupings that have been encountered frequently enough that they may have emerged as an approach to design. The majority slightly relax the International in some manner. Some add segmental vaults; others utilize several materials in combination for a decoupage effect rather than a smooth united surface. Some take advantage of the many new materials now available to clad a house, wrapping the house in new ways. Others are only a little askew—slight deviations from the orthogonal, just enough to tease the eye and show off how easy this is to do today. Finally, there are the singular statements—one-of-a-kind architect-designed landmarks, rarely encountered in the field (unless one has a special invitation) but comprising a great many of today's design awards and included in books on new houses.

The construction method most often observed in neighborhood examples is balloon- or platform-framed wood. In contrast, many landmark examples and experimental small houses utilize a broad range of structural possibilities.

21ST-CENTURY MODERN: SEGMENTAL VAULTS—A segmental vaulted roof is added to a house that otherwise would be thought of as either a late International or one of the other 21st-Century Modern house groupings. The vaulted element is often canted and contrasts significantly with the rectilinear lines of the rest of the house—and thus tends to become the dominant visual element. This feature is also found today on other building types.

21ST-CENTURY MODERN: DÉCOUPAGE—It appears that the most common 21st-Century Modern house is an orthogonal box, or boxes, designed with two, three, or more wall-cladding textures and materials. These are chosen from the great variety available today—metal siding, wood applied in many differing ways, concrete panels, HardieBoard, concrete block, and occasionally brick—all in combination with glass. The pattern created by these materials becomes a primary element of the home's design. Usually each material is in a slightly different plane, adding a three-dimensional element to even modest examples. High-style examples can have elaborate modeling of the house, approaching the look of an orthogonal sculpture.

21ST-CENTURY MODERN: UNIFYING MATERIAL—White stucco was in and of itself considered an important element of the International house. It was thought appropriate for any location, thus promoting International architectural unity rather than regional loyalties. While some mid-century examples used other materials, there was a 1970s and 1980s return to the white stucco roots that give center stage to the house form alone. By about 1990, architects had tired of exclusively using white stucco and instead began to design with the wide variety of other wall claddings that had been introduced. These included various types of enhanced glass, concrete panels, wood application techniques, polycarbonates, and many textures and colors of metals—including easily visible informal corrugated metal. Many of these could be applied as rain screens, a new method of applying sidings that increased air circulation and insulation (discussed on page 772).

Any of these could also provide a theme for an entire house, and architects have adopted and used these as an integral part of many designs. Sometimes the goal of using a material is to blend in, but equally likely the cladding is used almost as gift wrapping, enhancing and changing a boxy house with the decorative surface.[74]

21ST-CENTURY MODERN: SLIGHTLY ASKEW—While Deconstructivist houses are still being built today, one of the side effects of this movement has been that more simple rectilinear forms have been slightly loosened up. CAD programs make this far easier to do. This can be quite subtle—one tilted or canted wall, or even a prominent overhang with a slight angle. But the eye is challenged and the point is made—rich design opportunities are possible today because the house does not have to be completely rectilinear.

SEGMENTAL VAULTS

1. Seattle, Washington; 2007. A segmental vaulted roof, set at an angle, came to symbolize modernism on many building types during the last two decades.

2. Los Angeles, California; 1969. The tilted arched roof is likely part of a relatively recent remodeling.

3. Chicago, Illinois; ca. 2005. This is part of a large grouping of similar town houses where the arched roofs are level rather than canted.

4. East Hampton, New York; 1995. Highway House; Rafael Viñoly, architect. This house is a curved roof resting on a wall set at a right angle. Three poured-in-place concrete chimneys add a rhythmic element to the composition.

DÉCOUPAGE

1. Seattle, Washington; 2006. Note the use of smooth horizontal wood; concrete textured in a grid pattern; and vertical metal siding—each in a different wall plane. Both entrance facade and the side (view) facade (Figure 4) are shown.

2. Los Angeles, California; 2006. Horizontal boards, vertical metal and stucco (it appears)—in different planes, but less three-dimensional than in Figures 1 and 4.

3. Seattle, Washington; 2010.

4. Seattle, Washington; 2006. Note the broad roof overhang and walled garden on the side (view) facade of Figure 1.

5. Boston, Massachusetts; ca. 2000. Big Dig House. Multiple wall materials (salvaged when Boston's main interstate was buried in a tunnel) are used to create a Découpage effect.

6. Dallas, Texas; 2012.

7. Dallas, Texas; 2011. Cheatham House, Urban Reserve. There is a plan to eventually hang a shade screen from the boxed-in side of the roof. In the meantime, one can enjoy this sculptural form. The second floor forms a "T" at the rear and has a pool and large entertainment area overlooking a pond and the setting sun.

1

4

6

2

3

5

7

UNIFYING MATERIAL

1. Venice, California (Venice Beach); 1988. Snipper House; Miguel Angelo Flores & Associates, architects. The stair-stepped podium visible at left is lavender. The house has a glass brick and stucco cylinder for its core.

2. Chicago, Illinois (Hyde Park); 1996. Davis House; John Vinci, architect. Note entry deep in side of house and use of overall brick cladding. The traditional brick helps relate to its historic surroundings.

3. Fayetteville, Arizona; ca. 2005. "L-stack House"; Marlon Blackwell, architect. Responding to an irregular site, Blackwell utilized two rectangular boxlike shapes placed at right angles connecting them with a glassed-in stairway. The lower one bridges a small stream and forms a roof garden (maintaining the site's natural drainage). The upper box shelters an outdoor living space in the rear. The exterior cladding is a Brazilian redwood rainscreen with EPDM behind. The house is insulated with soy-based foam.

4. Long Island, New York; ca. 2008. House at Sagaponac. Flat board siding, no roofline cornice, and almost no windows on the front facade.

5. Los Angeles, California; 2005. Finkelstein Residence; Antony Unruh of Unruh Boyer, architect. The ways of building on a slope illustrated on page 634 are still being utilized today. The auto entry is at street level and is connected to the house inserted lower on the hill. The view facade faces away from the street. The house is unified by a handsome cladding of galvanized aluminum with a zinc coating called Corrugated Galvalume.

1

2

3

4

5

SLIGHTLY ASKEW

1. Pasadena, California; 1996. Dumbacher House; Hagy Belzberg, architect. Slight angles are introduced in the shape and upward tilt of the broad overhang above the second-floor outdoor living area.

2. Chicago, Illinois; 2005. Here there are three distinct sections of the house in three planes—the section on the left uses a diagonal parapet to create the appearance of a slanted roof; the central section is orthogonal and filled with windows; and rear one appears to have an outward slanting wall.

3. Beverly Hills, California; 1932 (rebuilt ca. 2012). Three materials on varied planes are accented by the slanted roof marking the entry—a combination of Découpage and Slightly Askew.

4. Los Angeles, California (Silver Lake); 1955 (later remodeling). Note the subtle wall cants and meticulous changes in material.

5. Los Angeles, California; 1948 (remodeled). The colored house walls (blue and brown), the textured wall finish, and the slightly Pueblo-esque elements mark this as a "desert" modern house. The cactus garden is added to further the theme.

SINGULAR STATEMENTS

1. Malibu, California; 2011. The 747 Wing House; David Hertz Architects. A new, and unique, example of how an unusual roof form can completely dominate a house—such houses were sometimes referred to as "roof architecture" in the 1950s and 1960s.

2. Los Angeles, California; 1988. Robert Bridges, architect. The street view on the other side of Figure 5 gives little hint of what lies behind.

3. La Jolla, California; 1990. Ocean view facade of Figure 4.

4. La Jolla, California; 1990. The street facade gives not a hint of the facade that faces toward downtown La Jolla and the ocean view (Figure 3).

5. Los Angeles, California; 1988. Robert Bridges, architect. Looking uphill one can see smooth wood sheathing meet huge concrete pylons. This two-sided house is located on an almost unbuildable site (see Figure 2).

6. Dallas, Texas; 1994. Rose House; Antoine Predock, architect. Morning sunlight shines through translucent doors in this two-sided house. The street side appears to grow out of the limestone bed of Turtle Creek, with stepped ledges planted with native plants. The private side opens up and steps up to the heavily shaded creek complete with a bridge for bird watching.

21ST-CENTURY MODERN: A NEIGHBORHOOD GROUPING—Throughout the 20th century, modern houses have generally been placed in neighborhoods of traditional houses, where the tendency is to think of them simply as a "modern" house in contrast to adjacent homes of historical styles. Modern homes have rarely been built in compelling modern streetscapes—in large enough concentration to easily display many different examples together. Thus it was difficult to appreciate either the many different kinds of modern houses or the subtle differences in related houses.[75]

Urban Reserve, a fourteen-acre project in Dallas, Texas, presents a timely example not only of how modern houses can be grouped together, but also of a green approach to site plan, landscape, and long-term sustainability—a rarity in the world where burying storm water underground in culverts is considered normal and large development sites are routinely cut and filled, scraped clean, wiping out native vegetation and obliterating wildlife habitat.[76]

Developer Diane Cheatham assembled the site (located along a hike and bike trail and close to a DART stop, yet for half a century a landfill and illegal dumping ground) and hired Robert Meckfessel of DSGN as the master planner and Kevin Sloan as the landscape architect. The goal was to create a neighborhood of fifty modern houses in a green and sustainable manner. All houses would be required to have some level of LEED certification.

First the team devised a pioneering approach to storm water. Runoff from about thirty-five offsite acres already drained here pours onto the site through a large culvert. The plan collected this into a pond, now used permanently to water the landscape of the development. A second pond collects any overflow as well as the runoff from the development itself, much of this flowing through rain gardens on its way. In all, fifty acres of storm water is naturally filtered on its way to White Rock Creek.

Second, there is an innovative street pattern. The street is but twenty-two feet wide, the minimum to handle a fire truck, rather than the thirty-foot city standard. A gently rounded curb line on the dry side eliminates curb cuts. The wet side has head-in parking spaces for guests, interspersed with long rectangular rain gardens filled with horsetail that not only filter water but also hide the cars. Native desert willows are planted on the dry side of the street and bald and pond cypress on the wet side.

Third, there is an inventive approach to lot size, house siting, and design criteria. The dry side of the street consists of forty-foot lots—twenty feet for construction and twenty for a side garden in the Charleston pattern (see illustration, page 682). The wet side of the street has larger lots set behind the rain gardens and pond. But how to create design criteria to regulate "modern" houses without tying architect hands? Eventually, it was decided simply to ban all historical styles, including Mid-century Modern (Contemporary in this guide) and create an architecture-review committee with a "we'll know it when we see it" definition of what constitutes a modern house. The result is that the houses built from 2007 to the present represent a broad range of the 21st-century modern houses groupings in this appendix.

GROUPINGS

1. Dallas, Texas; ca. 2008. Wise House; Jim Wiley, architect.

2. Dallas, Texas; 2010. Cube House; Russell Buchanan, architect. Built of integrally colored stucco, the struts in the awning highlight the slightly askew element.

3. Dallas, Texas; 2011. "Thyme to Be"; Robert Meckfessel, design architect. This LEEDS Platinum house has an eco shell of western red cedar shakes on a plastic backing—a cladding that saves labor by properly aligning the shakes, and creates a rain screen. Client and architect visited Sea Ranch and have captured some of its spirit in natural material and gently sloped shed roof. Solar panels on the roof and geothermal heat and cooling helped gain Platinum status.

4. Dallas, Texas; ca. 2010. This is a Découpage house. Note the wide boxed-in roof overhang used on the southwest corner.

5. Dallas, Texas; ca. 2010. This has a rust-tone metal cladding and a two-story plant-covered screening wall.

6. Dallas, Texas; ca. 2008. Chris Craft House; Vincent Snyder, architect. A singular statement clad in slate.

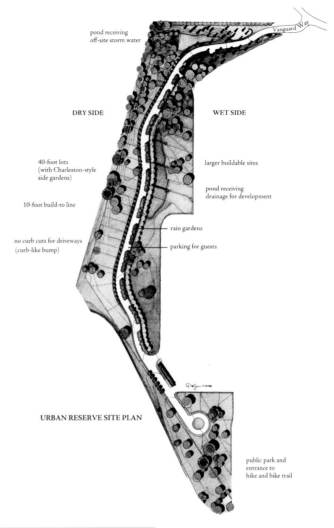

pond receiving off-site storm water

Vanguard Way

DRY SIDE

WET SIDE

40-foot lots (with Charleston-style side gardens)

larger buildable sites

pond receiving drainage for development

10-foot build-to line

rain gardens

no curb cuts for driveways (curb-like bump)

parking for guests

URBAN RESERVE SITE PLAN

public park and entrance to hike and bike trail

5

1

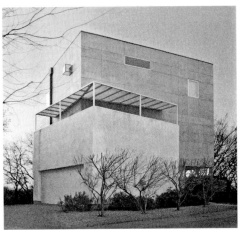

2

3

4

6

Styled houses with traditional designs that mimic the past have alternated with modern designs throughout the 20th century. World War II swiftly ended the Eclectic movement of the 1920s and 1930s as postwar tastes enthusiastically embraced modern styles throughout the 1950s and 1960s. Despite this overwhelming preference for modern styles during these decades, the very early beginnings of some late-20th-century-styled homes (such as Styled Ranch and American Vernacular) came as early as 1935. However, most of the late 20th-century styles did not emerge until the 1970s and 1980s, when a renewed taste for period styles based on earlier architectural traditions emerged, nurtured by the historic nostalgia created by the U.S. Bicentennial and a burgeoning nationwide preservation movement. At first there was little attempt to closely copy European or Colonial prototypes. Instead, distinctive historical details (for example, Tudor half-timbering, Georgian doorways, and Queen Anne spindlework porches) were applied to Ranch-house forms, producing the Styled Ranch. Those desiring a more formal look turned to the Mansard style.

But as the new millennium approached, home building boomed, and simply grafting historic details onto mid-century forms no longer sufficed. Three new kinds of styled houses emerged—Millennium Mansions, New Traditional houses, and American Vernacular—the broadest range of home styles ever before constructed at the same time. This was made possible by the Internet and its exploding content, giving immediate access to view historic precedents and to order reproduction details.

Millennium Mansions were an entirely new form with an even more complex version of a roof form seen only once before, on exuberant Queen Anne and Romanesque houses of the late 19th century. The roofs of Millennium Mansions practically explode above the house. It is almost as if the creative multi-part roof forms seen in both the late 19th and late 20th centuries presaged sensational fireworks displays to celebrate a new century mark. The exteriors of Millennium Mansions almost always include details borrowed from one or more historic styles and have a new signature feature—prominent (and largely non-historic) one-and-one-half- or two-story entries.

While some builders were massproducing Millennium Mansions, New Traditional houses began gaining favor elsewhere. Architect and educator Robert Stern led the way in making the design of New Traditional houses acceptable within the architecture profession.

With simple roof forms and unified sets of stylistic detailing, these houses now display an extraordinary range that includes almost all home styles found during the preceding three centuries of American home building. Designing and building New Traditional houses presented an enormous challenge when the public first became interested in

Styled Houses
Since 1935

the late 1970s. The architects, craftsmen, and builders who had been responsible for the design and construction of America's rich heritage of Eclectic-era styles were no longer active, if indeed they were still alive. The monographs of their work—and the great books with photographic views of European architecture they had used for ideas and guidance—were no longer in print. Architecture schools no longer taught historic architecture (even today, less than a handful of universities teach classical design). Thus, almost every New Traditional home one sees is designed by someone who decided to train himself or herself in historic architectural styles. The best of these architects, such as Stern, understand historic precedent well enough to reinterpret or generate new details, keeping the purpose of the original form but giving it a new integrity for today.

Some present-day residential developments include custom-written pattern books that designate architectural styles and specify architectural details.[1] Other developments utilize the approach of regulating house form, generally through form-based zoning. This method relies on creating a streetscape unified by similar size and shape, rather than governing a specific style. It is also possible to combine these two approaches for a high degree of regulation. Architect and planner Andrés Duany of Duany Plater-Zyberk & Co. (DPZ) has pioneered both concepts, designing style pattern books for some traditional neigh-

borhood developments and introducing form-based zoning to create simple harmonious new development in cities and towns.

A third "style"—American Vernacular (sometimes called Regionalism)—is favored by both builders and architects. Unadorned folk houses make up a large part of the nation's built environment, and American Vernacular houses emulate their simple forms. Because these new homes are carefully designed, they leave the realm of folk houses. Generally built of natural materials, American Vernacular houses emphasize the basic shape of any of the folk-house families, or traditions, and avoid style-associated decorative elements. The result is an understated yet familiar appearance created through careful choice of material and window placement, and the avoidance of high-style embellishment.

Together these three groups of houses, all with some historic precedent, make up the great bulk of homes built during the millennial housing boom that began about 1990 and was almost ended by the financial crisis of 2008.

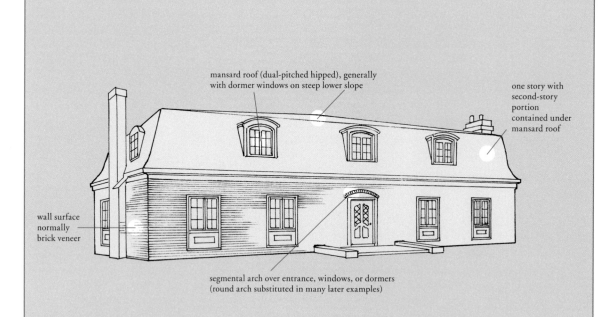

mansard roof (dual-pitched hipped), generally
with dormer windows on steep lower slope

one story with
second-story
portion
contained under
mansard roof

wall surface
normally
brick veneer

segmental arch over entrance, windows, or dormers
(round arch substituted in many later examples)

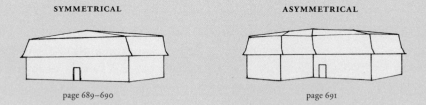

SYMMETRICAL

page 689–690

ASYMMETRICAL

page 691

PRINCIPAL SUBTYPES

Mansard

ca. 1940–1985

Identifying Features

Mansard roof (dual-pitched hipped roof) generally with dormer windows on steep lower slope; segmental arch over entrance, windows, or dormers (round arch substituted in many later examples); one story with a second story often contained under mansard roof; wall surface normally brick veneer.

Principal Subtypes

Two principal subtypes can be distinguished:

SYMMETRICAL—In this subtype the mansard roof dominates a symmetrical facade with centered entry. There are normally three or five ranks of windows; occasionally a side wing is added. In elaborate examples a small central wing may project forward from the front facade or two small wings project forward at either side.

ASYMMETRICAL—This is the most common subtype; its asymmetry is usually based on an L-shaped front-facade plan. The entrance is typically located on the recessed portion of the facade, with a main living space thrust toward the street. Elaborate examples may have a much more complex asymmetry.

Variants and Details

Entries, which are generally arched, grew in prominence and height from the style's inception circa 1940 until its demise circa 1985. Most early examples have an entry with a simple segmental arch above, often recessed into the main body of the house for shelter. A tall, slender, exaggerated entrance (sometimes called a Pullman door) was used by Los Angeles architectural designer John Elgin Woolf beginning in 1946, becoming widespread by 1970. These extended up through the cornice to form a one-and-one-half-story feature, with a one-story door below and tall arched element above. An unelaborated but deep entry surround provided shelter for the door.[2]

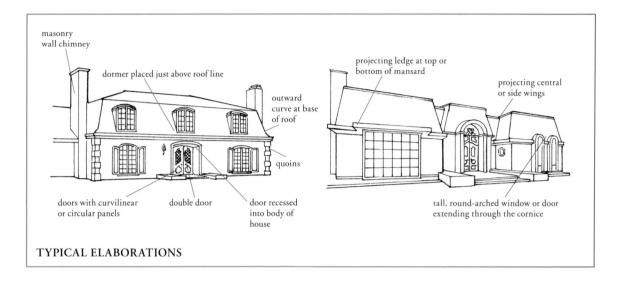

masonry
wall chimney

dormer placed just above roof line

projecting ledge at top or
bottom of mansard

projecting central
or side wings

outward
curve at base
of roof

quoins

doors with curvilinear
or circular panels

double door

door recessed
into body of
house

tall, round-arched window or door
extending through the cornice

TYPICAL ELABORATIONS

Paired front doors are the most common, usually wood panels in curvilinear design that occasionally incorporated a circular or elliptical panel. Stone quoins, or faux quoins shaped from brick, are often used at the corners of the house, or side wings.

Window features may extend to ground level or have an ornamental wood panel beneath the glass window. Roof dormers are almost always found in early versions and provide light to two-story sections of the house. After about 1975 roof dormers were sometimes replaced by very tall windows that extend upward through the cornice. Roof cladding was typically composition, wood shingles, or standing-seam metal.

Mansard houses of the 20th century typically are one story in height (not including whatever floor space might be behind the tall roof) and lack the molded cornices and decorative eave-line brackets frequently found on 19th-century Second Empire houses.

Comments

The Mansard style was the primary formal and "historic" house style built during an era dominated by more informal Ranch-style homes and Contemporary designs. Many of the subdivisions developed from the 1940s through the 1970s had deed restrictions and/ or zoning ordinances that dictated one-story structures or low roof heights. The Mansard style could follow many of these one-story, low-height regulations and still provide a two-story home, as up to a full story of living space was possible under the massive roof. Mansard roofs had historically provided an opportunity to squeeze in an extra story of living space; it is reported that original Second Empire houses in France allowed an extra story that was not taxed because of wording in the tax code.

Architect John Elgin Woolf (1908–1980) helped popularize the style with his Los Angeles–area homes, among them his 1958 Reynolds House in Hancock Park. His designs were embraced by those who yearned for traditional formality—and even drama—and rejected the more prevalent informality of the era. Shunned by the architectural press, Woolf's homes were built for a Who's Who of movie stars and were popularized by articles in shelter magazines.[3]

SYMMETRICAL

1. Atlanta, Georgia; ca. 1960s. The entry and the windows on the central house block have segmental arches.

2. Highland Park, Illinois; 1937. The central entry pavilion gives this a symmetrical feeling that is not completely correct. Each side wing has a different window and dormer pattern. Note the outward flare of the roof and the faux corner quoins.

3. Los Angeles, California; 1958. Reynolds House; John Woolf, designer. This tall, narrow entry design was widely imitated, leading to a new approach to Mansard as seen on page 691 in Figures 5 and 7, and perhaps even to the two-story arched entries found on Millennium Mansions.

4. Beverly Hills, California; 1949. This early example neither has dormers nor contains a second story under the roof.

5. Houston, Texas; ca. 1980s. For a brief period two-story front porte cocheres were popular, imparting a bit of a country club look.

ASYMMETRICAL

1. Prairie Village, Kansas; 1968. Note through-the-cornice windows and the recess of the paired front doors.

2. Lake Forest, Illinois; 1928 (and later). This is a high-style example with roof dormers on the left wing and wall dormers on the right wing. It has almost certainly been modified from its recorded construction date of 1928 and converted into a ca. 1960 Mansard house.

3. Oak Park, Illinois; 1940. Three similar, but not matching, Mansards, on the site of a former Congregational church.

4. Prairie Village, Kansas; 1958. A Tri-Level Split with the Mansard roof only on the two-level section.

5. Dallas, Texas; 1970. Dilbeck House; Charles S. Dilbeck, architect. The use of a boxy curb at the bottom of the Mansard roof was unusual.

6. San Marino, California; 1939. This appears to have had a major stylish update adding dramatic surrounds to the front door and windows.

7. Dallas, Texas; 1977. In this late example, John Woolf–influenced door and windows all are round-arched and extend through the cornice.

The Mansard could be a relatively inexpensive style to build, as only one story of masonry veneer was required, while the remainder of the wall surface was clad in roofing material. As such, it proved very popular for apartment complexes and other small-scale commercial construction.

The style fell from favor in the 1980s, but its exceptionally tall entry door topped by an arch, popularized by Woolf, was likely the genesis of the almost ubiquitous one-and-one-half- to two-story, round-arched entries found on Millennium Mansions until the mid-2000s.

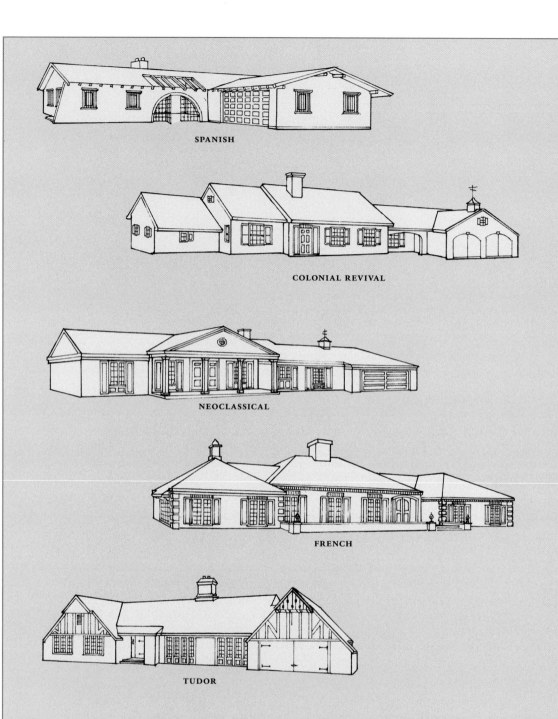

SPANISH

COLONIAL REVIVAL

NEOCLASSICAL

FRENCH

TUDOR

OTHER

Styled Ranch

1935–1985

S tandard Ranch houses frequently incorporate one or more common historic elements—shutters, wrought iron, paneled doors—because lending institutions felt comfortable with the traditional feeling these details impart. What sets a Styled Ranch apart is the presence of a more complete and unified set of stylistic details that spell out a distinct style, such as Spanish. It is a matter of judgment where the Ranch ends and the Styled Ranch begins. If one still wonders, after careful scrutiny, whether one is looking at a Styled Ranch, the answer is probably not.

Styled Ranch houses were built intermittently during the Ranch-house era (1935 to ca. 1975), but they became increasingly common during the 1970s and dominated new one-story homes in the 1980s. Five main styles are common: Spanish, French, Tudor, Colonial Revival, and Neoclassical. All of these styles have features similar to those found on the Eclectic versions of each style but were adapted to a wide, low, one-story form. There were also more exotic Character styles. Each of these could be found throughout the country, but some prevailed in a particular geographic location or time period.

Although Styled Ranches can be found from 1935 onward, before 1970 they were only common where a specific local building tradition or developer promoted their use—for example, in a Spanish Ranch subdivision in Arizona or Colonial Revival Ranches in Massachusetts. By 1970, however, buyers had begun to tire of simple Ranch homes and sought a different look. The 1976 U.S. Bicentennial celebration and a growing nation-wide preservation movement were both generating nostalgia for older styles. The easiest way to achieve a different look was to continue building the familiar one-story Ranch (the low height often required by deed restrictions) while adding strong stylistic details to the exterior.

Styled Ranch designs were prevalent in house pattern books of the 1970s and 1980s. The *Book of Successful Home Plans* by Richard Pollman (Structures Publishing Company, 1976), for example, had multiple plans for five subtypes (Tudor, Spanish, Colonial Revival, Neoclassical, and French). Other home plan books were devoted to a single house style (such as *Colonial Home Plans,* a Bantam/Hudson Plan Book first published in 1977, and *Tudor Houses,* by Home Planner, Inc., in 1989). These pattern books also included the beginnings of the New Traditional House, along with designs for regular Ranch houses.[4]

In general, Styled Ranch houses lack the broad overhanging eaves found on many Ranch houses and are more likely than the Ranch to have a dominant entry and traditional multi-paned windows, and omit short windows, corner windows, and often picture windows. Each Styled Ranch subtype has its own distinctive features, as seen on the following pages. One-and-one-half-story forms had roofs with a higher pitch than the earlier Ranch houses, and the dormers that provided light for the upper half-story were perfectly adapted to Ranch houses styled in the Tudor, Colonial Revival, Neoclassical, and French styles. The extra half-story helped create larger homes (to house master bedroom suites, large bathrooms, and closets) all within the same lot size. As with the Ranch style, split-level variations occur in all subtypes.

Rising land prices, desire for larger homes, and changing tastes gradually led to a new era of two-story houses. The year 1988 was the first time since the beginning of the Federal Housing Administration that a higher percentage of two-story houses were completed. As the one-story Ranch fell from favor during the 1990s, it was replaced by New Traditional houses and Millennium Mansions.

SPANISH RANCH—The earliest Styled Ranch subtype was Spanish. Cliff May, the prolific house designer and builder credited with popularizing the Ranch style, was a sixth-generation Californian. His 1946 book *Sunset Western Ranch Houses* identified the pitched-roof Spanish Colonial homes of southern California as the genesis of the Ranch house and included designs for them. Built throughout the entire Ranch era and into the 1980s, Spanish Ranches are most common in California and the Southwest.

Spanish Ranches are generally clad in stucco (or buff-colored brick) and topped with a tiled roof, most often red and of the types described on page 523. One or more round or parabolic arches are often present, usually at the front entry or porch, principal windows, or courtyard entry. Other decorative elements may include exposed roof rafters and beams, wood or metal window grilles and balconettes, and inward-slanting chimneys or wing walls.

COLONIAL REVIVAL RANCH—This subtype evolved from the broadly popular Minimal Traditional Cape Cod homes of the 1940s. Architect Royal Barry Wills helped keep alive interest in many forms of Colonial Revival with his *Houses for Good Living* (1946) and *More Houses for Good Living* (1968), which include examples of the one-story Ranch. Colonial Revival Ranch houses are often symmetrical or include a symmetrical central house block; the Ranch form may be achieved by adding clear house elements, often with slightly varied roof heights (page 698, Figures 3, 5, and 9). The main house block is most often side-gabled or hipped. Colonial Revival Ranches are commonly clad in one material, usually red brick or wood siding, while attached wings may be of a secondary material. The front door is typically prominent and may be centered and/ or enhanced with a Colonial Revival surround or entry porch. Other Colonial Revival detailing (such as dentils) may be present, as may dormers. The Colonial Revival Ranch was found throughout the Styled Ranch era and is more common along the Atlantic seaboard from Massachusetts south to Georgia.

NEOCLASSICAL RANCH—A less common subtype found more often in southern states, the Neoclassical Ranch style is characterized by a one-story porch supported by Classical columns. The porch may be present only at the entry (entry porch) or

SPANISH RANCH

1. San Diego, California; 1945. Cliff May, architect. This house has strong details, including the boxed wood window grille, deep diagonal-patterned molding on the front door, inward-slanting chimney, and tile roof with a handmade look.

2. Miami, Florida; 1970.

3. Montgomery, Alabama; ca. 1950s. Arched windows and openings to entry courtyard are coupled with "portales."

4. Claremont, California; ca. 1935. An early example that includes a picturesque water well in its imagery (in front of far-right window).

5. Dallas, Texas; 1947. Cox House. This includes a small two-story wing at far left.

6. Carlsbad, California; 1960. A Tri-Level Split with the entrance in a stair tower with two stepped windows.

1

2

3

4

5

6

COLONIAL REVIVAL RANCH

1. San Marino, California; 1948 and 1953. The recessed door has a single line of lights above and is crowned by a small segmental pediment.

2. Mission Hills, Kansas; 1955. Each of the pair of front-facing gables has a small bull's-eye window enhanced with large floral swags; oversized dentils line the cornice.

3. Baltimore, Maryland; 1957. This house has four distinct sections: a three-bay main block with a six-panel door, two-bay side wing, one-car garage, and wood-clad section connecting the house with the garage.

4. Phoenix, Arizona; 1936.

5. Boston, Massachusetts; 1962. Four side-gabled shapes of graduated sizes combine to create a very broad Ranch-house form.

6. Columbus, Georgia; 1953. A symmetrical five-bay center block has an entry with sidelights, a rounded entry porch, and oversized multi-pane double-hung windows.

7. Kansas City, Missouri; 1961. This Tri-Level Split has a second-story overhang clad in wood shingles that were laid close together and in straight lines.

8. Boston, Massachusetts; 1955. The side-facing garages in this wood-clad house are in a side-down section.

9. Prairie Village, Kansas; 1956.

10. Boston, Massachusetts; 1965. Bi-Level Splits like this one are well adapted to centered entries and symmetrical (or almost symmetrical) facades.

2

4

7

8

10

NEOCLASSICAL RANCH

1. Dallas, Texas; ca 1960s. This achieves the look of a five-part plan although it is actually a broad, single house block. The symmetrical gables have broken pediments over the windows.

2. Kansas City, Missouri; 1956.

3. Columbus, Georgia; 1948. A triangular-pedimented portico and double-hung windows dominate this front facade.

4. San Marino, California; 1947. Note the full-width porch and prominent chimney. The picture window is not common on Neoclassical Ranch houses.

5. Kansas City, Missouri; 1959. The red brick main house block has a full-width porch and is flanked by wood-clad side wings.

6. Alexandria, Virginia; 1963. A Bi-Level Split with a centered pair of front doors and a full-height, full-width porch. The columns are quite slender.

FRENCH RANCH

1. San Marino, California; 1947. The front door has matching sidelights.

2. Kansas City, Missouri; 1957.

3. St. Paul, Minnesota; 1972. This five-part composition has a symmetrical central block and hipped-roof wings. Note the tall vertical windows; these are often found on French Ranches.

4. Kansas City, Missouri; ca. 1960s. It is rare for a Tri-Level Split to have a single large hipped roof sheltering the entire house.

TUDOR RANCH

1. Seattle, Washington; 1979. A less common kind of Split—the garage is a half-story down, but a third level above it—that would make this house a Tri-Level Split—is not obvious.

2. Pasadena, California; 1940.

3. Dallas, Texas; ca. 1968. This broad Styled Ranch has a group of three leaded glass windows placed to the left of the nested gables with entry.

4. Dallas, Texas; 1978. Landsberger House. The entry is under the nested gables. At far right a small through-the-cornice dormer has leaded glass windows below.

OTHER STYLED RANCH

1. Phoenix, Arizona; 1960. There was a brief fad for storybook details, such as the entry roof and scalloped windows on this minimal example.

2. Pasadena, California; 1960. This large, cohesive Storybook Ranch shows how successful the fairy tale motif could be. Note the diamond-pane windows, and the pigeonnier in the peak of the asymmetrical gabled roof.

3. Chicago, Illinois; 1959. This house has dramatic upturned "pagoda" corners on the roof and calligraphic details on the garage.

4. Prairie Village, Kansas; 1957. More subtle Oriental imagery than Figure 3, this Tri-Level Split has a moon-gate picture window, an Oriental post-and-beam entry, and balcony railings with bamboo imagery.

extend the full width of the house. Generally there is a symmetrical main block. Often clad in brick, it is sometimes also accompanied by sections of wood frame. Traditional multi-pane windows are typically used, and roof dormers may be present.

FRENCH RANCH—Called "French Provincial" and "formal" in pattern books, French Ranches were most popular during the 1970s and 1980s. Generally, at least one portion of the house (commonly the central block) is topped by a high-pitched hipped roof. One or more segmental arches are usually present (on doors, windows, or dormers). Windows are usually tall and narrow, sometimes full height. The front entry is typically prominent and features a paneled front door (both paired doors and curvilinear panels are common). Tall narrow shutters generally enhance windows and/or entry. Walls are frequently clad with brick veneer.

French Ranches may be either symmetrical or asymmetrical. Symmetrical examples may have small side wings, either extending forward or set back from the main facade. (Some early survey books on Ranch houses assign the category French Provincial to most cross-hipped Ranch houses. In this guide, we look for a more complete set of style characteristics to categorize hipped and cross-hipped Ranch houses as French Ranch.)[5]

TUDOR RANCH—The Tudor Ranch style relied on half-timbering as a stylistic element and it is almost always present, generally attached to the exterior. *Tudor Houses* explained that half-timbering "evolved into a decorative device applied after the framing had been covered by a continuous wraparound surface of brick, wood, stucco or stone." In other words, the wood "timbers" were simply attached to the finished surface, rather than slightly recessed into the exterior, as in the Eclectic era.[6] While roughly one-third of Eclectic-era Tudors had half-timbering, it appears on almost all Tudor Ranches.

A second stylistic element often present are casement windows, sometimes with diamond-shaped panes. Occasionally, decorative garage doors are used. The roof form is typically gabled or cross-gabled.

The pattern books of the day referred to these as "Tudor adaptations" and "English styling." Like the French Ranches, these were most popular during the 1970s and 1980s.

OTHER RANCH—There were many decorative effects the builders of Ranch homes occasionally used to make a home recognizably different. One of the earliest was a "Hansel and Gretel" storybook look, resembling the Exotic Revival's Swiss Chalet, with an added vergeboard of deep scallops that swooped down across the front facade. Often accompanied by diamond-shaped windowpanes and copious window boxes, the Storybook Ranch sold well in the early 1950s but soon dropped from favor.[7]

Another early set of less common detailing was Oriental. Some were Japanese, with a pagoda form to the roof. Other Oriental-themed details could be added to enhance the effect—moon-gates, cast-iron hardware, Japanese-style gardens, etc. A Polynesian theme and details were also used.

One of the last of these to appear was Victorian. Growing out of the infatuation with old houses that emerged from the growing neighborhood preservation movement in the 1970s, it is easily identified by the broad low Ranch form with a spindlework porch and sometimes even a turret.

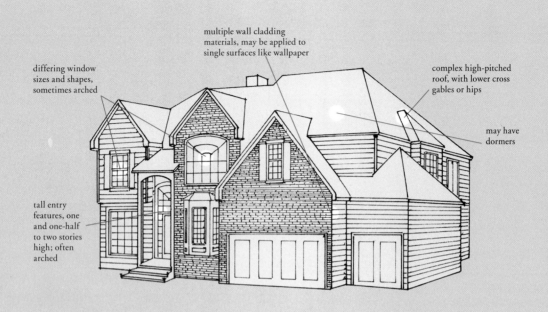

multiple wall cladding
materials, may be applied to
single surfaces like wallpaper

differing window
sizes and shapes,
sometimes arched

complex high-pitched
roof, with lower cross
gables or hips

may have
dormers

tall entry
features, one
and one-half
to two stories
high; often
arched

commonly asymmetrical

HIPPED ROOF WITH
LOWER CROSS GABLES

HIPPED ROOF WITH
LOWER CROSS HIPS

GABLED ROOF WITH
LOWER CROSS GABLES

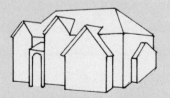

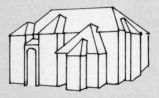

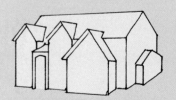

pages 710–11

pages 712–13

pages 714–15

PRINCIPAL SUBTYPES

Millennium Mansion

1985–Present

Identifying Features

Complex high-pitched roof, with lower cross gables or hips; tall entry features, one and one-half to two stories high and often arched; dormers; multiple wall-cladding materials, may be applied to single surfaces like wallpaper; differing window sizes and shapes, sometimes arched; commonly asymmetrical and with tall vertical appearance.

Principal Subtypes

The roofs of Millennium Mansions are quite varied. Here they are loosely grouped into hipped roof with lower cross gables (appears to be the most common), hipped roof with lower cross-hipped roofs, and gabled roof with lower cross gables.

Variants and Details

After half a century dominated by low, broad, one-story houses with simple uncluttered roof lines and underplayed entries, a dramatic new form of house virtually exploded from the drawing boards of building designers and spread quickly across the country during the 1990s. Sporting a roof form seen only once before—on exuberant Queen Anne and Romanesque houses just before the turn of the 20th century—Millennium Mansion roofs added even more complexity, as if to celebrate the new millennium with still more drama. Many Millennium Mansions have the high-pitched hipped roof with lower cross gables of the late 19th century (but with more gables per house), while others sport a roof rarely seen before—a hip-on-hip roof that sometimes expanded into cascading hips-on-hips-on-hips. Roof and wall dormers are both common and roof ridges are often discontinuous, adding more complexity to the roof line. These complicated roofs can be thought of as crowns, or, more satirically, as the Future Roofers of America Relief Act. The complex roof forms sometimes relate to bay windows, or other small extensions in the ground plan, that are expressed in the elevation of the house and continue into the roof form.[8]

The style's vertical appearance is not only a result of the typical two-story height. It also reflects taller interior ceiling heights (ten feet is now standard, and higher heights can be used) and taller floor joists engineered to allow more room for mechanical systems between the floors. Millennium Mansions are frequently built out to the limits of the zoning envelope (meaning they contain as much square footage as is legally allowed on a lot).

The entry into many Millennium Mansions assumed a new dominance—generally one-and-a-half or two stories tall and arched—a feature introduced by Hollywood architect John Wolff in his dramatic Mansard and Regency designs. Often an arched window is placed above the front door. This one-and-a-half- or two-story entry was not simply an exterior feature; it generally signals the presence of a two-story interior entry foyer that often leads into a two-story great room—a pair of interior features that became popular beginning about 1985.[9] Decades of the Ranch style's standardized eight-foot ceilings had led to a craving for very high ceilings. Ground-floor master bedroom suites injected a bit of interior practicality. By 2005, a tower—sometimes part of or adjacent to the entry—was being touted in real estate ads for new homes, and the earlier two-story entries were beginning to lose their broad appeal.[10]

Walls are often clad in several materials—sometimes applied as a thin sheet on a single surface, treating the cladding almost like wallpaper. Windows are typically of varied size and shape, and may not even be from the same design family.[11] Traditional detailing—French, Mediterranean, and English in derivation—is generally present on the exterior, and details may be a mixture of historic styles.[12] As this guide is going to press, Millennium Mansions appear to be growing less exuberant. In addition to entries shrinking to one story, windows are more likely to be from the same family, producing a more related design. Detailing is more frequently becoming associated with a single historic style—such as Tudor or French—with Mediterranean now gaining favor in Texas, California, and the Southwest.[13] The more tame and "proper" New Traditional house might gradually subsume the exuberant Millennium Mansion.[14]

Comments

The Millennium Mansion is the predominant style in many large subdivisions built from the late 1980s up to the present. They can be built on higher-priced land because their vertical massing allows far more square feet per lot than the horizontal Ranch house. It has been used as infill for older neighborhoods and, for a time, was also favored for huge custom-designed homes of five thousand to ten thousand square feet and up. These are generally built as a single massive structure, rather than broken down into visually distinct smaller additive elements, as is often the case with other contemporaneous styles (see illustration, p. 754). This penchant for size, particularly when interspersed amid small, earlier neighboring houses—or scattered on super-large far-flung rural lots—led to the nickname *McMansion*, initially used for Millennium Mansions but now referring to any new house deemed to be either oversized in comparison with adjacent homes or disjointed in style.

CASCADING HIPPED ROOFS: indicative of Millennium Mansions (uncommon before ca. 1985)

Seven cascading hipped roofs are visible from side facade

Five cascading hipped roofs (also called hip-on-hip roofs) and three lower cross-gables are visible from street

Regular ground-plans, with few extensions, allow simpler roof forms

ca. 1920s

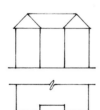

Irregular ground-plans, with shallow extensions added, allow create complex roof forms

ca. 2000

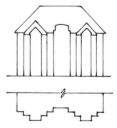

GROUND PLANS RELATED TO ROOF FORMS

LARGE WINDOW OFTEN ABOVE DOOR
commonly arched up to one-story in height

FRONT DOOR OFTEN PAIRED OR VERY WIDE
elaborate exterior decorative iron work common

TALL ENTRY PORCHES
(most popular ca. 1990–2005)

HIPPED ROOF WITH LOWER CROSS GABLES

1. Duluth, Minnesota; 1994. Note the three levels of the ridge of the main hipped roof (compare to the single long ridge on page 715, Figure 4). As in Figure 4 on this page, nested gables highlight both the garage entry and the front-door entry. However, in this example they are appropriate to the Tudor theme.

2. Kansas City, Missouri; 1997. This house appears to be clad in stucco board but with seams left exposed. This could indicate the boards are being used as a rain screen and the cracks are actually providing ventilation.

3. Naperville, Illinois; 2006. Millennium Mansions often incorporate Palladian-inspired windows as seen here above the entry and right wing; window on right is patched from three identical windows with an over-large round arch window above. The Palladian window motif, red brick and keystone lintels—even above the double garage door—evoke the Colonial Revival (see page 714, Figure 3). Note very closely spaced balusters (likely required by current building code).

4. Chicago, Illinois; 1996. Stone quoins, originally used to reinforce corners, assume a Postmodern look when used for two-story tall porch supports and to support gables on a garage wing. Note how nested gables relate to both garage bays and a two-story entry.

5. Naperville, Illinois; ca. 2006. Side automobile courts have recently become utilized as a way to handle multiple cars when alleys are not present to provide a rear automobile entrance.

6. Seattle, Washington; 2003. One-story Millennium Mansions are less common. Note how garages are placed in two different planes. At least eight roof levels and elements are present.

7. Duluth, Minnesota; ca. 2000. Note the five jerkinhead roofs.

8. Chicago, Illinois; ca. 1990s. Note the use of three completely different kinds of arched windows.

9. Naperville, Illinois; 2007. Each front-facing gable is different.

1

4

7

8

HIPPED ROOF WITH LOWER CROSS HIPS

1. Duluth, Minnesota; 1995. Cascading hipped roof, but otherwise calm details for a Millennium Mansion.

2. Dallas, Texas; ca. 1980. When this photo was published in the 1984 edition, the authors had no idea the cascading hip and two-story entry were harbingers of a style that would sweep the country.

3. Leawood, Kansas; 2005. The one-and-a-half-story entry seems short next to the adjacent two-story tower.

4. Leawood, Kansas; 2007. Part of the same developments as the two photos on page 709. This shows the shift to Mediterranean-style details with squared entries that occurred in some Millennium Mansion developments—even beyond Florida and the Southwest—in the 2000s.

5. Naperville, Illinois; 2005. An unusual stucco rectangle—with rounded arch in the center—provides the design theme for this house. Three different sizes are cut out and the fourth extends upward through a cornice. There is likely no historic structural precedent for this use of a rounded arch.

6. Naperville, Illinois; 2005. Nine separate hipped-roof forms are visible. Note the matching round arches above the entry and wall dormer, and the two large contrasting bay windows.

7. Lake Oswego, Oregon; 1989. Garages comprise more than one-half of the one-story facade. The roof is five cascading hips and is twice the height of the facade.

8. Dallas, Texas; 2005. This house has three easily visible hip-on-hip roof forms—one on each of the side wings and one above the front entry. Relatively consistent detailing, a single wall cladding, and an underplayed one-story entrance make this transitional to New Traditional French.

2

5

7

1

3

4

6

8

GABLED ROOF WITH LOWER CROSS GABLES

1. Duluth, Minnesota; 1996. Brick is used like wallpaper on the left side wing, the two-story entry, and the gabled double garage.

2. Baltimore, Maryland; ca. 1990s.

3. Alexandria, Virginia (vicinity); 2005. Small keystones are used throughout—over single windows, triple windows, garage doors, and two-story entry arches. These, along with red brick cladding on the front facade, impart a Colonial Revival flavor to this Millennium Mansion, despite the three front-facing gables.

4. Houston, Texas; 2004. Three heights are visible across the main roof ridge, and there are nine gables (including a small gabled roof dormer atypically nested in the left roof gable) and eight different sizes and types of windows. However, the single wall cladding, one-story entry, and similar segmental arched openings make this transitional to a New Traditional Tudor.

5. Carlsbad, California; 1970 with later additions. It appears that a 1970s house has had a Millennium Mansion remodeling. The original cross-gabled Ranch is in the middle. It seems to have been expanded by a double-gabled addition and pop-up on right, three dormers on the Ranch form, and new wing on left—attached to what may have been the original garage wing.

6. Phoenix, Arizona; ca. 2000. Multiple roof forms and a one-and-one-half-story-high entry mark this as a Millennium Mansion; the tile roof and stucco add a Mediterranean influence.

7. Chicago, Illinois; 2008. A familiar, yet unusual house. The complex cross-gabled roof and front porch might put it in New Traditional Queen Anne. The single wall material and lack of elaborate detail in the gables or along the porch could be a "more complex roof form" American Vernacular. But by the time one adds up nine different roof elements, it seems to approach being a Millennium Mansion—perhaps one marketed as a "new farmhouse."

1

3

6

NEW TRADITIONAL SHINGLE

NEW TRADITIONAL COLONIAL REVIVAL

NEW TRADITIONAL CLASSICAL

NEW TRADITIONAL ITALIAN RENAISSANCE

NEW TRADITIONAL TUDOR

NEW TRADITIONAL FRENCH

NEW TRADITIONAL VICTORIAN

NEW TRADITIONAL CRAFTSMAN

NEW TRADITIONAL PRAIRIE

NEW TRADITIONAL MEDITERRANEAN

New Traditional

After almost half a century dominated by modernism, the 1970s saw a renewed interest in historical styles that produced what today are called New Traditional houses. The first houses little resembled the earlier styled homes they sought to emulate. The 1984 edition of this guide had a brief chapter, "Neoeclectic," that illustrated builder examples of both Styled Ranch houses and two-story homes with relatively awkward proportions and details. Early architect-designed examples often featured abstracted Postmodern historic details. By the 1990s, however, New Traditional houses with more historically accurate proportions, forms, and details were being sought by clients and designed in nearly all the earlier styles.

Homes are commonly based on styles popular in the early 20th century—Colonial Revival, Tudor, Neoclassical, French, Italian Renaissance, Spanish, Craftsman, and Prairie. Romantic- and Victorian-era styles are also found, with Shingle style being by far the most common of these. The many styles of New Traditional are geographically spread throughout the United States; some styles, however, are favored locally, often with a bow to earlier traditions (for example, New Traditional Colonial Revival in New England, New Traditional Shingle on Long Island, and New Traditional Mediterranean in Arizona and southern California).

In traditional house design, both the overall composition and the individual details of each style are important. The earlier chapters of this guide have illustrations and photographs of the kinds of homes that have inspired New Traditional houses. Prior to 1930, traditional houses were most often constructed by builders who were familiar with these details. Today this is generally not the case—and careful study of precedents is important.[15]

The following pages of illustrations are not desirable details to emulate. Instead they are details that usually signal a recent construction date, making it easy to distinguish the majority of turn-of-the-millennium New Traditional houses from their earlier precedents. *It is to be emphasized that these are not desirable details to be used in constructing a new home or in a design review process;* rather, these are generally details to be avoided, as each immediately signals new construction. In the deftest of hands, it is difficult to distinguish a New Traditional from an earlier construction simply by looking at the exterior. The location and size of the house and the garage both provide clues, as do slightly inventive details—and the rear facade, if visible.

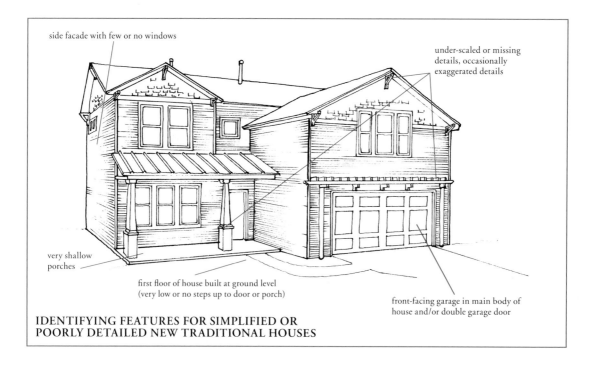

side facade with few or no windows

under-scaled or missing details, occasionally exaggerated details

very shallow porches

first floor of house built at ground level (very low or no steps up to door or porch)

front-facing garage in main body of house and/or double garage door

IDENTIFYING FEATURES FOR SIMPLIFIED OR POORLY DETAILED NEW TRADITIONAL HOUSES

Identifying Features for Simplified or Poorly Detailed New Traditional Houses

FRONT-FACING GARAGE INCORPORATED INTO MAIN BODY OF HOUSE— Side wings with garages might have been added later, but if you see a main house block that includes a front-facing garage, or a garage wing extending to the front, more often indicates a post-1935 house.

FEW OR NO WINDOWS IN SIDE FACADES—Pre-1935 houses generally lacked air-conditioning and required many windows that opened for summer temperature control and air circulation. Today's homes have no such restrictions, and although windows can be expensive to buy and install, when builders are urged to include more side windows they rarely mention cost and instead cite the advantages of arranging interior furnishings without interference from windows—providing a "sofa wall" and "bed walls"—and dismiss assurances from those who live in older homes that furniture actually can be arranged in front of windows.

PORCHES TOO SHALLOW TO BE REALLY USABLE—These look like a porch from the street (and on elevations presented for design review) but are not deep enough to accommodate porch swings, chairs, or chaises with space to walk past them—like the true living porches of homes built before air-conditioning.

BUILT ON SLAB FOUNDATION WITH FIRST FLOOR AT GROUND LEVEL; FEW OR NO STEPS UP TO FIRST FLOOR OF THE HOUSE—Slab foundations for houses gained popularity during the 1950s and 1960s and worked well for Ranch and Mid-century Modern houses where indoor spaces flowed outside. Even here, the slab

poorly scaled dormer windows

missing cornice board

few windows in side facade

missing glass in or around front door

under-scaled porch support

under-scaled, shallow roof overhangs

missing entablature or beam (roof sits directly on porch supports)

very shallow porches (three to six feet)

at ground level on slab foundation

SIMPLIFIED OR POORLY DETAILED NEW TRADITIONAL HOUSE

cornice board present

many windows in side facade

glass present in front door and sidelights

porch supports of early 20th-century proportions

historic roof overhang depth (often three feet or more in Prairie style)

entablature or beam present (porch roof separated from porch supports)

room-depth porches (seven to twelve feet)

raised foundation with steps to front-door level

WELL-DETAILED NEW TRADITIONAL HOUSE

COMPARISON OF DETAILING IN NEW TRADITIONAL HOUSES

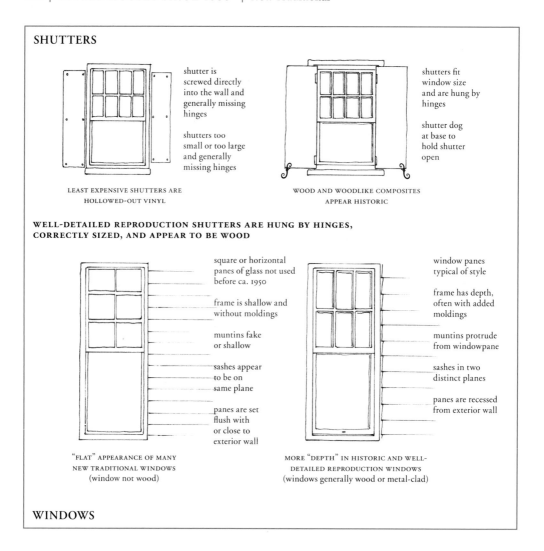

SHUTTERS

shutter is screwed directly into the wall and generally missing hinges

shutters too small or too large and generally missing hinges

LEAST EXPENSIVE SHUTTERS ARE
HOLLOWED-OUT VINYL

shutters fit window size and are hung by hinges

shutter dog at base to hold shutter open

WOOD AND WOODLIKE COMPOSITES
APPEAR HISTORIC

**WELL-DETAILED REPRODUCTION SHUTTERS ARE HUNG BY HINGES,
CORRECTLY SIZED, AND APPEAR TO BE WOOD**

square or horizontal panes of glass not used before ca. 1950

frame is shallow and without moldings

muntins fake or shallow

sashes appear to be on same plane

panes are set flush with or close to exterior wall

"FLAT" APPEARANCE OF MANY
NEW TRADITIONAL WINDOWS
(window not wood)

window panes typical of style

frame has depth, often with added moldings

muntins protrude from windowpane

sashes in two distinct planes

panes are recessed from exterior wall

MORE "DEPTH" IN HISTORIC AND WELL-
DETAILED REPRODUCTION WINDOWS
(windows generally wood or metal-clad)

WINDOWS

was often poured high enough to raise the house one or two shallow steps above grade. Many New Traditional houses do not even have this small amount of elevation.[16]

Variants and Details for Simplified or Poorly Detailed New Traditional Houses

The above items are the most obvious elements to look for. Finding under-scaled or missing elements is more challenging and may require referring back to the chapter on the style of the house being examined. Careful reproductions are almost impossible to distinguish from earlier homes, particularly from the street. Some of the most common differences follow.

WINDOWS—The majority of new windows are made from vinyl, fiberglass, aluminum, or metal-clad wood. In general, these are much flatter (have less depth) than earlier wood windows. This flatness can be observed in every part of the window: it is recessed

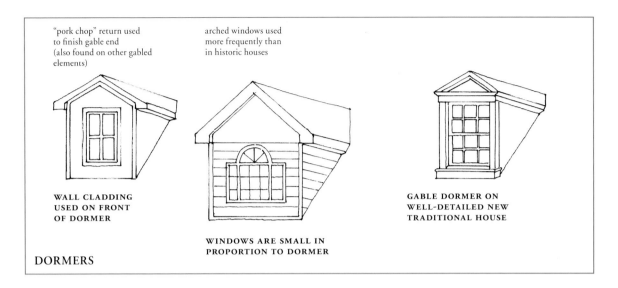

"pork chop" return used to finish gable end (also found on other gabled elements)

arched windows used more frequently than in historic houses

WALL CLADDING USED ON FRONT OF DORMER

WINDOWS ARE SMALL IN PROPORTION TO DORMER

GABLE DORMER ON WELL-DETAILED NEW TRADITIONAL HOUSE

DORMERS

from the front wall surface (this space is called the "reveal," because in old construction it revealed how thick the wall was), the thickness of the sliding sashes (if present), and the depth of the muntin bar that holds (or appears to hold) smaller glass panes in place. Window sashes originally had to be manufactured from many small panes of glass, and first leading, then later wood muntins, were used to assemble these panes into a single window sash. Since the late 19th century, when large panes of glass became readily available, windows with multiple lights have been a stylistic choice, not a necessity. Today, insulated double-glass panes are proportionately far less expensive in larger sizes, while there is an added cost for reproducing small-pane window patterns. Muntins can be emulated cheaply by tape or a shallow grid inserted between the double panes. Neither of these techniques produces a significant shadow or depth. More convincingly, molding is applied to the exterior and interior of a large double-glass pane to simulate individual panes (with an added charge for each pane thus).

SHUTTERS—Today a shutter of wood or a composite that resembles wood can cost ten times as much as a vinyl copy; thus the temptation to use vinyl is high. The least expensive vinyl shutters are only exterior "shells," applied with screws to the wall surface. Because these are easily available in prefab sizes, they often are slightly too short, too long, too narrow, or too wide to actually close over the window (which their method of attachment makes impossible anyway). Exposed attachment screw heads, visible vinyl bubbles covering attachment screws, and/or flexible shutter surface curving inward (from screws having been too tightly applied) are all giveaways.

DORMERS—Dormers are widely used, particularly where building codes define house height as the "mid-point" of the roof. Constructing a higher roof pitch and inserting multiple dormers for light and space can effectively add an extra story to a house. Simplified or poorly detailed new dormers include windows far smaller than the dormer they are placed in, wall cladding used on the front surface of a dormer, and dormers placed very close to the edge of the roof to provide more interior space. A "pork chop" eave

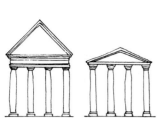

ENTABLATURE
missing or incorrectly proportioned

COLUMNS
too skinny and/or incorrectly placed

HISTORICALLY CORRECT PORTICO

PILASTERS
missing from typical locations

HISTORIC PILASTER LOCATION
against wall of porch with columns

PORTICOS

PILASTERS

tall Millennium Mansion style entry

dentils are exaggerated

entablature is missing

columns incorrectly placed (set in from the sides of the pediment)

pilaster is missing from wall behind columns

columns are too skinny

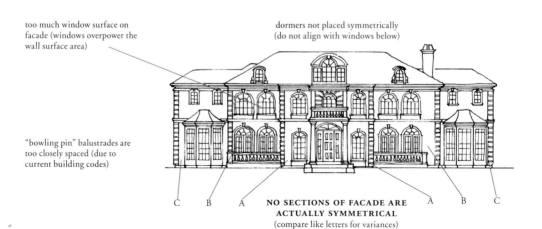

too much window surface on facade (windows overpower the wall surface area)

dormers not placed symmetrically (do not align with windows below)

"bowling pin" balustrades are too closely spaced (due to current building codes)

C   B   A

NO SECTIONS OF FACADE ARE ACTUALLY SYMMETRICAL
(compare like letters for variances)

A   B   C

MORE "CLASSICAL" DETAILS FOR SIMPLIFIED OR POORLY DETAILED NEW TRADITIONAL HOUSES

FEATURES:

1. tall entry elements, one and one-half to two stories, often arched

2. complex roof form with nonessential and/or many elements

3. multiple wall cladding materials used like wallpaper

4. many different window shapes and sizes, often including round-arched tops

MILLENNIUM MANSION FEATURES
(if two or more are present, consider Millennium Mansion as possible style)

return is very common on gabled dormers and is also used with other gabled elements of the house. This easily constructed detail, named for its pork-chop shape and widely used beginning in the 1950s, is today routinely substituted for a traditional gable return.

CLASSICAL DETAILS—A New Traditional house with Classical roots has many historic details. Each represents an opportunity to err; entire books illustrate these (see note 15, page 791). Most commonly, columns are too skinny, too few, or poorly spaced. The entablature (the horizontal-beam element placed atop columns supporting the triangular pediment or cornice above) may be omitted or incorrectly proportioned. Pilasters (flattened columns) may be omitted from common locations. These include placement against the back wall of a colonnaded porch or portico to visually connect it to the house, on each side of a door with a pediment or entablature above, and on elaborate Palladian windows. Most disconcertingly, houses that look symmetrical initially may be slightly asymmetrical in many small ways.

"half-timbering" does not relate to window placements; sometimes spaced to cover joints in four-foot-wide siding

"half-timbering" in historic houses relates to structural design and window placement

HALF-TIMBERING: not related to structure, like originals

MILLENNIUM MANSION–INFLUENCED FEATURES—These relate to common identifying features of Millennium Mansions: tall entries, one and one-half to two stories in height and often with an arched element; varied wall cladding materials, often applied to single surfaces like wallpaper; windows in many different shapes and sizes; and a complex roof form with nonessential elements. If there are two of these present, consider Millennium Mansion as the style.

HALF-TIMBERING CLUES—Today half-timbering is sometimes placed to cover the joints in sheets of four-foot-wide siding and does not relate to window placement or gable design. True half-timbering originally provided a home's structure and therefore naturally related to story changes, window placement, and gable design. Late 19th- and early 20th-century Tudor houses generally applied half-timbering to mimic historic structural patterns.

WALL CLADDING—Wall cladding materials are often intermixed, particularly in builder's houses. The development of thinner and less expensive stone cladding, shallow half-depth bricks for cladding, manufactured stone veneers, stucco board, and a wide variety of fabricated materials have led to greater use of masonry and stucco, often combined with imitation wood such as HardiePlank, HardieShingles, or vinyl siding. Today wall materials are often applied in vertical sections (a thin brick gable front might be found on an otherwise HardiePlank structure—a bit like applying brick wallpaper on the gable end). Historically, materials were built in horizontal layers (a solid structural masonry first floor with a wood second story).

GARAGES—The number and size of garages in new homes has grown dramatically, not uncommonly to three or more—with one often oversized. Garage access and placement is one of the first things that must be addressed when designing a New Traditional house. Garages facing the street deaden the public space; rear garages accessed from the alley or a front drive are ideal. When the illustrated street-accessed garage patterns appear, it likely means a New Traditional house rather than one from the Eclectic era.

REAR FACADES—Unlike front facades, rear facades vary significantly from historic precedents. Freed from many of the needs for utilitarian areas (such as a back porch with

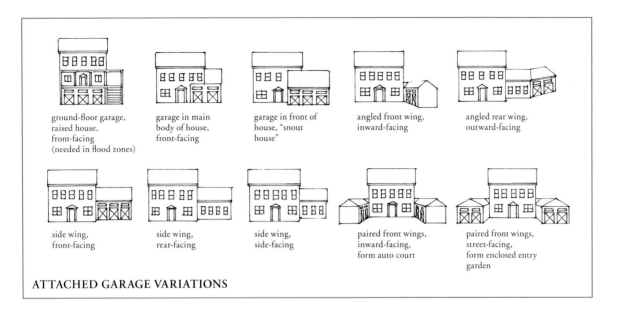

ground-floor garage,
raised house,
front-facing
(needed in flood zones)

garage in main
body of house,
front-facing

garage in front of
house, "snout
house"

angled front wing,
inward-facing

angled rear wing,
outward-facing

side wing,
front-facing

side wing,
rear-facing

side wing,
side-facing

paired front wings,
inward-facing,
form auto court

paired front wings,
street-facing,
form enclosed entry
garden

ATTACHED GARAGE VARIATIONS

icebox and space for washtubs) or access to exterior work areas (such as clotheslines), they can instead offer full interaction with rear gardens and views through large windows, complete window walls, porches, balconies, decks, and terraces.

ADDITIONAL DETAILS—The most obvious clue is a chimney that is not masonry but rather a rectangular box shape clad in wood or siding sometimes with metal flue caps exposed above. Arches also provide clues, among them three (or more) shapes of arch on the same house or arches not properly completed where they meet a pier or wall. Larger houses may be massive rather than composed of smaller additive sections (illustration, see page 754).

Comments

Architect Robert A. M. Stern (b. 1939), a faculty member of Columbia University and later dean of the Yale School of Architecture, has been a pivotal leader in this movement, beginning with his first Shingle-style houses in the late 1970s. His preeminent position and prolific publication has given his work a broad influence. Stern authored numerous books on his designs that by 1990 already included houses inspired by the Shingle, Italian Renaissance, and Georgian Revival styles; his stylistic inspirations have continued to broaden. It is important to note that Stern's work, and that of other talented New Traditional architects, is not completely derivative. Rather, they understand classical principles and architectural style well enough to subtly alter or rearrange elements to create New Traditional home designs, not copies—houses instantly familiar yet subtly different from the homes that inspired them. Architectural historian Vincent Scully describes this as a "conversation across the generations."[17]

At the neighborhood level, architect and planner Andrés Duany (b. 1949; Duany Plater-Zyberk & Company) and others have included stylistic guidelines in plans for traditional neighborhood developments since the 1980s—generally based upon local building traditions and styles. These can be very specific in requirements (or incentives) for use of certain styles, for elements such as front porches, and/or for certain colors or materials.

Today, New Traditional houses are constructed throughout the United States—as country houses on large estates, as infill for older neighborhoods, and in new developments, many of which require historic house styles. But there is an extraordinary disconnect between the styles of these widely built homes and the homes featured in most professional architecture periodicals. While prior to 1970 there was a general lineage from architecture-award-winning homes to those being built in typical American neighborhoods, today the AIA and time-honored publications such as *Architectural Record* rarely give even passing notice to New Traditional homes—despite the fact that a nationwide cadre of architects and building designers are creating them to fulfill strong consumer demand.

This disconnect led to the founding of the Institute of Classical Architecture and Art in 2002.[18] In addition, two periodicals originally focused on the preservation of older houses have specifically advocated New Traditional houses: *Clem Labine's Period Homes* and *Old House Journal's New Old House. Architectural Digest,* with its audience of affluent tastemakers and primary focus on interiors, has featured many New Traditional houses—as have a host of other widely distributed shelter magazines, such as *House Beautiful.*

Designing and building New Traditional houses presented an enormous challenge when interest in historic styles reemerged in the 1970s. When Robert Venturi's *Complexity and Contradiction in Architecture* was published in 1966, the body of knowledge needed to build houses with historic precedent had largely disappeared.[19] It had been more than thirty years since such houses were being built, and the architects and builders who had produced them were no longer active. The monographs of Eclectic architects' work and the books illustrating European precedents and details were no longer in print. Architecture schools were only teaching modernism—even today, with the exception of less than a handful of universities, this is still true. Some architects of New Traditional houses use the 1984 edition of this book to communicate with clients about the kind of house they would like.

Every early New Traditional house was designed by someone self-trained in appropriate forms and details. However, in the last fifteen years architecture books have been published, period reproduction products developed, and new websites launched to make building New Traditional houses easier. As a result, almost every earlier house style was built somewhere in the United States during the millennium housing boom.[20]

Shingle was the first New Traditional style broadly adopted by architects. Two late-modern styles, Shed and Postmodern, were often clad in shingles and sometimes published as new Shingle houses.[21] By 1990, Shingle houses with simpler forms and detailing were being designed by architects. In 1994, *Life* magazine began a new House of the Year program—because, they explained, so many people were having to just "settle" for a house, rather than really loving it. Their initial design was a fine New Traditional Shingle house, and the architect was, appropriately, Robert Stern.[22] The Shingle continues to be a favorite.

While Colonial Revival homes continued to be built occasionally during the 1950s and 1960s (primarily the Built-in Garage subtype), by the 1970s houses based on the complete range of English Colonial and Colonial Revival precedents sharply increased in popularity with builders. At first these New Traditional Colonial homes utilized a wide range of free adaptations and were often oddly proportioned (called Neocolonial in the 1984 edition of this book). By the 1980s better proportioned and architect-designed Colonial Revival houses were being built. Kentlands in Gaithersburg, Maryland, is an excellent example of a 1988 traditional neighborhood development that required Colonial Revival through its building codes.[23]

New Traditional Classical homes generally have the full-height columns or pilasters of earlier Classical styles; these were at first freely applied to a variety of house forms by builders with little concern for historically accurate detailing. By the 1990s, architects favored houses with Classical precedents and were designing a wide variety of beautifully detailed homes based on ancient Classical styles—as well as Renaissance Classical, seen primarily in New Traditional Italian Renaissance homes.

New Traditional Tudors have been a favorite since the late 1970s. Like their more correctly detailed pre-1935 predecessors, these have dominant, steeply pitched front gables, and far more commonly than their predecessors they have half-timbered detailing.

New Traditional French houses also appeared in the late 1970s and by the mid-1980s were among the most fashionable throughout the country, reaching a level of popularity never achieved by their quite varied pre-1935 French Eclectic forebears. These are typically characterized by high-hipped roofs and through-the-cornice-dormers (often with segmental arches). More recently these have been joined by houses inspired by French Colonial and more elaborate Chateauesque and Beaux Arts precedents. These all have been facilitated by stucco exterior boards and new types of stone and faux-stone cladding.

Around 1980 New Traditional versions of the various Victorian styles began to be built. Most New Traditional Victorian houses are Folk Victorian or Queen Anne with spindlework porch detailing. Other Victorian styles can also be found. In the 1990s New Traditional Craftsman began to gain in popularity, as did New Traditional Prairie houses.

Perhaps the most recent to be widely built are New Traditional Mediterranean homes. These include homes based on the Spanish Revival, as well as a newer source of inspiration, Tuscan (based loosely on the rural houses of Italy, often with squared towers). Most New Traditional Mediterranean houses have rounded arches, red tile roofs, and stucco walls that may include large sections clad with stone, a combination rarely if ever used in the Eclectic era.

New Traditional House Styles (page references to original style)

NEW TRADITIONAL SHINGLE—Generally based on precedents found on pages 373–84.

NEW TRADITIONAL COLONIAL—Generally based on precedents found in the Postmedieval English: pages 159–66, Dutch Colonial: pages 169–76, Georgian: pages 201–14, Federal: pages 217–32, and Colonial Revival: pages 409–32.

SHINGLE

1. Fishers Island, New York; 1985. Berkowitz House; Albert, Righter & Tittman, architects. Also inspired by the Low House (page 379, Figure 8), this design angles the main facade, bending it backward on the right.

2. Medina, Washington (vicinity); 2008. A rectilinear interpretation of a Palladian window in the gables. Note how the side of the garage wing (on right) is detailed as if it were simply part of the house.

3. Fishers Island; 1981. "Gable in a Square"; Albert, Righter & Tittmann, architects. The broad front-facing gable of the Low House (page 379, Figure 8) has inspired this creative geometry.

4. Boston, Massachusetts (vicinity); 2001. Note the shingles curving into the recessed window in the gable.

5. East Hampton, New York; 2005. Mullen House; John Mullen, architect. A home with handsome, understated details. The entry is actually onto a split-level a few feet below the first floor.

6. East Hampton, New York; 1999. Shope Rheno Wharton Architects. This house has a broad symmetrical facade. Note the bank of paired doors leading from the house to the garden.

7. Seattle, Washington; 2005. A front-gabled Shingle with a 21st-century interpretation of cottage windows on the first floor.

8. St. Paul, Minnesota; ca. 2000. This has a full-width porch and multiple shed dormers on a gable roof.

3

6

7

2

4

5

8

SHINGLE (cont.)

9. East Hampton, New York; 2004. A builder's interpretation of the entry porch Robert Stern used in Figure 11. The dead space in between the round arch and the gambrel roof could hold the family archives.

10. Annapolis, Maryland; ca. 2000.

11. Water Mill, New York; 1984–1987. Residence at Calf Creek; Robert A. M. Stern, architect. This gambrel roof example has deft detailing in the arched fanlight over the entrance.

12. Bedminster Township, New Jersey; 1985–1988. Residence at Pottersville; Robert A. M. Stern, architect. The faux window (opening without glass) in the pediment is a postmodern salute to the round and elliptical (oculus) windows sometimes found on pediments from the Federal style forward.

9

10

11

12

COLONIAL REVIVAL

1. Kansas City, Missouri; ca. 2006. The over-scaled broad triangular pediment gives what is actually a three-bay house with side wing the initial appearance of being a symmetrical five-bay house.

2. Chicago, Illinois; 1996. In this example the two-story entrance comes from the contemporaneous Millennium Mansion. The symmetry and simple roof are why it has been placed in the New Traditional category.

3. Dallas, Texas, ca. 1980. Note the wide spacing of the balusters above the front door and on the side wing—typical of 1980s examples. This saved money by using fewer balusters than the correct spacing seen in Eclectic-era houses. Today, stricter building codes require extremely close spacing that looks equally out of place. See page 711, Figure 3—no space can be wider than four inches.

4. Boston, Massachusetts; ca. 2000. This, like Figure 2, has a strong Millennium Mansion influence. Here the two front-facing gables with red brick "wallpaper" are an instant tip-off.

COLONIAL REVIVAL (cont.)

5. Kentlands, Maryland; ca. 1992. This 1990s side-gabled example had the benefit of Kentlands' building guidelines to keep it simple, like most original Colonial houses.

6. Stillwater, Minnesota; ca. 2003. A side-gambrel example with full-width porch and broad shed dormer.

7. Dallas, Texas; 2000. Weathers House; Ann Abernathy, architect. A small and understated main house block is part of a much larger house designed in an additive manner—as is partially visible at right.

8. Boston, Massachusetts; 2004. Here triple wall dormers above the garage echo triple roof dormers on the house. The house and garage connect in an additive manner.

9. Kansas City, Missouri; 1998. This house was closely modeled after Virginia Georgian mansions with the use of red brick, high foundation, steeply pitched hipped roof, and very understated entry.

10. Kentlands, Maryland; ca. 2000s. At Kentlands, a subtle mix of house size within a block face combines with slightly different setbacks of houses on the lots to create pleasingly irregular streetscapes.

11. New England; 2009. Federal House; PPA, Peter Pennoyer and Elizabeth Graciolo, architects. Designed for a historic district, this elegant house has historic details that are carefully and subtly reinterpreted in some places.

5

8

9

12

13

6

7

10

11

12. Pennsylvania; ca. 2005, Stone House (public facade); Albert, Righter & Tittmann, architects. This house is an excellent example of an additive composition; it has more stone and smaller windows on this public side.

13. Pennsylvania, ca. 2005, Stone House (meadow facade); Albert, Righter & Tittman, architects. Far more windows, including two bays, are on this private facade.

14. Stillwater, Minnesota; ca. 2003. The additive stepped-roof form is interesting.

14

CLASSICAL

1. Alexandria, Virginia; 2006. The two-story entry feature signals a house that is New Traditional rather than from the Eclectic era. Note that the entry porch and pediment are slightly out of scale.

2. Seaside, Florida (vicinity); ca. 2000. High foundation is required for possible floods. The small window size is less common on New Traditional houses.

3. Dallas, Texas; 2000–2004. Muse House; Quinlan Terry, architect. Larry Boerder, local architect. Solid masonry construction.

4. Dallas, Texas; 1975. This early example lacks an adequate entablature above the full-width porch and uses large windows more typical of Ranch houses.

5. Carillon Beach, Florida; 2000.

6. Seaside, Florida (vicinity); ca. 1990s. This front-gabled house is very similar to Figure 5. Compare the deeper entablature and more heavily molded cornice here to the much simpler one in Figure 5.

7. Highland Park, Texas; 2007. Gilliland House; Larry Boerder, architect. This house utilizes so many details of early 20th-century Neoclassical houses—including the South's beloved full-height entry porch with lower full-width porch subtype—that many neighbors think the house has been there for a century. Note the grouped windows, front door surrounded by lights, and the well-proportioned classical porches.

8. Carlsbad, California; 2006. Squared porch supports substitute for classical columns.

9. Cape Porch House; Albert, Righter & Tittmann, architects. This could be the country cousin of AR&T's Temple House (Figure 10). The Greek Revival elements here are simplified squared columns, corner pilasters, and a wide band of trim in the gable.

10. Concord, Massachusetts; 1991. Temple House; Albert, Righter & Tittmann, architects. This striking new interpretation of the Greek Revival has dramatic pilasters on the gable front and an exceptionally wide frieze band with windows.

11. Santa Rosa Beach, Florida; 1997. This house, inspired by the full-facade porch of the Greek Revival style, has a small temple-form room on the roof rather than a more typical cupola.

2

3

6

7

10

11

ITALIAN RENAISSANCE

1. Destin, Florida; ca. 1990s. Note the triple arched opening across the front entry porch.

2. Carillon Beach, Florida; 1998. Lloyd Vogt, architect. A very simple beach-house design with a triangular pediment. Note the checkerboard patterned paving and squared fence supports topped with round globe.

3. Beverly Hills, California; 1985. Styled houses with two-story entry features and large windows (as seen here) are almost certain to be post-1980 New Trads.

4. Atlanta, Georgia; 1995. Sloane House; William T. Baker, architect. It would take close examination to distinguish this refined design from an Eclectic-era example.

5. Dallas, Texas; 2001. Bramblett House; Allen Oliver, architect. This handsome but restrained house with projecting side wings likely inspired the larger more elaborate house in Figure 8, which is built nearby.

6. Dallas, Texas; 1988. Frank Welch, architect. Welch, renowned for his American Vernacular designs (called Texas Regional locally), distilled this simplified design to fit into a streetscape with many elaborate original 1910s and '20s Italian Renaissance houses.

7. Pasadena, California; 2005. There is a dramatic difference in the size of the small upper-story windows and tall arched first-floor windows. The seven-bay design requires a broad lot frontage.

8. Dallas, Texas: ca. 2010. Larry Boerder, architect. This larger relative of Figure 5 has a broader central section with room for a pair of oval windows, corner quoins, and a broad side balustraded terrace connecting to a two-story side wing on the right.

TUDOR

1. Lee's Summit, Missouri; 2005. A simple two-story side-gabled house has nested Tudor gables placed in front—similar to Figure 2, page 458.

2. Portland, Oregon; 2004. The garage wing forms a front automobile court that is as prominent from the street as the house proper.

3. Dalton, Georgia; ca. 2000. McEntire House; William T. Baker, architectural designer.

4. Portland, Oregon; 2009. A broad driveway and garage in the main body of the house dominate this Tudor design; the development likely lacks alleys.

5. Nashville, Tennessee; 1998–2000. Allen House; William T. Baker, architectural designer. This house utilizes clinker bricks and a roof clad with terra-cotta tile to blend with the older houses in the neighborhood.

6. Atlanta, Georgia; 2000–2003. Burfitt House; William T. Baker, architectural designer. An almost symmetrical stone-clad house with parapeted gables.

1

4

7

7. Hillsboro, Oregon; ca. 1996. Multiple-facade gables are far more common in today's New Traditional houses than they were in Eclectic-era Tudor houses.

8. Dallas, Texas; ca. 2000. Richard Drummond Davis, architect. The house as village—an approach seen in both Tudor and Colonial New Trad houses. Here one can imagine a half-timbered house at right, a parapeted gable house in the middle, and a Shingle house at left.

9. Dallas, Texas; 2011. Note the very high roof pitch and half-timbered box bay window. The owners voluntarily redesigned this infill house to conform with the historic setback line of the rest of the block, after they learned their new home would project 15 feet in front of it. This was very public-spirited, since they had a legal building permit and the forms for their foundation were already built.

9

2

3

5

6

8

FRENCH

1. Pasadena, California; 2000. The high-pitched hipped roof and through-the-cornice segmental arched windows identify this house's French origins.

2. Atlanta, Georgia; 1997. Smidt House; William T. Baker, architectural designer. This one-story example is the result of a total remodeling of a Neoclassical Ranch.

3. Duluth, Minnesota; 1993. The sloping site allows the garage of this one-story French to step down from the main house block.

4. Dallas, Texas; 2005. Larry Boerder, architect. This symmetrical house has a central block with side pavilions. Note the segmental pediment and diminutive roof dormers on the main block and segmental arched through-the-cornice dormers on the pavilions.

5. Naperville, Illinois; ca. 2005. Beginning about 2000, turrets and towers became popular on New Trads.

6. San Diego, California; ca. 2000s. A New Traditional version of a towered French Eclectic house.

7. Dallas, Texas; 2009. This New Traditional Chateauesque house has wall dormers with pinnacles and a turret.

8. Medina, Washington; 2007. Formal French houses favored stucco or stone walls with gray-slate roofs as seen here and in Figures 1 and 4.

9. Dallas, Texas; 2009. Larry Boerder, architect. This formal house has Beaux Arts roots. Note the roof-line balustrades, paired pilasters, and oval cartouche with swags in the triangular pediment.

10. Dallas, Texas; 2011. Larry Boerder, architect. The symmetrical facade of this French house is made less formal by the roof and wall materials.

1

4

7

9

2

3

5

6

8

10

QUEEN ANNE AND OTHER VICTORIAN

1. Seaside, Florida; 1985. This is based on Folk Victorian precedents, specifically, the pyramidal subtype that was prevalent in the South.

2. Dallas, Texas; 1976. Bicentennial House. Originally an American Four-Square, this was expanded and extensively remodeled in celebration of the nation's Bicentennial.

3. Minneapolis, Minnesota; 2003. A duplex with little added detail but two Romanesque arches and a broad, squat tower. This and Figure 5 both have lower automobile courts with arched entries.

4. Hillsboro, Oregon; ca. 2005. This and Figure 8 are both inspired by Free Classic Queen Annes with towers. Here the tower is broad and round.

5. Dallas, Texas; 2005. This elaborate house has many intricate masonry Richardsonian Romanesque details.

6. Stillwater, Minnesota; ca. 2003. Note the typical Queen Anne hipped roof with lower cross-gabled roof. This late 19th-century roof rarely is built today in this pure form and is quite simple when compared to the roofs of many new Millennium Mansions.

7. Highland Park, Chicago; 2003. This house has Queen Anne as its inspiration—the Free Classic subtype. Note the paired columns and the Palladian window above the entry.

8. Naperville, Illinois; 2004. Here the tower and the porch roof turrets both are hexagonal.

9. Hillsboro, Oregon; 1995. The huge porch roof turret dominates this facade and makes a *Mutt and Jeff* pair with the tall, narrow tower. The wing on the right, with an almost solid wall, appears to be the garage.

1

4

7

8

2

3

5

6

9

CRAFTSMAN

1. Seattle, Washington; 2000. This house has very shallow roof overhangs and diminutive exposed rafters with triangular braces. Unusual windows on the main floor mimic cottage windows but are double-hung and were photographed in the fully open position.

2. Portland, Oregon; 2006. A much higher percentage of New Traditional Craftsman houses are two-story than were their Early Modern predecessors.

3. Santa Rosa Beach, Florida; 2001. A one-story front-gabled New Trad Craftsman bungalow with a screened front porch.

4. Lee's Summit, Missouri; ca. 2005. Modeled after cross-gabled Craftsman houses, the porch support bases would likely have begun at ground level in an original.

5. Portland, Oregon; 2003. A side-gabled example with three dormers lighting the upper half-story.

6. Chicago, Illinois; 2005.

7. Carlsbad, California; 2001. Small one-car detached garages such as that on the left were very common in the 1910s and 1920s. This small TND has used these as a new way to get a third garage and at the same time create a small enclosed front garden behind it.

8. Los Angeles, California; ca. 2000. Look past the front garage and this New Trad Craftsman has a nice feel to it.

9. Portland, Oregon; 2001. Another newer house form—two wings extend almost to the street and are detailed with windows to look like part of the house even though both are garages.

1

4

5

8

2

3

6

7

9

PRAIRIE

1. Seattle, Washington; ca. 2000. A duplex with both entry porches recessed into the main body of the house.

2. Lisle, Illinois; 1989.

3. Dallas, Texas; ca. 2000. Note the use of corner windows.

4. Dallas, Texas; 2011. The broad roof overhang at the front distracts the eye from the many areas where the overlay is actually quite shallow.

5. Raytown, Missouri; ca. 2005. This house has the American Four-Square look of many more modest Prairie-era houses. The simple hipped roof with a single centered hipped dormer is quite typical, as is the full-width porch supported by heavy squared piers.

6. Dallas, Texas; ca. 2010.

7. Chicago, Illinois; 2001. Ribbon windows on both levels, combined with a change in wall cladding below the upstairs window line, give this a Prairie look.

8. Kansas City, Missouri; 2000. The broad overhang, the change in wall cladding, and the horizontal stone impart a Prairie feel to this house. The many single-spaced small square windows are atypical.

5

7

2

3

4

6

8

MEDITERRANEAN

1. Carlsbad, California; 2005. Examples with twisted columns and rounded towers have Spanish roots.

2. Dallas, Texas; 2001. New Mediterranean houses with an added squared tower, as seen here, are often called "Tuscan."

3. Dallas, Texas; 1996. Richardson Robertson III, architect. Note the raised terrace and the heavy squared tower.

4. San Antonio, Texas; 2000. Daniell House; Michael G. Imber, architect. This house is sited on a front motor court with a large fountain in the center.

5. Highland Park, Texas; 2011–2012. An unusually shaped corner lot facilitated this rambling shape.

6. Dallas, Texas; 2010. Larry Boerder, architect.

7. Carlsbad, California; 1989. The developer also finished this same house with a version of modest French details.

8. Dallas, Texas; 2008. This almost symmetrical example has Moorish details.

2

3

5

8

NEW TRADITIONAL CLASSICAL—Generally based on precedents found in the Neoclassical: pages 435–46, Early Classical Revival: pages 235–42, and Greek Revival: pages 247–64.

NEW TRADITIONAL ITALIAN RENAISSANCE—Generally based on precedents found on pages 497–508.

NEW TRADITIONAL TUDOR—Generally based on precedents found on pages 449–66.

NEW TRADITIONAL FRENCH—Generally based on precedents found in the French Eclectic: pages 485–94. More recently houses have been based on French Colonial: pages 179–86, Chateauesque: pages 469–74, and Beaux Arts: pages 477–83.

NEW TRADITIONAL VICTORIAN—Most commonly based on precedents in the Queen Anne: pages 345–70 and Folk Victorian: pages 397–405, but also occasionally in Second Empire: pages 317–30, Stick: pages 333–43, and Richardsonian Romanesque: pages 387–94.

NEW TRADITIONAL CRAFTSMAN—Generally based on precedents found on pages 567–78.

NEW TRADITIONAL PRAIRIE—Generally based on precedents found on pages 551–64.

NEW TRADITIONAL MEDITERRANEAN—Based on precedents found in the Spanish Revival: pages 521–34, joined by rural Italian elements, such as the squared towers in Italianate: pages 283–302, and in this form sometimes called Tuscan.

simple geometric forms

uncomplicated roofs

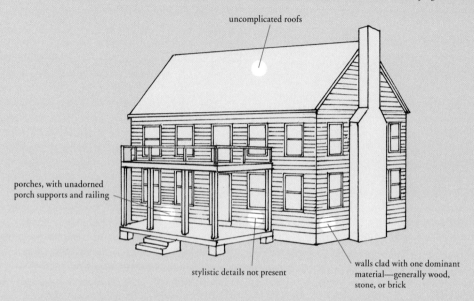

porches, with unadorned
porch supports and railing

walls clad with one dominant
material—generally wood,
stone, or brick

stylistic details not present

porch may be entry, partial-width,
or full-width and may be one or
two stories

FRONT-GABLED ROOF

page 757

SIDE-GABLED ROOF

pages 758–59

HIPPED ROOF

pages 760–61

CROSS-GABLED ROOF

page 762

COMPLEX ROOF FORMS

page 763

PRINCIPAL SUBTYPES

American Vernacular

ca. 1930–Present

Identifying Features

Simple geometric forms (the kinds of houses you could build with a set of blocks); covered porches and balconies, with unadorned porch supports and railings; uncomplicated roofs; walls clad with one dominant material—generally wood, stone, or brick; stylistic details not present.[24]

Principal Subtypes

FRONT-GABLED ROOF—Simple rectangular block with front-gabled roof; may have uncomplicated one- or two-story porch.

SIDE-GABLED ROOF—Simple rectangular block with side-gabled roofs; may have uncomplicated one- or two-story porch.

HIPPED ROOF—Simple hipped-roof form; may have uncomplicated one- or two-story porch.

CROSS-GABLED ROOF—Simple gable-and-wing form; may have straightforward one- or two-story porch.

COMPLEX ROOF FORM—This subtype includes a broad range of forms designed to evoke the qualities of slightly more complex American farmhouses. Some are designed to appear as if the house has grown over time, with basic shapes gathered or lined up together. Others add screened porches or incorporate familiar rural shapes like barns or silos. Some simply add roof or wall dormers, or a gable, to more basic forms.

Variants and Details

Porches are frequently the primary exterior embellishment on an American Vernacular house. In addition to the type of porch (one-story, two-story, partial-width, full-width, etc.), an interesting detail to note is the way a porch attaches to the house, as this can have a subtle but important visual effect. American Vernacular houses typically have porches deep enough to accommodate outdoor activity, not truncated ones that only appear to be real from the street. A screened porch is common. See illustrations and photographs of Pre-Railroad Folk and National Folk on pages 118 through 147 for a few of the wide variety of sources for American Vernacular. In addition, the porch variations of Folk Victorian on pages 397–405 provide sources for variations in form. American Vernacular examples, however, would generally have simple porch details and omit spindlework porch detailing or under-eave brackets.

Windows are typically double-hung, have simple frames, and may be multi-paned. The manner in which windows are arranged on the facades can sometimes distinguish an architect-designed example from one created from a pattern book or for a traditional neighborhood development. Architects are more likely to experiment with window size, spacing, and placement, while houses created by pattern books and design review are more likely to have window placement similar to that found on original folk houses.

ADDITIVE VS. MASSIVE—American Vernacular houses commonly achieve a large size in an "additive" manner—that is, with many smaller elements joined together—like a house that grew over time or one that was built as a central house block with hyphens and/or wings. By contrast, Millennium Mansions most often achieve their large size as a single massive element. Both approaches can be found in New Traditional houses, but using the additive avoids an overly large main-house block.

Occurrence

For decades the American Vernacular movement was limited to cerebral architects consciously designing a quiet house with good bones for clients preferring to be understated. Most were one-of-a-kind designs that fit easily into almost any setting. Beginning in the

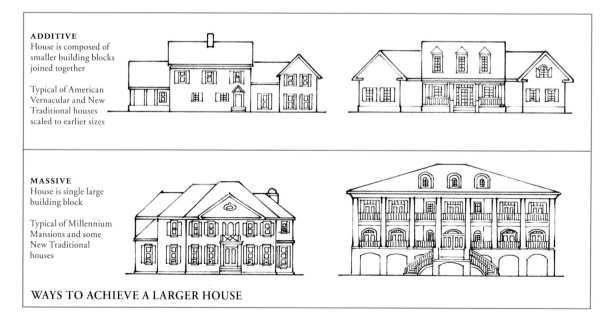

ADDITIVE
House is composed of smaller building blocks joined together

Typical of American Vernacular and New Traditional houses scaled to earlier sizes

MASSIVE
House is single large building block

Typical of Millennium Mansions and some New Traditional houses

WAYS TO ACHIEVE A LARGER HOUSE

1980s some TNDs had design guidelines written with the express purpose of creating new homes that recalled an area's architectural heritage—in effect legislating particular kinds of houses. Some of these guidelines concentrated on the form of the region's vernacular house (rather than a style) and created neighborhoods of American Vernacular houses.[25]

Comments

In the late 1920s most American architects were designing Eclectic English-, Spanish-, and French-influenced houses. A few architects, however, began to study regional folk-house traditions and emulated them in the homes they designed—simplifying houses rather than complicating them. Chief among these were William Wurster in California and O'Neil Ford and Dave Williams in Texas. As William Wurster explained the process, "Design up from the log cabin, instead of trying to compress the mansion." In 1928, Wurster designed the Gregory Farmhouse in Scotts Valley, California—a well-publicized early American Vernacular house—and his architecture continued to use a process of simplifying rather than creating new shapes and forms.[26]

In Texas, O'Neil Ford and his mentor and employer, Dave Williams, found inspiration in the folk houses that had been built in the Texas Hill Country by early German settlers. These sturdy, straightforward homes were simple shapes, built of native materials, and designed to take advantage both of their sites and the prevailing winds. Williams wrote two articles for the *Southwest Review* advocating a new regional architecture based on these Texas precedents.[27] In doing this, Williams and Ford joined Wurster

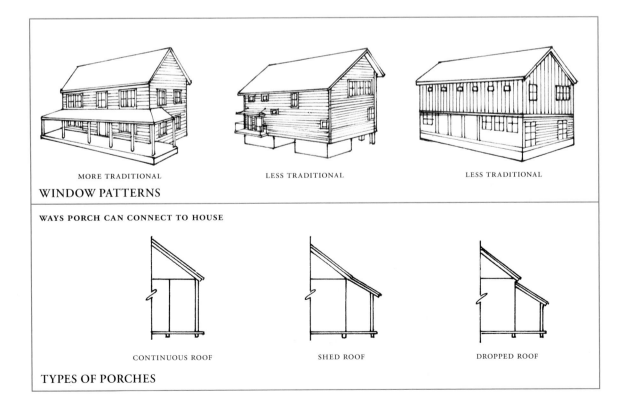

MORE TRADITIONAL   LESS TRADITIONAL   LESS TRADITIONAL

WINDOW PATTERNS

WAYS PORCH CAN CONNECT TO HOUSE

CONTINUOUS ROOF   SHED ROOF   DROPPED ROOF

TYPES OF PORCHES

SEA RANCH, CALIFORNIA In addition to folk houses (pages 118–147), the simple shapes of barns and outbuildings, such as these at Sea Ranch, provided inspiration for American Vernacular houses.

as early leaders of a nascent regionalist movement where architects looked to the folk architecture of their own regions and designed homes based on them.[28] In 1965 the Sea Ranch reinforced this with its use of simple vernacular forms, such as MLTW's Binker Barns with their predominant gabled shape.[29] In recent decades a growing number of architects have been designing these simple commonsense houses.[30]

Since the early 1980s, TNDs have adopted style- and/or form-based guidelines for new construction, many intended to re-create a region's heritage of vernacular architecture.[31] Recent pattern books have sometimes included regional patterns. An excellent example is *Louisiana Speaks: Pattern Book* by Urban Design Associates and Raymond L. Gindroz, FAIA, written after Hurricane Katrina destroyed so much of the rich vernacular architectural heritage of the Gulf Coast states. In addition, architects anxious to preserve the area's strong regional identity, such as Marianne Cusato and Duany Plater-Zyberk & Company, have designed plans for quite basic American Vernacular houses, such as Cusato's "Katrina Cottage."[32]

Finally, perhaps as a reaction to the spread of Millennium Mansions, "Farmhouse" became a favored style during the 1990s and 2000s and was featured in pattern and other books.[33]

FRONT-GABLED ROOF

1. Ocean Springs, Mississippi; ca. 2005. Katrina Cottage; Marianne Cusato, architect. With plans and materials easily available, many homes similar to this one have recently been built across the Gulf South. This plan features a 544-square-foot home. Groupings of similar small folk houses were found across the South until well after World War II.

2. Wyoming; ca. 2000. Duncker House; Paul and Peggy Duncker, architects. The windows are evidence that this is architect-designed and not a folk house. The decision to build a detached garage lets the house maintain a simple, straightforward shape.

3. Stillwater, Minnesota; ca. 2003. The front porch and the sunroom on the side balance each other.

4. Key West, Florida; ca. 1996. This is part of a large group of American Vernacular houses built on a former military base in the Truman Annex, near Harry Truman's Little White House. See also page 759, Figure 1.

SIDE-GABLED ROOF

1. Key West, Florida; ca. 1996. Here the porch is under the main roof of the house. Contrast this with the added porch in Figure 6.

2. East Hampton, New York; ca. 2005. Single windows are carefully spaced. A shed porch in front is joined by an apparent shed dormer in back.

3. Duluth, Minnesota; 2001. David Salmala, architect. A side-gabled house is joined to its front-gabled garage by an open breezeway. Note the square windows.

4. Sea Ranch, California; 1984. Binker Barn; MLTW Moore Turnbull, architects. Sea Ranch gave a huge impetus to American Vernacular houses inspired by the simple gable-roof shapes of farm buildings. The Binker Barn was developed as a stock plan that could be successfully sited in the different habitats at Sea Ranch. The large gable shape dominates but can be expanded and modified with the subordinate sheds. Construction was a heavy timber frame and block walls clad with redwood. Seventeen variations were built between 1968 and 1971. See also Figure 7.

5. Panama City Beach, Florida; 2000.

6. Charleston, South Carolina (vicinity); ca. 2000. Raised cottages like this are being built again to avoid floods in the Carolina Low Country. Note the small size of the Palladian windows in the center gable.

7. Sea Ranch, California; ca. 1970. Binker Barn; MLTW Moore Turnbull, architects. It sits in the right foreground of an American Vernacular grouping.

8. Dallas, Texas; 1939. Bromberg House, O'Neil Ford, architect. Ford was the father of Texas Regionalism. This sophisticated house with paired chimneys and a three-bay main house block feels symmetrical but with casually added additions. Porches and breezeways make up half the perimeter of the house. Note the use of large screened front porches downstairs on the left and upstairs on the right.[34]

1

5

6

8

HIPPED ROOF

1. Dallas, Texas; 2001. Dan Shipley, architect. This variation has a hipped-roof main block with asymmetrical side additions. The brick color and right-side stone wall are colors and materials used locally.

2. Destin, Florida; 2003. Cottages with full-width porches and pyramidal hipped roofs were widely built in the South and are now being built again along Florida's Gulf Coast.

3. Raytown, Missouri (vicinity); ca. 2005. Note the irregular size and placement of the upstairs windows.

4. Key West, Florida; ca. 1994. The form of the house is exaggerated by the full-width porch extending out on each side. Compare to Figure 3.

5. Mississippi; ca. 2000. Ken Tate, architect. This house was carefully planned to look like several smaller structures that were built earlier and then joined together.

6. Dallas, Texas; 1965. Field House; Frank Welch, architect. This house has an interior atrium. The roof was originally wood shingles, long since replaced with the standing-seam metal roofing now widely used on Texas regional houses.

7. Carillon Beach, Florida; ca. 2000. A row of American Vernacular houses with two-level porches.

2

5

6

CROSS-GABLED ROOF

1. Stillwater, Minnesota; ca. 2003.

2. Rhode Island; 1998. Wolf House; Estes/Twombly, architects. Scaled to fit into a neighborhood of small houses, a two-story gabled form sits behind a broad shed roof and chimney. The L-shape created by the two main elements holds a private garden.

3. Dallas, Texas; ca. 1980. John Mullen, architect. This house is designed with additive massing. The roof has understated parapets on the gable ends. Note how the chimney is subtly incorporated into the right wing.

1

2

3

COMPLEX ROOF FORMS

1. Annapolis, Maryland (vicinity); ca. 1970s. Paired windows on two front-gabled forms sheathed with what appear to be smooth wood boards.

2. Portland, Oregon; 1996. Note the three matching through-the-cornice gables.

3. Stillwater, Minnesota; ca. 2003.

4. Annapolis, Maryland; 1956. If the 1956 listed date is correct this might be a house that actually did grow in stages, rather than built to look like one.

5. North Carolina; ca. 2000. Dail Dixon, architect. Inspired by the tobacco barns of the region, this house resembles three barns connected with glass-walled links. The varying windows on each front-gabled element let you know this is an architect-designed house and also hint at the differing functions inside. An open breezeway pavilion connects the house to the side-gable garage.

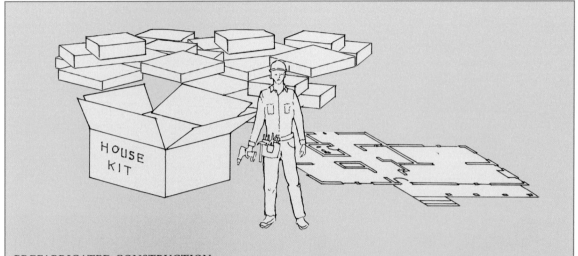

PREFABRICATED CONSTRUCTION

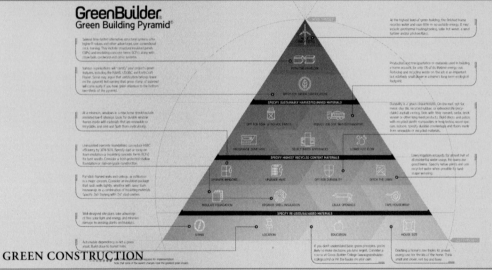

GREEN CONSTRUCTION

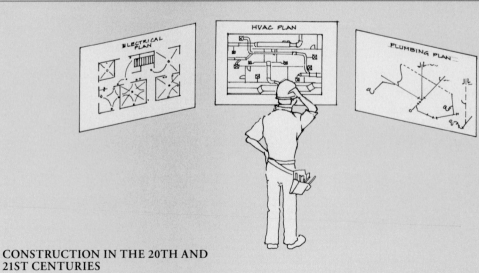

CONSTRUCTION IN THE 20TH AND 21ST CENTURIES

Approaches to Construction in the 20th and 21st Centuries

It seems astonishing that during the 20th century—when man went to the moon and lived on space stations circling the earth, and when computers became commonplace and phones were made mobile—the basic construction technique used for the vast majority of American houses continued to be wood, either 19th-century balloon-frame or a platform-frame variation of it (see illustration, pages 38–40).

Onsite stick construction has continued to dominate the construction of new American houses, despite an interest in prefab houses that was already under way in 1900, continued through the early 20th century, and that reached a near fever pitch after World War II, when multiple attempts were made to transform the factories left idle at war's end into housing production. And although a cadre of major architects—among them Frank Lloyd Wright, Carl Koch, Buckminster Fuller, and Le Corbusier—worked hard to design attractive and affordable prefab houses during the early and mid-20th century, the structural frames of houses in the U.S. are usually built onsite, and primarily with wood.

A concern for green, energy-efficient construction blossomed in the late 1960s. Yet forty years later wood construction, most of it not eligible for even the most basic of energy-efficiency ratings, continues to dominate. The need for green is great and this quest continues in full force today, with promise for the future.

What did evolve—and became a part of most American houses built today—are many of the materials that encase the stick structural frames, along with a great many technological innovations that enhance quality of life. Some of these changes are so fundamental and widespread that it is hard to imagine that at the beginning of the 20th century none were in place.

Prefabricated Construction

A prefabricated house is one that is made of pre-cut and pre-assembled parts manufactured offsite. The parts are delivered and expeditiously assembled on location. Some houses are constructed from individual pre-cut boards, while others are panelized or modular, meaning that entire wall panels or modular boxes are factory-built and then joined together on location. Any style of house can be prefabricated, either in part or in whole; in the United States houses were being shipped from New England to the West Coast as early as the mid-19th century.

By the early 20th century, mail order retailers like Montgomery Ward and Sears Roebuck were selling "kit houses" of pre-cut lumber, available in a wide range of styles and virtually indistinguishable from other houses of the same style that were not pre-cut.

It was the early-20th-century modernists, however, who began to seriously consider prefabrication as a way to meet the demand for affordable housing—a need particularly evident in Europe after World War I. Le Corbusier, Walter Gropius, Frank Lloyd Wright, and Buckminster Fuller had all designed prefabricated houses before 1929, when the Depression affected all types of construction. Although the housing market began to recover slowly during the 1930s, Sears stopped production in 1940.

During World War II, prefabrication methods were eagerly applied to defense and worker housing, with about 200,000 units of factory-built homes erected during the war.[1] In addition, the war led directly to one of the most widely used prefabricated units ever—the Quonset hut—built for housing and other purposes.[2] The efficacy of prefab in construction was even more clearly demonstrated after the war. The need to produce sixteen million homes for returning servicemen brought about a golden age in prefabrication, and it was utilized in four primary ways.

First, there was a broad postwar movement of individuals and companies trying to design and produce complete prefab houses—many of which mimicked traditional homes. These ran the gamut from Lustron, which manufactured innovative metal houses in a retooled World War II aircraft plant (supported by government grants) to Macy's, the revered New York City department store, which sold standardized homes completely furnished right down to color-coordinated bath towels and Melmac dinnerware.[3]

Second, there were those experimenting with very distinctive house forms that could be erected quickly and inexpensively, such as Buckminster Fuller's early Dymaxion House and his geodesic domes, the latter of which can still be ordered.

A third approach used standardized *parts,* as well as parts available from commercial catalogues, to build one-of-a-kind houses, such as the Eames House. This approach offered almost infinitely changeable designs, instead of a few standardized ones. These were rarely intended to mimic a traditional house but, rather, to look quite modern. Carl Koch's Techbuilt post-and-beam panelized houses were among the more successful of this approach.

Fourth, and undoubtedly most commonly, builders introduced prefabricated elements into traditional construction. For example, they set up shop areas to prefabricate large components, such as wood roof joists and wall panels, that were then used to construct large developments of balloon-frame houses.

Prefabricated houses experienced a decline in the 1980s and 1990s due to the increase in suburban developments and the public's association of prefab with inexpensive manufactured design. During this period, modular houses—almost identical to manufactured housing except for not being required to keep the moving chassis in place and being required to meet local building codes—filled a need for inexpensive prefab houses.

Recently, however, there has been a resurgence in high-end prefab housing due to affordability, an increase in companies offering this type of construction, the availability of more house designs (including both modern and traditional styles), and the inclusion of eco-friendly elements.[4] New technologies affording energy-efficient designs include: structural insulated panels (panels containing a foam core), insulated concrete forms

PRE-FAB

1. Montauk, New York; ca. 1964. Leisurama Home. Exhibited as the "Typical American House" at the American National Exhibition in Moscow in 1959, Macy's sold about two hundred of these for a second-home development in Montauk. The purchase included all of the furnishings, right down to Melmac dishes and color-coordinated sheets and towels.

2. Unidentified house; ca. 1960s. Buckminster Fuller, architect. Fuller patented this design consisting of a rigid geometric frame of metal or plastic covered by a structural skin on rigid panels. Fuller's own dome is one of the National Trust's "America's Treasures."

3. Boston, Massachusetts; 1999. Neighbors report that this Prefab house was manufactured in New Hampshire and erected in just a few days. It is New Traditional Colonial in style.

4. 1945 (designed 1920). Dymaxion House; Buckminster Fuller, architect. The only remaining example is at the Henry Ford Museum.

5. Madison, Wisconsin; 1957. Frank Lloyd Wright, architect. Wright believed that a well-designed Prefab house was possible and designed four plans for the Marshall Erdman Company. Only seven examples were built.

(concrete molds that create a continuous surface), and photovoltaic systems (that generate electricity). Prefabricated houses not only facilitate a shorter construction time but also produce half the material waste of onsite construction. In addition, prefabrication avoids exposure of building materials to natural elements, since production is in climate-controlled factories.

Green Construction

Green or eco-friendly houses focus on environmental impact and sustainability. While newly designed houses can incorporate green elements, the preservation and retrofitting (or "greening") of existing houses is the most eco-friendly action a community can take. The most efficient way to demonstrate sustainability is to preserve houses that are already built, as debris from building construction accounts for one-third of all waste generated in the United States. The amount of energy exhausted when a house is demolished and reconstructed can never be recovered within the generally shorter life span of new construction, regardless of green elements used and the amount of materials recycled.[5]

New discoveries and experiments with green architecture were largely a result of the environmental movement of the 1960s and 1970s, as well as the OPEC oil embargo of 1973. The first efforts toward new green construction generally relied on either the sun's energy or the stable temperature and insulating effects of the earth (or both) to reduce energy requirements. Some are passive solar houses (using no mechanical systems, only natural air flow; the vertical design of Figure 1 on page 769 was intended to facilitate this); others are active solar houses with mechanical distribution of heat and cooling, while still others stress thick coverings of earth for insulation. The solar collectors, air-flow systems, heavy insulation, lack of windows, and earth coverings used in these techniques sometimes created unique facade designs that bear little resemblance to traditional houses. These might be partially buried (as in Figures 2 and 3, page 769). Other green homes, often those built in the Contemporary and Shed styles, were designed with careful consideration to orientation, placement of window openings, shade structures, and plantings that facilitated passive solar energy.

By the 1990s, it was obvious that the real solution was to find ways to incorporate "green" into every style and type of house. Therefore, formal programs were set in place to promote ecological designs and materials, including the Committee on the Environment created by the American Institute of Architects and the Energy Star program by the EPA and the U.S. Department of Energy. Currently there are more than five hundred regional and national systems that rate energy efficiency and environmental impact. In 2000, the U.S. Green Building Council developed LEED (Leadership in Energy and Environmental Design), an excellent and inclusive rating system that evaluates energy use, water efficiency, air quality, overall design, and site selection for future construction. This program awards a silver, gold, or platinum rating to exemplary projects.

While an eco-friendly house of the mid- to late-20th century might be identifiable by a "space age" design, today green houses can appear traditional in style and still maintain equal environmental standards. Elements of green or eco-friendly houses may include Energy Star appliances, low-flow toilets, a tank-less water heater, solar-generated power, and native landscaping, all of which can be applied to both new and old houses. When retrofitting an older home, a green solution to aged windows is repair instead

GREEN

1. Lake Placid, Minnesota; ca. 1970s. Milo Thompson, architect. The vertical design was intended to facilitate natural air flow.

2. Sea Ranch, California; ca. 1970. Houses with earth roofs were designed to both fit into the landscape and provide ample natural insulation.

3. Phoenix, Arizona; 1979. Houses built underground in the 1970s were considered an ideal way to maintain year-round temperature without fuel expenditures.

1

2

3

of replacement. New wood, vinyl, or PVC windows have a shorter life expectancy and cannot be recycled or restored effectively. Original windows that have been properly restored could last for another one hundred years.

Alternative Construction Methods

There are a number of new construction methods that combine elements of prefabricated construction and green construction. They substitute different systems for the wood stick framing, assembled on site, that is most commonly used to build new houses today. Three are illustrated here.

The most familiar is Manufactured houses (or Modular)—completed houses built in factories, shipped to a site, and assembled. These can be either an entire pre-constructed house (a single-wide) or combinable sections of pre-constructed houses (double- and triple-wides). They are either placed on a foundation or have a skirt wrapped around their chassis, and the parts are sealed together.

A second method is to construct walls and roofs with large, relatively solid panels that have insulation as their core. Pre-cut panels are shipped and assembled onsite; doors and windows are added, and interior and exterior finishes are added.

A third method is to construct the walls from concrete forms that will remain permanently in place and have insulation built in. The forms are assembled and concrete is poured into them. Windows and doors are then added.

All three of these can have front or side porches, carports, or even enclosed garages added to the basic house.

Construction Changes in the 20th Century

While the basic way of constructing a house—balloon or platform framing created with two-by-four wood sticks and nailed joints—remained the same through the 20th century, much of what encased and served that wood structural skeleton evolved.

The most far-reaching transformation has been to the "guts" of houses: the interior systems that circulate heat, air conditioning, water, natural gas, and electricity; that drain sewage and waste water; and that—in the last few decades—allow various forms of television and internet access.[6] Many of these internal systems were in turn connected to much larger networks built and maintained by municipalities or utility companies. The room types and fixtures these various systems enabled have changed spatial allocations and costs of new construction in major ways. For example, bathrooms and kitchens as we know them today are quite new and their evolution in size and complexity during the 20th century is remarkable.[7]

Electrifying houses was perhaps the most momentous change, as it enabled so many other improvements. In 1907 only 8 percent of houses in the United States even had access to electric service, and not all of those homes were wired to take advantage of it. The spread of electric systems throughout the United States was amazingly rapid. By 1920, 34 percent of households had access to an electric supply, 63 percent by 1927 and 80 percent by 1941.[8] And while at first the new power source was used mainly for light, within only a few decades a legion of electric appliances, large and small, were introduced—and air conditioning became affordable.

Two major appliances—the refrigerator and the clothes dryer—greatly changed the character of rear facades and gardens in the mid-20th century. In 1923, there were only twenty thousand electric refrigerators in the United States (thus the almost ubiquitous exterior rear service porches that accommodated iceboxes and ice delivery). Made practical by Freon in the early 1930s, electrified refrigerators were quickly adopted. Only 5,000 refrigerators were manufactured in 1921, with that figure rising to 1 million in 1931 and then to 6 million in 1937. This was an astonishing number given that this was in the midst of the Depression.[9] The fact that the FHA would include the cost of major appliances in the home mortgages they insured undoubtedly helped; and a careful cost

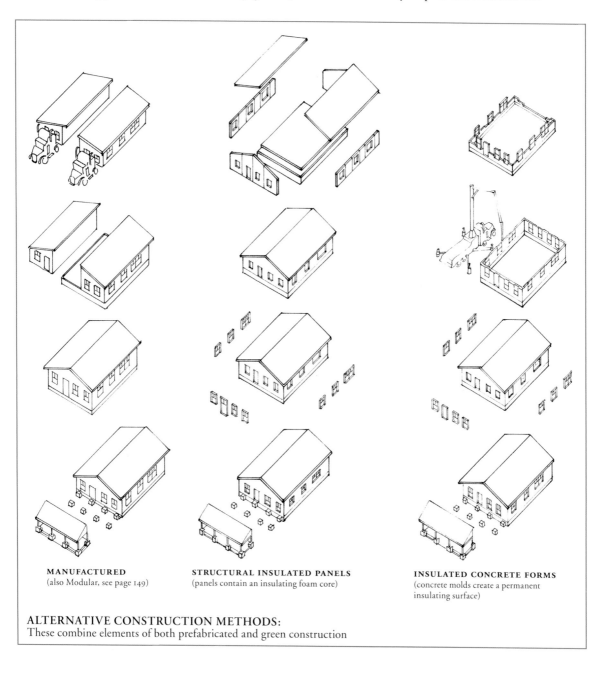

MANUFACTURED
(also Modular, see page 149)

STRUCTURAL INSULATED PANELS
(panels contain an insulating foam core)

INSULATED CONCRETE FORMS
(concrete molds create a permanent insulating surface)

ALTERNATIVE CONSTRUCTION METHODS:
These combine elements of both prefabricated and green construction

accounting would likely show that the refrigerator was no more costly than adding a back porch for the icebox. Similarly, the much later spread of clothes dryers allowed large areas of rear yards, previously dedicated to clothes lines, to be converted to other uses.

As municipal water systems and sanitary sewer systems were built throughout the country, it gradually became feasible to bring water into houses. Interior bathrooms, for example, are a remarkably modern innovation. In marveling over how many and how large bathrooms are in new houses built today compared to houses built in 1950, it is easy to lose sight of the real headline—in 1940, 45 percent of homes in the United States still lacked complete plumbing. Almost one-half of the houses in the United States did not even have all the *elements* common to a bathroom located anywhere inside. Complete plumbing was defined as hot and cold running water, a bathtub or shower, and a flush toilet—and it was *not* a requirement that these all be available in a single room, only somewhere within the house or dwelling unit.[10] By 1980 all but 2.7 percent of homes in the United States had complete plumbing, a remarkable transformation. Cable television and hard-wired internet access are recent examples of the rapid transformative spread of a service.

Less dramatic than the lifestyle changes enabled by new technical systems has been the gradual evolution of ways to encase the wood stick structural frame with new cladding and insulating materials for both interior and exterior walls. Originally, frame houses had lumber wall sheathing, sub floor, and roof deck. Brick and other veneers were applied directly to the wood sheathing. In the mid-20th century this lumber sheathing was replaced by plywood or various types of fiberboard on the outside and sheetrock on the inside. In the 1980s a product made from wood scraps, oriented strand board (OSB), began to be commonly used to sheath the exterior of the wood frame. It was typically wrapped with a breathable and waterproof membrane before the exterior cladding was attached. Today a fundamental change is being experimented with—particularly in 21st-Century Modern houses—the use of a rain screen that is not directly attached. First a waterproof membrane is applied to a structurally sound box, often OSB. Then a water-shedding (note, water-*shedding,* not necessarily waterproof) panel of cladding is added that is separated from the structural wall's waterproof membrane with spacers that allow an inch or more of space, providing air circulation. This allows the building to breathe, as well as providing an insulating space. It can also free the design of the exterior shell of a house from the actual structural systems, opening up possibilities that have begun to be explored in some civic buildings.[11]

Advances in glass technology have opened up yet another avenue of change: allowing large panes of plate glass and thermal-insulated glass to create larger and larger windows. And as the price of producing these products fell, soon entire walls of windows became feasible. The first house to demonstrate window walls was the House of Tomorrow exhibited at the 1933 Century of Progress (George Frederick Keck, architect)—where Keck discovered he had to use all kinds of screening devices on sunny days—from Venetian blinds to curtains.[12] However, it was not until interior air-conditioning became affordable after World War II that large window walls with sunny exposures were feasible. The ability to maintain the temperature of a house year-round not only allowed window walls to be placed without regard to orientation but also allowed solid walls without windows. It allowed house designs to abandon operable windows evenly placed on most wall surfaces to insure cross ventilation and instead made it feasible to design houses that located windows with greater attention to views, to privacy, and to furniture placement.

Notes

LOOKING AT AMERICAN HOUSES

1. Strict building codes enacted in wetlands or in earthquake-prone areas often have exceptions for a remodeled house (rather than a new house). This can lead to "remodeling" that essentially builds a new house on an old foundation. The same sort of rebuilding can be triggered by new and more restrictive zoning codes that apply only to a new house, not one deemed "remodeling" because it is built on the old foundation.

2. There are also business and retail neighborhoods, and these are generally beyond the scope of this book.

3. The census of 1800 defined an "urban" area as one with a population over 2,500. There were twenty-seven towns with populations between 2,500 and 10,000—and some, such as Newburyport, Massachusetts, and Alexandria, Virginia, still retain portions of their early rural and urban streetscapes. Of these, five already had individual populations exceeding 10,000 (New York, Philadelphia, Baltimore, Boston, and Charleston). By 1810, there were thirty-five towns with populations between 2,500 and 10,000.

4. John R. Stilgoe, *Common Landscape of America, 1580 to 1845* (New Haven, CT: Yale University Press, 1982), 82.

5. In much of the English Colonial South and Mid-Atlantic a pattern of larger and more self-contained plantations was common. Philip Pregill and Nancy Volkman, *Landscapes in History: Design and Planning in the Western Tradition* (New York, NY: Van Nostrand Reinhold, 1993), 329–30. See pages 328–32 for other colonial patterns.

6. Some small towns—particularly company towns or towns with origins in mining, forestry, and fishing—grew with great rapidity.

7. Regional patterns might include central green spaces (such as a town green in New England, a courthouse square in Texas, or a central plaza in Spanish towns), extensive use of regional materials, or distinctive patterns of streets, house sites, or block size (such as is found in Mormon-planned towns). For a few western towns with distinct regional variations see Virginia McAlester and A. Lee McAlester, *A Field Guide to America's Historic Neighborhoods and Museum Houses: The Western States* (New York, NY: Alfred A. Knopf, 1998): Butte, Montana, 372; Manti, Utah, 642; Nevada City, California, 127; Monterey, California, 115–123; Santa Fe, New Mexico, 441–452; Fredericksburg, Texas, 593–596; and others.

8. Only a few hundred inhabitants occupied many of the early rural neighborhoods. Today, areas with populations up to 10,000 are generally considered small towns. Even larger towns may still have a remaining core with "rural neighborhood" streetscapes. There is nothing magic about the figure 2,500 except that it was used by the census and is easily traceable as to how many towns had reached this size in census years. In 1880, there were 872 towns between 2,500 and 10,000. By 1890, there were 1,150. By 1900, there were 1,445, showing a steady increase of 270–300 towns established per decade.

9. Pregill and Volkman, 491–94. It is reported that between 1850 and 1870 approximately 7 percent of the total land area of the United Stated (129 million acres) was awarded to various railroad companies to incentivize the construction of transcontinental rail lines. "Land and Freedom," accessed August 15, 2010, http://www.landandfreedom.org/ushistory/us13.htm. By 1870, there were about 53,000 miles of railway in the United States. See table featured in *One Hundred Years of American Commerce 1795–1895*, ed. Chauncey Depew (New York, NY: D. O. Haynes),

143. It was essential to the railroads to establish small towns along these tracks—to add potential passengers and also to have maintenance facilities throughout their systems.

10. Dolores Hayden, *Building Suburbia* (New York, NY: Pantheon Books, 2003), 181–97; Julie Campoli, Elizabeth Humstone, and Alex MacLean, *Above and Beyond: Visualizing Change in Small Towns and Rural Areas* (Chicago, IL: Planners Press, American Planning Association, 2002), 37–45, 74–76, 153–61. In some cases, this has led to an old compact rural neighborhood adjacent to a newer neighborhood that looks like a post–World War II suburb. This was both enabled and exacerbated by the interstate highway system which connected more small towns and helped change the pattern not only of residential but also of small-town Main Streets by adding commercial nodes at highway interchanges. In addition, an arterial with strip development, often anchored by a WalMart, might develop along a road between Main Street and the interchange.

11. The distance considered "walkable" is often used in defining neighborhoods and their size. For a short illustrated history of neighborhood scale and walking radius, see "Sustainable Neighborhood Planning for the Region" (Treasure Coast Regional Planning Council, 2004), accessed September 22, 2011, http://www.tcrpc.org/orientation/02 _neighborhood_scale/2_neighborhood_scale_print. pdf. The area considered walkable is sometimes called a pedestrian shed and is typically considered today to be a five-minute walk or about a quarter-mile radius. In other countries and eras half-mile and one-mile radii have been used. For additional walkability planning elements, see Dhiru A. Thadani, *The Language of Towns and Cities: A Visual Dictionary* (New York, NY: Rizzoli, 2010), 731–35. To determine if an address is in a walkable neighborhood today visit www.walkscore .com (although changing retail patterns mean that this score may not accurately reflect the era in which a neighborhood was first planned).

12. Kenneth T. Jackson, *Crabgrass Frontier: The Suburbanization of America* (New York, NY: Oxford University Press, 1985), 33–35. Introduced in France, the first omnibus in the U.S. ran along Broadway in New York City beginning in 1829. Despite not running on tracks, and providing a rather rough ride over oft-rutted streets, by 1853 there were 653 omnibuses in New York City alone, and they were found in many other urban areas. Also see Clay McShane, "The Centrality of the Horse to the Nineteenth-Century American City," in *The Making of Urban America*, ed. Raymond Mohl (New York: SR Publishers, 1997), 110.

13. Hayden, 21–25; Henry C. Binford, *The First Suburbs: Residential Communities on the Boston Periphery, 1815–1860* (Chicago, IL: University of Chicago Press, 1985), 83–149.

14. Jackson, 25–33. In 1814, the first steam ferry service opened up locations for development across water bodies. Brooklyn Heights (ca. 1823), sometimes described as a suburb because of its remote location—a ferry ride across the East River from Manhattan—was actually developed as an urban-neighborhood type with narrow lots and attached houses accessed by foot. "Situated directly opposite the southeast part of the city, and being the nearest country retreat, and easiest of access from the center of business that now remains unoccupied; the distance not exceeding an average fifteen to twenty-five minute walk, including the passage of the river; the ground elevated and perfectly healthy at all seasons; as a place of residence all the advantages of the country with most of the conveniences of the city. Gentlemen whose business or profession require daily attendance into the city, cannot better, or with less expense secure the health and comfort of their families than by uniting in such an association" (32).

15. Jackson, 39–42; David L. Ames and Linda Flint McClelland, *Historic Residential Suburbs: Guidelines for Evaluation and Documentation for the National Register of Historic Places*, National Register Bulletin (Washington, DC: U.S. Department of the Interior, National Park Service, National Register of Historic Places, 2002), 17. Also see McShane, 111–12. In Boston, commuters rose from 6 percent in 1846 to 18 percent in 1860. Under ideal conditions, the area one could commute (about three square miles if walking for thirty minutes, and about twelve square miles with a four mile-per-hour omnibus) increased exponentially to about twenty-eight square miles with a horsecar going eight miles per hour.

16. For rural and urban population, see "Selected Historical Decennial Census Population and Housing Counts," U.S. Census Bureau, Table 4, http://www .census.gov/population/www/censusdata/hiscendata .html. Pittsburgh, for example, went from 47,000 in 1850 to 156,000 in 1880, Milwaukee from 20,000 to 116,000, Chicago from 30,000 to 503,000, and Boston from 137,000 to 363,000. Towns that had barely existed in 1850, like Denver and Kansas City, had populations of over 100,000 by 1890—thanks to the possibilities opened up by long-distance rail travel and shipping. The population of cities skyrocketed. Campbell Gibson, "Population of the 100 Largest Cities and Other Urban Places in the United States: 1790 to 1990," U.S. Census Bureau, *Population Division Working Paper No. 27*, Tables 8 and 12, June 1998, accessed July 14, 2010, http://www.census.gov/population/ www/documentation/twps0027/twps0027.html

17. Horsecars facilitated urban extensions in cities throughout the United States, creating areas like Dupont Circle and Capitol Hill in Washington, D.C., Lafayette Square in St. Louis, and Union Square and Franklin Square in Baltimore, Maryland.

18. Sam Bass Warner, *Streetcar Suburbs: The Pro-*

cess of Growth in Boston, 1870–1900 (Cambridge, MA: Harvard University Press, 1962), 76–78.

19. McAlester and McAlester, xxxii–xxxiii, 578–80.

20. Jackson, 41. New York City, where these were introduced in 1853, is a documented example of how rapidly the horsecar network grew. The city had 23 miles of track in 1856, expanding to 142 miles of track by 1860 when ridership reached about 100,000 per day. For an extensive survey, see Clay McShane, "The Centrality of the Horse to the Nineteenth-Century American City," in *The Making of Urban America,* ed. Raymond Mohl (New York, NY: SR Publishers, 1997), 105–30.

21. McShane, 116–25; Jackson, 105–07.

22. These three essentials were highlighted in an essay the author read but has not been successful in locating for this footnote.

23. Ames and McClelland, 34. Two primary books were Andrew Jackson Downing's *Cottage Residences, or a Series of Designs for Rural Cottages* (1842 and 1850) and Beecher's *Treatise on Domestic Economy* (1841). Both were widely read, frequently reprinted, and together had a huge effect on both the popular press and public consciousness. Hayden, 26–44; Jackson, 45–52.

24. "During the decade 1830–1840, the total length of completed railroad lines increased from 23 to 2,808 miles, and during the next ten years, more than 6,200 miles of railroad were opened, bringing the total network up to 9,021 miles in 1850. The most intensive growth during this period was in the Atlantic and Seaboard states." "American Railroads: Their Growth and Development," *Central Pacific Railroad Photographic History Museum,* last updated October 24, 2004, http://cprr.org/Museum/RR_Development.html. As a specific example, by 1850 Boston had eighty-three commuter stops within a fifteen-mile radius. Fifty-nine separate trains served these stops in 1849. As railroads expanded westward, track miles grew up to 28,920 by 1860, 49,168 by 1870, 87,801 by 1880, and 163,562 by 1890. Ames and McClelland, 16–17; Jackson, 35–38; Ann Durkin Keating, *Chicagoland: City and Suburbs in the Railroad Age* (Chicago, IL: University of Chicago Press, 2005), 7; United States Census Bureau, *Report on Transportation Business in the United States at the Eleventh Census 1890,* 4, and United States Census Bureau, *Report on the Agencies of Transportation in the United States at Tenth Census 1880,* 308–09.

25. McAlester and McAlester, xxv, xxvi–xxix. Each transcontinental railroad created new towns along their routes. The railroads also expanded existing cities; the first railroad in the country, the Baltimore & Ohio, was built to enlarge the trade area for Baltimore's harbor—in an attempt to counter the dramatic advantage that goods shipped along the Erie Canal had given the port of New York.

26. Keating, 7.

27. Jackson, 99–100.

28. Hayden, 54–61; Jackson, 76–86.

29. Jackson, 101–02.

30. Ibid., 87–100.

31. Ames and McClelland, 18; Jackson, 111; a shift from eight million in 1890 to twelve million in 1910, see U.S. Census Bureau, Table 4, http://www.census.gov/population/www/censusdata/hiscendata.html.

32. A related form of transit, cable cars had been invented in 1873 and proved particularly useful in areas with steep hills such as San Francisco. However, they were very expensive to install (requiring a central power plant) and never gained the broad popularity of horse-drawn and electric streetcars. See Jackson, 103–05, and McAlester and McAlester, 217–18, 514, 517.

33. John Stilgoe, *Metropolitan Corridor: Railroads and the American Scene* (New Haven, CT: Yale University Press, 1983), 289–93.

34. These could extend up to one hundred miles from a large city. The longest interurban line in the South connected Dallas and Fort Worth to a string of small towns located along the fertile blackland prairie—and once ran a few blocks from the author's home. Buildings associated with its relatively widely spaced stops still remain. See Hayden, 94, and Robert A. Rieder, "Electric Interurban Railways," *Handbook of Texas Online,* accessed January 18, 2011, http://www.tshaonline.org/handbook/online/articles/eqe12.

35. Hayden, 93–94; Jackson, 112–13; McAlester and McAlester, 313, 578, 671–72. The St. Charles Streetcar Line in New Orleans is the oldest continuously operated electric trolley in the country. After operating from ca. 1873 to 1893 as a horse-drawn line, it was electrified in 1893. In 1964 it became the only operating line in New Orleans. http://www.railwaypreservation.com/vintagetrolley/neworleans.htm (accessed 4/4/2013).

36. Trolleys also facilitated development around rural settlements by connecting them with cities. See Jackson, 118–20; Ames and McClelland, 18–20; McAlester and McAlester, xxxii–xxxiii, 45–46, 68, 106, 156, 191, 313, 403, 480, 519, 578–79, 584–85, 671–72.

37. See Prairie and Craftsman styles (particularly the American Four-Square), pages 551–78, for examples of these house styles.

38. Ames and McClelland, 20. Streetcar lines facilitated shopping downtown for major purchases (producing a golden age for downtown department stores). Shopping for daily necessities was accommodated by small commercial buildings located at intermittent streetcar stops.

39. Stilgoe, 299–305; Jackson, 112–13.

40. Jackson, 189.

41. Joel Tarr and Josef Konvitz, "Patterns in the Development of Urban Infrastructure," in *American Urbanism: A Historiographical Review,* ed. Howard Gillette, Jr., and Zane L. Miller (Westport, CT: Greenwood Press, 1987), 211; Ames and McClelland,

22; Virginia McAlester, Willis Winters, and Prudence Mackintosh, *The Homes of the Park Cities, Great American Suburbs* (New York, NY: Abbeville Press, 2008), 48, 87–89. Paving, as we know it today, was relatively rare prior to 1900. "Paving" at that time generally meant a gravel road, possibly with the dust subdued by oiling the gravel. New asphalt paving for streets of existing and developing neighborhoods was undertaken between 1910 and 1930. Post–World War II neighborhoods were almost always paved.

42. Examples include Highland Park West, see McAlester, Winters, and Mackintosh, 102; McAlester and McAlester, 76, 699 (Beverly Hills), 234–35 (St. Francis Wood), 575 (Highland Park West).

43. McAlester and McAlester, 416 (Fairacres in Omaha) and 337–38 (North End in Boise).

44. Joseph B. Mason, *History of Housing in the U.S. 1930–1980* (Houston, TX: Gulf Publishing Company, 1981), 13.

45. Ibid., 44–47.

46. FHA, *Successful Subdivisions: Principles of Planning for Economy and Protection Against Neighborhood Blight*, Land Use Planning Bulletin No. 1 (Washington, DC: GPO, n.d., ca. 1940).

47. Most common in large areas of previously vacant land that was not subdivided until after World War II. Post–World War II houses were built in many other settings: on still-vacant lots platted in earlier grid neighborhoods, and also in various subdivision patterns on small farms and large homesteads that were still present in built-up areas.

48. Cynthia L. Girling and Kenneth I. Helphand, *Yard, Street, Park* (New York, NY: John Wiley & Sons, 1994), 97–98.

49. Clarence Perry's principles for his "Neighborhood Unit," first published in 1929, included schools, parks, and nearby retail as important parts of a neighborhood. This had a significant effect first on the 1931 President's Conference on Housing and through this on the FHA's land-planning standards, in particular their recommendation for inclusion of these amenities in large-subdivision plans. Ames and McClelland, 47–48.

50. FHA, 13–14.

51. Hayden, 154–97.

52. Ames and McClelland, 23–24. During 1921–1936 alone more than 420,000 miles of road were built in the U.S., including intercity highways and farm-to-market roads, much of it with 50 percent federal subsidy from the 1916 Federal-Aid Highway Act. Jackson, 248–50. The interstate system was planned in the 1940s but did not receive their 90 percent federal funding until 1956. Earlier highways had been generally only 50 percent funded by the federal government.

53. Hayden, 168–71; www.alliemae.org/historyoffanniemae.html.

54. Thadani, 666. Also called DOT (development-oriented transit). For an excellent overview of "walkable urban" neighborhoods see Christopher B. Lionberger, *The Option of Urbanism: Investing in a New American Dream* (Washington, DC: Island Press, 2008), 86–137. While not all accessible by transit, a goal for sustainable development is to create walkable urban areas at select rapid-transit stops. This book also describes alternative "drivable suburban areas" and separates these two viable alternatives from the "Neverlands" that make up many edge nodes and are not enjoyable to either walk or drive.

55. Thadani, 664; Hayden, 201–29.

56. Thadani, 209–10; see illustrations on pages 211–12. See page 604 for density needed to support commercial uses; for example, it takes one thousand dwelling units for a corner store, two thousand dwelling units for a convenience store, six to eight thousand dwelling units for a supermarket plus ten to fifteen smaller stores.

57. Lionberger, 7. This is of a total package of U.S. assets that includes the value of natural resources, corporate equity, government bonds, and individual-citizen cash and even art collections.

58. Mason, 70; The interstate portion was engineered prior to strict interstate guidelines.

59. Richard O. Baumbach, Jr., and William E. Borah, *The Second Battle of New Orleans: A History of the Vieux Carré Riverfront-Expressway Controversy* (Tuscaloosa, AL: University of Alabama Press, 1981).

60. Jane Jacobs, *The Death and Life of Great American Cities* (New York, NY: Random House, 1961). It is a loss to not yet have books similarly describing early suburbs—streetcar, early automobile, and even post–World War II first-ring suburbs. These are not the dense, mixed-use urban neighborhoods of the Jacobs book but are quite distinct from the far-flung later post-suburban SLUG development (called "Neverlands" by Lionberger) that has proved so costly to the economy and the environment. Preserving the unique qualities of the excellent early suburban environments has high value, as they are often well-located and livable, drivable suburban neighborhoods.

61. National Historic Preservation Act of 1966, Community Reinvestment Act of 1977, Urban Renewal and Housing Act of 1949, National Housing Act of 1934. The National Historic Preservation Act of 1966 spurred surveys to list neighborhoods and landmarks on the National Register of Historic Places—the official listing that gave them protection against the use of federal funds for projects that would demolish them (or at least required a study of the alternatives to demolition). Because so little of the country had been fully surveyed, determining that an area was *eligible* for listing also gave some protection.

62. citiwire.net. Neal Peirce, Washington Post Writers Group, March 10, 2012. "What's easily forgotten is how the deep gashes in America's city fabric occurred. The highway planners of 1950s and 1960s seemed unfazed by pushing massive highways straight through cities, devastating black and other low-income

neighborhoods as well as cutting off waterfronts. It's a dark chapter in the American story. As my friend Peter Harnik writes in his Island Press book *Urban Green*: 'Waterfronts were blockaded in Portland, Cincinnati, Hartford, Cleveland, Philadelphia and San Francisco. Nooses of concrete were wound tightly around the downtowns of Dallas and Charlotte. Trenches of noise and smog cut through Boston, Detroit, Seattle and Atlanta. Stupendous elevated structures threw shadows over Miami and New Orleans. And wide strips of land were taken from large, iconic parks in Los Angeles, St. Louis, Baltimore and San Diego (*and San Antonio*).' Yet, as some of the intrusive roadways have collapsed, they've actually triggered amazingly rapid recovery and new prosperity. The collapse of a chunk of New York City's elevated West Side Highway in 1973 didn't, for example, cause the traffic Armageddon anticipated. As Streetsblog founder Aaron Naparstek noted at the Philadelphia Forum, substitution of a ground-level, more modest urban boulevard 'has made some of Lower Manhattan into some of the world's most valuable real estate.' " And the same has happened in Boston, Massachusetts, where the Big Dig put an elevated freeway underground. The Congress for the New Urbanism has a list of the Top Ten Possible Freeway Teardowns.

63. Michael Southworth and Eran Ben-Joseph, *Streets and the Shaping of Towns and Cities* (New York, NY: McGraw Hill, 1997), 84.

64. Hannah B. Higgins, *The Grid Book* (Cambridge, MA: MIT Press, 2009), 79–98; "Grid Plans," last modified on January 9, 2011, http://en.wikipedia.org/wiki/Grid_plan.

65. The original 1862 version gave out 160 acres, or a one-quarter section. Later versions of the act addressed less productive land moving west, and they gave away half-sections and full-sections. Lee Ann Potter and Wynell Schamel, "The Homestead Act of 1862," *Social Education* 61, no. 6 (October 1997): 359–64. "Teaching with Documents: The Homestead Act of 1862," National Archives, accessed July 3, 2010, http://www.archives.gov/education/lessons/homestead-act/; Milestone Documents (Washington, DC: National Archives and Records Administration, 1995), 55–56.

66. Government policy was to distribute sections of land to the railroads in a checkerboard pattern as incentive for private companies to build rail lines, particularly in the West.

67. For a remarkable overview of early town plans, see John William Reps, *The Making of Urban America: A History of City Planning in the United States* (Princeton, NJ: Princeton University Press, 1965).

68. Pregill and Volkman, 443–47. Denver, Kansas City, Boston, Brooklyn, Baltimore, Dallas, and Memphis are among the many cities that have streets with green medians linking neighborhoods together. In addition, many individual neighborhoods had streets with green medians included in their neighborhood

plans—a few examples are Riverhills in Houston, Munger Place in Dallas (today the portion with the median is part of the Swiss Avenue Historic District), Woodruff Place in Indianapolis, St. Francis Wood in San Francisco, Highland Park West in Dallas, and Guilford in Baltimore. After about 1940 planning generally shifted away from grand boulevards and turned to more utilitarian arterial streets coupled with large "efficient" highway systems and interior streets that did not invite outsiders. For a discussion of grand boulevards and side access lanes, see Allan B. Jacobs, Elizabeth Macdonald, and Yodan Rofé, *The Boulevard Book: History, Evolution, Design of Multiway Boulevards* (Cambridge, MA: MIT Press, 2002), 44–53.

69. Pregill and Volkman, 528–30.

70. Andrew Jackson Downing, *A Treatise on the Theory and Practice of Landscape Gardening, Adapted to North America, with a View to the Improvement of Country Residences* (New York, NY: Wiley and Putnam, 9th ed., 1875), 92–93. Downing contrasts the angular "Plan of a Common Farm, before any improvements" with a curvilinear "Plan of the foregoing grounds as a Country Seat, after ten years improvement." These same theories were further promoted by his equally successful Victorian cottage residences (Dover Architectural Series [New York, NY: Dover Publications, 1842]) and in *The Horticulturist*, a journal he edited during 1846–1852.

71. Downing's book was the popular American voice of a romantic landscape movement that began in England and was first implemented in the United States in Mount Auburn Cemetery outside Boston, as well as other cemetery projects that followed. Also see Pregill and Volkman, 394–98, and Reps, 325–31.

72. McAlester and McAlester, 698–99.

73. Norman T. Newton, *Design on the Land: The Development of Landscape Architecture* (Cambridge, MA: Belknap Press of Harvard University Press, 1971), 465–68; Hayden, 61–65; Jackson, 79–81. Olmsted's "Report" on Riverside also introduced the use of deed restrictions, tree planting, and other staples of neighborhood planning still used today. Olmsted (1822–1903) was widely considered the father of landscape architecture, and his son, Frederick Law Olmsted, Jr. (1870–1957), organized the country's first landscape design program at Harvard University in 1900. "Olmsted planted no fewer than 7,000 evergreens, 32,000 deciduous trees, and 47,000 shrubs in Riverside." The Frederick Law Olmsted Society of Riverside Illinois, http://www.olmstedsociety.org/.

74. Ames and McClelland, 37; McAlester and McAlester, 77.

75. FHA, 15, 18, 26–27.

76. Mason, 113. *The Community Builders Handbook: Prepared by the Community Builder's Council of the Urban Land Institute, 1947 (revised 1968)*. 1968. 218–22.

77. McAlester and McAlester, 698. In special circumstances, such as mining towns or the deepwater

port of San Francisco, it was necessary to build towns on less regular topography.

78. This might be a central town square, market square, courthouse square, neighborhood square, or, rarely, multiple squares. Circles also occurred. More irregular town greens were typical in parts of New England. A central plaza was considered so important by the Spanish that they actually legislated this space in their rules for building colonial settlements, the Laws of the Indies. See Reps for in-depth discussions of these and other plan types.

79. Pregill and Volkman, 423–47. Parks featuring active athletic areas such as baseball fields and tennis courts became increasingly common during the early 20th century but are not included in this simple matrix of green areas.

80. What happened to America's streetcar systems is an interesting topic with two hotly contested sides. It seems likely, based on both GM's desire to sell buses and the need to have broad arterial streets in existing cities, that GM played a strong, varied, and behind-the-scenes role in the conversion from electric streetcar to motor bus. By removing streetcar lines (a distinct advantage to motor bus sales), they gained more than ten thousand miles of broad paved city streets perfectly located to become automobile arterials with no expense beyond the removal of the tracks. There was no more cost-efficient or resource-conserving way to add automobile traffic into developed areas. This motivation is not discussed in the articles cited here that present two differing sides. "General Motors Streetcar Conspiracy," accessed August 18, 2010, http://www.fact-index.com/g/ge/general_motors_streetcar_conspiracy.html; Bradford C. Snell, "American Ground Transport: A Proposal for Restructuring the Automobile, Truck, Bus and Rail Industries," report presented to the Committee of the Judiciary, Subcommittee on Antitrust and Monopoly, United States Senate, February 26, 1974 (Washington, DC: U.S. Government Printing Office, 1974), 16–24; Cliff Slater, "General Motors and the Demise of Streetcars," *Transportation Quarterly* 51 (1997). General Motors seems to have used a revolving-fund concept, buying streetcar companies, converting the cars to buses, reselling them with guarantees they would never be converted back to streetcars, and then taking the funds and buying the next company.

81. McAlester and McAlester, 704–05.

82. Ibid., 699–700; "Variety of American Grids," *Discovering Urbanism,* last modified May 25, 2010, http://discoveringurbanism.blogspot.com/2010/05/variety-of-american-grids.html.

83. Ames and McClelland, 26; Marc A. Weiss, *The Rise of the Community Builders: The American Real Estate Industry and Urban Land Planning* (New York, NY: Columbia University Press, 1987), 1–6. Land intended for uses other than residential is also subdivided.

84. Warner, 37–38, 126–32; Hayden, 132.

85. Weiss, 2.

86. Ibid.

87. McAlester and McAlester, 8–10.

88. Weiss, 1–6.

89. McAlester and McAlester, 8–10; Jackson, 203–06.

90. United States Department of Veteran Affairs, "G.I. Bill History," last modified November 6, 2009, http://www.gibill.va.gov/benefits/history_timeline/index.html.

91. Mason, 12–14; McAlester, Winters, and Mackintosh, 163–64. The inclusion of all major appliances with the mortgage made purchase even more attractive.

92. Jackson, 197–218; Kristen B. Crossney and David W. Bartelt, "Residential Security, Risk, and Race: The Home Owners' Loan Corporation and Mortgage Access in Two Cities," *Urban Geography* 26, no. 8 (2005): 707; William J. Wilson, *When Work Disappears: The World of the New Urban Poor* (New York, NY: Knopf, 1996).

93. This was called "redlining" because maps were annotated with red ink, showing the undesirable areas. Inner-city neighborhoods throughout the United States were redlined, effectively starving them of funds for home purchases or restoration. In 1975 Munger Place, an early-20th-century streetcar suburb in Dallas, Texas, was effectively redlined. Preservation Dallas formed a nonprofit revolving fund (this was a volunteer project chaired by the author) and the fund purchased two dozen houses, most slated for demolition by the City of Dallas because of their poor condition. The question was how to resell the houses. We were able to work with Fannie Mae's national office and with the Lakewood Bank and Trust Company, then the area's neighborhood bank, to create a demonstration lending project. The goal was to show that such areas could be restored if mortgages were made available. The Lakewood Bank made construction loans to bring the houses up to code, and Fannie Mae agreed to provide "take-out" letters guaranteeing to purchase the banks' construction loans and provide typical 20- and 30-year mortgages to the homeowners. The program pioneered a completely new way of lending for Fannie Mae and became available nationally. The new program was actively promoted to lending institutions throughout the United States by Don Wright, who had been Lakewood Bank's president.

94. Board of Governors of the Federal Reserve System, "Community Reinvestment Act of 1977," last modified May 4, 2011, http://www.federalreserve.gov/communitydev/cra_about.htm.

95. This specific example is drawn from the deed restriction for the first plan of Munger Place in Dallas, Texas. Today many new high-end residential neighborhoods are also the most heavily governed, their

zoning enhanced by deed restrictions sometimes to obtain a certain look.

96. Ames and McClelland, 36. In 1924 the Standard State Zoning Enabling Act was written by Secretary of Commerce Herbert Hoover's Advisory Committee on Zoning, both to make it simpler for a state to allow zoning and to try to provide some legal continuity between the statutes of different states. Stuart Meck, AICP, *Model Planning and Zoning Enabling Legislation: A Short History,* vol. 1 of *Modernizing State Planning Statutes: The Growing Smart Working Papers* (American Planning Association, 1996) is a concise and understandable essay on this topic.

97. Meck, 2–4. William I. Goodman and Eric C. Freund, *Principles and Practices of Urban Planning* (Washington, DC: International City Managers' Association, 1968), 443–84. Comprehensive subdivision regulation spread almost as fast as zoning. By 1934, some 425 American cities had made subdivision regulation part of their planning departments.

98. Christopher Leinberger, "Sustainable Development and the Value of Urban Design," Dallas City Council briefing, January 2009. For a group of new walkable neighborhoods mostly built on former industrial sites, see Nate Berg, "Cutting Car Use at the Neighborhood Level," *Atlantic Cities Place Matters,* October 3, 2011, accessed September 27, 2011, http://www.theatlanticcities.com/commute/2011/10/cutting-car-use-new-developments/226/.

99. McAlester and McAlester, vi. This approach is introduced on page vi and used throughout.

100. Pregill and Volkman, 516–17.

101. McAlester and McAlester, 703. Evergreen trees with branches that grow to the ground, such as southern magnolias, are not desirable as street trees as they obliterate any view of historic houses.

102. Thadani, 239–40; Randall Arendt and Elizabeth A. Brabec, *Rural by Design: Maintaining Small Town Character* (Chicago, IL: Planners Press, American Planning Association, 1994), 10.

103. Girling and Helphand, 21–34; Residential Yard Typology chart, 29.

104. Ames and McClelland, 52–53.

105. Pregill and Volkman, 503–10.

106. Ibid., 594–96; Leonard H. Johnson, *Foundation Planting* (New York, NY: A. T. DeLa Mare Company, Inc., 1927), x–xi.

107. Ames and McClelland, 57–59; Rick Darke, *In Harmony with Nature: Lessons from the Arts and Crafts Garden* (New York, NY: Friedman/Fairfax Publishers, 2000); McAlester and McAlester, 705.

108. Ames and McClelland, 60 and 69.

109. According to geographer Terry G. Jordan's *Texas: A Geography* (Boulder, CO: Westview Press, 1984), there were four original types of western land surveys; see, in addition, accessed July 3, 2010, http://en.wikipedia.org/wiki/Public_Land_Survey_System,

for a good overview; McAlester and McAlester, 695–98; Pregill and Volkman, 328–44.

110. Jordan, 200–04. He goes on to say that southerners knew no other survey method prior to about 1800.

111. Under Spanish rule, Texas had land on waterways divided into long lots as early as 1731, according to Jordan, and in the 1830s independent Texas made "this pattern of survey mandatory for lands lying adjacent to major streams." The long-lot survey was not confined to the Spanish colonies; it also was used by the French in parceling out land in the Mississippi River Valley. In addition, the Dutch distributed land along the Hudson River in large "patroonships," with a sixteen-mile frontage along the Hudson and stretching as far back from the river as was "reasonable." Also see Pregill and Volkman, 331–32.

112. "The Public Land Survey System (PLSS)," last modified January 26, 2011, http://nationalatlas.gov/articles/boundaries/a_plss.html.

113. Where roads have been maintained along the one-mile lines, they are often obvious from the air. In some western cities the roads are broad arterials, lit at night with multiple rows of streetlights and clearly displaying the section lines first surveyed in accordance with the Land Ordinance of 1785.

114. California and New Mexico still had large areas of public lands that were surveyed under the Land Ordinance system after they became part of the United States in 1848. Texas surveyed its own land and (for lands not lying along rivers) at first followed Spanish/Mexican practice with an angled 45° southwest/northeast grid, later changing to a north-south system similar to the PLSS.

115. Jordan, 202.

116. Dell Upton, *Another City: Urban Life and Urban Spaces in the New American Republic* (New Haven, CT: Yale University Press, 2008), 33.

117. We understand this because of an unpublished 1990 paper by our friend Constance Adams titled "The Visible City: Tracing Memory and Character in Dallas' Historical Landscape." While at Yale Architecture School, she was able to trace the varying angles of in-town Dallas streets back to the original land grants. It should be noted that when Texas entered the U.S. it was an independent republic and was allowed to retain its right to assign out its own public lands; the state eventually chose to voluntarily follow the general precepts of the Land Ordinance of 1785.

FOLK HOUSES

1. Daniel D. Reiff, *Houses from Books: Treatises, Pattern Books, and Catalogs in American Architecture, 1738–1950: A History and Guide* (University Park, PA:

Pennsylvania State University Press, 2000), 304. The statement of continuity into later years is observational by the author.

2. Jay Dearborn Edwards, "Shotgun: The Most Contested House in America," *Buildings and Landscapes: Journal of the Vernacular Architecture Forum* 16 (2009): 62–96. Based on the aftermath of Hurricane Katrina, this paper traces the evolution of the shotgun houses of New Orleans.

3. John Fraser Hart, Michelle J. Rhodes, and John T. Morgan, *The Unknown World of the Mobile Home* (Baltimore, MD, and London: John Hopkins University Press, 2002), 1–35. This short history explains why definitive figures regarding manufactured housing vary from source to source. It includes excellent documented information that is used throughout this chapter, along with current statistics from the Manufactured Housing Institutes. See, accessed September 18, 2011, http://www.allmanufacturedhomes .com/html/vintage_mobile_homes.htm, for dated photos of mobile homes from the 1930s to 1975.

COLONIAL HOUSES

1. Reiff, 27–33.

2. A handful of urban-style houses were built in rural settings in the Albany region. These had the entrance on the long, non-gabled wall; in contrast, houses built in rows had the entrance in the narrow, gabled end, which always faced the street to conserve space on narrow, urban lots. Ironically, only these "rural" urban houses have survived, those of the larger towns having been destroyed by three centuries of urban growth.

3. Joseph Manca, "On the Origins of the American Porch, Architectural Persistence in Hudson Valley Dutch Settlements," *Winterthur Portfolio* 40 (2005): 95–96, 99–111.

4. Inspired by Native American traditions, folk houses with crude, half-timbered walls and thatched roofs are also common in Spanish America. Known as *jacal* or *palisado* construction, the walls consist of vertical posts set in the ground to provide support for a framework of twigs covered with clay. An example appears to the right of the masonry house in Figure 3, page 196.

5. David Gebhard, "Some Additional Observations on California's Monterey Tradition," *Journal of the Society of Architectural Historians* 46, no. 2 (1987): 170. This article traces the origin of these broad porches—both cantilevered and two-story—to the similar porches found in the "southeastern United States, the Gulf of Mexico, the Caribbean, and Bermuda." Gebhard suggests Monterey's porches be considered Southern/Caribbean elements, not "New England" ones, as has frequently been the case.

6. David Gebhard, "Some Additional Observations on California's Monterey Tradition," *Journal of the Society of Architectural Historians* 46, no. 2 (1987): 169–70. See also Monterey (the revival of this type of Spanish Colonial house) on pages 536–40.

7. Daniel D. Reiff, *Houses from Books: Treatises, Pattern Books, and Catalogs in American Architecture, 1738–1950: A History and Guide* (University Park, PA: Pennsylvania State University Press, 2000), 24. In some cases carved architectural details were imported from England.

8. Reiff, 23–33, 42–44.

9. Reiff, 25. This was the only house built before 1750 in the U.S. that closely followed a design published in a book (Palladio's Book II, plate 56).

10. Reiff, 31–32.

11. Fanlights are found in only a few high-style Georgian houses but become almost universal in the Federal house; they also occur in the closely related Early Classical Revival houses.

12. Reiff, 138–43.

13. The full flowering of this new concern for archeological classicism came in the contemporaneous Early Classical Revival and subsequent Greek Revival houses.

14. Reiff, 40–41.

ROMANTIC HOUSES

1. Reiff, 79–84. Latrobe also trained two pupils as architects, William Strickland and Robert Mills.

2. Reiff, 66.

3. A number of early-20th-century periodicals and books featured Swiss Chalets—and considered their exposed wood structure to be related to Craftsman houses. See http://www.dahp.wa.gov/styles/ swiss-chalet.

4. John H. Martin, "Orson Squire Fowler: Phrenology and Octagon Houses 1809–1887," *Crooked Lane Review* 137 (fall 2005).

VICTORIAN HOUSES

1. Reiff, 79.

2. Reiff, 133–35.

3. George L. Hersey, "Godey's Choice," *Journal of the Society of Architectural Historians* 18 (1959): 104–11. This survey of the architectural styles of the house design offered by *Godey's Lady's Book* and *Lady's Magazine* from 1851 to 1891 shows Mansard as most common during the 1870s.

4. Reiff, 86, 92–93.

5. The refinement and spread of factory techniques to shape raw wood into endless intricate variations made it progressively easier to provide an elaborated front facade as the late 19th century progressed.

6. Reiff, 86. Henry Hudson Holly, *Holly's Country Seats Containing Lithographic Designs for Cottages, Villas, Mansions, etc., with Their Accompanying Outbuildings, also country Churches, City Buildings, Railway Stations, etc., etc.* (New York, NY: D. Appleton, 1863). Designs Number 1 and 7 show applied horizontal and vertical stickwork. Robert P. Guter and Janet W. Foster, *Building by the Book: Pattern Book Architecture in New Jersey* (New Brunswick, NJ: 1992), 141–7.

7. For a detailed discussion of this movement and how it influenced Hunt and other American architects, see Sarah Bradford Landau, "Richard Morris Hunt, the Continental Picturesque, and the Stick Style," *Journal of the Society of Architectural Historians* 42 (1983): 272–89.

8. This term was introduced in Vincent Scully, *The Shingle Style and the Stick Style: Architectural Theory and Design from Richardson to the Origins of Wright* (New Haven, CT: Yale University Press, 1971).

9. Janet W. Foster, *The Queen Anne House: America's Victorian Vernacular* (New York, NY: Abrams, 2006), 16–17.

10. Henry Hudson Holly, *Modern Dwellings in Town and Country Adapted to American Wants and Climate with a Treatise on Furniture and Decoration* (New York, NY: Harper and Brothers, 1878). Holly began with a chapter titled "The Queen Anne Style" and proceeded not only to illustrate the style with plans but also to cover a range of topics related to the style, including a definitive illustration of the new type of entry—a living stair hall—a large roomy space, often with a fireplace and stairway designed so railings could be easily admired (pages 42 and 117).

11. Foster, 18. Guter and Foster, 147–56.

12. This preference was greatly encouraged by the 1893 World's Columbian Exposition in Chicago. Nothing was easier, after falling in love with the Classical columns that dominated the heart of the Exposition, than adding Classical detail to the shape and form of a house that was already being built with spindlework details.

13. Jay Dearborn Edwards, "Shotgun: The Most Contested House in America," *Buildings and Landscapes: Journal of the Vernacular Architecture Forum* 16 (2009): 62–96. This presents a scholarly overview of the evolution of all types of shotguns in New Orleans. Lloyd Vogt, *New Orleans Houses: A House-Watcher's Guide* (Gretna, LA: Pelican Pub. Co., 1985). This has excellent illustrations of the most common New Orleans Folk Victorian house forms and typical bracketed detailing.

ECLECTIC HOUSES

1. FHA. *Principals of Planning Small Houses* (1940), 28–29.

2. Gavin Edward Townsend, "The Tudor House in America: 1890–1930" (Ph.D. dissertation, University of California, Santa Barbara), 1, 264–65. Two studies are reported here. First, the results of a study in *Architectural Record*'s November 1925 issue that counts the styles of 571 houses published in architectural yearbooks and periodicals from 1923 to 1925. Second, Townsend's own count of the styles of 779 houses illustrated in *Architectural Record*'s annual country house issue between 1910 and 1932.

3. W. Barksdale Maynard, "Best, Lowliest Style! The Early Nineteenth-Century Rediscovery of American Colonial Architecture," *Journal of the Society of Architectural Historians* 59 (2000): 338–57. Maynard carefully traces the intellectual and nostalgic rediscovery of America's Colonial past during the early and mid-19th-century. He links it to both England's Picturesque movement and the 1876 Centennial.

4. See David Gebhard, "The American Colonial Revival in the 1930s," *Winterthur Portfolio* 22, no. 2/3 (summer/autumn 1987), 109–48; and David Gebhard, "Royal Barry Wills and the American Colonial Revival," *Winterthur Portfolio* 27, no. 1 (spring 1992), 45–74.

5. In England the word porch was used for an *entry* porch—a covered approach to the front door. In America the word porch has a far more inclusive meaning and often refers to a wider and deeper porch meant for use as an outdoor living space.

6. T. Matlack Price, "The Inherent Qualities of Building Materials: An Exposition of Considerations Governing Choice" *Arts and Decoration,* volume 5, number 11 (September 1915), 416. A builder estimated the cost of building a house from different materials. He began with a balloon-frame house clad with wood shingles that could be built at the base price of $10,000. Were the same house clad in clapboard it would cost $10,040. If it were covered in wire-lathe and stucco the cost would be $10,226. If it were constructed of hollow tile covered with stucco the price would be $10,681. If the house was instead constructed with solid brick walls the cost would be $11,272. Rough-finished stone walls would be $12,046—and true half-timbered construction would cost $12,546.

7. Gavin Edward Townsend, "The Tudor House in America: 1890–1930" (Ph.D. dissertation, University of California, Santa Barbara), 192–3.

8. Gavin Edward Townsend, "The Tudor House in America" (Ph.D. thesis, University of California, Santa Barbara, 1986), 1, 265. Townsend includes two separate studies that count the number of times houses of the most popular styles appeared in architectural publications during the 1920s. These are primarily large architect-designed houses. It seems likely that when one-story builder houses are also included that the Tudor style would likely be closer to the higher number given here.

9. Townsend, 103–10. This has a comprehensive

discussion of the many different types and titles of books that were available.

10. Townsend, 3–13 discusses the origins of these terms and others that are commonly used to describe Tudor houses.

11. For example, stone homes dominate suburbs near Philadelphia (where Wissahickon schist was quarried locally) and homes of ochre brick with iron-stone trim dominate Dallas (where local clays produced an ochre brick generally trimmed with reddish ironstone from nearby quarries).

12. McAlester and McAlester, 518, 674. In Seattle, Washington, the homes designed by Bebb and Mendel with stone first floors and extensive half-timbering in the upper stories likely led to the popularity of heavy half-timbering there. In contrast, in Portland, Oregon, architect Wade Pipes (1877–1961) designed many simple stucco-clad homes, unadorned by half-timbering, an approach widespread in that city. Pipes had studied in England and was familiar with, and favored designing, the "modern English home" designs of Voysey and Lutyens. Individual details, such as false thatched roofs or clipped gables, could also be locally favored. In the hands of master architects, such as Frank Lloyd Wright's Nathan Moore House in Oak Park, Illinois, and Greene and Greene's Robinson House in Pasadena, California, the style assumed intriguing Arts and Crafts qualities. See Lee Goff, *Tudor Style* (New York, NY: Universe Publishing, 2002), 177, 113. Most American architects practicing from 1890 to 1930 designed one or more houses in the Tudor style. This included both architects with a national reputation who were designing in many locations as well as architects whose work was generally confined to a single city or region.

13. Although a Beaux Arts house may look like it is all constructed of stone (both walls and decorative trim) or like it has brick walls with contrasting stone decorative trim, chances are very high that the trim and decorative elements are made of glazed terra cotta or possibly cast stone. Glazed terra cotta is a hard-fired clay product that could be glazed to look like most of the stones that were typically used on houses. Cast stone is a concrete product with less versatility in its finishes. Both offered relatively inexpensive ways to provide door and window surrounds and a broad range of decorative details that resembled carved stone. They were not limited to the Beaux Arts, but were also used for the decorative and trim elements of masonry houses in many other Eclectic and late Victorian styles. In fact, glazed architectural terra cotta is so versatile in its finishes, and can so closely resemble stone, that few people are aware of how widespread its use was in the early 20th century. It was not limited to trim, but was also used to clad entire buildings. It was particularly useful for disguising the steel skeletons of tall buildings built before World War II. According to the National Park Service's Preservation

Brief 7, below, many owners and architects today are "surprised to discover that what they presumed to be a granite or limestone building is glazed architectural terra cotta instead." The National Park Service's Technical Preservation Services Publications are available online and give excellent short histories of the materials and topics they cover—in addition to discussing preservation techniques. For more on terra cotta and cast stone see: Preservation Brief 7: De Teel Patterson Tiller, "The Preservation of Historic Glazed Architectural Terra Cotta," Technical Preservation Services of the National Park Service (http://www.nps.gov/tps /how-to-preserve/briefs/42-cast-stone.htm); and Preservation Brief 42: Richard Pieper, "The Maintenance, Repair and Replacement of Historic Cast Stone," Technical Preservation Services of the National Park Service (http://www.nps.gov/tps/how-to-preserve /briefs/7-terra-cotta.htm).

14. Townsend, 1, 264–6.

15. Townsend, 253–79. McAlester, Winters, and Mackintosh, 259–65, 325–29. Townsends's thesis has an excellent chapter on French Eclectic houses. *Homes of the Park Cities, Dallas* has excellent examples of how the style was interpreted by Dallas architects in the 1930s—as it likely was in other areas where construction continued during the 1930s. George N. Marble designed many French Eclectic houses for Dallas builders Dines & Kraft in the 1930s. In addition, Charles S. Dilbeck, who was, according to Willis Winters, "the most prodigious and popularly admired residential architect ever to practice in Dallas," designed many creative houses. He first designed French houses in Tulsa, Oklahoma, from 1929 to 1932. He then moved to Dallas in 1932 and partnered with several different builders as he designed a wonderful repertoire of French houses. Dilbeck also designed many creative Ranch houses.

16. Goodhue had encouraged the publication of and prepared the plans for *Spanish-Colonial Architecture in Mexico* (Boston, MA: J. B. Millet, 1901) and had already designed buildings with Mexico's elaborate Spanish Colonial precedents (Santísima Trinidad Cathedral in Havana, Cuba, and Hotel Colón in Panama).

17. Then called the Great War, it involved France, England, Italy, Austria, Russia, Germany, and others. Spain was not involved, protected by the Pyrenees Mountains. It made an excellent destination for a sketching trip after architecture school. This had been an important rite of passage for aspiring architects in the 19th century, when reproductions of photographs were prohibitively expensive. Traditionally, they filled sketchbooks with details they could use later in buildings they designed. Although in the 1910s books of photographs were becoming more widely available, such a trip was still of importance.

18. Elizabeth McMillian, *California Colonial: The Spanish and Rancho Revival Styles* (Atglen, PA:

Schiffer Publishing, Ltd., 2002), 37–57, has an overview of the Spanish architectural eras found in the quite varied Spanish Eclectic. For many years, this style was referred to as Spanish Colonial Revival, a correct term for buildings based on those of Mexico, Cuba, and South America. However, because most of the 1920s publications were of Spain itself and formed the basis of many houses, the 1984 edition of this book used the term Spanish Eclectic. Today, architecture historians are beginning to use the more inclusive Spanish Revival.

19. It is not unusual for Spanish features to be combined with Italian and even southern French details, creating houses that do not fit neatly into Spanish Revival, Mission, or Italian Renaissance. These are often called Mediterranean Revival, an even more inclusive name that covers a still wider range of variations and mixtures.

20. David Gebhard, "Some Additional Observations on California's Monterey tradition," *Journal of the Society of Architectural Historians* 46, no. 2 (June 1987): 157–70.

21. McMillian, 57–58; Mason, 14–15; Roland Coate, Sr., "The Early California House: Blending the Colonial and California Forms," *California Arts and Architecture* 35, no. 3 (1929): 22–23.

MODERN HOUSES

1. Larry Paul Fuller, ed., *The American Institute of Architects Guide to Dallas Architecture* (New York: McGraw-Hill Construction Information Group, 1999): 89

2. "The Cape Cod Cottage," *Architectural Forum* (March 1949), 101–06, author unknown. This example uses traditional balloon-frame wood construction.

3. Minimal Traditional houses are also called "small houses," "Depression-era cottages," "War Years cottages," "Victory cottages," "economical small houses," "FHA Houses," and "FHA Smalls." See "The American Small House," a presentation of The Historic Preservation Division of the Georgia Department of Natural Resources (pdf available at georgiashpo.org/historic/housing).

4. Joseph B. Mason, *History of Housing in the U.S. 1930–1980* (Houston, TX: Gulf Publishing Company, 1982), 6–7. The 1933 starts were down a stunning 90 percent from 1925.

5. McAlester, Winters, and Mackintosh, 164.

6. Among these were: Editors of *Architectural Forum, The Book of Small Houses* (New York, NY: Simon and Schuster, 1936); L. F. Garlinghouse Company, *Sunshine Homes* (Topeka, KS: L. F. Garlinghouse, 1938); National Plan Service, Inc., *Homes of Moderate Cost* (1941); *Home Builders Book of Low Cost Homes* (St. Paul, MN: Brown-Blodgett Company, 1941); *House-of-the-Month Book of Small Houses,* ed. Harold C. Group (Garden City, NJ: Garden City

Publishing Co., Inc., 1946); John P. Dean and Simon Breines, *The Book of Houses* (New York, NY: Crown Publishers, 1946); John S. Burrows, *Your New Home* (New York, NY: Archway Press, Inc., 1948).

7. *Principles of Planning Small Houses, Federal Housing Administration Technical Bulletin No. 4,* revised July 1, 1940, 12–25. There were many versions of this booklet. Its 1940 edition shows multiple ways to arrange interiors and slightly vary the exteriors of similarly shaped small houses. It was a less illustrated May 1, 1936, version that became available as construction of Minimal Traditional houses heated up in 1936. Starts grew to 336,000 in 1937, 406,000 in 1938, 515,000 in 1939, and 603,000 in 1940. This bulletin also showed how to efficiently add heating, plumbing, kitchens, and bathrooms to a house. These elements had not previously been a requirement for very small homes—and indeed had often not been the norm for them in earlier decades. Examples from the 1930s are shown in McAlester, Winters, and Mackintosh, 159–64, and discussed in McAlester and McAlester under Fairview, 10.

8. Mason, 31–41. Builders closed up their current projects to take up residence near planned industry and build large developments of urgently needed defense housing for the workers relocating to wartime industrial complexes. Wartime production was extraordinary: "71,000 naval ships; 300,000 aircraft; 100,000 tanks; 2.5 million trucks; 370,000 artillery pieces; 5.9 million bombs; 20 million small arms; 42 million rounds of ammunition; 5,400 cargo ships" were built in the U.S. for the Allies to use during World War II (Mason, 34). All of this varied production utilized the fastest production methods possible.

9. Mason, 41–44. Experience in rapid construction not only was taking place at home, it was also being gained on the front lines. The Seabees (the nickname of the Navy's Construction Battalion) had one thousand architects among its ranks. They were building bridges and assembling entire bases overseas in days to accommodate landing battalions, create instant airfields, and such. They used many ingenious approaches.

10. Mason, 46. Ten million servicemen returned right at the end of the war. The number of servicemen eligible for these no-down-payment GI Bill loans eventually totaled sixteen million.

11. Mason, 47, 49, 51, 53.

12. Levittown, New York, on Long Island, is the best known of the rapidly built postwar developments. Its developer, William Levitt, had built housing for defense workers during the war and learned to improvise rapid building techniques. When he applied these to his first postwar development, he was building side-gabled Minimal Traditional houses and small Ranchettes (early Ranch houses). While Levitt garnered much of the publicity, many other developers were doing the same thing in other parts of the United States. Mason, 48–49.

13. A very slightly revised version of *Principles of Planning Small Homes* was published in 1946, signifying continued support for these houses. The story of a Dallas couple who tried for a slightly more "modern" house is told in "The Mortgage Pattern Poses Problems: How a Texas Couple Stuck to Their Guns," *Living for Young Homemakers* (January 1951): 108–14.

14. The percentages stated here were derived from Ranch-style pattern book examples and from photographing suburbs of large cities. The following book counted house types in certain small towns and shows that the simple side-gabled and hipped-roof subtypes may be far more common particularly in rural areas. John A. Jakle, Robert W. Bastian, and Douglas K. Meyer, *Common Houses in America's Small Towns: The Atlantic Seaboard to the Mississippi Valley* (Athens, GA, and London: University of Georgia Press, 1989), 186–90.

15. Sometimes a grouping of several traditional double-hung windows is used in place of a picture window.

16. Patrick Sullivan, Mary Beth Reed, and Tracey Fedor, *The Ranch House in Georgia: Guidelines for Evaluation* (Stone Mountain, GA: New South Associates, 2010), 61. Richard Cloues has linked the widespread use of vine wrought-iron patterns to the real vines often photographed growing on the porch supports of California examples.

17. Exposed rafter tails in Craftsman homes often extended beyond the edge of the roof and might have decorative shapes cut into them. Exposed rafters in contemporary houses often had a single board attached that hid the rafter ends, producing a more sleek and unified appearance.

18. David Bricker, "Ranch Houses Are not All the Same," California Department of Transportation, accessed August 18, 2011, www.nps.gov/nr/publications/bulletins/suburbs/Bricker.pdf.

19. The cap on the loan amount that the FHA would insure determined the square footage of speculative homes.

20. *Principles of Planning Small Houses*, 39–43; Alan Hess, *The Ranch House* (New York, NY: Harry N. Abrams, Inc., 2004), 45. In addition, the *American Builder Magazine* had regular features in the 1940s and 1950s showing how a few designs could be easily modified to produce a varied appearance—by rotating the house orientation, flipping plans, varying the roof form, and using a variety of materials and/or stylistic detail. The FHA also recommended not siting houses in a row but rather varying the setbacks.

21. The Editorial Staff of *Sunset* magazine in collaboration with Cliff May, *Sunset Western Ranch Houses* (Menlo Park, CA: California Lane Publishing Company, 1946), 42. One of the magazine's illustrated house plans was presented with the headline, "Where there's room, let the house ramble."

22. Architects intensely studied the design of new, efficient floor plans for small houses during the 1930s and 1940s (there was little else to do during the Depression). Ranch-house interiors were designed for a more informal home life—with kitchens opening onto casual eating areas, generally with an adjoining family room or den, and a sliding glass patio door or French doors opening onto a rear patio. Formal living and dining rooms were generally minimized in size or simply omitted.

23. Among those who designed Ranch-style houses were California architects Cliff May, Paul R. Williams and William Wurster, and Dallas architect Charles S. Dilbeck. McAlester, Winters, and Mackintosh, 259–72.

24. Hess, 14–17. The introduction to *The Ranch House* eloquently expresses the need to fully understand and appreciate Ranch houses and the large neighborhoods they comprised. Builders played a far greater role than architects in designing Ranch houses, yet these houses were popular, and in many cases beloved, as family homes. The infrastructure and neighborhoods they created comprise a large part of our country's usable built environment.

25. Building Research Council, "The History of the Building Research Council," accessed October 2, 2011, http://brc.arch.illinois.edu/history.htm. The council was founded in 1944 at the University of Illinois to consider how the university could help meet the housing needs of returning World War II servicemen. They undertook decades of research and created the concept of the "kitchen work triangle," invented air-conditioning, and were the first to advocate roof truss construction. They have published more than two hundred highly respected pamphlets on many aspects of construction.

26. G. Lewis Craig and Rudard A. Jones, AIA, for Small Homes Council-Building Research Council, "Split-Level Houses," *University of Illinois Bulletin* 58 no. 24 (1960). Circular Series Index Number C2.5.

27. In 1946, there were only 17,000 televisions in the U.S. By 1949, the number of TVs purchased each month was 250,000. By 1953, 66 percent of Americans owned a TV; by 1960, 87 percent. See http://profcatcurrenthistory.wordpress.com/2011/05/03/television-ownership-drops-in-u-s-nielsen-reports-nytimes-com/.

28. See James Massey and Shirley Maxwell, "Split Decisions," *Old House Journal* (March–April 2002): 78; and also "On Long Island, Splits Outsell Ranches Four to One," *House and Home* (April 1954): 111–21.

29. "Here Is a New Kind of Two-Story House," *House and Home* (February 1954): 106–13, in a periodical for home builders, and in *Living for Young Homemakers* for the popular market. This design was a part of architect Carl Koch's (1912–1998) efforts to create a prefab building system for houses. It was promoted as an entirely new kind of two-story house that had the long, low silhouette of a Ranch, included

all the economies of a basement (but was livable as the ground floor), and had all the savings of an attic but was lighted and usable. This promotion was likely the reason that bi-level houses are often called "raised ranch" houses.

30. Henry-Russell Hitchcock and Philip Johnson, *The International Style: Architecture Since 1922* (New York, NY: Museum of Modern Art, 1932).

31. Steel structural systems were also used in Contemporary houses where the steel structural *skeleton* was more often emphasized, rather than the architectural *volume* of the early International. The Post-and-Beam illustration (page 635) shows how Contemporary houses were sometimes panelized—featuring panels set into the structural system rather than having a smooth volumetric stucco covering. International houses from the 1950s and 1960s were far more likely to have steel structure exposed in the Miesian manner.

32. Le Corbusier had incorporated much of the above in his Five Points of the New Architecture: 1) pilotis (columns) to raise the house above the ground, leaving free movement beneath; 2) a roof garden to replace the land lost beneath the house; 3) using the pilotis or columns to allow a free plan (plan libre) for the interior; 4) a free facade, responding to the needs of the interior; and 5) long, horizontal ribbon windows allowing even, generous exterior light and views outside.

33. Charles Moore, Gerald Allen, and Donlyn Lynch, *The Place of Houses* (New York, NY: Holt, Rinehart and Winston, 1974), 152–75.

34. The Case Study house program, sponsored by John Entenza and the *Arts and Architecture* magazine he edited, advanced similar principles—including the use of industrial materials, steel, glass, courtyards, and view windows—from 1945 until 1965. However, Case Study houses also were built of wood. Some Case Study houses were International, but others were Contemporary in style; they would all be called Mid-century Modern.

35. Richard Weston, *Twentieth-Century Residential Architecture* (New York, NY: Abbeville Press, 2002), 52. The term International architecture had been in use prior to the MOMA exhibit. Early International style architects, rebuilding Europe after World War I, believed the use of white stucco for a wall cladding material was very important. They were anxious to avoid the regional differences that they believed had led to that war. White stucco could be produced anywhere and was equally available internationally. Its use avoided the visible regional differences that were lent by nearby stone quarries, by brick colors produced from local clays, and by wood logged in timber-rich locales.

36. Henry-Russell Hitchcock and Philip Johnson were responsible for the instant dissemination of the name and when they used it as the title of their exhibition catalogue, *The International Style*.

37. Perhaps the first house in the United States to capture the essence of the America's International style was Rudolf Schindler's King's Road House, built in 1922. Although the house has a bit of added modern ornament, its complete indoor-outdoor integration through full window walls with view gardens outside (originally sliding glass was canvas doors so the canvas could be removed in the summer), its ground-level foundation permitting the indoors to flow out, and the tilt-slab concrete structure allowing an unconventional open floor plan all express the essential spirit of Mid-century Modernism, both International and Contemporary.

38. All of these industrial age "guts" of the building were relatively new in 1920, when only a fraction of the industrialized world even had access to electricity.

39. At the same time, some working in this style are minimizing everything in an attempt to lower consumption of energy and products.

40. The solid glass and steel columns of the Glass House and the Farnsworth House presaged the direction of International skyscrapers but rarely houses. The Glass House had a 50-acre site to provide the privacy needed to have such expanses of glass in a residence. The similar lack of privacy at the Farnsworth House was a constant trauma for Farnsworth, because her weekend home was far more open to public view.

41. Neil Jackson, *California Modern: The Architecture of Craig Ellwood* (New York: Princeton Architectural Press, 2002); 44–48. This was Craig Elwood's first house with a strong expression of structure; and architectural historian Reyner Banham considered it one of California's three seminal post–World War II houses.

42. Additional variations occur in architect-designed examples.

43. Massey and Maxwell, "Split Decisions," 78–83.

44. Sandy Isenstadt, *The Modern American House: Spaciousness and Middle-Class Identity* (Cambridge: Cambridge University Press, 2006), 198–214.

45. According to the exhibit, the Japanese garden itself was designed to be viewed from the house rather than to be used as an outdoor living area. Arthur Drexler, *The Architecture of Japan* (New York, NY: Museum of Modern Art, 1955), 262. Drexler explained: "A Japanese building was chosen by the museum for its third house in the garden because traditional Japanese design has a unique relevance to modern Western architecture. The characteristics which give it this relevance are post and lintel frame construction; flexibility of plan; close relation of indoor and outdoor areas; and the decorative use of structural elements." On the West Coast, Maybeck's early 20th-century description of architecture as "landscape gardening around a few rooms" anticipated the philosophy of the Contemporary style. Weston, 30.

46. Open grille materials such as metal and

unglazed terra cotta could be found, but concrete screen block was strong and the easiest to manufacture. Anthony Rubano, "The Grille Is Gone: The Rise and Fall of Screen Block," *Preserving the Recent Past 2* (Washington, DC: Historic Preservation Education Foundation, National Park Service, 2000), 3, 89–99.

47. It is believed that Wright created the name "carport," and that it was used first in connection with his first Usonian house, the Jacobs House.

48. While split-levels worked well with gently sloping sites, where a site had more than an eight- or ten-foot drop, or access only at the very base or very top of a steep slope, these required a great deal of site preparation. The many varied approaches to Contemporary houses on steep slopes were less expensive to build and allowed much of the rock and natural vegetation on a site to remain.

49. The width of roof overhang varies depending upon orientation and house design. Ideally, above window walls it is scaled to provide passive solar heating in winter and shading of glass surfaces in summer. Solid facades might not require this width.

50. All three had banner dates in 1934. This was the year Libbey-Owens-Ford purchased the patent for double-glass insulating Thermopane windows; this made it practical to have an entire window wall, rather than just a large window *placed in* a wall. In addition, thick plate glass was now manufactured by a more affordable method, placed in a variety of large view windows, and heavily promoted, particularly by Libbey-Owens-Ford, in print advertisements in professional journals. Their additional placement in shelter magazines was an early example of a "pull" ad campaign designed to get consumers to demand this product from design and building professionals. The campaign often emphasized the "view" as an important part of a room, and for the first time the view out of a house from primary windows began to have a monetary value. Sandy Isenstadt, *The Modern American House: Spaciousness and Middle-Class Identity* (Cambridge: Cambridge University Press, 2006), 198–210.

Second, the first plywood suitable for exterior use was introduced in 1934. See http://www.fs.fed.us/t-d/pubs/htmlpubs/htm07732308/index.htm. By the 1950s plywood was affordably available in a smooth finish (often used for overhangs) and in a K1–11 finish that mimicked wood siding and became a popular inexpensive wall cladding. And finally, 1934 marked the first glued laminated timber (GLULAM) structure in the United States, a research lab for USDA Forest Products. New glues soon enabled many engineered wood products, including: structural plywood; oriented strand board; GLULAM, which allows versatility in the shaping of beams; structural composite lumber; and prefabricated wood I-joists, which are commonly used in floor and roof framing. For more detailed definitions see http://www.apawood.org/level_b.cfm?content=srv_med_new_bkgd_gloss. Also see Thomas C. Jester, *Twentieth Century Building Materials: History and Conservation* (New York, NY: McGraw-Hill, 1995), 132, 137.

51. Pietro Belluschi had built a Contemporary house for a bachelor outside Portland that had a handsome front-facing gabled window wall and post-and-beam porch by 1937 and followed with others of the same ilk. This tradition followed him east when he became dean of MIT's architecture school in 1950. Pietro Belluschi and Jo Stubblebine, *The Northwest Architecture of Pietro Belluschi* (New York, NY: F. W. Dodge Corp., 1953), 66.

52. The feeling of interior spatial volume was accomplished through varying the ceiling's height, adding high clerestory windows, and using room dividers that did not reach the ceiling.

53. Paul Adamson, Marty Arbunich, and Ernest Braun, *Eichler: Modernism Rebuilds the American Dream* (Layton, UT: Gibbs Smith, 2002).

54. Many sources have noted that the FHA chose not to finance Contemporary houses for various reasons. One well-documented case is discussed in Patsy Swank's "The Mortgage Pattern Poses Problems: How a Texas Couple Stuck to Their Guns," *Living for Young Homemakers* (January 1952): 108–14.

55. James Duff Law coined the word "Usonian" in an attempt to create a term that, unlike "American," was more truly linked to the United States. Thus the suggested term "Usonian," derived from U.S.-onian, for the United States. Frank Lloyd Wright adopted the term, and it became alternatively identified with a particular set of his small houses.

56. He preferred carports, and a somewhat L form to the house that turned its back to the street, sheltering a private courtyard with the narrow end and allowing a long expanse of glass onto the courtyard on the long end. There was no dining room—instead incorporating this function into the large living area that was the heart of the house. The kitchen was in the heart of the house and allowed various degrees of interaction between the cook (now considered to be the mother), the main room, and views of the garden. He was to build more than sixty Usonians over the next twenty years in a wide variety of materials and design but always with the same principles.

57. In the 1910s and 1920s, the Prairie house was modifying floor plans of large houses to include more T and L plans. These plan types created more spaces that were one room deep and end rooms with light from many directions. In the 1930s the later one-story Usonian incorporated these principles and began to influence Ranch houses and then the Contemporary.

58. Frank Lloyd Wright, *The Natural House* (New York, NY: Horizon Press, 1954), 54–58. The interiors of Wright's small houses generally had a dominant

solid wall on one side (with windows floating above it) with open window walls on the other.

59. In some areas, overhanging eaves were used, often with exposed rafters. The use of an overhang was more practical in areas with snow.

60. Donlyn Lyndon and Jim Alinder, *The Sea Ranch* (New York, NY: Princeton Architectural Press, 2004), 13–31. Located on a former sheep ranch on the coast along California Highway 1, its four-thousand-acre site had been used for grazing and as timberland. The sheep ranch portion was divided into numerous separate pastures that swept from the sea cliff up to the forested area. Planted cypress hedgerows had been planted as windbreaks along the fence lines. Innovative landscape planning was designed to leave large portions of the meadows in their natural states and group structures toward the hedgerows. The forested parts of the sites had houses carefully placed within them. Natural materials (unpainted wood primarily) are used, and nonnative plants are only allowed inside a home's small fenced enclosure.

61. Ann Abernathy, AIA, interview, 2012 on recollections of MIT's design studio. "In the late '60s, early '70s, shed roof followed naturally from working with wood systems, unit masonry, even unit concrete systems, and so all our design projects had them. Only reinforced concrete did not imply the shed roof. MIT was not in the camp of Corbusier (Harvard) or Kahn (Penn). If anything, there was more of a Wrightian connection, but we studied vernacular architecture from all over, and primitivism in cultures from Mesoamerica and Africa. Pietro Belluschi (early work), Saarinen, Aalto, Mies (early work), Paul Rudolph, and the beloved Kevin Lynch had a strong influence. From California, we were influenced by Greene and Greene and Bernard Maybeck. We looked for examples of shed roofs in New England vernacular residential, farm, maritime, and warehouse buildings. In the Midwest and West, we looked at stockyards and mining structures, and grain elevators. Everyone was looking at 'architecture without architects.' "

62. Gerald Allen, *Charles Moore* (New York, NY: Whitney Library of Design, 1980), 30–37. Moore dramatized interior space within the tall slanted-roof vertical forms through use of varied levels and light.

63. "Building Types Study: Record Houses of 1967," *Architectural Record* (*New York City: The Record and Guide: 1967*): 42–47, 58–61, 72–75, 94–97, 100–03, 112–15.

64. John Mullen, FAIA, and Ann Abernathy, AIA, have independently reported the almost omnipresence of the Shed style and its formal principles during their respective graduate careers at Yale in the late 1960s and MIT in the 1970s.

65. "Architecture Without Architects" was an influential 1964 exhibition at New York's Museum of Modern Art. It was organized by architect Bernard Rudofsky, who also published a book on the same subject: *Architecture Without Architects: An Introduction to Non-Pedigreed Architecture.*

66. The organization Friends of Kebyar was founded in 1983. Its tours and its seventy-seven journal issues are one of the best ways to learn about the full breadth of the Organic architecture movement.

67. Chad Randl, *A-frame* (New York, NY: Princeton Architectural Press, 2004), 9–29. The A-frame house has many antecedents found in other cultures. It was Rudolf Schindler, however, who brought this form into the modern era with his Bennati House near Lake Arrowhead, California, in 1934–37. In this house Schindler introduced many features that would become typical of postwar A-frames, chief among them fully glazed gable ends.

68. While the A-frame was by far the most common of the alternative roof forms, other shapes occurred. Adding new roof form to otherwise simple houses was discovered to be a good way to create innovative modern designs—and win architectural awards! High-style roof variations included airplane, hyperbolic paraboloid, paper-fold, umbrella, inverted umbrella, and multi-arched roofs. While frequently included in architecture books, examples of these are rarely encountered in real life.

69. This was a challenge for all ceremonial buildings during the 1950s. Oscar Niemeyer used Formalism in many different forms for the buildings of Brasilia in 1956. His Itamaraty Palace there has attenuated arches of the type that came to adorn many different building types in the United States. Philip Johnson used this style for the Amon Carter Museum of Art (Fort Worth, 1961), where the segmented arches and "chicly tapered columns" helped coin the term "ballet classicism" for his Formalistic buildings. See Marcus Whiffen, *American Architecture Since 1780: A Guide to the Styles* (Cambridge, MA: MIT Press, 1969), 256–61.

70. See Whiffen, 275–9 for the midcentury view of Brutalism. Today there is a reaction against this style, making it endangered. Prince Charles has been very vocal about his disdain for Brutalist architecture. Speaking at the 150th anniversary of the Royal Institute of British Architects, he stated, "For far too long, it seems to me, some planners and architects have consistently ignored the feelings and wishes of the mass of ordinary people in this country. . . . To be concerned about the way people live, about the environment they inhabit, and the kind of community that is created by that environment, should surely be one of the prime requirements of a really good architect." To see the entire speech, see, "A Speech by HRH The Prince of Wales at the 150th anniversary of the Royal Institute of British Architects (RIBA), Royal Gala Evening at Hampton Court Palace, 29th May 1984," http://

www.architecture.com/TheRIBA/175thAnniversary
/AnnualLecture/speech.aspx#.UdW1JBZYndc.

71. A gambrel roofline visible from a distance does allow one to orient to the original house form.

72. K. Michael Hays, *Architecture Theory Since 1968* (Cambridge, MA: MIT Press, 2000), 379.

73. Frank Gehry, "A Jazz Riff, in Corrugated Steel," *The Wall Street Journal,* November 22, 2012.

74. Victoria Ballard Bell's *Materials for Design* (New York: Princeton Architectural Press, 2006) has sections on how glass, concrete, wood, metals, and plastics are used on building exteriors today.

75. In some places groupings developed by chance—such as second-home areas where experimentation seemed natural, near universities with architecture schools, or near an influential architect. In the 1950s and 1960s, some subdivisions were built by developers with an individual interest in modern design who chose to build and sell modern spec houses (mainly Contemporary). Today there are a number of new developments under way that are limited to modern houses. Incomplete citations from the Urban Reserve's website follow. David Sokol, "The Sagaponac Effect: Modernist Subdivisions Multiply," *Architectural Record* (March 25, 2008); Peter Hellman, "Modern Developments," *Metropolitan Home* (December 2005–January 2006); Gregory Ibanez, "Suburban Revolution," *Texas Architect;* David Dillon, "Urban Oasis," *Dallas Morning News,* FDluxe. com (October 2008), 17.

76. McAlester and McAlester, 24; Christine Hunter, *Ranches, Rowhouses & Railroad Flats* (New York and London: W. W. Norton, 1999), 117–19.

STYLED HOUSES SINCE 1935

1. Enforcement is generally through a public or private design review body, or occasionally comprised of city staff.

2. John Chase, *Glitter, Stucco & Dumpster Diving: Reflections on Building Production in the Vernacular City* (New York, NY, and London: Verso, 2000), 87–92.

3. Matt Tyrnauer, "Glamour Begins at Home," *Vanity Fair* (March 2009), accessed April 18, 2012, http://www.vanityfair.com/style/features/2009/03/ john-woolf200903?currentPage=1.

4. The transition to Styled Ranch and New Traditional Houses can be seen in pattern books in the early 1970s. For example, Andy Lang's *101 Select Dream Houses* (published in 1972 by Hammond, Inc., for the Associated Press) presents approximately 14 percent Styled Ranch designs along with 22 percent Ranch, 22 percent Contemporary, 22 percent two-story New Traditional, 8 percent Split-Level, 4 percent A-frame, 4 percent Mansard, 2 percent Cape Cod, 1 percent Shed, 1 percent Brutalist, and one unidentifiable house.

5. Cooper/Roberts Architects, AIA, and Phoenix (AZ), *Historic Homes of Phoenix: An Architectural & Preservation Guide* (Phoenix, AZ: City of Phoenix, 1992), 111.

6. Michael Walsh and Richard Toglia, *Tudor Houses* (Farmington Hills, MI: Home Planners, 1989), 9. This is particularly obvious when the timbers are used to cover over the seams left by four-foot-wide wall sheathing. It is important to remember that half-timbering in original early English precedents was created from the actual structural timbers that were infilled and left exposed. The patterns thus created were logical and structural.

7. Mason, 71.

8. Home Planners, LLC, *European Dream Homes* (2nd printing, 2001), and Don Sater, *European Classics* (Sater Design Collection, 2007). *European Classics* and Sater's other house plan books illustrate the specialized floor plans—with numerous angular, rounded, and squared bays—that are produced, and enabled by, the complex roof forms. Complex floor plans that produce complex roof forms are not limited to pattern-book examples. Even a few architects designing custom houses draw "ideal" floor plans first and then worry about the roof forms later. The author was sitting in a design review for a new home when suddenly the client turned to the architect and said, "Oh dear, I forgot to get you to include space for my exercise bike in the library." The architect said, "No problem, we will just make this little addition to the floor plan for it"—and proceeded to draw a small extension to the floor plan, just enough for an exercise bike. The architect then turned to the builder and said, "Can you just frame up some sort of roof over it?" The builder said, "Sure, I can frame up a little roof over it." And thus another cascading hip was added to an already complex roof plan—with the roof form being shaped by the complex floor plan.

9. David Dillon, "Big Mess on the Prairie," *Dallas Morning News* (October 2, 1994).

10. In many homes without a tall, arched one-and-one-half- or two-story added entry feature, it is possible to see the same general pattern expressed in the front door and a "feature" window above it. A *Wall Street Journal* real estate article reported on the new popularity of towers, and actually counted the number of references to towers in current real estate ads. Dan F. Sater, II, *European Luxury Homes* (Bonita Springs, FL: Sater Design Collection, 2003), and *Mediterranean Home Plans* (Bonita Springs, FL: Sater Design Collection, 2005), feature Millennium Mansion designs with towers. Square or rectangular towers are more common on Mediterranean designs; round or octagonal towers on others.

11. Historically, varied-size windows on houses are related by their details. Today, new window manufacturers typically offer a broad range of sizes for each window design they offer. Using windows from this

same design family gives a unity even when sizes vary. Some early Millennium Mansions used windows from different design families, giving them a less related overall appearance.

12. This free mix of historic details—that includes the application of flat details (such as a single-layer "wallpaper" wall of brick) and use of oversized details (such as overlarge Palladian windows)—may reflect builder attempts to produce postmodern architecture, with its witty use of symbolic architectural details.

13. It might soon be possible to have a Styled Millennium Mansions section in addition to simply having Millennium Mansions—much in the same way that Styled Ranch can be distinguished from Ranch. Tudor is easily applied to the subtypes of hipped roof with lower cross gables and gabled roof with lower cross gables, and French to the subtypes of hipped roof with lower cross-hipped roofs. Spanish Revival, with its highly varied roof forms, is also easily applied. The most problematic are Classical and Colonial styles—yet elements of these are clearly visible on some Millennium Mansions, particularly Palladian windows, red-brick keystone lintels, and occasionally a two-story entry with Classical columns.

14. Some municipalities have taken steps to ensure that this happens. The City of Beverly Hills, California, for example, in 2004 adopted the *Residential Design Style Catalogue* which describes a number of appropriate styles and incentivizes New Traditional houses rather than Millennium Mansions. The catalogue specifically stresses the importance of proper roofs, materials, and window design. See City of Beverly Hills, *Residential Design Style Catalogue* (Planning Division, March 2004), 87–88. Ironically the incentive for a "calmer" style is a slightly larger house.

15. Marianne Cusato, Ben Pentrath, Richard Franklin Sammons, and Leon Crier's *Get Your House Right* (New York, NY: Sterling, 2007) and Stephen A. Mouzon and Susan M. Henderson's *Traditional Construction Patterns* (New York, NY: McGraw-Hill, 2004) are two very useful references for those trying to understand or reproduce historically correct details for a new house or addition. Some of the early 20th-century books used by Eclectic era architects are available today as well.

16. An important exception are homes inspired by Colonial-era house styles, in particular early wood-clad New England homes, which would properly be placed quite low to the ground.

17. Dan Cooper, *New Classic American Houses: The Architecture of Albert, Righter & Tittmann* (New York, NY: Vendome Press, 2009), 10. The entire book is filled with examples of this process, often with excellent explanation (11, 17–24).

18. ICAA was originally two separate organizations that merged in 2002. Today it has strong education, publication, and advocacy programs that promote the Classical tradition in architecture and urbanism. It also works with non-architect home builders and Habitat for Humanity International to bring traditional design skills to a broad cross-section of the country's housing and neighborhoods.

19. It should be noted that Venturi was trying to add new dimensions of thought and ornamentation to modernism, likely not to encourage New Traditional architecture.

20. It is almost impossible to know the actual distribution of New Traditional styles. The following paragraphs are based on the author's observations; on notes from Larry Boerder, AIA; and on a survey of house styles built in Highland Park, Texas. McAlester, Winters, and Mackintosh, 216.

21. Vincent Scully, *The Shingle Style Today or the Historian's Revenge* (New York, NY: G. Braziller, 1974), illustrations 1, 63, 107, 112, 115. Scully writes about these early beginnings.

22. Many of the monographs of New Traditional architects include one or more Shingle houses, and handsome full-color books continue to appear on the Shingle style. For early examples see Peter Arnell and Ted Bickford, editors, *Robert A. M. Stern: Buildings and Projects: 1965–1980* (New York, NY: Rizzoli, 1981), 18, 72, 178; Leland M. Roth and Bret Morgan, *Shingle Styles: Innovation and Tradition in American Architecture 1874 to 1982* (New York, NY: H. N. Abrams, 1999), 212.

23. The Colonial Revival style works well with codes as there is a relatively simple set of rules, followed from the 17th until the early 20th centuries, that if followed ensure that such a house will fit in well with its predecessors. Kentlands was planned by Andrus Duany and Elizabeth Plater-Zyberk, and the neighborhood's first model homes were ready in 1990.

24. Willis Cecil Winters, FAIA, author of many books on Texas architects, developed a set of similar criteria that he shared with the author and on which these identifying features were based. His list includes the standing-seam metal roofs favored on American Vernacular houses in Texas.

25. Urban Design Associates, Louisiana Recovery Authority, and LRA Support Foundation, *Louisiana Speaks: Pattern Book* (Baton Rouge, LA: LRA Support Foundation, 2006). See also Urban Design Associates, Ray Gindroz, and Rob Robinson, *The Architectural Pattern Book: A Tool for Building Great Neighborhoods* (New York, NY: W. W. Norton and Company, 2004), 41–46, 77–78, 92–95, 112–13, 124–27.

26. Marc Treib, *An Everyday Modernism: The Houses of William Wurster* (Berkeley, CA, Los Angeles, CA, London: University of California Press, 1995), 98. Some have called this an early Ranch house, but it is more understated than the later Ranch style.

27. The articles were "An Indigenous Architecture" (1928), which featured Ford's sketches of German

folk houses and Williams's designs inspired by them; and "Towards a Southwestern Architecture" (1931).

28. In addition to Texas and California, Louisiana, the Carolinas, and the Pacific Northwest all had early regional architecture movements.

29. In addition to introducing what became the Shed style, with its prominent use of shed elements inspired by vernacular structures, simpler shapes were also built at Sea Ranch.

30. Among them, Frank Welch, John Mullen, William McDonald, and LakeFlato (particularly with their Porch Houses) in Texas; David Salmela and Sala Architects in Minnesota; Lloyd Vogt, Marianne Cusato, and Duany Plater-Zyberk & Company in the Gulf Coast states, and Estes/Twombly and Jeremiah Eck in New England. Hugh Newell Jacobsen, FAIA, of Washington, D.C., a master of American Vernacular forms, utilizes a highly additive approach.

31. Thadani, 267–68.

32. "Cusato Cottages," accessed November 16, 2011, http://cusatocottages.com.

33. Books include Jean Rehkamp Larson, *The Farmhouse: New Inspiration for the Classic American Home* (Newtown, CT: Taunton Press, 2004); William Morgan, *Yankee Modern: The Houses of Estes/Twombly* (New York, NY: Princeton Architectural Press, 2010); and Jeremiah Eck, *The Face of Home: A New Way to Look at the Outside of Your House* (Newtown, CT: Taunton Press, 2006). A pattern book example is Looney Ricks Kiss Architects, *Traditional Neighborhood Home Plans* (Tucson: Home Planners, LLC: 2000).

34. David Dillon, *The Architecture of O'Neil Ford: Celebrating Place* (Austin: University of Texas Press, 1999), 41.

APPENDIX: APPROACHES TO CONSTRUCTION IN THE 20TH AND 21ST CENTURIES

1. Mason: 56.

2. A Navy team had designed the versatile prefab Quonset huts in a one-month effort as the war was beginning. More than 150,000 Quonset huts were subsequently produced and used for a broad range of purposes during the war. Gwendolyn Wright, *USA: Modern Architecture in History* (London: Reakton Books, Ltd., 2008), 142–44.

3. A reported three hundred home builders of prefabricated homes were operating in 1946, many with federal subsidies as efforts were made to convert wartime plants to peacetime uses. See Andrew Blauvelt's essay for the Yale University School of Architecture's exhibition "Some Assembly Required: Contemporary Prefabricated Houses," October 27, 2006–February 2, 2007; Paul Sahre, *Leisurama Now: The Beach House for Everyone (1964–)* (New York, NY: Princeton Architectural Press, 2008); Alastair Gordon, *Weekend Utopia: Modern Living in the Hamptons* (New York, NY: Princeton Architectural Press, 2001).

4. Aaron Britt, Diana Budds, Jaime Gross, Jordan Kushins, and Miyoko Ohtake, "Special Report: The Next Generation of American Prefab," *DWELL* (December/January 2012): 72–114.

5. Donovan Rypkema, "Sustainability and Historic Preservation," from the Economic Benefits of Preservation Session at the Historic Districts Council Annual Conference in New York City, March 10, 2007, accessed October 5, 2011, http://www.preservation.org/rypkema.htm.
See http://www.census.gov/hhes/www/housing/census/historic/plumbing.html.

6. David P. Handlin, *The American Home: Architecture and Society—1815–1915* (Boston: Little, Brown: 1979): 452 ff. Most of these systems, in turn, connected a house to a larger system of distribution such as sewers, electric power lines, water service, cable TV, and internet. "By connecting a house to the surrounding community and eventually to the world at large, they did their part in destroying . . . isolation. . . . They disrupted age-old relationships and brought people into contact with one another in ways that they were not accustomed to or did not understand. The result was often not mutual enlightenment but consternation and even conflict."

7. Merritt Ierley, *The Comforts of Home: The American House and the Evolution of Modern Convenience* (New York: Clarkson Potter, 1999): 172. "Most Houses built before 1900 contained little if anything of twentieth-century technology. Well into the twentieth century many of these houses relied on kitchen and parlor stoves for heat, kerosene lamps for light, portable tubs for bathing and laundering, and outdoor privies for use as bathrooms."

8. Gerrylynn K. Roberts and Phillip Steadman, *American Cities & Technology: Wilderness to Wired City* (New York: Routledge, 1999): 99.

9. Barbara Krasner-Khait, "The Impact of Refrigeration," http://www.history-magazine.com/refrig.html. Accessed January 21, 2013.

10. http://www.census.gov/hhes/www/housing/census/historic/plumbing.html.

11. Richard Weston, *100 Ideas That Changed Architecture* (London: Laurence King, 2011): 186.

12. Lisa D. Schrenk, *Building a Century of Progress* (Minneapolis: University of Minnesota Press, 2007): 163–5.

For Further Reference

The selected works included here are those that I believe will be among the most helpful to readers seeking additional information about houses of a particular style or region, or about the neighborhoods in which they are located. The first section lists important references on the general topic of American houses. This is followed by nine lists of works treating more specific subjects (such as "House Form and Structure," "Colonial Houses," and "Styled Houses Since 1935"); these are arranged to parallel the generally chronological organization of the book. Four succeeding sections list selected "Regional and Local Guides," which cover a range of architectural styles as found in a particular part of the country. (Note that local works treating only a single style or period may be listed in the preceding chronological sections rather than with these guides of broader scope.) Only a few important examples of pattern books—works showing sample house plans and elevations—have been included from among the many thousands of such publications. These are labeled "[pattern book]" in the lists. A comprehensive survey of all such works published before 1895 can be found in Henry-Russell Hitchcock's *American Architectural Books* rev. ed. (Mansfield Centre, CT; Martino Press 2003). Daniel D. Reiff's *Houses from Books: Treatises, Pattern Books, and Catalogs in American Architecture, 1738–1950—A History and Guide* (University Park, PA: Pennsylvania State University Press, 2000) provides an excellent overview of the role such books have played in American domestic architecture; its appendices include selections of the numerous books covering the first half of the twentieth century. A final section, "House Preservation and Restoration," guides those wishing to conserve the original architectural character of older houses as they adapt them to contemporary living.

GENERAL WORKS

Alexander, Christopher. *The Timeless Way of Building.* New York: Oxford University Press, 1980.

Alexander, Christopher, Sara Ishikawa, and Murray Silverstein. *A Pattern Language: Towns, Buildings, Construction.* 1979, Reprint, New York: Oxford University Press, 2010.

Andrews, Wayne. *Architecture, Ambition, and Americans.* Rev. ed. New York: Free Press, 1979.

Blumenson, John J.-G. *Identifying American Architecture.* 2nd ed. Nashville, TN: American Association for State and Local History, 1995.

Brand, Stewart. *How Buildings Learn: What Happens After They're Built.* Rev. ed. New York, Viking, 1997.

Carley, Rachel. *The Visual Dictionary of American Domestic Architecture.* New York: Owl Book, 1997.

Chudacoff, Howard P., Judith E. Smith, and Peter C. Baldwin. *The Evolution of American Urban Society.* 7th ed. Boston: Prentice Hall, 2010.

Clark, Clifford Edward. *The American Family Home, 1800–1960.* Chapel Hill: University of North Carolina Press, 1987.

Corkin, Caitlin. *Surveying the Recent Past: The Challenge of Creating and Defining Context.* Paper presented at Looking Forward: Preservation in New England in the Twenty-first Century, Rhode Island, 2011.

Davidson, Marshall B. *Notable American Houses.* New York: American Heritage Publishing Co., 1971.

Eggener, Keith. *American Architectural History: A Contemporary Reader.* London and New York: Routledge, 2006.

Fitch, James Marston. *American Building 1: The Historical Forces That Shaped It.* 2nd ed. New York: Oxford University Press, 1999.

Foley, Mary Mix. *The American House.* New York: Harper & Row, 1981.

Foster, Gerald L. *American Houses: A Field Guide to the Architecture of the Home.* Boston: Houghton Mifflin, 2004.

Gelernter, Mark. *A History of American Architecture: Buildings in Their Cultural and Technological Context.* Hanover, NH: University Press of New England, 2001.

Gottfried, Herbert, and Jan Jennings. *American Vernacular Buildings and Interiors, 1870–1960.* New York: W. W. Norton, 2009.

Gowans, Alan. *Images of American Living.* New York: Harper & Row, 1983.

———. *The Comfortable House: North American Suburban Architecture, 1890–1930.* Cambridge, MA: MIT Press, 1989.

Handlin, David P. *The American Home Architecture and Society, 1815–1915.* Boston: Little, Brown & Co, 1979.

———. *American Architecture.* London: Thames & Hudson, 2004.

Harris, Cyril M. *American Architecture: An Illustrated Encyclopedia.* New York: W. W. Norton, 2009.

Harrison, Henry S. *Houses: The Illustrated Guide to Construction, Design, and Systems.* 3rd ed. New York: Kaplan, 1998.

Hilowitz, Beverley, and Susan Eikov Green. *Historic Houses of America.* Rev. ed. New York: Simon and Schuster, 1980.

Hopkins, Owen. *Reading Architecture: A Visual Lexicon.* London: Laurence King, 2012.

Howe, Barbara J. *Houses and Homes: Exploring Their History.* Walnut Creek, CA: AltaMira Press, 1997.

Hull, Brent, and Christine G. H. Franck. *Traditional American Rooms: Celebrating Style, Craftsmanship, and Historic Woodwork.* East Petersburg, PA: Fox Chapel, 2009.

Ierley, Merritt. *The Comforts of Home: The American House and Evolution of Modern Convenience.* New York: Three Rivers Press, 1999.

———. *Open House: A Guided Tour of the American Home, 1637–Present.* New York: Henry Holt and Co., 1999.

Jakle, John A., Robert W. Bastian, and Douglas K. Meyer. *Common Houses in America's Small Towns: The Atlantic Seaboard to the Mississippi Valley.* Athens: University of Georgia Press, 1989.

Jandl, H. Ward, John A. Burns, and Michael Auer. *Yesterday's Houses of Tomorrow: Innovative American Homes, 1850 to 1950.* Washington, DC: Preservation Press, 1991.

Kahn, Lloyd. *Home Work: Handbuilt Shelter.* Bolinas, Calif: Shelter Publications, 2004.

———. *Tiny Homes: Simple Shelter: Scaling Back in the Century.* Bolinas, CA: Shelter Publications, 2012.

Koeper, Frederick, and Marcus Whiffen. *American Architecture.* 2 vols. Cambridge, MA: MIT Press, 1981, 1984.

Lounsbury, Carl, and Vanessa Elizabeth Patrick. *An Illustrated Glossary of Early Southern Architecture and Landscape.* Rev. ed. New York: Oxford University Press, 1999.

Maddex, Diane. *Master Builders: A Guide to Famous American Architects.* Washington, DC: Preservation Press, 1996.

Martinson, Tom. *The Atlas of American Architecture: 2,000 Years of Architecture, City Planning, Landscape Architecture and Civil Engineering.* New York: Rizzoli, 2009.

Mason, Joseph B. *History of Housing in the U.S., 1930–1980.* Houston: Gulf Publishing, 1982.

Massey, James C., and Shirley Maxwell. *House Styles in America: The Old-House Journal Guide to the Architecture of American Homes.* New York: Penguin Studio, 1999.

McAlester, Virginia, and Lee McAlester. *Great American Houses and Their Architectural Styles.* New York: Abbeville Press, 1994.

Morgan, William, and Radek Kurzaj. *The Abrams Guide to American House Styles.* New York: Harry N. Abrams, 2008.

Packard, Robert T. *Encyclopedia of American Architecture.* 2nd ed. New York: McGraw-Hill, 1995.

Paradis, Thomas W. *The Greenwood Encyclopedia of Homes Through American History.* Westport, CT: Greenwood Press, 2008.

Pickering, Ernest. *The Homes of America.* New York: Thomas Y. Crowell, 1951.

Pollman, Richard B. *Book of Successful Home Plans* [pattern book]. Farmington, MI: Structures Publishing, 1976.

Poppeliers, John, S. Allen Chambers, and Nancy B. Schwartz. *What Style Is It?* Rev. ed. Washington, DC: Preservation Press, 2003.

Reiff, Daniel D. *Houses from Books: The Influence of Treatises, Pattern Books, and Catalogs in America, 1738–1950—A History and Guide.* University Park, PA: Pennsylvania State University Press, 2001.

Roth, Leland M. *A Concise History of American Architecture.* 2nd ed. Boulder, CO: Westview Press, 2003.

———. *Understanding Architecture: Its Elements, History, and Meaning.* 2nd ed. Boulder, CO: Westview Press, 2007

Saylor, Henry H. *Dictionary of Architecture.* 1967. Reprint: New York: John Wiley & Sons, 1994.

Schafer, Gil, Marc Kristal, and Bunny Williams. *The Great American House: Tradition for the Way We Live Now.* New York: Rizzoli, 2012.

Schweitzer, Robert, and Michael W. R. Davis. *America's Favorite Homes: Mail-Order Catalogues As a Guide to Popular Early 20th–Century Houses.* Detroit: Wayne State University Press, 1990.

Smith, Peter D. *City: A Guidebook for the Urban Age.* London: Bloomsbury, 2012.

Susanka, Sarah, and Kira Obolensky. *The Not So Big House: A Blueprint for the Way We Really Live.* 10th ed. Newtown, CT: Taunton Press, 2009.

U.S. Department of Commerce, Bureau of the Census. *Historical Statistics of the United States: Colonial Times to 1970.* Washington, DC, 1975.

Walker, Lester. *American Shelter.* Rev. ed. Woodstock, NY: Overlook, 1997.

Weston, Richard. *100 Ideas That Changed Architecture.* London: Laurence King, 2011.

Whiffen, Marcus. *American Architecture Since 1780: A Guide to the Styles.* 1969. Rev. ed. Cambridge, MA: MIT Press, 1993.

Williams, Henry Lionel, and Ottalie K. Williams. *A Guide to Old American Houses, 1700–1900.* San Diego, CA: Oak Tree, 1977.

Wiseman, Carter. *Twentieth-Century American Architecture: The Buildings and Their Makers.* New York: W. W. Norton, 2000.

Wright, Gwendolyn. *USA: Modern Architectures in History.* London: Reaktion Books, 2008.

In addition, a thorough bibliography of general works, "American Architecture, Architectural History & Historic Preservation: A Selected Bibliography," has been compiled by the Portland Bureau of Planning and Sustainability. It is available as a PDF file at www.portlandoregon.gov/bps/article/147430

HOUSE FORM AND STRUCTURE

Allen, Edith Louise. *American Housing.* Peoria, IL: Manual Arts Press, 1930.

Anderson, L. O. *Wood-Frame House Construction.* Rev. ed. Carlsbad, CA: Craftsman Book Company, 1992.

Blackburn, Graham. *The Parts of a House.* New York: Richard Marek, 1980.

———. *The Illustrated Book of Housebuilding and Carpentry.* Omnibus reprint edition of *Illustrated Housebuilding* and *Illustrated Interior Carpentry.* Woodstock, NY: Overlook Press, 2003.

DiDonno, Lupe, and Phyllis Sperling. *How to Design and Build Your Own House.* 2nd ed. New York: Knopf, 1987.

Dietz, Albert G. H. *Dwelling House Construction.* 5th ed. Cambridge, MA: MIT Press, 1992.

Kauffman, Henry J. *The American Fireplace.* New York: Galahad Books, 1972.

McKee, Harley J. *Introduction to Early American Masonry: Stone, Brick, Mortar and Plaster.* Washington, DC: Preservation Press, 1980.

Newcomb, Rexford, and William A. Foster. *Home Architecture.* New York: John Wiley & Sons, 1932.

Peterson, Charles E., ed. *Building Early America.* Radnor, PA: Chilton, 1992.

Townsend, Gilbert, and J. Ralph Dalzell. *How to Plan a House.* 3rd ed. Chicago: American Technical Society, 1965.

NEIGHBORHOOD GROUPINGS

Adams, Thomas. *The Design of Residential Areas: Basic Considerations, Principles, and Methods.* New York: Arno Press, 1934.

The American Collection: Craftsman Style: 165 New Home Plans in the Arts & Crafts Tradition of Fine Craftsmanship, Natural Materials, and Simple Elegance [pattern book]. Washington, DC: Hanley Wood, 2006.

Ames, David L., and Linda Flint McClelland. *Historic Residential Suburbs: Guidelines for Evaluation and Documentation for the National Register of Historic Places.* National Register bulletin. Washington, DC: U.S. Department of the Interior, National Park Service, National Register of Historic Places, 2002. Available at www.nps.gov/nr/publications/bulletins/pdfs/Suburbs.pdf.

Archer, John. *Architecture and Suburbia: From English Villa to American Dream House, 1690–2000.* Minneapolis: University of Minnesota Press, 2005.

The Architectural Pattern Book: A Tool for Building Great Neighborhoods. New York: W. W. Norton, 2004.

Arendt, Randall, and Elizabeth A. Brabec. *Rural by Design: Maintaining Small Town Character.* Chicago: Planners Press, American Planning Association, 1994.

Baumbach, Richard O., and William E. Borah. *The Second Battle of New Orleans: A History of the Vieux Carré Riverfront Expressway Controversy.* Tuscaloosa: University of Alabama Press, 1981. Published for the Preservation Press, National Trust for Historic Preservation in the United States.

Beasley, Ellen. *The Alleys and Back Buildings of Galveston: An Architectural and Social History.* Houston: Rice University Press, 2007.

Beveridge, Charles E., and Paul Rocheleau. *Frederick Law Olmsted: Designing the American Landscape.* Rev. ed. New York: Rizzoli, 2005.

Binford, Henry C. *The First Suburbs: Residential Communities on the Boston Periphery, 1815–1860.* Chicago: University of Chicago Press, 1988.

Campoli, Julie, and Alex S. MacLean. *Visualizing Density.* Cambridge, MA: Lincoln Institute of Land Policy, 2007.

Campoli, Julie, Elizabeth Humstone, and Alex S. MacLean. *Above and Beyond: Visualizing Change in Small Towns and Rural Areas.* Chicago: Planners Press, American Planning Association, 2002.

Church, Thomas D., Michael Laurie, and Grace Hall.

Gardens Are for People. 1955. 3rd ed. Berkeley: University of California Press, 1995.

Cigliano, Jan, and Sarah Bradford Landau. *The Grand American Avenue, 1850–1920.* San Francisco: Pomegranate Artbooks, 1994.

Clay, Grady, ed. *Landscapes for Living.* New York: McGraw-Hill, 1980.

Condon, Patrick M. *Seven Rules for Sustainable Communities: Design Strategies for the Post-Carbon World.* Washington, DC: Island Press, 2010.

Cooney, Loraine M., Hattie C. Rainwater, Florence N. Marye, and Phillip T. Marye. *Garden History of Georgia, 1733–1933.* 1933. Reprint, Atlanta, GA: Peachtree Garden Club, 1976.

Cory, Gregory L. *Golf Course Development in Residential Communities.* Washington, DC: Urban Land Institute, 2001.

Crawford, Margaret. *Building the Workingman's Paradise: The Design of American Company Towns.* London: Verso, 1995.

Darke, Rick. *In Harmony with Nature: Lessons from the Arts & Crafts Garden.* New York: Friedman/Fairfax, 2001.

Downing, A. J. *Landscape Gardening and Rural Architecture.* 1849. Reprint, New York: Dover Publications, 1991.

———. *A Treatise on the Theory and Practice of Landscape Gardening, Adapted to North America; with a View to the Improvement of Country Residences.* 1844. Reprint, New York: Wiley and Putnam, 2010.

Duany, Andres, Elizabeth Plater-Zyberk, and Robert Alminana. *The New Civic Art: Elements of Town Planning.* New York: Rizzoli, 2011.

Duany, Andres, Jeff Speck, and Mike Lydon. *The Smart Growth Manual.* New York: McGraw-Hill, 2010.

Easterling, Keller. *American Town Plans: A Comparative Time Line.* New York: Princeton Architectural Press, 1993.

Eckbo, Garrett. *Landscape for Living.* 1950. Reprint, New York: Architectural Record with Duell, Sloan, & Pearce, 2009.

Fishman, Robert. *Bourgeois Utopias: The Rise and Fall of Suburbia.* New York: Basic Books, 1999.

Ford, Larry R. *Cities and Buildings: Skyscrapers, Skid Rows, and Suburbs.* Baltimore: Johns Hopkins University Press, 1995.

Fox, Pamela W., and Sarah B. Gilman. *Farm Town to Suburb: The History and Architecture of Weston, Massachusetts, 1830–1980.* Portsmouth, NH: Peter E. Randall, 2002.

Garvin, Alexander. *The American City: What Works, What Doesn't Work.* 2nd ed. New York: McGraw-Hill, 2002.

Girling, Cynthia L., and Kenneth I. Helphand. *Yard, Street, Park: The Design of Suburban Open Space.* New York: J. Wiley and Sons, 1994.

Hayden, Dolores. *Building Suburbia.* New York: Pantheon Books, 2004.

Hayden, Dolores, and Jim Wark. *A Field Guide to Sprawl.* New York: W. W. Norton, 2006.

Hayward, Mary Ellen. *Baltimore's Alley Houses: Homes for Working People Since the 1780s.* Baltimore: Johns Hopkins University Press, 2008.

Hegemann, Werner, and Elbert Peets. *The American Vitruvius: An Architect's Handbook of Civic Art.* 1922. Reprint, s.l.: De Facto Publishing, 2008.

Herman, Bernard L. *Town House: Architecture and Material Life in the Early American City, 1780–1830.* Chapel Hill: University of North Carolina Press, 2005. Published for the Omohundro Institute of Early American History and Culture, Williamsburg, VA.

Higgins, Hannah B. *The Grid Book.* Cambridge, MA: MIT Press, 2009.

Hise, Greg. *Magnetic Los Angeles: Planning the Twentieth-Century Metropolis.* Baltimore: Johns Hopkins University Press, 1999.

Hunter, Christine. *Ranches, Rowhouses, and Railroad Flats: American Homes: How They Shape Our Landscapes and Neighborhoods.* Rev. ed. New York: W. W. Norton, 2005.

Jackson, Kenneth T. *Crabgrass Frontier: The Suburbanization of America.* New York: Oxford University Press, 2008.

Jacobs, Allan B., Elizabeth Macdonald, and Yodan Rofé. *The Boulevard Book: History, Evolution, Design of Multiway Boulevards.* Cambridge, MA: MIT Press, 2003.

Jacobs, Jane. *The Death and Life of Great American Cities.* 1961. Rev. ed. New York: Random House, 2011.

Johnson, Leonard H. *Foundation Planting.* New York: A. T. De La Mare Co., 1937.

Jordan, Terry G. *Texas: A Geography.* Boulder, CO: Westview Press, 1984.

Keating, Ann Durkin. *Chicagoland: City and Suburbs in the Railroad Age.* Chicago: University of Chicago Press, 2005.

Klaus, Susan L., and Frederick Law Olmsted. *A Modern Arcadia: Frederick Law Olmsted Jr. & the Plan for Forest Hills Gardens.* Amherst: University of Massachusetts Press, 2002.

Kunstler, James Howard. *The Geography of Nowhere: The Rise and Decline of America's Man-Made Landscape.* Rev. ed. New York: Simon & Schuster, 2004.

Lampl, Elizabeth Jo, and Kimberly Prothro Williams. *Chevy Chase: A Home Suburb for the Nation's Capital.* Crownsville, MD: Montgomery County Historic Preservation Commission, 2009.

Langdon, Philip. *A Better Place to Live: Reshaping the American Suburb.* Rev. ed. Boston: University of Massachusetts Press, 1997.

Leinberger, Christopher B. *The Option of Urbanism: Investing in a New American Dream.* Washington, DC: Island Press, 2009.

McAlester, Virginia, and Lee McAlester. *A Field Guide to America's Historic Neighborhoods and Museum Houses: The Western States.* New York: Knopf, 1998.

McAlester, Virginia, Willis Winters, and Prudence Mackintosh. *Great American Suburbs: The Homes of the Park Cities—Dallas.* New York: Abbeville Press, 2008.

McKeever, J. R. *The Community Builders Handbook.* 1968. 6th ed. Washington, DC: Urban Land Institute, 1988.

McKelvey, Blake. *The Urbanization of America, 1860–1915.* New Brunswick, NJ: Rutgers University Press, 1963.

McShane, Clay. "The Centrality of the Horse to the Nineteenth-Century American City." In *The Making of Urban America,* edited by Raymond Mohl. New York: SR Publishers, 1997.

Newton, Norman T. *Design on the Land: The Development of Landscape Architecture.* Cambridge, MA: Belknap Press of Harvard University Press, 1971.

O'Malley, Therese. *Regional Garden Design in the United States* Dumbarton Oaks Colloquium on the History of Landscape Architecture XV. Washington, DC: Dumbarton Oaks Research Library and Collection, 1995.

Peterson, Jon A. *The Birth of City Planning in the United States, 1840–1917.* Baltimore: Johns Hopkins University Press, 2003.

Pettis, Emily. *A Model for Identifying and Evaluating the Historic Significance of Post–World War II Housing.* Washington, DC: Transportation Research Board, 2012.

Pregill, Philip, and Nancy Volkman. *Landscapes in History: Design and Planning in the Western Tradition.* 2nd ed. New York: Van Nostrand Reinhold, 1999.

Punch, Walter T., and William Howard Adams. *Keeping Eden: A History of Gardening in America.* Boston: Bulfinch Press, 1992.

Rae, John Bell. *The Road and the Car in American Life.* Cambridge, MA: MIT Press, 1971.

Reps, John William. *The Making of Urban America: A History of City Planning in the United States.* 1966. Reprint, Princeton, NJ: Princeton University Press, 1997.

Rowe, Peter G. *Making a Middle Landscape.* Cambridge, MA: MIT Press, 1992.

Schroeder, Fred E. H. *Front Yard America: The Evolution and Meanings of a Vernacular Domestic Landscape.* Bowling Green, OH: Bowling Green State University Popular Press, 1993.

Schuyler, David. *Apostle of Taste: Andrew Jackson Downing, 1815–1852.* Baltimore: Johns Hopkins University Press, 1999.

Scott, Frank J. *Victorian Gardens: The Art of Beautifying Suburban Home Grounds—A Victorian Guidebook of 1870.* Rev. ed. Watkins Glen, NY: American Life Foundation, 1982.

Southworth, Michael, and Eran Ben-Joseph. *Streets and the Shaping of Towns and Cities.* New York: McGraw-Hill, 2003.

Stern, Robert A. M., and John M. Massengale. *The Anglo American Suburb.* London: Architectural Design, 1981.

Steuteville, Robert. *New Urbanism: Best Practices Guide.* 4th ed. Ithaca, NY: New Urban News Publications, 2009.

Stilgoe, John R. *Common Landscape of America, 1580 to 1845.* New Haven: Yale University Press, 1985.

———. *Metropolitan Corridor: Railroads and the American Scene.* New Haven: Yale University Press, 1985.

———. *Borderland: Origins of the American Suburb, 1820–1939.* New Haven: Yale University Press, 1990.

Teyssot, Georges. *The American Lawn.* New York: Princeton Architectural Press, 1999.

Thadani, Dhiru A. *The Language of Towns & Cities: A Visual Dictionary.* New York: Rizzoli, 2010.

Tishler, William H. *American Landscape Architecture: Designers and Places.* New York: John Wiley & Sons, 1996.

———. *Midwestern Landscape Architecture.* Urbana, IL: University of Illinois Press, 2004.

Treib, Marc. *The Architecture of Landscape, 1940–1960.* Philadelphia: University of Pennsylvania Press, 2002.

United States. *Successful Subdivisions: Principles of Planning for Economy and Protection Against Neighborhood Blight.* Washington, DC: Federal Housing Administration, 1940.

Upton, Dell. *Another City.* New Haven: Yale University Press, 2008.

Warner, Sam Bass. *Streetcar Suburbs: The Process of Growth in Boston, 1870–1900.* 3rd ed. Cambridge, MA: Harvard University Press, 1980.

Weiss, Marc A. *The Rise of the Community Builders: The American Real Estate Industry and Urban Land Planning.* Washington, DC: Beard Books, 2002.

Wilson, William H. *The City Beautiful Movement.* Baltimore: Johns Hopkins University Press, 1994.

Worley, William S. *J. C. Nichols and the Shaping of Kansas City: Innovation in Planned Residential Communities.* Columbia, MO: University of Missouri Press, 1993.

FOLK HOUSES

Brunskill, R. W. *Houses.* London: Collins, 1982.

———. *Vernacular Architecture: An Illustrated Handbook.* 4th ed. Retitled. London: Faber and Faber, 2000.

Driver, Harold E., and William C. Massey. "Comparative Studies of North American Indians." *American Philosophical Society Transactions* 47 (new series), pt. 2 (1957): 165–456.

Edwards, Jay Dearborn. "Shotgun: The most contested house in America." *Buildings and Landscapes: Journal of the Vernacular Architecture Forum* 16 (2009): 62–96.

Finley, Robert, and E. M. Scott. "A Great Lakes-to-Gulf Profile of Dispersed Dwelling Types." *Geographical Review* 30, no. 3 (July 1940): 412–19.

Glassie, Henry. *Pattern in the Material Folk Culture of the Eastern United States.* 1968. Reprint, Philadelphia: University of Pennsylvania Press, 1993.

Hart, John Fraser, Michelle J. Rhodes, and John Morgan. *The Unknown World of the Mobile Home.* Baltimore: Johns Hopkins University Press, 2003.

Hutslar, Donald A. *The Log Architecture of Ohio.* Columbus: Ohio Historical Society, 1977.

Jett, Stephen C., and Virginia E. Spencer. *Navajo Architecture: Forms, History, Distributions.* Tucson: University of Arizona Press, 1981.

Johnson, Wes. *The Manufactured Home Buyer's Handbook.* Jefferson, NC: McFarland & Co, 2005.

Jordan, Terry G. *Texas Log Buildings.* 1978. Reprint, Austin: University of Texas Press, 1994.

Kniffen, Fred. "Folk Housing: Key to Diffusion." *Annals of the Association of American Geographers* 55, no. 4 (Dec. 1965): 549–77.

Kniffen, Fred, and Henry Glassie. "Building in Wood in the Eastern United States: A Time-Place Perspective." *Geographical Review* 56, no. 1 (Jan. 1966): 40–66.

Lewis, Peirce F. "Common Houses, Cultural Spoor." *Landscape* 19, no. 2.

Marshall, Howard Wight. *Folk Architecture in Little Dixie.* Columbia: University of Missouri Press, 1981.

Montell, William L., and Michael L. Morse. *Kentucky Folk Architecture.* Lexington: University Press of Kentucky, 1995.

Pillsbury, Richard, and Andrew Kardos. *A Field Guide to the Folk Architecture of the Northeastern United States.* Hanover, NH: Geography Publications at Dartmouth, 1970.

Shortridge, James R. "Some Relationships Between External Housing Characteristics and House Types." *Pioneer America* 13, no. 2 (Sept. 1981): 1–28.

Swain, Doug, ed. *Carolina Dwelling.* North Carolina State University School of Design Student Publication, vol. 26. Raleigh: North Carolina State University, 1978.

Taylor, Steven V. *Manufactured Homes: The Buyer's Guide—How to Realize Your Dream in a Manufactured Home.* San Francisco: Cycle/Van der Plas, 2004.

Waterman, T. T. "North American Indian Dwellings." *Geographical Review* 14 (1924): 1–25.

Welsch, Roger L. *Sod Walls: The Story of the Nebraska Sod House.* 1968. Reprint. Lincoln, NE: J&L Lee Company, 1991.

Weslager, C. A. *The Log Cabin in America.* New Brunswick, NJ: Rutgers University Press, 1969.

Wilson, Eugene M. *Alabama Folk Houses.* Montgomery: Alabama Historical Commission, 1975.

COLONIAL HOUSES

Architects' Emergency Committee. *Great Georgian Houses of America.* 2 vols. 1933/1937. Reprint, New York: Dover Publications, 1970.

Baer, Morley, and Augusta Fink. *Adobes in the Sun.* San Francisco: Chronicle Books, 1972.

Bailey, Rosalie Fellows. *Pre-Revolutionary Dutch Houses and Families in Northern New Jersey and Southern New York.* 1936. Reprint, New York: Dover Publications, 1968.

Bunting, Bainbridge. *Early Architecture in New Mexico.* Albuquerque: University of New Mexico Press, 1976.

Bunting, Bainbridge, Jean Lee Booth, and William R. Sims Jr. *Taos Adobes: Spanish Colonial and Territorial Architecture of the Taos Valley.* Fort Burgwin Research Center Publication no. 2, 1964. Reprint, Albuquerque University of New Mexico, 1992.

Cummings, Abbott Lowell. *The Framed Houses of Massachusetts Bay, 1625–1725.* 2nd ed. Cambridge, MA: Harvard University Press, 1979.

Forman, Henry Chandlee. *The Architecture of the Old South: The Medieval Style, 1585–1850.* Cambridge, MA: Harvard University Press, 1948.

———. *Early Manor and Plantation Houses of Maryland.* 2nd ed. Baltimore: Bodine & Associates, 1982.

Garvan, Anthony N. B. *Architecture and Town Planning in Colonial Connecticut.* 1951. Reprint, New Haven: Yale University Press, 1982.

Gebhard, David. "Some Additional Observations on California's Monterey Tradition." *Journal of the Society of Architectural Historians* 46, no. 2 (June 1987): 157–70.

Giffen, Helen S. *Casas and Courtyards: Historic Adobe Houses of California.* Oakland, CA: Biobooks, 1955.

Gross, Geoffrey, Susan Piatt, Roderic H. Blackburn, and Harrison Frederick Meeske. *Dutch Colonial Homes in America.* New York: Rizzoli, 2002.

Guinness, Desmond, and Julius Trousdale Sadler Jr. *Mr. Jefferson, Architect.* New York: Viking Press, 1973.

Hamlin, Talbot. *Benjamin Henry Latrobe.* 1955. Reprint, New York: Oxford University Press, 1969.

Hannaford, Donald R., and Revel Edwards. *Spanish Colonial or Adobe Architecture of California, 1800–1850.* 1931. Reprint, Lanham, MD: Taylor Trade Publishing, 2012.

Harris, Eileen. *The Country Houses of Robert Adam: From the Archives of Country Life.* London: Aurum Press, 2007.

Howells, John Mead. *The Architectural Heritage of the Piscataqua: Houses and Gardens of the Portsmouth District of Maine and New Hampshire.* 1937. Reprint, Washington, DC: Whalesback Books, 1988.

———. *The Architectural Heritage of the Merrimack.* New York: Architectural Book Publishing, 1941.

Johnston, Frances Benjamin, and Thomas Tileston Waterman. *The Early Architecture of North Carolina.* Chapel Hill: University of North Carolina Press, 1947.

Katz, Ron, and Arielle de La Tour d'Auvergne. *French America: French Architecture from Colonialization to the Birth of a Nation.* New York: French Heritage Society, 2005.

Kelly, J. Frederick. *The Early Domestic Architecture of Connecticut.* 1924. Reprint, New York: Dover Publications, 2012.

Kimball, Fiske. *Domestic Architecture of the American Colonies and of the Early Republic.* 1922. Reprint, New York: Dover Publications, 2001.

Kirker, Harold. *The Architecture of Charles Bulfinch.* 1969. Reprint, Cambridge, MA: Harvard University Press, 1998.

Lane, Mills. *Architecture of the Old South: Colonial & Federal.* Savannah, GA: Beehive Foundation, 1996.

Manca, Joseph. "On the Origins of the American Porch." *Winterthur Portfolio* 40.23 (2006): 91–132.

McCall, Elizabeth B. *Old Philadelphia Houses on Society Hill, 1750–1840.* New York: Architectural Book Publishing, 1966.

Millar, John Fitzhugh. *The Architects of the American Colonies.* Barre, MA: Barre Publishers, 1968.

Morgan, William. *The Cape Cod Cottage.* New York: Princeton Architectural Press, 2006.

Morrison, Hugh. *Early American Architecture: From the First Colonial Settlements to the National Period.* 1952. Reprint, New York: Dover Publications, 2011.

Overdyke, W. Darrell. *Louisiana Plantation Homes.* New York: American Legacy Press, 1981.

Parissien, Steven. *The Georgian House in America and Britain.* 2nd ed. New York: Rizzoli, 2008.

Pierson, William H., Jr. *American Buildings and Their Architects: The Colonial and Neoclassical Styles.* New York: Oxford University Press, 1986.

Porterfield, Neil H. "Ste. Genevieve, Missouri." In *Frenchmen and French Ways in the Mississippi Valley,* edited by John Francis McDermott. Urbana, IL: University of Illinois Press, 1969.

Reiff, Daniel Drake. *Small Georgian Houses in England and Virginia: Origins and Development Through the 1750s.* Newark: University of Delaware Press, 1986.

Reynolds, Helen Wilkinson. *Dutch Houses in the Hudson Valley Before 1776.* 1929. Reprint, New York: Dover, 1965.

Richmond, Arthur P. *The Evolution of the Cape Cod House: An Architectural History.* Atglen, PA: Schiffer, 2011.

Schuler, Stanley. *The Cape Cod House.* Atglen, PA: Schiffer, 1982.

Stoney, Samuel Gaillard. *Plantations of the Carolina Low Country.* 1938. Reprint, New York: Dover Publications, 1990.

Tatum, George B. "Architecture." In *The Arts in America: The Colonial Period* by Louis B. Wright et al. New York: Charles Scribner's Sons, 1966.

Toledano, Roulhac, and Mary Louise Christovich. *New Orleans Architecture, Volume VI: Faubourg Tremé and the Bayou Road.* Gretna, LA: Pelican, 2003.

Toledano, Roulhac, Sally Kittredge Evans, and Mary Louise Christovich. *New Orleans Architecture, Volume IV: The Creole Faubourgs.* Gretna, LA: Pelican, 1996.

Waterman, Thomas Tileston. *The Mansions of Virginia, 1706–1776.* Chapel Hill: University of North Carolina Press, 1947.

———. *The Dwellings of Colonial America.* Rev. ed. New York: W.. W. Norton, 1999.

Whiffen, Marcus. *The Eighteenth-Century Houses of Williamsburg,* 2nd ed. Charlottesville, VA: University Press of Virginia, 1988.

ROMANTIC AND VICTORIAN HOUSES

Andrews, Wayne. *American Gothic.* New York: Random House, 1975.

Barber, George F. *Victorian Cottage Architecture: An American Catalog of Designs, 1891* [pattern book]. Reprint of *The Cottage Souvenir No. 2.* Mineola, NY: Dover Publications, 2004.

———. *Barber's Turn-of-the-Century Houses: Elevations and Floor Plans* [pattern book]. Reprint of *Modern Dwellings: A Book of Practical Designs and Plans, 3rd ed.,* 1901. Mineola, NY: Dover Publications, 2008.

Benjamin, Asher. *The American Builder's Companion* [pattern book]. 1827. Reprint, New York: Dover Publications, 1969.

———. *The Architect, or Practical House Carpenter* [pattern book]. 1830. Reprint, New York: Dover Publications, 1988.

Bicknell, A. J. *Bicknell's Village Builder and Supplement* [pattern book]. 1872. Reprint, Watkins Glen, NY: The American Life Foundation, 1976.

Brettell, Richard R. *Historic Denver, 1858–1893.* Denver: Historic Denver, 1973.

Cameron, Christina, and Janet Wright. *Second Empire Style in Canadian Architecture.* Canadian Historic Sites: Occasional Papers in Archaeology and History no. 24. Ottawa: National Historic Parks and Sites Branch, 1980.

Campen, Richard N. *Architecture of the Western Reserve, 1800–1900.* Cleveland: Case Western Reserve University Press, 1971.

Cochran, Gifford A. *Grandeur in Tennessee: Classical Revival Architecture in a Pioneer State.* New York: J. J. Augustin, 1946.

Comstock, William T. *Country Houses and Seaside Cottages of the Victorian Era* [pattern book]. Reprint of *American Cottages.* 1883. New York: Dover Publications, 1985.

Conover, Jewel Helen. *Nineteenth-Century Houses in Western New York.* Albany: State University of New York Press, 1971.

Cooper, J. Wesley. *Ante-Bellum Houses of Natchez.* Natchez, MS: Southern Historical Publications, 1983.

Cummings, M. F., and C. C. Miller. *Victorian Architectural Details.* Reprint of *Architecture* [pattern book], 1865, and *Architectural Details,* 1873. Watkins Glen, N.Y.: American Life Foundation, 1980.

Dana, William Sumner Barton. *The Swiss Chalet Book; A Minute Analysis and Reproduction of the Chalets of Switzerland, Obtained by a Special Visit to That Country, Its Architects, and Its Chalet Homes.* New York: William T. Comstock Co., 1913.

Delehanty, Randolph, and Richard Sexton. *In the Victorian Style.* San Francisco: Chronicle Books, 2006.

Denison, Allen, and Wallace Huntington. *Victorian Architecture of Port Townsend, Washington.* Seattle: Hancock House, 1978.

Downing, A. J. *The Architecture of Country Houses* [pattern book]. 1850. Reprint, New York: Dover Publications, 1969.

———. *Cottage Residences* [pattern book]. 1873. Reprint, New York: Dover Publications, 1981.

Early, James. *Romanticism and American Architecture.* New York: A. S. Barnes and Co., 1965.

Foster, Janet W. *The Queen Anne House: America's Victorian Vernacular.* New York: Abrams, 2006.

Fowler, Orson S. *A Home for All* [pattern book]. 1853. Reprint, New York: Dover Publications, 1973.

———. *The Octagon House: A Home for All* [pattern book]. 1853. Reprint, New York: Dover Publications, 1973.

Garvin, James L. "Mail-Order House Plans and American Victorian Architecture." *Winterthur Portfolio* 16 (1981): 309–334.

Gillon, Edmund V., Jr., and Clay Lancaster. *Victorian Houses.* New York: Dover Publications, 1973.

Girouard, Mark. *Sweetness and Light: The "Queen Anne" Movement, 1860–1900.* New Haven: Yale University Press, 1990.

Hackett, Cheryl, and Kindra Clineff. *Newport Shingle Style.* London: Frances Lincoln, 2010.

Hall, John, and Thomas Gordon Smith. *John Hall and the Grecian Style in America: A Reprint of Three Pattern Books Published in Baltimore in 1840.* New York: Acanthus Press, 1996.

Hamlin, Talbot. *Greek Revival Architecture in America.* 1944. Reprint, New York: Dover Publications, 1985.

Hammond, Ralph. *Ante-Bellum Mansions of Alabama.* 1955. Reprint, New York: Architectural Book Publishing Co., 1988.

Hersey, George L. "Godey's Choice." *The Journal of the Society of Architectural Historians* 18, no. 3 (1959): 104–111.

Hitchcock, Henry-Russell. *The Architecture of H. H. Richardson and His Times,* Rev. ed. Cambridge, MA: M.I.T. Press, 1970.

Holly, Henry Hudson, and Michael Tomlan. *Country Seats & Modern Dwellings: Two Victorian Domestic Architectural Stylebooks* [pattern book]. 1863 and 1878. Reprint, Watkins, Glen, NY: American Life Foundation, 1980.

Hussey, E. C. *Victorian Home Building* [pattern book]. 1875. Reprint, Watkins Glen, NY: American Life Foundation, 1976.

Kennedy, Roger G., and John M. Hall. *Greek Revival America.* New York: Stewart, Tabori & Chang, 2010.

Keyes, Margaret N. *Nineteenth Century Home Architecture of Iowa City.* Rev. ed. Iowa City: University of Iowa Press, 1993.

Lafever, Minard. *The Beauties of Modern Architecture* [pattern book]. 1835. Reprint, New York: Da Capo Press, 1968.

———. *The Modern Builder's Guide* [pattern book]. 1846. Reprint, New York: Dover Publications, 1969.

Lancaster, Clay. *Architectural Follies in America.* Rutland, VT: Charles E. Tuttle, 1960.

Landau, Sarah Bradford. "Richard Morris Hunt, the Continental Picturesque, and the 'Stick Style.'" *The Journal of the Society of Architectural Historians* 42, no. 3 (1983): 272–289.

Lane, Mills, and Van J. Martin. *Architecture of the Old South: Greek Revival & Romantic.* Savannah: Beehive Foundation, 1996.

Lewis, Arnold. *American Country Houses of the Gilded Age (Sheldon's "Artistic Country-Seats").* 1886–87. Reprint. New York: Dover Publications, 1982.

Lewis, Arnold, and Keith Morgan. *American Victorian Architecture.* 1886. Reprint, New York: Dover Publications, 1975.

Loth, Calder, and Julius Trousdale Sadler Jr. *The Only Proper Style: Gothic Architecture in America.* Boston: New York Graphic Society, 1975.

Maass, John. *The Victorian Home in America.* Reprint, New York: Dover Publications, 2000.

Major, Howard. *The Domestic Architecture of the Early American Republic: The Greek Revival.* Philadelphia: J. B. Lippincott, 1926.

Martin, John H. "Orson Squire Fowler: Phrenology and Octagon Houses, 1809–1887." *The Crooked Lane Review* 137 (2005).

McArdle, Alma de C., and Deirdre Bartlett McArdle. *Carpenter Gothic: Nineteenth-Century Ornamented Houses of New England.* New York: Whitney Library of Design, 1978.

Montgomery, Gladys. *Storybook Cottages: America's Carpenter Gothic Style.* New York: Rizzoli, 2011.

Ochsner, Jeffrey Karl. *H. H. Richardson: Complete Architectural Works.* Cambridge, MA: MIT Press, 1985.

Olwell, Carol, and Judith Lynch Waldhorn. *A Gift to the Street.* San Francisco: Antelope Island Press, 1978.

Palliser, George, and Charles Palliser. *The Palliser's Late Victorian Architecture* [3 pattern books]. 1878. Reprint, Watkins Glen, NY: American Life Foundation, 1978.

———. *Late Victorian Architecture* [pattern book]. Reprint of *Palliser's New Cottage Homes and Details,* 1887, and *American Architecture, or Every Man a Complete Builder.* 1888. Watkins Glen, NY: American Life Foundation, 1978.

Peat, Wilbur D. *Indiana Houses of the Nineteenth Century.* Indianapolis: Indiana Historical Society, 1969.

Pierson, William H., Jr. *American Buildings and Their Architects Volume 2: Technology and the Picturesque—The Corporate and the Early Gothic Styles.* New York: Oxford University Press, 1986.

Plymat, William, Jr. *The Victorian Architecture of Iowa.* 2nd ed. Mason City, IA: Palladian, 1997.

Robinson, Annie. *Peabody & Stearns: Country Houses and Seaside Cottages.* New York: W. W. Norton, 2010.

Roth, Leland M., and Bret Morgan. *Shingle Styles: Innovation and Tradition in American Architecture, 1874 to 1982.* New York: Abrams, 1999.

Saylor, Henry H. *Architectural Styles for Country-Houses: The Swiss Chalet Type.* New York: Robert M. McBride & Co., 1919.

Schmidt, Carl F. *The Octagon Fad.* Scottsville, NY: publ. by author, 1958.

Schmitt, Peter J., and Balthazar Korab. *Kalamazoo: Nineteenth-Century Homes in a Midwestern Village.* Kalamazoo, MI: Kalamazoo City Historical Commission, 1976.

Scully, Vincent J., Jr. *The Shingle Style Today, or the Historian's Revenge.* New York: Braziller, 1978.

———. *The Shingle Style and the Stick Style.* Rev. ed. New Haven: Yale University Press, 1979.

Shoppell, R. W. *Complete Collection of Shoppell's Modern Houses: Fifteen Hundred Illustrations* [pattern book]. New York: Co-operative Building Plan Association, 1886.

———. *Turn-of-the-Century Houses, Cottages and Villas: Floor Plans and Line Illustrations of 118 Homes from Shoppell's Catalogs* [pattern book]. Reprint, New York: Dover Publications, 1984.

Skjelver, Mabel Cooper. *Nineteenth Century Homes of Marshall, Michigan.* 3rd ed. Marshall, MI: Marshall Historical Society, 1982.

Sloan, Samuel. *The Model Architect* [pattern book]. 1852. Reprint, New York: Dover Publications, 1980.

Thomas, George E., and Carl Doebley. *Cape May, Queen of the Seaside Resorts.* Philadelphia: Art Alliance Press, 1976.

Vaux, Calvert. *Villas and Cottages* [pattern book]. 1864. Reprint, New York: Dover Publications, 1970.

———. *Villa and Cottage Architecture: The Style-Book of the Hudson River School.* 1867. Reprint, New York: Dover Publications, 1991.

Wilson, Samuel, Jr., and Bernard Lemann. *New Orleans Architecture, Volume 1: The Lower Garden District.* Gretna, LA: Pelican, 1991.

Woodward, George Everston. *Woodward's National Architect* [pattern book]. 1869. Reprint, American Life Foundation, 1977.

———. *Victorian City and Country Houses: Plans and Designs* [pattern book]. 1877. Reprint, New York: Dover Publications, 1996.

ECLECTIC HOUSES

American Builder Publishing Corporation. *Modern Homes: Their Design and Construction* [pattern book]. Chicago: American Builder Publishing Corporation, 1930.

Appelbaum, Stanley. *The Chicago World's Fair of 1893.* New York: Dover Publications, 1980.

Architectural Forum. *The Book of Small Houses* [pattern book]. New York: Simon and Schuster, 1936.

Axelrod, Alan. *The Colonial Revival in America.* New York: Norton, 1985.

Barnstone, Howard. *The Architecture of John F. Staub: Houston and the South.* Austin: University of Texas Press, 1979.

Blackburn, Bob L., and Jim Argo. *Heritage Hills: Preservation of a Historic Neighborhood.* Oklahoma City: Western Heritage Books, 1990.

Bricker, Lauren Weiss. *The Mediterranean House in America.* New York: Abrams, 2008.

Cardwell, Kenneth H. *Bernard Maybeck: Artisan, Architect, Artist.* Santa Barbara, CA: Peregrine Smith, 1977.

Clarke, Ann Brewster. *Wade Hampton Pipes: Arts and Crafts Architect in Portland, Oregon.* Portland: Binford & Mort, 1986.

Coate, Roland E. "The Early California House." *California Arts and Architecture* 35 (March 1929): 21–30.

Coffin, Lewis A., and James Ford. *American Country Houses of the Thirties, with Photographs and Floor Plans.* Mineola, NY: Dover Publications, 2007.

Edgell, G. H. *The American Architecture of To-day.* 1928. Reprint, New York: AMS Press, 1970.

Embury, Aymar II. *The Dutch Colonial House.* New York: McBride, Nast & Company, 1913.

Fox, Stephen, and Richard Cheek. *The Country Houses of John F. Staub.* College Station: Texas A&M University Press, 2007.

Frazer, Susan Hume. *The Architecture of William Lawrence Bottomley.* New York: Acanthus Press, 2007.

Garrison, James B. *Mastering Tradition: The Residential Architecture of John Russell Pope.* New York: Acanthus Press, 2006.

Gebhard, David. "The American Colonial Revival in the 1930s." *Winterthur Portfolio* 22, nos. 2–3 (summer–autumn 1987): 109–148.

———. "Royal Barry Wills and the American Colonial Revival." *Winterthur Portfolio* 27, no. 1 (spring 1992): 45–74.

Gebhard, Patricia. *George Washington Smith: Architect of the Spanish Colonial Revival.* Salt Lake City, UT: Gibbs Smith, 2005.

Gellner, Arrol, and Douglas Keister. *Storybook Style: America's Whimsical Homes of the Twenties.* New York: Viking Studio, 2001.

———. *Red Tile Style: America's Spanish Revival Architecture.* New York: Viking Studio, 2002.

Goff, Lee, and Paul Rocheleau. *Tudor Style: Tudor Revival Houses in America from 1890 to the Present.* New York: Universe, 2002.

Gordon–Van Tine Co. *117 House Designs of the Twenties* [pattern book]. 1923. Reprint, Philadelphia: Athenaeum, 1992.

Grady, James. *Architecture of Neel Reid in Georgia.* Athens: University of Georgia Press, 1973.

Hewitt, Mark A. *Carrère & Hastings Architects.* New York: Acanthus Press, 2006.

Hoffstot, Barbara. *Landmark Architecture of Palm Beach.* 3rd ed. Pittsburgh: History & Landmarks Foundation, 1991.

Hunter, Paul Robinson, and Walter L. Reichardt, eds. *Residential Architecture in Southern California.* 1939. Reprint, Santa Monica: Hennessey & Ingalls, 1998.

Jackson, Allen W. *The Half-Timber House.* 1912. Reprint. New York: Robert M. McBride, 2012.

J. D. Loizeaux Lumber Company. *Classic Houses of the Twenties* [pattern book]. 1927. Reprint, Philadelphia: Athenaeum, 1992.

Jones, Robert T. *Authentic Small Houses of the Twenties: Illustrations and Floor Plans of 254 Characteristic Homes* [pattern book]. 1929. Reprint, New York: Dover Publications, 1987.

Jordy, William H. *American Buildings and Their Architects, Volume 4: Progressive and Academic Ideals at the Turn of the Twentieth Century.* New York: Oxford University Press, 1986.

Kathrens, Michael C. *Newport Villas: The Revival Styles, 1885–1935.* New York: W. W. Norton, 2009.

Kathrens, Michael C., Richard C. Marchand, and Eleanor Weller. *American Splendor: The Residential Architecture of Horace Trumbauer.* Rev. ed. New York: Acanthus Press, 2011.

Kidney, Walter C. *The Architecture of Choice: Eclecticism in America, 1880–1930.* New York: George Braziller, 1974.

Kohler, Sue A., and Jeffrey R. Carson. *Sixteenth Street Architecture,* vol. 1. Washington, DC: Commission of Fine Arts, 1978–1988.

McKim, Mead & White. *A Monograph of the Works of McKim, Mead & White, 1879–1915.* 1915. Reprint, New York: Dover Publications, 1990.

McMillian, Elizabeth Jean, and Matt Gainer. *California Colonial: The Spanish and Rancho Revival Styles.* Atglen, PA: Schiffer, 2002.

Mizner, Addison. *Florida Architecture of Addison Mizner.* Ann Arbor: University of Michigan Press, 1993.

Mockler, Kim I. *Maurice Fatio: Palm Beach Architect.* New York: Acanthus Press, 2010.

Morrison, William. *The Work of Dwight James Baum.* New York: Acanthus Press, 2008.

Murphy, Kevin. *Colonial Revival Maine.* New York: Princeton Architectural Press, 2004.

Newcomb, Rexford. *The Spanish House for America.* Philadelphia: J. B. Lippincott, 1927.

———. *Mediterranean Domestic Architecture in the United States.* 1928. Reprint, New York: Acanthus Press, 1999.

Pennoyer, Peter, and Anne Walker. *The Architecture of Delano & Aldrich.* New York: Norton, 2003.

———. *The Architecture of Warren & Wetmore.* New York: W. W. Norton, 2006.

Pennoyer, Peter, Jonathan Wallen, and Robert A. M. Stern. *The Architecture of Grosvenor Atterbury.* New York: W. W. Norton, 2009.

Platt, Frederick. *America's Gilded Age: Its Architecture and Decoration.* Cranbury, NJ: A. S. Barnes, 1976.

Saylor, Henry H., ed. *Architectural Styles for Country Houses.* 1912. Reprint, Ithaca, NY: Cornell University Library, 2009.

Sclare, Liisa, and Donald Sclare. *Beaux-Arts Estates: A Guide to the Architecture of Long Island.* New York: Viking Press, 1980.

Skinner, Tina. *Radford's Artistic Homes: 250 Designs* [pattern book]. 1908. Reprint, Atglen, PA: Schiffer Publishing, 2002.

Smith, Henry Atterbury. *The Books of a Thousand Homes, Volume 1: 500 Small House Plans* [pattern book]. New York: Home Owners Service Institute, 1923.

———. *500 Small Houses of the Twenties* [pattern book]. 1923. Reprint, New York: Dover Publications, 1990.

Stamp, Gavin, and André Goulancourt. *The English House, 1860–1914: The Flowering of English Domestic Architecture.* Chicago: University of Chicago Press, 1986.

Stevens, John Calvin, and Earle G. Shettleworth. *John Calvin Stevens, Domestic Architecture, 1890–1930*. Portland, ME: Greater Portland Landmarks, 1995.

Stevenson, Katherine H., and H. Ward Jandl. *Houses by Mail: A Guide to Houses from Sears, Roebuck, and Company*. Washington, DC: Preservation Press, 1996.

Sully, Susan. *Casa Florida: Spanish-Style Houses from Winter Park to Coral Gables*. New York: Rizzoli, 2005.

Townsend, Gavin Edward. "The Tudor House in America, 1890–1930." Ph.D. diss. University of California, 1986, 1988.

Underwood, Francis H. *The Colonial House Then and Now*. Rutland, VT: Charles E. Tuttle, 1977.

Walsh, Michael, and Richard Toglia. *Tudor Houses* [pattern book]. Farmington Hills, MI: Home Planners, 1989.

Ware, William R. *American Vignola: Guide to the Making of Classical Architecture*. 1903. Reprint, Dover Publications, 1995.

Weitze, Karen J. *California's Mission Revival*. Santa Monica: Hennessey & Ingalls, 1984.

White, Samuel G., and Elizabeth White. *Stanford White, Architect*. New York: Rizzoli, 2008.

White, Samuel G., and Jonathan Wallen. *The Houses of McKim, Mead & White*. New York: Universe, 2004.

White, Samuel G., Elizabeth White, and Jonathan Wallen. *McKim, Mead & White: The Masterworks*. New York: Rizzoli, 2003.

Wilson, Henry L. *The Bungalow Book* [pattern book]. 1910. Reprint, New York: Dover Publications, 2006.

Wilson, Richard Guy. *McKim, Mead & White, Architects*. New York: Rizzoli, 1983.

———. *The Architecture of McKim, Mead & White in Photographs, Plans, and Elevations*. New York: Dover Publications, 1990.

Wilson, Richard Guy, and Noah Sheldon. *The Colonial Revival House*. New York: Abrams, 2004.

Wyllie, Romy. *Bertram Goodhue: His Life and Residential Architecture*. New York: W. W. Norton, 2007.

MODERN HOUSES

Adamson, Paul, Marty Arbunich, and Ernest Braun. *Eichler: Modernism Rebuilds the American Dream*. Layton, UT: Gibbs Smith, 2002.

Aladdin Company. *Aladdin Homes Built in a Day*, catalog no. 31 [pattern book]. 1919. Reprint, Watkins Glen, NY: American Life Foundation, 1985.

Allen, Gerald. *Charles Moore*. New York: Whitney Library of Design, 1981.

Baker, Geoffrey Harold, and Bruno Funaro. *Windows in Modern Architecture*. New York: Architectural Book Publishing Co., 1948.

Blake, Peter. *Marcel Breuer, Architect and Designer*. New York: Architectural Record [u.a.], 1954.

Bottomley, Myrl Elijah. *The Design of Small Properties; A Book for the Homeowner in City and Country*. New York: Macmillan Co., 1929.

Brooks, H. Allen. *The Prairie School: Frank Lloyd Wright and His Midwest Contemporaries*. 1972. Reprint, New York: W. W. Norton, 2006.

Brooks, Turner, et al. *Turner Brooks: Work*. New York: Princeton Architectural Press, 1995.

Brown-Blodgett Company (Saint Paul, MN). *100 Small Houses of the Thirties*. 1936. Reprint, Mineola, NY: Dover Publications, 2005.

Burrows, John S. *Your New Home*. New York: Archway Press, 1950.

Callender, John Hancock. *Before You Buy a House*. New York: Crown, 1953.

Cerwinske, Laura. *Tropical Deco: The Architecture and Design of Old Miami Beach*. New York: Rizzoli, 1991.

Clausen, Meredith L. *Pietro Belluschi: Modern American Architect*. Cambridge, MA: MIT Press, 1999.

Le Corbusier, and Frederick Etchells. *Towards a New Architecture*. 1946. Reprint, London: Architectural Press, 2011.

Craig, G. L., Rudard A. Jones, and William H. Kapple. *Split-level Houses*. Champaign, IL: Small Homes Council-Building Research Council, University of Illinois at Urbana-Champaign, 1960.

Current, William R., and Karen Current. *Greene & Greene: Architects in the Residential Style*. Dobbs Ferry, NY: Morgan & Morgan, 1977.

Cygelman, Adèle, and David Glomb. *Palm Springs Modern: Houses in the California Desert*. New York: Rizzoli, 2006.

Davies, Colin. *Key Houses of the Twentieth Century: Plans, Sections and Elevations*. London: Laurence King, 2006.

Dietsch, Deborah. *Classic Modern: Midcentury Modern at Home*. London: Simon & Schuster, 2001.

Dillon, David. *The Architecture of O'Neil Ford: Celebrating Place*. University of Texas Press, 1999.

Ditto, Jerry, Lanning Stern, and Marvin Wax. *Eichler Homes: Design for Living*. San Francisco: Chronicle, 1995.

Doan, Mason C. *American Housing Production, 1880–2000: A Concise History*. Lanham, MD: University Press of America, 2000.

Doubilet, Susan, and Daralice D. Boles. *American House Now: Contemporary Architectural Directions*. Rev. ed. New York: Universe, 2002.

Duchscherer, Paul, and Douglas Keister. *The Bungalow: America's Arts and Crafts Home*. New York: Penguin Studio, 1995.

Earls, William D. *The Harvard Five in New Canaan: Midcentury Modern Houses by Marcel Breuer, Landis Gores, John Johansen, Philip Johnson, Eliot Noyes & Others*. New York: W. W. Norton, 2006.

Ehrlich, Doreen. *Usonian Houses.* London: PRC, 2002.

Etter, Don D. *Denver Going Modern: A Photographic Essay on the Imprint of the International Style on Denver Residential Architecture.* Denver: Graphic Impressions, 1977.

Faibyshev, Dolly. *Palm Springs Mid-Century Modern.* Atglen, PA: Schiffer, 2010.

Flagg, Ernest. *Flagg's Small Houses: Their Economic Design and Construction, 1922.* Reprint of *Small Houses: Their Economic Design and Construction,* 1921. Mineola, NY: Dover Publications, 2006.

Ford, James, and Katherine Morrow Ford. *The Modern House in America.* New York: Architectural Book Publishing Co., 1940.

Frampton, Kenneth, and David Larkin. *The Twentieth Century American House: Masterworks of Residential Architecture.* London: Thames and Hudson, 1995.

Friedman, Avi. "The Evolution of Design Characteristics During the Post-Second World War Housing Boom: The U.S. Experience." *Journal of Design History* 8, no. 2 (1995): 131–146.

Gebhard, David, and Patricia Gebhard. *Purcell & Elmslie: Prairie Progressive Architects.* Salt Lake City, UT: Gibbs Smith, 2006.

George, Mary Carolyn Hollers. *O'Neil Ford, Architect.* College Station: Texas A&M University Press, 1992.

Gordon, Alastair. *Weekend Utopia: Modern Living in the Hamptons.* New York: Princeton Architectural Press, 2001.

Gorlin, Alexander, and Geoffrey Gross. *Tomorrow's Houses: New England Modernism.* New York: Rizzoli, 2011.

Graf, Jean, and Don Graf. *Practical Houses for Contemporary Living.* New York: F. W. Dodge, 1953.

Gregory, Daniel Platt, and Cliff May. *Cliff May and the Modern Ranch House.* New York: Rizzoli, 2008.

Group, Harold E. *Small Houses of the Forties, with Illustrations and Floor Plans* [pattern book]. 1946. Reprint, Mineola, NY: Dover Publications, 2007.

Hess, Alan. *Palm Springs Weekend: The Architecture and Design of a Mid-Century Oasis.* San Francisco: Chronicle Books, 2001.

———. *Organic Architecture: The Other Modernism.* Layton, UT: Gibbs Smith, 2006.

———. *Forgotten Modern: California Houses 1940–1970.* Layton, Utah: Gibbs Smith, 2007.

———. *Frank Lloyd Wright: Mid-century Modern.* New York: Rizzoli, 2007.

———. *Frank Lloyd Wright: The Houses.* New York: Rizzoli, 2007.

———. *The Ranch House.* New York: H. N. Abrams, 2008.

Historic Preservation Division, Georgia Department of Natural Resources. "American Small Houses." [N.d.] Retrieved from http://georgiashpo.org/sites/uploads/hpd/pdf/American_Small_House.pdf

———. "The Ranch House in Georgia: Guidelines for Evaluation." [N.d.] Retrieved from http://georgiashpo.org/sites/uploads/hpd/pdf/Ranch_House_Evaluation_revSept2010.pdf

Hitchcock, Henry-Russell. *In the Nature of Materials, 1887–1941: The Buildings of Frank Lloyd Wright.* 1942. Reprint, New York: Da Capo Press, 1975.

Hitchcock, Henry-Russell, and Philip Johnson. *The International Style: Architecture Since 1922.* 1932. Rev. ed. New York: W. W. Norton & Co., 1997.

Hodgson, Fred T. *Practical Bungalows and Cottages for Town and Country* [pattern book]. Chicago: Frederick J. Drake, 1916.

Home Planners, Inc. *The Essential Guide to Contemporary Home Plans* [pattern book]. Farmington Hills, MI: Home Planners, 1987.

Isenstadt, Sandy. *The Modern American House: Spaciousness and Middle-class Identity.* Cambridge: Cambridge University Press, 2006.

Jackson, N. *California Modern: The Architecture of Craig Ellwood.* New York: Princeton Architectural Press, 2002.

Jencks, Charles. *The Language of Post-Modern Architecture.* 6th ed. New York: Rizzoli, 1991.

———. *The Story of Post-Modernism: Five Decades of the Ironic, Iconic and Critical in Architecture.* 2nd ed. John Wiley & Sons, 2012.

Jensen, Robert, and Patricia Conway. *Ornamentalism.* New York: Clarkson Potter, 1982.

Johnson, Eugene J. *Charles Moore: Buildings and Projects, 1949–1986.* New York: Rizzoli, 1991.

Jones, Robert T. *Small Houses of Architectural Distinction* [pattern book]. 1929. Reprint, New York: Dover Publications, 1987.

Junior League of Tulsa. *Tulsa Art Deco: An Architectural Era, 1925–1942.* Tulsa, OK: Junior League, 1980.

Keil, Rob. *Little Boxes: The Architecture of a Classic Midcentury Suburb.* Daly City, CA: Advection Media, 2006.

Khan, Hasan-Uddin. *International Style: Modernist Architecture from 1925 to 1965.* Köln (Germany): Taschen, 1998.

Lambin, Jeanne, and Janine Duncan. "The Recent Past Is Groovy: Researching American Architectural Styles after World War II." *Alliance Review,* July–August 2008. http://www.landmarksil.org/pdfs/alliance_review.pdf

Lancaster, Clay. *The American Bungalow, 1880–1930.* 1983. Reprint, New York: Dover Publications, 1995.

Levine, Neil, and Frank Lloyd Wright. *The Architecture of Frank Lloyd Wright.* Princeton, NJ: Princeton University Press, 1998.

Luce, Henry R. *Form Givers at Mid-Century.* [New York]: Time, Inc. for American Federation of Arts, 1959.

Lyndon, Donlyn, James Alinder, Donald Canty, and Lawrence Halprin. *The Sea Ranch.* New York: Princeton Architectural Press, 2004.

Lyon, Hortense. *American Contemporary Houses.* Paris: Telleri, 1998.

Maddex, Diane. *Frank Lloyd Wright's House Beautiful.* New York: Hearst Books, 2000.

———. *Wright-Sized Houses: Frank Lloyd Wright's Solutions for Making Small Houses Feel Big.* New York: Abrams, 2003.

Maddex, Diane, and Alexander Vertikoff. *Bungalow Nation.* New York: Harry N. Abrams, 2003.

Maine Historic Preservation Commission. "Post World War II Architecture in Maine: A Guide for Surveyors." maine.gov.http://www.maine.gov/portal/index.html

Makinson, Randell L. *Greene & Greene.* Rev. ed. Salt Lake City: Gibbs Smith, 2001.

Martin, Harry, Dick Busher, and Warren Winther. *Contemporary Homes of the Pacific Northwest.* Seattle: Madrona Publishers, 1980.

Master Plan Service. *Encyclopedia of Home Designs.* Series. Mineola, NY: Master Plan Service, 1967–84.

May, Cliff, and Paul C. Johnson. *Western Ranch Houses by Cliff May.* 1946. Reprint, Santa Monica, CA: Hennessey & Ingalls, 1997.

May, Cliff, and Sunset Magazine. *Sunset Western Ranch Houses.* 1958. Reprint. Santa Monica, CA: Hennessey & Ingalls, 1999.

McCarthy, Muriel Q. *David R. Williams, Pioneer Architect.* Dallas: Southern Methodist University Press, 1984.

McCoy, Esther. *Five California Architects.* 2nd ed. Santa Monica, CA: Hennessey & Ingalls, 1975.

———. *The Second Generation.* Salt Lake City: Peregrine Smith Books, 1984.

Moore, Charles Willard, Gerald Allen, and Donlyn Lyndon. *The Place of Houses.* 1979. Reprint, New York: Holt, Rinehart and Winston, 2011.

Morand, François C. *Small Homes in the New Tradition* [pattern book]. New York: Sterling, 1959.

National Plan Service, Inc. *Homes of Moderate Cost* [pattern book]. Chicago: National Plan Service, 1941.

Nelson, George, and Henry Wright. *Tomorrow's House: A Complete Guide for the Home-Builder.* New York: Simon and Schuster, 1946.

Noever, Peter, and Regina Haslinger. *Architecture in Transition: Between Deconstruction and New Modernism.* Munich: Prestel, 1997.

Olsberg, R. Nicholas, and Jocelyn Gibbs. *Carefree California: Cliff May and the Romance of the Ranch House.* New York: Rizzoli International, 2012.

Pascal, Patrick, Julius Shulman, and David Sadofski. *Kesling Modern Structures: Popularizing Modern Design in Southern California, 1934–1962.* Los Angeles: Balcony Press, 2002.

Pearson, Clifford A., and Thomas Hine. *Modern American Houses: Four Decades of Award-winning Design in Architectural Record.* New York: Harry N. Abrams, 1996.

Pearson, David. *New Organic Architecture: The Breaking Wave.* Berkeley: University of California Press, 2001.

Peterson, Gary G. "Home off the Range: The Origins and Evolution of Ranch Style Architecture in the United States." *Design Methods and Theories* 23 (1989): 1040–59.

Randl, Chad. *A-frame.* New York: Princeton Architectural Press, 2004.

Rawlins, Christopher Bascom. *Fire Island Modernist: Horace Gifford and the Architecture of Seduction.* New York: Metropolis Books, 2013.

Reisley, Roland, and John Philip Timpane. *Usonia, New York: Building a Community with Frank Lloyd Wright.* New York: Princeton Architectural Press, 2001.

Riera Ojeda, Oscar, and Lucas H. Guerra. *The New American House: Innovations in Residential Design and Construction: 30 Case Studies.* 4 vols. New York: Whitney Library of Design, 1995–2003.

Rifkind, Carole. *A Field Guide to Contemporary American Architecture.* New York: Penguin, 2001.

Rosenbaum, Alvin. *Usonia: Frank Lloyd Wright's Design for America.* Washington, DC: Preservation Press, National Trust for Historic Preservation, 1993.

Samon, Katherine Ann. *Ranch House Style.* New York: Clarkson Potter, 2003.

Schulze, Franz. *Philip Johnson: Life and Work.* New York: Knopf, 2009.

Scully, Vincent Joseph, and Neil Levine. *Modern Architecture and Other Essays.* Princeton, NJ: Princeton University Press, 2005.

Sears, Roebuck and Co. *Sears, Roebuck Catalog of Houses* [pattern book]. 1926. Reprint, New York: Dover Publications, 1991.

Sergeant, John. *Frank Lloyd Wright's Usonian Houses: The Case for Organic Architecture.* 1976. Reprint, New York: Whitney Library of Design, 2009.

Serraino, Pierluigi. *NorCalMod: Icons of Northern California Modernism.* San Francisco: Chronicle Books, 2006.

Serraino, Pierluigi, Julius Shulman, and Peter Gössel. *Julius Shulman: Modernism Rediscovered.* Los Angeles: Taschen, 2009.

Shulman, Julius, and Gary Gand. *Julius Shulman: Chicago Mid-Century Modernism.* New York: Rizzoli, 2010.

Shulman, Julius, Michael Stern, and Alan Hess. *Julius Shulman: Palm Springs.* New York: Rizzoli, 2008.

Shulman, Julius, Sam Lubell, Douglas Woods, and Judy McKee. *Julius Shulman, Los Angeles: The Birth of a Modern Metropolis.* New York: Rizzoli, 2011.

Slaton, Deborah, and Rebecca A Shiffer, eds. *Preserv-*

ing the Recent Past. Washington, DC: Historic Preservation Education Foundation, 1995.

Slaton, Deborah, and William G. Fouls, eds. *Preserving the Recent Past 2,* Washington, DC: Historic Preservation Education Foundation, National Park Service, and Association for Preservation Technology International, 2000.

Smith, Bruce, and Alexander Vertikoff. *Greene & Greene: Masterworks.* San Francisco: Chronicle Books, 1998.

Smith, Elizabeth A. T., and Peter Gössel. *Case Study Houses, 1945–1966: The California Impetus.* Köln (Germany): Taschen, 2009.

Smith, Herbert L. *Twenty-five Years of Record Houses.* New York: McGraw-Hill, 1981.

Stickley, Gustav. *Craftsman Homes* [pattern book]. 1909. Reprint, New York: Dover Publications, 1979.

———. *Gustav Stickley's Craftsman Homes and Bungalows* [pattern book]. 1912. Reprint, New York: Skyhorse, 2009.

Storrer, William Allin. *The Architecture of Frank Lloyd Wright: A Complete Catalog.* 3rd ed. Chicago: University of Chicago Press, 2007.

Stubblebine, Jo, ed. *The Northwest Architecture of Pietro Belluschi.* New York: F. W. Dodge Corp., 1953.

Stubblebine, Ray, and Gustav Stickley. *Stickley's Craftsman Homes: Plans, Drawings, Photographs.* Layton, UT: Gibbs Smith, 2006.

Sutro, Dirk. *West Coast Wave: New California Houses.* New York: Van Nostrand Reinhold, 1994.

Trapp, Kenneth R., and Leslie Greene Bowman. *The Arts and Crafts Movement in California: Living the Good Life.* Oakland, CA: Oakland Museum, 1993.

A Treasury of Contemporary Houses. New York: F. W. Dodge, 1954.

Trulove, James Grayson, and Il Kim. *The New American Cottage: Innovations in Small-Scale Residential Architecture.* New York: Whitney Library of Design, 1999.

U.S. Federal Housing Administration. *Principles of Planning Small Houses.* Washington, DC: U.S. Federal Housing Administration, 1936, 1940.

Venturi, Robert. *Complexity and Contradiction in Architecture.* 1966. 2nd ed. New York: Museum of Modern Art, 2011.

Von Holst, H. V. *Country and Suburban Homes of the Prairie School Period, with 424 Photographs and Floor Plans* [pattern book]. N.d. Reprint, New York: Dover Publications, 1982.

———. *Modern American Homes, Etc.* [pattern book]. 1913. Reprint, American School of Correspondence: Chicago, 2008.

Wagner, Walter F. *A Treasury of Contemporary Houses.* New York: McGraw-Hill, 1978.

Webb, Michael, and Roger Straus. *Modernism Reborn: Mid-Century American Houses.* New York: Universe, 2001.

Weingarten, David, Lucia Howard, and Joe Fletcher. *Ranch Houses: Living the California Dream.* New York: Rizzoli, 2009.

Weston, Richard. *Twentieth-Century Residential Architecture.* New York: Abbeville Press, 2002.

Wickes, Molly, and Kate Irvin. *A Guide to Oak Park's Frank Lloyd Wright and Prairie School Historic District.* Oak Park, IL: Oak Park Historic Preservation Commission, Village of Oak Park, 1999.

Wilson, Henry L. *California Bungalows of the Twenties* [pattern book]. N.d. Reprint, New York: Dover Publications, 1993.

Winter, Robert. *The California Bungalow.* Los Angeles: Hennessey and Ingalls, 1980.

———. *Toward a Simpler Way of Life: The Arts & Crafts Architects of California.* Berkeley: University of California Press, 1997.

Winter, Robert, and Alexander Vertikoff. *American Bungalow Style.* New York: Simon & Schuster, 1996.

Wolfe, Tom. *From Bauhaus to Our House.* 1981. Reprint, New York: Farrar Straus Giroux, 2012.

Wright, Frank Lloyd. *The Natural House.* 1954. Reprint, New York: Horizon Press, 1982.

Zaleski, Caroline Rob. *Long Island Modernism, 1930–1980.* New York: Society for the Preservation of Long Island Antiquities, in association with W. W. Norton & Company, 2012.

In addition, Richard Longstreth's comprehensive "A Historical Bibliography of Architecture, Landscape Architecture, and Urbanism in the United States Since World War II" is updated regularly and is available through the following link: http://www.recent past.org/bibliography/RPPNbib2012.pdf

STYLED HOUSES SINCE 1935

Baker, William T., James R. Lockhart, and Beverly Means Dubose. *New Classicists.* Mulgrave (Australia): Images Publishing Group, 2004.

Bassenian, Aram, and Laura Hurst Brown. *Pure California: 35 Inspiring Houses in the New California Tradition.* Newport Beach, CA: Bassenian/Lagoni Architects, 2004.

Brostrom, Caitlin Lempres, William Wilson Wurster, and Richard C. Peters. *The Houses of William Wurster: Frames for Living.* New York: Princeton Architectural Press, 2011.

Carter, Thomas, and Elizabeth C. Cromley. *Invitation to Vernacular Architecture: A Guide to the Study of Ordinary Buildings and Landscapes.* Knoxville: University of Tennessee Press, 2005.

Chase, John. *Glitter Stucco and Dumpster Diving: Reflections on Building Production in the Vernacular City.* London: Verso, 2004.

Cooper, Daniel Robert. *New Classic American Houses:*

The Architecture of Albert, Righter & Tittmann. New York: Vendome Press, 2009.

Crosbie, Michael J., and John R. DaSilva. *Architecture of the Cape Cod Summer: The Work of Polhemus Savery DaSilva.* Mulgrave (Australia): Images Publishing Group, 2008.

Cusato, Marianne, Ben Pentreath, Richard F. Sammons, and Léon Krier. *Get Your House Right: Architectural Elements to Use & Avoid.* New York: Sterling, 2011.

DaSilva, John R. *Shingled Houses in the Summer Sun: The Work of Polhemus Savery DaSilva.* Mulgrave (Australia): Images Publishing Group, 2011.

Dillon, David. "Big Mess on the Prairie." *Dallas Morning News,* October 2, 1994.

Dowling, Elizabeth Meredith. *New Classicism: The Rebirth of Traditional Architecture.* New York: Rizzoli, 2004.

Eck, Jeremiah. *The Face of Home: A New Way to Look at the Outside of Your House.* Newtown, CT: Taunton Press, 2006.

Ferguson, Mark, Oscar Shamamian, and Joseph Giovannini. *New Traditional Architecture: Ferguson & Shamamian Architects—City and Country Residences.* New York: Rizzoli, 2011.

Gabriel, J. François. *Classical Architecture for the Twenty-first Century: An Introduction to Design.* New York: W. W. Norton/Institute of Classical Architecture and Classical America, 2004.

Home Planners, Inc. *Encyclopedia of Home Designs: 450 House Plans* [pattern book]. Farmington Hills, MI: Home Planners, 1987.

———. *Luxury Dream Homes* [pattern book]. Farmington Hills, MI: Home Planners, 1989.

———. *Arts & Crafts Home Plans: Showcasing 85 Home Plans in the Craftsman, Prairie, and Bungalow Styles* [pattern book]. Tucson, AZ: Home Planners, 2004.

Hopkins, George D. *Creating Your Architectural Style: Designing and Building a Fine Home.* Gretna, LA: Pelican, 2009.

House Plans: Custom-Designed Homes for the South. Birmingham, AL: Oxmoor House, 1988.

Ike Kligerman Barkley (firm), Robert A. M. Stern, and Marc Kristal. *Ike Kligerman Barkley: Houses.* New York: Monacelli Press, 2010.

Jacobsen, Hugh Newell, Paul Goldberger, Massimo Vignelli, and Robert C. Lautman. *Hugh Newell Jacobsen, Architect: Works from 1993 to 2006.* New York: Rizzoli International, 2007.

Kemp, Jim. *American Vernacular: Regional Influences in Architecture and Interior Design.* Washington, DC: American Institute of Architects Press, 1990.

Lang, Andy. *101 Select Dream Houses* [pattern book]. Maplewood, NJ: Hammond, 1972.

Larson, Jean Rehkamp, and Ken Gutmaker. *The Farmhouse: New Inspiration for the Classic American Home.* Newtown, CT: Taunton Press, 2006.

Looney Ricks Kiss Architects. *Traditional Neighborhood Home Plans: 170 Designs for Living in Villages & Towns* [pattern book]. Tucson, AZ: Home Planners, 2000.

McNamara, Sarah. "The Rise and Fall of the Mansard Roof." *The Old House Journal* 12, no. 7 (August–September 1984): 152–54.

Miers, Mary. *American Houses: The Architecture of Fairfax & Sammons.* New York: Rizzoli, 2006.

Morgan, William. *Yankee Modern: The Houses of Estes/Twombly.* New York: Princeton Architectural Press, 2010.

Mouzon, Stephen A., and Susan M. Henderson. *Traditional Construction Patterns.* New York: McGraw-Hill, 2004.

Mulvin, Paulette. *Western Home Plans: Over 200 Home Plans Specially Designed for California, Pacific Northwest, Rocky Mountains, Texas & Western Plains, Desert Southwest, Western Lovers Everywhere* [pattern book]. Tucson, AZ: Home Planners, 1992.

Prideaux, Jan. *European Dream Homes: 200 French, English and Mediterranean Designs* [pattern book]. Tucson, AZ: Home Planners, 2002.

Royal Barry Wills Associates. *More Houses for Good Living.* 1968. Reprint, New York: Architectural Book Publishing, 1976.

———. *Houses for Good Living.* 1946. Reprint, New York: Architectural Book Publishing, 1993.

Sagharchi, Alireza, and Lucien Steil. *New Palladians: Modernity and Sustainability for 21st-Century Architecture.* London: Artmedia, 2010.

Sater, Dan F. *European Luxury Homes* [pattern book]. Bonita Springs, FL: Sater Design Collection, 2003.

———. *Mediterranean Home Plans* [pattern book]. Bonita Springs, FL: Sater Design Collection, 2005.

———. *European Classics* [pattern book]. Bonita Springs, FL: Sater Design Collection, 2007.

Skurman, Andrew. *Contemporary Classicism: The Architecture of Andrew Skurman.* New York: Princeton Architectural Press, 2012.

Stern, Robert A. M. *New Directions in American Architecture.* Rev. ed. New York: G. Braziller, 1982.

Stern, Robert A. M., and Clive Aslet. *The American Houses of Robert A. M. Stern.* New York: Rizzoli, 1991.

Stern, Robert A. M., and Elizabeth Kraft. *Buildings and Projects, 1987–1992.* New York: Rizzoli, 1992.

Stern, Robert A. M., and Raymond Gastil. *Modern Classicism.* New York: Rizzoli, 1988.

Stern, Robert A. M., Peter Arnell, and Ted Bickford. *Robert A. M. Stern 1965–1980: Toward a Modern Architecture After Modernism.* New York: Rizzoli, 1987.

Toplin, Jim. *The New Cottage Home.* Newtown, CT: Taunton Press, 2000.

Treib, Marc, and David Gebhard. *An Everyday Modernism: The Houses of William Wurster.* San Francisco: San Francisco Museum of Modern Art, 1999.

Urban Design Associates, Louisiana Recovery Authority, and LRA Support Foundation. *Louisiana Speaks: Pattern Book.* [Baton Rouge, LA]: LRA Support Foundation, 2006. http://www.urbandesignassociates.com/services_pattern books_pg1.html

Versaci, Russell, and Erik Kvalsvik. *Creating a New Old House: Yesterday's Character for Today's Home.* Newtown, CT: Taunton Press, 2007.

Vetter, Cyril E., and Philip Gould. *The Louisiana Houses of A. Hays Town.* Baton Rouge: Louisiana State University Press, 1999.

Walker, Anne. *Peter Pennoyer Architects: Apartments, Townhouses, Country Houses.* New York: Vendome Press, 2010.

Watkin, David. *Radical Classicism: The Architecture of Quinlan Terry.* New York: Rizzoli, 2006.

APPROACHES TO BUILDING IN THE TWENTIETH CENTURY

Bergdoll, Barry, Peter Christensen, and Ron Broadhurst. *Home Delivery: Fabricating the Modern Dwelling.* New York: Museum of Modern Art, 2008.

Bletter, Rosemarie Haag. *Remembering the Future: The New York World's Fair from 1939 to 1964.* New York: Rizzoli, 1989.

Carroon, Jean. *Sustainable Preservation: Greening Existing Buildings.* Hoboken, NJ: Wiley, 2010.

Cowan, Ruth S. *A Social History of American Technology.* New York: Oxford University Press, 1997.

Gianino, Andrew. *The Modular Home.* North Adams, MA: Storey, 2005.

Graff, Raymond K., Rudolf A. Matern, and Henry Lionel Williams. *The Prefabricated House: A Practical Guide for the Prospective Buyer.* Garden City, NY: Doubleday, 1947.

Herbert, Gilbert. *The Dream of the Factory-Made House: Walter Gropius and Konrad Wachsmann.* Cambridge, MA: MIT Press, 1986.

Jester, Thomas C. *Twentieth-Century Building Materials: History and Conservation.* [New York]: McGraw-Hill, 1995.

Johnston, David, and Scott Gibson. *Green from the Ground Up: Sustainable, Healthy, and Energy-Efficient Home Construction.* Newtown, CT: Taunton Press, 2008.

Kaufmann, Michelle, and Catherine Remick. *Prefab Green.* Layton, UT: Gibbs Smith, 2009.

Koones, Sheri. *Prefabulous and Sustainable: Building and Customizing an Affordable, Energy-Efficient Home.* New York: Abrams, 2010.

Mouzon, Stephen A., and Robert Francis Kennedy. *The Original Green: Unlocking the Mystery of True Sustainability.* Miami: Guild Foundation Press, 2010.

Rydell, Robert W., Laura B. Schiavo, Robert Bennett, and Matthew Bokovoy. *Designing Tomorrow: America's World's Fairs of the 1930s.* Yale University Press, 2010.

Schrenk, Lisa Diane. *Building a Century of Progress: The Architecture of Chicago's 1933–34 World's Fair.* Minneapolis: University of Minnesota Press, 2007.

REGIONAL AND LOCAL GUIDES: NORTHEASTERN STATES

American Institute of Architects, Long Island Chapter, and Society for the Preservation of Long Island Antiquities. *AIA Architectural Guide to Nassau and Suffolk Counties, Long Island.* New York: Dover Publications, 1992.

Andrews, Wayne. *Architecture in New England: A Photographic History.* New York: Harper & Row, 1980.

Bassett, William B. *Historic American Buildings Survey of New Jersey.* Newark: New Jersey Historical Society, 1977.

Bronxville Centennial Celebration. *Building a Suburban Village: Bronxville, New York, 1898–1998.* Bronxville, NY: Bronxville Centennial Celebration, Inc., 1998.

Brown, Elizabeth Mills. *New Haven: A Guide to Architecture and Urban Design.* New Haven, CT: Yale University Press, 1976.

Buffalo Architectural Guidebook Corporation. *Buffalo Architecture: A Guide.* Cambridge, MA: MIT Press, 1981.

Bunting, Bainbridge. *Houses of Boston's Back Bay: An Architectural History, 1840–1917.* Cambridge, MA: Harvard University Press, 1967.

Burke, Bobbye, and Trina Vaux. *Historic Rittenhouse: A Philadelphia Neighborhood.* Philadelphia: University of Pennsylvania Press, 1985.

Cambridge Historical Commission. *Survey of Architectural History in Cambridge, Reports 1–5.* 5 vols. Cambridge, MA, 1965–1977.

Candee, Richard M. *Atlantic Heights: A World War I Shipbuilders' Community.* Portsmouth, NH: published for the Society by P. E. Randall, 1985.

Conry, Jaci. *A History Through Houses Cape Cod's Varied Residential Architecture.* Charleston, SC: History Press, 2010.

Dennis, Stephen Neal, and William J. Penberthy. *Historic Houses of the Sewickley Valley.* Sewickley, PA: White Oak Pub, 1996.

Diamonstein, Barbaralee. *The Landmarks of New York.* New York: Monacelli Press, 2005.

Dorsey, John, and James D. Dilts. *A Guide to Baltimore Architecture,* 3rd ed. Centreville, MD: Tidewater Publishers, 1997.

Downing, Antoinette F., and Vincent J. Scully Jr. *The*

Architectural Heritage of Newport, Rhode Island, 1640–1915. Rev. ed., New York: American Legacy Press, 1982.

Eberlein, Harold Donaldson, and Cortlandt Van Dyke Hubbard. *Historic Houses of the Hudson Valley*. 1942. Reprint, New York: Dover Publications, 1990.

———. *Historic Houses and Buildings of Delaware*. Dover, DE: Public Archives Department, 1962.

Fishman, David, Thomas Mellins, and Robert A. M. Stern. *New York: Architecture and Urbanism*. 5 vols. New York: Monacelli Press, 1983–2009.

Foerster, Bernd. *Architecture Worth Saving in Rensselaer County, New York*. Troy, NY: Rensselaer Polytechnic Institute, 1965.

Forman, H. Chandlee. *Maryland Architecture: A Short History from 1634 through the Civil War*. Cambridge, MD: Tidewater Publishers, 1968.

Fox, Pamela W. *North Shore Boston: Houses of Essex County, 1865–1930*. New York: Acanthus Press, 2005.

Gallery, John Andrew. *Philadelphia Architecture: A Guide to the City*. 3rd ed. Philadelphia: Paul Dry Books, 2009.

Garrison, James B., John Andrew Gallery, and William Morrison. *Houses of Philadelphia: Chestnut Hill and the Wissahickon Valley, 1880–1930*. New York: Acanthus Press, 2008.

Garvin, James L. *A Building History of Northern New England*. Hanover, NH: University Press of New England, 2001.

Goldberger, Paul. *The City Observed: New York—A Guide to the Architecture of Manhattan*. New York: Vintage Books, 1989.

Goldstone, Harmon H., and Martha Dalrymple. *History Preserved: A Guide to New York City Landmarks and Historic Districts*. New York: Schocken Books, 1974/1976.

Gowans, Alan. *Architecture in New Jersey*. The New Jersey Historical Series, vol. 6. Princeton, NJ: D. Van Nostrand, 1964.

Greiff, Constance M., Mary W. Gibbons, and Elizabeth G. C. Menzies. *Princeton Architecture*. Princeton, NJ: Princeton University Press, 1975.

Guter, Robert P., Janet W. Foster, and Jim DelGiudice. *Building by the Book: Pattern Book Architecture in New Jersey*. New Brunswick, NJ: Rutgers University Press, 1992.

Hardin, Evamaria, and Jon Crispin. *Syracuse Landmarks: An AIA Guide to Downtown and Historic Neighborhoods*. New York: Onondaga Historical Association, 1993.

Hartford Architecture Conservancy Survey. *Hartford Architecture*, vols. 1–3. Hartford, CT, 1978–1980.

Hayward, Mary Ellen, and Charles Belfoure. *The Baltimore Rowhouse*. New York: Princeton Architectural Press, 2001.

Historic American Buildings Survey. *Historic Buildings of Massachusetts*. New York: Charles Scribner's Sons, 1976.

Hitchcock, Henry-Russell. *Rhode Island Architecture*. 1939. Reprint, Cambridge, MA: MIT Press, 1968.

Howland, Richard Hubbard, and Eleanor Patterson Spencer. *The Architecture of Baltimore*. 1953. Reprint, Baltimore: Johns Hopkins Press, 1970.

Hubka, Thomas C. *Big House, Little House, Back House, Barn: The Connected Farm Buildings of New England*. Rev. ed. Hanover, NH: University Press of New England, 2004.

Huxtable, Ada Louise. *The Architecture of New York: A History and Guide*. 3 vols. Garden City, NY: Doubleday, 1964.

Jackson, Richard S., and Cornelia Brooke Gilder. *Houses of the Berkshires, 1870–1930*. Rev. ed. New York: Acanthus Press, 2011.

Jacobs, Stephen W. *Wayne County* [New York]: *The Aesthetic Heritage of a Rural Area*. New York: Publishing Center for Cultural Resources, 1979.

Junior League of Kingston. *Early Architecture in Ulster County* [New York]. Kingston, NY, 1974.

Kathrens, Michael C. *Great Houses of New York, 1880–1930*. New York: Acanthus Press, 2005.

Lancaster, Clay. *The Architecture of Historic Nantucket*. New York: McGraw-Hill, 1972.

———. *Old Brooklyn Heights: New York's First Suburb*. 2nd ed. New York: Dover, 1979.

Lancaster, Clay, Robert A. M. Stern, and Robert J. Hefner. *East Hampton's Heritage: An Illustrated Architectural Record*. New York: W. W. Norton, 1982.

Landscape Research (firm) and Somerville, MA. *Beyond the Neck: The Architecture and Development of Somerville, Massachusetts*. Rev. ed. Somerville: City of Somerville, 1990.

Lanier, Gabrielle M., and Bernard L. Herman. *Everyday Architecture of the Mid-Atlantic: Looking at Buildings and Landscapes*. Baltimore: Johns Hopkins University Press, 1997.

Larew, Marilynn M. *Bel Air* [Maryland]: *The Town Through Its Buildings*. Annapolis: Maryland Historical Trust, 1995.

Lawrance, Gary, and Anne Surchin. *Houses of the Hamptons, 1880–1930*. New York: Acanthus Press, 2009.

Lockwood, Charles. *Bricks & Brownstone: The New York Row House, 1783–1929*. 2nd ed. New York: Rizzoli, 2003.

Longstreth, Richard W. *Housing Washington: Two Centuries of Residential Development and Planning in the National Capitol* [sic] *Area*. Chicago: Center for American Places at Columbia College Chicago, 2010.

Malo, Paul. *Landmarks of Rochester and Monroe County*. Syracuse, NY: Syracuse University Press, 1974.

Maryland Historical Trust. *Inventory of Historic Sites in Calvert County, Charles County, and St. Mary's County.* Rev. ed. Annapolis, MD, 1980.

Mateyunas, Paul J. *North Shore Long Island: Country Houses, 1890–1950.* New York: Acanthus Press, 2007.

McGowan, Robert Harold. *Architecture from the Adirondack Foothills: Folk and Designed Architecture from Franklin County, New York.* Malone, NY: Franklin County Historical and Museum Society, 1977.

Morrison, William, and Michael C. Kathrens. *The Main Line: Country Houses of Philadelphia's Storied Suburb, 1870–1930.* New York: Acanthus Press, 2006.

Myers, Denys Peter. "The Historic Architecture of Maine." *Maine Catalog, Historic American Buildings Survey,* pp. 1–198. Augusta, ME: Maine State Museum, 1974.

New York State Office of Planning Coordination. *Long Island Landmarks.* Albany, NY, 1969.

Onorato, Ronald J., Warren Jagger, and Richard Guy Wilson. *AIA Guide to Newport.* Providence, RI: AIA RI Architectual Forum, 2007.

Pancoast, Patricia McGraw, and Josephine H. Detmer. *Portland.* Portland, ME: Greater Portland Landmarks, 1972.

Pratt, Richard. *A Guide to the Architecture of Hightstown Houses.* Hightstown, NJ: Stockton Street Solutions, 2012.

Preservation Worcester, Elliott B. Knowlton, and Sandra Gibson-Quigley. *Worcester's Best: A Guide to the City's Architectural Heritage.* Rev. ed. Worcester, MA: Preservation Worcester, 1996.

Prokopoff, Stephen S., and Joan C. Siegfried. *The Nineteenth-Century Architecture of Saratoga Springs.* New York: State Council on the Arts, 1970.

Raymond, Eleanor. *Early Domestic Architecture of Pennsylvania.* 1931. Reprint, Exton, Pennsylvania: Schiffer, 2007.

Reiff, Daniel D. *Architecture in Fredonia, 1811–1972: From Log Cabin to I. M. Pei.* Fredonia, NY: White Pine Press, 1997.

Rettig, Robert Bell. *Guide to Cambridge Architecture: Ten Walking Tours.* Cambridge, MA: MIT Press, 1986.

Rifkind, Carole, and Carol Levine. *Mansions, Mills, and Main Streets: Buildings and Places to Explore Within Fifty Miles of New York City.* New York: Schocken Books, 1975.

Sanchis, Frank F. *American Architecture: Westchester County, New York.* Croton-on-Hudson, NY: North River Press, 1977.

Schiffer, Margaret Berwind. *Survey of Chester County, Pennsylvania, Architecture: 17th, 18th, and 19th Centuries.* Exton, PA: Schiffer, 1997.

Schull, Diantha Dow. *Landmarks of Otsego County* [New York]. Syracuse, NY: Syracuse University Press, 1980.

Schwartz, Helen, and Margaret Morgan Fisher. *The New Jersey House.* New Brunswick, NJ: Rutgers University Press, 1990.

Shand-Tucci, Douglass. *Built in Boston: City and Suburb, 1800-2000.* Rev ed. Amherst: University of Massachusetts, 1999.

Southworth, Susan, and Michael Southworth. *AIA Guide to Boston.* 3rd ed. Guilford, CT: Globe Pequot, 2008.

Stotz, Charles Morse. *The Early Architecture of Western Pennsylvania: A Record of Building Before 1860.* 1936. Reprint, Pittsburgh: University of Pittsburgh Press, 1995.

Tatum, George Bishop. *Penn's Great Towns: 250 Years of Philadelphia Architecture Illustrated in Prints and Drawings.* Philadelphia: University of Pennsylvania Press, 1961.

Teitelman, Edward, and Richard W. Longstreth. *Architecture in Philadelphia: A Guide.* Cambridge, MA: MIT Press, 1981.

Thompson, Deborah, ed. *Maine Forms of American Architecture.* Camden, ME: Downeast Magazine, 1976.

Tolles, Bryant F. Jr., and Carolyn K. Tolles. *New Hampshire Architecture: An Illustrated Guide.* Hanover, NH: University Press of New England, 1979.

———. *Architecture in Salem: An Illustrated Guide.* Salem, MA: Essex Institute/Historic Salem, 2004.

University of Vermont Historic Preservation Program. *The Burlington Book: Architecture, History, Future.* Burlington, VT, 1980.

Van Trump, James D., and Arthur P. Ziegler Jr. *Landmark Architecture of Allegheny County, Pennsylvania.* Pittsburgh: Pittsburgh History and Landmarks Foundation, 1967.

Warner, Sam Bass. *The Private City Philadelphia in Three Periods of Its Growth.* 2nd ed. Philadelphia: University of Pennsylvania Press, 1996.

Webster, Richard J. *Philadelphia Preserved: Catalog of the Historic American Buildings Survey.* 2nd ed. Philadelphia: Temple University Press, 1981.

Weeks, Christopher. *The Building of Westminster in Maryland.* 2nd ed. Annapolis, MD: Fishergate Publishing Company, 1979.

Weeks, Christopher, and Alan Karchmer. *AIA Guide to the Architecture of Washington, D.C.* 3rd ed. Baltimore: Johns Hopkins University Press, 1994.

White, Norval, Elliot Willensky, and Fran Leadon. *AIA Guide to New York City.* 5th ed. Oxford: Oxford University Press, 2010.

Woodward, William McKenzie. *PPS/AIA RI Guide to Providence Architecture.* Providence, RI: Providence Preservation Society, 2003.

Yarnall, James L. *Newport Through Its Architecture: A*

History of Styles from Postmedieval to Postmodern. Newport, RI: Salve Regina University Press in association with University Press of New England, 2005.

REGIONAL AND LOCAL GUIDES: SOUTHERN STATES

American Institute of Architects, New Orleans Chapter. *A Guide to New Orleans Architecture.* New Orleans, 1974.

American Institute of Architects, Winston-Salem Section. *Architectural Guide, Winston-Salem, Forsyth County.* Winston-Salem, NC, 1978.

Andrews, Wayne. *Pride of the South: A Social History of Southern Architecture.* New York: Atheneum, 1979.

Behar, Roberto M., and Maurice Culot. *Coral Gables: An American Garden City.* Paris (France): Norma Editions, 1997.

Biloxi, City of. *The Buildings of Biloxi: An Architectural Survey.* Biloxi, MS, 2000.

Butchko, Tom. *An Inventory of Historic Architecture, Sampson County, North Carolina.* Clinton, NC: City of Clinton, 1981.

Caemmerer, Alex. *Houses of Key West.* Sarasota, FL: Pineapple Press, 2009.

Center for Planning Excellence. "Louisiana Speaks Deliverables." [n.d.] Retrieved from http://cpex .org/downloads/louisiana-speaks-deliverables

Chambers, S. Allen Jr. *Lynchburg* [Virginia]: *An Architectural History.* Charlottesville, VA: University Press of Virginia, 1981.

Cox, Ethelyn. *Historic Alexandria, Virginia, Street by Street: A Survey of Existing Early Buildings.* Alexandria: Historic Alexandria Foundation, 1976.

Cox, Warren Jr., and others. *A Guide to the Architecture of Washington, D.C.* 2nd ed. New York: McGraw-Hill, 1974.

Crocker, Mary Wallace. *Historic Architecture in Mississippi.* Jackson: University Press of Mississippi, 1988.

Dulaney, Paul S. *The Architecture of Historic Richmond* [Virginia]. 2nd ed. Charlottesville, VA: University Press of Virginia, 1976.

Eufaula Heritage Association. *Historic Eufaula: A Treasury of Southern Architecture, 1827–1910.* Eufaula, AL, 1972.

Gleason, David King. *Virginia Plantation Homes.* Baton Rouge, LA: Louisiana State University Press, 1989.

Gould, Elizabeth Barrett. *From Fort to Port: An Architectural History of Mobile, Alabama, 1711–1918.* Tuscaloosa, AL: University of Alabama Press, 1988.

Gournay, Isabelle, Paul G. Beswick, Dana F. White, and Gerald W. Sams. *AIA Guide to the Architecture of Atlanta.* Athens, GA: University of Georgia, 1993.

Gross, Steve, Sue Daley, John H. Lawrence, and James Conaway. *Creole Houses: Traditional Homes of Old Louisiana.* New York: Abrams, 2007.

Harris, Linda L. *An Architectural and Historical Inventory of Raleigh, North Carolina.* Raleigh: City of Raleigh, 1978.

Iseley, N. Jane. *Beaufort.* Beaufort, SC: Historic Foundation, 2003.

Iseley, N. Jane, William P. Baldwin, and Agnes LeLand Baldwin. *Plantations of the Low Country: South Carolina, 1697–1865.* Rev. ed. Greensboro, NC: Legacy Publications, 1987.

Jeane, D. Gregory, and Douglas Clare Purcell. *The Architectural Legacy of the Lower Chattahoochee Valley in Alabama and Georgia.* University, AL: University of Alabama Press, 1978.

Lancaster, Clay. *Eutaw: The Builders and Architecture of an Ante-Bellum Southern Town.* Eutaw, AL: Greene County Historical Society, 1979.

Lane, Mills, and Van Jones Martin. *Architecture of the Old South: Mississippi & Alabama.* New York: Abbeville Press, 1997.

Lane, Mills, Van Jones Martin, and Gene Carpenter. *Architecture of the Old South: Georgia.* Rev. ed. Savannah, GA: Beehive Press, 1996.

Lane, Mills, Van Jones Martin, Calder Loth, and Gene Carpenter. *Architecture of the Old South: Virginia.* Savannah, GA: Beehive Press, 1996.

Lane, Mills, Van Jones Martin, Gene Waddell, and Gene Carpenter. *Architecture of the Old South: South Carolina.* Savannah, GA: Beehive Press, 1996.

Linley, John. *Architecture of Middle Georgia: The Oconee Area.* Athens, GA: University of Georgia Press, 1972.

———. *The Georgia Catalog, Historic American Buildings Survey: A Guide to the Architecture of the State.* Athens, GA: University of Georgia Press, 1982.

Little-Stokes, Ruth, and Tony P. Wrenn. *An Inventory of Historic Architecture, Caswell County, North Carolina.* Yanceyville, NC: Caswell County Historic Association, 1979.

Loth, Calder. *Virginia Landmarks Register.* 4th ed. Richmond: Univerity of Virginia Press, 1999.

Lyle, Royster Jr., and Pamela Hemenway Simpson. *The Architecture of Historic Lexington* [Virginia]. Charlottesville, VA: University Press of Virginia, 1977.

Maddex, Diane. *Historic Buildings of Washington, D.C.* Pittsburgh: Ober Park Associates, 1973.

Millas, Aristides J., and Ellen J. Uguccioni. *Coral Gables, Miami Riviera: An Architectural Guide.* Miami: Dade Heritage Trust, 2004.

Mitchell, William R., and Van Jones Martin. *Classic Atlanta Landmarks of the Atlanta Spirit.* New Orleans: Martin–St Martin Publishing, 1991.

Mobile, City of. *Nineteenth-Century Mobile Architecture.* Mobile, AL, 1974.

Morrison, Mary L., ed. *Historic Savannah*. 2nd ed. Savannah, GA: Historic Savannah Foundation, 1979.

Nichols, Frederick Doveton, and Frances Benjamin Johnston. *The Early Architecture of Georgia*. Chapel Hill, NC: University of North Carolina Press, 1957.

———. *The Architecture of Georgia*. Savannah, GA: Beehive Press, 1976.

Ossman, Laurie, and Steven Brooke. *Great Houses of the South*. New York: Rizzoli, 2010.

Overdyke, W. Darrell. *Louisiana Plantation Homes*. New York: Architectural Book Publishing, 1965.

Patrick, James. *Architecture in Tennessee, 1768–1897*. Knoxville, TN: University of Tennessee Press, 1990.

Poston, Jonathan H. *The Buildings of Charleston: A Guide to the City's Architecture*. Columbia, SC: University of South Carolina Press, 1997.

Reeves, F. Blair. *A Guide to Florida's Historic Architecture*. Gainesville, FL: University of Florida Press, 1990.

Schezen, Roberto, and Shirley Johnston. *Palm Beach Houses*. New York: Rizzoli International, 1991.

Schuler, Stanley. *Mississippi Valley Architecture: Houses of the Lower Mississippi Valley*. Exton, PA: Schiffer Pub, 1984.

Schwartz, Nancy B. *District of Columbia Catalog, 1974, Historic American Buildings Survey*. Charlottesville, VA: University Press of Virginia, 1976.

Severens, Kenneth. *Southern Architecture: 350 Years of Distinctive American Buildings*. New York: E. P. Dutton, 1981.

Shulman, Allan T., Randall C. Robinson, and James F. Donnelly. *Miami Architecture: An AIA Guide Featuring Downtown, the Beaches, and Coconut Grove*. Gainesville, FL: University Press of Florida, 2010.

Simons, Albert, and Samuel Lapham Jr. *The Early Architecture of Charleston* [SC]. 1927. Reprint, Columbia, SC: University of South Carolina Press, 1990.

Starr, S. Frederick. *Southern Comfort: The Garden District of New Orleans*. Rev. ed. New York: Princeton Architectural Press, 2005.

Stoney, Samuel Gaillard. *This Is Charleston: A Survey of the Architectural Heritage of a Unique American City*, Rev. ed. Charleston, SC: Carolina Art Association, 1990.

Toledano, Roulhac. *A Pattern Book of New Orleans Architecture*. Gretna, LA: Pelican, 2010.

Urban Design Associates. *A Pattern Book for Gulf Coast Neighborhoods: Mississippi Renewal Forum*. Pittsburgh, PA: Urban Design Associates, 2005. http://www.mississippirenewal.com/documents/Rep_PatternBook.pdf

Virginia Historic Landmarks Commission. *Virginia Catalog: Historic American Buildings Survey*. Charlottesville, VA: University Press of Virginia, 1976.

Vogt, Lloyd. *New Orleans Houses: A House-Watcher's Guide*. Gretna, LA: Pelican, 1989.

Whitwell, W. L., and Lee W. Winborne. *The Architectural Heritage of the Roanoke Valley*. Charlottesville, VA: University Press of Virginia, 1982.

REGIONAL AND LOCAL GUIDES: MIDWESTERN STATES

American Institute of Architects, Kansas City Chapter. *AIA Guide to Kansas City*. Kansas City, MO: AIA/Highwater Editions, 2000.

Andrews, Wayne. *Architecture in Chicago and Mid-America*. New York: Harper and Row, 1973.

Bach, Ira J. *A Guide to Chicago's Historic Suburbs on Wheels and on Foot*. Chicago: Swallow Press, 1981.

Benjamin, Susan S., and Stuart Earl Cohen. *Great Houses of Chicago, 1871–1921*. New York: Acanthus, 2012.

Bigott, Joseph C. *From Cottage to Bungalow: Houses and the Working Class in Metropolitan Chicago, 1869–1929*. Chicago: University of Chicago Press, 2001.

Block, Jean F. *Hyde Park Houses, An Informal History, 1856–1910*. Chicago: University of Chicago Press, 1978.

Bryan, John Albury. *Missouri's Contribution to American Architecture*. St. Louis: St. Louis Architectural Club, 1928.

Campen, Richard N. *Ohio: An Architectural Portrait*. Chagrin Falls, OH: West Summit Press, 1973.

Cohen, Stuart Earl, and Susan S. Benjamin. *North Shore Chicago: Houses of the Lakefront Suburbs, 1890–1940*. New York: Acanthus Press, 2006.

Darbee, Jeffrey T., and Nancy A. Recchie. *The AIA Guide to Columbus*. Athens, OH: Ohio University Press, 2008.

Ehrlich, George. *Kansas City, Missouri: An Architectural History, 1826–1990*. Rev. ed. Columbia: University of Missouri Press, 1992.

Ferry, W. Hawkins. *The Buildings of Detroit*, Rev. ed. Detroit: Wayne State University Press, 2012.

Gebhard, David, and Gerald Mansheim. *Buildings of Iowa*. New York: Oxford University Press, 1993.

Gebhard, David, and Tom Martinson. *A Guide to the Architecture of Minnesota*. Minneapolis: University of Minnesota Press, 1977.

Hill, Eric J., and John Gallagher. *AIA Detroit: The American Institute of Architects Guide to Detroit Architecture*. Detroit: Wayne State University Press, 2003.

Hunter, Julius K., Robert C. Pettus, and Leonard Lujan. *Westmoreland and Portland Places: The History and Architecture of America's Premier Private Streets, 1888–1988*. Columbia, MO: University of Missouri Press, 1988.

Indiana Architectural Foundation. *Indianapolis Architecture.* Indianapolis, 1975.

Johannesen, Eric. *Cleveland Architecture, 1876–1976.* Rev. ed. Cleveland: Western Reserve Historical Society, 1981.

Johnson, Carl H. Jr. *The Building of Galena: An Architectural Legacy.* 3rd ed. Galena, IL: publ. by author, 1997.

Jones, Elizabeth F., and Mary Jean Kinsman. *Jefferson County: Survey of Historic Sites in Kentucky.* Louisville: Jefferson County Office of Historic Preservation and Archives, 1981.

Junior League of Evansville. *Reflections Upon a Century of Architecture: Evansville, Indiana.* Evansville, IN, 1977.

Kansas City, Missouri Landmarks Commission. *Kansas City: A Place in Time.* Kansas City, MO, 1977.

Kennedy, Roger. *Minnesota Houses.* Minneapolis: Dillon Press, 1967.

Kentucky Heritage Commission. *Ballard County: Survey of Historic Sites in Kentucky.* Frankfort, KY, 1978.

———. *Jessamine County: Survey of Historic Sites in Kentucky.* Frankfort, KY, 1979.

Kidney, Walter C. *Historic Buildings of Ohio: A Selection From the Records of the Historic American Buildings Survey.* Pittsburgh: Ober Park Associates, 1972.

Koeper, Frederick. *Illinois Architecture from Territorial Times to the Present: A Selective Guide .* Chicago: University of Chicago Press, 1975.

Lancaster, Clay. *Vestiges of the Venerable City: A Chronicle of Lexington, Kentucky.* Lexington: Lexington–Fayette County Historic Commission, 1978.

Magness, Perre. *Good Abode: Nineteenth-Century Architecture in Memphis and Shelby County, Tennessee.* Memphis, TN: Junior League of Memphis, 1983.

Mason City, City of. *Mason City, Iowa: An Architectural Heritage.* Mason City, IA, 1977.

McArthur, Shirley du Fresne. *North Point Historic Districts—Milwaukee.* Milwaukee: North Point Historical Society, 1981.

McCue, George. *The Building Art in St. Louis: Two Centuries.* 3rd ed. St. Louis, MO: Knight Publishing Co., 1981.

Meyer, Katharine Mattingly, ed. *Detroit Architecture: AIA Guide.* Rev. ed. Detroit: Wayne State University Press, 1980.

Millett, Larry. *AIA Guide to the Twin Cities: The Essential Source on the Architecture of Minneapolis and St. Paul.* St. Paul: Minnesota Historical Society Press, 2007.

———. *AIA Guide to the Minneapolis Lake District.* St. Paul, MN: Minnesota Historical Society Press, 2009.

———. *AIA Guide to St. Paul's Summit Avenue and Hill District.* St. Paul, MN: Minnesota Historical Society Press, 2009.

Millstein, Cydney, and Carol Grove. *Houses of Missouri, 1870–1940.* New York: Acanthus Press, 2008.

Newcomb, Rexford. *Architecture of the Old Northwest Territory.* Chicago: University of Chicago Press, 1950.

———. *Architecture in Old Kentucky.* Urbana, IL: University of Illinois Press, 1953.

Perrin, Richard W. E. *Historic Wisconsin Architecture.* Rev. ed. Milwaukee: Wisconsin Society of Architects, 1976.

———. *Historic Wisconsin Buildings: A Survey in Pioneer Architecture, 1835–1870,* 2nd ed. Milwaukee: Milwaukee Public Museum, 1981.

Sandeen, Ernest R. *St. Paul's Historic Summit Avenue.* 1978. Reprint, Minneapolis: University of Minnesota Press, 2004.

Schofield, Mary-Peale. *Landmark Architecture of Cleveland.* Pittsburgh: Ober Park Associates, 1976.

Scott, James Allen. *Duluth's Legacy,* vol. 1: *Architecture.* Duluth, MN: City of Duluth, 1974.

Shank, Wesley I. *Iowa Catalog: Historic American Buildings Survey.* Iowa City: University of Iowa Press, 1979.

Sinkevitch, Alice. *AIA Guide to Chicago.* 2nd ed. Orlando, FL: Harcourt, 2004.

Windle, John T., and Robert M. Taylor. *The Early Architecture of Madison, Indiana.* Madison, IN: Historic Madison, 1986.

REGIONAL AND LOCAL GUIDES: WESTERN STATES

Alexander, Drury Blakeley, and Todd Webb. *Texas Homes of the Nineteenth Century.* Austin: University of Texas Press, 1966.

American Institute of Architects, Dallas Chapter. *Dallasights: An Anthology of Architecture and Open Spaces.* Dallas, 1978.

American Institute of Architects, and Stephen Fox. *Houston Architectural Guide.* 3rd ed. Houston: American Institute of Architects, Houston Chapter, 2012.

Andree, Herb, and Noel Young. *Santa Barbara Architecture: From Spanish Colonial to Modern,* 3rd ed. Reprinted with corrections. Santa Monica: Hennessey & Ingalls, 2005.

Barnstone, Howard. *The Galveston* [TX] *That Was.* 1966. Reprint, College Station: Texas A&M Press, 1999.

Bernhardi, Robert. *The Buildings of Berkeley* [CA]. Berkeley: Lederer Street & Zeus, 1991.

Bracken, Dorothy Kendall, and Maurine Whorton Redway, *Early Texas Homes.* 1956. Reprint, Dallas: Southern Methodist University Press, 1982.

Brettell, Richard R., and Willis Winters. *Crafting*

Traditions: The Architecture of Mark Lemmon. Dallas: Meadows Museum, 2005.

Bruce, Curt, and Thomas Aidala. *The Great Houses of San Francisco.* New York: Knopf, 1974.

Burkholder, Mary V. *The King William Area* [San Antonio]: *A History and Guide to the Houses.* 2nd ed. San Antonio, TX: King William Association, 1977.

Butler, Phyllis Filiberti, and Junior League of San Jose. *The Valley of Santa Clara* [CA]: *Historic Buildings, 1792–1920.* 2nd ed. Novato, CA: Presidio Press, 1981.

Carter, Thomas, and Peter L. Goss. *Utah's Historic Architecture, 1847–1940: A Guide.* Salt Lake City: University of Utah Press, 1991.

Chase, John. *The Sidewalk Companion to Santa Cruz Architecture.* 3rd ed. Santa Cruz, CA: Museum of Art & History, 2005.

Clark, Anne. *Historic Houses of San Augustine* [TX]. Austin, TX: San Augustine Historical Society, 1972.

Cooper/Roberts Architects, AIA, and City of Phoenix (AZ). *Historic Homes of Phoenix: An Architectural & Preservation Guide.* City of Phoenix, 1992.

Culbertson, Margaret. *Texas Houses Built by the Book: The Use of Published Designs, 1850–1925.* College Station: Texas A&M University Press, 1999.

Dallas, Sandra. *Colorado Homes.* Norman, OK: University of Oklahoma Press, 1986.

Duchscherer, Paul, and Douglas Keister. *Victorian Glory in San Francisco and the Bay Area.* New York: Viking Studio, 2001.

Fairfax, Geoffrey W. *The Architecture of Honolulu.* Sydney (Australia): Island Heritage, 1972.

Fuller, Larry Paul, ed. *The American Institute of Architects Guide to Dallas Architecture, with Regional Highlights.* New York: McGraw Hill Construction Information Group, 1999.

Gebhard, David, and Robert Winter. *An Architectural Guidebook to Los Angeles.* Rev. ed. Salt Lake City: Gibbs Smith, 2003.

———. *A Guide to Architecture in Los Angeles and Southern California.* Santa Barbara, CA: Peregrine Smith, 1977.

Gebhard, David, et al. *A Guide to Architecture in San Francisco and Northern California.* Rev. ed. Salt Lake City: Peregrine Smith, 1985.

Gleye, Paul. *The Architecture of Los Angeles.* Los Angeles: Rosebud Books, 1981.

Goeldner, Paul. *Utah Catalog: Historic American Buildings Survey.* Salt Lake City: Utah Heritage Foundation, 1969.

———. *Texas Catalog: Historic American Buildings Survey.* San Antonio, TX: Trinity University Press, 1975.

Goins, Charles R., and John W. Morris. *Oklahoma Homes, Past and Present.* Norman, OK: University of Oklahoma Press, 1980.

Hart, Arthur A. *Historic Boise: An Introduction to the Architecture of Boise, Idaho, 1863–1938.* Auckland, NZ: Caxton Press, 1993.

Hawkins, William John, and William F. Willingham. *Classic Houses of Portland, Oregon, 1850–1950.* Portland, OR: Timber Press, 2005.

Henry, Jay C. *Architecture in Texas, 1895–1945.* Austin: University of Texas Press, 2010.

Historic Denver. "HD Guides and Publications." http://store.historicdenver.org/store/historic-denver-guides-series/

Kirker, Harold. *California's Architectural Frontier: Style and Tradition in the Nineteenth Century.* 3rd ed. Santa Barbara, CA: Peregrine Smith, 1986.

Lenggenhager, Werner, and Lucile McDonald. *Where the Washingtonians Lived.* Seattle, WA: Superior Publishing, 1969.

Masson, Kathryn, and Paul Rocheleau. *The California House: Adobe, Craftsman, Victorian, Spanish Colonial Revival.* New York: Rizzoli, 2011.

McDonald, William L. *Dallas Rediscovered: A Photographic Chronicle of Urban Expansion, 1870–1925.* Dallas: Dallas Historical Society, 1978.

McGrew, Patrick, and Robert Julian. *Landmarks of Los Angeles.* New York: Abrams, 1994.

Moore, Charles Willard, Peter Becker, and Regula Campbell. *The City Observed—Los Angeles: A Guide to Its Architecture and Landscapes.* Santa Monica, CA: Hennessey and Ingalls, 1998.

Neil, J. Meredith. *Saints and Oddfellows: A Bicentennial Sampler of Idaho Architecture.* Boise, ID: Boise Gallery of Art Association, 1976.

Noel, Thomas Jacob. *The Montclair Neighborhood.* Denver: Historic Denver, 1999.

Olmsted, Roger, and T. H. Watkins. *Here Today: San Francisco's Architectural Heritage.* San Francisco: Chronicle Books, 1995.

Paglia, Michael, Diane Wray Tomasso, and Kathleen Roach. *The Mid-Century Modern House in Denver.* Denver: Historic Denver, Inc, 2007.

Polyzoides, Stefanos, Roger Sherwood, and James Tice. *Courtyard Housing in Los Angeles: A Typological Analysis.* 2nd ed. New York: Princeton Architectural Press, 1992.

Regnery, Dorothy F. *An Enduring Heritage: Historic Buildings of the San Francisco Peninsula.* Stanford, CA: Stanford University Press, 1976.

Schwarzer, Mitchell. *San Francisco—Architecture of the San Francisco Bay Area: A History & Guide.* San Francisco: William Stout Publishers, 2007.

Shay, James, and Christopher Irion. *New Architecture San Francisco.* San Francisco: Chronicle Books, 1989.

Stoehr, C. Eric. *Bonanza Victorian: Architecture and Society in Colorado Mining Towns.* Albuquerque: University of New Mexico Press, 1975.

Swope, Caroline T. *Classic Houses of Seattle, High Style to Vernacular, 1870–1950.* Portland, OR: Timber Press, 2005.

University of Kansas Museum of Art. *Nineteenth Century Houses in Lawrence, Kansas.* Lawrence, KS: University of Kansas Museum of Art, 1968.

Vaughan, Thomas, and Virginia Guest Ferriday, eds. *Space, Style and Structure: Building in Northwest America.* 2 vols. Portland: Oregon Historical Society, 1974.

Watters, Sam. *Houses of Los Angeles.* New York: Acanthus Press, 2007.

Webb, Michael. *Brave New Houses: Adventures in Southern California Living.* New York: Rizzoli, 2003.

Welch, Frank D., Paul Hester, and Philip Johnson. *Philip Johnson & Texas.* Austin: University of Texas Press, 2000.

Wiberg, Ruth Eloise. *Rediscovering Northwest Denver.* 1976. Reprint, Niwot: University Press of Colorado, 1995.

Wilk, Diane. *A Guide to Denver's Architectural Styles and Terms.* Denver: Historic Denver/Denver Museum of Natural History, 1995.

Williamson, Roxanne Kuter. *Austin, Texas: An American Architectural History.* San Antonio, TX: Trinity University Press, 1973.

Woodbridge, Sally B., ed. *Bay Area Houses.* Salt Lake City: Peregrine Smith, 1988.

Woodbridge, Sally B., and Chuck Byrne. *San Francisco Architecture: An Illustrated Guide to the Outstanding Buildings, Public Artworks, and Parks in the Bay Area of California.* Rev. ed. Berkeley, CA: Ten Speed Press, 2005.

Woodbridge, Sally B., and Roger Montgomery. *A Guide to Architecture in Washington State.* Seattle: University of Washington Press, 1980.

Woods, Douglas, Melba Levick, and D. J. Waldie. *Classic Homes of Los Angeles.* New York: Rizzoli, 2010.

HOUSE PRESERVATION AND RESTORATION

Abramovitch, Ingrid. *Restoring a House in the City.* New York: Artisan, 2009.

Anderson Notter Associates. *The Salem Handbook: A Renovation Guide for Homeowners.* Salem, MA: Historic Salem, 1977.

Carroon, Jean. *Sustainable Preservation: Greening Existing Buildings.* Hoboken, NJ: John Wiley and Sons, 2010.

Ferro, Maximilian L. *How to Love and Care for Your Old Building in New Bedford.* New Bedford, MA: City of New Bedford, 1977.

Harris, Kip. *Confronting the Older House: A Homeowner's Guide.* Salt Lake City: Utah Heritage Foundation, 1979.

Hewitt, Mark Alan, and Gordon Bock. *The Vintage House: A Guide to Successful Renovations and Additions,* 2011.

Historic New England. "Surveying the Recent Past: The Challenge of Creating and Defining Context." http://www.historicnewengland.org/preservation/ regional-resources/looking-forward-symposium/ papers/surveying-the-recent-past-final.pdf

Howard, Cynthia. *Your House in the Streetcar Suburb.* Medford, MA: City of Medford, 1979.

Howard, J. Myrick. *Buying Time for Heritage: How to Save an Endangered Historic Property.* Raleigh, NC: Preservation North Carolina, 2007.

Hull, Brent. *Historic Millwork: A Guide to Restoring and Re-creating Doors, Windows and Moldings of the Late Nineteenth Through Mid-Twentieth Centuries.* New York: Wiley, 2003.

Hutchins, Nigel. *Restoring Old Houses.* Rev. ed. Toronto: Firefly Books, 1997.

Jackson, Albert, and David Day. *The Complete Home Restoration Manual: An Authoritative, Do-It-Yourself Guide to Restoring and Maintaining the Older House.* New York: Simon & Schuster, 1992.

Kitchen, Judith L. *Caring for Your Old House: A Guide for Owners and Residents.* Washington, DC: Preservation Press, 1995.

Labine, Clem, and Carolyn Flaherty, eds. *The Old-House Journal Compendium.* 1980. Reprint, Woodstock, NY: Overlook Press, 2007.

Leeke, John C. *Save America's Windows.* CreateSpace Independent Publishing Platform, 2009.

Legner, Linda. *City House: A Guide to Renovating Older Chicago-Area Houses.* Chicago: Commission on Chicago Historical and Architectural Landmarks, 1979.

Maddex, Diane, ed. *The Brown Book: A Directory of Preservation Information.* Washington, DC: Preservation Press, 1983.

Moss, Roger W. *Century of Color: Exterior Decoration for American Buildings, 1820–1920.* Watkins Glen, NY: American Life Foundation, 1981.

Murtagh, William J. *Keeping Time: The History and Theory of Preservation in America.* 3rd ed. Hoboken, NJ: John Wiley & Sons, 2006.

Nash, George. *Renovating Old Houses: Bringing New Life to Vintage Homes.* Newtown, CT: Taunton Press, 2003.

National Park Service–U.S. Department of the Interior. "Historic Preservation: Action Transforming our Thinking." http://www.nps.gov/history/ history/resedu/historic_preservation.pdf

———. "Technical Preservation Services: Preservation Briefs." http://www.nps.gov/tps/how-to-preserve/briefs.htm

New York Landmarks Conservancy. *Repairing Old and Historic Windows.* Washington, DC: Preservation Press, National Trust for Historic Preservation, 1992.

Phillips, Morgan W. *The Eight Most Common Mistakes in Restoring Houses (and How to Avoid Them).*

AASLH Technical Leaflet 118. *History News* 34, no. 8 (August 1979).

Poore, Patricia. *The Old-House Journal Guide to Restoration.* New York: Dutton, 1992.

Prentice, Helaine Kaplan. *Rehab Right: How to Realize the Full Value of Your Old House.* Berkeley: Ten Speed Press, 1986.

Rypkema, Donovan D. *The Economics of Historic Preservation: A Community Leader's Guide.* 2nd ed. Washington, DC: National Trust for Historic Preservation, 2008.

Seale, William. *Recreating the Historic House Interior.* Nashville, TN: American Association for State and Local History, 1979.

Shopsin, William C., and Grania Bolton Marcus, eds. *Saving Large Estates.* Setauket, NY: Society for the Preservation of Long Island Antiquities, 1977.

Shull, Carol D., and Beth L. Savage. "From the Glass House to Stonewall: National Register Recognition of the Recent Past." National Register of Historic Places Workshop. NCSHPO Annual Meeting, Washington, DC, March 25, 2001.

Stanforth, Deirdre, and Martha Stamm. *Buying and Renovating a House in the City.* Rev. ed. New York: Hippocrene Books, 1985.

Stephen, George. *Remodeling Old Houses Without Destroying Their Character.* New York: Knopf, 1972.

Stipe, Robert E. *A Richer Heritage: Historic Preservation in the Twenty-first Century.* Chapel Hill, NC: University of North Carolina Press, 2007.

Tyler, Norman, Ted J. Ligibel, and Ilene R. Tyler. *Historic Preservation: An Introduction to Its History, Principles, and Practice.* 2nd ed. New York: W.W. Norton, 2009.

U.S. Department of the Interior. *The Preservation of Historic Architecture: The U.S. Government's Official Guidelines for Preserving Historic Homes.* Guilford, CT: Lyons Press, 2004.

U.S. Department of the Interior, National Park Service, Preservation Assistance Division. *The Secretary of the Interior's Standards for Rehabilitation.* Rev. ed. Washington, DC, 1990.

U.S. National Park Service, Technical Preservation Services. *Respectful Rehabilitation: Answers to Your Questions About Old Buildings.* Washington, DC: Preservation Press, 1998.

Wagner, Richard. *Buyer's Guide to Older and Historic Houses.* Washington, DC: National Trust for Historic Preservation, 2000.

Young, Robert A. *Historic Preservation Technology.* Hoboken, NJ: J. Wiley & Sons, 2008.

WEB SITES

Architectural Record. archrecord.construction.com

Atlas Mobile Home Museum. Mobile Home / Trailer Coach Museum Archives. www.allmanufacturedhomes.com/html/vintage_mobile_homes.htm

Carnegie Mellon University. "Remaking Cities Institute." http://www.cmu.edu/rci/

Congress for the New Urbanism. http://www.cnu.org/

DOCOMOMO. www.docomomo-us.org

Institute of Classical Architecture & Classical America. http://www.classicist.org/

Marilyn and Ray Gindroz Foundation. http://www.marilynandraygindrozfoundation.org/

National Alliance of Preservation Commissions. napc.uga.edu/resources-links/preservation-links

National Park Service. "National Register of Historic Places Program: State Historic Preservation Officers (SHPO)." www.nps.gov/nr/shpolist.htm

National Trust for Historic Preservation. http://www.preservationnation.org/information-center/saving-a-place/modernism-recent-past/tools-resources/survey-designation/

Old House Journal. www.oldhousejournal.com

Period Homes. www.period-homes.com

Reconnecting America. http://www.reconnectingamerica.org/

Society of Architectural Historians. www.sah.org

Vernacular Architecture Forum. "Vernacular Architecture Newsletter Bibliography." http://resources.umwhisp.org/vafbib.htm

Acknowledgments

Many people have helped me in the preparation of this revision. Two were involved in almost every aspect—Steve Clicque, who took the vast majority of the new photographs, and Amanda Olson McCoy, who was my research assistant. Amanda did a wide range of things, chief among them preparing the preliminary layouts for the new materials and putting all of the corrections into a PDF of the original book. She also reviewed the materials I'd gathered for "Other 20th-Century Modern" and pulled the information together into a rough draft; some of her lively wording is found in the final text. Steve drove up and down streets of neighborhoods across the United States to gather photographs of visible examples; he cataloged and kept track of all the line art and photographs, doggedly pursuing some of the toughest final photo permissions. In addition, he restored many old photographs, kept the computers and programs running, providing virtually all IT-related tasks. I could not have completed the book without him.

Aleida Rodríguez, an experienced copy editor with a specialty in museum catalogs, helped edit all the text of the new changes, guiding me toward consistent style.

After the book was in production, both Jane Griffith Quinn and Julie Travis reviewed specific parts of the proofs, including the Notes, For Further Reference, and the numbering of photographs and captions. Sharon Dorsey, my office manager, kept everything else organized so that I could actually focus on writing the book.

Artist and architect Suzanne Patton Matty cheerfully and expertly prepared the line art for the new book chapters. She was recommended to me by William Seale and stuck with the project for over five years, even after she had returned to school full-time to earn a graduate degree. Dallas preservation architect Gary Scotnicki provided the additional drawings added to the Pictorial Key.

I particularly appreciate my longtime editor at Knopf, Jane Garrett, her belief that this revision was needed and her patience with the length of time it took to actually complete. When she retired from Knopf, Andy Hughes, who had overseen the production of the original edition in 1984, became my new editor. His expertise, friendship, and enthusiasm made the production of the revision a joy. Kevin Bourke was production editor of the new edition, and Kathleen Fridella and Maralee Youngs helped to round up some of the final pieces. Cassandra Pappas conceived and executed the beautiful, fresh design of the book's interior. North Market Street Graphics, the typesetter—

Dennis Bicksler, Tracy Pitz, Rhonda Stough, and Cindy Szili—contributed much to the quality of the book you see.

Because such a high percentage of mainstream modern homes are designed not to reveal themselves to the street, it was necessary to visit as many modern homes as possible. One of the best ways to do this is on organized tours. The Vernacular Architecture Forum hosts an annual conference that features numerous tours. Richard Longstreth organized a particularly helpful one of neighborhoods in the Washington, D.C., area that stressed the evolution of neighborhood planning during and after World War II and produced a well-researched companion book, *Housing Washington: Two Centuries of Residential Development and Planning in the National Captial Area.* The Frank Lloyd Wright Conservancy offers tours of Wright and Wright-influenced houses. I enjoyed attending their tours in Minneapolis–St. Paul, in Los Angeles, and in Palm Springs. The Palm Springs tour was led by Alan Hess, co-author of *Palm Springs Weekend: The Architecture and Design of a Midcentury Oasis* (and many other books on Mid-century Modern houses). The Society of Architectural Historians sponsored a tour of Paul Rudolph's work (as well as the work of other architects) in and around Sarasota, Florida, led by Joseph King, co-author of *Paul Rudolph: The Florida Houses.* Ken Turino organized an excellent conference with tours of mid-century modern houses for Historic New England. Dr. Mardges Bacon, Matthews Distinguished University Professor in the Department of Architecture at Northeastern University, gave the introductory speech. I was heavily influenced by her clear view of how the modern movement has evolved in America. Field trips to homes designed by Walter Gropius and Marcel Breuer near Boston and to iconic houses in New Canaan, Connecticut, made this tour invaluable— as did the talk by William D. Earls, author of *The Harvard Five in New Canaan.* And last but definitely not least, two tours of organic architecture offered by the Friends of Kebyar and led by its president, architect Nelson Brackin—one concentrating on Bruce Goff in Oklahoma and the other focusing on the work of Fay Jones in Arkansas—had a stunning cross-section of modern houses.

Good friends offered shelter and helped plan photo routes in their neighborhoods. Alice Ingraham and Tony Davies helped with Weston, Massachusetts, along with their friend Pamela W. Fox, author of *Farm Town to Suburb: The History and Architecture of Weston, Massachusetts, 1830–1980.* Nelson Brackin planned a day in Atlanta, Georgia, along with a two-day "Fox Trot," visiting the quite varied organic homes of James Fox in North and South Carolina. Dick and Kathy Kleinsasser Morris helped with Portland, Oregon, and James Sodeman shared his expertise on San Francisco, California. Anne and John Mullen invited me to spend several days in the New Traditional Shingle home that John had recently designed for the summers they spend in East Hampton, New York. The visit included the Museum of Modern Art's "Home Delivery: Fabricating the Modern Dwelling"; a tour of the original Levittown on Long Island; seeking out a new modern neighborhood being built in Sagaponack, New York; looking at Macy's 1950s pre-fab houses in Montauk; and visiting neighborhoods throughout the Hamptons.

And finally, great thanks to those who took the time to read large portions of the text and give me criticism and comments—New Orleans land-use attorney and preservationist William Borah, John Mullen FAIA, preservation architect Daron Tapscott, Willis Winters FAIA, and Ann Abernathy, architect in charge of the restoration of the Frank Lloyd Wright home and studio who, happily for me, ended up in Dallas. Marcel Quimby FAIA, Nancy McCoy FAIA, of Quimby McCoy Preservation Architecture, Larry Boerder, Kevin Sloan, Robert Meckfessel FAIA, Katherine Seale, and William Seale.

Many people have asked over the years about the roles that Lee and I respectively played in writing the 1984 edition of the book. It is unlikely that there would have been a 1984 *Field Guide* were it not for Lee McAlester. He had recently written two geology textbooks, *The Earth* and *The History of Life*, and firmly maintained that if he could research, write, and synthesize such massive topics certainly I could do the same for something as simple as houses—at least with his oversight and assistance. I needed this confidence to plunge forward with a book I very much wanted to write. I did the primary research, counted characteristics, wrote the initial drafts, gathered photographs, and prepared illustrations. He edited everything and pointed out the flaws in my research and logic (as I know he had done for the many Ph.D. students who studied under him at Yale). He also researched and wrote a few of the early chapters that particularly interested him. I do believe he soon discovered houses are not quite so simple.

The following were instrumental in obtaining photo permissions, digital prints, and pertinent information from their organizations and institutions:

Biltmore Hotel and Gardens, Asheville, North Carolina
Erica Walker
Bonneville House Association
Jeanette Falkner
Buffalo and Erie County Historical Society
Cynthia Van Ness
Catskill Center for Conservation
Lisa Rainwater
Cuyahoga County Archives
Judith G. Cetina
City of Dallas
Carol Roark
Dallas Historical Society
Jack Bunning
Susan Richards
Friends of the Cabildo
Kaitlin Ryan
Galveston Historical Foundation
Brian Davis
Dwayne Jones
The Gamble House
Bobbi Mapstone
Genesee Valley Council on the Arts
Kathryn Hollinger
Historic New England
Jeanne Gamble
Indiana Historical Society
Susan Sutton
Library of Congress, Historic American Building Survey

Louisiana State Museum
Tony Lewis, Curator of Visual Arts
Maryland Historical Society
Christopher Becker
Missouri History Museum
Ellen Thomasson
Museum of the City of New York
Robbi Siegel
National Anthropological Archives, Smithsonian Institution
Leanda Gahegan
Daisy Njoku
National Association of Historic Buildings
Paul Lopez
National Register of Historic Places and National Historic Landmarks
Jim Gabbert
Linda McClelland
Barbara Wyatt
Ricah Marquez
National Trust for Historic Preservation
Peter Brink
New York State Historical Association
Wayne Wright
Oak Court
Buchanan Architecture
Ohio Historical Society
Lisa Wood

Palm Harbor Homes
Howard Broughton, V. P. of Sales & Marketing
Preservation Dallas
Katherine Seale and Carol Roark, former Directors
Still National Osteopathic Museum & A. T. Still University
Jason Haxton
Robert Clement
Barb Magers
Syracuse University Press
Kelly Balenske
Texas Historical Commission
Mark Wolfe
University of Louisville, Ekstrom Library Special Collections: Photographic Archives
Bill Carner

University of Minnesota Libraries
Jennifer C. Torkelson
Barbara A. Bezat
University of Oklahoma
Alexandra Shadid
Westchester County Historical Society
Diana D. Deichert
Western Pennsylvania Conservancy
Clinton Piper
Fallingwater, PO Box R, Mill Run, PA 15464
fallingwater@paconserve.org
Western Reserve Historical Society
Ann Sindelar
Vicki Catozza

The following assistants, photographers, architects, and independent professionals provided additional photographs, assistance, and information:

Albert, Righter & Tittmann Architects, Inc.
William T. Baker & Associates
Brian Clicque
Chelsea Clicque
Heather Clicque
Bonnie Cochrane
Rick Brettell
Ian Cole
Al Cox
Marianne Cusato
Richard Drummond Davis
Jacqueline Decter
Eve Epstein
Stephen Fox

Patricia Gebhard
Mark Gunderson
Thomas Hahn
Tom Martinson
Keven McAlester
Alex McLean
Craig Melde, Architexas
Evelyn Montgomery
Robert A.M. Stern, Architects
Amy Talkington
Carty Talkington
Bonnie Wheeler
Willis Winters
Gloria Wise
David Woodcock

Although I very much appreciate the help and input of all of these individuals, they shouldn't be held responsible for my opinions stated within the text.

City of Hope

My last acknowledgment is one I never dreamed I would need to make. However, without City of Hope in Duarte, California, I could not have finished this book. A few months after turning in the manuscript, I was diagnosed with myelofibrosis, an unusual chronic leukemia. At first I didn't worry because the prognostic factors indicated I had about fourteen-years-plus life expectancy. But after correcting my first set of layouts, I suddenly felt much worse. The severe anemia produced by my rapidly dropping red-blood-cell count made it hard to focus (not enough oxygen makes it to the brain). During a consultation at City of Hope, I learned that in their opinion I needed an immediate stem-cell transplant. By some miracle, my sister, Dorothy "Dotsy" Savage, was a perfect match and willing to be my donor. I had hoped to be able to finish the second, third, and fourth layouts (not to mention the related e-book and documentary projects), but my primary physician, Dr. Eileen Smith, strongly encouraged that I schedule the transplant immediately.

It was an arduous process—including a two-week stint in the ICU—but knowing that I needed to finish this book helped get me through, along with the attentive care of Transplant Team 5—Dr. Stephen Forman, Dr. Smith, Dr. Ravi Bhatia, Dr. David Snyder, and Dr. Ahmed Aribi. Countless other generous nurses, caregivers, administrators, housekeepers, and indeed everyone I came in contact with at City of Hope, treated me with the highest level of professionalism and caring I possibly could imagine.

One special feature at City of Hope is The Village—two wonderful groupings of Mid-century Modern cottages that serve as housing for recuperating patients. So, as luck would have it, I found myself literally inhabiting my work. I finished this book while living in a Shed style cottage, the exact kind of space and grouping written about in the newly added Modern section of this book.

I had expected to spend the last four months (June to September 2013) gathering acknowledgments and double-checking facts, but instead I've had to spend great amounts of time simply recuperating. Despite my best efforts, I know there must be omissions to these acknowledgments and credits. I apologize to those of you who have helped me write this book and whom I may have omitted. I do intend to make corrections in the next printing.

Thus, my highest thanks go to City of Hope and, of course, to the production team at Knopf—always a joy to work with and incredibly understanding. Miraculously, the book is *almost* on schedule.

1. Hope Village, City of Hope, Duarte, California; 1958. This Contemporary (Mid-century Modern) was built for patients needing easy access to the hospital.

2. Parsons Village, City of Hope, Duarte, California; 1987. A Shed style similar to my temporary accommodations since July 2013.

3. Parsons Village, City of Hope, Duarte, California; 1987. Sidewalks wind through beautifully landscaped and friendly grounds.

About the Illustrations

All the final illustrations for the new chapters in this revision were drawn by architect and artist Suzanne Patton Matty. The author made a rough sketch for the artist to work from and in many cases provided additional visual materials. Often there were several rounds of corrections, with the final responsibility for the illustration content falling to the author.

The majority of the illustrations were based on photographs of houses or architectural details taken by the author or photographer Steve Clicque. In some cases, however, specific plans were only slightly modified, while in other cases a published plan or a specific location provided general inspiration for the illustration.

The only exception to the above is that preservation architect Gary Scotnicki drew all the small additions to the Pictorial Key.

Listed below are illustrations and locations that were particularly helpful to the author and artist.

Looking at American Houses

p. 61 inset map inspired by Woodstock, Vermont

p. 61 "New England village" inspired by Nantucket, Massachusetts

p. 61 "midwestern small town" inspired by Athens, Ohio

p. 62 inset map inspired by 19th-century plans of Philadelphia, Pennsylvania

p. 62 "Mid-Atlantic ship building district" inspired by Fells Point, Baltimore, Maryland

p. 62 "Upper South river port" inspired by South Lee Street, Alexandria, Virginia

p. 63 "Mid-Atlantic seaport" inspired by Union Park neighborhood, Baltimore, Maryland

p. 63 "midwestern river port" inspired by Lafayette Square, St. Louis, Missouri

p. 65 "along Chicago rail line" inspired by River Forest, Illinois

p. 71 "TOD" inspired by *Sprawl Repair Manual* by Galina Tachieva (Washington, DC: Island Press, 2010), 167

p. 71 "TND" inspired by Seaside, Florida

p. 73 "Rural Plan" inspired by *Rural by Design* by Randall Arendt (Chicago: American Planning Association, 1994), 39

p. 73 "Urban Plan" inspired by Philadelphia, Pennsylvania

p. 73 "Suburban: streetcar" inspired by *Seven Rules for Sustainable Communities: Design Strategies for the Post-Carbon World* by Patrick M. Condon (Washington, DC: Island Press, 2010), 26

p. 73 "Suburban: early automobile" inspired by Highland Park West, a Dallas suburb planned by George Kessler in 1918. Kessler was succeeded by planners Hare & Hare in the early 1920s.

p. 73 "Suburban: post–World War II" inspired by Levittown, Pennsylvania

p. 73 "Post-suburban: SLUG" inspired by *Rural by Design* by Randall Arendt (Chicago: American Planning Association, 1994), 39

p. 79 "Olmstedian plans" is a reproduction of the original plan for Riverside, Illinois (Frederick Law Olmsted, 1869).

p. 79 "Warped grids" modified from plan of St. Francis Wood, San Francisco, California (Olmsted Brothers, ca. 1912)

p. 79 "FHA-guided subdivisions" inspired by *Successful Subdivisions*, FHA, 1940, 12–21

p. 81 "Golf course developments" based on *A Field Guide to Historic Neighborhoods and Museum Houses* by Virginia and Lee McAlester (New York: Alfred A. Knopf, 1998), 9. Square-mile section developed with golf course green space

p. 81 "Geometric combinations" from McAlester and McAlester, *Field Guide to Historic Neighborhoods,* xxxix, based on plan of El Encanto subdivision, ca. 1928, Tucson, Arizona

p. 81 "Side-by-side combinations" based on Kessler Park and Kessler Square, Dallas, Texas

p. 86 "Effect of increasing block length" based on http://en.wikipedia.org/wiki/Grid_plan— Block Size and Street Lengths

p. 89 "Deed restrictions" based on Swiss Avenue and Munger Place Historic Districts, Dallas, Texas, 1905

p. 94 "Street enclosures" inspired by *Rural by Design* by Randall Arendt (Chicago: American Planning Association, 1994), 10

p. 95 "Rural southern farmstead" based on *Garden History of Georgia, 1733–1933* by Loraine Meeks Cooney, Hattie C. Rainwater, Florence Nisbet Marye, and P. Thornton Marye (Atlanta: Garden Club of Georgia, 1976), 79. Athens house built by John Thomas Grant

p. 95 "Rural villa or 'borderlands,'" inspired by Andrew Jackson Downing, *Cottage Residences,* 3rd ed. (New York and London: Wiley and Putnam, 1847), 50, fig. 16

p. 96 "Mini farm" from McAlester and McAlester, *Field Guide to Historic Neighborhoods,* xxxii, fig. 17

p. 96 "Railroad or horsecar suburb" inspired by *American Shelter: An Illustrated Encyclopedia of the American Home* by Lester Walker (New York: Overlook Press, 1981), 149

p. 97 "Post–World War II suburb (ca. 1950s)" inspired by *Yard, Street, Park: The Design of Suburban Open Space* by Cynthia L. Girling and Kenneth I. Helphand (New York: Wiley, 1997), 82

p. 97 "Post–World War II suburb (ca. 1960s)" inspired by *Case Study Houses* by Elizabeth Smith (Los Angeles: Taschen, 2009), 48

p. 99 "Underlying survey," from McAlester and McAlester, *Field Guide to Historic Neighborhoods,* 695. Adapted from *Texas: A Geography* by Terry G. Jordan Bychkov et al., (Boulder, CO: Westview Press, 1984)

p. 100 "Rigid rectangular surveys: Salt Lake City, Utah," http://upload.wikimedia.org/wikipedia/en/b/b5/Platslc.jpg—plan of Salt Lake City, Utah, Brigham Young

University, Harold B. Lee Library, Special Collections

p. 101 "Rigid rectangular surveys: Dallas, Texas" map from McAlester and McAlester, *Field Guide to Historic Neighborhoods,* 698. Inspired by "The Visible City: Tracing Memory and Character in Dallas' Historical Landscape" by Constance Adams (unpub.)

p. 102 "Long-lot surveys" inspired by historic map of New Orleans reproduced in *The Second Battle of New Orleans: A History of the Vieux Carré Riverfront Expressway Controversy* by Richard O. Baumbach Jr. and William E. Borah (Tuscaloosa: University of Alabama Press, 1981)

Folk Houses

p. 148 "Mobile home, before World War II" based on http://Allmanufacturedhomes.com—1937 Silver Dome. See also *The Unknown World of the Mobile Home* by John Frase-Hart, Michelle J. Rhodes, and John T. Morgan (Baltimore: The Johns Hopkins University Press, 2002), 34

p. 151 "Typical Siting of Manufactured Homes": "Rural siting," Key West, Florida vicinity, ca. 1980s
"Urban park siting," Phoenix, Arizona, ca. 1960s
"Urban park siting," Carlsbad, California vicinity, ca. 1980s

Victorian Houses

p. 344 Queen Anne sample house inspired by Martin Luther King, Jr., birthplace at 501 Auburn Avenue, Atlanta, Georgia

Eclectic Houses

p. 510 Mission sample house inspired by the Alhambra, 1923 Sears Roebuck Modern Homes (The Mission Type)

p. 536 Monterey sample house inspired by Williams House in Dallas, Texas, 1932, Dave Williams, architect

Modern Houses

p. 586 Minimal Traditional sample house based on "The Phelps," in *Homes of Moderate Cost* (National Plan Service, 1941), 12

p. 612 "Bi-Level Split" based on Design 47–1159 in *Contemporary Home Plans* (National Plan Service, 1990) p. 612 "Tri-Level Split" based on Plan 9783, "split level planning," Lester Cohen, architect, in *Foremost Home Plans* 4 (1970)

p. 621 "Bi-nuclear house," based on Bi-Nuclear House III, 1945, Marcel Breuer, architect, in

Marcel Breuer, Architect and Designer by Peter Blake (New York: Architectural Record/Museum of Modern Art, 1949), 86

p. 628 Contemporary sample house based on houses in Surrey Downs development, Bellevue, Washington

p. 633 "Elaborations commonly visible from street" modeled on real-estate ad for Kimmelman House, 8973 Wonderland Park Avenue, Los Angeles, 1957, Philip Kimmelman, architect (chief project architect for many Weldon Becket structures)

p. 633 "Decorative grilles, commonly concrete screen block" inspired by "Behold the Lowly Concrete Block . . . It Isn't Lowly Anymore," *House and Home*, March 1956, 142–49

p. 634 "Other typical elaborations" inspired by "Nine Hillside Houses," *House & Home*, April 1952, 82–83, 97

p. 635 "Some spatial configurations" modeled on Deck House, Inc., Series 5000 Marketing Kit—Interiors

p. 635 "Post-and-beam construction" inspired by "Post-Beam-Plank Construction," *House & Home*, June 1954, 98–115

p. 648 Shed sample house based on East Texas Residence, 1969, John Mullen, architect. Awarded Dallas AIA Best House of the Decade

p. 650 "How a gable roof is 'slipped' to create sheds" based on a sketch by Ann Abernathy, AIA

p. 651 "Some ways to organize shed-roof elements and rooms" lower left house based on Lake Dallas residence, Lewisville, Texas, John Mullen, architect

p. 651 "Some ways to organize shed-roof elements and rooms" lower right house based on house in Athens, Texas, by John Mullen, architect

p. 651 "Some ways to organize shed-roof elements and rooms" inspired by "some ways to organize rooms," *Charles Moore: Buildings and Projects 1949–1986,* edited by Eugene J. Johnson (New York: Rizzoli, 1986), 18

p. 651 "Typical elaborations" based on *Contemporary Home Plans* (New York: Bantam/Hudson Plan Books, 1977), 47

p. 654 Brutalism sample house modeled on *American Architecture Since 1780* by Marcus Whiffen (Cambridge, Mass: MIT Press, 1993)

p. 654 Deconstructivism sample house modeled on front facade of Blades House, Santa Barbara, California, 1995, Morphosis Architects (William Morgan, *The Abrams Guide to American House Styles*, 2004), 390

p. 654 Postmodern sample house modeled on Vanna Venturi House, Philadelphia, Pennsylvania, 1962, Robert Venturi, architect; Organic sample house modeled on Glen Harder House, Mountain Lake, Minnesota, 1970, Bruce Goff, architect

p. 672 Découpage sample house modeled on house in Urban Reserve, Dallas, Texas, ca. 2010

p. 672 Unifying Material sample house modeled on L-stack House, Fayetteville, Arizona, ca. 2005, Marlon Blackwell, architects

p. 672 Slightly Askew sample house modeled on Dumbacker House, Pasadena, California, 1996, Hagy Belzberg, architect

p. 682 "Urban Reserve site plan" modified from original site plan, provided courtesy Kevin Sloan (July 2009)

Styled Houses Since 1935

p. 688 "Typical elaborations" house on right based on Dilbeck House, Dallas, Texas, 1970, Charles S. Dilbeck, architect

p. 709 "Cascading hipped roofs" house photographed in new development near Kansas City, Missouri, ca. 2005

p. 709 "Tall entry porches" inspired by HPT 290139 by Fillmore Design Group, *Luxury Dream Homes* (Tucson, AZ: Home Planners, LLC, 2001), 151

p. 709 "Tall entry porches" inspired by Italian 8010 "Capucin," Don Sater, *Don Sater's European Classics* (Bonita Springs, FL: Sater Design Collection, 2007), 129

p. 719 "Comparison of detailing in new traditional houses" top, house in Dallas, Texas, ca. 2010

p. 719 "Comparison of detailing in new traditional houses" bottom, house in Munger Place Historic District, Dallas, Texas, 1985

p. 752 American Vernacular sample house modeled on Three Sides Farm in Bowie County, Texas, 1979, John Mullen, architect

p. 754 "Ways to achieve a larger house" additive house on left, from *New Classic American Houses: The Architecture of Albert, Righter & Tittmann* (New York: Vendome, 2009), Stone House, 99

p. 755 "Window patterns," left, from *The Farmhouse: New Inspiration for the Classic American House* by Jean Rehkemp Larson (Newton, CT: Taunton Press, 2004), 3. Based on the Marek House. In person, the full-width front porch includes a slightly deeper and handsome screened porch that would have been confusing at small scale.

p. 755 "Window patterns," center, from *Yankee Modern* by William Morgan (New York: Princeton Architectural Press, 2010), 105. Based on the Osprey House in Jamestown, Rhode Island, 2005, Estes/Twombly, architects.

p. 755 "Window patterns," right, from author's photo of the Arvold House in Duluth, Minnesota, David Salmela, architect

Appendix

p. 764 "Green construction," Green Building Pyramid, copyright *Green Builder Magazine*

p. 771 "Alternative construction methods" modeled on "Alternative Construction Methods," in *Louisiana Speaks: Pattern Book*, 26, prepared by Urban Design Associates for the Louisiana Recovery Authority and the LRA Support Foundation

Photo Credits

Ann Abernathy, 642–3:1; 656–7:5; 658–9:1; 732–3:3; 746–7:6; 767:5

Allison Abraham, 544–5:1, 2, 3, 4, 5

State of Alabama Bureau of Publicity and Information, 438–9:4

Alabama Department of Archives and History, 482–3:4

Architektursammlung, Technische Universitat Munchen from *L'Architecture Americaine,* 279:5; 356:5; 364–5:5, 8; 366–7:6, 7; 368–9:1; 471–3:4

Arkansas Historic Preservation Program, 441:3; 562–3:8. Bob Dunn, 288–91:15

Atlanta Historical Society, Peachtree-Cherokee Trust Collection, 418–19:8. Kenneth Kay, 427:5

William T. Baker, 736–7:4; 738–9:3, 5, 6

City of Biloxi, 351–5:1; 356:1; 404–5:3

Bentz-Thompson Architects, 769:1. Eric Sutherland, 626–7:5

Jean F. Block, *Hyde Park Houses* (Chicago: University of Chicago Press, 1978). Samuel W. Block Jr., 364–5:2

Larry Boerder, 734–5:7; 740–1:4, 9; 748–9:6

Bowdoin College Library, Special Collections, 274:4

Brian Vanden Brink, courtesy of Peter Pennoyer Architects, 732–3:7

R. Bruhn (© 1978), 326–7:7

Buffalo and Erie County Historical Society, 416–17:4, 8; 422–3:1; 465:3; 560–1:8. Roy Nagle Collection, 442–3:1

Cambridge Historical Commission, 428–9:1, 4; 622–3:2. Richard Cheek, 320–1:3; 322–3:5; 357:5; 362:1; 426:1; 622–3:5. Roger Gilman, 338–9:6. B. Orr, 320–1:4; 351–5:13; 414–15:1; 420–1:8; 428–9:2

Catskill Center for Conservation and Development, Arkville, New York. Mark Zeek, 351–5:11

John Chase, *The Sidewalk Companion to Santa Cruz Architecture* (Paper Vision Press), 351–5:14, 15

Steve Clicque, 138–9:7; 144–5:5; 151; 152–3:1, 2, 3, 4, 5; 154–5:1, 2, 3, 4, 6, 7; 206–8:6, 8; 212:4; 213:3; 298–9:1; 357:1; 358–61:11; 418–19:2, 5; 430–1:1, 2, 3, 4, 5, 6, 7, 8; 440:3; 457:1, 2; 458:1, 2; 459:1, 4; 460–1:1, 4, 6, 7, 9; 462:1; 463:3, 4; 465:1, 2, 4; 490–1:5; 504–5:1; 516–17:5; 528–9:8; 532:4; 538–9:4, 7; 544–5:6; 556–7:7; 558–9:5; 574–6:11; 584–5:4, 7; 590–1:2, 4, 6, 7; 592–3:1, 3, 5, 6, 7, 8; 594–5:1, 2, 3, 4, 5, 6; 604–5:3, 4, 5, 7, 9; 606–7:2, 3, 5, 6, 7, 8, 9; 608–9:2, 3, 4, 6, 8, 9, 10, 11; 610–11:1, 2, 3, 4, 5, 6, 7, 8, 10; 615:1, 2; 622–3:6, 8; 624–5:1, 4, 5, 6, 7, 8; 626–7:3, 4, 6, 7, 10; 636–7:1, 5, 6, 8, 9, 10; 638:4; 639:1, 2, 4, 5; 640–1:1, 3, 4, 5, 6, 8, 9; 642–3:2, 4, 5, 6, 7, 8, 10; 644–5:1, 2, 3, 4, 5, 6, 7; 652–3:3, 4, 5, 6; 658–9:2, 5, 7; 661:1; 662–3:1, 2, 3, 6; 666–7:1, 2, 5, 6, 7; 668–9:3, 5, 6; 670–1:2, 3, 5; 675:1, 2, 3; 676–7:2, 3, 6, 7; 678:1, 3, 5; 679:1, 2, 3, 4, 5; 680:2, 3, 4, 6; 682–3:1, 2, 3, 4, 5; 689:1, 2, 3, 4, 5; 690–1:1, 2, 3, 4, 5, 6; 697:1, 2, 4, 6; 698–9:1, 2, 3, 4, 5, 6, 7, 8, 9, 10; 700:1, 2, 3, 4, 5, 6; 701:1, 2, 3, 4; 702:1, 2; 703:1, 2, 3, 4; 710–11:1, 3, 4, 5, 6, 7, 9; 712–13:1, 3, 4, 5, 6, 7, 8; 714–15:1, 2, 3, 4, 5, 6, 7; 719; 724; 728–30:2, 4, 7, 8, 10; 731:1, 2, 4; 732–3:1, 2, 4, 5, 6, 10; 734–5:1, 2, 3, 5, 8; 736–7:1, 2, 5, 6, 7, 8; 738–9:1, 2, 4, 7, 8, 9; 740–1:1, 3, 5, 6, 7, 8, 10; 742–3:3, 4, 5, 6, 7, 8, 9; 744–5:1, 2, 3, 4, 5, 6, 7, 8, 9; 746–7:1, 2, 3, 4, 5, 7, 8; 748–9:1, 2, 3, 5, 7, 8; 756; 757:3, 4; 758–9:1, 3, 4, 5, 7, 8; 760–1:1, 2, 3, 4, 6, 7; 762:1, 2; 763:1, 3, 4; 767:3; 769:2, 3

Commission of Fine Arts. Jack E. Boucher, 482–3:3, 7; 490–1:7

Connecticut Historical Commission. Susan Babbitt, 340–1:2. Brian Pfeiffer, 123:4; 298–9:7; 324–5:1. Ellen Rosebrock, 351–5:7; 380–1:2

Courtesy of Biltmore House and Gardens, Ashville, North Carolina, 471–3:9

Courtesy of Palm Harbor Homes, 152–3:6, 8; 154–5:5

Al Cox, 209:5; 213:1, 2

Paul Crews, 400:2

Mary Wallace Crocker, *Historic Architecture in Mississippi* (1973). 274:3; 292–3:2

Marianne Cusato, 757:1

Cuyahoga County Archives, 358–61:5. David M. Thurn, 288–91:6

Dallas Historical Society, 358–61:4

Dallas Public Library, Texas/Dallas History and Archives Division, 376:1

Detroit Public Library, Burton Historical Collection, 279:2

James Fox, 656–7:1, 2, 3; 658–9:3

State University College at Fredonia, New York, Jewel Conover Archives in the Reed Library, 441:1

Galveston Historical Foundation, 401:4; 416–17:1

David Gebhard, 514–15:8; 516–17:6; 622–3:5

Robert C. Giebner, 196–7:1

Geoffrey Gross, 626–7:8

Julia Guice, editor, *The Buildings of Biloxi: An Architectural Survey,* 136–7:5

Ken Gutmaker, 757:2; 760–1:5; 763:5

Thomas Hahn, 254–5:6; 276–7:1; 288–91:2; 296–7:3; 298–9:5; 306–7:7; 338–9:2; 356:2, 3; 357:2; 358–61:15; 363:1, 2; 366–7:4, 5; 368–9:5 376:2; 399:4; 414–15:4; 438–9:7; 457:5; 460–1:2

Carol M. Highsmith, 624–5:2

Historic American Buildings Survey Office. Jack E. Boucher, 213:5

Historic Landmarks Foundation of Indiana, 326–7:5

http://creativecommons.org/licenses/by/2.0/deed.en, 392:1

Michael G. Imber, architects, 748–9:4

Illustration Inspirations, 151

Indiana Historical Society Library, 13:3; 254–5:8; 320–1:2; 351–5:6; 358–61:9

Warren Jagger, 762:2

Kansas City Landmarks Commission, 382–3:3

Kentucky Historical Society, 128–9:6

Margaret M. Keyes, *Nineteenth Century Home Architecture of Iowa City* (University of Iowa Press), 276–7:5; 298–9:8

The King William Association, San Antonio, Texas. Mary V. Burkholder, 404–5:1

Kirksville College of Osteopathy and Surgery, 358–61:14

Carleton Knight III, 212:2; 292–3:3; 298–9:6; 312–13:7; 324–5:3, 4; 340–1:5; 363:3; 392:4

Carson Leh, 680:1

Lexington-Fayette County Historic Commission, 140–1:9; 142–3:3; 294–5:2

Library of Congress, 258–9:3; 306–7:8; 402–3:2. American Press Assn., 500–1:5. George S. Cook, 210–11:3. Francis B. Johnston Collection, 164–5:1; 184–5:4; 210–11:6; 230–1:5; 238–9:7; 258–9:5; 262–3:7. National Photo Co., 577:2. W. H. Sutton, 326–7:8. Witteman Collection, 340–1:4; 463:5; 514–15:2. Marion Post Wolcott, 767:4

Library of Congress, Farm Security Administration Archives. Walker Evans, 128–9:4; 399:3; 402–3:6. Lange, 194–5:5. Russell Lee, 128–9:7; 459:3; 528–9:1. Carl Mydans, 144–5:6. Arthur Rothstein, 131:1, 4; 136–7:7; 196–7:4. John Vachon, 144–5:3. Marion Post Wolcott, 136–7:8; 142–3:2; 144–5:1; 146–7:1, 3; 458:3

Library of Congress, Historic American Buildings Survey, 146–7:2; 164–5:2; 194–5:6; 206–8:9, 10, 11; 240:2; 351–5:5; 368–9:7; 422–3:4; 480–1:8; 562–3:3. L. D. Andrew, 238–9:3. W. Harry Bagby, 164–5:4. Nelson E. Baldwin, 173:2; 174:1. John M. Beckstrom, 224–5:3. John O. Bostrup, 224–5:6. Jack E. Boucher, 125:2; 164–5:7; 173:1; 209:2; 210–11:5; 213:4; 230–1:8; 262–3:3; 276–7:2, 7; 288–91:5; 338–9:7; 378–9:3; 392:5; 393:4; 482–3:1. Branzetti, 123:1, 2; 209:1; 212:11; 228:4. James Butters, 238–9:5; 256–7:7; 278:1. Richard Cheek, 162–3:6. Clinedinst, 514–15:6. W. Collins, 590–1:5. C. O. Greene, 164–5:6, 8; 210–11:4, 7. Arthur C. Haskell, 224–5:1, 5; 226–7:1. Cortlandt Hubbard, 212:3. John A. Huffman, 402–3:1. Lester Jones, 123:5; 184–5:3, 6. Richard Koch, 182–3:1, 6; 184–5:7. R. Merritt Lacey, 175:1, 2, 4, 5. Leslie, 182–3:4. Jane Lidz, 272–3:1; 351–5:2; 358–61:12; 502–3:7; 532:1, 2; 572–3:2. E. P. MacFarland, 175:3; 262–3:6. Stanley P. Mixon, 174:2; 230–1:2. Eric Muller, 272–3:6. Frederick D. Nichols, 196–7:2, 6. Paul Piaget, 262–3:4. E. H. Pickering, 229:1, 3, 4; 230–1:1. James Rainey, 206–8:3. Cervin Robinson, 123:3; 206–8:4; 226–7:6, 8; 256–7:8; 312–13:2; 378–9:8. Sirlin Studies, 288–91:10; 300–1:4; 342:5. Roger Sturtevant, 194–5:1. Robert Thall, 326–7:6; 556–7:9; 584–5:5. Laurence E. Tilley, 206–9:2; 224–5:1; 226–7:4, 5; 288–91:8. Josiah Tully, 226–7:2. Thomas Waterman, 164–5:3; 174:5; 206–8:7. Carl F. White, 261:1. Henry F. Withey, 194–5:2

James R. Lockhart, courtesy of William T. Baker, 740–1:2

Louisiana State Museum, 275:3

University of Louisville Photographic Archives, 456:3. Brown-Doherty Collection, 393:2; 471–3:2. Caufield and Shook Collection, 15:5 (neg. 36593); 15:4 (neg. 41271); 136–7:6 (neg. 3909?); 241:5 (neg. 38025); 288–91:12 (neg. 40954); 378–9:1 (neg. 37097); 420–1:2 (neg. 72429); 420–1:3 (neg. 72425); 420–1:9 (neg. 41518); 424–5:1 (neg. 68196); 438–9:5 (neg. 79590); 444–5:1 (neg. 72648); 444–5:2 (neg. 5774A); 457:4 (neg. 41252); 490–1:1 (neg. 72687); 514–14:7 (neg. 2614); 528–9:3 (neg. 89283); 572–3:5 (neg. 41267); 574–6:4 (neg. 541259). Potter Collection, 427:2 (neg. 2523.5). A. B. Rue, 128–9:5. Standard Oil of New Jersey Collection, 128–9:2 (neg. 52483); 140–1:7 (neg. 48981); 144–5:2 (neg. 49832); 272–3:5 (neg. 51912); 272–3:7 (neg. 53953)

Louisville Landmarks Commission, 292–3:9; 306–7:4; 390–1:8; 393:1; 480–1:1; 500–1:9; 504–5:4

The Ohio Historical Society, Inc., Archives-Library Division, 140–1:1; 146–7:4; 196–7:3; 261:2; 324–5:6; 382–3:2; 418–19:3; 420–1:5; 424–5:4; 462:3; 570–1:1; 584–5:3

University of Oklahoma, Western History Collections. Bob Goins, 131:2

Amanda Olson-McCoy, 427:4

Oregon Historical Society, 294–5:5; 324–5:7; 342:1; 358–61:6

Pennsylvania Historical & Museum Commission, 376:5

Free Library of Philadelphia, 300–1:3

Historic Pittsford, Inc. Richard L. Turner, 256–7:4

William Plymat, Jr., *The Victorian Architecture of Iowa,* 296–7:5

Greater Portland Landmarks, Inc., Portland, Maine. Nicholas Dean, 296–7:7

Daniel D. Reiff, *Architecture in Fredonia* (Michael Rockefeller Arts Center Gallery), 322–23:4

Albert Righter & Tittmann Architects Inc, 668–9:1; 728–30:1, 3; 732–3:8, 9; 734–5:9, 10

Robert P. Ruschak, courtesy of Western Pennsylvania Conservancy, 656–7:4

Russell House Museum, 260:4

Historic Salisbury Foundation, Inc. Wayne Hinshaw, 164–5:5; 288–91:14; 358–61:1; 574–6:2

Santa Barbara Architecture (copyright © 1975, 1980 by Capra Press, Santa Barbara, CA 93120). Wayne McCall, 526–7:5; 528–9:2; 530–1:3, 4, 5, 7, 8; 533:1, 3; 538–9:2; 572–3:6

Dorothy Harris Savage, 440:1

Ben Schnall, 624–5:10

Mary-Peale Schofield, *Landmark Architecture of Cleveland* (Ober Park Assoc., Inc., Pittsburg, Pennsylvania), 368–9:8

Julius Shulman, 622–3:4, 7; 658–9:8

Roger B. Smith, *The Early Architecture of the Genesee Valley* (courtesy Milne Library, State University College of Arts and Sciences, Genesee, New York), 254–5:1; 312–13:3

Smithsonian Institution, National Anthropological Archives, 111:1, 2, 3, 4, 5; 113:1, 2, 3, 4; 115:1, 2, 3, 4

The Society for the Preservation of New England Antiquities, 162–3:1, 2, 3, 4, 5, 7, 8, 9; 206–8:5; 210–11:1; 228:3; 364–5:3, 6; 376:3; 377:4; 380–1:4; 414–15:2; 418–19:7; 471–3:1

James T. Sodeman, 300–1:5; 343:1, 2, 3

Roman Sokal, 570–1:8, 9; 574–6:10

South Carolina Department of Archives and History, 140–1:8; 351–5:16, 17; 400:5; 401:4; 402–3:4; 404–5:4, 5; 424–5:5; 427:1; 572–3:1

Robert A. M. Stern, Architects. Peter Aaron, 668–9:4. Steven Brooke, 728–30:12.

C. Eric Stoehr, *Bonanza Victorian* (University of New Mexico Press), 260:1; 275:1; 351–5:3

Syracuse University. Hans Padelt, 254–5:7

The Association for the Preservation of Tennessee Antiquities, Nashville Chapter, 258–9:8

Texas Historical Commission, 256–7:1, 2; 272–3:4; 296–7:8; 322–3:1; 351–5:8; 401:1, 3; 404–5:6; 584–5:1

Transylvania University, Lexington, Kentucky, The J. Winston Coleman Kentuckiana Collection, Francis Carrick Thomas Library, 128–9:8; 230–1:3; 256–7:5; 261:4; 278:2

United States Department of Housing and Urban Development, 228:5; 260:3; 562–3:9. David Valdez, 128–9:3

United States Department of the Interior—National Park Service, National Register of Historic Places, 210–11:2; 460–1:5; 462:2; 606–7:1; 622–3:3. G. G. George, 608–9:5. James R. Lockhart, 592–3:9; 604–5:6; 638:2. Paul Seder, 639:3. Mariann Seriff, 636–7:3. Ruth Williams, 622–3:3. Diane Wray, 642–3:3.

Urban renewable with Federal funds acquired by Knopf, 75:3

Utah State Historical Society, Historic Preservation Office, 390–1:4

Alexander Vertikoff, courtesy of The Gamble House, 572–3:9

Virginia Historic Landmarks Commission, 226–7:3; 238–9:2; 240:3, 5; 241:2, 4; 278:3; 326–7:1

Westchester County Historic Society by permission of The North River Press, Inc. Frank Sanchis. 516–17:8

Western Reserve Historical Society, 13:1; 15:3; 279:3; 380–1:5

Wichita/Sedgwick County Historical Museum, Wichita, Kansas, 342:3; 574–6:13

James F. Wilson, courtesy of Buchanan Architects, 662–3:5

State Historical Society of Wisconsin, 558–9:6. E. C. Hamilton, 312–13:6. James A. Sewell, AIA, 288–91:13. Mary Ellen Young, 558–9:8

Les Wollam photograph, courtesy of Daron Tapscott, 358–61:7

Index

Page numbers in *italics* refer to illustrations.